England 1868-1914

A History of England in eleven volumes

General Editor: **W. N. Medlicott**

Already published. Some of the titles listed above are provisional

England 1868-1914

The age of urban democracy

Donald Read

Longman
London and New York

Longman Group Limited London

*Associated companies, branches and representatives
throughout the world*

*Published in the United States of America
by Longman Inc., New York*

© Donald Read 1979

First published 1979

British Library Cataloguing in Publication Data

Read, Donald
   England, 1868–1914 – (A history of England).
   1. Great Britain – History – Victoria, 1837–1901
   2. Great Britain – History – Edward VII, 1901–1910
   3. Great Britain – History – George V, 1910–1936
   I. Title   II. Series
   942.081   DA560   78–41034

   ISBN 0–582–48278–X
   ISBN 0–582–48835–4 Pbk.

Set in 10/11 pt. Times
Printed in Great Britain by Richard Clay (The Chaucer Press) Ltd, Bungay, Suffolk

Introductory note

One of the effects of two world wars and of fifty years of ever-accelerating industrial and social revolution has been the growing interest of the citizen in the story of his land. From this story he seeks to learn the secret of his country's greatness and a way to better living in the future.

There seems, therefore, to be room for a rewriting of the history of England which will hold the interest of the general reader while it appeals at the same time to the student. This new presentation takes account of the recent discoveries of the archaeologist and the historian, without losing sight of the claims of history to take its place among the mental recreations of intelligent people for whom it has no professional concern.

The history will be completed in a series of eleven volumes. The volumes are of medium length, and are intended to provide a readable narrative of the whole course of the history of England and give proper weight to the different strands which form the pattern of the story. No attempt has been made to secure general uniformity of style or treatment. Each period has its special problems, each author his individual technique and mental approach; each volume is meant to stand by itself not only as an expression of the author's methods, tastes, and experience, but as a coherent picture of a phase in the history of the country.

There is, nevertheless, a unity of purpose in the series; the authors have been asked, while avoiding excessive detail, to give particular attention to the interaction of the various aspects of national life and achievement, so that each volume may present a convincing integration of those developments – political, constitutional, economic, social, religious, military, foreign, or cultural – which happen to be dominant at each period. Although considerations of space prevent minute investigation it should still be possible in a series of this length to deal fully with the essential themes.

A short bibliographical note is attached to each volume. This is not intended to supersede existing lists, but rather to call attention to recent works and to the standard bibliographies.

W. N. Medlicott

Acknowledgements

We are grateful to the following for permission to reproduce a photograph: The Three Magnets:— Syndics of Cambridge University Library.

We are grateful to the following for permission to reproduce copyright material:

George Allen and Unwin Ltd, for a table from *The Treasury* by H. Roseveare; Allied Services Ltd., and the author, Professor Peter Mathias for a table from *Retailing Revolution* by Professor Mathias, published by Longman Group Ltd.; Associated Book Publishers Ltd., for a table p. 268 from *Sociology History and Education* by D. W. Musgrave, published by Methuen & Co. Ltd.; Associated Book Publishers Ltd., for a table p. 112 from *The Conservative Party from Peel to Churchill* by Robert Blake, published by Eyre and Spottiswoode; the authors, Professor T. C. Barker and R. M. Robbins, and London Transport for a map from *History of London Transport Vol II*; The Bodley Head for 2 tables from *National Income and Expenditure of the United Kingdom* by J. B. Jeffreys and Dorothy Walters from *Income and Wealth*, published by Bowes and Bowes; Cambridge University Press for 3 tables from *Wages and Incomes Since 1860* by A. L. Bowley; 3 tables from *Industrial Growth and World Trade* by A. Maizels; material from 11 tables from *British Economic Growth 1688–1959* by P. Deane and W. A. Cole; material from 1 table from *Occupation and Pay in Great Britain 1906–1960* by G. Routh; a map from *A New Historical Geography of England* edited by H. C. Darby; material from 5 tables from *Migration and Economic Growth* by B. Thomas and material from one table from *Abstract of the British Historical Statistics* by B. R. Mitchell and P. Deane; The Harvester Press Ltd., and Augustus M. Kelley for a table p. 82 from *Home and Foreign Investment 1870–1913* by A. K. Cairncross; Her Majesty's Stationery Office for the Board of Trade Wholesale Price Indices for 1871–1895; Institute of Economic Affairs for 2 tables from *The Long Debate* on Poverty by R. M. Hartwell; the author's agent for 3 lines from *The Lesson* by Rudyard Kipling, 6 lines from *Recessional* by Rudyard Kipling and 4 lines from *The White Man's Burden* by Rudyard Kipling, by permission of the National Trust and the Macmillan Co. of London and Basingstoke; MacGibbon & Kee/Granada Publishing Ltd., for 2 tables from *The British Political Elite* by W. Guttsman;

Macmillan, London and Basingstoke for a table p. 42 from *The Myth of the Great Depression* by S. B. Saul (1969); a table from *English Rural Communities* by Dr Mills; 2 tables p. 53 from *The Relief of Poverty* by M. E. Rose; and a table from *Trends in British Society Since 1900* by A. L. Halsey; the author's agent for 7 tables from *The First Industrial Nation* by Peter Mathias, reprinted by permission of A. D. Peters & Co. Ltd.; Thomas Nelson & Sons Ltd., for a table from *The Rise of the Public Schools* by T. W. Bamford; Oxford University Press for 2 tables from *The Struggle for Mastery in Europe* by A. J. P. Taylor; a table from *Regional Wage Variations in Britain 1850–1914* by E. H. Hunt; Routledge and Kegan Paul Ltd., for a table from *The Changing Social Structure of England and Wales 1871–1916* by D. C. Marsh; Weidenfeld and Nicolson for a table from p. 135 *Industrial Retardation in Britain 1880–1914* by A. L. Levine.

Preface

1

This is a social and political history of England during the late-Victorian and Edwardian years. It is not a history of Great Britain, still less of the United Kingdom (including Ireland), though these wider horizons are sometimes appropriately included in discussion. England's 'Irish Question' demands notice, as does England's 'British Empire'. Recognized too are the contributions made by some famous Scotsmen, Irishmen, and Welshmen. But this is England's history, even though not all the participants were Englishmen, and even though many imperial adventures were conducted far from England's corner of the globe.

How best then to survey this complex period of rapid change? Discussion of the years between 1868 and 1914 has been divided into three chronological sections – 1868–80, 1880–1900, 1901–14. These successive sub-periods – 'the Victorian Turning Point', 'Fin de Siècle', and 'Edwardian England' – each had their own distinctive moods, which were expressed partly through passing fashions but partly also through important fresh responses to the underlying long-term shifts and problems of the age. Some of the characteristics of these moods are outlined by way of introduction to the three sections. The same sequence of topics is then discussed in turn through each section. Brief notice of the economic background – before, during, and after the 'great depression' – is followed by assessment of the social scene, with especial emphasis upon class divisions and upon the wide extent and dismal reality of late-Victorian and Edwardian poverty. The rapid progress of urbanization is surveyed in separate chapters, as are the decline of religion and the expansion of culture (broadly defined). Late-Victorian England witnessed a concentration – unequalled in the Western world – of its inhabitants into cities and towns. Even though the United States already possessed a much larger total population than either England or the whole United Kingdom, a much smaller proportion of Victorian Americans were town dwellers compared with Victorian Englishmen. In 1890 the population of the United States stood well over 62 million and that of England and Wales about 29 million: yet the numbers living in cities and towns with a minimum of 8,000–10,000 inhabitants totalled roughly 18 million in each country. Moreover, nearly one-third of the people of England and Wales lived in cities with more than 100,000 population, whereas only half this proportion were city dwellers in the

United States. This new intensity of English urbanization – with all its economic, social, and political causes and effects – helps to make the history of late-Victorian England of major significance, not only in the context of national history but also against the canvas of world history.

Such a concentration of population in towns made possible the rise of a mass culture – especially a reading culture; and also the development of mass democracy in politics. In less than twenty years the parliamentary electorate of England and Wales grew from little more than 1 million voters in 1866 to over four times that number by 1885. Mass political techniques which the twentieth century has taken for granted – competing party programmes, constituency organization, frequent public meetings, continuous political reporting and discussion through the press – all first extended nationally and permanently between the 1860s and the 1880s. And much of this political debate centred upon problems which themselves had arisen out of the new urban, industrial way of life – problems of public health, housing, working conditions, popular education, unemployment. How far should government, central or local, seek to intervene in such matters? This key question for late-Victorians and Edwardians is discussed in the first parts of the three chapters on 'Government'. Separately considered in the same chapters are the rapid progress and remaining incompleteness of contemporary political 'democracy'. Particular reference is given in this connection to the Second and Third Reform Acts, to the new techniques of political communication, and to the rise of independent working-class Labour politics. 'One man one vote' had not been achieved by 1914, and no women at all were yet allowed the parliamentary suffrage. Nevertheless, many contemporaries rightly believed that the political system had become sufficiently responsive to the wishes of the many to make it 'democratic' in practice. The urban lower-middle and working-classes could now influence their rulers as never before, not only through the ballot box but also (whether they possessed votes or not) through trade unions, through pressure groups, through religious and secular organizations, even through the unpredictable urban crowd, and perhaps through the popular press which grew up to reflect their interests and aspirations. A social revolution had created the environment for a political revolution: England (as the subtitle to the present book suggests) had entered 'The Age of Urban Democracy'.

But the new democracy remained ready to follow charismatic political leaders. Separate parts within the chapters on 'Government' introduce the rival political personalities, who competed eloquently and strenuously for the support of the new mass electorate – Gladstone for Liberalism, first against the Conservative Disraeli, then against Lord Salisbury and Lord Randolph Churchill, and finally also against Joseph Chamberlain. During the first decade of the twentieth century H. H. Asquith, David Lloyd George, and Winston Churchill dominated the political platforms. They were the admired and hated spokesmen of the 'new Liberalism'. The policies and the legislation promoted by the various party leaders are discussed within each section in successive chapters on domestic, imperial, and foreign affairs. Public interest was usually greater in domestic reform than in imperial or foreign questions – except when these led to war, as happened in 1899 with the Boer War and again in 1914 with the First World War. The final chapter of the book, 'Crisis', describes the diverse and culminating tensions of the years 1911–14, as surviving Victorians and their Edwardian children and grandchildren drew near to catastrophe. How much (or little) was the outbreak of the First World War expected? To what extent was the Edwardian world dissolving even before it felt the terrible impact of 'total' war?

2

The source materials available for the study of this crucial period are vast in quantity and rich in quality. Lytton Strachey went so far as to quip that the history of the Victorian age would never be written: 'we know too much about it'. Certainly, a leading feature of the times was the communications revolution, which involved an unprecedented diffusion of the written word. The books, pamphlets, newspapers, and printed ephemera of the Victorians have survived in huge quantities for historians to read. So have the private papers of hundreds of Victorian public men, whose readiness to communicate in writing was only slightly affected by the introduction of the telephone during the last quarter of the nineteenth century. The British Library holds 750 volumes of Gladstone documents. John Morley, who served as Chief Secretary for Ireland and who subsequently became Gladstone's official biographer, is said to have remarked that only two things in life had ever frightened him – his first sight of Dublin Castle, and his first sight of the Gladstone papers. The printed Parliamentary Papers constitute another major source. They total over 50,000 titles for the nineteenth century, and contain a mass of both factual information and contemporary comment. The *Daily Telegraph* (3.7.1872) wrote of 'our passion for Blue Books – of the John Bull belief that whatever can be labelled is safe, and the national faith that figures and facts act as a counter-charm to sentiment and revolution'.

During the 1960s about half the researchers into central government records preserved at the Public Record Office were interested in the nineteenth and twentieth centuries. As a result, many outstanding books and articles have been published during the last few years which have greatly deepened our understanding of late-Victorian government, politics, and society. We now know more about many vital Victorian features than did the Victorians themselves. Nevertheless, it remains essential to remember that meaningful generalizations can be made only in appropriate contexts. One important feature of recent research has been to emphasise the contrasts and variations within Victorian England – between places, between years, and between classes. For most of their time the Victorians and Edwardians were not acting together as Englishmen but were moving separately (sometimes conflictingly) as townsmen or countrymen, Anglicans or Nonconformists, coalminers or coalowners, ladies or ladies' maids. And within each category lay the personal experience of hundreds or thousands or millions of individuals Most of them lived very ordinary lives. But the ordinary was at least as important as the extraordinary; and in the nick of time 'oral historians' have recently begun to collect and to analyse the recollections of the last survivors from this hitherto mainly silent Victorian and Edwardian majority.

3

For help in writing this book I am glad to thank the following scholars who have saved me from many errors of fact, interpretation, and expression – the late Professor R. T. Anstey, Dr A. Armstrong, Mr S. P. Bayley, Dr H. St.C. Cunningham, Dr G. M. Ditchfield, Dr D. Fraser, Mr R. T. B. Langhorne, Dr J. C. Lovell, Professor B. Keith-Lucas, Dr F. S. L. Lyons, Dr F. C. Mather, Professor G. E. Mingay, Professor H. J. Perkin, Professor A. J. Taylor, Dr D. M. Turley, Dr A. B. Wilkinson. I owe a particular debt to Professor W. N. Medlicott, the general editor of the series, for his encouragement and advice at every stage. Mrs Yvonne Latham has cheerfully helped with the typing. My wife has willingly carried more than her fair share in the home and in the garden while the book was being written. Responsibility for errors of commission or omission remains, of course, mine alone.

Donald Read   Darwin College
                                         University of Kent
                                               Canterbury

Contents

The Victorian turning point, 1868–1880

Chapter 1

Introduction: *'The revolution of our times'*

1

The chronological mid-point of Queen Victoria's long reign fell in 1869 –
more than thirty years on the throne, over thirty still to pass. Of course,
the Victorians did not know that the reign still had so much time to run.
But long before its ending they were to become aware that the
lengthening span of years from the queen's accession in 1837 possessed a
unity only through the accident of her longevity. At the time of her
Golden and Diamond Jubilees in 1887 and 1897 the great changes which
had taken place since the start of the reign were frequently described.
Lord Salisbury remarked as prime minister in 1897 how Queen Victoria
had 'bridged over that great interval which separates old England from
new England'. This transition from the 'old' to the 'new' had been not
only continuous but also accelerating, so that each Victorian generation
seemed to be the more separated from its predecessor. Society, industry,
agriculture, religion, ideas, politics – everything seemed to be in flux.
James Baldwin Brown, a leading Congregationalist minister, tried in
First Principles of Ecclesiastical Truth (1871) to measure 'the revolution
of our times'. Society (he wrote) seemed to be seeking a new basis
'instead of expanding on the old bases. Compare the throng of things
which now press upon you daily, the crowd of interests which demand
attention, and force themselves into the council chamber of your
thoughts, with the narrower circle of pursuits, pleasures and ideas which
occupied our fathers little more than a generation ago'. 'The real power
of the revolution,' continued Brown, was mental more than material.
'The submission of every thing and every method to the free judgement
of reason, by the menstrum which a free Press, a free Platform, and a
free Parliament supply.' Certainly, the power of traditional authority in
church and state had been receding since the seventeenth century. Now
it was being rapidly displaced by the power of inquiry, observation, and
opinion. In intellectual and scientific fields the numbers engaged were
still small; but the interested audience was growing fast. And the public
opinion which could influence political decisions was becoming larger
with every year.

   Yet where was all this leading? Belief in progress, in 'improvement',
had waxed strong during the first half of the reign, 'age after age, making
nicer music from finer chords'. But confidence seemed to be weakening
by the late 1860s. 'We shall "improve" still faster than we have done for

the last thirty years. And how much better shall we be for it at the end?' (*Leeds Mercury*, 25.8.1869). Uncertainty was increasingly to characterize the whole period from 1868 to the outbreak of the First World War in 1914. 'It is the year of grace 1868,' wrote Anthony Trollope, the novelist, in the March number of *St. Paul's* magazine; 'the roar of our machinery, the din of our revolutions, echoes through the solar system; can we not, then, make up our minds whether our progress is a reality and a gain, or a delusion and a mistake?'

As foreign economic and political competition intensified, the relative decline of British power was to become indisputable. The victory of the Federal forces in the American Civil War (1861–5) had left the United States ready at last to exploit its huge potential in men and resources. Bismarck was working through the 1860s to unify Germany, and the German Empire was proclaimed in 1871 after the swift collapse of the French Second Empire during the Franco–Prussian War. Imperial Germany was to prove a much stronger rival than Imperial France. It was rightly recognized as the end of an era when Lord Palmerston – the veteran protagonist of a confident foreign policy – had died in 1865. The Second Reform Act, which almost doubled the electorate, followed in 1867; and the Education Act, which opened the way for national elementary education, was passed in 1870. In 1871 appeared Charles Darwin's *The Descent of Man*, which reinforced the impact already made upon old scientific and religious ideas by his *Origin of Species* (1859). Walter Pater's *Renaissance* was published in 1873, the herald of 'aestheticism' in England. And finally, the 'great depression' – which was to last a generation – threatened agriculture and industry from the mid 1870s.

Thomas Hardy, the novelist, claimed in *The Return of the Native* (1878) that concern had begun to show itself not only in the thoughts of contemporaries but even in their faces. 'People already feel that a man who lives without disturbing a curve of feature, or setting mark of mental concern upon himself, is too far from modern perceptiveness to be a modern type.' The steam-engine word 'pressure' began to be much used to describe disorder both in institutions and in individual lives. In 1875 appeared *Social Pressure* by Sir Arthur Helps, and W. R. Greg's article in the *Contemporary Review* for March on 'Life at High Pressure.' Greg quoted statistics from the *British Medical Journal* which showed how the number of deaths from heart disease among men aged between twenty and forty-five had risen from 0.553 per 1,000 per year in 1851–5 to 0.709 in 1866–70. The faces in Gustave Doré's famous drawings for *London* (1872) were certainly animated and urban, very different from the round and comfortable visage of traditional John Bull. In 1866 the editor of *Punch* asked his leading artist 'to modernize the John Bull he draws'.[1] A more representative Englishman was now 'the man on the top of a Clapham omnibus'. But was this new town type less healthy in body and more volatile in temperament than old farmer Bull? England was changing and so perhaps were Englishmen, as the second half of Victoria's reign began.

Notes

1. R. G. G. Price, *History of Punch* (1957), pp. 107, 119.

Economic life: *'The full morning of our national prosperity'*

1

Statistics of population, occupation, and location revealed a society which was becoming extended, urbanized, and industrialized as never before. At the 1871 census the population of England taken by itself totalled almost 21,300,000 men, women, and children. The population of England and Wales taken together had grown more than two-and-a-half fold since the start of the century:

	England and Wales	United Kingdom
1801	8,900,000	15,900,000
1831	13,900,000	24,000,000
1851	17,900,000	27,400,000
1861	20,000,000	28,900,000
1871	22,700,000	31,500,000
1881	26,000,000	34,900,000

The *Preliminary Report* upon the 1871 census remarked complacently how during Queen Victoria's 'happy reign' 5,900,000 people had been added to the total of her subjects, 'not by the seizure of neighbouring territories, but mainly the enterprise, industry, and virtue of her people'.

The industry of the Victorians in reproduction was certainly impressive:[1]

	Births per thousand	Deaths per thousand
1861–5	35.8	22.6
1866–70	35.7	22.6
1871–5	35.7	22.0
1876–80	35.4	20.8

In 1871 births in England and Wales totalled 797,000, deaths 515,000. Concealed within the high overall death rates were even higher rates of infant and child mortality:

| | Deaths per thousand, England and Wales | | | | | |
	Males			Females		
	0–4	5–9	10–14	0–4	5–9	10–14
1861	71.8	6.7	4.3	62.0	6.8	4.4
1871	71.7	8.3	4.4	62.4	7.5	4.5
1881	56.6	5.8	3.2	48.0	5.7	3.2

The infections which were the greatest killers of Victorian infants and children showed no respect for social class. In 1856 Bishop Tait of Carlisle lost five young daughters in one single scarlet fever epidemic. The sombre realities of Victorian life and death were forcefully illustrated in the Registrar-General's *Annual Report* for 1872, which contained a survey by Dr William Farr, Superintendant of the Statistical Department, entitled 'March of an English Generation through Life'. This survey showed what would happen to every million children born if their life experience proved to be the same in each age group as it had been for those same age groups during the 1860s. At ages 0–4 over a quarter (263,182) would die, chiefly from infectious diseases such as measles, scarlet fever, whooping cough, and from pneumonia or bronchitis. 141,387 boys would die and 121,795 girls, to leave the sexes almost equal in numbers. 'Nearly every one of the 736,818 survivors has been attacked by one disease or another; some by several diseases in succession. There is one fact in their favour: the majority of zymotic diseases rarely recur.' Yet 34,309 would still die aged 5–9 – 8,743 from scarletina, 'the principal plague of this age'. This would leave 702,509 to enter puberty. Another 17,946 would die aged 10–14: 'the deaths are fewer than at any other age'. 684,563 would then enter the 15–19 age group, of whom 5,263 females and 3,811 males would die of consumption. Tight-lacing was suggested as a reason for the significant excess among girls. Within the 20–24 age group 'large numbers' would marry. There would be 28,705 deaths, 13,785 from consumption. 1,100 women would die in childbirth. 634,045 people would then reach their twenty-fifth birthday, 571,993 their thirty-fifth. 'The prime of life; two-thirds of the women are married; and now at its close is the mean of the period (33–34) when husbands become fathers, wives become mothers, the new generation is put forth.' 2,901 women would die in childbirth. Consumption would cause 27,134 deaths, more among women than among men. And at this age total deaths among women (31,460) would outnumber those among men (30,592).

Over the ages 35–44 deaths would total 69,078 (men 35,142, women 33,936). Consumption 'still predominates'. 'It is the age of fathers and mothers.' The original million would have been halved a few months after entering the 45–54 age group. At this stage there would be 81,800 deaths. 'The centres of life are the sources of death' – heart, lungs, liver, stomach. Cancer would take 4,583 lives. There would be equal numbers of men and women surviving at age 53; but from 55 the number of surviving women would be greater than that of men. 421,115 men and women would enter the 55–64 age group; only 309,029 would attain their sixty-fifth birthday. Over the ages 65–74 this number would be sharply cut to 161,124. At the end of the 75–84 range the total of survivors would be down to 38,565. A mere 2,153 would reach 95; 223 would attain 100, and the last would die at 108.

This survey was dealing in averages, and so could not reveal the many local variations in mortality rates. But elsewhere in the report it was noted how in Liverpool – parts of which were grossly overcrowded – not even a quarter but nearly one-half of all children died before reaching the age of 5. Only one in four of Liverpudlians reached the age of 45. 'Every great city has in it a bit of Liverpool.'

2

In terms of numbers Victorian society was dominated by children and young people. Throughout the 1850s and 1860s the average age of the population stayed constant at 26.4 years. In 1871 out of a total population of just over 22,700,000, almost 10,400,000 were aged under 20; less than a quarter (4,400,000) were aged over 45. The predominant youthfulness of the population meant that in 1871 (even leaving aside widows and widowers) as many as 61.3 per cent of males and 58.7 per cent of females were unmarried. The marriage rate – corrected for the proportion of marriageable persons in the population – fluctuated through most of the 1860s and 1870s about 18.0–19.0 per thousand, with a peak of almost 21.0 in the prosperous year of 1873.[2] By the 1860s rising costs or aspirations of living were often said to be leading to more postponement of marriage by middle-class men. But they had always tended to marry late. In 1871 the mean age of marriage among manual workers stood about 24.0 years, whereas among shopkeepers and farmers it was 27.0 and among professional men and managers it reached nearly 30.0. The mean age of marriage for brides varied much less between classes than for bridegrooms, ranging between a working-class mean of 22.0 to a middle-class mean about 25.0.[3]

In most years 'swarms of emigrants' (in the words of the Registrar-General) were drawn off overseas, chiefly to the United States and to the colonies. Only approximate emigration statistics can be calculated; but it has been estimated that England lost 1,355,000 people by emigration over the period 1871–1911, roughly 10 per cent of her natural increase.[4] Nine out of ten of these emigrants were aged under 40:

	Total	USA	British North America	Australia/ New Zealand	South Africa	Total Empire	All other countries
1861–70	157	113	13	27	1	41	3
1871–80	168	109	18	30	5	53	6
1881–90	256	172	30	37	8	75	9
1891–1900	174	114	19	13	17	49	11
1901–10	284	126	85	23	28	136	22
1911–13	464	123	189	85	28	302	39

Emigration from the United Kingdom Annual averages (nearest thousand)

Though large numbers were moving overseas, much greater numbers were migrating within the United Kingdom, especially from the countryside to work in the towns.[5] Except in the 1880s – when overseas emigration was particularly heavy – the towns absorbed at least half a million migrants per decade during the second half of the nineteenth century:[6]

	London	Other towns	Colliery districts	Rural areas
1851–61	+244	+272	+103	—743
1861–71	+262	+271	+ 91	—683
1871–81	+307	+297	+ 84	—837
1881–91	+169	— 31	+ 90	—845
1891–1901	+226	+294	+ 85	—660

Net gain or loss by migration in England (in thousands)

The *General Report* upon the 1871 census had explained how the new mobility offered by the railways and by improved roads had encouraged 'the flow of people'. Nevertheless, apart from the Irish, most migrants moved only short distances. They did so, however, within a ripple effect, as an important paper on 'The Laws of Migration' explained to the Statistical Society in 1885. 'The inhabitants of the country immediately surrounding a town of rapid growth flock into it; the gaps thus left in the rural population are filled up by migrants from more remote districts, until the attractive force of one of our rapidly growing cities makes its influence felt, step by step, to the most remote corner of the kingdom.'

Women were even more mobile than men. Domestic service attracted them in large numbers to the towns, but they also migrated for factory and shop work. 'The workshop is a formidable rival of the kitchen.' The magnetism of the provincial towns tended to fluctuate as their trade expanded or stagnated: the pull of London was both the strongest and the steadiest. Rather more than one in three of London's inhabitants had been born outside the capital. The majority had come from surrounding rural areas; but significant numbers were drawn from the rest of England, as well as from Ireland and Scotland.[7]

To what sort of work did these migrants move? The occupied population of England and Wales has been estimated at:[8]

1871		1881	
Male	Female	Male	Female
7,100,000	3,200,000	7,800,000	3,400,000

By 1871 the Industrial Revolution had been continuing for about a century; but the rise of industry had not meant the fall of agriculture, except in relative terms. England, as the *General Report* upon the 1871 census emphasised, was 'still a great agricultural country':

	Numbers employed, 1871		
	Male	Female	Total
Agriculture	1,351,000	85,000	1,436,000
Mining	371,000	6,000	377,000
Manufacturing	2,089,000	1,269,000	3,358,000
Building and roadmaking	663,000	1,000	664,000
Transport	511,000	12,000	523,000
Dealing	656,000	182,000	838,000
Banking and insurance	117,000	2,000	119,000
Public Service and professions	429,000	149,000	578,000
Domestic service	196,000	1,488,000	1,683,000

Within these general categories were some large and very large occupations:

Farmers	250,000	Blacksmiths	112,000
Labourers and farm servants	957,000	Carriage and harness makers	79,000
Coalminers	320,000	Woodworkers	81,000
		Furniture makers	75,000
Building workers	562,000		
Machine-makers	130,000		
Toolmakers	64,000		

These were almost entirely men's jobs, but in some other activities women outnumbered men:

	Male	Female
Cotton workers	188,000	279,000
Woollen workers	121,000	125,000
Dress and footwear workers	354,000	545,000
Dress retailers	63,000	25,000
Food retailers	229,000	45,000
Indoor home domestic service	68,000	1,204,000

Domestic service was thus the biggest single employment for women; agricultural labouring the biggest single job for men. Both were traditional occupations, very different from work in industry. Industrial employment, broadly defined and taken as a whole, was certainly now the biggest occupational category; but its importance was not overwhelming. Moreover, within large parts of industry small workshops rather than factories remained the centres of production. The ready-made clothing industry of east London even contrived to expand rapidly during the last quarter of the century on a basis of small workshop and domestic outwork manufacture. The cotton factory inspectors' returns for 1871 showed that even the average cotton mill employed no more than 177 people. The overall tendency was indeed towards larger units of production. This process had been encouraged by the Limited Liability Acts of 1856 and 1862. It was fastest in heavy industry, where economies of scale were greatest, but slower in textiles.[9]

3

The British economy in 1868 was still recovering from the memory of the great Overend Gurney failure of 1866, which had greatly contributed to a collapse of business confidence. At the start of 1868 money could be borrowed at the remarkably low rate of 2 per cent; and yet there were few takers. Happily, morale was about to revive. By the end of the 1860s Britain was entering one of the greatest boom periods of the whole century. This boom was based upon a great surge of international investment, which lasted at full force from early 1871 until the summer of 1873.

The 1850s, 1860s, and early 1870s, though not years of continuous and ubiquitous prosperity, certainly constituted an era of great overall economic growth.[10] But progress was shared unevenly between industries, between localities and between years. In textiles, for example – the largest industrial sector – the fierceness of competition checked profit-making but stimulated innovation and investment. The American Civil War (1861–5) added a 'cotton famine', which meant an unprecedented disruption of work in Lancashire. For the iron, shipbuilding, and coal industries, on the other hand, the needs of war – Crimean, American, and Franco-Prussian – created an extra demand. But most industries did well for much of the time, and especially in the mid-Victorian boom years: 1851–3, 1856–7, 1863–5, 1871–3.

The Times of 26 September 1871 – writing with the latest boom well established, and with the experience of the recent Franco-Prussian War and of the Paris Commune in mind – welcomed prosperity as the best protection against the infection of either Prussian militarism or of French Communism. *The Times* regarded the steady growth in tea, coffee, and cocoa imports as clear evidence that the masses were sharing in the benefits of booming trade. It also discounted fears about the increasing costliness of extraction, and even of the prospective exhaustion, of national coal stocks, which now provided nearly all the power (through steam-engines) for British industry. These fears had been strongly voiced by W. S. Jevons, a rising young economist, in his book on *The Coal Question* (1865). In 1872 Gladstone, as Prime Minister, remarked excitedly in a widely-quoted speech how trade had 'advanced within these last few months not by steps, but by strides – not by strides, but by leaps and bounds'.[11] In full activity the British economy, the strongest in the world, certainly represented a remarkable achievement. 'We are now in the full morning of our national prosperity,' Jevons had written in his book on coal, 'and are approaching noon.'

British exports were growing very fast decade by decade:[12]

	Textiles		Cottons		Iron and Steel		Machinery		Coal		Total
	£m.	%	£m.	%	£m.	%	£m.	%	£m.	%	£m.
1850–9	59.9	60	35.6	36	17.9	18	2.4	2	2.3	2	100.1
1860–9	98.5	62	57.6	36	24.0	15	4.6	3	4.5	3	159.7
1870–9	118.6	55	71.5	33	34.9	16	7.7	4	8.8	4	218.1

(At current prices: annual averages)

Imports even outran exports in rate of growth:[13]

	Grain and flour		Groceries		Meat, dairy produce		Textile raw materials		Other raw materials		Manufactured goods		Total imports
	£m.	%	£m.	%	£m.	%	£m.	%	£m.	%	£m.	%	£m.
1855–9	19.6	12	24.7	15	5.0	3	50.4	30	26.3	16	2.8	2	169.5
1860–9	31.9	12	33.9	13	12.0	5	90.7	35	32.1	12	5.0	2	260.9
1870–9	52.0	14	49.4	14	23.4	7	95.8	27	44.2	12	9.9	3	360.6

(Annual averages)

These figures showed how Britain was becoming increasingly dependent upon imported food. By the late 1870s about half of cheese and butter requirements were imported, over one-third of cereals and one-fifth of meat.[14]

The United Kingdom's balance of payments ran as follows:[15]

	Balance of visible trade	Net shipping earnings	Profits, interest, dividends	Insurance, brokerage, commissions	All other	Balance of invisible trade	Net balance
1851–5	− 33	+19	+24	+ 6	− 8	+ 41	+ 8
1856–60	− 34	+26	+33	+ 8	− 8	+ 60	+26
1861–5	− 59	+34	+44	+11	− 8	+ 81	+22
1866–70	− 65	+45	+57	+13	− 9	+106	+41
1871–5	− 64	+51	+83	+16	−12	+139	+75
1876–80	−124	+54	+88	+16	− 9	+149	+25

(Annual averages in £m.)

The adverse balance on visible trade was thus beginning to grow rapidly; but so was the favourable balance on invisibles – from shipping services, from interest and dividends upon overseas investments, from the profits of foreign trade and services, and from insurance charges, brokerage fees and the like. These all resulted from the City of London's position as the world financial centre. At the beginning of his book on *Lombard Street* (1873) Walter Bagehot, the great Victorian political and economic analyst, described the City as 'by far the greatest combination of economical power and economical delicacy that the world has ever seen'. Between 1870 and 1914 about £350 million was raised in London through the issue of foreign securities.[16]

Both the importance of these services to the world economy, and their profitability, continued to increase during the last quarter of the nineteenth century at the very time when the predominance of British industry was slipping away under pressure from foreign rivals. It had long been realized that Britain could not expect to keep indefinitely the great economic lead which she had won as the pioneer of the Industrial Revolution. But need the foreign challenge demolish the whole of her advantage? Mid-Victorian Britain regarded itself – with only small exaggeration – as 'the workshop of the world'. This expression had been coined by Disraeli in 1838. But it was usually forgotten that he had used it in a warning sense: 'The Continent will not suffer England to be the workshop of the world.' Richard Cobden had emphasized the prospective strength of foreign competition when arguing for free trade in the 1830s; but by the 1850s warnings of the foreign danger were beginning to take the present rather than the future tense. By 1864 Cobden was describing the 'fabulous increase of every kind of production' in the United States.[17] It was noted with concern that whereas Britain had won nearly all the scientific, technological, and industrial awards at the Great Exhibition of 1851 she secured less than one in ten at the Paris Exhibition of 1867.

Yet while the boom of 1871–3 lasted optimism prevailed. Even after the onset of financial crisis throughout the Continent and in the United States during the summer of 1873 there was no general economic crisis in Britain. Some firms failed heavily, prices fell, and so did the demand for labour. But only after several years did it begin to be feared that British industry and agriculture had become trapped in what was to be known, rightly or wrongly, as the 'great depression'.

4

By the 1860s Britain had become a country of free trade. Repeal of the Corn Laws in 1846 had been the most dramatic moment in this advance, which was substantially completed by Gladstone's budgets of 1853, 1860, and 1861. The Anglo-French Commercial Treaty was signed in 1860, and other European powers soon followed its lead. The Continentals lowered their tariff barriers to promote freer trade, but they stopped short of full free trade. British markets, however, were now open to foreign goods and materials with a freedom unprecedented among civilized powers. The effects of this upon the British economy were difficult to identify. Contemporary free traders claimed that increased imports under free trade would stimulate the growth of exports by way of return. Yet British markets were not now flooded with foreign goods, while British exports to Europe grew steadily but not dramatically – from about 30 per cent by value of all exports in the early 1850s to about 40 per cent in the early 1870s. On the other hand, freer trade may have stimulated multilateral exchange within the international economy to the benefit of demand for British goods outside Europe.

Certainly, repeal of the Corn Laws did not ruin British agriculture, as protectionists had forecast.[18] Of course, in relative terms agriculture became less important as the revolution in trade and industry gained momentum. In the first decade of the century agriculture and related activities had contributed about one-third of the national product, but by 1851 this was down to one-fifth and by 1871 to one-seventh:[19]

	Industrial distribution of the national income of Great Britain			
	Agriculture, fishing, forestry	Manufacture, mining, building	Trade and transport	Total national product
1801	75.5	54.3	40.5	232.0
1851	106.5	179.5	97.8	523.3
1871	130.4	348.9	201.6	916.6

(£m. at current prices)

Yet home wheat growers were in no difficulties after the free opening of British ports to foreign grain. The Crimean War (1854–6) interfered with Russian grain exports, and high transport costs made the huge potential output of the American mid-West expensive to import. Foreign wheat imports did indeed double between 1850 and 1870, coming to provide about one-half rather than one-quarter of British consumption. But this still left a sufficient market for home-grown wheat. Wheat prices in Britain during the 1850s and 1860s fluctuated about moderate levels – down to 40s. 2d. per quarter in 1864, up as high as 64s. in 1867 – and thereby falsified both the fears of protectionists and the hopes of those free traders who promised 'cheap bread' after Corn Law repeal.

More and more wheat was grown, with a peak of 3,688,000 acres under cultivation in Great Britain during 1869. Yet market conditions ought to have encouraged expansion of livestock farming rather than wheat growing, to meet the demand from the expanding and increasingly affluent (and therefore increasingly meat-eating) urban market. In *The Landed Interest and the Supply of Food* (1879) James Caird, a leading authority on agriculture, estimated that consumption per head of animal food (meat, cheese, and butter) had doubled in thirty years. With population growth taken into account, this meant a trebling in demand. But agriculture in the south and east of England persisted with its traditional emphasis upon arable and corn. When diversification did take place it was often only to mixed farming – grain production plus stock fattening. Widespread livestock farming remained concentrated in the north and west.

These northern districts proved best able to withstand agricultural depression when it came from the mid-1870s. The mid-Victorian prosperity of corn growing and even of mixed farming was always precarious, though contemporaries did not realize the fact. 'High farming' was pursued with dedication, often requiring heavy expenditure upon drainage, new fertilizers and machinery. The profit return on these investments frequently remained low even before the depression. Steam-threshing became common from the 1850s; steam-reaping also came in; but steam-ploughing was tried only by large farmers. The introduction of machinery varied in extent from area to area, partly depending upon the availability or otherwise of cheap hand labour.[20] Labour was becoming short in some rural areas even during the prosperous 1850s and 1860s, as the population began to fall because of overseas emigration and migration to the towns:[21]

Urban and rural populations, England and Wales		
Population		
Rural	Urban	Rural percentage
1851	8,900,000	9,000,000	49.8
1861	9,100,000	11,000,000	45.4
1871	8,700,000	14,000,000	38.2
1881	8,300,000	17,600,000	32.1

The cultivation of land was largely in the hands of tenant farmers. In general, as Caird explained in his book on *The Landed Interest*, England was farmed through a tripartite division of ownership and effort between landowners, tenant farmers, and agricultural labourers. 'The landowners make the permanent works on their estates, their income being paid in rent by tenant-occupiers; the tenants in their turn direct the cultivation, provide the farm stock and implements and all the necessary capital and skill, and employ and pay the agricultural labourers by whose work the land is cultivated.'

Some land was owned by comparatively many, but most land was owned by comparatively few.[22] Large landowners, with estates of 10,000 acres or more, were shown in John Bateman's *Great Landowners of Great Britain and Ireland* (4th edn, 1883) to possess about one-quarter of all the soil of England. In Rutland and Northumberland they held as much as one-half of the respective county areas. Gentry and squires, with estates of 1,000–9,999 acres, owned another 29.5 per cent of the country. These great or large landowners totalled only 4,217 persons: yet they controlled over half the territory of England. 9,585 larger yeoman owned 12.5 per cent; and 217,049 small proprietors had 12 per cent. At the bottom of the landownership scale 703,289 cottagers each possessed less than one acre.

Ownership of a large estate brought with it high social status, much higher than success in commerce or manufacture. The *Economist* (16.7.1870) remarked that it would 'pay' a millionaire in England to sink half his fortune in land, even though the profit return would be small, rather than to live upon his whole wealth without land: 'he would be a greater person in the eyes of more people'. The biggest peer-landowners, such as the Dukes of Northumberland, Devonshire, or Buccleugh, owned hundreds of thousands of acres and drew six-figure annual incomes, though admittedly a decreasing amount came from the profits of agricultural ownership. Landowning aristocrats and gentry formed the dominant element in English high 'Society', both in the counties and during the London 'season'. Not all members of a landed family resided under the roof of the family 'seat'; but all lived under the protection of the estate and its income. *The Times* (4.2.1864) explained how the eldest son inherited the estate and family title (if any); how each younger son went into the army (much more probably than the navy), the law, the civil service, the Church of England, 'or for some trade in which he may speculate all the more boldly because his family will rescue him if it be possible'. Daughters usually hoped to marry into other landed families of at least equal rank. Sometimes, however, both sons and daughters married – from necessity or from choice – into moneyed 'new' families. There were families in every locality with recently-bought estates and with aspirations of gaining acceptance by the old landed elite.

The *Cornhill Magazine* for March 1873 claimed that the three rural orders of landed proprietor, farmer, and peasant were joined together by 'bonds of ancient kindness and traditional loyalty . . . which none but a very blind utilitarian, or a very fanatical democrat, could wish to snap asunder'. Such represented the ideal view of rural relationships. Harsh pressures, personal and legal, were sometimes employed to sustain this hierarchical system. But, on the whole, the leadership of landlords was welcomed by tenant farmers, and the leadership of farmers was at least accepted by labourers. Outbreaks of organized discontent during the 1870s, first among the labourers and later among the tenant farmers, were the more striking for being exceptional. Many landlords were motivated by a sense of service to the rural community. They invested in estate improvements which, judged by commercial standards, could not pay but which benefited their tenants. They often served as magistrates at quarter sessions, where until the creation of the county councils in the late 1880s they dealt not only with crime and punishment but with many aspects of local government. And at the village level local farmers served as overseers of the poor, churchwardens, or surveyors of the roads.

Over 60 per cent of all farms covered less than 100 acres. Larger farms were most frequently found in the cereal-growing counties of the east and south-east. The 'incentive income' of farmers – their return for management, initiative, and risk – has been estimated to have doubled between the early 1850s and the early 1870s.[23] The *Cornhill Magazine* for February 1873 noted how this prosperity had narrowed the gap between farmers and squires, but had widened that between farmers and their labourers. Old-style farmers had eaten plainly in their kitchens; but now they were said to dine upon rich food, wear fashionable clothes, and drive smart dog-carts.

The condition of the agricultural labourers and their families varied from place to place, season to season, and year to year.[24] Day labourers could earn well at harvest time; but during the rest of the year the advantage lay with regular 'farm servants' who enjoyed security, regular weekly wages, and often cottages. Carters, cattlemen, and shepherds constituted a specialist elite among these annually-hired workers. But many countrymen perforce varied their jobs according to season or demand. Workmen of all grades in East Anglia and in the southern counties had to accept a lower standard of living than among the agricultural workers of the livestock-farming north. During the 1850s and 1860s, though, there had been some improvement in all wages as emigration and townward migration drew off surplus labour. The total of day labourers and farm servants enumerated in England and Wales reached a peak of 1,241,000 at the 1851 census; by the 1871 census this number had dropped to 957,000. Over this same period average money wages rose about one-third:[25]

Weekly cash wages of English agricultural labourers							
	Northern Counties *s. d.*	East Midlands *s. d.*	West Midlands *s. d.*	South-West *s. d.*	South-East Midlands *s. d.*	South and South-East *s. d.*	East Anglia *s. d.*	Average *s. d.*
1850–1	12 2	10 1	8 4	7 9	8 8	9 1	7 10	9 7
1860–1	12 3	12 6	10 4	9 7	10 7	11 10	11 1	11 7
1867–71	15 1	13 4	11 4	10 6	11 7	11 8	11 0	12 5

These figures take no account of additional family earnings of wives or children, nor of unavoidable periods of unemployment. Nor do they allow for payments in kind, which in some districts added considerably to money wages, nor for the value of food grown on labourers' allotments. Finally, they do not set a value upon residence in tied cottages.

The standard of housing for English agricultural workers was another widely varying feature of rural life. Cottages in 'closed' villages, where building had usually been supervised by the local landowner, were usually of good or adequate quality; but such homes were often restricted to a few key estate workers. In some closed villages cottages had even been pulled down for fear of creating settlements for ordinary labourers under the Poor Law. The Union Chargeability Act of 1865 countered this by giving labourers rights of relief through residence within the wide area of their Poor Law unions rather than merely within their native parishes. But long before 1865 'open' villages had grown up for the overflow of population from closed villages, and to meet the general increase in rural numbers. Unfortunately, cottages in such places were often much inferior to the model cottages of the closed villages – built too cheaply, lacking adequate sanitation, and too small for large families. Yet such properties found willing tenants because of a widespread housing shortage.

Young men did not willingly leave good homes, as one Norfolk rector explained in the *Nineteenth Century* for August 1881. 'They *do* run away from the odious thought of living and dying in a squalid hovel with a clay floor and two dark cabins under the rafters.' Migration never reached the point (as some alarmists began to claim) where the countryside was becoming generally 'depopulated'; but the movement away was noticeable and persistent. The 957,000 labourers and farm servants counted at the 1871 census, already a fall of more than one-fifth since 1851, had dropped further to 848,000 by 1881. Countrymen moved to the towns or overseas for two sets of reasons. On the one hand were the bad conditions, limited opportunities, and the dullness of country life: on the other were what seemed to be better-paid jobs, shorter hours, and the greater excitement of life in expanding towns at home or in new countries abroad.

Agricultural labourers were characterized as slow-witted. Certainly, they were often under-educated. Rural elementary schools were numerous by mid-century, usually run by the Church of England; but labourers' sons were commonly taken away to work by the age of eight. Yet the slowness of mind and speech of some labourers was probably only a result of their conditions of work. Moreover, there were always younger labourers with enough spirit to make a new start. Unfortunately, those with the greatest need to leave the land were the nearest to demoralization – workers in the lowest-wage counties, such as Dorset and Devon. To encourage migration from such areas Canon Edward Girdlestone, vicar of Halberton in north Devon, promoted a private but widely-publicized scheme of assisted migration between 1866 and 1872. Some 500 labourers were involved, many with families. Some went to town jobs, but most to higher-wage rural areas, especially in the north of England. Some were so ignorant of geography that they asked if they were being taken 'over the water'.[26]

These simple people were obviously descendants of the feudal peasantry of the middle ages. As late as 1891 the Liberal *Daily News* found it necessary to attack the economic, social, and political control exercised over the Berkshire village of Lockinge by Lord Wantage. The estate was well run; there were two churches and an excellent village school. It was 'a little self-contained world in which nobody is idle, nobody is in absolute want'. But such feudalism, concluded the *Daily News*, was now unacceptable. 'Materially, the result on the face of it is delightful . . . But for all the purposes of political life and social progress and human development it is utterly bad.'[27]

5

Total social domination of this kind was becoming rare by the 1890s. There had been signs of change in countrymen's attitudes and expectations since mid-century. In May 1870 the *Cornhill Magazine* complained of the substitution of London clothes and music-hall songs for traditional country dress and tunes. Thirteen years later Thomas Hardy, the novelist, agreed that a Dorsetshire gathering was now 'as dark as a London crowd', with the labourers and their wives dressed (as were the urban poor) in the cast-offs of the upper and middle classes. Yet Hardy believed that changes for the good outweighed those for the bad. Labourers were now better-paid and freer in their lives than a generation earlier. He showed in his novels that he shared no illusions about the harshness of life in the old 'Wessex'. The rural artisans lovingly portrayed in *Under the Greenwood Tree* (1872), millers, blacksmiths, carpenters, and the like, had enjoyed a measure of independence and prosperity; but he described in *Far From the Madding Crowd* (1874) and elsewhere how the lot of ordinary Dorset labourers had been depressed and subservient. Hardy was glad that labourers could now more easily change farms, or even leave the district rather than accept exploitation. The result, he believed, had been a more balanced relationship between masters and men.[28]

This new position had been won, continued Hardy, thanks in significant part to the efforts from the early 1870s of Joseph Arch, the pioneer agricultural trade unionist. Arch had raised wages at least temporarily, and had raised expectations permanently. The agricultural labourers had long lagged far behind the town workers in organizing trade unions. The famous affair of the 'Tolpuddle martyrs' in 1834 had been only a passing special case. Traditionally, the agricultural labourers had preferred rioting and rick-burning to continuous organization and pressure. But at last in the early 1870s they proved able to sustain a widespread trade union movement.[29]

Behind this new union activity lay the general prosperity of agriculture during the 1850s and 1860s. The improvements in wages and conditions during these years encouraged the desire for further and more rapid advance. Old-style rioting had been a product of ignorance and desperation: new-style unionism was the product of awareness and hope. Cheap newspapers, railways, the penny post were now available both to stimulate rural opinion and to assist the organizing efforts of union leaders. The wide dispersion of rural workers no longer prevented combination, even though it continued to make unions more difficult to maintain in the countryside than in the towns. The example of the nine-hour movement also helped to rouse rural unionists (see below, p. 185). Conversely, the 'Revolt of the Field' (as it became known) attracted widespread urban interest because of its novelty and its scale. Many industrial trade unions gave both moral and financial support, as did radical Members of Parliament and sympathetic clergymen headed by Archbishop Manning, the Roman Catholic leader.

Small-scale and short-lived attempts at trade union organization were being made in Kent as early as 1866. Other efforts followed during the next few years in Leicestershire, Buckinghamshire, Lincolnshire, and

Norfolk. Then on 7 February 1872 Joseph Arch suddenly sprang to the fore at a meeting in the Warwickshire village of Wellesbourne. He quickly rallied the local labourers to demand a weekly wage of 16*s* instead of their current 12*s*. Within a few weeks his campaign had spread from these tiny beginnings to a wide extent of rural England. Arch was a persuasive speaker and organizer; but the speed of this upsurge showed that he was appealing to feelings which were already formed and only waiting to be given expression. Arch's union demanded a 'living wage' at all times, not one fixed by demand and supply: 'if demand and supply regulate the price of labour, if because a few men are out of work a farmer takes advantage of this and screws down the labourers' wages, I maintain it is not just to do so'. The new unionists were also interested in promoting overseas emigration and migration to the towns – as ways of increasing the security of those left on the land. Arch impressed his hearers (including Thomas Hardy) with his mixture of firmness and restraint. He made no impossible demands, and he gave no encouragement to violence. His motto was 'United to protect, but not combined to injure.' He was a Wesleyan lay preacher, and many other rural union leaders were also active in the democracy of the Nonconformist chapels. As a result, the movement developed a strong moral and political side – with much emphasis upon education and temperance, upon the granting of the vote to agricultural labourers, and upon the need for land reform. Few union leaders were themselves ordinary labourers. Arch, for example, possessed a wide range of country skills.

His National Agricultural Labourers' Union was formed at the end of May 1872. It brought together various local unions, mainly from low-wage counties south of the Trent. By its peak in 1874 it was said to have over 86,000 members. This was a remarkable total to achieve among previously non-unionized workers dispersed over hundreds of villages. Nevertheless, not all local combinations accepted Arch's lead. The Lincolnshire League, for example, wanted a minimum wage of 18*s*. per week, compared with Arch's demand for 16*s*., which had been framed with the lower wage levels of Warwickshire in mind. At the end of 1873 the Lincolnshire League joined a loose Federal Union, formed with the encouragement of the London Trades Council.

Up to this date the 'Revolt of the Field' had made considerable gains for the agricultural labourers. The market for labour was strong, and local strikes quickly forced up wages. The example of one area stimulated pressure and concession in another, sometimes without a strike. By 1874, however, the unions were running into stiffer resistance from the farmers, partly on grounds of principle and partly because farmers had begun to find themselves able to manage with fewer workers if they used machinery or less intensive methods of cultivation. In many villages non-union workmen could still be hired, for in no county had the unions enrolled even half the total number of labourers. Union members could also be intimidated by evictions from tied cottages and by lock-outs. During 1874 a prolonged lock-out in East

Anglia was resisted both by Arch's National Union and by the Federal Union. This confrontation became a crucial trial of strength. £18,000 was subscribed by the town unions and by the general public, and as much as £29,000 was apparently spent on strike pay and upon the Promotion of migration from the affected areas. But by August 1874 all available funds were exhausted, and the farmers had won.

From 1875 the demand for labour was affected by bad harvests and by the slump in grain prices. By the early 1880s the National Union was reduced to 15,000 members; and Arch was turning increasingly to political agitation. The wage gains of the early 1870s had often been quickly lost; but the trade union upsurge had at least proved that the rural labourers possessed minds of their own. This was an important demonstration. Liberal politicians had previously feared that, if rural workers were given the suffrage, they would simply vote as told by Conservative squires and parsons. At last in 1884 many rural householders were enfranchized; and at the 1885 general election Arch himself became Member of Parliament for North-West Norfolk.

Notes

1. N. L. Tranter, *Population since the Industrial Revolution* (1973), p. 53.
2. G. U. Yule, 'On the Changes in the Marriage- and Birth-Rates in England and Wales during the Past Half Century', *Journal of the Royal Statistical Society*, LXIX (1906), pp. 90–1.
3. D. V. Glass, *Numbering the People* (1973), p. 192.
4. See B. Thomas, *Migration and Economic Growth: A Study of Great Britain and the Atlantic Economy* (2nd edn., 1973), esp. Ch. V.
5. See A. K. Cairncross, *Home and Foreign Investment, 1870–1913* (1953), Ch. IV; and R. Lawton, 'Population Changes in England and Wales in the Later Nineteenth Century', *Transactions of the Institute of British Geographers*, Vol. 44 (1968).
6. Phyllis Deane and W. A. Cole, *British Economic Growth, 1688–1959* (2nd edn., 1967), p. 10.
7. See H. A. Shannon, 'Migration and the Growth of London, 1841–91', *Economic History Review*, V (1934).
8. W. A. Armstrong, 'An Industrial Classification, 1841–1891', in E. A. Wrigley (ed.), *Nineteenth-Century Society* (1972), Ch. 6, part 2.
9. See H. A. Shannon, 'The Coming of General Limited Liability' and 'The Limited Companies of 1866–1883', in Eleanora M. Carus-Wilson (ed.), *Essays in Economic History*, I (1954). Also J. H. Clapham, *Economic History of Modern Britain*, II (1932), pp. 114–19, 137–43.
10. See R. A. Church, *The Great Victorian Boom, 1850–1873* (1975), and references there.
11. *The Times*, 25.7.1872.
12. P. Mathias *The First Industrial Nation* (1969), p. 468.
13. Ibid., p. 467.
14. See J. Caird, *The Landed Interest and the Supply of Food* (4th edn., 1880; reprinted 1967), esp. Ch. I.
15. Phyllis Deane and W. A. Cole, *British Economic Growth, 1688–1959* (2nd edn, 1967), p. 36.

16. See A. R. Hall (ed.), *The Export of Capital from Britain, 1870–1914* (1968); and P. L. Cottrell, *British Overseas Investment in the Nineteenth Century* (1975).
17. D. Reed, *Cobden and Bright* (1967), pp. 12–14, 229.
18. See E. L. Jones, *The Development of English Agriculture, 1815–1873* (1968), and references there.
19. Phyllis Deane and W. A. Cole, *British Economic Growth, 1688–1959* (2nd edn, 1967), p. 166.
20. J. Caird, *The Landed Interest and the Supply of Food* (4th edn, 1880: reprinted 1967), pp. 15–17, 28–9; R. Samuel (ed.), *Village Life and Labour* (1975), pp. 18–19, 61–6.
21. R. Lawton, 'Rural Depopulation in Nineteenth Century England', in D. R. Mills (ed.), *English Rural Communities* (1973), p. 195. See also J. Saville, *Rural Depopulation in England and Wales, 1851–1951* (1957).
22. See especially F. M. L. Thompson, *English Landed Society in the Nineteenth Century* (1963).
23. J. R. Bellerby, 'National and Agricultural Income 1851', *Economic Journal*, LXIX (1959), p. 103.
24. See especially G. E. Mingay, 'The Transformation of Agriculture', in R. M. Hartwell (ed.), *The Long Debate on Poverty* (1974); and R. Samuel (ed.), *Village Life and Labour* (1975).
25. R. M. Hartwell (ed.), *The Long Debate on Poverty* (1974), p. 44.
26. F. G. Heath, *The English Peasantry* (1874), Ch. V.
27. M. A. Havinden, *Estate Villages* (1966), pp. 113–18.
28. T. Hardy, 'The Dorsetshire Labourer', *Longman's Magazine*, July 1883, in H. Orel (ed.), *Thomas Hardy's Personal Writings* (1967). See also P. Bull, 'Thomas Hardy and Social Change', *Southern Review*, III (1969).
29. See J. Arch, *The Story of His Life* (1898); Pamela Horn, *Joseph Arch* (1971); and J. P. D. Dunbabin (ed.), *Rural Discontent in Nineteenth-Century Britain* (1974).

Chapter 3

Social life: *'Every man has somebody beneath him'*

1

'It matters not at what class you begin, or however low in the social scale, you will find that every man has somebody beneath him.' So wrote Samuel Smiles, the best-selling mid-Victorian social commentator, in his book on *Thrift* (1875). The Victorians and Edwardians made no attempt at reticence about social and economic differences. Railway trains were divided into three classes of accommodation; church and chapel seating was often segregated into rented pews and free pews 'for the poor'; and public houses were divided into public and saloon bars.

'Class' had grown out of the Industrial Revolution.[1] Landed society had been based upon 'rank', 'degree', 'order'. These assumed the existence of a God-given hierarchy; but one in which a 'chain of connection' ran through society, thereby allowing the fulfilment of obligations both upwards and downwards. Industrial society, by contrast, began to separate individuals instead of linking them. 'Men and women even of moderate means in our large towns lead a life altogether apart from the poor. How many of them ever speak to a working man or woman except in the way of business? . . . What does the large manufacturer know of the vast majority of his hands outside of the factory?' So asked William Rathbone, a leading Liverpool merchant and philanthropist, in *Macmillan's Magazine* for May 1867. Henry Maine in his book on *Ancient Law* (1861) had welcomed – in an immediately famous phrase – the movement 'from Status to Contract' as the foundation of modern social and legal relationships. Maine believed that 'progressive societies' could not have arisen without this shift.

During the early years of the nineteenth century men of business had begun to think and to speak of themselves as 'the middle classes', and then sometimes as 'the middle class'; and those whom they employed in more or less manual work began to be described, and then began to describe themselves, as 'the working classes' or 'the working class'.[2] These new social groupings soon began to develop separate political outlets. Their separation in politics was most strikingly expressed in the contemporaneous but almost rival Chartist and Anti-Corn Law League movements of the 1840s. The middle-class Leaguers sought free trade: the Chartists asserted that working men most of all needed the vote. Even so, only a minority of Chartists were motivated by ideas of social levelling, and only a handful were ready to use violence to gain their ends. A French Revolution never came near to eruption in England during the 1830s and 1840s, despite the clamour of agitation. Alexis de Tocqueville, the brilliant French political scientist, concluded that, unlike the French, the English were not offended by the existence of social superiors. 'This effect – has it not come about because the Englishman, unlike the Frenchman, is accustomed to the idea that he can rise in the social scale?'[3]

The possibility of rising within nineteenth-century English society was often remarked upon. It was praised as a safety-valve, which allowed individuals of ability and enterprise to make their way rather than to remain without hope. Queen Victoria was fond of pointing out how she had known two archbishops, one the son of a butcher and the other the son of a grocer. Yet such marked upward social mobility remained only a remote possibility. Indeed, the opportunities for workmen to become owners or managers of large firms were probably declining during the late-Victorian years as industry grew more settled. In 1871 only 16 per cent of leaders of the hosiery industry and 4 per cent of leaders of the steel industry were the sons of manual workers, and even these low proportions had further declined by the end of the century. Joint-stock companies, which were becoming numerous, were more likely to give promotion to already middle-class office workers than to manual workers from the factory floor.[4] But was movement to a higher social class necessarily a desirable objective? Not every Victorian accepted that it was. Thomas Wright, who wrote under the pseudonym of 'the journeyman engineer', argued more than once that it ought to be the aim of intelligent and active workmen to raise the level of their class rather than 'to improve themselves *out* of the working classes'. John Morley, the Liberal intellectual and politician, agreed in 1876 that it was 'of questionable expediency to invite the cleverest members of any class to leave it – instead of making their abilities available in it'. Such questioning of the whole idea of a social (and educational) 'ladder' was to become increasingly strong among late-Victorian and Edwardian socialists and radicals.[5]

But the majority of Victorians and Edwardians did not aspire to rise. They were content to accept their social status as they found it. One American visitor of the 1860s complained that if a shopkeeper were conducting the same business in the same place as his grandfather he announced the fact 'as a matter of congratulation, not seeing that, with his superior advantages, he ought to feel it a disgrace that he has advanced no farther'.[6] The expression 'I know my place and I keep it' was commonly heard. 'Deference', to use Walter Bagehot's word in his famous book on *The English Constitution* (1867), worked as a powerful social and political sedative. It led those of lower rank to accept the leadership of those above them, especially when the latter possessed titles or land or (best of all) both. 'It is well', concluded Anthony Trollope in *The Claverings* (1867), 'that some respect should be maintained from the low in station towards those who are high, even when no respect has been deserved.'

The Tichborne case of the early 1870s illustrated not only how Englishmen were prepared to love a title, but also how much they valued the right of a poor man to inherit one.[7] Arthur Orton, a butcher's son from Wapping, pretended to be Roger Tichborne, who had been presumed drowned off South America in 1854. When Orton claimed to be the rightful possessor of the Tichborne estates and baronetcy, the Dowager Lady Tichborne – who disliked the Tichborne family – accepted him as her son. Two long and celebrated trials in the High Court between 1871 and 1874 made popular heroes of 'The Claimant' – whose grossly rotund figure added to his fascination – and of Dr Kenealy, his turbulent counsel. The *Annual Register* for 1871 recorded how the country became divided between believers and unbelievers, and how 'The Case' was the first topic at every dinner-table. By the time of Orton's 188-day trial for perjury (1873–4) the fraudulent nature of his assertions had become clear to many; but his humbler supporters still insisted upon believing that he was a poor man excluded from his birthright by a papistical conspiracy. As *The Times* remarked in its annual summary for 1875, 'the uneducated multitude' had ended by demanding 'with an explicable confusion of thought, that justice should be done to one of the commonalty who by the very assumption was admitted to be an imposter'. Orton served ten years in prison for perjury, but popular interest was slow to subside. At a Stoke-on-Trent by-election in 1875 Kenealy, standing as an independent, easily defeated both Liberal and Conservative opponents.

2

Dudley Baxter's book on *National Income* (1868) provided the first satisfactory statistical analysis of Victorian society. He compared its shape to that of the Atlantic island of Teneriffe, 'with its long low base of labouring population, with its uplands of the middle classes, and with its towering peaks and summits of those with princely incomes'. Baxter estimated the total number of the upper and middle classes in England and Wales at 4,870,000, and the 'manual labour class' at 16,130,000. His definition of the middle class was actually too wide, since it included (for example) all foremen and supervisory workers and their families. Yet even with this misplacement, his figures set the upper and middle classes at no more than one-fifth to one-quarter of the total population.

The gap in money and real incomes between some of the middle and the working classes was also tending to widen. According to one calculation, average business profits taxed under schedule D of the income tax rose by as much as 60 per cent between 1850 and 1880; whereas money wages grew by only some 47 per cent (or 39 per cent allowing for unemployment).[8] Baxter estimated that the upper and middle classes included 2,053,000 income-earners. 7,500 of these enjoyed 'large incomes' over £5,000 per annum; another 42,000 had £1,000 to £4,999; 150,000 possessed 'middle incomes' of £999 down to £300; while 850,000 had 'small incomes' of £100 to £299. About another 1 million, though middle-class, fell below the income-tax threshold of £100.

Baxter's totals were only approximations; but clearly a great contrast of incomes existed within the middle class. Significantly, the terms 'upper middle class' and 'lower middle class' came into use – the latter about mid-century, the former a little later. The lower middle class could be taken as including all those whose incomes did not exceed about £300 per year but who shared pretensions to 'respectability'. These included shopkeepers and small businessmen, plus those 'white collar' workers whose numbers grew rapidly during the second half of the century as the structure of Victorian society became more complicated. School-teachers, clerks, and shop assistants formed the largest 'white collar' groups:[9]

	Schoolteachers		Clerks	
	Men	Women	Men	Women
1871	32,901	94,029	129,271	1,446
1881	46,074	122,846	229,705	6,420

Although the census returns did not provide separate totals of shop assistants, by the end of the century they had visibly become the biggest single category of middle-class women workers.

Clerks separated into two income-groups. Higher-grade men clerks, chiefly found in banking, insurance, the civil service, and large firms, could earn £200 a year. This was sufficient to maintain a modest middle-class way of life without strain, including the employment of one general servant. Few clerks could hope to rise beyond this level to become employers on their own account. Many remained as lower-grade clerks, always struggling to live upon £100 a year or less. With the growth of large-scale business, division of labour was spreading through shops and offices so that most clerks and shop assistants found themselves employed in only routine tasks. Even so, the spread of education was increasing the supply of clerks faster than the demand was growing. Bright boys from aspiring artisan families, and girls too by the end of the century, competed eagerly for office jobs, because this was one way into the middle classes. Or they might make the transition even more precariously by becoming shop assistants. These were not always accepted as belonging to the middle class at all; but they were addressed at work as 'Mr' or 'Miss', not (like domestic servants or factory hands) merely by their surnames.

'Bow, bow, ye lower middle class! Bow, bow, ye tradesmen, bow, ye masses.' So ran the social rollcall in Gilbert and Sullivan's *Iolanthe* (1882). Two figures in fiction, Mr Pooter, the pretentious yet engaging head clerk of *The Diary of a Nobody* (1892) by George and Weedon Grossmith; and Kipps, the shop assistant hero of the H. G. Wells novel (1905), belonged to this social area. As Wells indicated, the very long hours and low wages of shop workers made theirs virtually a sweated trade; but this was tolerated in the name of 'respectability'. An article on 'The Teacher Problem' in the *Fortnightly Review* for May 1899 described an elementary schoolteacher as 'a small middle-class person – knowing hardly anything well, parochial in sympathies, vulgar in accent and style of his talking, with a low standard of manners'; but 'withal extremely respectable, correct morally, with a high sense of duty, as he understands it'. All the middle class was busy 'keeping up appearances', but especially the lower middle classes – who were fearful of the working class just below, from which many of them had risen and down into which all feared they might fall. Leonard Bast in E. M. Forster's *Howards End* (1910) lived 'at the extreme verge of gentility'; he was 'not in the abyss, but he could see it, and at times people whom he knew had dropped in, and counted no more'.

Marriage, followed by the birth of children, could push a man closer to this social abyss. B. G. Orchard's book on *The Clerks of Liverpool* (1871) discussed the wisdom of marrying on £80 per annum, the salary of the lowest-paid clerks. Orchard printed budgets which showed conflictingly how it was possible and impossible to marry wisely on £80 a year, or even on £150. Some artisans earned as much or more than £80 a year. To be middle-class – or to aspire to be middle-class – was not entirely a matter of income. A *Spectator* article (30.11.1872) on 'The Numbers of the Comfortable' calculated that only 60,000 families in Great Britain could be called 'comfortable' – they could afford to buy *The Times*, price 3*d.*, without feeling extravagant. But a further 650,000 families (out of 4,600,000 altogether) were 'respectable' even though they were 'always struggling to make ends meet'. Such people followed a middle-class way of life. 'A clerk lives an entirely different life from an artisan – marries a different kind of wife – has different ideas, different possibilities, and different limitations.' So explained Charles Booth in his late-Victorian social survey of London. It was not only a question 'of the wearing or not wearing of a white shirt every day, but of differences which invade every department of life'. More was expected socially from a clerk than an artisan; 'but the clerk's money goes further and is on the whole much better spent'.

Acceptance as a 'gentleman' or 'lady' depended upon an elusive combination of income, occupation, and personal characteristics. Mr Salteena, the hero of nine-year-old Daisy Ashford's revealingly ingenuous *The Young Visiters* (sic), written in the 1890s, was the son of a butcher and lacked social polish. He admitted that he was (in a much used expression) 'not quite a gentleman', even though 'you would hardly notice it'. Alfred Marshall, the economist, tried in 1873 to establish the connection between occupation and class. 'If a man's daily task tends to give culture and refinement to his character, do we not, however coarse the individual man may happen to be, say that his occupation is that of a gentleman? If a man's daily task tends to keep his character rude and coarse, do we not, however truly refined the individual man may happen to be, say that he belongs to the working classes?'[10] The extent to which personal qualities, apart from occupation or income, could qualify an individual as a 'gentleman' much exercised the Victorians. An article in the *Cornhill Magazine* for March 1862 by Fitzjames Stephen, a leading lawyer, entitled simply 'Gentlemen', argued that the basic test was how much an individual contributed to 'social pleasantness'. But many Victorians assumed that such pleasantness required the backing of a minimum of income to finance an education and a way of life which would encourage the social graces. The problem for the lower middle classes was how to earn that minimum.

For the more solid middle classes, too, social status made financial demands.[11] The expected standard of living was rising fast. J. H. Walsh's *Manual of Domestic Economy; suited to Families spending from £100 to £1,000 a Year* had first appeared in 1857. When a new edition was published in 1873 Walsh raised the income levels for all his four middle-class categories – from £100 to £150, from £250 to £350, from £500 to £750, and from £1,000 to £1,500. Middle-class outlay on food, drink, domestic service, and household goods seems to have increased over these years by about one-half. W. R. Greg's *Contemporary Review* article of March 1875 on 'Life at High Pressure' complained how the style of living had become exaggerated. Mrs Beeton's famous *Book of Household Management* had first appeared in 1861, price 7s. 6d; and it had sold nearly 200,000 copies by 1868. The quantity of food offered at middle-class tables, under Mrs Beeton's guidance, was generous; its range less so. Her menus were abundant in meat, fish, and solid foods, deficient in fresh fruit, vegetables, and salads. Condensed versions of her book were soon published for every level of the middle class, as well as Beeton cookery booklets at 6d. and 1d. for the working classes.

Booth's *Life and Labour of the People in London* and Seebohm Rowntree's pioneering social survey of York (1901) both accepted employment of at least one domestic servant as a sure sign of middle-class status.[12] The greater the number of servants kept the higher the standing of the family within the middle class. Between the censuses of 1851 and 1871 the total of indoor female servants in England and Wales grew twice as fast as the population as a whole – from just over 750,000 to just over 1,200,000. Within these aggregates general servants increased from about 575,000 to 780,000; but in proportionate terms the biggest expansion was in the numbers of more specialised staff employed in larger households – housekeepers, cooks, nursemaids, and (among menservants) grooms and coachmen. Domestic service provided much the largest single occupation for women. In 1881 one female in nine, and one girl in three aged 15–20, was an indoor domestic:

Indoor domestic servants

1871		1881		1901		1911	
Male	Female	Male	Female	Male	Female	Male	Female
68,300	1,204,500	56,300	1,230,400	47,900	1,285,100	42,000	1,296,000

Country houses, run by large domestic staffs, were at their most flourishing about 1870, just before the onset of agricultural depression. But most female servants worked in urban middle-class households with only a few staff, and most families employed only one servant. The 1861 first edition of Mrs Beeton's *Household Management* suggested that an income of £1,000 a year could support a cook, upper housemaid, nursemaid, and under housemaid, plus a male servant; £750 a year justified employment of a cook, housemaid, nursemaid, and footboy; £500 a cook, housemaid, and nursemaid; £300 a maid-of-all-work, and nursemaid; and £200 a year a maid-of-all-work, plus 'a girl occasionally'. The servant population varied in density from one urban locality to another. The upper middle-class suburb of Hampstead led the way in 1911 with 737 servants per 1,000 population.

The wage costs of domestic service constituted a major charge upon the national economy, yearly adding 10–11 per cent to the national wage bill between 1851 and 1911. The wages of individual servants varied widely from household to household, grade to grade, and place to place. In the 1860s Mrs Beeton suggested that a maid-of-all work would earn £9–14 per year, a cook up to about £30. To these figures must be added the value of free board and lodging. Servants' sleeping quarters might be cramped or damp; but most servants were immigrants from the countryside, probably well used to poor living conditions. In 1871 a half to three-quarters of domestic servants had been born in the countryside.

The routine of domestic service was physically demanding, most severely so in single-servant households where the (aptly named) maid-of-all-work was expected to labour from early morning to late evening. Victorian middle-class houses were not designed for easy running. Their vertical plan meant that servants spent much time and energy climbing stairs. Family and servants perforce lived closely together, a proximity made tolerable for the middle classes only by the enforcement of strict rules of servant conduct and routine. Turnover of staff was rapid. One survey of the 1890s showed that, though a minority of servants fitted the stereotype of the long-standing family retainer, the majority stayed less than two years in each employment.[13]

3

At the top of the Victorian class hierarchy stood 'Society'.[14] Aristocratic and wealthy families participated in a more or less fixed round of entertainment which came to a summer climax with the London 'season'. These families owned country houses in different counties, but they acted together (in the expression of the time) as 'the upper ten thousand'. Members of the estimated 4,000 families 'in Society' at the end of the nineteenth century were often connected by relationship or by association at public school or at Oxford or Cambridge. Indeed, into the 1860s 'Society' remained sufficiently small and exclusive for it to be almost literally true that 'everyone who was anyone' knew everyone else. The social round was dominated by the mistresses of a few great political and territorial mansions in the capital and in the country. After the death of Lord Palmerston in 1865, however, the great political salons of Lady Palmerston, Lady Molesworth, and Lady Waldegrave soon lost their sway. Political life was becoming more 'democratic' at the same time as more trivial interests were beginning to flourish within 'the best circles'. The 'best' circle of all was the Prince of Wales's Marlborough House set, which was devoted to boisterous good living, practical joking, and sexual exchanges. Queen Victoria lived in semi-retirement; but the ceremony of presentation at court remained an essential ritual for every debutante.

Beatrice Webb remembered the heavy demands made upon mental and physical energy by the social round: 'the presentation at Court, the riding in the Row, the lunches and dinners, the dances and crushes, Hurlingham and Ascot, not to mention amateur theatricals and other sham philanthropic excrescences'. For young girls the purpose was to find a husband, a search carried out by mothers 'sometimes with genteel surreptitiousness, sometimes with cynical effrontery'.[15] Beatrice Webb survived to become a socialist. She suggested that the test of fitness for membership of 'Society' was possession of some form of power over others. A title could give this, but so also could command of great wealth. And by her day 'plutocrats', millionaires and near-millionaires with fortunes made more or less reputably in business, on the stock exchange, or in the colonies, had gained entry into 'Society' in noticeable numbers. Mrs Webb recollected that South African gold and diamond millionaires possessed 'neither manners nor morals'. George du Maurier began in the 1870s to publish his *Punch* cartoons of Sir Gorgius Midas, a Jewish *nouveau riche* vulgarian. Anthony Trollope's novel *The Way We Live Now* (1875) deplored the extent to which 'commercial profligacy' had begun to compromise the standards of the old gentry and aristocracy. In 1879 Gladstone publicly complained of the new willingness of men of title to sell themselves in support of 'speculations which they neither understand nor examine'.[16] By 1896, 167 noblemen – over a quarter of the peerage – held company director-ships. And if the peerage was moving into business, so businessmen were moving into the peerage. Titles were given in these years to great bankers, brewers, ironmasters, armaments manufacturers, and others.

'Society' was thus broadening its intake, perhaps with some damage to its standards of behaviour and polish. But the glitter of the London 'season' from late-April to the end of July ('the party that lasted a hundred days') formed a fascinating part of the Victorian scene, fascinating not only to those who participated but also to the middle-class millions who read eagerly in the press about the doings of the fashionable. Every day during the season they paraded on horseback or in carriages down Rotten Row. Then at the end of July the Marlborough House ball brought the London round to an end. 'London is deserted; only some three million and a half people remain to await the coming of next season. All the houses round Regent's Park are shut up.'[17] 'Society' was on the move – first to the Cowes week of yachting in the Isle of Wight, then to the grouse moors of the north of England and Scotland, where shooting started on the 'glorious twelfth' of August. In later autumn country house parties gathered for partridge shooting or hunting. Guests might stay for a week or more; but the practice was also spreading of spending a 'weekend' (a new word of the 1870s) at country houses which had been built with large gardens but without an estate. In such houses the interest lay more in card-playing, in conversation more or less serious, and perhaps in love affairs more or less discreet than in traditional country pursuits.

The coming of the railways had made possible this round of country house visiting. The *Cornhill Magazine* suggested in December 1863 that to sustain country hospitality required an income of £10,000 a year. A country house could then become 'a little world complete'. In his autobiography A. J. Balfour, the Conservative prime minister, lovingly remembered 'weekending' at such houses as Stanway and Clouds. H. G. Wells was allowed to join Edwardian country house weekends because of his brilliance. There were just two unwritten rules, remembered Wells: no subsequent reporting of the free speech that was customary, and no attempts to profit later from the friendly contacts that were made. 'On these conditions, nobody felt on show, nobody posed.'[18]

A few members of the upper middle classes found their way into 'Society', and into country house circles. One such was H. H. Asquith, a successful barrister and the first prime minister not to own a landed estate. Upper middle-class families were more or less self-made, in the sense that their fortunes were usually based upon success in business or the professions. Among businessmen the rise of large public limited companies produced a new breed of managing directors, whose four-figure salaries put them into the upper middle class. At the same time, the old professions of the Anglican Church, the law, and medicine were expanding fast, and new professions were emerging – all to meet the increasingly sophisticated demands of Victorian life. The earnings of professional men could vary widely, from £5,000 a year or more for top barristers to very little for the unsuccessful. But an income round about £1,000 has been suggested as the average Victorian reward for moderate professional success.[19]

Measured by the census returns, seventeen professional occupations in England and Wales increased their membership more than two-and-a-half fold between 1841 and 1881 – from 125,000 to 317,000. This compared with only a two-thirds rise in total population. For example, numbers of dentists rose from 522 to 3,583, of civil engineers from 853 to 7,124, of architects from 1,486 to 6,898. Not all these totals were either complete for each profession, or strictly comparable between censuses; but the scale of overall growth was plain enough. Some professions, and branches of professions, were more prestigious than others. Barristers, for example, ranked socially higher than solicitors, and upper clergy were treated differently from lower clergy. This was defended by one contemporary on the ground that the lower professions appeared to depend upon a command of narrow expertise, whereas the work of a barrister or a bishop could make a general impact upon the public mind.[20] Moreover, solicitors received money directly from their clients, which was considered vulgar. Retail shopkeepers were especially looked down upon for this reason. No matter how large their establishments, they were 'in trade'. Doctors also charged their bills directly, and into the 1880s Queen Victoria followed the old custom of not making her new doctor, James Reid, a member of her 'household'. He was supposed to dine apart, until his geniality at table ('I hear Dr Reid has dinner parties!') caused a royal change of mind.[21]

Most professions became increasingly organized during the Victorian years, not only with the practical aim of raising standards but also with the social intention of achieving higher status. A royal charter was often eagerly desired as a mark of recognition; and beyond this an Act of Parliament, which conferred more or less monopolistic powers on qualified practitioners. The Royal College of Surgeons (1800) led the way in the quest for recognition, followed by the Law Society (1825), the British Medical Association (1832), the Royal Institute of British Architects (1834), the Institution of Mechanical Engineers (1847), and many more during the rest of the century. But new professions found it hard to gain full social acceptance. Engineering, despite its remarkable achievements, was long regarded as somehow only a development of the blacksmith's craft, almost a form of physical labour. The engineers reduced their own general acceptability by inventing snobberies between themselves – civil engineers, for example, looked down upon mechanical engineers. As late as 1891–2 architects were likewise squabbling with each other. Under the cry 'Architecture, A Profession or an Art', Norman Shaw and other architectural nonconformists led an attack upon the plans of the Royal Institute of British Architects to take control of the profession through a system of examination and registration. 'Give up all anxiety to have initials, many or few, after your name; devote yourself with all your power to the study of your art.' But despite this plea, architecture was now well on its way to becoming a typical 'respectable' middle-class profession.[22]

4

The working classes (estimated by Baxter in 1867 to total over

16 million people in England and Wales) were perhaps even more
elaborately graded than the middle classes above them. Baxter
calculated that 7,785,000 manual workers earned independent incomes;
but these workers were spread over a wide range of skilled and unskilled
jobs:

	Average weekly wage for men (s.)	Numbers (thousands)			
		Men	Women	Juveniles	Total
Most highly skilled	35	42	2	12	56
Highly skilled	28–30	799	38	230	1,067
Lower skilled A	25	582	93	201	876
Lower skilled B	21–23	1,030	988	925	2,943
Unskilled A	15–20	260	45	114	419
Agricultural and rural labour	14	1,149	127	401	1,676
Unskilled B	12	108	47	47	202
Unskilled C (all female)	12	—	447	97	545

Baxter's 'lower skilled B' category included over 1,200,000 adult and
juvenile domestic servants; and his table consequently tended to
exaggerate the proportion of skilled workers within the labour force.
Only about one in seven workers were 'highly skilled'; about one-third
were 'lower skilled'; and over half were either unskilled, or agricultural
labourers, or domestic servants. Baxter placed in the highly skilled
category men such as watch makers, printers, ship workers, building
workers – mostly in apprenticeship trades. Some of these trades had
hardly been affected by mechanization, and all of them required a high
degree of individual capacity and dexterity. Such artisans formed an
aristocracy of labour, especially noticeable in London. 'Between the
artisan and the unskilled labourer a gulf is fixed,' wrote Thomas Wright,
'the journeyman engineer'. 'Any clever or ambitious labourer who
shows a desire to get out of his place, by attempting to pick up or creep
into "the trade" to which he is attached as an unskilled assistant, is guilty
of deadly sin.'[23]

The artisans separated themselves from the rest of the working classes
not only by occupation and income but also by their expenditure
patterns, by their higher level of elementary education and literacy, by
their commitment to craft trade unionism, and often also by their
involvement in religious, social, or political movements. Mrs Josephine
Butler praised the artisans who supported her campaign against the
Contagious Diseases Acts. They were (she said) usually temperance
men, often members of chapels, secretaries of trades councils, and
presidents of working men's clubs. They could express their opinions
clearly in writing, and they took pains (she claimed) to get their evidence
first-hand by reading the relevant statutes and blue books.[24] Such
artisans could hope to lead comfortable lives, more or less secure in
employment, and protected by their union unemployment benefit if they

did lose work. They enjoyed some spare time, and they could earn incomes higher than those of some hard-pressed members of the lower middle classes. As one bookbinder explained, an artisan with a good trade and steady employment was 'better off than many curates', easier not only financially but also in his mind because he was 'not obliged to keep up an appearance'.[25]

United Kingdom money wages have been estimated to have increased 41 per cent between the early 1850s and the mid-1870s, and real wages 32 per cent.[26] But skilled workers gained more than their share of this improvement, and unskilled workers less. The wage levels of top artisans could reach double those of the unskilled. However, among both the skilled and unskilled, large wage differentials persisted between regions right up to 1914, even for identical work. Fitters' rates in central London, for example, reached twice those in Cornwall. London, the industrial north, and parts of the midlands (including Birmingham) were the areas where high wages were most likely to be paid. Employers in prosperous trades in these parts were always on the lookout for good labour rather than for cheap but inefficient labour.

London paid high wages, but it also paid low wages. It was a city of government, finance, and commerce, of clerks and shopkeepers, of small workshops and skilled artisans; but it was also a centre of expanding 'sweated' trades, such as the production of ready-made clothing, which employed immigrants and women who were prepared to accept very low rates. Not more than one-sixth of London's adult labour force worked in factories. Factory workers were more characteristic of provincial industrial districts, such as the textile belts of Lancashire and Yorkshire. In the absence of factory work to provide a social band of lower skilled operatives, contrasts of earnings and status between the artisans and most other working men remained very noticeable in London. Yet even among the unskilled a hierarchy of status operated. Ship workers in the London docks looked down upon shore workers, and permanent labourers despised casual labourers. English costers rejected Irish costers, and all unskilled workers felt entitled to dismiss the grimy chimney sweeps, 'treated with contumely by those who were but little better than themselves'.[27]

Nevertheless, workers below the artisan level constituted 'the poor'. They were not always destitute, but they lived in fear of destitution – through unemployment, illness, accident, or old age. They did not lack homes, but often they could afford to live only in slums or almost slums. Among the working classes only artisans stood much chance of passing all their lives above the poverty line. Even factory workers could be laid off in thousands at times of bad trade. Yet 'the poor' were not to be confused with 'the residuum' at the very bottom of society. This name was first applied by John Bright in the 1850s to the lowest social category of demoralized people in 'almost helpless poverty and dependence' – the only Victorians without 'somebody beneath' them.[28] The same people were later described by William Booth, founder of the

Salvation Army, in his book *In Darkest England* (1890) as 'the submerged tenth'. He estimated their number at about 3 million, roughly one-tenth of the population of England and Wales.

The Victorians rightly believed that the permanent existence of distress and demoralization encouraged disease and crime. They also feared that it might breed red revolution on the Continental model. Sir James Kay-Shuttleworth, the pioneer educationist, warned in 1866 of 'the dangerous classes who prey upon property, or sell their virtue, or are ready to take advantage of any tendency to tumult . . . the classes who stagnate, like the lees of society, in the obscure and unhealthy parts of great cities'.[29] Not all, indeed, lived obscurely. Every night from its opening in the 1860s the seats and arches of the Thames Embankment provided sleeping quarters for thousands of down-and-outs, as Doré illustrated in his *London* (1872).

The machinery of the Poor Law was designed not so much for this 'residuum' of people almost past help, as for those who needed support in sickness, unemployment, or old age but who were not demoralized:[30]

	Indoor paupers		Outdoor paupers		Total	
	Mean number	Percentage of population	Mean number	Percentage of population	Mean number	Percentage of population
1865	131,312	0.63	820,586	3.9	951,898	4.5
1870	156,800	0.71	876,000	3.9	1,032,800	4.6
1875	146,800	0.62	654,114	2.8	800,914	3.4
1880	180,817	0.71	627,213	2.5	808,030	3.2

These figures represented the mean of the numbers under relief in England and Wales on 1 January and on 1 July preceding. About twice as many received relief during the course of each year. The New Poor Law of 1834 had clearly not ended outdoor relief, as was its original intention. It had, however, made Poor Law administration more cost effective. Even so, the burden of London poor relief first exceeded £1 million in 1867, and £2 million in 1882; expenditure for England and Wales outside London passed £5 million in 1862, and £6 million in 1868.[31] The poor rate therefore constituted a major local tax. Paradoxically, it was most felt in poor districts, since these contained many ratepayers who were themselves of small means and yet who were living alongside large numbers of potential paupers. The Union Chargeability Act of 1865 placed the cost of poor relief upon the Poor Law unions as a whole and thereby removed inequalities of burden between rich and poor parishes within the same union. But great inequalities continued between unions.

The New Poor Law principle of 'less eligibility' had required that conditions for paupers within workhouses should always remain harsher than the worst conditions for those workers and their families who doggedly contrived to maintain themselves outside. But this grim standard was gradually modified, since it proved undesirable within 'mixed' workhouses to place the young, the sick, and the aged – the largest pauper categories – under the same strict disciplines as the able-bodied. By mid-century workhouse conditions were again as variable as under the unreformed Poor Law. Much depended upon the generosity and efficiency of local boards of guardians, and upon the capacity and humanity of workhouse masters and matrons.

The opening of special institutions outside the Poor Law, such as reformatories, led to an absolute fall during the 1870s in the number of paupers aged under 16. But in the absence of old-age pensions, aged paupers remained a continuing large group into the twentieth century:[32]

	Paupers under 16	Paupers, 60 plus	Per cent Paupers, 60 plus on Population, 60 plus
1861	322,612	322,612	21.6
1871	392,245	369,128	21.7
1881	271,937	291,867	15.2
1891	235,478	298,356	14.0
1901	208,941	333,616	13.8
1905	222,690	368,483	14.7

From the 1860s the sick poor began to receive improved medical attention.[33] The 1867 Metropolitan Poor Act allowed the establishment of new institutions for the care of the ill, infirm, and insane poor in London, and also for the creation of dispensaries to administer outdoor medical relief. By 1883 all but three of London's thirty Poor Law areas had opened infirmaries; and the provincial towns had begun to follow suit. A Local Government Board census of 1896 revealed that 58,550 sick paupers were under hospital treatment, 22,100 of them in separate infirmaries, the rest in sick wards of general workhouses. In 1885 the Medical Relief Disqualification Act removed the stigma of pauperism, with consequent loss of voting rights, from those who were receiving medical relief under the Poor Law.

The number of paupers did not nearly measure the full extent of Victorian poverty. Dudley Baxter emphasized how 'a large proportion' of the poor bore great hardships rather than apply for relief. 'They exhaust their savings; they try to the utmost their trade unions or benefit societies; they pawn little by little all their furniture; and at last are driven to ask for relief.' After waiting in crowds under humiliating publicity, the men were then set to work breaking stones, 'with 6d. a day, and a loaf per week of bread for each of their family. Sometimes, rather than accept the relief, they die of starvation.' Widespread unemployment in times of bad trade was accompanied by extensive under-employment within some occupations even in better times. About 10 per cent of the population of London (perhaps 400,000 people in the 1890s) consisted of casual workers in the docks and elsewhere, plus their families. London dock labourers, noted Baxter, earned a miserable 15*s*. per week in full work; but so overgrown were their numbers that in ordinary years they worked little more than half time.

5

Victorian working-class men and women were easily distinguishable from the classes above them by their physical appearance and by their clothes. Working-class families, living in crowded homes perhaps with only minimal water supplies, could not maintain middle-class standards of privacy and personal cleanliness. Unsuitable or inadequate food also left its pinching mark upon the faces of the poor from childhood. They had perforce to buy in very small amounts from local shopkeepers, which usually meant that they were paying higher prices than the middle classes, who could shop selectively and purchase in larger quantities. Food costs absorbed as much as three-quarters of working-class budgets. This was proportionately half as much again as the middle classes spent, and yet the standard of working-class diet remained widely unsatisfactory. About 1860 as many as one-quarter of the population may have been under-nourished, even at the low dietary standard of 3,000 calories per day.[34]

This low level of diet was frequently aggravated by bad household management and by lack of cooking skill among working-class women. T. H. Huxley, the scientist, remarked that poor Frenchwomen could make their housekeeping money go twice as far as poor English women, 'and at the same time turn out twice as palatable a dinner'. The nearness of agricultural labourers' wives to the food-growing process did not make many of them better cooks than their urban sisters. 'The soddened cabbage', complained Richard Jefferies, was the symbol of much cottage cookery.[35] The London school board introduced cookery teaching for girls from 1874, and subsequently lessons also in laundry work and housewifery. But the report of the Inter-Departmental Committee on Physical Deterioration in 1904 was still emphasizing the need for instruction in the proper selection and preparation of food. The committee also recommended that every dwelling let for family occupation should be required by law to include a cooking grate.

Into Edwardian times the English working classes were notorious for the bad state of their teeth. They were said to use neither toothbrushes nor handkerchiefs. The upper and middle classes took greater care of their teeth, and also of their speech. William Morris, the socialist, regretted in 1883 that most people were 'doomed by accident of their birth to misplace their aitches'; he heard two languages talked in England, 'gentleman's English and workman's English'.[36] Under the influence of public school education the upper and upper middle classes were eliminating their local speech. Three Victorian Prime Ministers – Peel, Lord Derby, and Gladstone – spoke with Lancashire accents; but they had all been educated long before the Arnoldian transformation of the public schools. Their sons and grandsons were taught a standard 'Oxford' English, which perhaps lacked vigour but which had the merits of clarity and smoothness, and which could be everywhere understood by all classes. Local working-class accents could be so strong, as well as so incorrect in grammar, as to be hardly intelligible to outsiders of any class. London cockney was perhaps the most unpolished speech of all. Yet cockney itself was changing. The confusion of *v* with *w* (as practised by Dickens's Sam Weller) disappeared soon after 1875, to be replaced by an insistence upon substituting *y* for *a*. The large numbers of immigrants moving into London from the countryside may have contributed to this speech change.[37] Bernard Shaw's Eliza Doolittle in *Pygmalion* (1912) had been anticipated in Richard Whiteing's novel *No. 5 John Street* (1899):

'Oh, I'm no good for a lidy, I ain't! Oh, why didn't yer ketch me when I was a kid?'
'... I can't speak proper. I can't be'ave proper ...'
'I ain't a-goin' to no Flower Gals' Mission – not me!'
'... You don't even 'old yer tongue same way as we do ...'
'... you'll git the 'ump, an' cuss the dye you tried to mike a lidy out of a fightin' flower-gal.'

By 1912 it was said to be getting difficult to tell from their appearance to what class people belonged – 'until they open their mouths'.[38] But fifty years earlier it had been easy to recognize a working man by his clothes. Hippolyte Taine's *Notes on England* found dress to be 'a badge of social rank'. Clothes worn by the working classes were often second (or more) hand. Mistresses passed on their dresses to servants, and these cast-offs might ultimately find their way to old clothes markets. Taine complained how the Derby day crowds wore 'tatterdemalion attire', in contrast to the peasants and labourers of France whose garb was always first-hand. But the wives and daughters of skilled workers in England did often make their own dresses; and the importation of the first cheap and efficient sewing-machines from the United States in the late 1860s encouraged more lower middle-class women to do the same. In Lewis's popular Manchester department store the velveteen section soon became its biggest.[39]

An article in the *Cornhill Magazine* for June 1873 on 'Our Civilisation' by Eliza Liston, a novelist, attacked the absurdities of contemporary upper and middle-class fashion, both for men and for women. Men wore stiff shirt collars 'which rasp their necks', and showed a wide expanse of shirt-front 'which the very act of fastening rumples'; and their coats ended in 'meaningless swallow tails'. Different sets of male clothing were needed for every occasion – at business, at home, in town, or in the country. But all varieties of men's attire lacked colour.[40] It was the role of Victorian women to provide colour in clothes; and the dresses of the 1860s and 1870s, making full use of the new aniline dyes, ventured upon especially vivid colour contrasts. To colour they often added elaboration, and sometimes exposure. 'Our highest efforts,' complained the *Cornhill* lady author, 'culminate in partial nakedness in the middle of winter if we are women, in black broad-cloth in the dog-days if we are men.' From the mid 1860s to the end of the century female dress sought to emphasize and even to create curves – crude intimations of sexuality. The crinoline, impractical but graceful, was replaced by the bustle, which persisted in various shapes through the 1870s and 1880s. Ladies seem to have been wearing drawers since about the start of Victoria's reign, and by the 1860s working-class women had begun to adopt them. All classes and both sexes wore hats at all times outdoors.

6

A queen reigned at the apex of Victorian society, but women in general remained second-class citizens.[41] Nevertheless, within working-class households wives and mothers were usually the key figures who maintained the minimum of comfort and routine essential for family life, even while living through an unending round of drudgery, pregnancy, and more or less ill-health. The vital part played by working-class wives did not save large numbers of them from violence at the hands of their husbands. Wife-beating constituted a major Victorian social problem. The Matrimonial Clauses Act of 1878 allowed badly-used wives to obtain legal separation, with maintenance paid by their husbands. The act was gradually strengthened, and between 1897 and 1906 magistrates' courts in England and Wales granted over 87,000 separation and maintenance orders.[42]

Domestic service provided much the largest field of female employment. But numerous women practised prostitution, part or full-time. Many prostitutes were indeed former servants, who had lost employment or been 'ruined', perhaps by a son of the house.[43] Counts of London prostitutes in the 1850s and 1860s varied from a few thousands to a hundred thousand. Certainly, visitors often commented upon the numbers who pestered men in the streets. Gladstone's innocent forays in hopes of saving 'fallen' women caused his friends much concern lest his motives be misinterpreted. He helped to found several rescue homes.[44] Dr William Acton's book on *Prostitution* (1857: 2nd edn, 1870) dismissed the belief that all prostitutes came to a bad end: 'prostitution is a transitory state, through which an untold number of British women are ever on their passage'. Many became satisfactory wives and mothers.

Legislation to clear the streets was slow to come because the 'social evil' (as prostitution was euphemistically named) was widely regarded as a necessary safety-valve. Only thus could the system of late marriages for middle-class men and frequent pregnancies for middle-class wives be made to work. W. E. H. Lecky's *History of European Morals* (1869) contained an often cited defence of the prostitute. 'Herself the supreme type of vice, she is ultimately the most efficient guardian of virtue. But for her, the unchallenged purity of countless happy homes would be polluted.' So the 'double standard' of sexual morality operated – a flexible standard for 'respectable' men, but a rigid code of purity for 'respectable' women.[45] The assumption was that married middle-class women would devote themselves to husbands, homes, and families. Women were regarded as the weaker sex, physically and mentally unfitted for full involvement in the world. Menstruation was thought to undermine both their strength of body and balance of mind. It was also asserted by doctors that such fragile creatures were unlikely to enjoy the physical side of marriage. Certainly, middle and upper-class girls were often told nothing about this before marriage. How many of them remained sexually unresponsive can never be known; but perhaps not as many as convention assumed. Queen Victoria hinted to her married eldest daughter in 1859 how women were 'poor creatures', 'born for man's pleasure and amusement'. Yet enquiries made by a doctor among forty-five American middle-class women born before 1890 (thirty-three of them before 1870) suggested that most had felt sexual desire and a majority had experienced orgasm.[46]

It was a man's world in part because of the marked surplus of females in England (though not in Wales):[47]

| | 1871 | | 1901 | |
	Males	Females	Males	Females
England	10,353,000	10,946,000	14,718,000	15,798,000
Wales	706,000	707,000	1,011,000	1,001,000

In a society supposedly centred upon the institution of the family one in three of adult Victorian women were unmarried at any one time, and one in four never married. It was especially middle-class unmarried women who found themselves 'superfluous', without a role. 'Paterfamilias at his office all day, and reading his newspaper all the evening; Materfamilias fuming about her servants; the young brothers all driven away to seek some less tiresome spot, and four or five hapless young women, from twenty to forty, without professions or pursuits, or freedom of time or money, and with only a few miserable make-believe accomplishments of pseudo-music, pseudo-art, pseudo-reading.'[48] Middle-class women might become governesses, a 'respectable' but often ill-rewarded outlet in terms both of income and fulfilment. A governess was not one of the servants, yet not one of the family. Fortunately, during the second half of the century a wide range of alternative employment opportunities gradually became available within the new urban society – thousands of middle-class women became schoolteachers, shop assistants, clerks, post office workers, nurses:[49]

	Numbers of occupied females, England and Wales	
	1881	1901
Professions and administration	150,000	236,000
Commerce, clerks, and miscellaneous	52,000	151,000
Dealers and assistants	182,000	343,000
Employed not included above	23,000	27,000
Farmers	20,000	22,000
Total	427,000	779,000
Others occupied	2,976,000	3,393,000
All occupied	3,403,000	4,172,000
Percentage middle-class of all	12.6	18.7

Women schoolteachers increased from under 100,000 in 1871 to over 170,000 by the end of the century; women clerks grew in numbers from less than 1,500 in 1871 to well over 50,000 by 1901, and to nearly 125,000 by 1911. From the 1880s the widespread introduction of shorthand into business use, and the invention of the typewriter, had given women their great opportunity to enter office work. The General Post Office became the largest single employer of middle-class females. By 1911, 14,328 women were engaged as telegraphists and telephone operators, 20,337 as counter assistants or clerks.

Florence Nightingale had led the way in the transformation of nursing into a respectable career for women. 'Daughters of clergymen, military and naval officers, of doctors, of farmers, of tradesmen and artisans are found side by side in all the great metropolitan hospitals. Many of those who would formerly have sought places as music teachers or nursery governesses have been absorbed in this way.'[50] However, of the 63,500 female nurses in England and Wales in 1901 only about 25,000 could be described as trained, and less than half of these reached Florence Nightingale's set standard. Less than 5,000 were both 'ladies' and trained. Should women also be allowed to become doctors? In 1865 Elizabeth Garrett took the Licence of the Society of Apothecaries, and became the first woman to gain a registrable English medical qualification. To its chagrin, the rules of the society spoke of 'persons', and no grounds could be found for excluding a female. In 1874 the London School of Medicine for Women was founded, and in 1876 an Act was passed which required suitably qualified women to be placed on the medical register. Thereafter the existence of women doctors gradually became accepted, though they did not become numerous. Twenty-five women doctors were recorded at the 1881 census, 477 in 1911.[51]

Male clerks complained that increasing competition from women was forcing down salaries to levels which men with families found inadequate. But in all fields of employment women's average rates were fixed well below men's:[52]

| | Average annual earnings, 1913–14 | |
	Men (£)	Women (£)
Higher professional	328	—
Lower professional	155	89
Managers	200	80
Foremen	113	57
Clerks	99	45
Skilled manual	99	44
Semi-skilled manual	69	50
Unskilled manual	63	28

Women cotton factory workers were especially well-paid. They earned average wages of 18s. 8d. per week in 1906, which was less than for male cotton operatives but more than for most male agricultural labourers.[53]

Queen Victoria always remained cautious about the process of middle-class women's emancipation. Women, she thought, should be 'sensibly educated – and employed whenever they can be usefully, but on no account unsexed and made doctors (except in one branch), lawyers, voters, etc. Do that, and you take at once away all their claim to protection on the part of the male sex.'[54] During the mid-Victorian years education for middle-class girls tended to concentrate upon instruction in superficial man-catching 'accomplishments' rather than upon the serious development of mind and knowledge. The report of the Taunton Commission on secondary education (1864–8) deplored this emphasis. Pressure for a more serious approach was already strong, not only from feminists, but from others who believed that national well-being required middle-class wives and mothers to be properly taught. Expert witnesses called before the Taunton Commission included Miss Frances Buss and Miss Dorothea Beale, the outstanding headmistresses respectively of the North London Collegiate School and of Cheltenham Ladies' College. They set new standards, which were increasingly copied in other late-Victorian girls' public schools. Thirty-six such schools were founded between 1871 and 1880, thirty-four between 1881 and 1890.[55]

Both Miss Buss and Miss Beale remained spinsters from choice, not from lack of offers of marriage. Both agreed that marriage would remain the most satisfactory outlet for most women. But they believed that all middle-class women should have the right to an education which would enable them to lead full lives even if they did not marry. This was emphatically the belief of the late-Victorian feminists, who were demanding women's rights from the 1860s, though the word 'feminist' itself seems to date from the 1890s.[56] The electoral aspect of feminism – the demand for 'votes for women' in parliamentary elections – became persistent from 1865, when John Stuart Mill, the political philosopher, made it part of his platform while winning the Westminster constituency at the general election.

Early nineteenth-century radical movements had sometimes included women in their demand for universal suffrage, but not with much prominence. The new demand of the 1860s was middle-class, and not for universal suffrage but for the vote 'on the same terms as for men'.[57] Continuous organization can be traced from the creation in 1866 of a committee which prepared the way for the formation of the London National Society for Women's Suffrage in 1867. Societies were also formed in Manchester and elsewhere, which eventually federated with the London society. Over the next thirty years various new bodies were started, until in 1897 a consolidated National Union of Women's Suffrage Societies was formed. Up to her death in 1890 the campaign was largely controlled by Miss Lydia Becker, secretary of the Manchester society. Thereafter Mrs Millicent Fawcett, president of the NUWSS, became the leading figure among Victorian suffragists. These 'suffragists' were non-violent in their methods, and not to be confused with militant Edwardian 'suffragettes'. Miss Becker and Mrs Fawcett pursued the usual pressure-group round of public meetings, journalism, and lobbying. Both single and married women became involved in the movement; but its demand for the vote was formulated especially with the needs of 'surplus' single women or widows in mind. The suffragists differed among themselves whether to press in the first instance for votes for married women. Yet the Married Women's Property Act of 1870 and subsequent legislation gave women rights to ownership of property after marriage, which made it logical to demand votes for them in respect of that property. As formulated about the time of the passing of the Second Reform Act in 1867, women's suffrage on the same terms as for men would have added some 300–400,000 spinsters and widows to the electoral registers, compared with a United Kingdom male electorate of nearly 2,500,000.

A spate of press discussion about women's suffrage came to a climax when Mill moved an amendment to the 1867 Reform Bill which would have substituted 'person' for 'man' in the text. His persuasive speech attracted seventy-three votes in support. Private members' bills for women's suffrage were debated in the Commons every year but one during the 1870s. Four pages were devoted to arguments for and against in the 1881 edition of Sidney Buxton's *Handbook to Political Questions of the Day*. Opponents argued that women were mentally and physically unsuited 'to face the rough and tumble of the polling-booth': 'men's respect and reverence for women would be fatally undermined if they were enabled to assert themselves in political matters; while the finer edge of women's nature would be blunted'. Mill's essay on *The Subjection of Women* (1869) provoked great antagonism by asserting that even within the happiest of marriages wives without full rights were suppressed: 'even with true affection, authority on the one side and subordination on the other prevent perfect confidence'.

Women's suffrage remained a non-party question in Parliament. The successive Conservative leaders (Disraeli, Salisbury, Balfour) inclined to be favourable; but a majority of their followers were opposed. Among the Liberals the opposite applied. Gladstone became increasingly hostile. He did not want to ask any woman 'unwittingly to trespass upon the delicacy, the purity, the refinement, the elevation of her own nature, which are the present sources of its power'.[58] In 1884 he firmly resisted an attempt to amend the Third Reform Bill in favour of female suffrage. Even so, the amendment attracted 135 votes. But this proved to be the high point in the women's suffrage campaign until Edwardian times. The very fact that the question was a non-party matter weakened it in parliamentary terms. The 1867 and 1884 opportunities for amendments to Government bills were exceptional. Usually the suffragists had to depend upon bills introduced without Government support by private members, a hazardous procedure which always led to failure.

Opponents could justly claim that the majority of women had not yet demanded their own enfranchisement; also that women now stood in less need of the vote because they were being given protection and opportunities in other ways. The Married Women's Property Act of 1870, as developed by amendments into the Edwardian period, allowed a married woman to retain ownership of her property even while she continued to live with her husband. He no longer automatically gained control of her estate on marriage. The Matrimonial Causes Act of 1857 set up the divorce court, and so made divorce available at least to the better-off.[59] The double standard was, however, written into the Act, for whereas a husband could divorce his wife for adultery alone, in the case of an erring husband the law still required proof of incest, rape, bigamy with a married woman, an unnatural offence, or adultery accompanied by cruelty and desertion. The number of divorces in England and Wales quadrupled from an annual average about 150 in the 1860s to nearly 600 in the 1890s.

The progress of middle-class women's social emancipation was much helped by the growing availability in towns of 'respectable' tea-rooms and cafés where they could meet and eat, and not least by the provision of public lavatories for women. Middle-class girls were also becoming emancipated through bicycling and sport. *Punch* (18.7.1891) showed 'the girl of the period' advancing from decorous croquet-playing in a crinoline during the 1860s to much more vigorous roller-skating in the 1870s, to lawn tennis in the 1880s, and to golf in the 1890s. By the 1890s the 'new woman' had arrived. A *Fortnightly Review* article of August 1892 on 'The Working Lady in London' emphasized how fewer middle-class girls now simply waited at home before marriage. Another article on 'The Evolution of Daughters' (*Contemporary Review*, April 1894) reminded its middle-class readers that their daughters were only catching up with working-class girls, who had always worked and had long enjoyed greater personal freedom. The vast majority of girls still hoped to end up married. An article by Grant Allen called 'Plain Words on the Woman Question' (*Fortnightly Review*, October 1889) warned that the women's movement had been too much dominated by the problem of surplus spinsters. They were a special case; the main problem lay in ensuring women's emancipation in marriage.

A symptom of the increasing recognition of women was the proliferation of magazines specially written to meet their interests.[60] These gradually moved down the social scale from *The Lady* (1885) to *My Weekly* (1910) and *Woman's Weekly* (1911), both of which were published for working-class women. The ambiguous motto of *Woman* (1890) was 'Forward, but not too fast'. A correspondent to *The Queen* in 1900 revealingly discussed her state of mind as an 'intermediate woman'. She had been better educated than her predecessors; she recognized that women's sphere must be extended. Yet in common with the majority of late-Victorian and Edwardian women of all classes she confessed her preference for the small and the personal rather than for the general. Her overwhelming desire was to be 'a quite unillustrious, more or less hampered and dependent wife and mother'.

Notes

1. See especially H. Perkin, *The Origins of Modern English Society, 1780–1880* (1969); and A. Briggs, 'The Language of "Class" in Early Nineteenth Century England', in M. W. Flinn and T. C. Smout (eds.), *Essays in Social History* (1974), Ch. 7.
2. See R. Williams, *Keywords* (1976), pp. 51–9.
3. Ada Zemach, 'Alexis de Tocqueville in England', *Review of Politics*, XIII (1951), p. 338.
4. H. Perkin, *The Origins of Modern English Society, 1780–1880* (1969), pp. 425–6.
5. T. Wright, *The Great Unwashed* (1868), p. 11; T. Wright, *Our New Masters* (1873), p. 101; J. Morley, *Miscellanies* (1886), III, p. 27.
6. S. Fiske, *English Photographs* (1869), p. 244.
7. See especially D. Woodruff, *The Tichborne Claimant* (1957).
8. H. Perkin, *The Origins of Modern English Society, 1780–1880* (1969), pp. 414–21.
9. See Lee Holcombe, *Victorian Ladies at Work* (1973); G. Anderson, *Victorian Clerks* (1976); and G. Crossick (ed.), *The Lower Middle Class in Britain, 1870–1914* (1977).
10. A. C. Pigou (ed.), *Memorials of Alfred Marshall* (1925), p. 103.
11. See especially J. A. Banks, *Prosperity and Parenthood* (1954), Chs. III–VII.
12. See especially Pamela Horn, *The Rise and Fall of the Victorian Servant* (1975); and M. Ebery and B. Preston, *Domestic Service in Late Victorian and Edwardian England, 1871–1914* (1976).
13. Miss C. E. Collet, *Report on the Money Wages of Indoor Domestic Servants*, C. 9346 (1899).
14. See Leonore Davidoff, *The Best Circles* (1973); and Hilary and Mary Evans, *The Party That Lasted 100 Days* (1976).
15. Beatrice Webb, *My Apprenticeship* (1926), pp. 45–54.
16. W. E. Gladstone, *Midlothian Speeches, 1879* (1971 ed.), pp. 237–8.
17. A. and E. Gissing (eds.), *Letters of George Gissing to Members of His Family* (1927), pp. 164–5.
18. W. W. Wager (ed.), *H. G. Wells, Journalism and Prophecy* (1964), p. 251.
19. See A. Carr-Saunders and P. A. Wilson, *The Professions* (1933); and W. J. Reader, *Professional Men* (1966).
20. T. H. S. Escott, *England, Its People, Polity, and Pursuits* (1879), II, pp. 39–48, Ch. XXX.
21. A. Ponsonby, *Henry Ponsonby* (1942), p. 60.
22. R. N. Shaw and T. G. Jackson, *Architecture, A Profession or An Art* (1892), p. 13. See also B. Kaye, *The Development of the Architectural Profession in Britain* (1963), Chs. 7–8.

23. T. Wright, *Our New Masters* (1873), pp. 5–6. See also E. J. Hobsbawn, *Labouring Men* (1964), Ch. 15.

24. *Report of the Royal Commission upon the Administration and Operation of the Contagious Diseases Act*, II, C. 408 (1871), p. 441.

25. F. Rogers, *Labour, Life and Literature* (1913; reprinted 1973), p. 298.

26. G. H. Wood, 'Real Wages and the Standard of Comfort since 1850', *Journal of the Royal Statistical Society*, LXXIII (1909), reprinted in E. M. Carus Wilson (ed.), *Essays in Economic History*, Vol. 3 (1962). See also E. H. Hunt, *Regional Wage Variations in Britain, 1850–1914* (1973).

27. H. Mayhew, *London Labour and the London Poor* (n.d.), II, p. 409. See also G. Stedman Jones, *Outcast London* (1971).

28. D. Read, *Cobden and Bright* (1967), pp. 175–6.

29. Sir J. Kay-Shuttleworth, *Thoughts and Suggestions on Certain Social Problems* (1873), p. 31.

30. See M. E. Rose, *The Relief of Poverty, 1834–1914* (1972), and references there. Also D. Fraser (ed.), *The New Poor Law in the Nineteenth Century* (1976).

31. *Royal Commission on the Poor Laws and the Relief of Distress*, appendix volume I, Minutes of Evidence, Cd. 4625 (1909), appendix V (17).

32. C. S. Loch, 'Statistics of Population and Pauperism in England and Wales, 1861–1901', *Journal of the Royal Statistical Society*, LXIX (1906), pp. 291–2.

33. See B. Abel-Smith, *The Hospitals, 1800–1948* (1964).

34. A. L. Bowley, *Wages and Income since 1860* (1937), p. 36. See also T. C. Barker *et al.*, *The Dietary Surveys of Dr. Edward Smith, 1862–3* (1970).

35. T. H. Huxley, *Critiques and Addresses* (1873), pp. 46–7; R. Jefferies, *Toilers of the Field* (1892), pp. 107, 213–14; W. Besant, *London in the Nineteenth Century* (1909), pp. 164–5.

36. *Collected Works of William Morris*, XXIII (1915), pp. 153–4.

37. C. L. Graves, *Mr. Punch's History of Modern England* (n.d.), III, pp. 196–7; J. Franklyn, *The Cockney* (1953), pp. 22, 251–2.

38. Daily Mail, *What the Worker Wants* (1912), p. 158.

39. A. Briggs, *Friends of the People* (1956), p. 129; Patricia Branca, *Silent Sisterhood* (1976), pp. 51–3, 149–50.

40. See especially C. W. Cunnington, *Feminine Attitudes in the Nineteenth Century* (1935); C. W. and Phillis Cunnington, *The History of Underclothes* (1951); and C. W. and Phillis E. Cunnington, *Handbook of English Costume in the Nineteenth Century* (3rd edn, 1970).

41. See Martha Vicinus (ed.), *Suffer and Be Still* (1972); plus the bibliography at Ch. 10; and Martha Vicinus (ed.), *A Widening Sphere, Changing Roles of Victorian Women* (1977), plus the bibliography at Ch. 10.

42. O. R. McGregor, *Divorce in England* (1957), pp. 22–4.

43. See especially S. Marcus, *The Other Victorians* (1966), pp. 128–36; E. Trudgill, 'Prostitution and Paterfamilias', in H. J. Dyos and M. Wolff (eds.), *The Victorian City* (1973), II, Ch. 29; and E. Trudgill, *Madonnas and Magdalens* (1976).

44. P. Magnus, *Gladstone* (1963), pp. 105–10, 305, 345.

45. See K. Thomas, 'The Double Standard', *Journal of the History of Ideas*, Vol. 20 (1959).

46. R. Fulford (ed.), *Dearest Child* (1964), p. 205; C. N. Degler, 'What Ought to Be and What Was: Women's Sexuality in the Nineteenth Century', *American Historical Review*, Vol. 79 (1974); Patricia Branca, *Silent Sisterhood* (1975), pp. 124–6.

47. D. C. Marsh, *The Changing Social Structure of England and Wales, 1871–1961* (2nd edn, 1965), p. 60.

48. Josephine E. Butler (ed.), *Woman's Work and Woman's Culture* (1869), pp. 13–14.

49. A. L. Bowley, *Wages and Income in the United Kingdom since 1860* (1937), p. 129. See especially Lee Holcombe, *Victorian Ladies at Work* (1973).

50. C. Booth, *Life and Labour of the People in London*, VIII (1896), p. 87. See especially B. Abel-Smith, *History of the Nursing Profession* (1960).

51. See W. J. Reader, *Professional Men* (1966), Ch. 11.

52. G. Routh, *Occupation and Pay in Great Britain, 1906–60* (1965), p. 104.

53. E. H. Hunt, *Regional Wage Variations in Britain, 1850–1914* (1973), p. 116.

54. R. Fulford (ed.), *Darling Child* (1976), p. 51. See especially Josephine Kamm, *Hope Deferred, Girls' Education in English History* (1965), Chs. XII–XV.

55. J. A. Banks, *Prosperity and Parenthood* (1954), pp. 191, 229–30.

56. See especially R. J. Evans, *The Feminists* (1977).

57. See especially R. Fulford, *Votes for Women* (1957); and Constance Rover, *Women's Suffrage and Party Politics in Britain, 1866–1914* (1967).

58. *Female Suffrage, A Letter from the Right Hon. W. E. Gladstone, M.P. to Samuel Smith, M.P.* (1892), p. 7.

59. See O. R. McGregor, *Divorce in England* (1957), esp. Chs. I, II; and Griselda Rowntree and N. H. Carrier, 'The Resort to Divorce in England and Wales, 1858–1957', *Population Studies*, XI (1957–8).

60. See Cynthia L. White, *Women's Magazines, 1693–1968* (1970), Ch. 2.

Chapter 4

Town life: *'Where will London end?'*

1

When Victoria became queen in 1837 most of her English subjects were still countryfolk: when she died in 1901 most of them were townspeople. Here was one of history's great social and economic transformations. England had become the world's first predominantly urbanized industrial nation.[1] Some types of town and some forms of commerce and industry had, of course, existed since ancient times; but never before had large urban areas constituted the everyday environment of most citizens of a large state. This novel development forced the Victorians to learn how to live a new urban way of life. 'Possibly the life of England is changing, perhaps has already changed, far more than we realize', sensed an article in the *Quarterly Review* for April 1873. 'The growth of enormous cities, the ease of travelling and the taste for travelling, the largeness and organization of commercial energy, the disappearance of those local attachments and local peculiarities, which used to hold us so strongly because they had bound our fathers and grandfathers before us – these imply, it may be, a more rapid transition from one state of national development to another than can be made clear to those in whose unconscious presence the process has accomplished itself.'

Already by 1871 about two-thirds of the population of England and Wales lived in cities, large towns, and small towns, each with 2,500 or more people.[2] England was 'still a great agricultural country,' explained the 1871 census *General Report*, 'but its cities are extending beyond their ancient borders ... Villages and small places are rising up to the importance of large towns.' The number of inhabitants per square mile had grown from 27.0 in 1801 to 73.0 in 1871. The 1871 census report named six categories of town: the metropolis; 65 county and assize towns; 56 watering places; 42 seaports (excluding London); 72 manufacturing towns; and 97 mining towns. The most heavily urbanized counties in 1871 were Durham and Lancashire in the north, Staffordshire and Warwickshire in the midlands, and London. By the end of the century much of the north and of the midlands had become one more or less continuous urban area, which stretched upwards from Birmingham left and right of the Pennines. At each successive census the towns, and especially cities and towns with over 100,000 inhabitants, were seen to be extending their influence as they absorbed a steadily larger percentage of the increasing population:

	Total population of 100,000 towns	Percentage of total population
1871	7,400,000	32.6
1881	9,400,000	36.2
1891	11,400,000	39.4
1901	14,200,000	43.6

In 1871 the London registration district contained a population of 3,250,000 people; Liverpool had over 400,000, Manchester and Birmingham each over 300,000, Leeds and Sheffield each more than 200,000, and eight other towns each over 100,000.

Hippolyte Taine, the French writer, visited Manchester – the original shock city of the Industrial Revolution.[3] It had become above all the office and warehousing centre of the cotton trade; but into the 1860s cotton mills could still be found at work within its boundaries. At six o'clock these discharged noisy crowds of men, women, and children to swarm 'in the turgid air'. Their clothes were soiled, and their faces looked drawn and dismal; many of the children were bare-footed. Taine followed them home. 'Through half-open windows we could see wretched rooms at ground level, or often below the damp earth's surface. Masses of livid children, dirty and flabby of flesh, crowd each threshold and breathe the vile air of the street, less vile than that within.' Taine then moved on towards the suburbs, where rows of small, cheap houses had been built by speculators. 'The black streets were paved with ironstone slag. Lines of red roofs were ruled against the universal grey of the sky. But at least each family has its own home, and the fog they breathe there is not so contaminated.' Nevertheless, Taine felt 'all the fearful weight with which this climate and the industrial system press down upon men'.

What could, or should, be done to ease this pressure? The *Pall Mall Gazette* (1.7.1871) explained that it was no use bewailing the emergence of the new urban way of life. Its continuance must be accepted, and action taken to remedy its worst effects. 'The truth is that town life hitherto has been mainly co-existent with utter absence of provision for certain necessaries of life which are indispensable to healthy existence anywhere. Air, light, wholesome water, good drainage, and sufficient house-room ought, under good government, to be fairly obtainable in towns as in the country.' Much town pollution, dirt, and disease arose from shortcomings in the disposal of waste – human and animal urine and excrement, domestic and industrial smoke and refuse. This problem of waste in a material sense was seen to create a problem of waste in a moral sense. The second report of the Royal Sanitary Commission, published in 1871, emphasized 'the close connexion between physical and moral pollution'. It believed many causes of death to be removable; 'and much chronic weakness, and incapacity for work' to arise from 'sanitary negligence'. A large proportion of the population both in town and country drank polluted water; in many places 'accumulations of filth' were 'widely vitiating the air'; the working classes were thrown into sickness and poverty 'by a tainted atmosphere and unhealthy dwellings'; overcrowding was 'the cause of much physical as well as moral evil', and smoke pollution was widespread because of 'unpunished neglect' of means of control.

Though reformers dwelt upon the moral aspect of 'public health' (which was, significantly, a new term), what chiefly moved middle and upper-class ratepayers and taxpayers to countenance the expenditure of some of their taxes upon control of the new urban environment was their own personal sense of exposure. Urban dirt and disease did not only affect the poor. 'No classes are exempt from these evils.' The cholera epidemic of 1831–2 had made a deep impression, and from the 1830s public health legislation began to be passed, albeit hesitantly. Edwin Chadwick's brilliant *Report on the Sanitary Condition of the Labouring Population* – a statement of the need for national action – appeared in 1842. The 1848 Public Health Act, inspired by Chadwick, created local boards of health in certain areas with a General Board of Health at the centre. The Act represented an important step towards centralization and standardization, although in many matters it was permissive, not mandatory. It required tactful application. But Chadwick was decidedly not tactful, and in 1854 he was removed from the General Board, which was wound up four years later. The man who in effect succeeded Chadwick as the leading civil servant in the field of sanitary reform was Sir John Simon, the first medical officer for the City of London (1848–55) and then medical officer successively (1855–76) of the Board of Health, the Privy Council, and the Local Government Board.[4] Simon possessed an eye for publicity, and his spirited annual reports as medical officer sometimes sold out and were even reprinted. He was more conciliatory and less doctrinaire than Chadwick, and he began by working as far as possible through co-operation with the local authorities. The 1858 Local Government Act left these authorities free to form local boards of health. Standards suggested by Simon could then be enforced through local action. But such piecemeal progress proved too slow; and in 1866 – under pressure both from Simon and from another cholera visitation – a further Sanitary Act was passed. Local authorities were now required to undertake sanitary regulation. The Act failed to provide adequate machinery for directing those authorities which refused to take action, but the principle of compulsory regulation had been established.

Alongside such general legislation, numerous special acts were being tried during the 1850s and 1860s. Successive Nuisance Removal Acts allowed the establishment of a national network of nuisance authorities, and their powers grew as the definition of 'nuisance' was gradually enlarged. The 1855 Act was the first measure to speak of houses 'unfit for human habitation'. The 1848 City of London Sewers Act was followed in 1865 by the Sewage Utilization Act, which created sewer authorities. This measure was the first public health legislation to reach into rural areas, and also the first to apply to the whole United Kingdom. Specific housing legislation began with two Lodging Houses Acts in 1851. As many as eight Burials Acts were passed between 1850 and 1861, an indication of the increasing problem of the disposal of the dead. Disease Prevention Acts were passed under pressure from epidemics in 1848 and 1855. As well as national legislation, a host of local Acts were passed which sometimes gave local authorities much stronger powers than were nationally available. A striking example of this had been the 1844 Manchester Borough Police Act, which from this early date prevented further building of back-to-back houses in the borough. New back-to-back building was not prohibited nationally until 1909, and even then the Act contained loopholes.

A Royal Commission on the Sanitary Laws sat during 1869–71. Its reports were drafted by Simon, and some of its recommendations were put into legislation over the next few years. The 1871 Local Government Act brought together within one new department the functions of the Local Government Act Office, the Registrar-General's Office, the Medical Department of the Privy Council, and the Poor Law Board. Unfortunately, these many responsibilities made the new Local Government Board not more but less enterprising, and Simon retired in despair in 1876. The 1872 Public Health Act covered the country with sanitary authorities (town councils and local boards in urban areas, guardians in rural areas), which were given obligatory sanitary duties. All authorities were now required to appoint medical officers of health, following the example set by Liverpool as early as 1847. The consolidating 1875 Public Health Act laid down clearly and comprehensively the public health responsibilities of local authorities. This Act made sanitary law much easier to enforce, and it provided the basis for administration well into the twentieth century. But it added little new to policy. Further progress awaited changes in attitudes towards urban society, looking beyond 'public health' to 'social welfare'.

2

This piecemeal early legislation, consolidated in 1875, had been successful only in the sense that without it urban sanitary conditions would have been even more grim than they still were. The death rate of 22.9 per thousand for England and Wales in 1870 was exactly the same as in 1840. Yet it was an achievement that the rapid spread of town life had not forced the rate markedly higher. Even so, the water supply of Stafford in 1866 was taken from wells close to 'receptacles of filth'; and it was said only half in jest that 'the persons living at No. 6 drink the water that is *made* at No. 7'.[5] Piped water was needed not only for drinking but also for sanitation. The increasing use of water closets solved the domestic problem of sewage, but only by flushing it away to become a public problem. Smelly drains, both within the home and outside, were so commonplace that many Victorians – such as the child Daisy Ashford in the 1890s – tended to accept them as normal. 'I shall put some red ruge [sic] on my face said Ethel because I am very pale owing to the drains in this house.'[6] Along with odours from the drains went smoke pollution from chimneys, domestic and industrial. New buildings in cities such as London or Manchester were smoke-blackened within a year. And a daily battle had to be fought to keep Victorian homes clean from dust.

Where dirt was hard to check so was disease. Two rival theoretical explanations of how diseases spread were current in England during the second quarter of the nineteenth century.[7] The miasmatic theory asserted that epidemics were caused by corruption of the atmosphere through exhalations from organic putrefaction. Edwin Chadwick and Florence Nightingale shared this view. The germ theory contended that specific contagia, probably animate, were the sole causes of infections and epidemic diseases. Sir John Simon came to accept that contagia caused disease, but he held that they could only spread in bad environments. Not until the early 1880s were the specific organisms of various diseases isolated by Robert Koch, and the germ theory vindicated.

Hospitals themselves constituted major centres of infection.[8] The first requirement of a hospital, emphasized Florence Nightingale in her *Notes on Hospitals* (1859), was 'that it should do the sick no harm'. But not until the end of the century could it be claimed that hospitals were of positive benefit to large numbers of patients. The better-off subscribed charitably to local voluntary hospitals, but they usually preferred to be ill at home rather than risk entering even the best of them. In London St Bartholomew's and St Thomas's dated back to the Middle Ages. The infirmaries, which were being opened under the Poor Law, offered simple medical treatment exclusively for the lower orders.

Was crime a form of psychological sickness caused by town life? This was often asserted.[9] An article by the Reverend W. D. Morrison, chaplain of Wandsworth prison, on 'The Study of Crime' (*Mind*, 1892) pointed out that whereas the counties required only one policeman to 1,134 population, provincial towns needed one to 672 and London one to 349. The second report of the Royal Sanitary Commission (1871) thought it significant that the Black Country with its grim appearance also presented 'the blackest calendars to our assizes', a conjunction which illustrated 'the effect of filth and sunless atmosphere on the minds as well as the bodies of the sufferers'. Another view held that over-indulgence in alcohol was the main cause of crime. The effects of drink were believed to reach far beyond the offence of drunkeness itself, since drinking encouraged a lowering of moral standards at the same time as it spread poverty. Stealing to overcome poverty then followed. Whether the volume of crime increased at times of trade depression has remained a matter of dispute. But it seems that offences against property, much the most common form of crime, rose in times of depression and fell in times of prosperity. Drunkenness and crimes of violence, by contrast, increased in prosperous times. High wages and steady employment apparently led to more drinking, which encouraged a higher incidence of violence. But professional criminals continued active at all times.

Crime statistics were influenced by variations in the effectiveness of law enforcement by the police, both between places and between years. The appointment of an active chief constable could make a measurable difference. Crime was always markedly above the national average in London, and also in Lancashire. Indictable offences known to the police in England and Wales reached a peak of 101,369 in 1868 but fell to 81,000 to 82,000 in 1871–2 (years of very good trade) before gradually rising again to 98,440 in 1880.

Provincial police forces were reorganized and made more efficient under the 1856 County and Borough Police Act.[10] The Act provided central police grants to local authorities and set up an inspectorate. The spread of towns meant that the number of borough police forces increased to as many as 231 by 1888. Policemen were often unpopular with the working classes, especially in the towns. When in 1864 a group of young men at Pudsey, near Leeds, beat up two constables, the magistrate observed that the district was 'well known for this sort of thing'.[11] The middle classes looked favourably upon the police as protectors of their property, and referred to them affectionately as 'bobbies' – in memory of Sir Robert Peel, creator of the Metropolitan Police. But the working classes spoke less affectionately of 'coppers' and 'rozzers'.

3

As damaging in its physical and moral effects as a bad water supply was bad housing. Disraeli even claimed in his novel *Lothair* (1870) that pauperism was 'not an affair so much of wages as of dwellings. If the working classes were properly lodged, at their present rate of wages, they would be richer. They would be healthier and happier at the same cost'. At the 1871 census the number of inhabited houses in England and Wales was 4,520,000, an increase of almost 600,000 since 1861. 37,803 houses were under construction on census day. The volume of house building moved in long cycles, with peaks in the later 1870s and about 1900 balanced by troughs in the mid-1880s and just before 1914:[12]

	Annual average of houses built in Great Britain
1860–4	54,800
1865–9	64,300
1870–4	88,500
1875–9	113,500
1880–4	81,700

Building peaks and troughs in each locality, however, could vary from the national pattern by several years.

The housebuilding cycle in the United States moved roughly in opposition to the British cycle; and this has encouraged the contention that the two were directly linked through high emigration and capital outflow from the United Kingdom at times of prosperity and intensified housebuilding in the United States.[13] Emigration, it has been argued, reduced the supply of building labour, and also the demand for houses. Conversely, when overseas demand for immigrants and capital declined, the United Kingdom demand for housing revived and more labour and finance became available for builders to meet this demand. But was this inverse relationship really so pronounced? Though emigration at certain periods was certainly very heavy, the growth in United Kingdom urban population and household numbers – and therefore in potential building demand – continued even at times of large exodus. The British housebuilding cycle was probably more shaped by such domestic factors as the rate of growth of real incomes, or by the timing of the introduction of electric tramcars which opened up the suburbs.[14]

In general, Victorian housing supply seems to have met effective demand. Indeed, in London during the last quarter of the nineteenth century empty houses usually comprised at least 4 per cent of the total. Most houses, middle-class as well as working-class, were rented. Rents were tending to rise, except during the 1880s when heavy over-building occurred in some London suburbs. Almost all houses were built by speculative builders, many of them small-scale. Their 'jerry building' (a description which gained currency in the 1870s) was often denounced by contemporary critics. One architect answered that jerry building was unavoidable because people demanded more accommodation than they could afford. Builders were expected to work miracles on the cheap. 'In no other way could the citizen house himself in a "villa" for a rent which would only provide a superior cottage if built substantially.' Many late-Victorian houses, moreover, must have been at least passably well built, for they have stood for a century and more.[15]

Certainly more extensive than shoddy housebuilding was un-progressive design, even of homes for the better-off. Domestic heating, lighting, and sanitation remained much more primitive than the state of contemporary technical knowledge required. Servants laboured to fill jugs, basins, and bathtubs with hot water, and buckets with coal. The English preference for open coal fires rather than for central heating amazed American visitors. J. J. Stevenson's book on *Home Architecture* (1880) admitted that fires produced dust and lost most of their heat up the chimney. 'But it has the advantage that we are used to it.' Into the 1870s bathrooms remained rarities in London, though they were beginning to be installed in larger new suburban houses.

If the middle classes lived less comfortably than they might have done, many of the working classes lived squalidly in slums or almost slums.[16] At least one-fifth of London working-class wages was absorbed by rent; but the very poor could afford only single rooms in slum tenements at perhaps 2*s.* 6*d.* per week. At the other end of the working class, artisans could pay three or four times this amount, and were housed comparatively well. Inability to pay more than a low rent compelled many of the poor to crowd together. The Registrar-General defined 'overcrowding' as more than two persons per room. A study of Sultan Street, Camberwell, built about 1870, has shown how one too-populous slum was created. Some of its seventy six-roomed houses, though not badly built, became slums almost from new, and the rest then inevitably followed suit. In 1871 Sultan Street's houses were filled by 661 persons. By 1881 the street's population had risen to 1,038, and two-thirds of the inhabitants were now living more than two per room. Not all slums developed as quickly as this. Many had begun as respectable central residential areas. But from mid-century and earlier these were beginning to be abandoned by the middle classes of London and the big towns in favour of residence at a distance in new suburbs. The poor then moved in. Even so, working-class accommodation in central city areas was often in short supply. The destruction of working-class homes to make room for street improvements, for new public buildings, and for the construction of railway lines and stations – plus the factories, warehouses, and offices which tended to cluster near the railway – added significantly to the overcrowding problem. Some 800 acres of land in central London were taken for railway purposes during the nineteenth century, displacing at least 120,000 people. Casual labourers – 680,000 in central London by 1860 – needed to live by their work. Demolition for 'improvements' therefore only forced them to live still closer together.[17]

Who then was to provide sufficient and satisfactory housing for the poor? An article on 'The Indigent Class – their Schools and Dwellings' in *Fraser's Magazine* for February 1866 was ready to contemplate 'even millions of expenditure' to give England 'that which, with all her grandeur and power, she sorely lacks – a healthy and virtuous population as the base of her mighty pyramid'. Once again the moral as well as the physical aspect was emphasised. 'It is *their* souls as well as *our* bodies which are to be saved.' But few Victorians accepted that either the state or the local authorities should spend money on housebuilding or renovation. The 1851 Lodging Houses Act had given local authorities powers to build for the working classes; but over the next thirty years only Liverpool, Huddersfield, and Nottingham made even small use of the Act. Almost all Victorian housebuilding was left to private speculative enterprise, which was accepted as the most effective means of providing sufficient mass housing at low cost. The *Leeds Mercury* (4.4.1874), for example, insisted that the only duty of the state was to require observance of the health regulations and the demolition of unfit buildings. 'Those who ask Mr Disraeli to introduce some enactment which will at once take away the evils of which we now complain overrate the powers of the state and even mistake its functions.' In the next year Disraeli's Government did sponsor the Artisans and Labourers Dwellings Improvement Act. This developed McCullagh

Torrens's 1868 Artisans and Labourers Dwellings Act, which had widened the permissive powers of local authorities to order the renovation or demolition of property 'unfit for human habitation'. Whereas the 1868 Act had only allowed action house by house, the 1875 Act permitted overall clearance schemes. Yet neither measure provided for re-housing; and under the 1875 Act extensive and expensive clearance schemes in London eventually drove 22,868 persons from 5,555 separate tenements without offering alternative accommodation. Though the slums were reduced, overcrowding was only increased. In two senses, this was not a constructive housing policy.

Blocks of 'model dwellings' were erected in London by charitable bodies such as the Peabody Trust. This was started in 1862 by George Peabody, a banker, who eventually gave a total of £500,000. Their barrack-like tenements still stand round inner London as monuments to Victorian faith in charitable effort.[18] The hope was that the commercial success of the model dwellings movement would prove to speculative builders that construction for the poor could yield a reasonable return – at least 5 per cent. But builders always sought to make more profit by building for the middle classes and artisans. And the quest for even a 5 per cent return meant that the really poor could not afford the rents which had to be charged. Average weekly wages of Peabody tenants in the late 1870s reached 24s, which was quite a high figure. Rents paid averaged more than 4s. Moreover, in relation to the large size of the housing problem it was pointed out in 1875 that even after thirty years' endeavour the accommodation provided barely equalled six months' increase in London population.

A less ambitious approach to housing provision for the working classes was tried with Octavia Hill's system of strict personal management of converted houses, which began in 1864 with financial help from John Ruskin among others. Miss Hill accepted that small families of unskilled workers could afford to live only in single rooms, and that larger families (with two or three children earning at work) might aspire to no more than two or perhaps three rooms. She advocated state intervention for slum clearance because slums were consequences of the 'dulled conscience' of the community, and clearance could never be made to pay. But beyond this stage she strongly preferred private enterprise. She believed not only that single-room accommodation could be built on cleared slum sites without subsidy, but that it could make a profit. Yet Miss Hill's ventures were made to work only because of their very small scale, which allowed close supervision of poor families and their rooms.

The powers allowed under the 1875 Artisans Dwellings Act for the enforcement of comprehensive clearance were applied with best effect in Birmingham.[19] Here Joseph Chamberlain (mayor 1873–6), promoted a scheme to clear over fifty acres of mainly slum property in the city centre at a cost of £1,500,000. Other provincial cities had already begun reshaping their centres, but Chamberlain was determined that by 'sagacious audacity' Birmingham should have the best centre of all. The main feature of his scheme was an imposing new street – Corporation Street – designed as the main street of the midlands, lined with well-built shops. The local authority undertook no construction itself, resting content with regulation of the efforts of private contractors. As the scheme came to fruition during the 1880s it stood as visible evidence of the success of Birmingham methods. As well as launching the improvement scheme, Chamberlain had municipalized the gas and water supplies. He was enough of a 'socialist' to believe that services which by their nature best functioned as monopolies should be under public control. Birmingham council borrowed heavily to buy out the local gas companies; but, as Chamberlain had forecast, a rising yearly profit was made. In all this work Chamberlain and his supporters were consciously promulgating a new civic gospel. 'What folly it is,' exclaimed Chamberlain, 'to talk about the moral and intellectual elevation of the masses when conditions of life are such as to render elevation impossible! What can the schoolmaster or the minister of religion do, when the influences of the home undo all he does?' Yet, as critics pointed out, 'the denizens of crowded courts and alleys' who had been displaced by his improvement scheme wanted new homes much more than they wanted a new shopping-centre. Chamberlain wrongly assumed that re-housing could be left to speculative builders in the suburbs. Even under his dynamic leadership Birmingham remained without a positive working-class housing policy.

Birmingham's new council house was opened in 1879. Two years earlier Manchester had completed its huge town hall, which was described as 'thirteenth century Gothic, suffused with the feeling and spirit of the present age'.[20] Increasingly during the late-Victorian years, English cities and towns acquired more or less impressive new public buildings – not only town halls, but also public libraries, public baths, police stations, fire stations, and (most numerous of all) board schools. By Edwardian times central London had been covered with public and commercial piles thought appropriate and proportionate to the capital of a world empire. Unfortunately, this rebuilding had proceeded piecemeal, and it followed a confusion of architectural styles which ranged from the Gothic of the early-Victorian Houses of Parliament to the grandiloquence of Edwardian Whitehall.

How much civic pride did the Victorians feel for their newly-built cities and towns? When the Prince of Wales visited Middlesbrough in 1887 to open the new town hall, the mayor expressed satisfaction even in his town's pall of smoke – it was 'an indication of plenty of work'. The Reverend R. W. Dale, a Congregational minister in Birmingham from 1854 to 1895 and a leading supporter of Chamberlain's municipal programme, exclaimed on a visit to Lake Lucerne and its mountains that there was nothing so magnificent there to make him 'feel half the thrill I sometimes felt when I have looked down on the smoky streets of Birmingham from the railway'.[21] These, however, were leading citizens with a personal sense of commitment. It has been suggested that a large proportion of nineteenth-century town dwellers were urbanized in the residential sense without being fully urbanized in the social sense. So long as they were still operating with rural reference groups – if they were comparing their lot favourably with relatives or friends in the villages which they had left – then their mental world was not yet completely that of the town.[22] Certainly, about a third of the inhabitants of London had been born in the countryside. Such people would not immediately or entirely adopt urban attitudes or values. 'Somewhere, half in memory and half in fact, there lies for each of us the little country town, a Milby, a St Ogg's, a Middlemarch: such spots surely, though no longer the representative and typical seats of English life, retain still immense general influence and importance; they are the haunts of our earliest and dearest reminiscences.' So admitted one *Quarterly Reviewer* of George Eliot's *Middlemarch* in April 1873.

Yet every year spent in the city dimmed these memories. And for the majority born into an urban environment they had never existed. But the reference group still did not become the whole urban mass. Cities and large towns were found to be too big and diverse for this. Urban horizons became formed by the physical and mental limits of each working-class neighbourhood or middle-class suburb. Robert Roberts has remembered his almost self-contained community in Edwardian Salford: 'some thirty streets and alleys locked along the north and south by two railway systems a furlong apart. About twice that distance to the east lay another slum which turned on its farther side into a land of bonded warehouses and the city proper. West of us, well beyond the tramlines, lay the middle classes, bay-windowed and begardened. We knew them not'.[23]

4

It was often remarked how, as the working classes continued to move into the towns in search of economic and social betterment, the middle classes were 'moving out' (to use the expression of the time) in search of residential improvement. 'Those who had means were perpetually trying to get out from London, those who were destitute were always trying to find their way in.'[24]

'The rise of the suburbs', as it was called in a *Contemporary Review* article of October 1891, formed an essential part of late-Victorian urbanization. People became spread over increasingly extensive areas round the old centres of English cities and large towns, a spread which in the case of London eventually reached out many miles. In 1851 outer London contained only 322,000 people, compared with 2,363,000 within inner London; but thereafter the balance started to change, slowly at first but rapidly by the end of the century:

	Inner London	Outer London
1861	2,808,000	419,000
1871	3,261,000	628,000
1881	3,830,000	940,000
1891	4,228,000	1,410,000
1901	4,536,000	2,050,000

By 1900 London was reaching from Barnet, Enfield, and Loughton in the north to Croydon and Sutton in the south, from Hounslow and Kingston in the west to Barking, Woolwich, and Bromley in the east.[25]

The mid-Victorian hope was that suburban life would enable families to enjoy the best of both town and country living – still near enough to urban centres to share in the economic and social benefits of concentration, yet far enough out to find fresh air and open space. Charles Kingsley, the novelist and social critic, speaking in 1857 on 'Great Cities and their Influence for Good and Evil', held out hope that suburbs would permit 'a complete interpenetration of city and of country, a complete fusion of their different modes of life, and a combination of the advantages of both, such as no country in the world has ever seen.' The reality was not destined to work out so well. Kingsley did not foresee how city centres would lose much of their vigour once

London-built up area

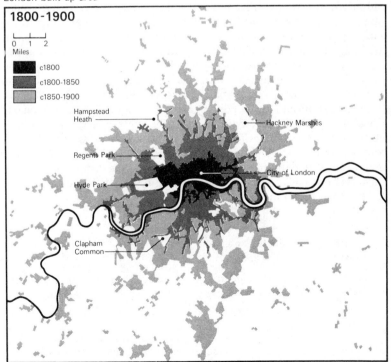

they had become places only of daytime employment, with many streets left lifeless each evening and at week-ends. Furthermore, the common social and cultural life of the city was to be weakened without necessarily being replaced by a fully developed community life in each suburb. Walter Bagehot anticipated these shortcomings as early as 1868 (*Economist*, 12 September). 'London spreads literally into distant suburbs, where friends are scattered, where acquaintances are forgotten, where there are no local pleasures and no local instruction, and which are miles from the central foci.' Significantly, the residential population of the old City of London had fallen from 112,000 in 1861 to 75,000 ten years later. Yet in 1866 over 170,000 non-residents were working in the City during daytime.

It was remarked in 1873 how the railways had 'set us all moving far away from London – that is to say, the special middle class of Londoners', people with incomes of £300–£500 per year. 'The upper ten thousand and the abject poor still live and sleep in the metropolis.' The solid middle classes were moving to captured suburban villages such as Richmond, Croydon, and Slough, while 'the smaller fry content themselves with semi-detached boxes at Putney, Kilburn, New Cross, or Ealing'.[26] The steady rise in real incomes made it economically possible for tens of thousands of London clerks and artisans to rent suburban houses and to travel back daily to work in central London. Rows of suburban streets were still a novelty to the *Architect* in 1873; it looked in some dismay upon 'another kind of housebuilding going on in the country, beside the railway stations in the vicinity of London ... the building of small houses in streets – actually in close rows along one side of the way and the other – with little back yards or so-called gardens such as people possess at Battersea or Islington'. Annual rents of £28–£40 were paid for such small houses. The *Builder* noted in 1885 how London's suburban growth during the first half of Victoria's reign had consisted of ribbon development along the exit roads as far as three or four miles out; but how since about 1867 'the intervals between the lines shot out in the earlier period' had been 'busily filled up'. Three or four miles constituted the maximum practicable walking distance from home to work and back. The London building boom of the late 1870s was especially a boom in suburban construction:

> The richest crop for any field
> Is a crop of bricks for it to yield.
> The richest crop that it can grow
> Is a crop of houses in a row.

This revealing jingle appeared in Tarbuck's *Handbook of House Property* (1875). 'Where will London end?' was being asked as early as 1870. 'Goodness knows' came the reply. 'Building plots are snapped up as if they were so many gold nuggets.'

The appearance of late-Victorian suburban housing in London and elsewhere – terraced, semi-detached, and detached – remains familiar from surviving examples. Roofs were usually of Welsh grey slate, often topped with ornamental ridge tiles, and with walls of dark red, grey, or yellow stock bricks, sometimes in a patterned mixture. Bay windows were now usual, at least downstairs, and embellishments such as fancy railings, plaster mouldings, and coloured tiles or glass were much favoured. Window dressings and garden layouts reflected the class, or aspirations to class, of the neighbourhood. Aspidistras half-concealed by draped lace curtains, privet hedges, and tiny flower beds were ubiquitous.

It was easy to laugh at this associated pretentiousness and conformism of suburban living. But millions of suburban Victorians remained happy to live as they did. Suburban life was willingly dominated by domesticity and dullness. It was inward-looking, centred round the family and the home, even though the head of the household probably travelled to the city centre daily. The standard of social and cultural expectation was established by interaction between neighbouring families, in terms of competition as much as contact. 'Keeping up with the Joneses' could be attempted even while 'keeping oneself to oneself'. As incomes rose, families moved up the housing scale (renting assisted mobility) by migration to a better house in another street or another suburb. A railway line could divide a suburb strikingly, one side 'superior' the other not. 'The leading ambition of every rightminded Ilfordian,' it was written in 1907, 'is to migrate as speedily as possible from one side of the line to the other.'[27] The railways which divided the suburbs also carried the most affluent commuters to houses deep in the country or by the sea, at such places as Brighton or Hastings. With an atrocious pun characteristic of the period *Punch* (1.8.1874) wondered 'whether people take to living at Redhill because it is so redhilly accessible by railway?'

5

The answer to *Punch*'s question was in the affirmative. Improvements in transport played a vital part in the suburban revolution.[28] A traffic census in 1866 showed that about 680,000 people were entering the City of London each day between 5 a.m. and 9 p.m. on foot or in vehicles. The great majority in London and elsewhere, especially of working men, were still walking to work; but the numbers travelling by train, horse bus, or horse tram were growing rapidly from the 1860s. The following tentative Edwardian estimates gave some idea of the rate of growth:[29]

Passenger traffic in Greater London			
	Railway (local companies)	Tramways	Bus (LGOC and LRCC)	Journeys per head
1867	40,547,398	—	41,424,428	22.7
1880	133,877,485	64,817,361	57,722,231	54.8
1902	273,767,648	358,119,754	279,466,557	136.0

It had now become possible to talk of 'the man on top of the Clapham omnibus' as a representative middle-class figure. Clapham had become a leading south London suburb, to which the horse buses plied regularly. These buses were always middle-class vehicles. The fares were high (a minimum of 2*d.* or 3*d.*, at about 1*d.* per mile), and most services started too late (normally about 8 a.m.) to suit working people. The London General Omnibus Company had been formed, at first under French control, in 1856. By 1890 it constituted the largest bus company in the world, with some 860 vehicles and 9,000 horses. Each bus was served by five pairs of animals, plus a spare. The 'General's' only serious rival was the London Road Car Company, formed in 1880, which set new standards of comfort.

'The working man is rarely seen on the sophisticated cushions,' explained an article on 'The Bus' in the *Cornhill Magazine* for March 1890. 'The tramcar is *his* familiar vehicle, and he can ensconce himself there in his mortar-splashed clothes without restraint.' A tram could carry about fifty passengers compared with only half that number on a bus. Tram fares were therefore much lower than bus fares, and this began to encourage the movement of artisans out of central London. Even so, London's tramlines stopped at the fringes of the City and West End, leaving passengers to walk the rest of their way or to take an expensive bus. The buses enjoyed a monopoly in central London. In 1869 Liverpool had led the way in laying down grooved tram track, rather than the L-shaped rails used by several tramway ventures earlier in the decade which had caused unacceptable interference with other road traffic. In London successful grooved tramway operation began from 1870. The Tramways Act of that year gave local authorities powers of veto over construction, but not until 1882 did a local authority (Huddersfield) itself to run a tramway. This Huddersfield example encouraged extensive municipalization during the next two decades. By the end of the century about a thousand miles of tramway were in operation.

The harness jingling and hoof clopping of hansom cabs has been remembered as the characteristic street sound of late-Victorian London. But cab travel was expensive (with a minimum charge of 1*s.*), and it was confined to the well-to-do. London possessed about 7,800 cabs in 1870, and over 10,500 by 1884 (more than half of which were hansoms). Horse transport dominated the streets of large towns, and it was ruthless in claiming right of way. At rush hours the main streets of London became heavily congested, as well illustrated by Doré's *London* drawing of 'A City Thoroughfare'. Street accidents were frequent, and some 200 people per year were being killed in the capital about 1870. Moving traffic generated a high volume of penetrating noise from iron-shod horses' hooves, and from the running of iron-rimmed wheels on hard, often granite road surfaces. Wood-block surfacing was sometimes laid for quietness in busy city streets, but it was not sufficiently extensive to subdue what Tennyson as early as 1852 was calling 'streaming London's central roar'. Coventry Patmore, another poet, complained on a visit to London that never less than three barrel-organs were playing beneath his windows. 'The incessant varying roar of carts, carriages and organs, to me, who have never lived in London, is indescribably maddening.'[30] Street noise was so intrusive that straw was often laid outside the homes of sick people. But the smell and dirt from horse droppings could be equally offensive. Rain converted the manure into a morass which was then splattered by passing traffic upon the pavements. At busy points crossing sweepers plied their lowly but necessary trade. The paths which they cleared through the mess were especially needed by ladies, whose long skirts were always skimming the ground.

Each town horse produced three to four tons of droppings per year. The horse population of Great Britain has been conservatively estimated at well over 2 million about 1871, on its way to a peak over 3,275,000 about 1901:[31]

	1871	1901	1911
Trade horses, goods	286,000	702,000	832,000
Buses and trams	35,000	308,000	25,000
Stage carriages, post horses, other Hackneys	125,000	156,000	138,000
Private carriage horses	201,000	400,000	537,000
Riding horses, hunters	74,000	200,000	—
Used in agriculture	940,000	1,089,000	1,087,000
On farms, unbroken	314,000	422,000	408,000
Total commercial	444,000	1,166,000	995,000
Total private or pleasure	414,000	600,000	537,000
Horses on farms	1,254,000	1,511,000	1,495,000
	2,112,000	3,276,000	3,017,000

The number of town horses grew especially fast during the last quarter of the century, reaching a maximum of perhaps 1,500,000 at its end. The spread of the railways, far from removing the need for horses, had made them necessary in new ways for short-distance transport, even while putting an end to long-distance horse carriage. The railway stations and goods yards themselves generated much horse-drawn traffic.

The number of private carriages in England and Wales increased from some 205,000 in 1851 to 460,000 in 1881. Here was one measure of rising middle-class affluence and aspiration, for it needed a minimum income of about £600 a year to maintain even a modest two-wheeler.[32] But the total of carriage owners did not continue to grow thereafter. Especially in London, it was proving more and more difficult and expensive to find stabling. Moreover, street congestion made city driving unpleasant, at the same time as cabs and buses – while themselves adding to congestion – were providing satisfactory alternative transport.

6

Many more horses were pulling many more vehicles on England's roads during the late-Victorian heyday of the railways than had been employed in the pre-Victorian heyday of the stagecoach. By the 1870s the main railway network was almost completed.[33] The Settle and Carlisle line, thrust by the Midland Railway through the northern Pennines between 1869 and 1875, represented the last example of 'heroic' main-line construction. The United States – not Britain – was now the pioneering railway nation. The Great Central line built in the 1890s to London's last new main-line station, Marylebone, was unnecessary and never a commercial success. It stood as a monument to the megalomania of Sir Edward Watkin, who aspired to control a route all the way from Manchester to Paris. Short-cuts for main lines, suburban branches, and cross-country links were also added to the network during the late-Victorian years. Total railway mileage in Great Britain amounted to about 13,500 miles in 1870, and over 20,000 miles by 1913. But more significant than this extension was the much intensified use of the network. Whereas nearly 360,000 passengers and 166,500,000 tons of freight were being carried in 1871, over 1,423,000 passengers and 561,500,000 tons of freight were transported in 1913. *Bradshaw's Railway Guide* contained 270 pages in 1864, but 1,000 pages more in 1914.

An estimate has been made of the social saving brought to the economy by the construction of the railways.[34] In 1865 extra resources totalling 4.1 per cent of the national income would have been needed to replace railway freight services in England and Wales; plus a further 2.6 or 7.1 per cent to provide alternative means of passenger carrying, depending upon the degree of comfort to be offered. Thus over 10 per cent of national income would probably have been sacrificed if the railways had not become available.

The *Final Report* of the Royal Commission on Railways (1865–7) praised the British preference for private enterprise in railway building under private Acts of Parliament. About 1,800 such Acts to sanction new railway construction had been passed by 1867, plus 1,300 amending Acts. The commission advised that nationalization – as allowed from 1866 under Gladstone's Railways Act of 1844 – should not be undertaken. Nor was it. But the many small companies of the first railway generation were now merging with the bigger names. By 1914 the British railway system was dominated by just eleven companies.

These years of amalgamation also saw the introduction of powerful new locomotives, of restaurant cars, sleeping coaches, Pullman cars, and corridor coaches with lavatories, of gas and then of electric lighting in carriages, and of steam heating. Heavier, faster, and more frequent trains could not be run without expensive track, bridge, and station rebuilding. All this was undertaken to make the system serve the economic and social needs of the new urban, industrial society.

Diminishing returns on capital invested were to be expected at this stage of railway development; but some late-Victorian operating techniques did become outdated and wasteful compared with contemporary American practice.

The railways found it difficult to raise charges, especially freight rates, even when national price levels were rising. At times of depressed trade businessmen readily complained of railway rates, and Parliament inclined to be sympathetic. The 1873 Railway and Canal Traffic Act had created the Railway Commission to oversee the railways and to secure the enforcement of railway legislation. This represented a significant intervention, even though the powers of the commission were incomplete. The 1894 Railway and Canal Traffic Act provided that if any trader complained to the commission of the unreasonableness of any freight charge increase, the burden of justification lay with the railway company. This was often difficult to prove statistically, and the unexpected effect of the act was largely to hold standard rates at the 1892 levels. These were not generally raised until 1913, when another Act allowed the companies to lift charges by 4 per cent to cover costs of a wage award.[35]

Suburban railway travelling had become an important feature of London life and work by the last quarter of the century. The early-Victorian trunk routes out of London had not at first been lined with many suburban stations; but by the 1870s almost all the mass of local lines and local stations had been opened, with the exception of the Edwardian tube lines. The intensity of this suburban construction was greater south of the Thames than north of it, mainly because the southern lines had less freight and long-distance traffic to accommodate. Suburban commuters did not like to travel for much longer than one hour; but in that time trains could reach far beyond the limits of horse-drawn transport.

The railways had transformed thinking about time. They had speeded up communication, both mental and physical, to an extent that could hardly again be repeated. Richard Cobden, the statesman, put this point strikingly in 1862. He had just travelled by train from London to Edinburgh in ten and a half hours. 'The last time I made this journey without stopping was in 1825, when I started from Edinburgh on the *outside* of the Mail coach on 1 February, and rode to London in two days and two nights, which was then considered a marvellously rapid journey.' The fare plus cost of meals on the road came to about £5 15*s*. '*Now* I make the same journey in about a quarter of the time for £3 10*s*. and a dinner at York, travelling in an arm chair in a little carpeted drawing room without fatigue and almost without motion ... Our successors can have no such gain on our present travelling even if they are shot like a cannon ball through a pneumatic tube.'

In Cobden's day long-distance trains averaged about forty miles per hour. But by the end of the 1880s speeds had been improved. Journey times to Manchester from London fell from five hours to four hours and a quarter. The well-publicised 'railway races' to Edinburgh in 1888 along the east and west coast routes brought the normal journey times down to about eight and a half hours. The new speed and reliability was praised by a veteran Manchester businessman in the 1890s.

Nowadays you do not ask men *how* they can move this or that weight of material; but what it will cost, and which is the best company to send it by. You do not ask the distance from town to town; but how long will it take by such a train. We do not discuss about the time *when* we shall be able to see such and such a book or paper; but it is ordered to be here or there in the morning.[36]

The railways gradually standardized timekeeping throughout the country as 'railway time' – which was Greenwich mean time – became accepted. The 1880 Statutes (Definition of Time) Act finally made Greenwich time the legal standard for Great Britain. Watches were ceasing to be expensive status symbols, as they became cheap enough to be bought 'for as many shillings as it used to cost pounds'.[37] But concern with time was one symptom of that 'high pressure' of which many late-Victorians complained. Time dominated even Alice's Wonderland (1865), where the White Rabbit was constantly consulting his watch, fearful lest he be late. In 1868 Dr Alfred Haviland published '*Hurried to Death': or A Few Words of Advice on the Danger of Hurry and Excitement, Especially Addressed to Railway Travellers.*

The railways' concern with time and speed helped to produce a high accident rate.[38] The Royal Commission on Railway Accidents (1874–7) reported that between 1872 and 1875 an average of over 1,300 passengers and railwaymen had been killed each year in the United Kingdom. Charles Dickens was involved in an accident at Staplehurst in 1865 which killed ten people, and which left him nervous of railway travelling for the rest of his life. The 1868 Regulation of Railways Act compelled the fixing of communication cords, while another Railways Act of 1889 at last made block signalling and continuous brakes on passenger trains compulsory. On balance, the Victorians accepted that railways had brought much more good than harm to society. Gladstone in an article on 'Free Trade, Railways and Commerce' (*Nineteenth Century*, February 1880) set 'Improvement of Locomotion' alongside free trade as the twin bases of national progress. Revealingly, the big city railway stations were designed in a celebratory style as secular cathedrals. London's Broad Street, Cannon Street, Charing Cross, Victoria, Holborn Viaduct, and St Pancras stations were all built during the 1860s.[39]

Railways had benefited all classes. The fact that even the artisans (though not the poor) used them was evidenced by the need to provide three classes of accommodation. From 1872 the Midland Railway began to offer third-class seats on all trains, not just on those mandatory cheap (and slow) trains run under Gladstone's 1844 Railways Act. In 1875 the Midland abolished second class entirely, and soon afterwards it began to upholster its third-class compartments. The other companies gradually followed suit. The growth of third-class traffic had been dramatic. In 1845 over 40 per cent of passengers held first-class tickets, over 42 per cent second-class, and only 17 per cent third-class; by 1875 these proportions had changed to 9 per cent, 14 per cent, and 77 per cent respectively. By 1911 almost 96 per cent of all passengers travelled third-class.[40]

The Times Golden Jubilee retrospect (21.6.1887) praised the part played by the railways during the reign, not least in revolutionizing the transmission of correspondence and news.[41] Letters delivered in England and Wales increased from 132 million in 1840 (the year of the penny post) to 704 million in 1870, and to 2,827 million by 1913. According to *Whitaker's Almanack*, twelve letter deliveries were made each day in the City of London in 1890, and six to eleven elsewhere in the capital. 'Letters properly directed, and properly posted, should be delivered in from two to four hours.' Postcards had been introduced by Gladstone's Government in 1870, at a postage of $\frac{1}{2}d$. Gladstone himself – economical in all things – became a heavy postcard user. Numbers delivered in England and Wales rose from 64 million in 1872 to 1,069 million in 1913. Picture postcards were allowed from 1894, and immediately achieved great popularity. A general parcel post was started from 1883. And thanks to persistent advocacy by John Henniker Heaton, penny postage throughout the British Empire was introduced in 1898, and penny postage to the United States in 1908.

The electric telegraph was taken over by the General Post Office in 1870, a striking early example of nationalization but not an encouraging one.[42] The private companies were compensated over-generously, and the service invariably ran at a loss under the Post Office. One reason for this, however, was the commendable desire to make the service widely available by opening telegraph offices all over the country. The number of telegrams sent in England and Wales grew from 7,100,000 in 1870 to ten times that number each year during the Edwardian period. The effect of the telegraph upon communication of information was as revolutionary as the effect of the railways upon the movement of goods or people. What had taken hours or days to communicate during the early part of the century could now be said by telegraph in minutes.

The telephone came into use from the end of the 1870s; more at first for business than for private calls.[43] The GPO started a small service; but the National Telephone Company, which absorbed many other private companies, became much more important. A few municipalities also ran their own local services. Not until 1912 did the Post Office take over the National Telephone Company, and acquire a near monopoly of the whole system. United Kingdom trunk calls numbered 5,900,000 in 1898, but 36 million by 1913.

7

Alfred Marshall, the economist, remarked in his *Principles of*

Economics (1890) how improvements in manufacturing techniques had cheapened production, but how they had not in themselves directly increased the amount of raw material obtained in return for the product of a given amount of capital and labour. He suggested that probably more than three-quarters of the benefit derived by England from the progress of manufactures during the century had come 'through its indirect influences in lowering the cost of transport of men and goods, of water and light, of electricity and news: for the dominant fact of our own age is the development not of the manufacturing, but of the transport industries'. In terms of direct economic effects, new British railway construction was ceasing to be a major factor by 1870; but replacement and maintenance of rolling stock was continuous, and iron rails were being replaced by steel during the 1870s. The railway companies built their own large engineering works, and Crewe emerged as a town entirely created by the railways and their needs. Overseas demand for British railway manufactures remained high. An average of almost £1 million worth of locomotives was exported each year during the 1860s.[44]

Railway shares became a leading investment field for the middle classes. On their marriage in 1869 T. H. Green, the Oxford philosopher, and his wife placed in joint settlement eleven different railway securities, which yielded a comfortable return of about £600 per annum. As company rivalries were reduced by amalgamations, and as interference by Government and Parliament increased, the 'railway interest' became more united and organized. In 1867 the Railway Companies' Association was formed as a permanent pressure group. Within the 1868 Parliament about 125 railway directors sat in the Commons and about 48 in the Lords, though railways were not the primary business concern of all of these men.[45]

The spread of railways even had direct effects upon shipping. In 1867 coal imported by rail into London exceeded traditional seaborne imports from the north-east for the first time. Within ten years railborne supplies had reached double those carried by sea. Though in terms of scale Britain had ceased to be the world's leading railway nation, she remained the predominant maritime power. Into Edwardian times the United Kingdom was still building about 60 per cent of all ships launched. In 1914 the British mercantile fleet – at well over 12 million tons – was about four times as large as the German, the next largest:[46]

	Shipping tonnage registered in the United Kingdom (average net tons per annum per decade)	
	Sailing ships	Steamships
1860–9	4,590,000	724,000
1870–9	4,240,000	1,847,000
1880–9	3,435,000	3,783,000
1890–9	2,784,000	5,993,000
1900–9	1,710,000	8,921,000

Net shipping earnings from the rest of the world doubled from a yearly average of £37,500,000 in the 1860s to £75,700,000 during 1900–8.[47]

By the 1860s steamships were displacing sailing ships in the short-distance trade between Britain and the Continent. During the late 1860s and 1870s they took the Atlantic trade; and in the 1870s and 1880s, assisted by the opening of the Suez Canal in 1869, the trade with India and the Far East. But sailing ships still continued on round-the-world routes, and in grain carrying from Australia and the west coast of America.[48]

Jules Verne's *Around the World in Eighty Days* was first published in 1873. Eighty days still seemed remarkable; but a ninety-day world tour was being offered as a normal tourist trip before the end of the decade – fare from £200.

The route will be over the Great Union and Central Pacific Railway to San Francisco, passing through some of the grandest and most interesting scenery in the world. From San Francisco the tourist will be taken to Japan and China by the Pacific Mail Steamship Company, and thence by the Peninsular and Oriental Company, via Galle, Madras, Calcutta, and Bombay (over the Great Indian Railway), to Southampton, or London via Brindisi.[49]

With steamships hurrying about the oceans regardless of winds, and with railways penetrating all the continents, the world was coming to seem a very much smaller place during the last quarter of the nineteenth century.

Notes

1. See especially A. Briggs, *Victorian Cities* (1963); and H. J. Dyos and M. Wolff (eds.), *The Victorian City* (1973).
2. See especially C. M. Law, 'The Growth of Urban Population in England and Wales, 1801–1911', *Transactions of the Institute of British Geographers*, XLI (1967); D. Friedlander, 'The Spread of Urbanization in England and Wales, 1851–1951', *Population Studies*, XXXV (1970); and R. Lawton, 'Rural Depopulation in Nineteenth Century England', in D. R. Mills (ed.), *English Rural Communities* (1973).
3. H. Taine, *Notes on England* (1957), pp. 219–20.
4. See R. Lambert, *Sir John Simon* (1963); and O. MacDonagh, *Early Victorian Government* (1977), Ch. 8. Also A. P. Stewart and E. Jenkins, *The Medical and Legal Aspects of Sanitary Reform* (2nd edn, 1867: reprinted 1969).
5. A. P. Stewart and E. Jenkins, *The Medical and Legal Aspects of Sanitary Reform* (2nd edn, 1867: reprinted 1969), p. 47.
6. Daisy Ashford, *The Young Visiters* (1919), p. 22.
7. See G. Rosen, 'Disease, Debility and Death', in H. J. Dyos and M. Wolff (eds.), *The Victorian City* (1973).
8. See B. Abel-Smith, *The Hospitals, 1800–1948* (1964).
9. See especially J. J. Tobias, *Crime and Industrial Society in the 19th Century* (1967); J. J. Tobias (ed.), *Nineteenth-Century Crime* (1972); and V. A. C. Gatrell and T. B. Hadden, 'Criminal Statistics and their Interpretation', in E. A. Wrigley (ed.), *Nineteenth Century Society* (1972).
10. See T. A. Critchley, *A History of Police in England and Wales* (1967), Chs. 4, 5; and H. Parris, *Constitutional Bureaucracy* (1969), pp. 234–40.

11. See R. D. Storch, 'The Policeman as Domestic Missionary: Urban Discipline and Popular Culture in Northern England, 1850–1880', *Journal of Social History*, Vol. 9 (1976).
12. P. Mathias, *The First Industrial Nation* (1969), p. 490.
13. See B. Thomas, *Migration and Economic Growth: A Study of Great Britain and the Atlantic Economy* (2nd edn, 1973), esp. Chs. XI, XIII.
14. See S. B. Saul, 'House Building in England, 1890–1914', *Economic History Review*, second series, XV (1962); and H. J. Habbakuk, 'Fluctuations in House-Building in Britain and the United States in the Nineteenth Century', in A. R. Hall (ed.), *The Export of Capital from Britain, 1870–1914* (1968).
15. R. N. Shaw and T. G. Jackson (eds.), *Architecture, A Profession or an Art* (1892), pp. xii–xiii. See also H. J. Dyos, 'The Speculative Builders and Developers of Victorian London', *Victorian Studies*, XI supplement (1968).
16. See A. Sutcliffe, 'Working-Class Housing in Nineteenth-Century Britain: A Review of Recent Research', *Bulletin of Labour History*, no. 24 (1972), and references there. Also H. J. Dyos and D. A. Reeder, 'Slums and Suburbs', in H. J. Dyos and M. Wolff (eds.), *The Victorian City* (1973); and A. S. Wohl, *The Eternal Slum* (1977).
17. See H. J. Dyos, 'Railways and Housing in Victorian London', *Journal of Transport History*, II (1955); H. J. Dyos, 'Some Social Costs of Railway Building in London', ibid., III (1957–8); J. R. Kellett, *The Impact of Railways on Victorian Cities* (1969), Ch. X; and G. Stedman Jones, *Outcast London* (1971), Ch. 8.
18. See W. Ashworth, *The Genesis of Modern British Town Planning* (1954), Ch. IV; G. Stedman Jones, *Outcast London* (1971), Ch. 9; J. N. Tarn, *Five Per Cent Philanthropy* (1973), Chs. 2–4; and A. S. Wohl, *The Eternal Slum* (1977), Ch. 6.
19. See A. Briggs, *History of Birmingham* (1952), II, Ch. IV; A. Briggs, *Victorian Cities* (1963), Ch. V; and E. P. Hennock, *Fit and Proper Persons* (1973), pp. 111–30.
20. W. E. A. Axon (ed.), *An Architectural and General Description of the Town Hall, Manchester* (1878), pp. 2–3.
21. A. W. W. Dale, *Life of R. W. Dale* (1899), p. 196.
22. R. E. Pahl, *Patterns of Urban Life* (1970), p. 32. See also J. A. Banks, 'The Contagion of Numbers', in H. J. Dyos and M. Wolff (eds.), *The Victorian City* (1973).
23. R. Roberts, *The Classic Slum* (1971), p. 3.
24. D. A. Wells, *Recent Economic Changes* (1891), p. 432.
25. J. T. Coppock, 'The Changing Face of England: 1850–*circa* 1900', in H. C. Darby (ed.), *A New Historical Geography of England* (1973), pp. 667–73.
26. See especially D. J. Olsen, *The Growth of Victorian London* (1976), Ch. 5. Also H. J. Dyos, *Victorian Suburb* (1961).
27. A. A. Jackson, *Semi-Detached London* (1973), p. 64.
28. See, in general, C. E. R. Sherrington, *A Hundred Years of Inland Transport* (1934); and P. S. Bagwell, *The Transport Revolution from 1770* (1974), Chs. 4–8. In particular, see T. C. Barker and M. Robbins, *A History of London Transport* (1975–6), Vol. I.
29. *Royal Commission on London Traffic, Appendices to the Evidence*, Cd. 2752 (1906), appendix no. 6, p. 127. See also *The Times*, 16 July 1881.
30. B. Champneys, *Memoirs and Correspondence of Coventry Patmore* (1900), II, p. 108.
31. See especially F. M. L. Thompson, *Victorian England: The Horse-Drawn Society* (1970); and F. M. L. Thompson, 'Nineteenth-Century Horse Sense', *Economic History Review*, second series, XXIX (1976).
32. J. A. Banks, *Prosperity and Parenthood* (1954), Ch. VI.
33. See especially M. Robbins, *The Railway Age* (1962); H. Perkin, *The Age of the Railway* (1970); and H. J. Dyos and D. H. Aldcroft, *British Transport, An Economic Survey from the Seventeenth Century to the Twentieth* (1974), Chs. 4–7.
34. See G. R. Hawke, *Railways and Economic Growth in England and Wales, 1840–1870* (1970); and D. H. Aldcroft, *Studies in British Transport History, 1870–1970* (1974), Chs. 1–2.
35. See P. J. Cain, 'Traders versus Railways, The Genesis of the Railway and Canal Traffic Act of 1894', *Journal of Transport History*, new series, II (1973); and R. J.

Irving, 'The Profitability and Performance of British Railways, 1870–1914', *Economic History Review*, second series, (1978).

36. Cobden to H. Ashworth, 21 August 1862 (British Library Add. Mss. 43,654); R. Spencer, *A Survey of the History, Commerce and Manufactures of Lancashire* (1897), p. 164.
37. F. Harrison, *The Choice of Books* (1886), p. 422.
38. See O. S. Nock, *Historical Railway Disasters* (2nd edn, 1969).
39. See J. Betjeman, *First and Last Loves* (1952), Ch. 9; and J. Summerson, *Victorian Architecture* (1970), Ch. II.
40. H. J. Dyos and D. H. Aldcroft, *British Transport, An Economic Survey from the Seventeenth Century to the Twentieth* (1974), p. 213.
41. See H. Robinson, *The British Post Office* (1948), Chs. 25–9.
42. See J. Kieve, *The Electric Telegraph* (1973).
43. See F. G. C. Baldwin, *History of the Telephone in the United Kingdom* (1925); and A. Hazlewood, 'The Origin of the State Telephone Service in Britain', *Oxford Economic Papers*, new series, V (1953).
44. See B. R. Mitchell, 'The Coming of the Railway and United Kingdom Economic Growth', *Journal of Economic History*, XXLV (1964).
45. See G. Alderman, *The Railway Interest* (1973).
46. P. Mathias, *The First Industrial Nation* (1969), p. 489.
47. Phyllis Deane and W. A. Cole, *British Economic Growth, 1688–1959* (2nd edn, 1967), p. 234.
48. See G. S. Graham, 'The Ascendancy of the Sailing Ship, 1850–85', *Economic History Review*, second series, LX (1956); and C. K. Harley, 'The Shift from Sailing Ships to Steamships, 1850–1890', in D. N. McCloskey (ed.), *Essays on a Mature Economy* (1971).
49. R. H. Langbridge (ed.), *Life in the 1870s* (1974), p. 53.

Chapter 5

Religious life: *'Very hard to come at the actual belief of any man'*

1

Religion occupied a central place in the minds of most middle and upper-class Victorians.[1] The defence and promotion of Christian belief – or at least the observance of Christian worship – were regarded as vital to society. As population grew, and as cities and towns fast extended, thousands of churches and chapels were put within reach of the new urban millions. Between 1840 and 1876 the Anglicans alone built 1,727 new churches in England and Wales, and rebuilt or restored 7,144 more, at a total cost of £25,548,703. The Christian message remained available to all; and until near the end of the century religious leaders shared a sense of uplift. Yet relative to growth of population, attendance was only holding its own. In absolute terms, therefore, although more people were attending church or chapel than ever before, unprecedented numbers were also remaining outside their doors.

The 1851 census of religious worship provided evidence which allowed a calculation of the numbers attending service on 30 March 1851.[2] These totalled: Church of England 3,773,474; Nonconformists 3,153,490; Roman Catholics 305,393; others 28,685. Fully committed participation in religious observance was spread between the leading denominations as follows:[3]

	Church of England in England		
	Easter-Day communicants	Churches	Clergy
1851	875,000	14,077	16,194
1871	1,110,000	15,522	19,411
1881	1,225,000	16,300	20,341

	Methodist membership in England					
	Wesleyan	New Connexion	Primitive	Bible Christian	United	Total
1851	285,000	16,962	106,074	13,894	—	421,930
1871	319,495	22,870	148,597	18,050	61,924	570,936
1881	349,695	25,797	168,807	21,209	65,067	630,575

Congregational and Baptist membership in England

	Congregational	Particular Baptist	General Baptist
1851	165,000	122,000	18,277
1863	180,000	132,000	20,714
1880	—	176,500	24,489

Roman Catholics in England and Wales

	Estimated Catholic population	Churches	Priests	Mass attenders
1851	900,000	597	826	482,000
1871	—	947	1,551	—
1881	—	1,175	1,979	—

The Presbyterian Church of England was formed in 1876 with 46,540 communicants. Membership of the Society of Friends revived from a low point near 13,800 in the early 1860s to over 15,000 by 1881.

Support for each denomination varied widely from place to place, and also between types of people.[4] Percentage attendance was in general higher in country than in town; and both town and country attendance tended to run above average in eastern England, the east midlands, and the south-west, and to fall below it in the north, west midlands, and south-east. The Church of England was active in the country districts, where its parochial organization suited the local situation, weaker in the industrial towns where the parish system was less effective. But no Nonconformist sect could match the Church of England's national spread, for each sect drew its main support from certain areas. Nevertheless, in 1851 Nonconformists of all types provided more sittings than the Anglicans in Cornwall and Bedfordshire, and in all counties east of the Pennines from Nottingham and Derby northwards. The Bible Christians and Primitive Methodists were strong among agricultural workers; the Wesleyans remained more town-centred, the sect of shopkeepers and small businessmen. The Congregationalists played the leading Nonconformist part in London, notably in the middle-class suburbs. The Baptists flourished especially in the east midlands, East Anglia, and the west country. The Presbyterians were strongest in the border counties, near to Scotland; the Catholics in Lancashire, nearest to Ireland. The Unitarians and Quakers – comparatively few numerically – constituted the wealthiest Nonconformist bodies, abounding with merchants, manufacturers, and bankers.

The bigger the town usually the greater the extent of non-attendance at church or chapel. According to the 1851 religious census, in a score of the largest towns less than one person in ten attended any place of worship on census Sunday. Over the whole country, and over all classes, at least one-quarter of the population were voluntary absentees. Among the working classes this proportion stood much higher. 'More especially in cities and large towns it is observable how absolutely insignificant a portion of the congregation is composed of artizans.' Many working men did not regard church or chapel as open to them. Clergymen were 'gentlemen'. Both in church and chapel middle-class worshippers often laid claim to rented pews. Where 'free' pews were available, they seemed to be provided as an act of social condescension. Moreover, middle-class worshippers were universally well-dressed. Working class men and women knew that they would be marked out by their clothes. They were most likely to attend services for the great festivals – at Christmas, Easter, harvest festival, and watch night. They also attended for family marriages, funerals, and christenings. Ninety per cent of all English and Welsh marriages were performed under religious auspices in 1870, and still over 78 per cent in 1913.[5]

2

'Church' and 'chapel' were rival organizations, even though they professed Christianity in common. 'Almost every village of any size has two distinct sets of apparatus for doing good – the one worked by Churchmen, the other by Dissenters. Every town has its exclusive circles of social intercourse – the one appropriated to Churchmen, the other to Dissenters.' So admitted Edward Miall, a leading Congregationalist, in the House of Commons (9 May 1871). The Church of England always remained confident about its superiority both in social terms and as an institution. 'The Church of England is the religion of the higher classes, most of the middle, and, in the rural districts, of the labouring classes.' So claimed *The Times* (9.5.1871), with some exaggeration. 'It deals far more easily and comfortably with an ordinary man of average character, doing his duties after a fashion, than the Nonconformists, who, according to their theology, try to persuade him that he is utterly lost, or graceless, or superstitious, or a fool. All feel that they can live under the shelter of the Church of England, safe from wind and wave, whether they agree with it or not.' As the established institution, the Church of England was supposedly open to all. People 'went' to Church, whereas they 'joined' a chapel. Yet the 1851 religious census had shown that the number of Nonconformist worshippers in England and Wales then stood not far short of the Anglican total. The Church of England was becoming one denomination among many, albeit still the leading and the largest one.

  Small Nonconformist sects with strange-sounding names abounded, sometimes confined to one chapel, and often to one locality – the Hallelujah Band, the Free Grace Gospel Christians, the Christians Who Object to be Otherwise Designated, and many more. The main Nonconformist bodies were divided by their origins into the Old Dissent of the seventeenth century – the Presbyterians, Congregationalists, Baptists, and Quakers; and the New Dissent of the eighteenth-century evangelical revival – notably Methodism in its several forms. All were self-made and in varying ways self-governing organizations, which owed nothing to state help and had indeed long suffered from state hostility. By early-Victorian times they enjoyed toleration; but so long as the Church of England remained the privileged established denomination Nonconformist militants continued to feel dissatisfied and combative. The chief journalistic mouthpiece for this discontent was the *Nonconformist*, a weekly journal founded by Edward Miall in 1841, with the uncompromising motto 'The Dissidence of Dissent and the Protestantism of the Protestant Religion'. 'Look at the life imagined in such a newspaper as the *Nonconformist*,' complained Matthew Arnold in *Culture and Anarchy* (1869), '. . . a life of jealousy of the Establishment, disputes, tea-meetings, openings of chapels, sermons; and then think of it as an ideal of a human life completing itself on all sides.' John Morley answered that a history of persecution and under-privilege had made it difficult for Nonconformists to acquire the social and cultural graces. 'Dissent is not picturesque, but it possesses a heroic political record.'[6]

Many Nonconformists were not militant. The Wesleyans, for example, usually inclined towards conservatism in both religion and politics. But all shades of Nonconformity showed increasing self-assurance as Queen Victoria's reign progressed – reflected in the replacement of the old word 'Dissenter', which carried defensive overtones, by 'Nonconformist' with its more confident assertion of difference. One strength of Nonconformity was believed to be its readiness fully to involve its laymen. 'They have more offices, deaconships and visitors and tract distributors: and in these ways the chapels manage to employ their people very much better than the Church. This is an attraction to small shopkeepers and mechanics, who find they are looked upon as somebody in the congregation.' Typical middle-class Nonconformists hoped to do well for their chapel, and also for themselves. 'There are several who have made money and a great many intend and expect to make it before long. They are a pushing, active, restless, enterprising class of people, intent on religion, and determined to make the best of both worlds.' In such terms was one Sheffield United Methodist congregation described in 1869.[7]

The Nonconformists became closely associated with the temperance movement, and also with the 'frozen Sunday'. They insisted that it was not their temperance programme but the absence of temperance which was keeping many of the working classes from attending service: 'many millions of our people deaden their spiritual nature by drink'.[8] The ultra-Sabbatarians wanted prohibition of all public non-religious Sunday activities – all shops shut, all public transport stopped, and all public houses closed. Most working men – with few pleasures but drinking, and little leisure time except on Sundays – were unlikely to be attracted by such a negative social programme.

The political demands of Nonconformity were more positive.

Nonconformists had first been forced to fight for religious toleration under the law, and then for civil equality with Anglicans. This second struggle was still continuing during Victoria's reign. Nonconformist influence was considerable within the Liberal Party. In 1868 the Compulsory Church Rate Abolition Act was promoted by Gladstone as Opposition leader.[9] The Society for the Liberation of the Church from state Patronage and Control (usually known as the Liberation Society) demanded abolition even of voluntary church rates. But Gladstone's measure, which was backed by moderates on both sides of the Commons, simply declared that henceforth no lawsuit could be started to compel payment. In other words, the grievance was removed without removing church rates themselves. The 1880 Burials Act ended another old grievance. In country districts – where often only Church of England burial grounds were available – Nonconformists had been required to be buried according to Anglican rites.[10] The 1880 Act allowed any 'Christian and orderly' form of service, or no service at all. Church property in the shape of churchyards was thereby recognized as national property, not under the exclusive control of the Established Church. Some Anglicans warned that this represented a step towards the disestablishment and disendowment of the Church of England.

Disestablishment and disendowment were certainly the main demands of the Nonconformist militants in the Liberation Society.[11] They contended that true religious equality required that the Anglican Church be put upon the same unprivileged footing as the Non-conformist sects. 'No idea has now to wage such war with those that seek its downfall,' wrote Charles Buxton in *Ideas of the Day on Policy* (3rd edn, 1868), 'as the idea that the State, as a State, must hold, and uphold the true Faith'. The arguments for and against disestablishment filled more than twenty pages of his son's *Handbook to Political Questions of the Day* (8th edn, 1892). Some arguments for disestablishment were professedly in the best interests of the Church of England itself – 'there is much more vitality in a religion voluntarily supported than in one largely endowed'. One Anglican curate, the Reverend Francis Kilvert, attended a Liberation Society lecture at Chippenham in 1876. The lecturer began by emphasizing the advantages of the Church fulfilling its mission unhampered by establishment. 'But by degrees the cloven hoof peeped out and we heard more of the rights of the Nation, National rights, the *parish* Church, the intolerable monopoly of the Church, the social disadvantages of Dissenters, the arrogance of the Church and clergy, and the usual rigmarole.'[12] A few high Anglicans were indeed themselves prepared to accept disestablishment because they feared political interference with their forms of worship. But the majority followed Gladstone, who argued that though it was right to remove disabilities which affected individual Nonconformists, they were not oppressed as individuals by the existence of the Anglican Establishment. On the contrary, a connection between Christianity and the state was claimed as strengthening the practice both of religion and of government. The disestablishment question was complicated by its link with disendowment. Some militants argued that all pre-Reformation Church property should be seized, because it had not been intended for the Church of England; others contended that all property granted before 1662 should be taken, since before that date only one legal Church had existed and its property belonged to the nation.

The disestablishment and disendowment of the Church of Ireland by Gladstone's Government in 1869 gave great encouragement to the Liberationists. Gladstone stressed, however, that the Irish Church had represented only a small minority of Irishmen, whereas the Church of England remained the largest denomination for Englishmen. Nevertheless, the disestablishment movement seemed to be gaining ground during the early 1870s.[13] In 1871 Edward Miall, the Congregationalist leader of the Liberation Society, introduced a disestablishment motion in the Commons (9 May) with probably the most effective speech in favour ever heard in Parliament. He emphasized how the recent tendency had been 'to sweep away class distinctions, and, as far as law can do it, to remove the causes of social divisions and discords'. Disestablishment, he argued, would represent action in this liberating spirit. Miall's motion was defeated by 374 votes to 89; but the minority had become large enough to make Liberationists very hopeful that within a few years steady pressure from outside Parliament would gain them a majority inside. Motions by Miall in 1872 and 1873 attracted 94 and 61 votes respectively. Yet the majority of Nonconformists in the country never felt so strongly as the Liberationists. The 1868 Church Rate Act; the 1871 act which abolished university tests (see below, p. 180); and the 1880 Burials Act all seemed to lessen the need for disestablishment. Advocates were themselves divided between those who wanted instant English disestablishment, and those who recommended a gradualist approach by pressing first for disestablishment in Wales and Scotland.

The English disestablishment issue returned to prominence during the 1885 general election; but mainly because of a Conservative decision to raise the cry of 'the Church in danger'. By this date Joseph Chamberlain, the radical leader, had come to accept that disestablishment lacked sufficient support to make it present practical politics, and he relegated it to 'the remoter distance'. Gladstone soon afterwards made Irish Home Rule the dominating political issue. By 1894 Chamberlain's friend R. W. Dale, the prominent Birmingham congregational minister, was remarking how disestablishment had seemed closer to achievement twenty years earlier: 'the popular passion has all run into the channels of the various labour questions'.[14]

The coldness – sometimes flaring into antagonism – between Anglicans and Nonconformists was surpassed in intensity by the distrust – sometimes flaring into hatred – of both Anglicans and Nonconformists for Roman Catholics, especially during the first half of Victoria's reign.[15] 'Popery' was doubly suspected. It was associated in

English minds with tyranny in politics and religion, and with abnormality in private life. The celibacy of Roman Catholic priests was regarded as unnatural, probably leading to sexual irregularities. The confessional was seen as an excuse for prurient prying. When Lord Ripon became a Catholic convert in 1874 *The Times* (5.9.1875) announced that he had forfeited the confidence of the English people because he had renounced his moral and intellectual freedom. The proclamation of papal infallibility in 1870 convinced Gladstone that Catholics could not now be trusted in their political allegiance, since the Pope might order them to act against it. Gladstone's pamphlet on The *Vatican Decrees in their bearing on Civil Allegiance* (1874) quickly sold 145,000 copies.

In 1868 Disraeli had assured the House of Commons (3 April) that 'High Church Ritualists and the Irish followers of the Pope have long been in secret combination'. Queen Victoria feared that the Anglo-Catholics might take over the Church of England. 'I am sure there will have to be a new Reformation.'[16] Royal pressure privately helped to persuade Archbishop Tait of Canterbury to promote – and Disraeli's cabinet to countenance – the 1874 Public Worship Regulation Act. Tait feared not that the ritualists would capture the Church but that they would provoke its break-up, through internal dissension and through consequent weakened resistance to pressure for disestablishment. The Act gave bishops extra powers to control the ceremonial practices of their clergy. Yet attempts to use the machinery provided by the Act only added to the obstinacy of the ritualists, who continued to flourish within the Church of England. Legislation had proved to be an unsatisfactory method of regulating an established Church in modern times.[17]

3

'A desire to flee from the wrath to come, and a probation of three months.' Such were the terms of membership of one Hackney Wesleyan chapel given in *Dickens's Dictionary of London, 1879*. Amidst all the religious bustle of late-Victorian England, how deep was religious belief? Anthony Trollope remarked in his *Clergymen of the Church of England* (1866) that it was 'very hard to come at the actual belief of any man'. Observance did not necessarily mean faith. Regular church and chapel attendance was accepted by many of the middle and upper classes as necessary for social reasons, whether they believed or not. A good example had to be set to the lower orders. One 1911 study of an old country squire remarked that 'he does not ask whether he needs the comforts of religion, he is sure that society needs religion, and if society needs religion he, as one of the first in the social organization, must be there at his post'. C. H. Spurgeon, Baptist minister of the London Metropolitan Tabernacle and the most popular preacher of the 1860s and 1870s, remained under no illusions about his congregations o thousands. 'In these days men are strongly tempted to believe that to look like a Christian will certainly be as useful as to be a Christian at heart.'[18]

Certainly, sermons by leading preachers were enjoyed as entertainment whether or not they were also welcomed for their spiritual guidance. Styles of preaching varied; some preachers expounded the Bible, some taught doctrine, some were polemicists. All were expected to preach at length.[19] Nonconformists admitted that exciting sermons could sometimes take even too much attention. But hymn singing, which most Nonconformists relished, provided a strong counter-attraction. At intervals religious revivals swept over the middle classes, notably during 1874–5 when the American evangelistic preacher Dwight L. Moody and singer Ira D. Sankey toured the country.

Just as sermons were much heard and read, so accounts of deathbed scenes were much in demand. A 'good deathbed' set an example. A good funeral was also expected. All classes lavished freely on funeral display, and working-class families often spent well beyond their means.[20] *The Times* (2.2.1875) complained about the spread of 'prodigious funerals', 'awful hearses drawn by preternatural quadrupeds, clouds of black plumes, solid and magnificent oak coffins instead of sepulchral elm, coffin within coffin, lead, brick graves and capacious catacombs'. Degrees and duration of mourning among the middle and upper classes had become elaborately graded. Widows moved through a cycle of gradually reduced mourning which lasted for three years.

The custom of elaborate mourning did not exclude continuing 'doubt'. Doubt was indeed very much part of Victorian religion, well exemplified in the career of Tennyson who was tortured by uncertainty right until his old-age expression of faith in *Crossing the Bar* (1889). Queen Victoria herself admitted to 'flashes of doubtfulness'; but (she added) it was impossible to believe that lives cut short, such as Prince Albert's, could really have come 'to an utter end'. The queen regretted that fear of eternal damnation had disappeared as a spur to faith.[21] With the gradual abandonment of acceptance of the literal truth of the Bible, theologians were emphasizing the subjectivity of the concepts of heaven and hell, describing them as states of mind not as physical entities. But Victoria was unhappy about the unsettling effects of the new biblical scholarship, and also about the impact of new scientific ideas (including Darwin's theory of evolution) upon religious belief. 'Science is greatly to be admired and encouraged, but if it is to take the place of our Creator, and if philosophers and students try to explain everything and to disbelieve whatever they cannot prove, I call it a great evil instead of a great blessing.'

'Most men who call themselves Christians would say that they believed the Bible, not knowing what they meant, never having attempted – and very wisely having refrained from attempting amidst the multiplicity of their worldly concerns – to separate historical record from inspired teaching.' So explained Anthony Trollope in 1866. The fierce theological conflict over the publication of *Essays and Reviews* in 1860 remained rather remote from the average man in the pew.[22] The seven Broad Church Anglican contributors included Frederick Temple, later Archbishop of Canterbury, Mark Pattison, later Rector of Lincoln College, Oxford, and Benjamin Jowett, later Master of Balliol. Aware of the progress of German biblical criticism, the essayists set out to read the Bible 'like any other book'; but in the confident belief that in so doing its value, especially that of the New Testament, would be not weakened but strengthened. They were wrongly suspected, however, of inclining towards deism – 'Seven against Christ'.

Biblical criticism was well advanced long before Charles Darwin's *Origin of Species* (1859) added the evidence of evolution to the case against a literal acceptance of the Old Testament story of the creation.[23] By the late 1870s the *Origin of Species* had been absorbed by most Christians, and also *The Descent of Man* (1871), in which Darwin first explicitly applied the idea of evolution to human beings. *Punch* (8.12.1877) sang his praises in verse:

> Though dogmatists and dullards long opposed
>   His theory with venomous persistence,
> Darwin may now consider it has closed
>   Its – 'Struggle for existence'.

The Book of Genesis, it was agreed, should be read as allegory. The process of evolution, as explained by Darwin, was as wonderful an expression of God's power as the old creation story.

The problem remained, though, of how to accept man as part of nature – not a special creation – and yet to keep man special in the sight of God, and therefore capable of immortality. It was rightly emphasized that Darwin's book was misnamed. The very thing which he had *not* explained was the ultimate origin of species. Darwin spoke of 'chance', but that could be regarded as the hand of God. Lord Salisbury emphasized in his 1894 presidential address to the British Association for the Advancement of Science how science could never establish ultimate causes.

Few men are now influenced by the strange idea that questions of religious belief depend on the issues of physical research. Few men, whatever their creed, would now seek their geology in the books of their religion, or, on the other hand, would fancy that the laboratory or the microscope could help them to penetrate the mysteries which hang over the nature and the destiny of the soul of man.[24]

Benjamin Jowett admitted in 1871 that there were 'degrees of the belief in immortality'. 'Some persons will say no more than that they trust in God, and that they leave all to Him. It is a great part of true religion not to pretend to know more than we do.' Winwood Reade's widely-read *The Martyrdom of Man* (1872), on the other hand, dismissed the desire for immortality as misplaced – 'belief in property after death'. Reade believed in God, but God so great 'that he cannot be defined by us'.[25] Reade had moved further perhaps than he realized towards 'agnosticism'. This word was coined by T. H. Huxley, the scientist and Darwinian publicist, in 1869. In an immediately famous article on 'The Physical Basis of Life' in the *Fortnightly Review* for February 1869 he explained the agnostic position, how it stopped short of atheism. 'If a man asks me what the politics of the inhabitants of the moon are, and I reply that I do not know; that neither I, nor any one else, have any means of knowing; and that, under these circumstances, I decline to trouble myself about the subject at all, I do not think he has any right to call me a sceptic.' Huxley became a leading member of the Metaphysical Society, a remarkable discussion group of over sixty leading figures of all shades of belief and non-belief – including Gladstone, Archbishop Manning, Archbishop Thomson of York, Ruskin, and Tennyson. It met regularly between 1869 and 1880 to hear and discuss papers by members on such problems as 'Is God Knowable?', 'What is Death?', 'What is Matter?', 'The Soul before and after Death', 'The Absolute', and so on.[26]

Most members of the Metaphysical Society held their opinions firmly; but by the end of the 1870s this was beginning to seem old-fashioned. John Morley in his important essay *On Compromise* (1873) denounced 'light-hearted neutrality', which was not to be confused with hard-thought-out agnosticism. But the light-hearted attitude was spreading.[27] Did any opinions matter? 'What do you do then in this perplexity – this halting between two opinions? Why, you do this. You try to persuade yourselves that neither opinion is of much moment – that the question cannot be decided absolutely – that it should not be decided absolutely – in fact, that it is one of your chief glories that you leave it undecided.' So explained, and complained, W. H. Mallock in *The New Republic* (1877), another key book of the decade. Why spend time on religious argument or 'doubt'? Why spend time even on religious observance? By the 1880s the range of secular alternatives to Sunday churchgoing was extending fast.

4

The majority of Victorian working men were not active in the practice of religion. But they shared a vague belief in God. The London working man, explained C. F. G. Masterman, a close observer, 'faithfully believes in a Deity whose fundamental characteristic is a general tolerance, and who will assuredly compensate him in the next world for the many good things denied him in this'.[28] The number of active atheists always remained tiny. An organized secularist movement had existed since the 1840s, directed from 1866 by the National Secular Society with Charles Bradlaugh as president.[29] Bradlaugh, a solicitor's clerk, ran a weekly paper – the *National Reformer* (1861) – to voice his heterodox opinions. He advocated not only atheism but also birth control and republicanism. Bradlaugh was a brilliant speaker, pugnacious but not offensive in his manner. Even so, he attracted very much more attention than support. At its peak about 1885 the National Secular Society had still only attained perhaps 100 branches with some 4,000 members. Most supporters of the society seem to have been working men, chiefly lapsed Roman Catholics and Nonconformists, who had reacted against their family faiths or against the absurdities of the Bible; or who had been converted by Tom Paine's classic *Age of Reason* (1793), which continued a bestseller among radical workmen throughout the nineteenth century. Bradlaugh died in 1891, by which date socialism with its positive policies (which he opposed) was proving stronger than secularism with its negatives.

By the 1880s and 1890s not only socialist working men were demanding that more notice be paid to social conditions at home. Even some religious leaders were heard wondering why, with massive non-attendance in the cities and towns of England, quite so much attention had been given to missionary work overseas.[30] In the 1860s and 1870s, when David Livingstone was a popular hero, missionary self-confidence and self-sacrifice had reached their height. Livingstone was strongly motivated by faith in the future of Africa, and by confidence in his own role of promoting 'commerce and Christianity' as a way of emancipating the Africans. During the last quarter of the century, however, missionary work became more specialized and less heroic. Missionaries began to serve as teachers, doctors, and pastoral guides. This greater social emphasis risked diverting attention from the spiritual role of the churches. But this risk was bound to be run both in 'darkest Africa' and in 'darkest England', if Christianity was to remain a living creed.

Notes

1. See R. A. Soloway, 'Church and Society: Recent Trends in Nineteenth Century Religious History', *Journal of British Studies*, XI (1972), and references there; especially O. Chadwick, *The Victorian Church*, Vols. I (3rd edn, 1971) and II (2nd edn, 1972). Also A. D. Gilbert, *Religion and Society in Industrial England* (1976).
2. See K. S. Inglis, 'Patterns of Religious Worship in 1851', *Journal of Ecclesiastical History*, XI (1960).
3. A. D. Gilbert, *Religion and Society in Industrial England* (1976), Ch. 2; R. Currie *et al.*, *Churches and Churchgoers* (1977).
4. See J. D. Gay, *The Geography of Religion in England* (1971); A. Everitt, *The Pattern of Rural Dissent: The Nineteenth Century* (1972); and H. McLeod, 'Class, Community and Region: The Religious Geography of Nineteenth-Century England', *Sociological Yearbook of Religion in Britain*, Vol. 6 (1973).
5. R. Currie *et al.*, *Churches and Churchgoers* (1977), pp. 223–4.
6. J. Morley, *The Struggle for National Education* (1873), p. 7. See especially K. Young, *Chapel* (1972); D. M. Thompson (ed.), *Nonconformity in the Nineteenth Century* (1972); and I. Sellers, *Nineteenth-Century Nonconformity* (1977).
7. E. R. Wickham, *Church and People in an Industrial City* (1957), pp. 116, 130.
8. G. Haw (ed.), *Christianity and the Working Classes* (1906), p. 87.

9. See especially Olive Anderson, 'Gladstone's Abolition of Compulsory Church Rates', *Journal of Ecclesiastical History*, XXV (1974).

10. See P. T. Marsh, *The Victorian Church in Decline* (1969), Ch. 10; and W. H. Mackintosh, *Disestablishment and Liberation* (1972), Ch. 21.

11. See especially W. H. Mackintosh, *Disestablishment and Liberation* (1972); and D. A. Hamer, *The Politics of Electoral Pressure* (1977), Ch. VIII.

12. W. Plomer (ed.), *Kilvert's Diary* (1971), III, pp. 296–7.

13. See especially S. M. Ingham, 'The Disestablishment Movement in England, 1868–74', *Journal of Religious History*, Vol. 3 (1964); and P. T. Marsh, *The Victorian Church in Decline* (1969), Ch. 6.

14. A. W. W. Dale, *Life of R. W. Dale* (1899), p. 672. See especially N. J. Richards, 'Disestablishment of the Anglican Church in England in the late Nineteenth Century: Reasons for Failure', *Journal of Church and State*, Vol. 12 (1970); and A. Simon, 'Church Disestablishment as a Factor in the General Election of 1885', *Historical Journal*, XVII (1975).

15. See especially G. F. A. Best, 'Popular Protestantism in Victorian Britain', in R. Robson (ed.), *Ideas and Institutions of Victorian Britain* (1967); and E. R. Norman, *Anti-Catholicism in Victorian England* (1968).

16. R. Fulford (ed.) *Your Dear Letter* (1971), p. 161. See especially P. T. Marsh, *The Victorian Church in Decline* (1969), Chs. 5, 7, 9.

17. See J. Bentley, *Ritualism and Politics in Victorian Britain* (1978).

18. W. L. Burn, *The Age of Equipoise* (1964), p. 277; H. McLeod, *Class and Religion in the Late Victorian City* (1974), p. 201.

19. See especially H. Davies, *Worship and Theology in England*, IV (1962), Ch. X.

20. See J. Morley, *Death, Heaven and the Victorians* (1971); and J. S. Curl, *The Victorian Celebration of Death* (1972).

21. H. Nicolson, *Tennyson* (1960), pp. 247–53; Elizabeth Longford, *Victoria R.I.* (1964), pp. 340–5; R. Fulford (ed.), *Darling Child* (1976), pp. 292–4. See also G. Rowell, *Hell and the Victorians* (1974).

22. See especially M. A. Crowther, *Church Embattled, Religious Controversy in Mid-Victorian England* (1970).

23. See especially A. Ellegård, *Darwin and the General Reader, 1859–1872* (1958); Gertrude Himmelfarb, *Darwin and the Darwinian Revolution* (1959); and B. M. Young, 'The Impact of Darwin on Conventional Thought', in A. Symondson (ed.), *The Victorian Crisis of Faith* (1970).

24. G. Basalla (ed.), *Victorian Science* (1970), p. 353.

25. Sir A. Quiller-Couch (ed.), *The Oxford Book of English Prose* (1925), p. 755; J. C. Masterman, *Bits and Pieces* (1961), pp. 83–7.

26. See A. W. Brown, *The Metaphysical Society* (1973).

27. W. E. Houghton, *The Victorian Frame of Mind, 1830–1870* (1957), pp. 179–80; A. Briggs, 'The Eighteen Seventies', *University of Leeds Review*, Vol. 17 (1974–5).

28. C. F. G. Masterman, *From the Abyss* (1902), pp. 59–60. See especially J. Kent, 'Feelings and Festivals, An Interpretation of Some Working-Class Religious Attitudes', in H. J. Dyos and M. Wolff (eds.), *The Victorian City* (1973).

29. See especially F. B. Smith, 'The Atheist Mission, 1840–1900' in R. Robson (ed.), *Ideas and Institutions of Victorian Britain* (1967); E. Royle, *Radical Politics, 1790–1900, Religion and Unbelief* (1971); and Susan Budd, *Varieties of Unbelief* (1977).

30. See especially O. Chadwick, *Mackenzie's Grave* (1959); and M. Warren, 'The Church Militant Abroad: Victorian Missionaries', in A. Symondson (ed.), *The Victorian Crisis of Faith* (1970).

Chapter 6

Cultural life: *'To morally transform the world'*

1

The new dominant town environment was being developed chiefly for the promotion of work. But socially-aware Victorians recognized that facilities for play and recreation – mental and physical – would be needed by the new urban millions. Matthew Arnold had become greatly concerned by what he regarded as the shallow and misguided values of the new urban England. In *Culture and Anarchy* (1869) he divided society into three categories: Barbarians (aristocrats), Philistines (the middle classes), and Populace (the rest). He argued that all lacked 'culture'; but he was particularly critical of the middle classes, who were (he claimed) too much interested in profit-making and materialism. Arnold called upon Englishmen to abandon their sectional interests, to seek instead a social consensus through the lifetime pursuit of 'sweetness and light', of 'a national glow of life and thought'. Some were trying to give the masses 'an intellectual food prepared and adapted'; but Arnold did not want his culture-bearers to offer any substitutes. 'Culture works differently. It does not try to teach down . . . It seeks to do away with classes and sects; to make the best that has been thought and known in the world current everywhere.'[1]

Arnold made little impression upon the masses themselves, and not much upon the middle classes, though they enjoyed his ironical style. But as a persistent voice from the intellectual minority he was at least pointing the way towards 'culture' as a continuing pursuit for all. 'In every generation,' wrote his niece, Mrs Humphry Ward, the novelist, 'while a minority is making or taking part in the intellectual process itself, there is an atmosphere, a diffusion produced around them, which affects many, many thousands who have but little share – but little *conscious* share, at any rate – in the actual process.'[2] In its Golden Jubilee survey *The Times* (22.6.1887) described the interaction between public opinion and the arts. During Victoria's reign they had gained attention 'rather by their violence, vigour, variety, and adaptation to the everyday wants of mankind, than by the attainment of supreme excellence'. Great work in art or letters was usually the product of periods of repose, which the Victorian age was not. But the growth of a wide audience, claimed *The Times*, had at least encouraged a high overall standard of competence among both writers and painters. Victoria's reign 'need not fear comparison with earlier periods in any achievement that falls within the scope of conscientious industry, patient effort, and thoroughgoing investigation'.

During the first half of the reign the arts had been expected to provide moral instruction at least as much as to give pleasure. Subtlety in a book or painting was not highly valued, since it might impede understanding. The hidden depths found by modern critics in the works of Dickens, George Eliot, Tennyson, and others were not noticed by the contemporary reading public. Favourite poets and painters were set alongside favourite preachers. In this spirit the most popular Victorian paintings told a story or pointed a moral.[3] W. P. Frith's meticulous, moralizing depictions of such scenes as *Derby Day* (1856) or *The Railway Station* (1862) won remarkable acclaim. 'All those who believe that the art of a time is then most vital when it occupies itself with what belongs to that time,' exclaimed *The Times* (19.4.1862) of the latter picture, 'stamps it, interests it, makes it of importance to the world, must rejoice in Mr Frith's achievement.' John Ruskin, the Victorian art sage, taught how the whole quality of life was shaped by the presence or absence of beauty or morality in everyday surroundings or relationships. He believed that both art and religion needed enthusiastic support in the fight against the spreading squalor and materialism of urban industrial society. Neither religion nor art could be separated from everyday existence. For Ruskin the concept of aesthetic man was as false and dehumanizing as the idea of economic man.[4]

By the 1870s, however, the heyday of moralizing in paint was passing; and one commentator upon 'The State of English Painting' (*Quarterly Review*, April 1873) even dared to suggest that Frith was not an artist at all but merely an illustrator. The same critic contended that painters had foolishly been trying to match the new medium of photography upon its strongest ground. Certainly, the camera had become a significant social influence by the 1860s. The *Photographic News* claimed in 1861 that photography was 'the best feature of fine arts for the million'.[5] Studios had been opened by photographers in every town, and people of small means could now command likenesses which equalled those painted exclusively for the well-to-do in previous generations.

Victorian inventiveness in technology was not paralleled by innovation in terms of style. Aesthetically, complained one contemporary, 'the sole original feature of the epoch' had been the crinoline. In architecture was fought about 1860 'the battle of the styles', none of them new.[6] Most Victorians of the 1850s and 1860s were agreed in disliking the classical simplicities of early nineteenth-century architecture. This meant that they disliked much of the building which they had inherited. Parson Kilvert described in his diary for 4 May 1876 a church 'built in the Dark Ages of fifty years ago ... ugly as it appeared externally the interior was worse'.[7] Church 'restoration' was pursued with entire confidence, under the inspiration of Ruskin. Venetian Gothic – taken from the Middle Ages – was good because Christian: classical was bad because pagan. Ruskin did not indeed advocate mere copying; but he did recommend that contemporary Gothic should take care to retain the medieval harmony between form and spirit. And such Christian harmony seemed appropriate not only for churches but also for secular buildings. During the late 1860s versions of the Gothic were being boldly used for such important edifices as the Law Courts, St Pancras Hotel, Keble College, and many lesser buildings. The leading Gothic practitioners were Sir Gilbert Scott, William Butterfield, G. E. Street, and Alfred Waterhouse. Waterhouse's Manchester town hall was rightly praised as 'a Gothic that is a natural development from the architecture of the Middle Ages, not a repetition of it'. But, as the same observer regretted, lesser architects tended to produce uninspired imitations, and their work was to be found all over the country. By 1872 Ruskin himself was beginning to despair at the insensitive application of Gothic ideas. This, he admitted, had 'dignified our banks and drapers' shops with Venetian tracery, and pinched our parish churches into dark and slippery arrangements for the advertisement of cheap coloured glass and pantiles'.[8]

From about this date Gothic was beginning to lose favour. It remained the customary form for churchbuilding; but in other spheres the 'Queen Anne' style began to be adopted. The leading Queen Anne architect was Norman Shaw, himself a former Gothicist.[9] Despite its name the new mode – which was to flourish with modifications for the rest of the century – owed much more to the Renaissance than to the early eighteenth century. It showed a liking first for red-brick and then for terracotta exteriors, ornamented in the bourgeois style of the English seventeenth century but with gables and dormers of Flemish inspiration. It was a middle-class style especially suited to dainty domestic housebuilding – notably in the London garden suburb of Bedford Park, erected from the late 1870s; but it was adaptable also for office and public building.

2

An article by James Buchanan in the *New Quarterly Musical Review* for November 1895 on 'The Education of Audiences' discussed the great extension of musical interest during the Victorian period.[10] Leisure had increased, and the teaching from the 1840s of the tonic-sol-fa system – the substitution of syllables for notes on a conventional musical stave – had helped to spread a simple musical understanding among working-class adults and children. It enabled amateur choirs to sing ambitious choral works with at least passable competence. The best working-class choirs – to be found in the West Riding and in north Staffordshire – did possess real musical knowledge in their performances of cantatas and oratorios. These were the favourite Victorian musical forms, satisfyingly pious both in words and music. The first (1880) edition of Grove's *Dictionary of Music and Musicians* was sure that oratorio gave 'to the Musician the exact analogy of what the Cathedral is to the Architect – the highest Art-form'. Every year big new oratorios were announced; but the favourites remained Handel's *Messiah* and Mendelssohn's *Elijah*. It has been argued that the diversion of talent into oratorio writing – a form which encouraged note-spinning – rather than into symphonic composition was one reason for the low standard of serious musical output in England during the Victorian period.[11]

On the Continent England was known as 'the land without music'. Certainly, all the best new serious music played in England came from the Continent itself; but most popular songs were English compositions. Not that many Victorians drew a sharp distinction between serious and popular music. Middle-class taste ranged easily from religious arias to popular tunes. And music was heard everywhere, not only in public performance but at home and (not least) on the streets. The Monday Popular Concerts at St James's Hall, London, offered a high level of performance for forty years from 1859. In Manchester the Hallé Orchestra gave its first concert in 1858, conducted by Charles Hallé, a German expatriate. German immigrants into the Lancashire cotton trade helped to provide the nucleus of a dedicated audience, which Hallé gradually educated up to his own high musical standard.[12] But though the Manchester middle classes were perhaps especially musical, attendance at concerts was increasing both in London and in the provinces through the 1860s and 1870s. In the capital an essential part of the fashionable 'season' was to be seen at the Covent Garden opera house. Italian opera – especially Verdi – was preferred. Wagner's work aroused strong feelings both for and against.

Among the middle classes 'musical evenings' provided a favourite form of relaxation, with family and friends expected to play an instrument or sing. Good manners demanded that the standard of performance should be not less than tolerable. Ownership of an upright piano became a status symbol among working-class families with aspirations to rise into the lower middle class. The most popular of all songs sung at home itself celebrated the appeal of the domestic hearth – *Home Sweet Home*.[13] Those who did not play or sing were expected at least to recite. Tennyson was a favourite – with *The Charge of the Light Brigade, Locksley Hall*, and other suitable poems. But the heavily sentimental pieces of some lesser rhymsters were also much heard. Mrs Hemans's *Casabianca* long continued perhaps the most popular recitation of all:

> The boy stood on the burning deck
> Whence all but he had fled . . .

Yet many parodies of *Casabianca* went into circulation. The Victorians always remained ready to laugh at their own sentimentality, or at their own social formality. Hence their liking for practical jokes, a liking shared by the Royal Family itself. The popularity of the nonsense verse of Edward Lear, Lewis Carroll, and others may have reflected a subconscious desire to escape from the restraints of society into the laughter of release.[14] Puns and riddles were much loved, the more forced and therefore nonsensical apparently the better. *Punch* – a merciless printer of puns – was selling about 40,000 copies per week in 1870, and well over 100,000 in 1913.

The Victorian love of play on words perhaps also confirmed that theirs was a literature-centred culture. 'Literature is at once the cause and effect of social progress ... Books have become our dearest companions, yielding exquisite delights and inspiring lofty aims.' So exclaimed G. H. Lewes – whose mistress was George Eliot, the novelist – in articles on 'The Principles of Success in Literature' which appeared in the *Fortnightly Review* of 1865. Not that serious books were the reading of all. Many people read only newspapers or magazines. But at some level most Victorians seem by the last quarter of the century to have been avid readers of something.[15] Literature, continued Lewes, had now become a profession, or at least a trade. The world of struggling writers was powerfully described by George Gissing – who was himself one of them – in his novel, *New Grub Street* (1891).

The numbers employed in the paper, printing, book, and stationery trades of Great Britain grew from under 94,000 in 1871 to 212,000 by 1901. The annual output of books rose from about 2,000 per year at mid-century to 10,000 by its end. In 1868, 4,581 new books and new editions were published – 984 titles were devoted to theology, 408 were novels.[16] In total the Victorians have been estimated to have published over 40,000 novels. The rapid expansion in the numbers of white-collar workers (and their wives) created a large new reading public both for fiction and non-fiction, and for journalism. Middle-class women – with time to spare – were said to be the main readers of novels. But Charles Dickens sold so well that he must have been read by both sexes and all classes. In 1882 the total home sales of his works since his death in 1870 were reported as 4,239,000 copies. No other novelist could match Dickens in popularity, though Thackeray, Trollope, and George Eliot all had their followers. Thackeray estimated his audience at 15,000. George Eliot's great novel, *Middlemarch* (1871), sold 5,250 copies of a cheaper 7s. 6d. edition in three months. Her work was both symptomatic and influential: 'the first great *godless* writer of fiction that has appeared in England ... the first legitimate fruit of our modern atheistic pietism.'[17]

Yet 'sensational' novelists such as Mrs Henry Wood could outsell all the serious novelists except Dickens. Mrs Wood's *East Lynne* (1861) had sold 430,000 copies by 1898, when total circulation of her novels exceeded 2,500,000. Ouida, whose *Under Two Flags* was published in 1867, became equally popular. Her descriptions of gilded interiors and her exaggerations of plot exerted a curious fascination. Ruskin complained in an article on 'Fiction – Fair and Foul' in the *Nineteenth Century* for June 1880 that the liking for sensation was a reaction against the artificial and monotonous town environment to which most readers were now condemned. Down the scale of literacy still lighter fiction was available in the form of penny weekly journals. These contained stories full of melodrama and sentiment, read by what Wilkie Collins once called 'The Unknown Public' (*Household Words*, 21.8.1858). Here, concluded Collins, lay a huge audience, already literate but in need of a wider and deeper education.

Two-thirds to three-quarters of the English working class could probably read at least passably well by mid-century, with men more likely to be literate than women, and with the lowest percentage of reading in the manufacturing towns of the north and midlands.[18] A return in 1865 of the educational standards of men in the navy and marines found that over 61 per cent could read well and only 11 per cent could not read at all. Perhaps three people could read for every two who could also write. In the early 1840s a third of all men and a half of all women were signing the marriage registers with marks; but by the late 1870s only about one man in seven and one woman in five was doing so. The system of national elementary education set up under the famous 1870 Education Act and subsequent legislation did not (as soon came to be believed) create an entirely new working-class reading public. Such a public already existed. What the new education did achieve was gradually to raise the standard of reading, writing, and general knowledge, at the same time as it ensured that even the hard-core last few per cent of working-class illiterates had almost disappeared by the end of the century.

A chapter on 'Very Cheap Literature' in *The Great Unwashed* (1868), by Thomas Wright, the journeyman engineer, described how not only cheap newspapers but also cheap reprints of books were read easily and eagerly by London artisans. Shakespeare's complete works could be bought for one shilling. Wright also noted how the surplus lists of Mudie's and other circulating libraries offered a cheap way of obtaining books. Yet such buyers would presumably have been lower middle-class people rather than workmen. Mudie's was the great middle-class circulating library, with hundreds of thousands of volumes on its shelves but strongest of all in three-decker novels.[19] Mudie's had about 25,000 subscribers in 1890, and W. H. Smith's circulating library about 15,000. The number of public libraries was still limited. The 1850 Public Libraries Act had been only a permissive measure for the building of libraries, not for the buying of books. Subsequent legislation was more positive; but even by 1886 only about a hundred local authorities in England were running libraries.[20]

C. E. Mudie cast a strict eye over the new novels about to go on his shelves. He sometimes banned books entirely – as with George Moore's early novels. By the 1870s perhaps a slightly less prudish attitude to literature was gaining ground. But when in January 1875 Wilkie Collins's *The Law and the Lady* was being serialized in the *Graphic*, the editor timidly substituted 'He caught my hand in his and covered it with kisses' where Collins had written 'He caught my hand in his, and devoured it with kisses. His lips burnt me like fire.' In poetry, attacks by Robert Buchanan on what he called 'the Fleshly School of Poetry' achieved notoriety in the early 1870s.[21] The offending sensualists were Alfred Swinburne and D. G. Rossetti. But Buchanan was not widely supported by other critics. Swinburne had become the inspiration of most younger English poets, even while Robert Browning was achieving late recognition after publication of *The Ring and the Book* (1868–9); and while Alfred Tennyson, the poet laureate, was progressing to a peerage (1883). By the 1880s Tennyson was well past the peak of his popularity. The public had grown sated with Arthurian *Idylls of the King*, masterly in versification but sugary in sentiment.

Until about 1870 the drama (unlike the opera) had been regarded as morally dangerous. Theatres were equated with brothels, and actresses with prostitutes.[22] Audiences were predominantly working-class and uncouth. Crude melodramas were much liked, which offered colour, action, sentiment, and poetic justice all in simple terms. Melodramas such as *Lost in London* (1867) provided escape from the dreary round of urban struggle, and many plays directly contrasted a rural dream village with the miseries of city life.

Two men in particular contributed to winning back a large 'respectable' audience for the theatre – Tom Robertson, the playwright, and Henry Irving, the actor-manager. Robertson's comedies of everyday life, such as *Society* (1865) and *Caste* (1867), though stilted by later standards, began to win a public by their realism, especially as it was a realism which avoided impropriety of situation or language. Robertson's characters, moreover, were conceived as individuals, not as melodramatic stereotypes. Irving's *Hamlet* was the theatrical highlight of 1874. His magnetic stage personality was allied to intelligent interpretation of character; and he abandoned the old artificial declamatory delivery, though his elocution was still mannered. His most famous part, to which he returned many times, was not in a great play but in *The Bells*. Translated French plays became popular in the 1870s. These were allowed to be much more frivolous and 'improper' than plays by English writers. At a higher level of French drama, the visit of the Comédie Française, including Sarah Bernhardt, to the Gaiety Theatre in 1879 turned into a triumph. In an article on 'The French Play in London' (*Nineteenth Century*, August 1879) Matthew Arnold welcomed the influx of the middle classes into the theatres: 'this great class, having had the discipline of religion, is now awakening to the sure truth that the human spirit cannot live right if it lives by one point only'.

3

In its Golden Jubilee survey *The Times* (22.6.1887) remarked that the Victorian age had been not only the age of railways but also the age of newspapers. The main medium for the mass dissemination of news and of ideas consisted of newspapers and other journalism. The 'taxes on knowledge' had been gradually removed after mid-century – advertisement duty (1853), stamp duty (1855), and paper duty (1861). Finally, in 1869 the security system was ended, whereby a newspaper proprietor had been required to enter into a bond to cover the costs of any fines imposed for the publication of blasphemous or seditious libels. These reforms made possible a rapid transformation and expansion of the Victorian newspaper press.[23] Many new papers were started; daily newspaper prices fell to 1*d.*; and circulations increased greatly. For the first time daily publication by local papers became economically viable in provincial towns. Important established titles such as the *Manchester Guardian* and the *Leeds Mercury* now appeared each morning, as did new papers such as the *Birmingham Post* (1857) and *Yorkshire Post* (1866).

Newspaper printing was being much speeded up by the development of rotary presses. But newspaper design remained dull and solid. No attempt was yet made to break up the text to permit rapid reading. It was still assumed that readers were earnest seekers after truth for whom the daily search through the columns constituted confirmation of their own seriousness. And the assumption persisted that such readers were interested above all in politics, ready every day to peruse long and often verbatim reports of political speeches, along with many items of political news and full leading articles of political comment.[24] The development of the electric telegraph from the 1840s had made news equally available everywhere, so that local papers could now hold their own in their localities against the London press. The Press Association was formed in 1868 to provide a joint news service for provincial papers at low rates of telegraphic transmission. Thanks to the national and international spread of the telegraph, all papers, local and London, could by the 1870s bring world news to their readers only a few hours old. Previously it had taken days or weeks. This much faster spread of news made possible a much quicker public response. It strengthened the hope that the press might play an important part in creating greater understanding both between classes at home and between nations throughout the world. James Grant, editor of the *Morning Advertiser*, boldly claimed in his standard history of *The Newspaper Press* (1871–2) that the 'Mission' of the press was 'to Enlighten, to Civilize, and to Morally Transform the World'. Nevertheless, newspapers sold most copies at times of war or rumours of war.

H. R. Fox Bourne, editor of the *Weekly Dispatch*, claimed in his *English Newspapers* (1887) that during the early 1870s the press reached a period of optimum quality. Competition had become keen enough to encourage improvements, but not yet so keen as to encourage 'unworthy ways of attracting and amusing readers'. Nevertheless, newspaper proprietors were in business to make profits through sales or from advertising revenue. In 1882 it was estimated that the *Daily News* was making £30,000 per year, the *Standard* £60,000, and the *Daily*

Telegraph £120,000. On the other hand, failing newspapers could lose equally large sums. Grant noted in his history how the circulation of United Kingdom newspapers stood thirty times higher about 1870 than in 1830. In 1870 the London daily press consisted of seven morning dailies and five evenings:[25]

			Estimated circulation
Daily Chronicle	Liberal	½d.	—
Daily News	Liberal	1d.	90,000
Daily Telegraph	Liberal	1d.	190,000
Morning Advertiser	Liberal	3d.	6,000
The Times	Independent	3d.	63,000
Morning Post	Conservative	3d.	3,500
Standard	Conservative	1d.	140,000
Echo	Liberal	½d.	80,000
Evening Standard	Conservative	1d.	—
Pall Mall Gazette	Liberal	2d.	8,000
Sun	Liberal	4d.	—
Globe	Conservative	1d.	7,000

Though published in London, these papers were not national in circulation, for their sales were largely confined to the capital and the home counties. Subscribers in midland and north of England towns, or in the countryside, could not expect to read morning papers such as *The Times* or *Daily Telegraph* at their breakfast tables, even after the introduction of special newspaper trains during the late 1870s. *The Times* was also losing its unique status as the nationally and internationally accepted voice of ruling opinion.[26] Until repeal of the newspaper stamp duty in 1855 it had dominated the press, with a circulation exceeding that of all its metropolitan morning rivals put together. But with the emergence of the penny dailies it was deprived of this pre-eminence, falling far behind the *Daily Telegraph* in circulation. *The Times* did retain considerable influence in high political circles until the retirement in 1877 of J. T. Delane, its great editor; but thereafter it carried much less weight. And its publication of the Pigott forgeries in 1887 (which it unwisely accepted as evidence that Parnell, the Irish leader, had given encouragement to the Phoenix Park murders of the Irish Chief Secretary and a colleague in 1882) cost the paper a crippling £200,000 in legal expenses and much more in reputation. By the beginning of the twentieth century it was in serious danger of collapse.

The most successful daily paper of the 1870s was the *Daily Telegraph*, started in 1855. In general, it reflected the middle-class mind of the time. Its contents were still heavily political, but it also gave extensive coverage to crime reporting. In addition, it carried numerous job advertisements, which attracted middle-class readers. It began as a strong Liberal paper; but it abandoned Gladstone for Disraeli in the late 1870s at the time of the Eastern crisis with Russia. Its news coverage was unequalled; and it was the *Telegraph*, in association with the *New York Herald*, which sent the explorer H. M. Stanley to find Livingstone in

Africa (1871). The faithful Gladstonian organ among the London morning papers was the *Daily News*. The *Standard* became the paper of business Conservatism, while the *Morning Post* continued as the mouthpiece of 'Society'.

The leading provincial morning papers were now entering upon their golden age, under able editors such as C. P. Scott of the *Manchester Guardian*, T. Wemyss Reid of the *Leeds Mercury*, and J. T. Bunce of the *Birmingham Post*.[27] The Liberal *Manchester Guardian* was selling 30,000 copies daily in 1880, the Conservative *Yorkshire Post* 47,000 in 1885, and the Liberal Unionist *Birmingham Post* 27,000 in 1889. The big provincial papers now published daily; but in country areas weekly papers remained important organs of news, advertisements, and sometimes of opinion.

Very different from newspaper journalism was the 'higher journalism' of the weeklies, monthlies, and quarterlies. Most of these were journals of great earnestness, which made no concessions to their readers in terms either of the length or depth of their articles. Yet the *Fortnightly Review* was estimated by its editor, John Morley, to have 'about 30,000 readers in the most influential classes'.[28] A major article such as T. H. Huxley's 'On the Physical Basis of Life' (*Fortnightly Review*, February 1869) could arouse deep but informed conflict of opinion among readers In terms of circulation the weekly politico-literary *Saturday Review* (1855) led the way with a sale of perhaps 20,000 weekly in 1870. The leading monthlies were the *Fortnightly Review* (1865), the *Contemporary Review* (1866), and the *Nineteenth Century* (1877).

Few working men read the reviews, and not many read the new penny dailies. Most workmen, at least until the introduction of halfpenny evening papers from the late 1870s, preferred to concentrate their newspaper reading upon more or less sensational and salacious Sunday papers.[29] The most successful were *Lloyd's Weekly News*, with a circulation as high as 500,000 in 1870; *Reynolds's Weekly News* with a sale of about 200,000; and the *Weekly Times* with a circulation about 150,000. In 1896 *Lloyd's* became the first newspaper to reach a million sale. In its reporting of sex, crime, and violence it was as solid in appearance as the middle-class newspapers.

The high circulation of the leading newspapers was helped by intensive advertising. 'No dead-wall in London is without its sign-board, no fence without its announcement of unparalleled circulation.'[30] Advertising was becoming a vital factor in selling the many new branded goods which were being offered on the new mass market. The most profitable newspapers were those which could fill a half or more of their space with advertisements, large and small. Spreads grew bigger and bigger until by the Edwardian period full-page newspaper advertisements were regular features. The concentration of population in towns also encouraged a great development of poster advertising. Letterpress posters began to give way to illustrated posters. The Pears' soap firm made notable use of Millais' famous *Bubbles* painting (1886); and also of the *Punch* cartoon (26.4.1884) which showed a dirty vagrant writing a letter over the caption, 'Two years ago I used your soap, since when I have used no other'. Advertisements appeared not only on hoardings and buildings but also on buses and trams. Sandwich-board men walked the streets. All this contributed colourful contrast to the surrounding urban dirt and drabness. But when in 1900 the white cliffs of Dover were disfigured with a huge advertisement for Quaker Oats, it was recognized that even in free-trade England commercial publicity could not be allowed unlimited extension. Dover council secured a local Act of Parliament, which served as a model for local authority control of unsuitable advertising.

4

The growth of mass advertising had proceeded alongside the development of mass education; the two were obviously related. The famous Education Act of 1870 marked a turning point; but it was a turning point in a progression already begun.[31] Its enactment did not mean that the English working classes received no elementary education before 1870. Nor, on the other hand, did it establish a complete system of state education. Probably two-thirds to three-quarters of the English working classes could already read passably well by mid-century. They had attended school through at least some of their childhood years; childhood was usually taken as ending at 13. Nevertheless, a large minority of illiterates remained untaught, and this minority included the very noticeable 'street arabs' of London and other large towns, who hung about looking for odd jobs and often drifted into crime. Contemporaries disagreed widely about the pre-1870 statistics of elementary education, and historians have followed suit. One estimate has suggested that of the working-class 3–12 age group in 1869 1,420,000 children were attending inspected schools, almost 1 million were on the books of unaided schools, and over 1,500,000 (39 per cent) were not attending school at all. No elementary school places existed for about 1 million children. In the capital alone in 1871 the new London school board found a deficiency of 100,000 places.[32]

Most of the better early-Victorian elementary schools were run by the Anglican or Roman Catholic churches or by the Nonconformist sects. Private schools made up the total. The state supplied its first grant of £20,000 per annum for school building in 1833, increased to £30,000 in 1839. This money was distributed indirectly, through the National Society for Promoting the Education of the Poor in the Principles of the Church of England (1811) and the undenominational but Nonconformist-supported British and Foreign School Society (1808). Grants were given to match local effort, which meant that in practice the already rich Church of England received three-quarters of the money. From 1853 the state, anxious to encourage full use of the voluntary schools, also began to pay capitation grants based upon the numbers of children who attended with reasonable regularity. By 1859 these grants had reached over £723,000. Her Majesty's Inspectors of Education, first appointed in 1839, ensured that grants paid to inspected schools were well used. But the inspectorate itself (62 strong by 1870) cost further money, as did the training of teachers which the state had begun to subsidize. Thirty-eight training colleges with 2,826 students were inspected during 1860. About three-quarters of college income came from the state.

In these various ways central government already exercised considerable indirect control over elementary education well before 1870. But should the state involve itself more directly? Should national or local government build or run schools? If so, should such government-provided schools be spread nationwide, or should they simply fill gaps in coverage left by the denominations? And what form of religious instruction (if any) should be given in government schools? Bitter argument over the best answers to these key questions continued through the whole first half of Queen Victoria's reign.

Religion stood at the centre of the disputes, as Richard Cobden mournfully remarked in 1852. 'It is the old story, Church and Dissent, and rival sects. If you propose to teach religion, they object to anything being taught but their own, or they insist upon none being taught at the public expense. If you propose to leave out religion, they denounce you as an atheist.'[33] The Church of England was convinced that as the Established Church it ought to receive preferential treatment. It wanted to be given taxpayers' money so that Anglican elementary schools could be put within the reach of all children. Both as sectarians and as taxpayers the Nonconformists rejected this vehemently. Why should they pay taxes to subsidize schools which would give Anglican instruction? A noisy minority of Nonconformists – led by Edward Baines, Congregationalist proprietor of the *Leeds Mercury* and Member of Parliament for Leeds (1859–74) – became 'voluntaryists'. They argued (against all appearances) that educational provision for the working classes in the industrial districts was extending satisfactorily, and that therefore state intervention was not needed. 'Voluntaryist' schools refused all government aid. Other Nonconformists however, came out in favour of state-run schools in which religious instruction would be non-sectarian. By 1867 even Edward Baines, while not quite admitting that voluntaryism had always been inadequate, did concede that it had failed to keep voluntaryist schools up to the standard of those schools which had taken state grants. Baines announced that he was now prepared to support acceptance of government aid for Congregational schools, admitting that he had 'over-strained a religious scruple'.[34]

Opposition to state interference in education on grounds of *laissez-faire* political theory was now declining. Interference had proved necessary to protect public health; and just as vaccination had become compulsory against smallpox, 'so we are bound to employ measures as stringent against ignorance which is fatal to the material and moral prosperity of the country'.[35] But the cost of state intervention still gave many middle and upper-class Victorians pause, even if they were ready to accept the principle. They were already paying an array of local rates and of direct and indirect taxes. To encourage cost effectiveness the Revised Code of 1862 introduced 'payment by results' as an integral part of English elementary education. Government grants were now varied in the light of the inspectors' reports. The regrettable result was excessive concentration in schools upon rote-learning of the main grant-earning 'three R's', ready for a parade of superficial knowledge on inspection day. Two-thirds of the maximum capitation grant of 12s. per child per year depended upon this examination, one-third upon sufficient attendance. The author of the Revised Code was Robert Lowe, Vice-President of the Committee of the Privy Council on Education. He told the Commons (13.2.1862) that though he could not promise that elementary education would henceforth be both efficient and economical, 'it shall be either one or the other. If it is not cheap it shall be efficient, if it is not efficient it shall be cheap'.[36] The Revised Code was accepted by the 1870 Education Act, and though gradually modified it continued to exercise a constricting influence until the end of the century.

The 1870 Education Act brought improved education to the working classes not so much at their own demand as at the behest of the middle and upper classes. Many middle-class people hoped that improved education of the lower orders would reduce drunkenness or crime or both. It might achieve this positively by educating children in self-restraint, negatively at least by taking the street arabs into school. Another argument was political. Now that many working men had been given the vote under the 1867 Reform Act it was felt necessary to 'educate our masters'. This famous expression was an adaptation of words used by Robert Lowe in the Commons on 15 July 1867. 'I believe it will be absolutely necessary that you should prevail on our future masters to learn their letters.' Lowe was motivated not by liking for the new 'democracy', but by fear of it in power. Sir James Kay-Shuttleworth, a veteran educational administrator, remarked how 'the old-fashioned alarm of the tyranny of the mob, if they learned to read and write, has changed into a dread of the ignorance, brutality, and misery of an untaught people'.[37] The growing strength of foreign competition in trade and industry also encouraged belief in the need for an educated workforce. 'We must make up the smallness of our numbers by increasing the intellectual force of the individual.' So ended W. E. Forster's speech introducing the 1870 Education Bill to the Commons.

Another line of argument suggested that the working classes possessed a natural right to equality of educational opportunity compared with other classes. Thomas Burt, one of the first two labour Members of Parliament, put this view in its broadest terms. 'We say educate a man, not simply because he has got political power, and simply to make him a good workman; but educate him because he is a man.'[38] But what did equality of educational opportunity mean in terms of structure? In 1871 T. H. Huxley, the scientist and a leading member of the new London school board, remarked that no education system would be worthwhile or truly national 'unless it be one which establishes a great educational ladder, the bottom of which shall be the gutter, and the top of which shall be Universities'.[39] This 'ladder' concept, given prominence by Huxley, with its implications of educational selection and social rising, was to influence thinking about education for the rest of the century and beyond. But even in Huxley's day socialists and others were already pointing out how equality of opportunity would work against egalitarianism; instead of raising the level of working people as a whole, the ladder would work quite oppositely by drawing off the most able boys and girls. In *The Return of the Native* (1878) Thomas Hardy described how Clim Yeobright believed 'that the want of most men was knowledge of a sort which brings wisdom rather than affluence. He wished to raise the class at the expense of individuals rather than individuals at the expense of the class'.

5

The need to ensure that all the nation's children received at least a basic education was now widely agreed. But the problem of religious instruction in schools wholly or partly supported by the state remained a cause of deep differences. Two rival organizations were formed, the National Education League and the National Education Union.[40] The National Education League was started at Birmingham early in 1869 by Joseph Chamberlain and other local Nonconformist radicals 'to rouse the whole country to a sense of our present educational destitution; to create and guide a strong public opinion; and thus to make possible a bold and comprehensive measure'. By this the league meant the creation of a network of state schools which would make free and compulsory elementary education available to all children. Such schools were to be provided in all places, even where existing denominational provision was educationally sufficient. On the question of religious instruction in state schools the league began by advocating what it called 'unsectarian' teaching, which would have allowed use of the Bible without commentary. But from 1872 it changed to a secularist position, which demanded that religious education should be given only outside regular school hours.

From its Birmingham headquarters the National Education League conducted its campaign on the model of the Anti-Corn Law League. Over a hundred branches were soon established throughout the country, which organized a multitude of meetings. A monthly journal with an average sale of 20,000 copies per week helped to give unity to the movement; and 250,000 pamphlets were distributed within a few months of the League's formation. It secured an annual income of £6,000, thanks especially to the backing of wealthy Birmingham manufacturers, of whom Chamberlain was only one. The National Education League was an anti-Anglican body, but not all Nonconformists supported it. Edward Baines, and others who could not accept the exclusion of religion from state schools, even turned to the Anglican-led National Education Union. This was formed in Manchester in November 1869 with the object of 'judiciously supplementing the present system of denominational education'. Feelings ran high between the rival organizations. Manchester town hall had to be cleared when fighting broke out at an education meeting in March 1870. The Union claimed that League policy hoped to force the gradual running down of existing voluntary denominational schools. The League certainly expected that a comprehensive state system would reduce the need for such schools.

Gladstone's new Liberal Government of 1868 listened to the rival arguments, but it produced an education scheme which was very much its own.[41] Feeling was widespread that some measure was required, and with the national economy entering one of the great boom periods of the century the prospect of increased educational taxation and expenditure was not regarded as insupportable. In his Commons speech introducing the Education Bill (17.2.1870) W. E. Forster, Vice-President of the Council, explicitly rejected the Education League approach. It would undermine existing schools, would relieve parents of all payment, would entail 'enormous expense', and 'would drive out of the field most of those who care for education, and oblige the Government to make use solely of official or municipal agency'. Intervention and innovation were to be kept to the inescapable minimum. 'Our object is to complete the present voluntary system, to fill up gaps.'

The Education Bill was intensely debated and much amended during its passage through the Commons. As eventually enacted, it provided that elected school boards should be formed in localities which were short of schools; new board schools could then be opened with financial support from an education rate levied in each district. To circumvent the militant Nonconformist complaint of 'the Church on the rates', existing voluntary schools were to have no connection with the school boards, but were to receive aid directly from central government. Ministers accepted an amendment (the Cowper-Temple clause) which laid down that 'no religious catechism or religious formulary which is distinctive of any particular denomination shall be taught in the school'. This was not so 'undenominational' as it sounded, for Cowper-Temple was chairman of the National Education Union, and (as he himself emphasized) it left every teacher free 'to explain the Bible according to his own views'. In voluntary schools parents were to be allowed to withdraw their children from religious instruction on grounds of conscience, and such instruction was to be timetabled at the beginning or end of the day.

Punch (16.7.1870) showed Forster standing in school before Britannia in the guise of a schoolmistress:

'Please, M'm, I've done it, M'm.'
'And *how* have you done it, William?'
'Please, M'm, I've reduced all the fractions to the lowest common denomination.'

The provisions of the 1870 Act certainly meant that, though the Church of England remained the established Church, the idea of a national faith was no longer to be given openly preferential treatment by the state. And yet the Nonconformist militants of the National Education League remained deeply upset by aspects of the 1870 Act. Where existing denominational provision was 'sufficient', no board schools were to be built, which meant that in many country areas existing Anglican schools would retain their monopoly. Nor was elementary education made everywhere compulsory or free. The Act simply allowed permissive compulsion. Local school boards could compel attendance in their districts if they wished.

Gladstone's Government was able to carry the 1870 Education Act with the help of the Conservatives despite opposition from its own side. But Joseph Chamberlain and the National Education League now set out to force amendment of the Act.[42] During 1872-3 the League began a campaign of intervention at by-elections, in an attempt to ensure that all Liberals elected were favourable to its demands. In the most publicized of these interventions at Bath in June 1873 the official Liberal candidate – under threat of opposition from the League – pledged himself to support compulsion and universal introduction of school boards, and also to back repeal of clause twenty-five of the Act, which permitted payment of the school fees of poor children out of the rates. Clause twenty-five could mean local payments to sectarian schools. The amount involved was small (only £5,000 in 1872), but to excited militants the principle seemed large. In 1876 responsibility for aiding children of poor parents was simply transferred from the school boards to the boards of guardians.

Despite much clamour, the National Education League failed to change the 1870 Act to suit its sectarian prejudices, which was fortunate for the development of English education. Though the Act had not tried to create a national network of state schools, it did put together a national patchwork. This approach was unheroic but sufficiently effective. The campaign of the National Education League did good in publicizing the moral and social case for compulsory and free education. Yet even here other influences probably carried most weight in bringing about the eventual introduction of general compulsion. Anglican schools in country districts where attendance had not been made compulsory found their chances of earning good government grants affected, since only regular attenders could hope to examine well. This moved the Conservative Government in 1876 to set up local school attendance committees, which could make by-laws for compulsion. Finally in 1880 the new Liberal Government, with Conservative support, required both school boards and attendance committees to make by-laws for compulsory attendance of all children aged 5–10. Attention now concentrated upon school fees, which averaged about 3*d*. per week per child. Many school boards waived these for needy children. Finally the 1891 Fee Grant Act allowed 10*s*. per year for each child in average attendance, and all schools were allowed the option of settling for this or of still making charges if they wanted more income than the grant would provide. By 1895 fewer than 800,000 children in England and Wales were paying fees, and nearly 4 million were attending school free.

6

The 1870 Education Act did not touch secondary education. As early as 1859 Matthew Arnold was urging the Government to 'regard the necessities of a not distant future and organise your secondary instruction'. Arnold was the first to use the word 'secondary' in this connection; but many others were beginning to share his concern, as foreign competition in business grew stronger. Secondary education meant middle-class education – for few working-class children could hope to stay at school beyond 13. Yet the Victorian middle classes refused to have their education organized for them from above. They believed in liberty, even to the point of confusion, as Arnold complained. The Taunton Commission (1864–8), which enquired into endowed and other schools, concluded that they required 'thorough concert among themselves'. The Endowed Schools Act of 1869 did lead to reorganization and improvement of the old grammar schools; but the creation of a system of national secondary education had to wait until the passing of the 1902 Education Act. The instruction of Victorian boys class by class about 1865 has been categorized as follows:[43]

Type of School	Leaving age	Parents	Kind and purpose of education	Curriculum	Schools	Children 8-15 (per 1,000 population)
1st grade (A)	18 or 19	Aristocracy, gentry, gentlemen of independent means	Cultural. Boarding. Leading to university. Some private-tutoring	Classical	The Seven. High fees. Graduate clerical staff	2–3
		Professionals, businessmen. Large manufac- turers, etc.	Cultural and professional. Leading to learned professions. Boarding and/or day	Modern sides, Latin, maths, modern languages, some science.	Proprietary and endowed. Moderate fees. Graduate staff. Clerical Headmaster	
2nd grade (B)	16	Tradesmen in considerable business, farmers, agents, managers, upper clerks, etc.	Training for trade and agriculture	English, maths, modern languages, geography, science, some Latin	Day grammar schools. Com- mercial academies, day and boarding†	3–5

Type of School	Leaving age	Parents	Kind and purpose of education	Curriculum	Schools	Children 8-15 (per 1,000 population)
3rd grade (C)	14	Small tradesmen, shopmen, clerks, upper artisans, 'decayed tradesmen'	The essentials well done	3 R's plus some show of the above	Private schools. Low fees. Some overlap above and below	6-8
—	12, 13 or none	Artisans, labourers, etc.	The rudiments	3 R's	National school type. Dame schools. Often no school at all	
Work-house	—	Paupers	The barest rudiments	—	Workhouse schools	

The great public schools had been investigated by the Clarendon Commission (1861–4). It found that the moral and religious training was good; but that on the academic side the teaching of classics was excessively favoured, though the commission accepted that it deserved priority. The amount of time given to mathematics and science teaching was found to be very inadequate in most schools. As a result, only a tiny minority of public schoolboys followed careers in science or technology. Upper and upper middle-class Victorians who sent their sons to public school expected them above all to acquire good personal qualities. Adolescence was now recognized as a difficult period for boys, during which they required firm control and strong example. Significantly, most public schools were boarding institutions.[44] Within this closed environment Victorian public schoolboys were trained first to control themselves, and then to control others. They submitted to authority, not least by 'fagging' for other boys; then they themselves came to share in the exercise of authority through the prefectorial system. Gradually they were moulded into more or less stereotyped Christian gentlemen, and into potential leaders of others in politics, in the armed forces, and in the government of the British Empire.

The number of public schools had grown rapidly during the first half of Victoria's reign. This matched the growth in the numbers and aspirations of the upper middle classes. They might not be able to afford entry for their sons into such old aristocratic foundations as Eton or Harrow, but most of them could afford one of the newer schools such as Rossall (1844), Wellington (1853), Haileybury (1862), and many more. By the Edwardian period it cost about £300 a year to maintain a boy at a major public school, at least £200 at a minor school. Not all boarding schools were of sufficient calibre to be accepted into the Headmasters' Conference, started in 1869. By the end of the century perhaps 100 schools enjoyed undoubted public school status. Only a handful were non-Anglican foundations, and most were High Church.[45]

Thomas Arnold, headmaster of Rugby school from 1828 to 1842 – and himself an Anglican clergyman – had provided a model to which later Victorian headmasters always referred. But in Arnold's Rugby the emphasis had been upon a combination of 'Godliness and good learning', whereas in late-Victorian public schools Godliness became increasingly coupled with 'manliness', and manliness often came to be too readily interpreted as prowess at organized games.[46] 'Muscular Christianity' had arrived; and games-playing at public schools became compulsory, which it had not been at Arnold's Rugby. Henry Newbolt's public school verse reflected the prevailing mood. *Vitai Lampada* celebrated a simple ideal of service throughout life based upon the code of the school playing field:

> The Gatling's jammed and the Colonel dead,
> And the regiment blind with dust and smoke.
> The river of death has brimmed his banks,
> And England's far, and Honour a name,
> But the voice of a schoolboy rallies the ranks:
> 'Play up! play up! and play the game!'

But by the turn of the century criticism was mounting, as reflected in an article on 'Our Gentlemanly Failures' in the *Fortnightly Review* for March 1897. 'Grown and growing up, we see them everywhere: bright-eyed, clean-limbed, high-minded, ready for anything, and fit for nothing.' In *The Public Schools and the Empire* (1913) H. B. Gray, an experienced schoolmaster, argued against public-school standardization, against 'exaltation of conventional virtues'. Daringly, he suggested that the upper classes must no longer be trained to rule inferior peoples but to share in an imperial partnership. This would require encouragement of 'foresight, sagacity, and adaptability' rather than predictability.

A common emphasis upon teaching classics kept the public schools closely linked with the Universities of Oxford and Cambridge.[47] University reform meant that many closed scholarships and fellowships were thrown open; but since most of these were for classics this apparently liberal change only strengthened the public-school grip. As with the public schools, the two ancient universities became open to the sons of the upper middle classes, including Nonconformists. From the 1850s Nonconformists were allowed to take bachelor of arts degrees; and nineteen times between 1860 and 1889 a Nonconformist was senior wrangler in mathematics at Cambridge.[48] From 1871 religious tests were abolished for college fellowships, and after 1878 college fellows could marry without losing their fellowships. New houses for married dons then spread rapidly over north Oxford. The range of studies did broaden after mid-century – natural sciences, moral sciences, law, and modern history all appeared as degree courses; but the number of fellowships remained heavily in favour of classics at Oxford and of classics and mathematics at Cambridge. College teaching was transformed in quality and quantity under the influence of such notable tutors as Benjamin Jowett at Oxford and Oscar Browning at Cambridge. The complaint was indeed raised by Mark Pattison, Rector of Lincoln College, Oxford, that the ancient universities made insufficient contribution to high scholarship because of the attention now being diverted to college teaching and to the encouragement of college spirit.

The complaint was also heard that the ancient universities still lacked contact with everyday Victorian life. Yet not all dons wanted them to remain remote. From the late 1860s the university extension movement, officially recognized at Cambridge in 1873, brought some distinguished Oxbridge lecturers to provincial and East End audiences.[49] In places such as Sheffield, Nottingham, and Exeter their work helped to encourage the opening of local colleges, which were later to grow into provincial universities. Jowett's Balliol played a prominent part in the extension movement. The motivation behind it was not entirely altruistic. Fear of the spread of 'socialism' spurred some dons to participate in an intellectual counter-attack. Yet some of the lecturers were themselves radicals, notably the Oxford group of the 1880s which taught in the East End and included Arnold Toynbee. In the peak year of 1891–2 Oxford and Cambridge together provided 722 extension classes attended by nearly 47,000 people. But only a minority of these came from the working classes. The extension groups had to be self-supporting, and fees had to be charged.

7

Education in late-Victorian grammar schools, public schools, and universities remained the preserve of a minority. What, in an age of increasing urbanization and 'democracy', about the cultural levels of the majority? The growth of towns, wrote Alfred Marshall, the economist, in 1900, made it doubly urgent 'to turn music and painting and other fine arts to account in filling the void in man's life caused by the want of the free light and freshness and beauties of nature'.[50] The working week was reduced for many skilled workmen by several hours during the early 1870s; but the average remained about fifty-five hours, which meant that most workmen were still very tired after work.[51] They looked in their new spare time for relaxing amusement rather than for cultural edification. Significantly, the very word 'sport' – in the sense of organized games-playing – only came into use after mid-century. The railways made it possible for cricket and football teams to travel many miles to matches, and for spectators to begin to follow their sides as 'supporters'.

Cricket was ahead of football in becoming an organized national game.[52] The first number of the *Yorkshire Post* (2.7.1866) promised to report 'every kind of national Sport' – horse racing, field sports, coursing, cricket, rowing, 'and athletic amusements in general'. But football was not thought worthy of mention by name. This first number contained a quarter-column report of the Gentlemen v. Players cricket match, won by the Gentlemen thanks largely to 'superb bowling' by young W. G. Grace. Overarm bowling had been legalized in 1864, though Grace seems to have still bowled roundarm. The performances of Grace, a Gloucestershire doctor, as a superlative batsman and very good bowler were backed by his forceful personality and eventually by his impressively large and bearded figure. In terms of late-Victorian public awareness 'W.G.' became an equal personality with 'W.E.G.', Gladstone, the Liberal statesman.[53] The regular county championship began in 1873; the first Australian touring team visited England in 1878; in 1880 was played the first England–Australia test match in England. In 1882 the Australians won their first (highly exciting) victory in England, by seven runs. At the end of the week the *Sporting Times* mourned the demise of English cricket. 'The body will be cremated, and the Ashes taken to Australia.'

Upper-class amateurs from the public schools and ancient universities set the tone of cricket in the 1860s and 1870s; but from the 1880s a succession of successful professional players began to emerge. Social distinctions remained strong, however, for every amateur was addressed as 'Mr', every professional by his surname. In football also amateurs at first dominated the game in its several forms.[54] The Football Association was formed in 1863 by a group of enthusiasts who codified the rules, including the vital rule which was to distinguish 'soccer' from 'rugby' – 'No player shall run with the ball.' Public-school amateurs consciously set out to introduce the game into urban communities in the hope that it would counteract the feared tendency towards national physical deterioration in the new environment. In its early years therefore the Football Association comprised a mixture of public-school old boys' clubs with working-class sides, chiefly from the industrial midlands and north. The F.A. challenge cup competition was started in 1871, and the victory of Blackburn Olympic over the Old Etonians in the 1883 final marked a significant shift. Thereafter the working-class sides came to dominate the game, and increasingly their players became professionals, who were paid much more than genuine expenses. Efforts were made at first to check the spread of professionalism, but from 1885 it was reluctantly accepted. Clubs became limited companies, which meant that crowd attendance and takings became all-important. The Football League was started in 1888 to provide a focus for continuous support of local professional sides. Football crowds, which by the 1890s could run to tens of thousands, seem to have consisted chiefly of artisans and lower middle-class white collar workers, who now had some time and money to spare. Support was local, but professional soccer players were increasingly bought and sold on the transfer market.

The handling version of football (rugby) followed its own course from the 1860s. It remained a strong public-school and amateur game, controlled from 1871 by the Rugby Union. In parts of industrial Lancashire and Yorkshire working-class professionalism did creep in; but the Northern Union, formed in 1895, became sharply separated from the middle-class amateur game.

Horse racing was also much developed from mid-century. The open meeting at Epsom for the running of the Derby had long provided a holiday for the London working classes, well described in George Moore's novel *Esther Waters* (1894). The watching of the race itself constituted only one part of the festivities. An American found it in 1869 a 'bewildering combination of a drive, a race, a picnic, a fair, a mass-meeting, and a festival'.[55] But horse racing was about to adopt new rules and forms of organization. The Jockey Club gradually eliminated corruption, and thereby made racing acceptable to the less puritanical members of the middle class. Enclosed courses began to be set up, starting with Sandown Park in 1875, which offered improved facilities but which charged entrance money. Such meetings lacked the carnival element, but provided better racing. By the end of the century only the greatest of the traditional open meetings still prospered – at Epsom, Ascot, Goodwood, Doncaster, and York.

Horse racing provided a major occasion for gambling. The moral tensions caused by this connection were revealed in an essay written by one west-country schoolboy, the son of a groom. 'Races are very bad places. None but wicked people know anything about races. The last Derby was won by Mr I. Anson's Blinkbonny, a beautiful filly, rising four. The odds were twenty to one against her; thirty started, and she won only by a neck.'[56] The upper and middle classes were allowed by law to bet off course on credit. Working men could bet by cash on course, but cash betting outside was illegal. Nevertheless, such betting was endemic in towns. Bets were placed via newsagents' or barbers' shops, in public houses, or on the streets – little restricted by a steady number of prosecutions. The extent and alleged spread of gambling was often deplored; and a House of Lords Select Committee on Betting reported in 1902. About £5 million per year was then being spent on gambling. The annual Oxford and Cambridge boat race on the Thames provided a great excuse for wagers; and it almost matched the Derby as an excuse for a London public holiday.

Each decade brought some games novelty. Croquet became highly popular in country houses and middle-class suburban gardens in the 1860s, the more attractive because both sexes could play together. Roller-skating became the craze ('rinkomania') of middle-class young people in the mid 1870s. Then in 1877 the All-England Croquet Club at Wimbledon became the All-England Croquet and Lawn Tennis Club, and held its first lawn tennis tournament. The game had been invented in 1874 by Major Walter Wingfield under the unappealing name of 'sphairistike'; but it was quickly renamed and modified into a game which the young and not-so-young of both sexes could easily learn to play with more or less seriousness in suburban gardens and tennis clubs.

In the countryside the aristocracy and gentry followed the old field sports. Fox hunting, noticed one American visitor, came 'next to the British constitution and the Church of England'; 'to ride well to hounds' was regarded as 'an accomplishment like the mastery of an art or of a science'.[57] In Edwardian times, when large numbers of farmers were riding to hounds alongside the gentry and aristocracy, fox hunting probably had over a quarter of a million followers. Shooting was equally popular. Game preservation and slaughter were claimed by the Edwardian period to have absorbed £45 million in investment and to require £40 million expenditure each year. The introduction of the breech-loading rifle from the 1860s much increased the size of bags – on the Prince of Wales's Sandringham estate, for example, from 7,000 to 30,000 birds per year. The Prince was himself a good shot, and his son, the future George V, an outstanding one.[58]

8

About the middle of the nineteenth century the music hall was born. It grew out of tavern entertainment, and drinking long retained a prominent part in the proceedings, with a chairman to keep order. By 1868, according to one contemporary count, London already possessed twenty-nine larger and ten smaller halls; and over the United Kingdom there were said to be about 300. The *Beehive*, the organ of artisan trade unionism, attacked music halls in 1868 as 'glaring temples of dissipation' where the minds of young men were 'debased by the low songs and vulgar exhibitions' and where their morals were corrupted by prostitutes.[59] Yet the halls undoubtedly fulfilled a function within working-class culture. With their blaze of light and surface opulence, their laughter and chorus singing, they encouraged working-class solidarity. Favourite songs often commented upon working-class experience – courtship, marriage ('She was one of the early birds and I was one of the worms'), family life, and old age. It formed an essential part of Albert Chevalier's rendering of *My Old Dutch* ('We've been together now for forty years') that it was sung in front of a backdrop which depicted the workhouse with its separate entrances for men and women. At each hall twenty or thirty songs were sung each evening. The most successful – such as the nonsensical *Ta-ra-ra-boom-deay*, made popular by Lottie Collins from 1891 – became known everywhere, played on barrel organs, whistled by street boys, and heard even in the villages.

By the 1880s new West End halls were attracting a large better-off audience of gentlemen out for amusement, guards' officers, young clerks, university students, and the like. *The Times* (5.10.1883) wrote condescendingly of the recent increase in the number of music halls. 'A clerk, or journeyman, or petty tradesman did not crave formerly for music, and brilliantly lighted rooms and the companionship of his equals. He had not the money to spend or the time. Now that he has both, he is still without the training, or perhaps only without the means, to take his pleasure intellectually.' From 1878 music halls had to secure a 'certificate of acceptability' from their local authorities, and this was said to have led to the closure of some 200 inferior halls. Certainly, accommodation was becoming much less rough by the 1880s. The halls were ceasing to be glorified taverns, and were becoming 'theatres of variety'. In Bristol, where the People's Palace opened in 1892, a local newspaper was soon praising it for having popularized 'a variety entertainment altogether free from vulgarity . . . Such a success would have been impossible twenty years ago.'[60]

The music-hall tunes of the day were increasingly performed by bands on bandstands in public parks or at the seaside. A national brass-band movement flourished from the 1840s, with bands of working-class musicians from industrial towns – Black Dyke Mills band, Leeds Railway band, and many more – competing at great contests mounted at Belle Vue, Manchester, the Crystal Palace, London, and elsewhere.[61] 'Shall we permit bands to play in the parks on Sundays?' asked the *City Press* of 11 June 1870. 'Shall we compel people, who roam about the parks, and throng the suburban highways, to go to Church, and make an exhibition of sham piety?' The growing demand for Sunday amusement made 'Sunday Opening of Museums, etc.' into one of the main social questions of the time, contentious enough to claim a whole section in successive editions of Sydney Buxton's *Handbook to Political Questions of the Day*. The Lord's Day Observance Society was countered from 1855 by the National Sunday League, started by London artisans. The League argued that the ancient Jewish concept of the Sabbath was unsuited to an urban industrial society. Bradlaugh, the secularist, proclaimed 'a free Church in a free State, and a free Sunday for a free People'.[62] But some working-class leaders, such as George Potter and Henry Broadhurst, supported restrictions on Sunday amusements – not only on religious grounds, but also for fear that workmen would be allowed no rest. Sunday opening of national museums and art galleries in London was finally allowed from 1896. But elements of the Victorian 'frozen Sunday' were to survive far into the twentieth century.

The number of traditional full-day holidays taken by town workers had fallen markedly during the early nineteenth century. Bank of England staff, for example, had enjoyed forty-two holidays in the eighteenth century; by 1830 this was down to eighteen, and by 1834 to Christmas Day and Good Friday only, 'to prevent the interruption of business'. On the other hand, artisans led the way in still worshipping 'St Monday', 'that greatest of small holidays'. A Saturday half-holiday was being introduced in many factory towns from mid-century by employers who hoped thereby to check the taking of Monday.[63] And the number of public holidays was once again increased by the Bank Holidays Act of 1871. This measure, promoted by Sir John Lubbock, passed with unexpected ease, despite the rejection of a less generous bill only three years earlier. Lubbock's Act made Easter Monday, Whit Monday, the first Monday in August, and Boxing Day into 'bank holidays'. *The Times* (6.8.1872) reported that, since the artisans had always taken 'as many Mondays as they pleased', the chief beneficiaries in London were clerks, shopworkers, and the like. *The Times* praised bank holiday behaviour. 'Rational, sober, and modest amusements are more and more supplanting all others, and the riot which made some old-fashioned folks doubt whether Holydays could do people any good has become all but a thing of the past.'

Salaried employees were now beginning to receive one or two weeks' paid holiday each year, and this enabled them to spend at least a week at the seaside. For example, Mr Pooter of *The Diary of a Nobody* (1892) went every summer to Broadstairs. The Pooters seem to have followed the prevailing middle-class practice whereby food was bought by the visitors but then cooked by their landladies.[64] Only 48 seaside resorts had been listed at the 1871 census, but over 200 were included in the 1896–7 edition of *Seaside Watering Places*. Into the 1870s nude sea-bathing by men was still permitted in some places; but it was ceasing to be acceptable as numbers of holiday-makers increased. 'If ladies don't like to see men naked', complained Francis Kilvert in his diary (12.6.1874), 'why don't they keep away from the sight?' Heavy bathing costumes were soon to become obligatory at every resort for both sexes. Walking formed a major part of a Victorian holiday, along the promenade or on one of the many new pleasure piers. Nearly every Victorian resort with any pretensions built at least one pier.[65] Blackpool finished up with three, a measure of its primacy among northern resorts. Working men were rarely given paid holidays, but in the textile towns unpaid wakes weeks, spread town by town through the summer, began to be taken. And Blackpool became the favourite wakes-week resort. Young C. P. Scott, editor of the *Manchester Guardian*, described the scene there in 1873. 'A strawberry garden which, together with a bowling green, dancing room, croquet ground and swings, constitutes a centre of attraction . . . Out-door dancing goes on at as many as five or six places . . . The high wages are producing a wonderful development of popular amusements.'[66] These still simple facilities were eventually to be supplemented by the wonders of electric tramcars along the seafront (1885), Blackpool tower (1894), and the big wheel (1896). Uniquely, Blackpool obtained powers in 1879 to levy a $2d$ rate to advertise its attractions. During the last quarter of the century the populations of the two main Lancashire resorts of Blackpool and Southport grew from only a few thousands to 47,000 and 48,000 respectively. The south coast towns were led by Brighton ('London by the sea'), an all-class resort with over 123,000 inhabitants by 1901. Bournemouth (47,000) and East-bourne (43,000) had grown rapidly into planned middle-class resorts from almost nothing at mid-century.

Workmen who could not afford a week's holiday might take day trips by cheap excursion trains. The Great Exhibition of 1851 had given a big stimulus to such excursions. Wills, the Bristol tobacco firm, took its workers to London by train in 1851; and every year thereafter the whole workforce travelled for a day's outing, usually by the sea.[67] By the end of the century 'excursions in brakes' were being reported in Charles Booth's London survey as too many to count. By 1914 motor-driven charabancs had become commonplace.

The middle classes were now travelling to Europe in large numbers. Thomas Cook started his Continental tours in the 1850s. The English pioneered mountaineering and winter sports in the Alps from the 1860s, and by the end of the century the French and Italian Rivieras were swamped with English tourists. The number of travellers from England to Europe through ports with regular railway connections grew from 165,000 in 1850 through 351,000 in 1869 to 951,000 by 1899.[68]

9

For those many Mancunians who still could not afford an excursion ticket from Victoria station to Blackpool drink was (in the familiar expression of the time) 'the shortest way out of Manchester'.[69] Public houses constituted the social centres for the poor in town and country alike, an escape from the limited space and perhaps also the squalor of life at home. In London and other big cities, where many walked long distances to and from work, the pub provided a tempting resting place on the way. Just over 100,000 on-licences were in force in England and Wales during the last third of the nineteenth century, which meant that the number of persons per licence rose from 201 in 1871 to 316 in 1901. Licence numbers were then deliberately cut during the Edwardian period to just over 90,500 by 1911, 398 persons per licence. Even so, the number of public houses remained very high by later twentieth-century standards.

The deeper the poverty of a town district the higher the proportion of public houses to population. Most were small and rough, but an increasing number of larger and well-fitted pubs were being opened in London and other large towns during the 1880s and 1890s – decorated with glittering mirrors and elaborately worked glass, with coloured and patterned tiling, and with extravagant woodwork. The late 1890s witnessed a pub building boom, which eventually collapsed in a spate of bankruptcies among publicans. Most London publicans were tough characters, out to make money fast, who overworked their staffs and hoped to sell out within a few years. By the end of the century mild ale at 4*d* per quart had replaced porter as the favourite drink in London's public bars. Saloon bar customers preferred bitter beer at 3*d* or 4*d* a pint. The best bitter was brewed in Burton-on-Trent, where the Bass brewery was producing almost 1 million barrels a year by 1890 compared with only 100,000 in 1850.

Consumption of alcohol in the United Kingdom reached its all-time peak per head during the mid 1870s. In 1875 the official returns indicated a national average consumption of 1.30 gallons of spirits per head. 1876 was the peak year for beer, with average consumption of 34.4 gallons. These were three or four times the figures of a century later. Charles Booth suggested that one-quarter of London working-class earnings were spent on drink; Seebohm Rowntree accepted one-sixth as the proportion for York in the 1890s.[70] Obviously, consumption varied widely between individuals; but many and probably most working-class families spent more on alcohol than they could afford. Taxes on drink plus the licensing duties contributed well over one-third of national taxation revenue until the end of the century. Robert Lowe in 1873 even described the habitual drunkard as 'the sheet anchor of the British Constitution'.

Drunkenness certainly constituted a major Victorian social problem. William Hoyle, a leading prohibitionist, claimed in *Our National Resources and How They Are Wasted* (1871) that England had at least 600,000 drunkards. But this was guesswork. Statistics of prosecutions for drunkenness varied according to the intensity of local police zeal, and therefore did not measure the extent of the problem. The amount of middle-class alcoholism remained even more uncertain. Charles Booth suggested in his 1902 volume that London middle-class women took to 'secret bottles' out of boredom. The Victorian medical profession was divided over the causes of alcoholism – whether it arose from pressure of circumstances, or from hereditary predisposition.[71]

At last during the Edwardian period drink consumption began to fall fast even while, or perhaps because, other expenditure was rising:[72]

	United Kingdom consumer expenditure as percentage of total expenditure				
	Food	Alcoholic drink	Tobacco	Durables	Clothing and footwear
1900	27.3	20.8	3.7	2.5	10.0
1913	28.3	16.2	4.1	2.9	10.6

The range of consumer goods available to the working classes had become much wider than in the 1870s. Some spending seems to have switched from drinking to smoking, as cigarettes became popular. Cigarette expenditure rose from £5,500,000 in 1900 to £21,500,000 in 1913. Improved supplies of pure water may have helped to reduce beer consumption. The number of mineral water manufacturers in England and Wales grew from 1,360 in 1861 to 6,691 by 1891. In London Charles Booth noted how the pubs had begun to sell ginger beer, and even tea, coffee, and Bovril. 'These things are new, and though trifles in themselves, they serve as straws to show the way of the wind.'

Ought the state to intervene to regulate, and even to restrict, the sale of alcoholic drink? John Stuart Mill thought not: he contended that free trade produced the best publicity for temperance in the shape of the miserable drunkard. T. H. Green, on the other hand, argued that opponents of strict licensing legislation failed to distinguish between 'that liberty of the subject which is compatible with the real freedom of others, and that which merely means freedom to make oneself a social nuisance'. Temperance legislation, he claimed in 1881, represented 'the next great conquest which our democracy, on behalf of its own true freedom, has to make'.[73] Three possible types of intervention were open to the Victorians – restriction, insulation, and prohibition. Restriction of opening hours was opposed by working men, who pointed out that drink was always available in gentlemen's clubs. Up to 1914 public houses remained open in London on weekdays from 5 a.m. to half-past midnight; and outside London only slightly less long. Sunday opening was confined to two hours about midday and then again during the evening. Insulation against this tempting availability could be contrived by working men who signed and kept 'the pledge' to abstain from alcohol. During the 1870s five main temperance organizations were active: the British Temperance League (1835); The Band of Hope (1847), which worked to persuade adults and children to sign the pledge; the United Kingdom Alliance (1853); the National Temperance League (1856); and the Church of England Total Abstinence Society (1862).

The United Kingdom Alliance led an energetic and persistent campaign for permissive temperance legislation.[74] A favourite version of this 'local option' wanted voters in every locality to be given power to choose by a two-thirds majority to close down the public houses for a period of years. The Alliance claimed that the moral persuasion tried by the Band of Hope was too slow-working. The state needed to act like a father with children, 'keeping temptation out of their way'. Arguments for and against alteration of the liquor laws filled thirty-two pages of Sydney Buxton's *Handbook to Political Questions of the Day* (8th edn, 1892). At every general election and many by-elections from the 1850s to the end of the century the United Kingdom Alliance sought to secure promises of support for local option from candidates in return for the votes of local temperance electors. The Alliance usually, although not always, came out in favour of Liberal candidates; but it claimed to stand above party politics. In the 1850s and 1860s it had connections with working-class radicals and trade unionists, such as George Potter and George Howell. By the 1870s, however, the whole temperance movement was becoming more middle class. The impressive target of £100,000 was set for Alliance funds in 1871, and eventually raised.

This was the peak period for the United Kingdom Alliance in terms of agitation. Sir Wilfred Lawson's 1869 Permissive Bill for local option was backed by nearly 800,000 petitioners, and it won 87 votes in the Commons. Gladstone's Government now promised its own measure. But its 1871 Licensing Bill provoked vociferous opposition from the drink interest, at the same time as the Alliance denounced the measure for not proposing local option. It was therefore withdrawn. The 1872 Licensing Act was much more modest in its attempt to limit the number of liquor licences; but once again the Alliance attacked the Government for not proposing local option. From 1879 Lawson changed his approach in Parliament, no longer himself introducing bills but proposing resolutions which called upon the Government to sponsor local option legislation. In 1883 the Commons approved Lawson's resolution by 288 votes to 141, with Gladstone voting in support for the first time. But no Government proposals followed. Local option became one item among many in the 1891 Liberal Newcastle Programme; but by now neither the Liberal party nor the United Kingdom Alliance were so strong as twenty years earlier. After the general election defeat of 1895 the Liberal leaders began to withdraw from commitment to local option. The Royal Commission on the Licensing Laws (1897–9) reported against local option, at least for England; but it recommended a large reduction in the number of liquor licences, with compensation to be paid out of funds raised by the drink trade itself, not by taxpayers. Proposals on these lines were eventually enacted in the Conservative 1904 Licensing Act, and the reduction in excess numbers of public houses was accelerated.

Did drinking cause poverty, or was poverty a cause of drinking? Many middle-class commentators too readily accepted that drunkenness was the main, even the sole, cause of poverty. But more perceptive observers recognized that working people mostly turned to drink to escape from their miserable circumstances, 'the shortest way out of Manchester'. Booth's London survey at last offered some firm statistics to deflate the exaggerated claims of causal links between drink and poverty. He found that only 13 per cent of the poor and 14 per cent of the very poor owed their misfortune directly to drink. Illness, unemployment, and family size, concluded Booth, were the main causes of working-class poverty. But heavy drinking was likely to persist until poverty came under control, and until the mental horizons of the poor had been widened. 'You or I take a book, and so get into a new world and change of thought; the poor have very little of this, therefore they drink.'

Notes

1. See *Passages from the Prose Writings of Matthew Arnold Selected by the Author* (1880: reprinted 1963). Also R. Williams, *Culture and Society, 1780–1950* (1958), Ch. 6; R. Williams, *Keywords* (1976), pp. 76–82; and P. J. Keating, 'Arnold's Social and Political Thought,' in K. Allott (ed.), *Matthew Arnold* (1975).
2. Mrs Humphry Ward, *Recollections* (1918), pp. 231–2. See also G. Saintsbury, *Matthew Arnold* (1899), Ch. IV.
3. See especially R. Lister, *Victorian Narrative Painting* (1966).
4. See especially K. Clark (ed.), *Ruskin Today* (1964).
5. H. and Alison Gernsheim, *Concise History of Photography* (1965), p. 119.
6. Frances Power Cobbe, *Studies New and Old of Ethical and Social Subjects* (1865), pp. 391–2. See especially P. Ferriday (ed.), *Victorian Architecture* (1963); R. Furneaux Jordan, *Victorian Architecture* (1966); and J. Barnard, *The Decorative Tradition* (1973).
7. See D. J. Olsen, *The Growth of Victorian London* (1976), esp. Ch. 3. Also C. L. Eastlake, *A History of the Gothic Revival* (1872; reprinted 1970).
8. *British Almanac and Companion*, 1871, p. 201; K. Clark, *The Gothic Revival* (3rd edn, 1962), pp. 208–13.

9. See A. Saint, *Richard Norman Shaw* (1976); and M. Girouard, *Sweetness and Light* (1977).
10. See especially E. D. Mackerness, *A Social History of English Music* (1966), Chs. IV–VI; and R. Pearsall, *Victorian Popular Music* (1973).
11. P. Scholes, *The Mirror of Music, 1844–1944* (1947), pp. 65–95.
12. See M. Kennedy, *The Hallé Tradition* (1960).
13. See M. R. Turner (ed.), *The Parlour Song Book* (1974); M. R. Turner (ed.), *Parlour Poetry* (1974); and Jacqueline S. Bratton, *The Victorian Popular Ballad* (1975).
14. See D. J. Gray, 'The Uses of Victorian Laughter', *Victorian Studies*, X (1966); and R. Pearsall, *Collapse of Stout Party* (1975).
15. See V. E. Neuburg, *Popular Literature* (1977), Ch. 4.
16. *Annual Register, 1868*, pp. 307–8. See also R. D. Altick, *The English Common Reader* (1957).
17. D. Carroll (ed.), *George Eliot* (1971), pp. 453–4.
18. R. K. Webb, 'Working Class Readers in Early Victorian England', *English Historical Review*, LXV (1950); and R. K. Webb, 'The Victorian Reading Public', in B. Ford (ed.), *From Dickens to Hardy* (1958).
19. See Guinevere L. Griest, *Mudie's Circulating Library and the Victorian Novel* (1970).
20. See T. Kelly, *History of Public Libraries in Great Britain* (1973), book I.
21. See E. Trudgill, *Madonnas and Magdalens* (1976), esp. Ch. 9. Also C. K. Hyder (ed.), *Swinburne* (1970); B. Litzinger and D. Smalley (eds.), *Browning* (1970); and J. D. Jump (ed.), *Tennyson* (1967).
22. See especially G. Rowell, *The Victorian Theatre* (1967); and M. R. Booth, *English Melodramas* (1965). Also M. Savin, *Thomas William Robertson* (1950); and L. Irving, *Henry Irving* (1951).
23. See especially A. J. Lee, *The Origins of the Popular Press, 1855–1914* (1976).
24. See S. Morison, *The English Newspaper* (1932), Ch. XIV; and A. Hutt, *The Changing Newspaper* (1973), Chs. 3, 4.
25. See A. P. Wadsworth, 'Newspaper Circulations, 1800–1954', *Transactions of the Manchester Statistical Society*, 1955; A. Ellegard, 'The Readership of the Periodical Press in Mid-Victorian Britain', *Acta Universities Gothoburgensis*, LXIII (1957); and A. J. Lee, *The Origins of the Popular Press, 1855–1914* (1976), tables.
26. See H. W. Massingham, *The London Daily Press* (1892); and *The History of The Times*, II (1939), III (1947).
27. See especially D. Ayerst, *Guardian, Biography of a Newspaper* (1971); and M. Milne, *The Newspapers of Northumberland and Durham* (1971).
28. See especially C. Kent, 'Higher Journalism and the Mid-Victorian Clerisy', *Victorian Studies*, XIII (1969); and J. Gross, *The Rise and Fall of the Man of Letters* (1969), Ch. 3.
29. See T. Wright, *Our New Masters* (1868), pp. 333–47; and H. J. Perkin, 'The Origins of the Popular Press', *History Today*, VII (1957).
30. S. Fiske, *English Photographs* (1869), p. 117. See especially Diana and G. Hindley, *Advertising in Victorian England* (1972).
31. See Gillian Sutherland, *Elementary Education in the Nineteenth Century* (1971), and references there. Also J. Hurt, *Education in Evolution* (1972); and D. W. Sylvester, *Robert Lowe and Education* (1974).
32. W. P. McCann, 'Elementary Education in England and Wales on the Eve of the 1870 Education Act', *Journal of Educational Administration and History*, II (1969); and D. Rubinstein, *School Attendance in London, 1870–1904* (1969), p. 22. See also E. G. West, *Education and the State* (2nd edn, 1970), esp. Chs. 10, 11; and E. G. West, *Education and the Industrial Revolution* (1975), esp. Ch. 8.
33. D. Read, *Cobden and Bright* (1967), pp. 180–1.
34. D. Read, *The English Provinces, c.1760–1960* (1964), pp. 165–9.
35. 'School Boards and Primary Education', *Quarterly Review*, October 1873, p. 378.
36. D. W. Sylvester, *Robert Lowe and Education* (1974), Chs. 3–5.
37. Sir J. Kay-Shuttleworth, *Social Problems* (n.d.), p. 183. See also A. E. Dyson and J. Havelock (eds.), *Education and Democracy* (1975), parts two and three.

38. A. Watson, *A Great Labour Leader* (1908), p. 104.
39. C. Bibby, *T. H. Huxley* (1959), p. 157.
40. See especially F. Adams, *History of the Elementary School Contest in England* (1882: reprinted 1972); and S. E. Maltby, *Manchester and the Movement for National Elementary Education* (1918).
41. See especially E. E. Rich, *The Education Act, 1870* (1970); J. Murphy, *The Education Act, 1870* (1972); and D. W. Sylvester, *Robert Lowe and Education* (1974), Ch. 6.
42. See F. Adams, *History of the Elementary School Contest in England* (1882; reprinted 1972), esp. Chs. VI, VII; and D. A. Hamer, *The Politics of Electoral Pressure* (1977), Ch. VII.
43. T. W. Bamford, *The Rise of the Public Schools* (1967), p. 172.
44. See especially R. Wilkinson, *The Prefects* (1964); T. Weinberg, *The English Public Schools* (1967); and J. R. Gillis, *Youth and History* (1974), Ch. 3.
45. A. Ponsonby, *The Decline of Aristocracy* (1912), p. 225; B. Simon and I. Bradley, *The Victorian Public School* (1975), pp. 30–1.
46. See D. Newsome, *Godliness and Good Learning* (1961).
47. See especially J. Roach, 'Victorian Universities and the National Intelligentsia', *Victorian Studies*, III (1959); S. Rothblatt, *The Revolution of the Dons* (1968); M. Sanderson (ed.), *The Universities in the Nineteenth Century* (1975).
48. H. S. Skeats and C. S. Miall, *History of the Free Churches in England* (1891), p. 625.
49. See T. Kelly, *A History of Adult Education in Great Britain* (1961), Ch. 14; J. F. C. Harrison, *Learning and Living, 1760–1960* (1961), Ch. VI; and B. Simon, *Education and the Labour Movement, 1870–1918* (1965), pp. 86–92.
50. A. C. Pigou (ed.), *Memorials of Alfred Marshall* (1925), pp. 409–10.
51. See M. A. Bienefeld, *Working Hours in British Industry* (1972), Ch. 4.
52. See especially W. F. Mandle, 'Games People Played: Cricket and Football in England and Victoria in the Late Nineteenth Century', *Historical Studies*, Vol. 15 (1973).
53. See R. Bowen, *Cricket* (1970), esp. Chs. 8, 9.
54. See M. Marples, *A History of Football* (1954); P. M. Young, *A History of British Football* (1968); and J. Walvin, *The People's Game* (1975).
55. S. Fiske, *English Photographs* (1869), pp. 158–9. See especially W. Vamplew, *The Turf* (1976), Chs. 2–4, 13.
56. J. Hurt, *Education in Evolution* (1972), p. 61.
57. R. G. White, *England, Without and Within* (1881), pp. 330–1. See especially R. Carr, *English Fox Hunting* (1976); and D. C. Itzkowitz, *Peculiar Privilege, A Social History of English Foxhunting, 1753–1885* (1977).
58. A. Ponsonby, *The Camel and the Needle's Eye* (1910), p. 64; C. Chenevix Trench, *The Poacher and the Squire* (1967), pp. 171–83.
59. C. L. Graves, *Mr. Punch's History of Modern England* (n.d.), I, p. 296. See especially F. Anstey, 'London Music Halls', *Harper's Monthly Magazine*, January 1891; G. Stedman Jones, 'Working-Class Culture and Working-Class Politics in London, 1870–1900: Notes on The Remaking of a Working Class', *Journal of Social History*, VIII (1974); R. Mander and J. Mitchensen, *British Music Hall* (2nd edn, 1974); and P. Bailey, *Leisure and Class in Victorian England* (1978), Ch. 7.
60. Kathleen Barker, *Entertainment in the Nineties* (1973), p. 12.
61. See J. F. Russell and J. H. Elliot, *The Brass Band Movement* (1936); and E. D. Mackerness, *A Social History of English Music* (1966), pp. 166–9.
62. See B. Harrison, 'Religion and Recreation in Nineteenth-Century England', *Past & Present*, no. 38 (1967).
63. J. Guiseppi, *The Bank of England* (1966), pp. 35, 100. See especially A. Reid, 'The Decline of St. Monday, 1766–1876', *Past & Present*, no. 71 (1976).
64. See especially J. A. R. Pimlott, *The Seaside Holiday* (1947), Chs. VIII–X; and A. Horn, *The Seaside Holiday* (1967).
65. See S. H. Adamson, *Seaside Piers* (1977).
66. J. L. Hammond, *C. P. Scott* (1934), pp. 39–40- See also H. J. Perkin, 'The "Social Tone" of Victorian Seaside Resorts in the North-West', *Northern History*, XI (1975).
67. Helen E. Meller, *Leisure and the Changing City, 1870–1914* (1976), p. 212.

68. R. J. Croft, 'The Nature and Growth of Cross-Channel Traffic through Calais and Boulogne, 1870–1900', *Transport History,* Vol. 6 (1973).
69. See B. Harrison, *Drink and the Victorians* (1971); and B. Harrison, 'Pubs', in H. J. Dyos and M. Wolff (eds.), *The Victorian City* (1973). Also B. Spiller, *Victorian Public Houses* (1972); and M. Girouard, *Victorian Pubs* (1975).
70. See A. E. Diggle, 'Drink and Working-Class Living Standards in Britain, 1870–1914', *Economic History Review,* second series, XXV (1972).
71. R. M. MacLeod, 'The Edge of Hope: Social Policy and Chronic Alcoholism, 1870–1900', *Journal of the History of Medicine,* XXII (1967).
72. A. H. Halsey (ed.), *Trends in British Society Since 1900* (1972), p. 89.
73. B. Harrison, *Drink and the Victorians* (1971), pp. 208–9.
74. See D. A. Hamer, *The Politics of Electoral Pressure* (1977), Chs. IX–XIII.

Chapter 7

Government

Developments: *'A country successful in politics'*

1

'As I write for Englishmen', remarked Walter Bagehot casually in 1874, 'I need not draw out a formal proof that England is a country successful in politics.'[1] Even foreigners accepted this claim, as they compared the uncertainties of their own government with the stability, even in change, of the British system. Tolstoy noticed in *War and Peace* (1868–9) how an Englishman was 'self-assured as being a citizen of the best organized state in the world'. Yet Victorian England possessed no written constitution. Practice in government and politics had been formed and reformed little by little since the middle ages, and especially since the civil war and 'Glorious Revolution' of the seventeenth century. Matthew Arnold quoted in *Culture and Anarchy* (1869) what he described as the 'thoroughly British' thoughts of *The Times* of 7.7.1868. 'Art is long and life is short; for the most part we settle things first and understand them afterwards.' This pragmatic approach still predominated in 1914. A history book published in that year emphasized how Britain had produced no Rousseau, no Marx. 'The dominant feature of British public life has been the growth not of philosophic schools, but of political parties and social expenditure.'[2]

Even the writings of Victorian political thinkers played down theory, in the sense that they made only limited claims for the role of government. This attitude can be traced back to Locke, the philosopher of the 1688 revolution, with his emphasis upon reason, individual liberty, and the rights of private property. Bentham and the philosophic radicals of the early nineteenth century had produced fresh arguments but had retained Locke's priorities. The persuasive prose of John Stuart Mill's famous essays *On Liberty* (1859) and *Representative Government* (1861) continued the discussion. Mill argued that individuals could generally serve their own interests better than governments; and that even where this might not be the case, it was often desirable that the initiative should be left with individuals 'as a means to their own mental education'. This was not to be taken as a charter for mere permissiveness; the assumption was that such liberty would benefit the state best by promoting self-discipline and prudent action among its citizens. The individual stood at both the beginning and the end of Mill's attention. 'The worth of a State, in the long run, is the worth of the individuals composing it.' Yet Mill did not believe that the lowest classes of citizens could be trusted with the vote. Their ignorance might lead to confiscation of property, even to anarchy or dictatorship. The idea of a natural right to a vote was firmly rejected by Mill and the Liberals as much as by Conservatives. From the Conservative side, Lord Salisbury claimed in the *Quarterly Review* for July 1864 that natural right could never justify equal suffrage 'so long as there is not equal property to protect'. A day labourer should not be put on an equality with a Rothschild. From the Liberal side, a *Fortnightly Review* article on 'Democracy in England' (June 1865) by Sheldon Amos, a leading jurist, explained how Bentham and Mill had banished 'the indefinite word *right* from political science'. The only good reason for recognizing a right was 'general utility'.

What role then was left for the state in Mill's individual-centred society? Government must obviously provide a framework of internal law and order, and of defence from outside attack. But should, or could, it do more? It was not possible, concluded Mill in his *Principles of Political Economy* (1848), to restrict the interference of the state by any universal rule, 'save the simple and vague one that it should never be admitted but when the case of expediency is strong'. Mill's conclusion therefore was characteristically English. Notwithstanding apparently firm assertions that the principle of *laissez-faire* was best, in the last resort he applied the test not of principle but of expediency. Mill did try to test expediency by drawing a distinction between 'self regarding' actions, which did not affect others and which could be left uncontrolled; and 'other regarding' actions which might affect the community and which might require control. But this contrast was too artificial to be convincing. Not many actions clearly fell wholly within Mill's first category. His *Political Economy* contents page proclaimed:

Laisser-faire the general rule – but liable to large exceptions. Cases in which the consumer is incompetent judge of the commodity. Education. Case of persons exercising power over others. Protection of children and young persons ... Cases in which public intervention may be necessary to give effect to the wishes of the persons interested. Examples: hours of labour; disposal of colonial lands.

And so Mill went on, leaving a wide area of uncertainty behind him as part of his legacy to his Liberal admirers.

2

Mill's essays *On Liberty* and *Representative Government* became basic texts for Victorian Liberals. Also widely read was John Morley's essay *On Compromise* (1874), which sought to apply Mill's ideas in a spirit of political gradualism. Morley was to become one of Gladstone's closest colleagues. What then was meant by 'Liberalism' in British politics in the Gladstone era? A book was published in 1885 with the title *Why I am a Liberal: being Definitions and Personal Confessions of Faith by the Best Minds of the Liberal Party*. Pride of place was given to Gladstone's combative comparison:

The Principle of Liberalism is TRUST IN THE PEOPLE, qualified by Prudence.
The Principle of Conservatism is MISTRUST OF THE PEOPLE, qualified by fear.

Gladstone had repeated this definition of Liberalism many times down the years. During his 1880 election campaign he emphasized how 'emancipation and enfranchisement' were the objectives of the Liberal Party. 'Progress qualified by prudence; trust in the people above all, qualified only by that avoidance of violent . . . ill-considered change, which is really necessary in order to give due effect to the principles of Liberalism.'[3]

Clearly, this was Gladstone's considered definition of Liberalism. But whom did Gladstone mean by 'the people'? In his youth both whigs and tories had equated 'the people' with the middle classes. 'If there is a mob,' exclaimed Lord Brougham during the First Reform Bill debates, 'there is the people also. I speak now of the middle classes.' This old usage drew a careful distinction between 'the people' or 'the public', who were trustworthy, and 'the mob' or 'the populace', who were not. The free trade victory, explained the Liberal *Cambridge Independent Press* (5.9.1850), 'though a triumph of the people and for the people, has not been a triumph of the populace'. It reflected 'the Monarchy of the Middle Classes'. In his *Letters on a Regicide Peace* (1796) Edmund Burke had numbered 'those who, in any political view, are to be called the people . . . not declining in life, of tolerable leisure for such discussions, and of some means of information more or less, and who are above menial dependence' as about 400,000 in England and Scotland. In 1852 Richard Cobden, whose reputation had been made as an organizer of public opinion, realistically recognized the limited size of that public opinion as a continuous force. 'In Burke's day he put down the public at 400,000. If we double that number, it will be a liberal estimate of those who actually trouble themselves habitually about affairs of state.'[4]

Gladstone was only five years younger than Cobden and ten years older than Queen Victoria. 'The people' were always to him a limited – even though eventually a much increased – number. Admittedly, in 1886 when he found upper-class opinion almost unanimously against his new Home Rule policy, he made his long-remembered contrast between opponents and supporters of Home Rule as 'class against the mass, classes against the nation . . . all the world over I will back the masses against the classes'. But though euphony had here tempted Gladstone into praise of the masses, he still did not mean this to refer to 'the populace'. In conversation in 1881 he had expressed his continuing hostility to the extension of political influence down to such a level: 'when I am gone younger men who may take my place will either be far more advanced than I ever have been, or will be forced on by the extreme liberalism of the masses'.[5] Possession of the vote was to Gladstone, as to Mill, a privilege for which men might show themselves qualified, not a right to which all were by nature entitled. In this spirit he came to support the urban householder franchise of 1867, and its extension to the counties in 1884. What were the qualities, he asked in 1864, 'that fit a man for the exercise of a privilege such as the franchise? Self-command, self-control, respect for order, patience under suffering, confidence in the law, regard for superiors'. He argued that such qualities had been shown by the Lancashire operatives during the 'cotton famine' caused by the American Civil War (1861–5). Eventually, Gladstone even persuaded himself that such men were more, not less, likely to make good voters than their social superiors. In an article which asked 'Is the Popular Judgement in Politics more just than that of the Higher Orders?' (*Nineteenth Century*, July 1878) he explained how possession of property tended to encourage selfishness. Electors with little property could more easily make political judgements on grounds of high principle. 'Did the Scribes and Pharisees, or did the shepherds and fishermen, yield the first, most, and readiest converts to the Saviour and the company of His apostles?'

Gladstone justified the extension of the householder franchise to the agricultural labourers in 1884 on the ground that, like the cotton operatives, each rural householder was 'a skilled labourer . . . a man who must do many things which require in him the exercise of active intelligence'. He still regarded these franchise extensions not as giving the vote to the unthinkable mob, but on the contrary as reinforcing a system which deliberately kept the rootless and unintelligent without the vote. The skilled workmen now enfranchised had shown themselves, in Gladstone's view, if not middle class in material terms, clearly middle class or better than middle class in moral terms. 'The people' were now much more numerous than in his youth, but still they were not the unlimited 'populace'.

When charged by Ruskin in 1878 with thinking 'one man as good as another and all men equally competent to judge aright on political questions', Gladstone replied that on the contrary he was 'a firm believer in the aristocratic principle – the rule of the best. I am an out-and-out *inequalitarian*'.[6] He was always eager to appoint whig peers to high positions. 'England is a great lover of liberty, but of equality she has never been so much enamoured.' This did not mean that Gladstone was motivated by snobbery. It was the essence of his admiration that aristocrats were especially likely – because of their education, leisure, and independence – to make sound rulers.

Gladstone's trust in the people qualified by 'prudence' deliberately left the last word with the Liberal leaders. He himself expected to be followed, not to follow. He deferred only to the stirrings of his own conscience. Freedom of conscience both in politics and in religion was a vital right to Victorian Liberals. Many of the most active were Nonconformists, who had endured civil disabilities on account of their religion. Such men might often follow Gladstone, but they always knew their own minds in doing so. They were necessarily sometimes restless under party discipline. In *Why I am a Liberal* James Stansfeld, a Nonconformist and Gladstonian cabinet minister, claimed this as a virtue among Liberals rather than a weakness, as 'evidence that their party remains faithful to its true character'.

3

Liberal principles had traditionally been translated into objectives under the slogan 'Peace, Retrenchment, and Reform'. This cry dated from the First Reform Bill agitation of 1830–2. In a speech of 1879 Gladstone pointed approvingly to 'the inscription which faces me on yonder gallery'. 'We try to diminish the sin and sorrow of the world . . . to alleviate a little the burden of life for some, to take out of the way of struggling excellence those impediments at least which the folly or the graver offence of man has offered as obstacles in his progress.'[7] This passage cast light on Gladstone's sense of 'reform'. It was the most flexible word in the Liberal vocabulary, meaning much more to radicals on the left of the party than to whigs on the right. In its most restricted application it could refer solely to reform of Parliament, in the spirit of the three Reform Acts. In pressing for wider representation most Liberals persuaded themselves that they were doing no more, nor less, than returning to the temper of the old Anglo-Saxon constitution. E. A. Freeman, the historian and an ardent Liberal, claimed in his *Growth of the English Constitution* (1872) that contemporaries had 'advanced by falling back on a more ancient state'. The Anglo-Saxon system, he claimed, had been democratic, though not purely so. All freemen had a voice, but not an equal voice. The continuing limited range of the Victorian franchise even after 1884 could therefore be defended historically. 'Our ancient history is the possession of the Liberal.'

A wider Liberal definition of 'reform' also included the removal of disqualifications, restrictions, or impositions which affected political, religious, or economic life. By his budgets of 1853, 1860, and 1861 Gladstone had played a leading part in completing the great Victorian movement towards free trade. Sir Robert Peel had secured repeal of the Corn Laws in 1846; Gladstone had followed by removing the last protective duties upon articles of everyday consumption. Victorian Liberals were sure that freedom in buying and selling was the best way to prosperity both for individuals and for states. And commercial progress during the 1850s and 1860s seemed so strikingly to confirm this that even Victorian Conservatives abandoned their support for economic protection.

The Liberals were committed to free trade in religion as well as in trade. They opposed the enjoyment of civil advantages by members of the Church of England, though they differed among themselves whether it should continue as the established Church. Landmarks in the achievement of religious equality were repeal of the Test and Corporation Acts (1828), Catholic Emancipation (1829), the opening of Oxford and Cambridge to Nonconformists in the 1850s, the abolition of compulsory church rates (1868), and the Burials Act of 1880. Liberals contended that all protections and privileges depressed the unprotected or unprivileged on the one hand, and tended to corrupt the privileged on the other. 'The danger is not that a particular class is unfit to govern. Every class is unfit to govern. The law of liberty tends to abolish the reign of race over race, of faith over faith, of class over class.' So explained Gladstone's friend Lord Acton, the historian, to Gladstone's daughter.[8]

In international affairs this attitude meant sympathy for nationalities struggling to free themselves from foreign rule. Liberals had been especially enthusiastic about the achievement of Italian unification by the expulsion of the Austrians. 'The conduct of Austria towards Italy at large,' wrote Gladstone in the *Quarterly Review* (April 1859), 'has involved a glaring and systematic contempt of liberty and of public right.' The Austrians had ruled 'without the check of free institutions, over a race much more advanced'. Differences over the extent of desirable 'reform' for Ireland eventually split the Liberal Party. Gladstone convinced even Anglican Liberals that the disestablishment of the Church of Ireland was right (1869) because it was an alien Church. He also carried many of his party in acceptance of two Irish Land Acts (1870, 1881) even though these seriously undermined landlords' property rights. But the party split finally over his 1886 Home Rule proposals. The Liberal Unionists refused to regard Ireland as a 'nation' almost like Italy, which deserved at least qualified independence.

Just as the condition of Ireland posed difficult questions for Liberals so did the condition of England. On matters of social reform, touching upon poverty, employment, living and working conditions, radical Liberals were much more eager for positive state and municipal intervention than were Gladstonians. The latter tended to be mesmerized by the freedom which had been given to individuals through the removal of restrictions and privileges. Everyone could now find his own happiness: the state should not try to make people happy by legislation. 'Till Parliament can give health, strength, providence, and self-control, how can it deal with the evil of pauperism?' Free men, in this Liberal definition, expected neither charity from other men nor patronage from the state. 'Manliness' was all. In the sphere of the state, concluded Gladstone (*Nineteenth Century*, January 1887), 'the business of the last half-century has been in the main a process of setting free the individual man, that he may work out his vocation without wanton hindrance, as his Maker will have him do. If, instead of this,

Government is to work out his vocation for him, I for one am not sanguine as to the result.' But radicals, such as Joseph Chamberlain, had begun to argue that the poor and unprivileged in modern society could not always help themselves. To assist such people the radicals were ready to venture as far as the boundaries of 'socialism'. Chamberlain explicitly contrasted the facts of poverty in 1885 with Britain's reputation for success in government. There was 'reason to doubt the perfection of our system' which left one in thirty in the richest country in the world dependent upon poor relief and one in ten upon the verge of starvation.[9]

One factor which made Gladstonians suspicious of social reform was its prospective high cost. They were deeply attached to the cry of 'retrenchment' in government, for they believed that good government meant cheap government. Gladstone, Chancellor of the Exchequer through much of the 1850s and 1860s, believed ardently that money should be left to 'fructify in the pockets of the people'. Taxation should be kept as low as possible; waste in administration should be rooted out. This was a moral as well as an economic duty. To waste was sinful – to waste public money while acting in stewardship was doubly sinful. Hence Gladstone's suspicion of all schemes for social reform. 'The optional expenditure has more than trebled within fifty years,' he complained in 1887, 'while the population has less than doubled . . . the State and the nation have lost ground with respect to the great business of controlling the public charge.'

Economy in naval and military expenditure was one ground for pursuing 'peace' in Liberal foreign policy. Though only a small minority of Liberals were pacifists, most believed that a Christian foreign policy should use force only as a last resort, even against uncivilized races. 'Remember the rights of the savage, as we call him. Remember that the happiness of his humble home, remember that the sanctity of life in the hill villages of Afghanistan among the winter snows, is as inviolable in the eye of Almighty God as can be your own.'[10] Gladstone was an enthusiast for the settlement of disputes between the major powers by arbitration. But he believed that the number of such disputes which involved Britain could be minimized by the avoidance of assertive policies. Practical benefit as well as moral satisfaction could be expected to follow from such restraint. Peace brought prosperity, whereas war brought increased taxation and upset trade.

4

In *Culture and Anarchy* (1869) Matthew Arnold made a spirited attack upon the 'anarchy' and vulgarity of contemporary Liberalism. His concern was not directly with economics and politics but with cultural tone. He found the lives and minds of provincial English middle-class Nonconformist Liberals, of whom he took John Bright as representative, to be decidedly imperfect, despite their success in business. He blamed this upon the Hebraic inspiration of Nonconformity with its neglect of the Hellenic tradition of humanism. Growth of business and population were 'mechanically pursued by us as ends precious in themselves'. More influential than Arnold were two older critics, Thomas Carlyle and John Ruskin.[11] Both feared that democracy might lead to disorder, but both gave inspiration to late-Victorian reformers and even to socialists. Into the twentieth century Carlyle's *Sartor Resartus* (1838) and *Past and Present* (1843), and Ruskin's *Unto This Last* (1862) and *Fors Clavigera* (1871–84) were widely read as calls for change. Ruskin's art criticism and his social criticism each reflected a striving towards perfection. His concern was with 'felicitous fulfilment of function in living things'. He protested against the separation of work and enjoyment through the excessive competition and specialization of modern industry. Work must remain creative and satisfying. 'Honest production, just distribution, wise consumption.'

From the Conservative side the outstanding contribution to the debate about democracy after the passing of the Second Reform Act came from Fitzjames Stephen's *Liberty, Equality, Fraternity* (1873). Stephen contended that Mill and the Liberals expected too much from human nature. Men and women did not act as rationally as Mill, 'a book in breeches', imagined. Men were so diverse in character and circumstances that fraternity or equality could have little meaning. Nor could men be improved by liberty and free discussion. Most were ignorant or indifferent; many were selfish and venal. They could not be governed by appeals to their reason, only by coercion, more or less covert. 'Force is always in the background.' And upon this basis of force the wise minority must rule, benevolently but firmly.

By the date of the publication of Stephen's book the Conservative Party was on the brink of its first election victory for over thirty years. Conservatism depended upon instinct rather than upon any elaborate set of principles of political action. In his *Vindication of the English Constitution* (1835) the young Disraeli had maintained that the only principles upon which government should be based were 'principles of ancestral conduct'. Conservatives tended to be satisfied with things as they were. In particular, they cherished those national institutions which had been handed down from earlier times – the monarchy, the established Church, the Lords and Commons, the social hierarchy. They shared a strong sense that British 'success' in government could be easily undermined, and that it could best be protected by calm and caution. They claimed to be especially 'loyal' to the monarchy, because it provided both a social apex and valuable continuity in government above party. The romantic view of the sovereign personally in touch with the people as expressed in Disraeli's 'Young England' novels of the 1840s was hardly to be taken seriously even then, and certainly not thirty years later. But as Prime Minister (1874–80) Disraeli did encourage Queen Victoria to take the glamorous title of Empress of India, and he did convert the Queen into a Conservative partisan. The Conservatives also attached great value to the House of Lords, both for the social leadership of the peers and because of the power of their house to check rash legislation. The Church of England was also regarded as another key Conservative institution. As the established Church it offered stability and continuity. Conservative voters were much more likely to be Anglicans than Nonconformists. 'Gentlemen, I say it with reverence, the most Conservative book in the world is the Bible, and the next most Conservative book in the world is the Book of Common Prayer.' So claimed Archdeacon Wordsworth in 1865. Liberals believed that history was on their side: Conservatives were sure that God was on theirs.[12]

The British Empire became another institution which Conservatives chose to place under their particular care. Disraeli's widely publicized Crystal Palace speech of 1872 promised 'to uphold the Empire of England', and soon thereafter the Conservatives became the party of 'imperialism'. Linked with concern for the empire was Conservative emphasis upon 'patriotism'. The officer class was chiefly Conservative. Liberals were regarded, by implication and sometimes explicitly, as unpatriotic in their policies, neglectful of the armed forces, even pacifists.

Yet Conservatism overlapped with Liberalism in one important emphasis. Both party creeds agreed that government existed especially to protect the right of private property. The Conservatives were traditionally the party of landed property; but under Disraeli and Lord Salisbury the party successfully widened its appeal to include the defence of urban middle-class property. How far then should individual property rights be limited by government in order to help the working classes? Conservatives took much of the awkwardness out of this question by caring so little for theory. They sometimes referred to old landed traditions of paternalism, but not to any more abstract 'ism'. This pragmatic approach was underlined in Lord Hugh Cecil's book on *Conservatism* (1912). 'Any scheme for enlarging the function of the State must be judged by Conservatives merely on its merits without reference to any general formula, but from a standpoint prudently distrustful of the untried, and preferring to develop what exists rather than to demolish and reconstruct.'

In his Crystal Palace speech of 1872 Disraeli had named 'the elevation of the condition of the people' as another 'great object' of the Conservative Party '*Sanitas sanitatum, omnia sanitas*'. The limited character and extent of the social reform measures promoted by his 1874–80 Ministry showed that his intentions in this field were more modest than his language suggested (see below, p. 186). Yet it was clearly necessary for Disraeli to offer the working classes something if the Conservative Party was to sustain its claim to be the party of social union. Such a claim was increasingly made. Social union in this Conservative definition did not mean social equality. On the contrary, it carried with it acceptance of social differences, recognition of the class system in general even though individuals might rise within it. Sir Stafford Northcote claimed in 1876 that the 'great principle' of the Conservative Party was its connection not with any one class but with all, 'endeavouring to teach each class that it should respect the rights and privileges of the other'. The Conservatives regarded themselves as uniquely the 'national' party. Liberalism was sectional: Labour was to be sectional. 'We are not for the classes or the masses, for their interests are one. We are not for Individualism or Socialism, for neither is founded on fact.'[13]

5

For both Conservatives and Liberals the question of state intervention arose most persistently in connection with the problem of poverty. Poverty continued on a huge scale despite unparalleled commercial progress. In his 1864 budget statement Gladstone praised the 'astonishing development of modern commerce' under free trade. And yet, he admitted, 'an enormous mass of paupers' remained; and many more people were 'struggling manfully but with difficulty' to avoid pauperdom. One East End clergyman had told him that 12,000 out of 13,000 parishioners in his charge lived always on the verge of want. Gladstone seemed surprised to learn that there were whole East End districts 'in which you cannot find an omnibus or a cab, and in which there is no street music, nor even a street beggar'.

'Poverty in the midst of plenty.' 'The rich grow richer, the poor grow poorer.' These clichés were repeated not just by malcontents but by 'respectable' observers. Who then was to blame? Anthony Trollope, writing his *Autobiography* in the mid 1870s, was far from sure that it was sufficient to shift the blame on to providence. 'We acknowledge the hand of God and His wisdom, but still we are struck with awe and horror at the misery of many of our brethren.' Some political economists admitted that they had been better at offering explanations of poverty than at proposing solutions for it. W. S. Jevons told the British Association in 1870 how 'during the last thirty or forty years we have tried a mighty experiment, and to a great extent we have failed'. Free trade, reduction of taxation, Poor Law reform, emigration – all had brought great benefits to the working classes, and yet the slightest relapse of trade still threw 'whole towns and classes of people' into destitution.[14]

The effects of 'poverty in the midst of plenty' may have been perplexing, but the traditional view accepted that 'ye have the poor always with you' (Matthew, xxvi, 11). God had given poverty with the good purpose of spurring men on to work and to create wealth. Such was the argument, for example, of Patrick Colquhoun's *Treatise on Indigence* (1806). But Colquhoun had distinguished between stimulating poverty and debilitating 'indigence'. Destitution – lack of the means to live – was socially and economically damaging, and justified the provision of relief and charity. If the existence of the poor was necessary for progress, so was the existence of the rich. The idea of natural selection came to reinforce this belief. 'Moderate accumulation of wealth', explained Charles Darwin in *The Descent of Man* (1871), assisted the process of natural selection. 'When a poor man becomes moderately rich, his children enter trades or professions in which there is struggle enough, so that the able in body and mind succeed best.'

The view that the best help for the poor consisted in self-help was given its most persuasive expression in the works of Samuel Smiles. His *Self-Help* (1859) sold 150,000 copies in thirty years. Smiles emphasized the especial importance of four qualities: energy, cheerfulness, prudence, and industry. In a book revealingly entitled *Mistaken Aims and Attainable Ideals of the Artizan Class* (1876) W. R. Greg repeated the Smiles formula in its strictest form. Greg agreed that the conditions of the poor were bad. But they were misled by their leaders, who would not tell them that their sufferings were chiefly caused by their own 'ignorance, perversity, insobriety, improvidence and unthrift'. Greg quoted figures from Smiles to show that the working classes spent at least 10 per cent of their earnings on drinking and smoking, and lost 15 per cent through wasteful buying and poor housekeeping.

Greg urged working men to develop further institutions of working-class thrift which had been growing since about mid-century.[15] Co-operation both in manufacturing and in retail distribution was praised by many middle-class observers. By 1872 co-operative retail societies had over 300,000 members in England and Wales, and in that year they paid £716,000 in dividend to members. One attraction of the 'co-ops.' to thrifty working men – and their wives – was that the societies could serve as savings banks. Members whose shares were fully paid up could continue to allow their interest, plus their dividend on purchases, to accumulate as additional shares. When the maximum share limit was reached, money could still be credited as loan capital, earning interest. Thus members' money could steadily grow without any savings being made out of wages. Many Victorian working people did indeed begin to save directly in the new Post Office Savings Bank, set up by Gladstone in 1861. By the 1890s there were over 5,700,000 accounts with total deposits of £83 million. More than 10,000 branches were on hand. This was therefore the most accessible institution of Victorian thrift, with the result that over half the depositors in 1896 were women and children.

Another important expression of self-help in action were the friendly societies. At the end of the century the Chief Registrar praised them as 'one of the great glories of the Victorian era ... welfare has been established in a very large degree by the labours and the sacrifices of working men themselves'. Friendly societies offered at least two benefits – sickness benefit at about 10s. per week, and death benefit of about £10, which was enough to pay for a 'respectable' funeral. Registered friendly societies in the United Kingdom had 2,750,000 members in 1877 and

5,600,000 by 1904; funds grew during the same period from £12,700,000 to £41 million. This high membership probably meant that nearly all artisans and other superior working men were covered. But by the end of the century even the large friendly societies, such as the Manchester Unity of Oddfellows, with over 700,000 members, were becoming aware of financial difficulties. Recruitment of young, healthy members could no longer easily balance demands for benefit payments; the proportion of elderly members was growing, and they were living longer than in the past and were drawing virtual old-age pensions from the societies in the guise of sickness benefit.

Friendly society members had usually been in more or less continuous employment. Among the less steadily employed the urge to thrift was often turned into waste. Insurance salesmen talked poor families into taking out burial and other insurance which they could not afford. When wage-earners fell out of work even payments of a few pence per week could not be maintained, and the policies lapsed. Gladstone drew attention in 1864 to the high proportion of lapses – 70,000 out of 135,000 insured by the Royal Liver Society in one year.

Building societies offered yet other opportunities for thrift and enterprise, especially among tradesmen and the lower middle classes. The first such societies had been formed in the eighteenth century with the aim of assisting members to build houses for themselves; but by the middle of the nineteenth century these small terminating societies were beginning to be overshadowed by larger permanent building societies which provided opportunities for investment without limit of time, as well as making advances upon houses. In 1869 some 1,500 societies were in existence with membership over 300,000; by 1903, 2,124 societies had over 600,000 members. The Chief Registrar estimated in 1896 that during the previous sixty years at least 250,000 people had been helped by building societies to become owners of their homes.

6

All these worthy institutions of thrift and self-help shared the limitation that they could not assist the chronically poor. A regular wage was needed to permit saving, or even to support steady spending at co-operative stores. The only institution upon which the really poor could depend was the Poor Law, and to ask for poor relief carried with it the stigma of being known as a pauper. Yet it was beginning to be suggested about 1870 that though Smilesian self-reliance might be keeping tens and hundreds of thousands of working men from applying for poor relief, it patently was not rewarding them with decent livelihoods. On 17 June 1870 McCullagh Torrens, a Liberal with a strong interest in social questions, introduced in the Commons a motion for 'special consideration' of the problem of unemployment in the great towns. Recent rapid urban growth, Torrens suggested, had created new conditions of employment and unemployment. Those now out of work were not necessarily bad characters, deficient in self-reliance. 'What the House had to provide for and deal with was not the class which, being from various circumstances broken down, came upon the rates for relief, but those who were able to work, who wished for work, and who had not work to do.' Torrens directly denied three of the favourite assertions of the Smiles school. Trade union strikes and restrictive practices, he contended, could not be largely blamed for prevailing unemployment, since most men were still not trade unionists. Nor did most workmen fall out of work because of excessive drinking; they usually drank too much only because they were depressed by lack of employment. Nor was gambling a major cause of poverty, since it was heavily pursued only when work was plentiful and wages high. Torrens, in other words, was moving towards realization that the main causes of Victorian poverty were not drunkenness nor idleness but low wages and irregular employment, plus large families, sickness, widowhood, and old age. Another generation was to pass, however, before the investigations of Charles Booth and Seebohm Rowntree began to provide statistical proof of these realities.

What more then might be done for the unemployed? Torrens was not so bold in his remedies as in his analysis. 'He did not ask the Government to provide work for a single man, or to do anything which could in any way be regarded as bordering on Socialism.' He only pressed for Government assistance towards the emigration of surplus workmen to Canada and Australia. This idea of assisted emigration was often canvassed; but it could be no more than one palliative. The Victorians had already decided that what they needed was more knowledge about social problems, and also improved organization of the large but apparently still inadequate efforts of private philanthropy. With these ends in view they formed, first, the National Association for the Promotion of Social Science (1857); and, second, the Charity Organisation Society (1869).

The Social Science Association was committed to the belief that social communities were not mere haphazard collections of human beings, and that the 'science of society' could be discovered and explained.[16] With this end in view the association began to collect and to publicize social facts and ideas. The need to gather information about their rapidly changing society had been increasingly felt by the Victorians. 388 Royal Commissions were appointed between 1830 and 1900. The Statistical Department of the Board of Trade dated from 1832, the General Register Office from 1837. The Manchester Statistical Society was formed in 1833, the Statistical Society of London in 1834. Pioneer statisticians such as Drs William Farr and W. A. Guy made the most of still far from complete data. Farr wrote large parts of the annual reports of the Registrar-General, while elaborate annual reports were also produced by the Poor Law Commissioners, the Factory Inspectors, and others.[17]

The Social Science Association held its annual meeting in a different town each year. Its most active sections were those dealing with law reform, education, crime and punishment, public health, and social conditions. As well as shaping opinion through public discussion, the association pressed its views upon politicians and civil servants behind the scenes. Its greatest successes were the appointment of the Royal Commission on Sanitary Laws (1869) and the passing of the Married Women's Property Act (1870). The association thought in terms of 'improvement' rather than of radical social reform. In this spirit it won support from a wide range of middle-class opinion without reference to party political attitudes. But the economic and social pressures which built up from the mid 1870s gradually forced this non-political approach through 'social science' to give way to the approach through social politics. In 1886 the Social Science Association dissolved itself.

The urge among middle- and upper-class Victorians to support philanthropy was impressive both in its intensity and extensity.[18] They were well aware that St Mark's version of Christ's words was fuller than St Matthew's, carrying with it additional exhortation. 'For ye have the poor with you always, and whensoever ye will ye may do them good' (xiv, 7). Of course, those most active in good works were not always disinterested. Snobbery and ambition played their parts. Through philanthropic organizations and subscriptions social climbers could advertise their wealth, associate with the aristocracy, and achieve public notice. Newly-risen members of the middle class could reassure themselves about their social progress by making gestures of generosity and condescension towards the working classes. 'And there was the opportunity for discussing subjects which under conditions of contemporary prudery had acquired all the fascination of the forbidden.'[19]

Statistics of the large extent of Victorian philanthropy were never complete. *The Times* of 11 February 1869 published a survey of over 200 London charities, which estimated their annual income at £2 million. Sixteen years later (19.1.1885) *The Times* counted over 1,000 London charities, with an income of nearly £4,500,000. This large number covered a great diversity of philanthropic activities, at home and abroad, including causes such as Sabbatarianism, which the twentieth century has hardly continued to accept as philanthropic but which many Victorians thought important for social progress. Not all help for the poor was material; it could also be moral, as in the Girls' Friendly Society or the Mothers' Union. Nor were all charities directed towards the working classes; decayed gentlefolk also had their own provision. Well over 200 religious and philanthropic bodies were represented at the memorial service in 1885 for Lord Shaftesbury, the social leader of Victorian philanthropy. These included not only such major foundations as the Young Men's Christian Association or Dr Barnardo's Homes, but also many lesser bodies such as the Pure Literature Fund, the Cabmen's Shelter Fund, the Flower Girls' Mission, and the Metropolitan Drinking Fountain Association.[20]

The stream of money for charity was still flowing strongly at the end of the century. A sample of 466 wills which were proved in the 1890s disposed of £76 million in personalty; £20,200,000 of this was bequeathed to charitable institutions. By the Edwardian period London charities were enjoying an annual income of about £8,500,000. All this was admirable; but there was always too much division of effort for either efficency in service or economy in administration. This weakness began to be strongly criticized in the 1860s, especially in London, where poverty was at its most extensive. Business methods, explained William Rathbone, needed to be introduced into charity work, not (he emphasized firmly) to displace voluntary enthusiasm but to organize it. In Liverpool he had secured the amalgamation of three societies into one Central Relief Society. London's need for the 'organization of charity' was even greater than Liverpool's, and out of this climate of concern emerged the Charity Organisation Society, formed in 1869.[21] The COS established itself as a federation of district committees, ultimately forty-two in number, which matched the Poor Law divisions of metropolitan London. A central office provided co-ordination and guidance, and a council (which included representatives of the districts) was the governing body. This proved to be an efficient administration; but what gave especial force to the COS was its simple yet strongly held guiding philosophy. It was the enemy of all indiscriminate alms-giving. It insisted that each case of poverty required to be assessed individually in terms of the situation and motivation of applicants and their families; assistance was to be offered only to those who were likely to use it to restore themselves to independence. The COS drew a stern distinction between 'charity' for the deserving, which it took as its own sphere, and 'relief' for the rest, which it left to the Poor Law. Its annual report for 1875 described its aim as 'to improve the condition of the poor' by:

1. 'systematic co-operation with the Poor Law authorities, charitable agencies, and individuals';
2. by 'careful investigation of applications';
3. by 'judicious and effective assistance in all deserving cases';
4. by 'the promotion of habits of providence and self-reliance';
5. by 'the repression of mendicity and imposture'.

The report emphasized that the chief intention was 'to deal with the causes of pauperism rather than its effects, and permanently to elevate the condition of the poor'.

The COS achieved recognition with remarkable speed, collecting a host of prominent vice-presidents and securing the patronage of the Queen. The Poor Law Board minute of November 1869 on 'The Relief of the Poor in the Metropolis' amounted to official endorsement of the ideas and methods of the COS. The minute advised a clear separation between the spheres of the Poor Law and of private charity, and it also encouraged the exercise of charity through district offices. To most Londoners, rich and poor alike, its district offices represented the visible reality of the COS. All applicants for charity were interviewed by district office workers. Those poor judged deserving could be given grants or loans, or be provided with work, or be given letters to hospital. This, however, marked only a beginning. Regular visits were then made to the families until it was clear that independence had been regained. To treat charity in this personal way required an array of skilled social workers, and the COS quickly found itself laying down guidelines for a new profession of social casework. As early as 1871 the district committees were handling over 12,500 cases per year, a number more than doubled by 1887 – after which it gradually declined.[22]

Alongside this local work the COS central office conducted a steady national publicity campaign. Frequent pamphlets were published, and also a number of major reports – printed to look like official blue books. Meetings and conferences were called, deputations met Ministers, and *The Times* was plied with letters. This pressure became especially persistent after 1875 when C. S. Loch was appointed secretary. Loch, who remained in office until 1913, came to personify the COS. Yet not all was success. Social casework itself only came to be directly undertaken by the COS when it rapidly became clear that the society was failing in the hope of arranging co-operation between existing bodies. The COS could not stop the multiplication of other, more or less inefficient, charitable institutions. Eventually the COS, like the Social Science Association, found itself falling behind the times. Into the Edwardian period it still resisted all proposals for state provision of welfare, other than through the grim last resort of the Poor Law; and it vigorously opposed the famous Liberal social reforms of 1906–14.

7

The contrast between the atmosphere of the 1860s, which produced the COS, and the atmosphere of the new century, which produced the Liberal reforms, was very marked. Yet even about 1870 the potential power of the state positively to encourage social happiness was beginning to be discussed with a fresh interest. An article on 'Technical Education a National Want' in *Macmillan's Magazine* for April 1868 noticed how the passing of the more or less 'democratic' 1867 Reform Act, plus the Paris Exhibition of the same year – which had publicized the strength of the foreign challenge to British industrial supremacy – had started a significant, albeit uncertain, shift in public opinion:

Hitherto the question for a Ministry on its trial has been – 'what is the state of accounts of exports and imports? Has the nation under your guidance bought and sold more than under the Opposition? Are the funds higher or lower than when you took office, and do you leave the turn of trade against us?' For the future it seems as if new questions would be asked – 'Do you leave the English people a happier, wiser, more skilled, more refined, and more contented people than you found them when you took office? Has the social condition of the various classes become more equal under your administration, or are the extremes of luxury and misery as wide as before?' These are awkward and uncomfortable questions; but they seem likely to be the questions of the future.

These were indeed the questions for the future. By October 1874 Joseph Chamberlain thought the time right for an article in the *Fortnightly Review* on 'The Next Page in the Liberal Programme'. Chamberlain reminded his readers that 4 million people had received poor relief in England and Wales in 1872. Any reforms, wrote Chamberlain, which would 'tend by natural causes to a more equal distribution of wealth' would do more to secure the greatest happiness of the greatest number 'than all the provident and benefit societies which have ever been started by those who have no need to practice thrift for the benefit of those who have no opportunity'.

Chamberlain was, of course, still regarded at this date as a very advanced politician. He was prepared to use state and municipal power with a new boldness. Nevertheless, intervention in social and economic affairs was already extensive. The idea that during the first half of Victoria's reign her subjects were unqualified adherents of *laissez-faire* in government was misrepresentation, which gained wide currency after the publication of A. V. Dicey's *Law and Public Opinion in England during the Nineteenth Century* (1905). Dicey, an Oxford jurist of high reputation and clear style, was too eager to separate in his chapter headings the years 1825–70 as a 'Period of Benthamism or Individualism'; from the years 1865–1900, the 'Period of Collectivism'. He did modify this crude contrast in his detailed analysis; but his book was remembered for its simplifications, not for its qualifications. Dicey himself knew that the famous Benthamite objective of 'the greatest happiness of the greatest number', though it certainly expected the maximization of individual liberty as the end of government, never excluded the possibility of state intervention as a means to promote and to protect such liberty. The *laissez-faire* 'general rule' was never presented by John Stuart Mill or by his Benthamite predecessors as a natural law, such as (say) the economic law of supply and demand. *Laissez-faire* always required to be tested for its 'utility' in promoting the greatest happiness. Thus the predominant social and political thinking of the first half of the reign left the Victorians with considerable freedom of action. Moreover, the direct influence of theory upon busy ministers and civil servants may have been less than their sense of the need for action against 'intolerable' evils. Whether principle or pragmatism carried the more weight – and this varied from case to case – both could sometimes point in the same direction of more state involvement.[23]

British government was transformed during the nineteenth century in order to retain control of an industrializing society. By the 1860s 'experts', within the civil service and outside it, had been active for a generation in influencing administration and legislation. The foremost among the first generation of experts was Edwin Chadwick, secretary to the Poor Law Commission (1834–46) and one of the three members of the Board of Health set up by the 1848 Public Health Act. Controversy over the public health question became intense; but it was not so much over whether intervention was needed to regulate urban sanitary conditions – which were often appalling – as over the form which such intervention should take. Chadwick was a strong believer in central control for the sake of efficiency; but his opponents preferred local autonomy. Traditionally, Englishmen had regarded central bureaucracy with suspicion as 'foreign' and therefore potentially authoritarian.

Government growth was already tending to be self-sustaining. Once machinery had been created – with boards, officials, inspectors – the experts were likely to discover how still more intervention and still more machinery were needed. One such expert, Sir Arthur Helps, Clerk of the Privy Council, explained in his book on *Social Pressures* (1875) why an advancing civilization required not less but more government. Individuals were now caught in the great urban mass: 'does not a human being living in a great town like London require that the State should fight his battle against a thousand opposing interests?'

A *Westminster Review* article on 'Dangers of Democracy' (January 1868) pointed out how the Victorians had convinced themselves that free trade was best in commerce; but how in other spheres authority, central and local, had long played the leading part – in religion through the established Church, in the provision of poor relief, and (a notable piece of early public monopoly enterprise) in running the General Post Office. The whig Government of the 1830s had made the first Exchequer grant for education, and had sponsored a Factory Act, drafted for them by Chadwick. This Factory Act was limited in application to children and young persons, and it applied only to textile factories. Moreover, it proved easy to circumvent. The education grant was small. Yet those modest beginnings remained crucial. Parliament had recognized that conditions of labour, and likewise conditions of education, could concern the state; and to express this concern it imposed a system of inspection. Four factory inspectors were appointed in 1833, and two education inspectors in 1839. Factory legislation was gradually extended after 1833 down to the great consolidating Factories and Workshops Acts of 1878 and 1901. Conditions of work for seamen were regulated by legislation which culminated in the Merchant Shipping Act of 1854. And a whole range of detailed labour legislation began to be passed from the 1860s, covering bakehouses, chimney sweeps, matchmakers, women and children in agriculture, and so on. Such detailed legislation required expert drafting and expert enforcement. Perhaps significantly, the word 'expertise' seems to date from the 1860s.

Fear of infection exerted a stronger influence upon public health regulation than any political theory. Samuel Smiles himself was an interventionist on sanitary questions; and in *Thrift* he made a direct attack upon *laissez-faire* advocates who said that 'nobody' could be blamed for sanitary evils.

Nobody adulterates our food. Nobody fills us with bad drink. Nobody supplies us with foul water. Nobody spreads fever in blind alleys and unswept lanes . . . Nobody has a theory too – a dreadful theory. It is embodied in two words – *Laissez faire* . . . it becomes us to unite, and bring to bear upon the evil the joint moral power of society in the form of a law.

Local 'improvement' Acts had been passed since the eighteenth century, and the English preference for local action was still recognized in the important 1866 Sanitary Act. But central government was now given the authority to compel, although adequate machinery for enforcing insistence had still to be provided.[24] In 1890 Sir John Simon published his *English Sanitary Institutions*, at the end of which he listed the four forms of central intervention which had been developed by that date:

1. Where central government worked directly in a locality through its own officials (as under the Factory Acts).
2. Where central government operated as an umpire between local interests, or as an agent in Parliament.
3. Where central government wielded the power of the purse, and so could impose conditions (as in education).
4. Where it had positive control, 'very often in the form that this or that act of the local authority is not valid till the central authority confirms it'.

The 1866 Sanitary Act was passed at the instance of a civil servant by politicians who were hardly aware of the significance of the measure in terms of intervention. Equally significant was the enforcement by an Act of 1853, strengthened in 1867, of compulsory vaccination against smallpox for every infant born in England and Wales. This was the first continuous public health responsibility undertaken by the state. Vaccination was provided free, yet without any sense of Poor Law stigma; and it was made compulsory and universal. By 1872–83 over 85 per cent of children were being vaccinated. The Anti-Compulsory Vaccination League cried out in the name of individual liberty against such 'absolute invasion of the sacred right of the parent'; but relaxations in compulsion were not secured until 1898 and 1907, by which time the smallpox scourge had been conquered.[25]

Still more uncompromising than the Vaccination Acts were the Contagious Diseases Acts of 1864, 1866, and 1869. These Acts required prostitutes in certain naval and garrison towns to be registered, and allowed special police to lay information that a woman was a common prostitute. She could then be compelled to undergo medical examination for venereal disease, and if found infected could be consigned to hospital under near prison conditions. A national agitation against the Acts (on the grounds that they were interfering, and yet seemed to countenance immorality) persisted through the 1870s. The campaign was led by the National Anti-Contagious Diseases Acts Association, and by the Ladies' National Association. The formidable secretary of the latter body was Mrs Josephine Butler. She believed that prostitutes should remain free even to be prostitutes, and that they should be reclaimed voluntarily through education. The Contagious Diseases Acts, she contended, were 'depriving God's creatures of free-will, of choice and of responsibility'. Moreover, they interfered with women's liberty yet not with men's. Here again the 'double standard' showed itself in relations between the sexes, and also in relations between classes. If a general licensing system were adopted, as on the Continent, poor women who were not necessarily prostitutes might be hounded to protect 'rich profligates' from the consequences of their own dissipation. In his standard work on *Prostitution* (2nd edn, 1869) William Acton claimed that the Contagious Diseases Acts had found a middle way between too much and too little intervention. They tried to control vice by telling prostitutes 'we cannot force you to abstain from vice; but we can and will take care that your shameful lives shall no longer work injury to the health of others, or outrage public decency'. But Mrs Butler refused even to discuss the working of the Acts, in the belief that they were wrong in principle. As early as 1871 the *Annual Register* was remarking that 'the days of a most useful sanitary reform appeared already numbered'. Medical opinion remained strongly in favour; but politicians began to fear that their alleged support for 'immorality' might cost votes. The Acts were suspended in 1883 and repealed in 1886, a perverse victory for individual liberty.[26]

Even government intervention to prevent adulteration of food was resisted by some ultra-libertarians. John Bright's alleged remark that 'adulteration is a legitimate form of competition' was often quoted, but usually to be denounced. Mill's *Liberty* recognized that public control was necessary to check adulteration. The alarming extent of the problem was first revealed in the 1850s, thanks to an investigation promoted by the *Lancet* which was followed by a House of Commons select committee of inquiry. Large and often dangerous additions or substitutions were commonplace in London (water in milk, alum or chalk in flour, sulphate of lime in sugar, and hundreds of other malpractices) often for the sake of profit, sometimes for appearance. The Adulteration of Foods Act (1860) proved ineffective, but Acts of 1872 and 1875 were more successful. Public analysts were appointed under the Acts, and these new local officials began to secure numerous prosecutions for adulteration. Between 1877 and the turn of the century the percentage of bread samples found to be adulterated fell from 7.4 to almost nil, and the percentage of all sampled articles found adulterated dropped from 19.2 to less than 9.0. Dilution of liquids with water remained difficult to detect; but dangerous adulteration had been almost eliminated by a major exercise in public health intervention.[27]

Transport provided another sphere where government intervention became extensive. To protect the 7,750,000 emigrants who left the British Isles during the first three-quarters of the nineteenth century (most of them poor people, easily exploited by the shippers and others) a series of Passenger Acts was passed between 1803 and 1855.[28] An emigration officer was stationed at Liverpool in 1833, even before the first factory inspectors had been appointed under the Factory Act. The growth of railways produced a steady flow of legislation, concerned especially with safety but also with charges and services.[29] The Railway Department of the Board of Trade was formed as early as 1840. Gladstone's Railway Act of 1844 required the running of at least one train per day which offered covered third-class accommodation at a maximum fare of a penny a mile. It also reserved to the state the possibility of nationalization after twenty-one years. Railway nationalization was not undertaken during the nineteenth century; but regulation through the Board of Trade and through the Railway Commission (1873) was developed to an extent exceeded only by the amount of regulation of the mining industry, where the safety aspect was even more imperative. The first mining inspector was appointed under the 1842 Mines Act, which entirely forbade the employment underground of women and of boys below the age of ten.

8

As the purposes of government extended and became more complicated so the civil service grew in size and sophistication. By the Edwardian period it was being claimed as an essential contributor to the 'success' of British government. Graham Wallas, the political scientist, remarked how in Britain the real constitutional check against autocratic rule was provided neither by the House of Lords nor by the monarchy, but by the existence of a permanent civil service, appointed independently of politicians and holding office during good behaviour. Wallas described this as 'the one great political invention in nineteenth-century England, and like other inventions it was worked out under the pressure of an urgent practical problem'.[30]

The reshaping of the civil service to meet the problem of Victorian government began with the famous Northcote–Trevelyan *Report on the Organization of the Permanent Civil Service* (1855). Significantly, the very term 'civil service' only came into general use at this time. Gladstone rightly regarded the Northcote–Trevelyan report as formulated in the spirit of the 1832 Reform Act. Just as the 1832 Act had opened up the franchise but left it still very limited, so the Northcote–Trevelyan proposals aimed to open up the civil service but with no intention of making it 'democratic'. The proposals – most of which were gradually adopted over the rest of the century – were designed

(a) to lessen the cost and increase the effectiveness of government;
(b) to divide higher administrative work from clerical work;

(c) to lessen aristocratic control of the civil service by reducing patronage;

(d) to introduce open competition and promotion by merit.

It was not expected that open competition would greatly widen the range of intake beyond the upper and upper-middle classes, only that it would give a sounder basis of choice than the method of patronage. Gladstone welcomed the prospect that the best public-school brains might be drawn into competition for entry, thereby raising the standard of efficiency. At the same time, he expected that more efficient administration would permit savings in cost. There was no realization yet that the civil service would soon greatly expand, and that it needed to be reformed in order to undertake the drafting and application of an increasing volume of legislation.

In 1855 the Civil Service Commission was created, a step towards the structural unification of the service. Some qualifying examinations for nominees were introduced from this date, and a handful of higher places were filled from the 1860s by open competition.[31] An Order In Council of 1870 introduced more general open competition for higher posts, though this still did not apply to the Foreign or Home Offices. But appointment through patronage and nomination was coming to need exceptional justification within an increasingly professional and politically neutral group. Top civil servants were still numbered by hundreds, but figures for the permanent non-industrial civil service at all levels showed a steady growth: 32,000 (1861), 50,000 (1881), 116,000 (1901). In 1876 a grade (the Lower Division) was created common to all departments. This helped to lessen traditional departmentalism, though at the same time it reinforced the sense of civil service hierarchy. In this tightening structure there ceased to be room for semi-independent figures such as a Chadwick or a Simon, who had been personalities in the public eye. The top civil servants of the late-Victorian generation were hardly known, even as names, to the general public.

The central department of government was the Treasury.[32] It tended to avoid recruitment by competitive examination, absorbing instead men of proved capacity from other offices. It tried to develop a watchdog role over the expenditure of other departments, not so much in the name of better government – for it did not itself make positive proposals – as in the interests of economy. Gladstone's Exchequer and Audit Department Act (1866), by creating the first effective machinery for a retrospective annual audit of expenditure, gave the Treasury good reason for enforcing strict standards of financial practice throughout Whitehall. The Treasury was also generally successful in insisting that its prior approval be obtained for new expenditure. But to the end of the century 'Treasury control' remained uncertain. It did restrain expenditure upon departmental establishments, but not where expansion proposals were based upon 'expert' advice. As one Permanent Secretary of the Treasury wrote despairingly, 'I do not know who is to check the assertions of experts when the government has once undertaken a class of duties which none but such persons understand'. Nor was the Treasury able to resist major policy proposals, if they were pressed by a forceful minister. It could, however, always insist upon full written justification for new expenditure plans, and it could (and did) make the pursuit of its assent a laborious matter.

The Admiralty and the War Office were the biggest spenders, and they engaged in repeated tussles with the Treasury. At the time of the Boer War the shortcomings of the British army were unfairly linked with the workings of Treasury control; not least by Lord Salisbury, the Prime Minister. In a speech on 30 January 1900 he delivered a remarkable public attack upon the system: 'much delay and many doubtful resolutions have been the result'. This was wartime hysteria. Treasury resistance may have prevented the services getting all the money which they asked for, but it had never cut so deep that they were left with less than they needed.

In 1870 central government expenditure totalled £67,100,000, the greater part of which was directed towards the costs of war – past, present and future. Debt charges absorbed £27,100,000; the army, navy, and ordnance almost as much (see below, p. 196). The whole cost of central civil government was about £11 million, of which less than half could be attributed to social welfare broadly defined. Local welfare provision was still much greater than national provision. In England and Wales gross local authority spending amounted to £30,200,000 in 1868, equivalent to about 26s. per head of population. The United Kingdom equivalent for central government civil expenditure was only 7s. per head. Local outlay upon poor relief (£7,400,000 in 1868) made up a quarter of local authority spending.

Central government gross income in the 1870s came much more from indirect than from direct taxation:

	Direct taxation		Indirect taxation			
	Income and property tax	Land and assessed taxes	Death duties	Customs	Excise	Stamps
1871	6.4	2.7	4.8	20.2	22.8	3.6
1876	4.1	2.5	5.8	20.0	27.6	4.4
1880	9.2	2.7	6.2	19.3	25.3	4.2

(£ m.)

Income tax was the most flexible Victorian tax. The standard rate was reduced from 6d. in the £ in 1869 to 2d. in 1875 and 1876. Thereafter it rose to 5d. in 1879 and 1880 to meet the costs of Disraeli's foreign and colonial policies. Gladstone long hoped to abolish income tax entirely. He retained the early nineteenth-century view that it should be a tax to meet wartime emergencies, not a routine revenue tax. He regarded its continuation in peacetime as a temptation to wasteful expenditure. Finally, at the general election of 1874, with revenue buoyant,

Gladstone promised to secure speedy abolition of income tax if confirmed in power. But the Liberals lost the election. Disraeli took office, and he decided that there was little demand for abolition of a tax which at that date weighed so lightly with and upon the electorate.[33]

The abolition of income tax would have thrown the revenue bias still further towards indirect taxation. The mid-Victorian assumption was that the rich, middling, and poor should all stand on the same 'manly' footing, paying the same rates of indirect taxation to provide the main source of national revenue. The effect of this was analysed by the economist W. S. Jevons for the Treasury in 1869:[34]

Taxes	Family expenditure			
	£40	£85	£500	£10,000
	(per cent per annum)			
On necessaries	2.1	1.7	0.8	0.1
Rates and tolls	2.5	2.4	1.9	1.6
Direct taxes	—	—	2.7	3.7
Legacy, probate duty	—	—	0.8	2.7
Stimulants	5.5	4.1	1.8	0.5
	10.1	8.2	8.0	8.6
Other taxes, say	—	—	1.0	1.0
	10.1	8.2	9.0	9.6

9

By the late 1880s 'socialism' had become a force in British politics; but about 1870 it was still feared as a prospect rather than as a present reality. The progress of the International, formed in 1864, was discussed regularly in the press, including the part played by its secretary, 'a mischievous, hot-headed and intemperate German named Karl Marx'.[35] English trade unions affiliated to the International shared a total membership of not more than 50,000 out of a total union membership claimed at 800,000. The International failed to interest those trade unionists who worked in the heavy industries of the provinces. The largest affiliated union was the Amalgamated Society of Carpenters and Joiners. Even among affiliated unions little red revolutionary spirit showed itself. The passing of the 1867 Reform Act had reassured English workmen that peaceful pressure could bring major reforms. Marx himself admitted that in England the labour movement lacked 'the spirit of generalisation and revolutionary ardour'. His hope was only that English workers might be drawn into an international revolution once it had started upon the Continent. It looked as if this revolution might have arrived with the outbreak of the 1871 Paris Commune, and for a few weeks this aroused great concern in English political circles. But the *Annual Register* subsequently remembered how the manifestations of coming revolution in England had turned out to be 'singularly weak, and even laughable'.[36]

English socialism was not revolutionary, but it had become decidedly interventionist. In a lecture on 'Modern Socialism', given in 1872, Henry Fawcett, the economist and politician, explained how the aspirations of English socialists had changed since the days of Robert Owen, with his dreams of self-sustaining ideal communities. Socialists were now 'beginning to place their chief reliance upon State intervention. They seem to think that if individual efforts have been unable to achieve success, this provides the most cogent argument in favour of an appeal to the State'. Workmen saw that, though self-help might have assisted to increase wealth, it had conspicuously failed to reduce poverty. Poverty in the midst of plenty remained the pressing problem, not only because of its moral importance but also because of its social and political challenge. 'The more wealthy the nation is admitted to be the more perilous does it become, and the more ominous of future trouble that one out of twenty of the nation should be a pauper . . . Ought it not to be regarded as almost incredible that a social structure resting on such a basis should have stood so long?'[37] Yet the very fact that English trade unionists, who might or might not call themselves 'socialists', were seeking more intervention by the state rather than violent revolution, amounted to acceptance of that state and of much of the existing social order.

Notes

1. N. St John-Stevas (ed.), *Collected Works of Walter Bagehot*, VII (1974), p. 226.
2. G. H. Perris, *Industrial History of Modern England* (1914), p. 312.
3. W. E. Gladstone, *Political Speeches in Scotland, March and April 1880* (1880), pp. 145-6; A. Bullock and M. Shock (eds.), *The Liberal Tradition* (1967), pp. 143-4.
4. Cobden to J. B. Smith, 28 December 1852 (Smith Papers, Manchester Reference Library).
5. A. Ponsonby, *Henry Ponsonby* (1942), p. 256.
6. J. Morley, *Life of William Ewart Gladstone* (1906), II, p. 190.
7. W. E. Gladstone, *Midlothian Speeches, 1879* (1879; reprinted 1971), p. 90.
8. A. Bullock and M. Shock (eds.), *The Liberal Tradition* (1967), p. 126.
9. J. L. Garvin, *Life of Joseph Chamberlain*, II (1933), Ch. XXVII.
10. W. E. Gladstone, *Midlothian Speeches, 1879* (1879; reprinted 1971), p. 94.
11. See especially B. E. Lippincott, *Victorian Critics of Democracy* (1938). Also R. J. White (ed.), *The Conservative Tradition* (1950).
12. O. Chadwick, *The Secularization of the European Mind in the Nineteenth Century* (1975), p. 108.
13. *The Times*, 18 September 1876; F. E. Smith, *Unionist Policy* (1913), pp. 45-6.
14. R. L. Smyth (ed.), *Essays in Economic Method* (1962), p. 27.
15. See especially P. H. J. H. Gosden, *Self-Help, Voluntary Associations In the 19th Century* (1973).
16. See B. Rogers, 'The Social Science Association, 1857-1886', *Manchester School*, XX (1952).

17. See Ruth G. Hodgkinson, 'Social Medicine and the Growth of Statistical Information', in F. N. L. Poynter (ed.), *Medicine and Science in the 1860s* (1968); and M. J. Cullen, *The Statistical Movement in Early Victorian Britain* (1975).

18 See D. Owen, *English Philanthropy, 1660–1960* (1964), part 3; and B. Harrison, 'Philanthropy and the Victorians', *Victorian Studies*, IX (1966).

19. Margaret B. Simey, *Charitable Effort in Liverpool in the Nineteenth Century* (1951), pp. 56–7.

20. E. Hodder, *Life and Work of the Seventh Earl of Shaftesbury* (1887), appendix.

21. W. Rathbone, *Social Duties* (1867), pp. 53–5, 128–9. See especially C. L. Mowat, *The Charity Organisation Society, 1869–1913* (1961).

22. See Kathleen Woodroofe, *From Charity to Social Work* (1962), part I. Also Helen Bosanquet, *Social Work in London, 1869–1912* (1914; reprinted 1973).

23. See especially H. Parris, *Constitutional Bureaucracy* (1969), Ch. IX; A. J. Taylor, *Laissez-Faire and State Intervention in Nineteenth-Century Britain* (1972); Gillian Sutherland (ed.), *Studies in the Growth of Nineteenth-Century Government* (1972); and O. MacDonagh, *Early Victorian Government, 1830–1870* (1977).

24. See R. M. Gutchen, 'Local Improvements and Centralization in Nineteenth-Century England', *Historical Journal*, IV (1961).

25. See R. J. Lambert, 'A Victorian National Health Service: State Vaccination 1855–71', *Historical Journal*, V (1962).

26. See G. Petrie, *A Singular Iniquity, The Campaigns of Josephine Butler* (1971); F. B. Smith, 'Ethics and Disease in the Later Nineteenth Century: The Contagious Diseases Acts', *Historical Studies*, XV (1971); and Patricia Hollis (ed.), *Pressure From Without in Early Victorian England* (1974), pp. 312–15.

27. See J. Burnett, *Plenty and Want* (1966), Ch. 10.

28. See O. MacDonagh, *A Pattern of Government Growth, 1800–60* (1961).

29. See H. Parris, *Government and the Railways in Nineteenth-Century Britain* (1965).

30. G. Wallas, *Human Nature in Politics* (1908), p. 249. See especially E. Hughes, 'Civil Service Reform 1853–5', *Public Administration*, XXXII (1954); Emmeline W. Cohen, *The Growth of the British Civil Service, 1780–1939* (1965), part two; and O. MacDonagh, *Early Victorian Government, 1830–1870* (1977), Ch. 11.

31. See J. Roach, *Public Examinations in England, 1850–1900* (1971), Chs. 8, 9.

32. See H. Roseveare, *The Treasury* (1969), Chs. 5–7; M. Wright, *Treasury Control of the Civil Service, 1854–74* (1969); and M. Wright, 'Treasury Control 1854–1914', in Gillian Sutherland (ed.), *Studies in the Growth of Nineteenth-Century Government* (1972).

33. See B. E. V. Sabine, 'The Abolition of Income Tax (A Dream of 1873–74)', *British Tax Review*, 1973.

34. H. Roseveare, *The Treasury* (1969), pp. 191–2.

35. W. R. Greg, *Mistaken Aims and Attainable Ideals of the Artizan Class* (1876), pp. 261–2. See especially H. Collins and C. Abramsky, *Karl Marx and the British Labour Movement* (1965).

36. See especially R. Harrison (ed.), *The English Defence of the Commune, 1871* (1971).

37. H. and Millicent G. Fawcett, *Essays and Lectures on Social and Political Subjects* (1872), Ch. 1.

Personalities: *'Not in all respects well qualified'*

1

'Not the defeat of a principle, but the defeat of a leader and his "side" is the really mortifying thing.' So explained one standard Edwardian account of English government and politics.[1] Victorian and Edwardian Englishmen were little interested in political theory, not only because they preferred results to ideas, but also because in the realm of government and politics they liked to give their support or opposition to nationally known personalities.

The foremost personality of all was, of course, Queen Victoria (1819–1901).[2] She had succeeded to the throne in 1837, and already by the late 1860s it was coming to seem as if she had always been queen. This sense of an increasingly long reign was not everywhere a cause of loyal enthusiasm. The English republican movement reached a peak about 1870.[3] Republicanism had been stimulated by the belief in general that an elected head of state would be more appropriate to the 'democratic' spirit of the times; and by feeling in particular that taxpayers' money was financing the idleness and dissipation of the Prince of Wales, and by hostility to the withdrawal of the queen herself from public functions. Victoria had gone into perpetual mourning for Prince Albert, who had died in 1861. Republicans ranged from Sir Charles Dilke, a young radical baronet, to trade unionists who wanted better opportunities and conditions for working men. The cost of providing for Victoria's eight children as they grew up offered easy ground for republican complaints – in 1870 ten royalties were receiving annuities worth £111,000; by 1900 sixteen were getting £168,000. But the nearly fatal and widely publicized illness of the Prince of Wales from typhoid at the end of 1871 suddenly destroyed the always limited popularity of the republican movement.

Gladstone, the Liberal Prime Minister, although himself a convinced royalist, shared the concern about the queen's withdrawal and the prince's idleness. Victoria refused to give her heir any responsible work, partly because she did not trust his discretion, partly because she subconsciously feared that his popularity might rival her own. When Gladstone persisted in proposing that the prince might become Viceroy of Ireland, the queen grew angry; and the episode contributed to a permanent frosting of her relationship with the Liberal leader. Disraeli had found himself equally unsuccessful with a similar proposal in 1868. But Disraeli's relationship with the queen grew closer as Gladstone's cooled. Disraeli was a genuine romantic in his attitude to the throne. In addition, he was skilful in dealing with women. He cultivated a colourful manner of speech and writing to Victoria which contrived to be both respectful and intimate, informative and amusing, and to which the lonely queen gladly responded. In general, Victoria agreed with Disraeli's policies, whereas she increasingly believed Gladstone's politics to be dangerous and the man himself to be more or less deranged. By 1885 Gladstone was privately wishing that the queen would abdicate in favour of the Prince of Wales; but there was never any likelihood of abdication.

While critics complained about Victoria's withdrawal, the queen herself emphasized how little the public knew about the heavy load which she carried in private. But much of this was routine or minor paper work. The political influence of the sovereign declined during the second half of the reign, as party differences and cabinet government solidified.[4] The firmer the party majority in the House of Commons, linked to an election programme, the less scope remained for royal influence or intervention. Victoria still insisted upon being consulted in advance with regard to foreign policy initiatives, a sphere in which her European royal family connections gave her a unique position. In general, she liked to regard Her Majesty's Government as still personally hers; but only in circumstances where the ruling political party did not know its own mind could the monarch now hope to choose a prime minister (as perhaps with Rosebery in 1894), and then only from a limited range. With regard to selection of individual cabinet ministers, royal recommendation carried little weight, though a royal veto could sometimes be pressed, as over Labouchere in 1892.

Public opinion continued to assume that the queen possessed more power than was really the case. But Victoria's popularity was gradually restored during the last twenty-five years of her reign by the development of the symbolic and ceremonial side of monarchy, which provided a new role for British sovereigns in place of the old exercise of political power and influence. Victoria's position as ceremonial head of the empire was given recognition at the Golden and Diamond Jubilees of 1887 and 1897, the like of which had never been known before. The queen was being seen again, and this helped to convince her subjects that she was a 'good' queen, both in performance of her functions and as a person. 'Good sovereign – no Change required.' She did indeed possess an attractive personality – hard working, shrewd yet sincere, religious in a simple way, kind even though sometimes obstinate, regal but without pride. She disliked the aristocracy as dissipated, and her tastes and reactions were in many respects middle-class. Lord Salisbury, her last prime minister, remarked that when he knew the queen's opinion on any issue he 'knew pretty certainly what view her subjects would take, and especially the middle class of her subjects'.[5]

2

William Ewart Gladstone (1809–98) continued active in British politics from the 1830s to the 1890s, and for fifty years he played a leading part.[6] He first entered the cabinet under Peel in 1843, and he spent most of the next thirty years in high office, notably as Chancellor of the Exchequer (1852–5, 1859–66) and as Prime Minister for the first time from 1868 to 1874. He began as a Peelite Conservative, but by the late 1860s he was accepted as the leader of the Liberal Party. The hardening of the party system was forcing politicians to take sides. But to the end Gladstone regarded all his policies as 'conservative' – in the sense that they were designed to preserve or to promote social and political order at home and abroad through timely acceptance of necessary improvement. Gladstone liked single 'great' issues, which he could present to the

Liberal Party in moral, Christian terms with the expectation that his followers would then put aside all sectional interests. In this spirit he advocated Irish Church disestablishment in the late 1860s, campaigned against Disraeli's foreign policy in the late 1870s, and advocated Irish Home Rule from 1885. In connection with these two last causes he returned from retirement to serve three more times as prime minister – 1880–5, 1886, 1892–4.

During this long career Gladstone became both deeply admired and deeply hated – 'the People's William' or 'the Grand Old Man' to his supporters: power-hungry, unpatriotic, mad, 'God's One Mistake', according to his opponents. It was difficult not to feel strongly one way or the other about 'Mr Gladstone'. Yet neither his supporters nor his opponents really understood him, for his personality was both complex and not readily revealed. One Liberal minister remembered him as two characters in one. 'Passionate and impulsive on the emotional side of his nature, he was cautious and conservative on the intellectual. Few understood the conjunction.'[7] Gladstone's greatest defect was his insensitivity in dealing with people. He paid little attention to humouring the vanities and idiosyncrasies of his colleagues and followers, a fault which in the case of Joseph Chamberlain cost him vital support. Yet his persuasive oratory gave him great power over the House of Commons as a whole and over public opinion outside Parliament. He managed to appeal to different sections of opinion at the same time, encouraging each section to construct its own image of him. In the 1860s urban working-class radicals came to associate Gladstone with ideas of democratic parliamentary reform. Yet he had set up as a landowner at Hawarden in Flintshire, and he always emphasized the importance of maintaining social hierarchy, especially in the country-side. During the 1870s the Bulgarian agitation built him up as a model politician in the eyes of Nonconformists; and yet in his private devotions he continued as a dedicated high Anglican.

Did Gladstone stay in politics too long? He became increasingly an old man surrounded by perhaps over-deferential, younger lieutenants. It had always been difficult to hold out against him in argument, such was his articulateness in general and his mastery of detail in particular; yet he was not always right. His immense mental and physical energy endured well into old age, so that he could work for sixteen hours a day; but by the 1880s his mind was narrowing. Two topics came to absorb most of his attention: Homer and Home Rule. His many Homeric writings were all directed towards demonstrating – with wilful ingenuity – his theory that God had made a double revelation of Himself through the Jews and through the Greeks.[8] These Homeric studies reflected Gladstone's strong European sense, which had been shaped by his Oxford classical education and which recognized a great tradition extending from ancient Greece and Rome down to the nineteenth century. Gladstone's interest in Homer also formed an important part of his intense religious concern. As a young man he might well have become an Anglican clergyman, until his father, John Gladstone, a Liverpool merchant, directed him not to follow this vocation but to enter public life instead. Young Gladstone therefore took into politics the moral earnestness and purpose which he would have shown as a clergyman. At the end of 1868, only a few days after forming his first Government, he confided to his diary the hope that he would eventually be able to retire from politics and be spared for a few years 'to live that kind of work which perhaps (I have never lost the belief) more specially belongs to me . . . as a doorkeeper in the house of my God'. One of his private secretaries even contended that he was 'not in all respects well qualified' for politics. 'His affections were set on another and a very different world, in which he lived and moved and had his being.'[9] Certainly, Gladstone regularly sought guidance from private prayer. Not that this made him always solemn in public. He enjoyed dining out, and he could be an entertaining and amusing companion. And, paradoxically, one element in the complexity of his make-up was his engaging simplicity. As a septuagenarian Prime Minister he was only restrained from taking a turn on the roundabout at Deal fair by the reminder that the Opposition papers would make fun of him. Yet by the 1860s Gladstone was becoming a world personality, viewed in his day alongside such international contemporaries as Bismarck and Lincoln.

3

The career of Gladstone's great political rival, Benjamin Disraeli, Earl of Beaconsfield from 1876 – Chancellor of the Exchequer 1852, 1858–9, 1866–8, and Conservative Prime Minister 1868 and 1874–80 – was summed up by Lord Randolph Churchill in 1883. 'Failure, failure, failure, failure, partial success, renewed failure, ultimate and complete triumph.'[10] Disraeli was born into an upper middle-class Jewish family, but he was baptised a Christian. To his decidedly Jewish features he added during his younger days a dandified affectation of dress and manner which made him noticed but hardly respected. The influence of Byronic romanticism upon him was obvious, but he emerged during the 1830s as a unique personality. His father was a well-known literary figure, and young Disraeli himself first achieved brief success with his novel *Vivian Grey* (1826). Thereafter to the end of his life he wrote a succession of highly characteristic novels of social and political life, the most significant of which were *Coningsby* (1844), *Sybil* (1845), and *Tancred* (1847), which gave expression to the 'Young England' ideas of his group within the Conservative Party. Disraeli had first entered Parliament in 1837, and he was bitterly disappointed not to be given office by Peel in 1841. Thereafter he grew increasingly critical of his leader, and his biting speeches in 1846 against Peel's sudden switch to advocacy of Corn Law repeal confirmed Disraeli's position as a major House of Commons figure. Despite his origins, he slowly came to be accepted as a leader of the landed interest. He regarded Jews as natural aristocrats, and he did not find it strange that he should become the friend of great landed proprietors. Landlord friends set him up as a country gentleman at Hughenden in Buckinghamshire, for which he had become a county Member of Parliament in 1847. Disraeli believed that the aristocratic principle and the territorial system provided guarantees of freedom. True aristocrats could neither be frightened by the mob nor overawed by kings. Yet he also genuinely admired the principle of monarchy, an admiration which he expressed with calculated exaggeration to Queen Victoria. The company of women brought out the best in him; and in congenial company he could be amusing and fanciful. Yet he remained a 'mystery', a word often applied to him – 'the mystery man', 'an Asian mystery'. The character of Sidonia in *Coningsby* could have been a self-portrait. 'Though unreserved in his manner, his frankness was strictly limited to the surface. He observed everything, thought ever, but avoided serious discussion. If you pressed him for an opinion, he took refuge in raillery, or threw out some grave paradox, with which it was not easy to cope.'[11]

At the heart of the Disraeli mystery lay the question: was he a sincere and serious statesman? Or had he entered politics simply to satisfy ambition, to enjoy success and excitement? Excitement came early, but real success came (as Randolph Churchill indicated) very late, so late that when he took office as prime minister for the first time with a majority in 1874 he was already too old and ailing to pursue a fully active course. In retrospect after his death in 1881 Conservative admirers much exaggerated Disraeli's contribution towards the progress of 'Tory Democracy' and of social reform. His influential posthumous reputation was only loosely related to the facts of his career. His legislative achievement was certainly small compared with Gladstone's; but then at Disraeli's death Gladstone had held office for nearly twenty years compared with Disraeli's eleven, of which almost half had been spent in weak minority administrations.

Both Gladstone and Disraeli were elusive personalities, never fully understandable. But the course of the contest between them became a matter of public observation.[12] From the time of Disraeli's Corn Law attacks on Peel – when Gladstone, who was temporarily not a member of the Commons, found himself unable to speak in defence of his leader – Gladstone distrusted Disraeli as unscrupulous and unprincipled. He believed that Disraeli's lack of scruples had permanently lowered the standard of Victorian political conduct. In 1852 he ruthlessly demolished Disraeli's budget in the Commons. Disraeli was now alerted, and henceforth he returned Gladstone's hostility. He thought Gladstone a hypocrite, or at least a humbug. As party heads their formal personal confrontation lasted only from 1868 to Gladstone's first retirement in 1875; but their rivalry had been apparent long before 1868, and it was to continue in spirit even after Disraeli's death in 1881. Both men could dominate the House of Commons, where the honours in debate were evenly shared between them. Disraeli never tried to counter Gladstone on his strongest ground, preferring the rapier to the bludgeon, employing oblique arguments or making unexpected sudden thrusts. After Disraeli's death Gladstone was much troubled how he could honestly pay the customary tribute in the Commons. He chose to remember Disraeli's readiness to risk political unpopularity in advocating full political equality for the Jews; he also praised his rival's tenacity and self-control, and 'his great Parliamentary courage'. In short, he praised Disraeli for possessing admirable qualities; but not for the purposes to which he had chiefly put those qualities.

4

Lord Salisbury (1830–1903), the next Conservative Prime Minister after Disraeli, served in the highest office much longer than his better-remembered predecessor – 1885–6, 1886–92, 1895–1902.[13] Late Victorians came to accept him as a comfortable bearded symbol of continuity. As with Disraeli and Gladstone, the image differed from the reality. Neither in personality nor in his policies did Salisbury feel comfortable. He was an aristocratic survival into an age of democratic politics, a great landowner at a time of rapid urbanization, aloof even neurotic by temperament, an intellectual at the head of an unintellectual party with a crisp literary style and great quickness of mind. In religion, however, he made a complete intellectual surrender, committed to Anglican faith rather than reason. He especially needed the support of religion because in secular matters he was deeply pessimistic, with little confidence in 'progress'. In both home and foreign politics he pictured himself in charge of a long rearguard action. He was too shrewd to resist change totally; but he tried hard to slow it down. He feared on historical grounds that the rule of democracy would lead perhaps to violence, at least to confiscation of property – not because the masses were worse than other classes, but because they were no better. 'Come the revolution' remained a serious private expression with him. 'We are in a state of bloodless civil war,' he lamented in 1889. 'No common principles, no respect for common institutions or traditions, unite the various groups of politicians, who are struggling for power. To loot somebody or something is the common object under a thick varnish of pious phrases.'[14]

Yet this remote and pessimistic aristocrat who feared the tyranny of the majority served the new democratic electorates as Prime Minister with success and popularity. In part he was lucky. He benefited from the efforts of J. E. Gorst and of Lord Randolph Churchill to modernize the machinery and the reputation of the Conservative Party, to extend its appeal to the urban middle classes and even to working men. As a result, Salisbury found himself popular almost in spite of his wish, in demand as a straightforward but effective public speaker to large audiences. Yet he hardly came to respect, though he came to accept the need to organize, what he once disdainfully described as 'Villa Toryism'.[15]

Salisbury served as Foreign Secretary from 1878 to 1880, and during most of his time as prime minister. Foreign affairs constituted his special interest, the more attractive to him because he was able for long periods to control British policy with little reference to public opinion or even to his cabinet colleagues. Yet he was little more hopeful abroad than at home. He was very conscious of Britain's declining relative power in the world. He became chiefly responsible for British participation in the 'scramble for Africa'; but his huge territorial acquisitions there reflected concern rather than confidence. He sought to ensure that the British Empire would be able to survive in the twentieth century. He hated 'jingoism', even when it expressed support for his policies. By temperament he would have much preferred to be the servant not of a popular electorate but of an autocratic ruler – to have worked under Queen Elizabeth (as did his famous ancestor, Lord Burleigh) rather than under Queen Victoria.

5

The urban business middle classes were not only coming to vote for Lord Salisbury, they were also joining his cabinets. The leading late-Victorian middle-class politician was Joseph Chamberlain (1836–1914).[16] He first came into prominence about 1870 as one of the leaders of the Birmingham-based National Education League. Chamberlain was a Unitarian, who first made a fortune as a screw manufacturer and who then retired from business to give his time to politics. As Mayor of Birmingham (1873–6) he initiated a pioneering programme of local reforms which attracted international notice. In 1876 he became a local Liberal Member of Parliament; and Birmingham was to remain the Chamberlain family power-base through his parliamentary career and through those of his two sons, Austen and Neville. He entered Gladstone's cabinet as President of the Board of Trade in 1880. In 1885 he revealed his 'unauthorized programme' of radical reforms; but his hopes were frustrated by Gladstone's adoption of Irish Home Rule as the first priority for the Liberal Party. Chamberlain refused to accept Home Rule, and left the Liberals to become a Liberal Unionist. From 1895 to 1903 he served as Colonial Secretary in the Salisbury and Balfour Conservative/Liberal Unionist coalitions. With enthusiasm and determination he applied his great energies behind policies designed to protect and to develop the British Empire. In Chamberlain's mind the idea of empire was simply a world expression of the idea of 'community', which he had first promoted in Birmingham. In 1903 he left office to campaign for 'tariff reform' as a means both of uniting the empire and of ensuring markets for British manufacturers in an increasingly competitive and protectionist world. As in his National Education League days, he was once more acting as a 'movement' politician, eager to press public opinion upon Government and Parliament from outside.

Chamberlain's immaculate but cold exterior constituted a mask. He always appeared before the public with an eyeglass glinting in his right eye, and nearly always with an orchid in his buttonhole. He seemed to have hardened himself to accept tragedy in private life and frustration in politics. His first two wives both died in childbirth. Yet the man beneath the mask was not nearly so temperate as he seemed. George Wyndham, a Conservative cabinet colleague, remarked how Chamberlain was completely misunderstood by the public, which 'judging by his face, thought him a cool, unimpassioned calculator. He was just the reverse, being rash and impulsive in his decisions, to a great extent a political gambler, anything but a safe man to be at the head of affairs'.[17] Was Chamberlain then a gambler in the sense that he was unprincipled? Certainly his dramatic moves in 1886 over Home Rule and in 1903 over tariff reform were imperfectly considered; but they were founded upon sincerely-held principles. In the event, neither manoeuvre worked out as Chamberlain had hoped. He lost the almost certain prospect of becoming Liberal Prime Minister after Gladstone. The man who looked the picture of self-made Victorian success conducted a career of at least half failure in politics.

Notes

1. S. Low, *The Governance of England* (2nd edn, 1914), p. 128.
2. See especially A. Ponsonby, *Henry Ponsonby* (1942); and Elizabeth Longford, *Victoria R.I.* (1964).
3. See R. Harrison, *Before the Socialists* (1965), Ch. V.
4. See F. Hardie, *The Political Influence of Queen Victoria, 1861–1901* (3rd edn, 1963); J. P. Mackintosh, *The British Cabinet* (2nd edn, 1968), Ch. 9; and H. J. Hanham (ed.), *The Nineteenth-Century Constitution* (1969), pp. 24–60.
5. Lady Gwendolen Cecil, *Life of Robert, Marquis of Salisbury*, III (1931), pp. 186–7.
6. See especially J. Morley, *Life of William Ewart Gladstone* (1903); P. Magnus, *Gladstone* (1960); S. G. Checkland, *The Gladstones* (1971); and E. J. Feuchtwanger, *Gladstone* (1975). Also M. R. D. Foot and H. C. G. Matthew (eds.), *The Gladstone Diaries* (1968 in progress); and M. R. D. Foot, 'Morley's Gladstone: A Reappraisal', *Bulletin of the John Rylands Library*, Vol. 51 (1969).
7. J. Bryce, *Studies in Contemporary Biography* (1903), p. 412. See also G. M. Young, *Victorian Essays* (1962), pp. 90–110; and D. A. Hamer, 'Understanding Mr. Gladstone', *New Zealand Journal of History*, Vol. 6 (1972).
8. See J. L. Hammond, *Gladstone and the Irish Nation* (1964), Ch. V; and H. Lloyd-Jones, 'Gladstone on Homer', *Times Literary Supplement*, 3 January 1975.
9. Lord Kilbracken, *Reminiscences* (1931), p. 128.
10. Lord Randolph Churchill, 'Elijah's Mantle; April 19th, 1883', *Fortnightly Review*, May 1883, p. 614. See especially R. Blake, *Disraeli* (1966); and R. W. Davis, *Disraeli* (1976).
11. R. Palmer, *Memorials*, part II (1898), Vol. I, pp. 478–9.
12. See especially R. Blake, *Disraeli and Gladstone* (1969).

13. See especially Lady Gwendolen Cecil, *Life of Robert, Marquis of Salisbury*, 4 vols. (1921–32); M. Pinto-Duschinsky, *The Political Thought of Lord Salisbury, 1854–1868* (1967); P. Smith (ed.), *Lord Salisbury on Politics* (1972); and R. Taylor, *Lord Salisbury* (1975).
14. Lord Chilston, *W. H. Smith* (1965), p. 296.
15. J. P. Cornford, 'The Transformation of Conservatism in the Late Nineteenth Century', *Victorian Studies*, VII (1963), p. 52.
16. See especially J. L. Garvin and J. Amery, *Life of Joseph Chamberlain*, 6 vols. (1932–69); P. Fraser, *Joseph Chamberlain* (1966); and D. Judd, *Radical Joe* (1977).
17. W. S. Blunt, *My Diaries* (1932), p. 439.

Democracy: *'The Niagara leap'*

1

The basis of the enduring success of the Victorian political system was its adaptability, its capacity for self-reform, for strengthening itself by becoming ever more representative of the population as a whole. Sometimes, as with the Reform Acts of 1832, 1867, and 1884–5, such reform was enacted by statute; but reform also proceeded continuously through changes in the conduct and conventions of government and politics. Did the late-Victorians seek then to create a 'democracy' in Britain after the passing of the Second Reform Act in 1867? In his speech introducing the measure Disraeli had hoped that it would 'never be the fate of this country to live under a democracy'. But his proposals had been drastically amended during the passage of the bill through the Commons; and opponents such as Robert Lowe were sure that it was ultra-democratic in tendency, and that a new breed of Jacobin working-class leaders must soon emerge who would begin by seeking the confiscation of property and end by throwing the country into anarchy. Many others – including Lord Derby, prime minister until February 1868 – simply hoped for the best. It was, he admitted in a famous phrase, 'a leap in the dark'; but not, he trusted, a leap into darkness.[1]

A month after the passing of reform Thomas Carlyle published an article entitled 'Shooting Niagara and After'. In 1859 Charles Blondin had caught the imagination of the world by twice crossing the Niagara Falls on a tightrope, the second time blindfold. Englishmen now found themselves crossing a political Niagara equally blindly. 'That England would have to take the Niagara leap of completed Democracy one day,' explained Carlyle, 'was also a plain prophecy, though uncertain as to time.'[2] Yet on no acceptable definition of 'democracy' could the British system of government and politics after 1867 be accurately described as 'completed'. A movement had certainly been started towards rule by numbers; but under the reformed system still only about one adult male in three enjoyed the parliamentary franchise in England and Wales. Nevertheless, the 1867 Reform Act had produced a striking increase in electoral numbers:[3]

| | England and Wales | | United Kingdom |
	County electors	Borough electors	Total electors
1866	542,633	514,026	1,364,456
1869	791,916	1,203,170	2,445,847
1883	966,721	1,651,732	3,152,912

The English and Welsh borough electorate had thus been broadened much more than the county electorate, by about 134 per cent as against 45 per cent. The townsmen newly enfranchised in 1867 consisted chiefly of skilled workmen. The Act extended the franchise down to urban householders with a one-year residential qualification, and to lodgers who had occupied for a year lodgings worth at least £10. It also created an occupation franchise in the counties for occupiers of land worth £12 per annum, and a property franchise for those owning lands worth £5 per annum.

The Second Reform Act was important not only in itself, but also because it was virtually certain to be followed before long by further reform – in favour, for example, of agricultural labourers and others still denied the vote. After the passing of the First Reform Act in 1832 its authors had hoped for 'finality'; neither the friends nor the enemies of reform expected the 1867 Act to be a final measure. Parliamentary reform had become progressive. The general elections of 1868, 1874, and 1880 were each conducted within larger and wider electorates. Numbers of voters were rising steadily as a result of adult population growth. In addition, the 1878 Registration Act increased the gap between the borough and county electorates by providing much fuller preliminary lists of borough voters and by reducing opportunities for frivolous objections. In some constituencies more names were added to the registers after 1878 than after 1867. Personal payment of rates was quietly abandoned as a qualification by the time of the 1874 general election, which was also the first to be conducted with secret voting under the terms of the 1872 Ballot Act.

The Second Reform Act was obviously a far from final measure with regard to redistribution of seats. The changes agreed in 1867 were modest. Seven English seats were made available through the disfranchisement of corrupt boroughs, and 45 further seats were taken from small boroughs. Twenty-five of these were allotted to counties; 13 went to new boroughs; 6 were given as extra seats to large boroughs; London University received a seat; and the remaining 7 seats were added to the representation of Scotland. The House of Commons now contained 658 members, shared among the constituencies as follows: England 463, Wales 30, Scotland 60, Ireland 105; County 283, Borough 366, University 9.

Representation remained very uneven. Over seventy boroughs with populations under 10,000 kept representatives, even though many larger places still had no borough members of their own. London, Lancashire, and Yorkshire continued to be notably under-represented in proportion to population. Wiltshire and Dorset elected 25 borough and county members for 450,000 people, whereas London's 3 million inhabitants were represented by only 24 members, and the West Riding's 2 million by only 22.

The landed interest remained the largest social group in the Commons, at least until the 1880 Liberal election victory:[4]

	Occupations of Members of Parliament		
	1874	1880	1885
Landowners, rentiers	209	125	78
Army and Navy officers	116	86	58
Professional	157	167	154
Commerce/industry	157	259	186

Landowners yielded their predominance within the late-Victorian cabinets even more slowly:[5]

	Occupations of cabinet ministers	
	Pre-1868 Ministers	Entrants, 1868–86
Landowners	12	9
Rentiers	3	3
Civil Service	2	2
Professional	2	10
Entrepreneurs	1	5

The number of contested elections was growing:[6]

	Number of constituencies	Number uncontested
1865	401	194
1868	420	140
1874	416	122
1880	416	67
1885	643	39

But this increasing total of contests was not necessarily a sign that constituency 'influence' had given way to democracy. It might mean only that – with larger numbers of local electors – more contests were needed to decide whose influence was paramount. The Ballot Act had added to this uncertainty. Gladstone had previously advocated open voting as more English and 'manly'; but he came to accept that working-class electors needed the protection of secrecy so that their votes could be cast 'freely as respects the landlord, freely as respects the customer, freely as respects the employer, freely as respects the working class itself'. Yet as late as 1883 Sir Frederick Pollock's monograph on *The Land Laws* explained how political support for landlords from their tenant farmers was 'not unfrequently reckoned on with as much confidence as the performance of the covenants and conditions of the tenancy itself'.

The Ballot Act meant the end of the hustings, which had been centres of tumult in many constituencies. The 1868 general election had perhaps marked a high point in constituency violence, stimulated by the combination of old-style open voting with a much increased number of voters. *The Times* (22.6.1868) cynically described a typical nomination day. 'Unceasing clamour prevails; proposers, seconders, and candidates speak in dumb show, or confide their sentiments to the reporters; heads are broken, blood flows from numerous noses, and the judgement of the electors is generally subjected to a severe training as a preliminary to the voting of the following day.'[7] Elections also remained more or less corrupt. Twenty-two successful petitions for bribery were presented after the 1868 general election. Anthony Trollope described his unhappy experience as a candidate for the notoriously venal small borough of Beverley. Of its 2,700 voters over a third were ready to be bribed. Indeed, to these electors (as Trollope explained) there was 'something absolutely mean and ignoble in the idea of a man coming forward to represent a borough in Parliament without paying the regular fees'.[8] Beverley was duly disfranchised after the 1868 election; but only the most blatant cases ended with disfranchisement or even with election petitions alleging corruption. In the absence in most places of any elaborate constituency organization, candidates could hardly avoid spending freely to rally support. 'Treating' was expected, especially the provision of much free drink, and candidates were assumed to be men with the means to treat. 'The first condition of getting into the English Parliament is to be rich,' declared the *Fortnightly Review* (July 1879), 'and the second to seem rich.' Candidates had to meet the returning officers' expenses as well as their own; and if elected they served as Members of Parliament without salary. One 1868 account put election costs at about £2,000 per candidate, win or lose, without recourse to bribery. The cost of a borough contest could be less than this; but the cost of a county contest would probably be higher. 'Hustings, placards, advertisements, committee rooms, messengers, cabs, hotel-keepers, publicans, and, above all, lawyers,' explained *Macmillan's Magazine* (September 1868); 'in the phrase appropriate to such occasion, you have set money going.'

Working men could not hope to meet the high costs of politics, unless trade unions were prepared to subsidize election expenses and to pay maintenance for successful candidates. No working men were returned in 1868. At the 1874 general election the first two workmen, both miners, entered the Commons – Thomas Burt for Morpeth, and Alexander McDonald for Stafford. After the 1880 election they were joined by Henry Broadhurst, a stonemason, secretary to the parliamentary committee of the Trades Union Congress. By living frugally, Broadhurst was just able to manage upon his union salary of £150 per year.

2

Broadhurst, Burt, and McDonald were 'Lib-Labs', still prepared to accept a lead from the Liberal Party even though it was dominated by the middle and upper classes. The Liberal Party in the House of Commons was a grand coalition, which ranged from whigs on the right to radicals on the left.[9] Most of the whigs came from landed families, but only a few of the radicals. Neither the whigs nor the radicals constituted a majority within the Liberal ranks. The whigs were indeed little more, but no less, than a great family connection. Most of the principal whigs sat under the leadership of Lord Granville in the Lords; but (like him) they had often first served in the Commons before succeeding to a title. Their numbers in the upper house included some of the richest landed magnates in the country, topped by an array of dukes – Argyll, Bedford, Devonshire, Norfolk, Sutherland, and Westminster. Devonshire's heir, Lord Hartington, emerged in the 1870s as the foremost member of the band of some thirty whig members of the Commons, most of them relatives of peers. In 1883 Hartington outlined what he regarded as the traditional whig role within the Liberal Party. This was, he suggested, not to initiate popular movements but 'to direct, and guide, and moderate' them; for the whigs 'formed a connecting link between the advanced party and those classes which, possessing property, power and influence, are naturally averse to change'. The radicals found this moderating role of the whigs increasingly exasperating, as Joseph Chamberlain made clear in a tart private comment on Hartington's explanation. Chamberlain complained that, if the radicals were 'fortunate enough to kindle the fire of national enthusiasm', then the whigs claimed the right to cut in and to dampen down the fire.[10]

The radicals numbered about eighty members in the 1874–80 House of Commons, one-third of the Liberal total. But in action they tended to separate in pursuit of their particular enthusiasms – such as disestablishment, local option, educational reform, and land reform. The majority were Nonconformists, and many were more or less self-made businessmen. But a greater number of Liberal businessmen in the Commons were moderates of less adventurous opinions; well content with membership of 'the best club in the world', and ready to blend into its still aristocratic atmosphere.

The social, religious, and political contrasts within the Liberal ranks tended to mean that the parliamentary party lived in a state of tension. Lord Granville recognized this when trying to persuade Gladstone to continue as party leader in 1875. 'A great party should have a recognised leader in Parliament, more especially the party favouring progress but not unanimous as to the rate at which that progress should be made.' Lord Hartington admitted that there was hardly any important question (disestablishment, household suffrage for the counties, education, land reform) on which the whigs and radicals would not vote against each other. Gladstone was the one man who could hope to hold these contrasting elements together by force of personality.[11]

3

'The old lines of a general election do not serve us now,' admitted the Liberal whip to Gladstone in 1868 just before the first general election under the reformed system; 'all is new and changed.'[12] All indeed was not to be 'new', for in many agricultural counties and smaller boroughs the old oligarchical spirit continued strong as late as the 1880 election. But in many larger boroughs new constituency party associations were formed after 1867, which became linked within the National Union of Conservative and Constitutional Associations, on the one hand, and within the National Liberal Federation, on the other.

The National Union began obscurely in London in 1867. In 1870, however, Disraeli appointed J. E. Gorst, a vigorous administrator, as national party agent. Gorst immediately established a Conservative central office, and in 1871 he also became secretary of the National Union. The union now came rapidly into prominence as the propaganda arm of central office, calling conferences and publishing a stream of pamphlets intended for popular reading. Gorst gave particular attention to winning support from middle and working-class voters in the boroughs. 'We are generally strong in counties and weak in boroughs, and we shall never attain stable political power till the boroughs are conquered. The only boroughs where we are really the stronger party are the Lancashire boroughs.' Gorst's efforts were believed to have contributed significantly to the big Conservative election victory in 1874. By then over 400 local Conservative Associations were affiliated to the National Union, and Conservative candidates contested every winnable constituency. Of 74 English and Welsh constituencies where the Conservatives gained seats, 65 were said to possess local Conservative Associations. After 1874, however, this successful organization was allowed to run down, and Gorst (admittedly a difficult personality) resigned. Following the heavy Conservative defeat of 1880 a second beginning had to be made, with Gorst once more as party agent.[13]

The Conservative initiative had come from the centre. Gorst's local associations were designed to collect votes, not to play much part in the shaping of policy, which was dutifully left to the party leaders at Westminster. By contrast, the National Liberal Federation was largely the product of constituency activism; and it aimed to rally support round policy proposals which were intended for presentation to the national party leaders as the authentic voice of Liberal democracy. The course of Liberal reorganization ran continuously from the formation of the Birmingham Liberal Association in 1865. This body was strongly centralized, but it was democratic in the sense that from 1867 membership was extended to all Liberals ready to pay a nominal annual subscription of 1s. Birmingham, with its system of small-scale workshop industry, had enjoyed a long tradition of class co-operation in support of radical reform, which went back to the days of the First Reform Act agitation and earlier. Under the Second Reform Act it was one of the large towns given a third Member of Parliament, though its electors could still cast only two votes each. The hope was that this provision would assist the election of third members who might represent minority opinion. But the Birmingham radical leaders saw that with careful prearrangement of voting they might spread the votes of the Liberal majority so that all three seats could be captured. This was duly achieved in the 'vote as you are told' parliamentary election of 1868. Then came the 1870 Education Act. Elections to the new local school boards were conducted on a system which gave electors each as many votes as there were members of the board. These votes – fifteen in Birmingham – could, however, be distributed as desired. At the first school board election the Liberal Nonconformists ran fifteen candidates and spread their vote so much that the Conservative Anglicans, who ran eight candidates, actually secured a majority of seats from a minority of votes. This bitter lesson encouraged a further tightening of local Liberal organization; and at the 1873 school board elections the Liberals took great care to concentrate their vote behind the eight candidates needed to give them a bare but sufficient majority. In this same year Frank Schnadhorst, a master political wirepuller, became secretary of the Birmingham Liberal Association; and in the 1874 general election all three Liberal candidates were returned unopposed.[14]

In 1876 Joseph Chamberlain, the leader of the radicals, was elected without opposition as a Birmingham Member of Parliament at a by-election. He went to Westminster convinced of the need to revivify the Liberal Party through the adoption of Birmingham methods of constituency organization and of a Birmingham radical programme. By 1873, as Gladstone's first ministry gradually disintegrated, Chamberlain was already arguing that it was foolish for radicals to pursue their desired reforms through separate organizations – the National Education League, the Liberation Society, the United Kingdom Alliance, and so on. 'There are Leagues and Associations and Unions but no party; and there never will or can be till we choose out the most important of all the questions debated, and weld them into a connected scheme which all or most of us may accept as our programme.' The idea of a party adopting a 'programme', which the electorate would endorse and ministers would then implement, was still regarded by traditional politicians as too democratic, an American conception which threatened the independence of Government and Parliament. Even the old radical John Bright, Chamberlain's colleague in the representation of Birmingham, held this view. Chamberlain and his fellow new radicals were determined to give the enlarged electorate the opportunity of participating in a national debate on policy. The new mass electorate ought not to rest content with choosing Members of Parliament in the old way simply on account of their 'sound principles'.

In September 1873 and October 1874 – before and after the heavy Liberal election defeat – Chamberlain published two important articles in the *Fortnightly Review*. The first was entitled 'The Liberal Party and its Leaders', the second 'The Next Page of the Liberal Programme'. Many Liberals, wrote Chamberlain, acted as if possession of the vote were enough in itself. 'They expect the people who have been enfranchised to hoard their newly acquired influence as a child may treasure a bright new shilling, and they shrink from the conclusion that it is wanted for use.' The Liberal Party should offer a programme of 'Free Church, Free Land, Free Schools, and Free Labour.' Earlier provincial leaders – such as Richard Cobden from Manchester or Thomas Attwood from Birmingham – had stood apart from the parliamentary parties, exerting pressure through outside 'movement'. The National Education League had been a movement of this type. But now Chamberlain was moving away from single-purpose agitation to the detailed politics of social reform. To pass complicated measures of social reform through Parliament would require the commitment of a major party and its leaders. And the instrument through which Chamberlain hoped to draw the Liberal Party into such a commitment was the National Liberal Federation.

The National Education League was wound up early in 1877, and on 31 May the National Liberal Federation was launched at a delegate meeting in Birmingham, presided over by Chamberlain. Representatives attended from over 100 places, and forty-seven English and Welsh borough associations immediately affiliated themselves to the NLF. By 1884 eighty-eight local associations had joined. Conservative and even whig critics attacked this American-type 'caucus' organization at both the constituency and national levels. They claimed that Chamberlain and his friends were seeking to manipulate local and national opinion to feed their own ambitions for power and office. The elaborate structure of the Birmingham Liberal Association, and of other associations more or less modelled on the Birmingham pattern, could certainly be presented as showing a wish to manipulate. Chamberlain replied, however, that the detailed organization down to street level only showed the democratic spirit of the new approach. The Birmingham Association was basically organized by wards, each with an elected committee; the executive committee for the whole association was composed of ward leaders, plus a considerable number of co-opted members; and there was also a larger general committee, which comprised the executive committee and members elected at ward meetings ('the six hundred'). The actual running of the association was left to a small sub-committee of prominent members, mostly middle-class businessmen such as Chamberlain himself. These members could be influenced by the two big committees; but in practice most of the influence went the other way, down from the leadership to the executive and general committees and thence to the ward committees and to individual members. Yet this cannot fairly be called manipulation. As the *Manchester Guardian* (6.6.1879) pointed out, with many constituencies now 'so unwieldy in size and so complex in character' it was 'impossible for any improvised machinery to ascertain the wishes or be answerable for the votes of the electors'. Centralized and permanent constituency party organization could not be avoided.[15]

Not all new-style Liberal associations were as radical as that at Birmingham; but the fact that the National Liberal Federation headquarters were established there helped to ensure that, until the Home Rule split of 1886, the national body tended to follow Chamberlain's lead. Chamberlain was well content that the NLF should show a marked provincial bias. He was especially contemptuous of the London of the governing classes, of 'that club management and Pall Mall selection which has been going on for so long and which has made the Liberal Party the molluscous, boneless, nerveless thing it is'. The new Liberal organization, by contrast, reached down to every provincial backstreet. Every party enthusiast was given a role in campaigning at ward meetings and on doorsteps. Many of these activists were Nonconformists, already used to the participatory democracy of their chapels. Shopkeepers, tradesmen, schoolmasters, and artisans seem to have been particularly prominent. Elementary schoolmasters were 'marginal men', still unsure of their status in society and therefore the more likely to be militant.[16]

Social life also began to be organized after 1867 along political lines. Thousands of Liberal and Conservative clubs were opened all over the country. In each big town a central club was formed to attract men of money and influence, who might hope to fraternise there on occasion not only with local Members of Parliament but also with some of the national party leaders. Much more modest clubs were also formed in small towns and in the wards of large towns for lower middle-class types. In London six new Conservative and three new Liberal clubs were established between 1868 and 1885. The most important were the National Liberal Club and the Constitutional Club, each intended to provide provincial political leaders and clubmen with a base in the capital.[17]

For the majority of working men the club function was served by the public houses, which offered a nightly escape from overcrowded homes. Gladstone sweepingly attributed the Liberal defeat of 1874 to the publicans' strong dislike of the 1872 Licensing Act. He claimed that thereafter the pubs had become committee rooms for the Conservative Party. In fact, the drift of publicans from the Liberal to the Conservative side was not completed till the 1890s. Moreover, conversation in Victorian public houses can hardly have been controlled by the licensees. At most, the landlords can only have exerted an influence similar to that of newspaper editors, able to reinforce but not to create a trend of public opinion.[18]

Very different from informal public-house discussion of politics was that of the local 'Houses of Commons'. More than a hundred such debating societies existed by 1883, with a total membership over 35,000. Each had its own Government and Opposition, and debate followed parliamentary rules. The proceedings were often reported in the local press. Bonar Law, a future Prime Minister, joined the Glasgow parliament in 1879. Commenting in the same year upon a congress of these mock parliamentarians at Liverpool, one local paper remarked how 'only an insatiable appetite for participation in positive party strife' could account for the willingness of sober Englishmen to masquerade as legislators. Here was striking evidence of 'the modern fascination of politics' in the new era of mass electorates.[19]

4

Since the days of the First Reform Act agitation – followed in 1846 by the Conservative split over Corn Law repeal – the Liberals had seemed to be the natural party of government. From 1867, however, Disraeli led the Conservatives in a strong challenge to this Liberal predominance, a challenge which was continued by Lord Randolph Churchill in the 1880s. At the 1868 general election the Conservatives still appeared as predominantly the country party; but after the 1885 election they were to owe half their seats in the Commons to urban and suburban constituencies. Here was a crucial shift. During the last quarter of the century the Conservatives were able to take from the Liberals much urban business middle-class support, along with a significant share of the working-class vote. In this way the old party of the landed interest was able not merely to survive but greatly to flourish in the new age of urban democracy.

The urban business middle classes had generally supported and benefited from the great Liberal reforms of the second and third quarters of the century – from the two Reform Acts, from the introduction of free trade, and from the nearly complete achievement of religious and educational equality. By the 1870s, however, increasing numbers of the middle classes found themselves no longer so eager for 'reform', since reform beyond what had now been gained was likely to mean a radical (even a 'socialist') threat to the rights of property. 'Until the last few years the owners of new wealth were usually dissatisfied,' explained Walter Bagehot in the *Economist* (10.1.1874). 'They had not the place in the world they wished to have, and they tried to gain it by political agitation . . . But now at last there is nothing more of this kind to be won . . . a most potent force which used to be restless and for change is now contented and against change.' Lord Salisbury had shrewdly noticed in a *Quarterly Review* article of October 1869 on 'The Past and Future of the Conservative Party' how 'the army of so-called reform, in every stage of its advance necessarily converts a detachment of its force into opponents'.

Smaller men of property, such as shopkeepers, managers, or clerks, could become at least as cautious and defensive in their politics as larger property owners. Disraeli sensed that electors of this type might well now be persuaded to vote Conservative. The lower middle classes were very conscious of their social separation from the working class, separation which was becoming emphasized by the spread of middle-class suburbs. The middle classes often feared that working men would try to use their new-given votes to attack property rights. Yet in many urban constituencies the Conservatives needed to attract a significant number of working-class votes to supplement their middle-class support. Disraeli boldly aimed to gloss over the urban social gap by persuading both classes to vote together, and to vote moreover for what had traditionally been the party of the landed interest.

His first task was to restore the credibility of the Conservatives as a party of government. The three Conservative administrations formed since the party split over repeal of the Corn Laws – the Derby Governments of 1852, 1858–9, and 1866–8 – had all been minority ministries. They had been formed more or less with the permission of the Liberals, who felt strong enough sometimes to quarrel among themselves and to allow the Conservatives to take office without power. But by unexpectedly steering so bold a measure as the Second Reform Act through Parliament Disraeli had snatched the political initiative from the Liberals for the first time in a generation. 'I have seen in my time several monopolies terminated and recently I have seen the termination of the monopoly of Liberalism ... the Tory Party has resumed its natural functions in the government of the country.'[20]

Disraeli set out to persuade the electors not merely that the Conservatives were once more *a* party of government but that they should be accepted as *the* party of government. 'For what is the Tory Party unless it represents national feeling?' In his carefully mounted and widely publicized Manchester and Crystal Palace speeches of 1872 he developed in very bold terms the idea of the Conservatives as the 'national' and natural ruling party, which stood far above the Liberal Party with its many factions. He described the Conservative Party as 'not a confederacy of nobles' and 'not a democratic multitude'; but 'a party formed from all the numerous classes in the realm – classes alike and equal before the law'. The Conservative Party existed to protect and to promote existing institutions at home and existing British interests overseas. But the test of the soundness of political institutions lay in the state of the country. Conservatives must always therefore bear in mind the condition of the people. On taking office with a large majority in 1874 Disraeli countenanced a limited but useful policy of social reform at home. He left the details of such reform to his colleagues, who were careful to stop well short of arousing middle-class fears of 'confiscation'. It became a stock Conservative point that redistribution of the property of the rich would not benefit the poor; that their best security lay in the prosperity of the rich. 'What is of all things important to them is that capital should flow, that employment should exist, that wages should fertilise the channels of commerce.'[21]

Such was the 'national' policy of the late-Victorian Conservative Party, which won its first great election victory in 1874. But even in its general election defeats of 1868 and 1880 there were signs of a turn of opinion towards the Conservatives in some of the big cities and towns. In the twenty-nine largest boroughs (with electorates over 17,500) the Conservative share of the poll rose from 33.5 per cent to 44.3 per cent between 1868 and 1880. The Conservatives made particular progress in the greater London area, with its expanding suburbia, and in Lancashire and Cheshire. By contrast, they made much less progress in Yorkshire:[22]

The Conservative breakthrough, 1859–1900
Conservative Members only: total seats in brackets

	1859	1865	1868	1874	1880	1885	1886	1892	1895	1900
London	(18) 0		0	(22)3	10	8	(59)35	47	36	51	51
Lancashire and Cheshire	(36)15	(38)18	(46)31	34	19	(69)46	58	45	60	56
Yorkshire	(37)14	(39)14	(40)13	(38)17	8	(52)16	20	16	21	26

A swing to the Conservatives had begun in Lancashire even before the Second Reform Act. No conclusive explanations for this trend were apparent. Were working-class voters in Lancashire deliberately voting against their Liberal employers? Perhaps. But in Yorkshire the operatives showed no such tendency. The strongest Conservative areas in Lancashire, moreover, were on the western side away from most of the cotton towns, places where Irish Catholic immigrants were more numerous than anywhere else in England. The Church of England was rabidly evangelical in Lancashire, and closely linked to the Conservative Party. Dislike of the papist, quarrelsome, and dirty Irish – and fear of their competition for jobs – probably exerted a major influence. The Fenian outrages, which had included the killing of a prison guard at Manchester, were a recent memory in 1868.[23]

The attitude of Lancashire in 1868 was simply the most striking illustration of how any constituency or region could move against the national trend. Gladstone had made the question of Irish Church disestablishment the main national election issue in 1868; but many of the electors of Lancashire chose to evaluate it in the light of their feelings about the Irish around them, not on the basis of its merits in Ireland or in principle. Gladstone was himself a candidate for South-West Lancashire in 1868, a mixed urban and rural constituency. The rural voters were traditionally Conservative, but the Liberals had hopes of the townsmen. Yet despite Gladstone's prestige, and despite the overall Liberal election victory, he was soundly beaten. 'Lancashire has gone mad,' complained the Liberal whip, 'and the contest there has been one of race, Saxon against Celt.' 'The issues which occupy the thoughts of professional politicians,' concluded *The Times* annual summary, 'are not always the determining causes of local triumphs or defeats.'

5

Gladstone may have been distrusted in parts of his native county in 1868 and afterwards, but nationally he made a powerful appeal to many middle-class and working-class voters. He became the first party leader and Prime Minister to emerge as a mass public speaker. He has already been quoted as defining Liberalism as 'Trust in the People, qualified by Prudence'. How then did he seek to communicate with 'the people'? Even before the passing of the Second Reform Act he had begun a dialogue, as he talked himself (in two senses) into the Liberal leadership during the mid-1860s through a succession of speeches in and out of Parliament. In 1862 he had made a speech-making visit to Tyneside, and in 1864 he ventured upon a tour of Lancashire. 'I hope I do not rest on them,' he confided to his diary after the latter excursion. 'It is, however, impossible not to love the people from whom such manifestations come . . . Somewhat haunted by dreams of halls, and lines of people, and great assemblies.' In an immediately famous Commons speech on 11 May 1864 he had asserted that 'every man who is not presumably incapacitated by some consideration of personal unfitness or of political danger is morally entitled to come within the pale of the constitution'. A later passage explained how he was thinking only of 'a reasonable extension, at fitting times and among *selected* portions of the people'. But these qualifications were generally ignored by both supporters and opponents of reform, and from 1864 Gladstone found himself becoming a popular politician regardless of his hesitations and reservations. When at the 1865 general election he lost his seat for Oxford University, he was returned instead for the important county constituency of South Lancashire. 'At last, my friends,' he exclaimed in Manchester's Free Trade Hall, 'I am come among you, and I am come among you "unmuzzled".' This at once became another widely noticed Gladstonian expression. And yet to the end of his life more than thirty years later Gladstone tried to minimize the constitutional novelty of these speech-making forays. He was to claim that until his Midlothian campaign of 1879 'I never, except in explanation to constituents, pursued Parliamentary action except within the walls of Parliament'.[24]

But during the 1868 election Gladstone's 'explanations' to his Lancashire constituents extended to seven major speeches delivered within ten days, and these orations can be seen as an early version of the later Midlothian campaigns. Gladstone now followed the traditional practice of addressing constituents with such intensity both of language and of publicity that charges of demagoguery fell upon him not only from Conservatives but from some Liberals. 'It seemed to them derogatory to a great statesman,' explained Charles Kingsley (*Macmillan's Magazine*, February 1869). 'They were mistaken. No lawful act can be derogatory to a representative of the people by which he comes into contact with them without flattering or cringing.' After his Lancashire defeat in 1868 Gladstone became the representative for

Greenwich, and in this constituency three years later he delivered a great open-air oration on Blackheath (28 October), which represented a further important step in his developing relationship with 'the people'. He was now openly addressing not only his own constituents but all the electorate – defending the national policy of his Government as well as successfully explaining to the many laid-off dockyard workers in his audience how the reduction in dock employment had been a non-party economy agreed in the time of the Conservative Government. Walter Bagehot emphasized in the *Economist* (4.11.1871) the novelty of Gladstone's feat in restoring his position inside Parliament through an oratorical triumph outside. 'It marks the coming of the time when it will be one of the most important qualifications of a Prime Minister to exert a direct control over the masses – when the ability to reach them, not as his views may be filtered through an intermediate class of political teachers and writers, but *directly* by the vitality of his own mind, will give a vast advantage in any political race ... Parliament fully appreciates this reserve power in a Prime Minister, which secures him, as it were, a separate and private appeal to the people.'

In making his appeals to the people Gladstone came to pride himself on his sense of right timing. In an autobiographical note written about 1896 he described this as a 'striking gift', though his description of it was characteristically clouded.[25] 'This must not be considered as the simple acceptance of public opinion ... It is an insight into the facts of particular eras, and their relations one to another, which generates in the mind a conviction that the materials exist for forming a public opinion, and for directing it to a particular end.' Gladstone then suggested four occasions when he thought he had shown a right sense of timing: the renewal of income tax in 1853, his proposal of 'religious equality for Ireland' in 1868, his Home Rule plan of 1885–6, and his attempt to secure a dissolution of Parliament in 1894 to settle the conflict with the Lords. The proposals which Gladstone timed with such care were not strikingly original in content. As Bagehot pointed out (*Economist*, 7.2.1874), Victorians were usually more startled than impressed when first exposed to new ideas. 'I never heard of such a thing' was an expression of disapproval. New ideas needed to become old ideas before any politician could hope successfully to commend them to the public. Gladstone's reforms were usually schemes which, in principle if not in detail, had been some time under discussion. He liked to present them, moreover, as measures not so much of innovation as of conservation.

6

The progress of the newspaper press now made it possible for Gladstone's speeches to be read by a wide national audience. The leading London and provincial daily papers – with their long leading articles and more or less verbatim reports of parliamentary debates and political meetings anywhere in the kingdom – helped to promote a steady level of high political controversy. By 1868 sixteen English towns possessed at least one daily (morning or evening) paper; by 1885 this total had grown to fifty, and by 1901 to seventy-one. Towns which possessed two or more rival morning papers, Liberal and Conservative, were usually treated to a spirited conflict of political opinion. The Liberals held a large lead until the 1880s:[26]

	Political distribution of English provincial dailies (morning and evening)			
	1868	1886	1900	1910
Liberal and Allied	26	66	71	57
Conservative and Allied	9	40	40	35
Independent	1	19	35	14
Neutral	8	13	25	15

Newspaper leading articles could reinforce a tendency of opinion, but they could not stifle one, nor could they create one unassisted. In the *Cornhill Magazine* for March 1870 Leslie Stephen compared press influence with the process of natural selection. 'It is constantly raising all manner of discordant and disconnected war-cries. If they happen to fall in with the humour of the time, a general rush is made with immense vigour in the direction indicated. If they do not meet with sympathy they drop out of notice.' At the 1886 general election both the *Scotsman* and the *Glasgow Herald* withdrew their support from Gladstone because of his conversion to support for Home Rule. In Yorkshire and Lancashire, on the other hand, leading Liberal journals such as the *Leeds Mercury*, *Bradford Observer*, and *Manchester Guardian* remained with him. Yet Gladstone held much of his ground in Scotland, but lost seats in Lancashire and Yorkshire.[27]

Newspapers played a vital part through their reports of public meetings. When Lord Carlingford found in 1885 that *The Times* and other major papers would not report his speeches he knew that his political career was over. 'That kind of speech is wasted when not allowed to reach the public.'[28] Readers who had sometimes heard the party leaders speak locally could recreate similar occasions in their own minds as they read the long, often first-person newspaper reports, peppered with 'cheers' and 'groans', 'laughter' and 'interruptions'. In this way the press reinforced the primacy of the platform. A book entitled *The Platform, Its Rise and Progress* appeared in 1892. It was a survey by Henry Jephson of the steadily increasing political influence of public meetings since the time of Wilkes. In a review of the book (*Nineteenth Century*, April 1892) Gladstone agreed that 'the Platform at its maximum of power is stronger than the Press . . . three P's have denoted the instruments by which British Freedom has been principally developed and confirmed. These three P's are PETITION, PRESS, and PLATFORM.'

Gladstone's own great powers as an orator were often discussed. John Morley, his official biographer, emphasized his rich tones and his clear articulation, which enabled him (long before the days of microphones) to be heard by audiences far larger than the five or six thousand usually accepted as the maximum number who could hope to hear in the open air. Gladstone's language and phraseology were not especially polished, nor did he coin many striking phrases. Indeed, his sentences tended to be prolix and involved, though in his best speeches he kept this tendency in check. Moreover, his manner and presence – his earnestness, his flashing eye, expressive face, broad gestures, and wonderful voice – could take his audiences with him through many convolutions of language. An account, published after his death, of Gladstone in action in 1879 showed how he could rouse an audience:[29]

'Gentlemen, this has been a liquid, an aqueous Government. You remember what it came in upon?' 'Beer,' we shouted and the orator bowed with a gesture of infinite smiling consent. 'And you see what it is going out upon?' 'Water,' we yelled, remembering Mr. Cross's Bill [to buy the London water companies], and again he bowed in acquiescence ... All through a speech of long tortuous sentences he endowed us with a faculty of apprehension we did not know we possessed. And then the peroration: 'You are shortly to pronounce your verdict, you and the people of these isles; and, whatever that verdict may be, as I hope it will be the true one, I trust it will be clear.' We leaped to our feet and cheered; decidedly we should make it clear. 'I trust it will be emphatic.' We waved our sticks and hats in emphasis. 'I trust it will be decisive; and that it will ring' (here, with a swing of the arm clear round his neck, and a superb uplifting of the whole frame, he sent his trumpet voice into every cranny of the hall till it rang again) 'from John O'Groats to the Land's End;' and a frantic mass of humanity roared themselves hoarse for a full two minutes.

Such meetings could express in visible form that class harmony which Gladstone's speeches were always recommending. He hoped that responsible working men, while accepting their station in life, would welcome political initiatives from their social superiors in celebration of a Liberal faith which joined the classes morally without disturbing their social separateness.

Gladstone's plan of exposition when 'on the stump' – to use the mid-Victorian Americanism – was simple and well arranged. Each series of speeches was aimed at a national audience; but all were delivered within a comparatively small radius of towns so that they could acquire unity of purpose. The major theme was always supported by a second theme to add variety. Each speech developed the argument of both themes, so that the series overall flowed like a course of lectures. 'The two themes were almost invariably the same: first the iniquity, injustice and depravity of some institution and of his opponents' policy in supporting that institution, and secondly, the financial extravagance of his opponents and their inability to appreciate the principles of good government.'[30]

The most dramatic of Gladstone's agitations was his long campaign of the late 1870s against the pro-Turkish policy of the Disraeli Government (see below, p. 205). On 6 September 1876 he published a pamphlet which immediately became famous – *The Bulgarian Horrors and the Question of the East*. By the end of the month it had achieved the remarkable sale of 200,000 copies. Gladstone's written style was usually far less persuasive than his oratory, but this pamphlet was sufficiently readable to sweep him to the head of the agitation. A spate of protest meetings followed during the autumn of 1876. Jephson's *The Platform* drew attention to their novelty. 'Hitherto the Platform had exercised its influence on the Government through the House of Commons; now, as Parliament was not sitting, it endeavoured to influence without such intervention.' Gladstone's Flintshire home, Hawarden, became a centre of pilgrimage for thousands of Liberal excursionists, who presented eulogistic addresses and expected impromptu speeches from him in reply. *The Times* (21.8.1877) described these occasions as a 'new invention in the way of political agitation'.

Gladstone himself felt uncomfortable about them. But he grew increasingly sure that the Conservatives could be defeated at the next general election. He persuaded himself that the iniquities of the Government's Eastern policy made it his Christian duty to mount his attack with the maximum of drama and publicity. This could best be secured by himself contesting a Conservative-held seat. At the beginning of 1879 he therefore decided to contest the Midlothian constituency, near Edinburgh, at the next general election. Lord Dalkeith, heir of the Duke of Buccleugh, had represented Midlothian since 1853, except during the 1868–74 Liberal Parliament. The seat was thus normally Conservative, but winnable by a Liberal. Gladstone realized that the local Conservatives were intensely partisan, and he therefore looked forward to a spirited contest.[31]

No one knew when Disraeli would call a general election; but Gladstone resolved to make a series of full-dress speeches over a two-week period at the end of November and beginning of December 1879. 'It seems to me good policy to join the proceedings of 1876–9 by a continuous process to the dissolution.' Excitement ahead of the campaign was intense, and demand for tickets far outran supply. But excitement was not confined to Midlothian. National attention followed Gladstone as he travelled north by train from Liverpool. He spoke wherever the train stopped en route for Edinburgh, and he continued to give impromptu addresses at every opportunity throughout his fortnight in the area – in churches, town halls, even from hotel windows. *The Times* (26.12.1879) could not imagine a Pitt or a Castlereagh 'stumping the provinces, and taking into his confidence, not merely a handful of electors, but any crowd he could collect in any part of the island'. But Gladstone hoped that his every word, to however insignificant an audience, would achieve an effect through national press coverage. He delivered his first great oration at Edinburgh on 24

November, his second the next day at Dalkeith, his third at West Calder on 27 November; two more major speeches followed at Edinburgh on 29 November, another at Perth on 1 December, and a last at Glasgow four days later. Any one of these addresses would have satisfied a lesser politician. Their number was the more striking since Gladstone was almost seventy years old.

Disraeli had become Earl of Beaconsfield in 1876, and Gladstone fulminated against the immoralities of 'Beaconsfieldism'. Disraeli himself rarely made public speeches. His famous Manchester and Crystal Palace orations of 1872 were the more noteworthy for being exceptional. In response, however, to Gladstone's Eastern Question agitation Disraeli's Conservative colleagues (though not Disraeli himself) were finally drawn during 1879 into platform controversy. The *Annual Register* estimated that during the 1879 recess 'more speeches had been made by Cabinet Ministers than in all the recesses of other Parliaments put together'. *The Times* (26 December) complained that there was now 'not very much to choose between the political parties in the matter'. *Punch* (13 December) portrayed Gladstone as 'the Colossus of Words'. Verbal conflict became even more widespread during what Jephson called 'the great autumn Platform campaign' of 1884, which centred round the question of the Lords' resistance to parliamentary reform. Gladstone as Prime Minister made nine important speeches and several lesser ones, while Lord Salisbury spoke eight times. The two leaders were supported by cabinet and ex-cabinet ministers to a total of some eighty-five speeches. The *Annual Register* counted 1,512 Liberal meetings in England and Scotland, against 195 called by the Conservatives. But the Conservative leaders were now speaking often enough outside Parliament to give the overall spread of meetings a quasi-deliberative character. As Jephson remarked, the party rivals now contended beyond Westminster 'just as thoroughly and effectively as if they met on one Platform'.

7

In the spring of 1880 Disraeli suddenly called a general election, and Gladstone returned to Midlothian for a second two-week campaign. This was hardly less vigorous than his first agitation, and he duly captured the seat by a safe margin (Gladstone 1,579 votes; Dalkeith 1,368). The Conservative majority of fifty seats in the Commons was replaced by an overall Liberal majority of fifty-four.

Disraeli had remained unimpressed by Gladstone's Midlothian speeches, which he dismissed as 'drenching rhetoric'. His best-remembered (albeit laboured) attack on Gladstone's oratory was delivered in 1878: 'a sophistical rhetorician, inebriated with the exuberance of his own verbosity, and gifted with an egotistical imagination that can at all times command an interminable and inconsistent series of arguments to malign an opponent and to glorify himself'.[32] This personalization of the party political struggle was reflected and encouraged by the soubriquets given to Gladstone. First he was dubbed 'the People's William' by the *Daily Telegraph* in the 1860s then about 1879 someone (probably Sir William Harcourt) first called him 'the Grand Old Man', a flattering description that stayed with him for the rest of his career:

> God bless the People's William
>   Long may he lead the van
> Of Liberty and Freedom,
>   God bless the Grand Old Man.

The press often described the Gladstone–Disraeli rivalry in sporting terms – as a horse race, a boxing match, and the like. Organized sport was itself only just coming into popularity, and politics could provide an outlet for partisanship. Many more or less cheap artifacts began to be produced for enthusiastic supporters – Gladstone and Disraeli busts, plates, tiles, plaques, handkerchiefs, etcetera. But pairs of salt (Gladstone) and pepper (Disraeli) pots suggested that not all buyers were one-party men. Demand and supply seem to have been still expanding during the 1880s. Disraeli, though dead, was remembered in many forms; and representations of Salisbury, Chamberlain, and Randolph Churchill were now added to the market. But Gladstone items remained the biggest sellers.[33]

Political partisans were sufficiently numerous and noisy for it to seem as W. S. Gilbert exclaimed in *Iolanthe* (1882):

> That every boy and every gal
>   That's born into the world alive,
> Is either a little Liberal
>   Or else a little Conservative!

Yet many Victorians, perhaps a majority, were not in fact political partisans. Jesse Collings, Chamberlain's lieutenant, emphasized in 1886 the importance of 'the non-demonstrative, stay-at-home, non-thinking, arm-chair, timid, etc.' without whose votes success was impossible.[34] The very existence of the party system could produce guilt feelings, or seem to require a defence. It was noticed how Englishmen were ready to applaud loudly at meetings when told that an issue was not a party question. Erskine May's standard *Constitutional History of England* (5th edn, 1875) included a review of 'the evils and merits of party'. May concluded that party government was necessary for the security of representative institutions, since rulers without opposition could become despots.

8

The 1880 election put Disraeli firmly out of office for the last time. Traditionalists in both parties expressed concern at this second big 'swing of the pendulum', following that of 1874. Significantly, the pendulum figure of speech itself first came into common use in 1880. Did the large turnover of seats mean that the new electorate was dangerously volatile? Before the passing of the Second Reform Act certain parties or shades of opinion had tended to continue in government for decades. 'Is every election henceforth to be a leap in the dark?'[35]

If the Commons majority was to be changed at almost every general election did this give the House of Lords a new role to play? Should the upper house act as a brake, rejecting what it believed to be unwise reforms proposed by a transient majority in the Commons? Alternatively, should it act as a brake not against 'democracy' but in the very name of 'democracy', resisting the tyranny of a Commons majority by rejecting measures which the peers believed the voters might wish to repudiate at a general election? Both these roles were played by the House of Lords at various times during the late-Victorian and Edwardian periods.

The number of adult members of the House of Lords rose steadily: 399 (1830), 411 (1850), 462 (1870), 500 (1880), 539 (1890), 577 (1900). In the mid-Victorian years the numbers of Liberal and Conservative peers in frequent attendance were fairly evenly balanced. Moreover, the Liberals were in a continuous (even though sometimes divided) majority in the Commons. From 1867, however, the position changed in two important respects. Firstly, the Conservatives showed in 1874 that they could now win an outright majority in the Commons; and secondly, they found themselves in an increasing majority in the Lords. They could now readily reject measures sent up from the Commons when the Liberals were in government. They could justify this either in the name of 'democracy' or against 'democracy'. Or they could do it in a partisan spirit, in hopes of forcing a general election which the Conservatives might win.

By the time of the debates on Gladstone's bill for the disestablishment of the Irish Church in 1869 the Liberals had slipped into a clear minority in the Lords. Peers who had been prepared to follow Lord Palmerston until his death in 1865 were suspicious of Gladstone. Lord Granville estimated the Conservative majority in the upper house as about sixty to seventy, without counting bishops 'or Liberals who vote oftener for the Opposition than for the Government'. It seemed likely that the Lords would reject the 1869 Irish Church Bill. Eventually, however, a compromise was reached at the instance of the Queen. But it was obvious that conflict between the two houses would recur. Lord Salisbury (17 June) had urged his fellow peers to make bold claims for their role under the reformed parliamentary system. Most of the time, claimed Salisbury, the House of Commons did not represent the nation 'because in ninety-nine cases out of a hundred the nation, as a whole, takes no interest in our politics ... In all these cases I make no distinction – absolutely none – between the prerogative of the House of

Commons and the House of Lords.' In addition, Salisbury contended that in certain instances 'the nation must be called into council and must decide the policy of the Government'; it was the duty of the Lords 'to insist that the nation shall be consulted'. In this spirit Salisbury recommended the peers to reject the 1872 Ballot Bill, on the ground that it had not been put to the electorate at the 1868 general election. He was coming close to asserting that a Liberal Government should always be forced to seek a 'mandate' for legislation from the electorate. Liberals complained that this amounted to advocacy of direct democracy. 'Lord Salisbury was the first to introduce into English politics that essentially Jacobinical phrase' (*Daily News*, 27.3.1901).[36]

With the aim of avoiding a constitutional crisis, Gladstone's 1868–74 Government had acquiesced in frequent Lords' amendments and delays to its major bills. Though increasingly annoyed by upper-house interference, Gladstone's innate conservatism made him still eager to retain a significant role for the peerage. He was much impressed by the 'deference' felt towards peers, which helped to maintain the stability of society. After the 1869 differences, he wrote a memorandum which recommended the creation of many more peers, including life peers, to help sustain the quality of the upper house. Yet the Lords had themselves rejected life peerages in 1856 and again in 1869. Walter Bagehot feared that the two houses of Parliament were growing more and more unlike, as the Commons became more 'popular'. 'The younger and more energetic body will speedily and inevitably be at fatal issue with the old and graver one' (*Economist*, 5.8.1871). The final confrontation did not come so fast as Bagehot expected; but it was to remain in prospect for forty years before erupting when the Lords rejected the 'people's budget' of 1909.

9

How democratic was late-Victorian local government? The very expression 'local government' had only come into use about mid-century. This reflected a growing realization that administration at the local level was becoming increasingly complex and important.[37] The Victorians much preferred local action to central government control. They believed that local rule could be more easily checked, and could be kept as cheap as possible. 'The theory is that all that can should be done by local authority, and that public expenditure should be chiefly controlled by those who contribute to it.' So explained the second report of the Royal Sanitary Commission in 1871. Yet in their desire to avoid elaborate and expensive bureaucracy the early Victorians ended up by creating a host of local bodies with particular powers, which amounted to neither the most effective nor the least expensive system of local government. It was – as G. J. Goschen remarked while President of the Local Government Board in 1871 – 'a chaos as regards authorities, a chaos as regards rates, and a worse chaos than all as regards areas'.[38] The confusion reached its highest point with the passing of the 1870 Education Act, which added local school boards to the boroughs, parishes, improvement districts, sanitary districts, Poor Law unions, highway districts, and the rest which were already in existence.

Separate elections were necessary for the running of many of these bodies. Before the great Municipal Corporations Act of 1835 very few elected local authorities had existed in England; after the passing of the Local Government Act of 1894 every town and village found itself governed by councils chosen by large numbers (though still not by all) of their citizens. About 1870 the vote was confined in general to those who owned or were connected with property in the locality, with plural voting allowed in proportion to assessed property values for elections to such bodies as local boards of health and Poor Law guardians. The Assessed Rates Act of 1869, amended in 1878, extended the municipal franchise to tenants of properties of sufficient rateable value even if their landlords were paying the rates. This allowed significant numbers of the working classes to vote in municipal elections for the first time. Women with appropriate property qualifications were enfranchised under a little considered amendment to the Municipal Franchise Act. A court ruling of 1872 held, however, that this Act did not apply to married women. In that year there were just over 800,000 male municipal voters in England and Wales, and just over 100,000 females.

One argument against women's enfranchisement at both the local and national levels claimed that they were unsuited for participation in the turmoil of elections. The degree of party political colour and of consequent clamour in local elections varied widely from place to place.[39] Political activity showed itself with the maximum of organization in Birmingham, which offered a striking example to other towns during the late 1860s and 1870s. The Birmingham radicals operated at all political levels. They organized support in elections for the Poor Law guardians and school boards, in borough council elections, and in parliamentary elections; and they expressed their national political aspirations through the National Education League and the National Liberal Federation. The Birmingham leadership group, mainly Nonconformist businessmen and ministers, developed a 'civic gospel' to explain and to justify their municipal activity. This gospel was first articulated by George Dawson, a local Baptist minister and a persuasive preacher. It was translated into notable effect by Joseph Chamberlain during his mayoralty (1873–6). In a sermon upon 'The Evils and Uses of Rich Men' the Reverend R. W. Dale, Birmingham's leading Congregationalist minister, urged middle-class big businessmen to give their time and their talents to municipal work, to feel 'called of God' to ensure adequate provision of poor relief, good drainage and lighting, good schools, 'harmless public amusement', and honest administration. The eleventh commandment, suggested Dale, should be 'that thou shalt keep a balance sheet'. He believed that such involvement in applied

Christianity was essential for the well-being both of the new urban society and of the religious bodies themselves. During the last decades of the century a quarter of the membership of Birmingham town council consisted of large-scale businessmen who had answered Dale's call.[40]

Local government in the Victorian countryside contrasted with that of the towns both in form and in spirit. Here the institutions and influence of the landed interest still predominated. County administration was controlled by the county justices of the peace meeting at quarter sessions. Justices were appointed upon the recommendation of the county lord lieutenants. In practice the magistrates were largely self-perpetuating groups, drawn chiefly from local landed families. As late as 1887 four out of five county magistrates seem to have been peers or their heirs, gentry, or clergy.[41] J. S. Mill's essay on *Representative Government* (1861) had attacked this non-elective quarter sessions system as 'the most aristocratic in principle which now remains in England; far more so than the House of Lords, for it grants public money and disposes of important public interests, not in conjunction with a popular assembly, but alone'.

In Birmingham rateable values rose fast during the 1870s, and this, plus the accident of cheap terms of borrowing, greatly assisted the translation of the radical civic gospel into action. In other places and at other times, however, municipal improvement could only be financed by significant increases in rates. In 1870 local authority spending in England and Wales stood at £27,300,000. By 1882 this had more than doubled. Local rates yielded £16,500,000 in 1868, £23,900,000 in 1882. Grants-in-aid from central government remained comparatively small, though they grew from under £1 million in the late 1860s to £2,900,000 in 1882. G. J. Goschen, the energetic young President of the Local Government Board in Gladstone's 1868 cabinet, wanted major reforms of local taxation and administration, especially in the counties. In 1871 he introduced bills to reform local taxation and the machinery of county government. But opposition from the landlords, who still dominated the House of Commons, forced the withdrawal of both proposals. The creation of county councils had to wait another seventeen years. By then reformers had gone beyond concern simply for sound finance and good administration to demand recognition of the claims of democracy in the countryside.

10

At the time of the 1874 general election Walter Bagehot (*Economist*, 17 January) was pleased to report that his earlier fears for the collapse of 'deference' in politics had proved groundless. The new household electors were voting 'much like the old £10 householders'; they had left political control 'in the hands of leisure, of property, and of intelligence'. A. V. Dicey, another expert observer, in an article on 'Democracy in

England' written for American readers of the *Nation* (3.6.1880), emphasized the still limited extent of this deferential electorate compared with that of the United States. He noted too how the elected House of Parliament could still be restrained by the Crown or by the House of Lords. The British electorate continued 'conservative' even though it had just rejected a Conservative ministry. 'None of the traditions of English political sentiment have been broken by the mass of the Liberal party . . . An English radical loves a lord when he sees him, and does not object to tell him so to his face . . . Democracy in England is as yet, it should be noticed, by no means wholly democratic.'

Notes

1. See A. Briggs, *The Age of Improvement* (1959), Ch. 10; and F. B. Smith, '"Democracy" in the Second Reform Debates', *Historical Studies, Australia and New Zealand*, Vol. 11 (1964).
2. See M. Wolff, 'The Uses of Context: Aspects of the 1860s', *Victorian Studies*, IX (1965), supplement.
3. See H. J. Hanham, *Elections and Party Management, Politics in the Time of Disraeli and Gladstone* (1959).
4. W. L. Guttsman, *The British Political Elite* (1963), p. 82.
5. Ibid, p. 84. See also H. J. Laski, 'The Personnel of the English Cabinet, 1801–1924', *American Political Science Quarterly*, Vol. 22 (1928); and W. L. Arnstein, 'The Survival of the Victorian Aristocracy', in F. C. Jaher (ed.), *The Rich, The Well Born, and The Powerful* (1973), esp. pp. 207–12.
6. See T. Lloyd, 'Uncontested Seats in British General Elections, 1852–1910', *Historical Journal*, VIII (1965).
7. See D. Richter, 'The Role of Mob Riot in Victorian Elections, 1865–1885', *Victorian Studies*, XV (1971).
8. A. Trollope, *Autobiography* (1883), Ch. XVI. See especially W. B. Gwyn, *Democracy and the Cost of Politics in Britain* (1962); and C. O'Leary, *The Elimination of Corrupt Practices in British Elections, 1868–1911* (1962).
9. See especially D. A. Hamer, *Liberal Politics in the Age of Gladstone and Rosebery* (1972); T. W. Heyck and W. Klecka, 'British Radical M.P.s, 1874–1895', *Journal of Interdisciplinary History*, IV (1973); and J. Vincent, *The Formation of the Liberal Party, 1857–1868* (2nd edn, 1976).
10. D. Southgate, *The Passing of the Whigs, 1832–1886* (1962), p. 417.
11. Agatha Ramm (ed.), *Political Correspondence of Mr. Gladstone and Lord Granville, 1868–1876* (1952), I, pp. 140, 150.
12. See A. F. Thompson, 'Gladstone's Whips and the General Election of 1868', *English Historical Review*, LXIII (1948).
13. See R. T. McKenzie, *British Political Parties* (2nd edn, 1963), Chs. IV, V; and E. J. Feuchtwanger, *Disraeli, Democracy, and the Tory Party* (1968).
14. See A. Briggs, *History of Birmingham* (1952), Vol. II, Ch. VI; A. Briggs, *Victorian Cities* (1963), Ch. V; and E. P. Hennock, *Fit and Proper Persons* (1973), pp. 131–8.
15. See H. J. Hanham, *Elections and Party Management, Politics in the Time of Disraeli and Gladstone* (1959), esp. Ch. 7.
16. H. J. Hanham, *The Reformed Electoral System in Great Britain, 1832–1914* (1968), p. 20.
17. R. T. McKenzie, *British Political Parties* (2nd edn, 1963), pp. 161–3; J. A. Garrard, 'Parties, Members and Voters after 1867', *Historical Journal*, Vol. 20 (1977).
18. See B. Harrison, *Drink and the Victorians* (1971), esp. Ch. 13.

19. See B. Jerrold, 'On the Manufacture of Public Opinion', *Nineteenth Century*, June 1883.
20. R. J. White (ed.), *The Conservative Tradition* (1950), pp. 171–2.
21. Lady Gwendolen Cecil, *Life of Robert, Marquis of Salisbury*, III (1931), pp. 65–6.
22. See J. P. Cornford, 'The Transformation of Conservatism in the late 19th Century', *Victorian Studies*, VII (1963); and R. Blake, *The Conservative Party from Peel to Churchill* (1970), Ch. IV.
23. See H. J. Hanham, *Elections and Party Management, Politics in the Time of Disraeli and Gladstone* (1959), Ch. 14; and J. Vincent, 'The Effect of the Second Reform Act in Lancashire', *Historical Journal*, XI (1968).
24. J. Morley, *Life of William Ewart Gladstone* (1903), book V; P. Guedalla (ed.), *Gladstone and Palmerston* (1928), pp. 279–87.
25. W. E. Gladstone, *Autobiographica* (1971), p. 136. See also G. M. Young, *Victorian Essays* (1962), pp. 107–8.
26. A. J. Lee, *The Origins of the Popular Press in England, 1855–1914* (1976), p. 287.
27. See J. P. Mackintosh, *The British Cabinet* (2nd edn, 1968), Ch. 8; and N. Blewett, *The Peers, The Parties and The People* (1972), Ch. 15.
28. A. B. Cook and J. Vincent (eds.), *Lord Carlingford's Journal* (1971), pp. 135, 139.
29. Lord Kilbracken, *Reminiscences* (1931), pp. 109–12. See also W. E. H. Lecky, *Democracy and Liberty* (1899), pp. xx–xxiii.
30. H. J. Hanham, *Elections and Party Management, Politics in the Time of Disraeli and Gladstone* (1959), pp. 204–5.
31. See R. Kelley, 'Midlothian: A Study in Politics and Ideas', *Victorian Studies*, IV (1960). Also W. E. Gladstone, *Midlothian Speeches, 1879* (1879; reprinted 1971).
32. *The Times*, 29 July 1878; A. E. Gathorne Hardy, *Gathorne Hardy, First Earl of Cranbrook* (1910), II, p. 126.
33. See H. J. Hanham, 'Politics and Community Life in Victorian and Edwardian Britain', *Folk Life*, Vol. 4 (1966).
34. Edith H. Fowler, *Life of Henry Hartley Fowler* (1912), p. 217.
35. T. E. Kebbel, 'A Conservative View of the Elections', *Nineteenth Century*, May 1880, p. 910.
36. Lady Gwendolen Cecil, *Life of Robert, Marquis of Salisbury*, II (1921), pp. 24–6; H. J. Hanham (ed.), *The Nineteenth Century Constitution* (1969), pp. 183–8.
37. See especially B. Keith-Lucas, *The English Local Government Franchise* (1952); and K. B. Smellie, *A History of Local Government* (4th edn, 1968).
38. J. Redlich and F. W. Hirst, *The History of Local Government in England* (ed. B. Keith-Lucas, 2nd edn, 1970), p. 213.
39. See especially E. P. Hennock, *Fit and Proper Persons* (1973); and D. Fraser, *Urban Politics in Victorian England* (1976).
40. E. P. Hennock, *Fit and Proper Persons* (1973), pp. 34–5, and part II. See also A. Briggs, *History of Birmingham* (1952), Vol. II, Ch. IV; and A. Briggs, *Victorian Cities* (1963), Ch. V.
41. See C. H. E. Zangerl, 'The Social Composition of the County Magistracies in England and Wales, 1837–1887', *Journal of British Studies*, Vol. 11 (1971).

Chapter 8

Domestic policy: *'My mission is to pacify Ireland'*

1

Benjamin Disraeli became Prime Minister in February 1868, upon the resignation of Lord Derby through ill-health. Disraeli had thus beaten his great rival, Gladstone, to what he called 'the top of the greasy pole'.[1] But the Conservative Government remained a minority administration, and an election was bound to come as soon as the new voters enfranchised under the Second Reform Act had been registered. No one knew what the new electors wanted; but Gladstone was determined to offer not material benefits but a great moral cry – 'justice for Ireland'. This might seem surprising in view of the recent Fenian outrages. In September 1867 two Fenian prisoners had been rescued and a prison guard killed in an attack upon a prison van in Manchester; and in December an attempt to rescue Fenian prisoners by blowing up the wall of London's Clerkenwell prison killed twelve innocent people. But Gladstone regarded the Fenian outrages not as reason for pursuing a course of negation in Ireland, but for promoting a policy which would seek to remove the grievances exploited by the Fenians. This seemed the more necessary because of the sympathy shown in the United States for the Fenian cause, which had even led to Fenian forays across the Canadian border. Gladstone remarked in December 1867 that the British Empire faced 'but one danger. It is the danger by the combination of the three names, Ireland, United States and Canada'.[2]

On 1 May 1868 Gladstone carried in the Commons a series of resolutions in favour of the disestablishment and disendowment of the Anglican Church of Ireland. The occasion confirmed him as prime minister in the next Liberal Government. All sections of the Liberal Party, which had become seriously divided over the Second Reform Act, were glad to rally round this proposal. It represented an attack upon privilege in the Liberal tradition. At the 1861 census Ireland had contained less than 700,000 Anglicans, compared with 4,500,000 Roman Catholics. Yet the Irish Church was established and endowed as if it served all the population. Nonconformist Liberals were especially glad to support the removal of such an anomalous establishment. Anglicans on the Conservative side were divided – high Churchmen were entirely opposed to disestablishment, but broad Churchmen less so.

Disraeli was able to remain in office only by securing the queen's consent to a dissolution of Parliament, in the knowledge that the new

registers would not be ready for a general election until November 1868.
The course of this election showed little anticipation of the important
reforms which were soon to follow, although Gladstone's campaign in
south-west Lancashire did introduce the innovation of a series of
speeches intended for a national audience.[3] But these orations
concentrated upon Irish Church disestablishment, supported by some
guarded mention of Irish land reform. Conservatives claimed credit for
initiating the Second Reform Act, the Liberals for transforming it.
Disraeli hoped for an anti-Catholic upsurge against Gladstone's Irish
Church policy; but this did not occur, except in Lancashire. In general,
the Conservatives could not change their image as the permanent
minority party. The Liberals increased their majority by about forty,
gaining especially well in the smaller English boroughs, and in Scotland,
Wales, and Ireland:[4]

	Liberals	Conservatives	Liberal majority
England	243	217	26
Wales	23	10	13
Scotland	53	7	46
Ireland	65	40	25
	384	274	110

Victorian and Edwardian elections were conducted over a period of
about three weeks. As soon as the last results were declared, Disraeli
established an important constitutional precedent by resigning
immediately, without waiting to meet the new House of Commons.
Here was recognition that the electorate was now consciously choosing
a ministry, rather than simply electing representatives in Parliament
who would only then decide what government to support. Disraeli was
to repeat the same action in 1880, and Gladstone followed suit more
hesitantly in 1874.

Gladstone selected a cabinet which represented a careful balance of
whigs (who provided caution and continuity), former Peelites of good
administrative ability (including himself), and new men. The whig Lord
Granville became Colonial Secretary, and then from 1870 Foreign
Secretary. The Peelite Edward Cardwell was made War Secretary. John
Bright was persuaded to take office for the first time as President of the
Board of Trade. Robert Lowe became Chancellor of the Exchequer.
W. E. Forster served as Vice-President of the Council, with a seat in the
cabinet from 1870.

The measures which this cabinet decided to promote were chiefly
institutional reforms, inspired by the idea of 'liberation' and the curbing
of privilege. They had been mostly under discussion for years, and
especially since the Crimean War (1854–6) had brought the shortcomings
of aristocratic government into prominence. Gladstone himself gave
most of his attention to Ireland. He received the news that the queen was
about to invite him to become Prime Minister while he was tree-felling

on his Hawarden estate. After continuing his blows for several minutes, he looked up: 'and with deep earnestness in his voice, and great intensity in his face, exclaimed: "My mission is to pacify Ireland"'.[5]

2

English public opinion was both baffled and bored by the Irish question. Only under the spur of violence were most Victorians ready to show interest. Few Englishmen had accepted that–quite apart from any specific grievances – the Irish wanted to be treated as a separate nation. This aspiration was both unbelievable to the English (why should the Irish want more than the Scots or the Welsh?) and unacceptable, because it was seen as a threat to the security of the United Kingdom. This failure to understand arose both from ignorance of Irishmen in Ireland, and from prejudiced awareness of Irishmen in England. Even Gladstone paid only one visit to Ireland – for three weeks in 1877. At the 1871 census the number of Irish-born immigrants in England and Wales was 567,000. Over one-third lived in Lancashire and Cheshire; London contained 91,000. To these totals must be added the many children of immigrants, born in England but very Irish in upbringing. The Irish tended to take the lowest paid, least skilled jobs. They were none the less disliked for supposedly driving down wage rates, for their alleged readiness to act as blacklegs during strikes, for their disorderly behaviour, and for their tenacious Catholicism. Englishmen, including English working men, openly regarded themselves as racially superior. By the 1860s – the decade after publication of Darwin's *Origin of Species* – cartoon representations of Irishmen in *Punch* and elsewhere regularly portrayed the Irish with ape-like features.[7] The Fenian violence of the 1860s and the Land League outrages of the 1880s were regarded as confirmation of Irish racial under-development. It thus became easier for Englishmen to assume that they were bound to continue in the government of Ireland because of Irish inadequacy.

Even one of Gladstone's ministers, Lord Kimberley, a whig, privately justified 'remedial measures' for Ireland in unflattering terms. 'England must for her own safety hold Ireland, come what may, and it is her duty to leave no remedial measures untried. Past misgovernment, though not the main cause of the misery of the Irish, has no doubt aggravated the ills which they suffer. It is possible therefore that a long course of wise and just government may produce at last some decided improvement. But the true source of Irish unhappiness is the character of the Irish race.'[8] Gladstone was much more sensitive than Kimberley. As early as 1845 he had described Ireland as 'that cloud in the west, that coming storm, the minister of God's retribution upon cruel and inveterate and but half-atoned injustice!'[9] He had been slow to offer 'justice' to Ireland; but his sense of right timing correctly told him that English public opinion was now at last prepared to accept some bold Irish legislation.

The Irish Church Act of 1869 aimed to remove what Gladstone described in the Commons (1.3.1869) as 'the token and the symbol of ascendancy'. Erskine May's standard *Constitutional History* (5th edn, 1875) described the Act as 'the boldest measure of modern times'. It reflected 'the extraordinary power of a Government representing the popular will under an extended franchise'. It seemed momentous not only because it disestablished an Anglican church but also because of its disendowment provisions.[10] It vested the property of the Church of Ireland in a Temporalities Commission. The state took some £16 million as its own, but paid about £10 million back in various forms of compensation. By judicious management the remaining 'church surplus' yielded about £13 million over the next fifty years, which was used for the relief of poverty, the encouragement of agriculture and fisheries, the endowment of higher education, and other good purposes.

But had the disendowment provisions dangerously opened the way to further state interference with property rights? 'Revolutions commence with sacrilege and go on to communism; or to put it in the more gentle and euphemistic language of the day, revolutions begin with the Church and go on to the land.' So contended the Irish Bishop Magee of Peterborough in the House of Lords (15.6.1869). And so they did, for in 1870 Gladstone skilfully piloted through cabinet and Parliament his first Irish Land Act.[11] Not that the measure was especially bold in itself; but it represented as much as contemporary English opinion would accept. Ulster tenant right was granted the force of law where it existed. Elsewhere, Irish tenants were given greater rights to compensation for improvements if they moved or were evicted. Eviction, other than for non-payment of rent, was itself discouraged by requiring landlords to pay compensation for disturbance. A land purchase scheme – inspired by John Bright – allowed tenants to borrow from the state two-thirds of the cost of their holdings with repayment over thirty-five years.

The Act proved disappointing in operation. Ulster tenant right was found to be difficult to define; landlords could still raise rents and then evict for non-payment; and leaseholders were not protected for improvements. The 'Bright clauses' were little used because the cost of purchase was too high. It may even have been that eviction, which the Act tried to limit, was not in reality such a major problem. But more important for the political future than the shortcomings of the measure was the spirit in which Gladstone had devised it – what Robert Lowe described as its 'idea of restitution'. Gladstone had come to feel that the Irish people ought to be offered compensation for the ancestral wrongs done by the confiscations of earlier generations. He was trying to respond to the Irish mentality as no previous English minister had attempted to do. 'What the Irishman may think with great semblance and perhaps with the full reality of historic truth is this – that, without at all questioning the landlord's title, he too had by the old customs of the country his share in a tribal property.'

How near was Gladstone to understanding that, regardless of the resolution of specific grievances, the Irish wanted recognition of their nationhood? In an important speech in 1867 he had emphasized that he would 'not for a moment listen to any plans whatever for separate institutions and a separate policy for England, Scotland or Ireland'; but 'in all matters except that, no man ought to be able to say that any one of these nations is governed according to the traditions, the views or the ideas of another'. Ten years later he was remarking that on Irish government he went 'much farther than the "average" Liberal'.[12] He was already prepared to recognize Irish national claims to some form of self-government, though he assumed the continued supremacy of the imperial Parliament at Westminster. He was never to admit that the aspirations of Irish nationalism might require not merely internal self-government but total independence from Great Britain.

The 'Home Rule' movement was just beginning during the years of Gladstone's 1868–74 Government. At the 1874 general election, helped by the secret ballot, a group of fifty-nine Irish Home Rulers were returned. This marked the beginning of the end of old-style Liberal–Conservative party politics in Ireland outside Ulster. In 1875 the Home Rule group gained a new recruit after a by-election – Charles Stewart Parnell, a Protestant Irish landlord but a strong nationalist, who soon revealed compelling powers of leadership. The rise of Home Rule had been helped by the fierce opposition of the Irish Roman Catholic hierarchy to Gladstone's Irish University Bill of 1873. This had been intended as another step in 'restitution'. Gladstone proposed a new University of Dublin as a teaching and examining body, to be associated with existing institutions such as the Protestant Trinity College and the Catholic Maynooth College. The Irish Catholic bishops, however, opposed mixed education, as did radical English secularists. As a result, the bill was defeated in the Commons, with thirty-five Irish Liberal members voting against. Gladstone wanted to resign; but Disraeli refused to form another minority Conservative administration, and the Liberals limped along in office for another year.

3

Gladstone's Government was more successful with its famous 1870 Act for the development of elementary education in England, though even this led to divisions among the Liberals. The Prime Minister was personally involved in the drafting of the original Education Bill; but he did not quite share W. E. Forster's sense of social urgency.[13] As a staunch Anglican, he would have preferred state schools to give only secular instruction; but in the end he had to accept the more or less undenominational religious teaching provided under the Cowper-Temple amendment.

Gladstone was much more deeply committed to civil service reform. He welcomed this both as a way of reducing privilege and of increasing efficiency in government. The Order in Council of 1870, which exposed most of the civil service to entry through open competition, marked the completion of the first phase of reform inspired by the Northcote-Trevelyan report. Cardwell's army reforms likewise reflected a Gladstonian desire for greater efficiency (see below, p. 196). But Gladstone gave only reluctant backing to the Universities Tests Act of 1871, which abolished religious tests for holders of teaching posts at Oxford and Cambridge.[14] It seemed enough to him that since the 1850s the two universities had been open to non-Anglican undergraduates; and he would have preferred teaching to remain under religious influence. He accepted, however, that reform was necessary to forestall attempts to abolish all clerical fellowships. Gladstone was only mildly interested in Lord Selborne's 1873 Supreme Court of Judicature Act.[15] This merged the two English legal systems – common law and equity – which still existed side by side, each with their own courts. A High Court was created, eventually divided into three divisions, along with a Court of Appeal. The 1873 Act was passed as a non-party measure; but it was soon to be modified by the Disraeli Government's 1875 Judicature Act and by the 1876 Appellate Jurisdiction Act. The latter restored the powers of the House of Lords as a final appeal body.

Two reforms enacted in 1872 (the Ballot Act and the Licensing Act) had reached the statute book only after earlier bills had failed because of strong opposition. Gladstone had been a late convert to support for the ballot; but he became angry at the rejection by the House of Lords of the 1871 bill. On the other hand, he showed little interest in licensing legislation; for he felt no sympathy with the temperance interest, even though this was becoming linked with the Liberal Party.

The legislative achievement of Gladstone's first administration meant that it was one of the most successful ministries of the century. Neither Gladstone himself nor his ministers were equally enthusiastic about every measure passed; but all proposals were presented to Parliament in the belief that they were desirable or unavoidable reforms which, though sometimes far-reaching, never went further than was necessary for the encouragement of good government and social harmony. The most valuable reforms were those which affected institutions – the Irish Church Act, the University Tests Act, the Ballot Act. Less satisfactory were the ventures into social reform – the Irish Land Act, the Licensing Act, and the trade union legislation of 1871.

4

In the 1860s trade unionism was still confined to a small minority of the working classes, and was strongest among skilled artisans.[16] The leading craft union was the Amalgamated Society of Engineers, with nearly 35,000 members in 1870. Other prominent craft unions had been formed by the stonemasons, carpenters and joiners, the ironfounders, and the boilermakers. A particular concern of these unions was to maintain restricted entry into their trades, so as to protect wages and standards. Most wage settlements were still negotiated at local branch level, and rates and hours varied between different parts of the country. During the boom of the early 1870s – which stimulated a strong demand for labour – trade unions spread widely within some large-scale semi-skilled industries, notably among the coalminers, cotton workers, and railwaymen. The agricultural workers also formed effective unions for the first time. Much of this expansion faded with the collapse of the boom, but an underlying growth trend remained. The membership of twenty-eight important unions rose from 142,530 in 1870 to 266,321 in 1875, fell to 227,924 in 1880, but was back to 267,907 by 1885. Total United Kingdom trade union membership stood at 750,000 about 1888, perhaps 10 per cent of all adult male manual workers.[17] Trade unionism in short involved only a minority of Victorian workers from the 1860s to the 1880s; but it was a growing minority which included a high proportion of the skilled and semi-skilled whose labour was essential to the national economy.

The skilled workmen started not only trade unions but also local trades councils. These provided mutual support between trades during strikes. In many large towns they proved to be more enduring than particular unions, and so they contributed the element of continuity to working-class organization. The London Trades Council was very active politically. Attitudes towards political involvement varied widely among trade unionists; but a majority probably welcomed the prominent parts played by the Reform League and by the London Working Men's Association during the Second Reform Act agitation. The LWMA was led by George Potter, a joiner and founder of the trade union weekly paper, the *Bee-Hive*. The Reform League counted among its leaders Robert Applegarth, general secretary of the Amalgamated Society of Carpenters and Joiners; George Odger, shoemaker secretary of the London Trades Council; and George Howell, a bricklayer who became the League's secretary.

The Reform League and the London Working Men's Association exerted much less influence than had been expected during the 1868 general election, the first contest to be conducted under the extended franchise.[18] The Liberals, both at national and local level, were not accommodating; and the Reform Leaguers were too deferential to press working-class claims hard. They rallied working-class support for middle-class candidates in some thirty constituencies; and yet no working-class candidates were put forward for winnable seats. After the election the Reform League broke up. A new Labour Representation League undertook the placing of working men as candidates for Parliament. Meanwhile, the parliamentary committee of the new Trades Union Congress, with George Howell as its secretary, set out to persuade ministers and members of Parliament of the need for fresh and sympathetic trade union legislation.

The *Hornby v. Close* judgement of January 1867 had ruled that, since the purposes of a union were not (as previously thought) analogous to those of a friendly society, trade unions could not recover money from defaulting officials. The financial security of trade unions was thus threatened. A few months later came an equally serious challenge when in *R. v. Druit* three working tailors were found guilty of criminal conspiracy for picketing the workshops of master tailors. Trade unionists had assumed that peaceful picketing had been legalized under the Molestation of Workmen Act of 1859.

The need for new legal protection was thus apparent. But at this same period the reputation of trade unions was being damaged by the 'Sheffield outrages' – the revelation of a long history of force and intimidation in the Sheffield cutlery trades, especially by the saw grinders' union under its secretary, William Broadhead. Similar practices were found to have been followed in the Manchester area and elsewhere. As a direct result of these revelations, a Royal Commission of inquiry was appointed into trade unionism in general and into the Sheffield and Manchester cases in particular (1867–9). Rival trade union committees were quickly formed, each claiming to represent organized labour. The Conference of Amalgamated Trades, which consisted of the full-time secretaries of the main craft trade unions, was allowed to give evidence to the commission through Robert Applegarth. The other committee had been set up under the influence of George Potter at a conference held in London in March 1867 at which provincial workmen were strongly represented. Though this committee soon faded away, it proved to be the forerunner of the Trades Union Congress, which dates its inception from a meeting at Manchester in June 1868.[19] Thirty-four delegates, who claimed to speak for 118,367 members, attended this foundation meeting. Delegates from provincial trades councils were prominent, whereas the London craft unions did not participate. The main achievement of the first congress was simply to agree upon the desirability of coming together again every year 'for the purpose of bringing the trades into closer alliance, and to take action in all Parliamentary matters pertaining to the general interests of the working classes'. A second congress duly met at Birmingham in August 1869. The third congress, called in London for March 1871, was the first truly national gathering, attended by delegates from forty-nine societies with 289,430 members. At the Sheffield congress of 1874 delegates attended from 153 societies with nearly 1,200,000 members. Thereafter the impact of trade depression broke up many unions, and by the early 1880s the represented membership had fallen to about 500,000.

The main concern of the 1871 Trades Union Congress was with the Gladstone Government's proposals for trade union legislation. These had awaited the final reports of the Royal Commission. The commission had included three members favourable to trade unions – Frederic Harrison, the positivist writer; Thomas Hughes, a radical Member of Parliament and well-known author; and the Earl of

Lichfield. Harrison worked hard in the commission to counter the commonly held view that trade unions operated in restraint of trade – often through restrictive practices, and sometimes by violence and intimidation as at Sheffield. The positivists did not reject the teaching of classical political economy that trade unions could not alter aggregate wages, the wage fund. But they believed that unions could influence wage rates in particular trades, and could prevent drastic wage falls. Harrison concentrated the attention of the commission upon the large craft unions, and in so doing contrived to give the impression that trade unions, far from being dangerous to society, were organizations largely concerned with providing benefits to members in unemployment and old age. The majority report of the Royal Commission came out much more favourably to the trade union idea than might have been expected; but Harrison, Hughes, and Lichfield still signed a minority report. This turned the arguments of opponents of trade unions upside down by claiming that violence only occurred where unions were weak or non-existent. Effective unionization brought 'an increased sense of order, subordination and reflection'. Workers should be left free to bargain as they thought fit under the law, for there was 'no logical halting place between the old system of compulsion and that of entire freedom'.

Within a month of the publication of the Royal Commission reports Harrison had drafted a bill for Parliament, which was introduced by Hughes and A. J. Mundella. This closely followed the minority's proposals for removing statutory restrictions on combination, for protecting trade union funds, and for abolishing special offences in trade disputes. The bill was eventually withdrawn; but it had helped to shape 'respectable' opinion, which was shifting from hostility towards cautious acceptance. 'Like thunder-clouds, they advance against the wind, and can boast of converts of the class of Mr. Mill.' So noted *Blackwood's Magazine* for May 1870. In the *Fortnightly Review* exactly a year earlier John Stuart Mill, in a notice of W. T. Thornton's book *On Labour*, had dramatically abandoned the classical wage-fund theory, with its dispiriting assertion that wages could not be permanently raised either by legislation or by combination, and that they must always tend to fall to subsistence level. 'The right and wrong of the proceedings of Trades' Unions becomes a common question of prudence and social duty, not one which is peremptorily decided by unbending necessities of political economy.' In the 1862 edition of his *Principles of Political Economy* Mill had already added a section which defended trade unions and strike action as necessary to keep wage rates up with what the market could pay. Within a few years of 1869 the wage-fund theory had become largely discredited.

The Gladstone Government secured the passing of a temporary Trade Unions' Funds Protection Act in 1869; but not until February 1871 was its main trade union bill introduced. This followed the Hughes and Mundella proposals in giving protection to funds of registered unions, and it covered them against charges of criminal conspiracy because their purposes were in restraint of trade. Trade unions were thus now finally recognized as lawful organizations. But the Gladstone Government remained suspicious of trade unionism in practice. While the cabinet was discussing the 1871 bill Gladstone made a significant jotting: 'principle to punish violence; and in all economical matters the law to take no part'.[20] Trade unionists were deeply disappointed by clauses which proposed to retain as criminal offences 'molestation', 'obstruction', 'intimidation', and 'threat'. These were vague expressions which could be interpreted by the courts restrictively. The TUC protested; but the Government would only agree to placing these clauses in a separate Criminal Law Amendment Act.

It now became urgent TUC policy to secure alteration of this second Act. During the 1874 general election the Conservatives showed a willingness to re-open the question, and after coming to power the Disraeli Government appointed another Royal Commission. Its report proved to be unhelpful, but skilful parliamentary lobbying finally persuaded the cabinet to promote the Conspiracy and Protection of Property Act (1875). Under this act no one became liable for criminal conspiracy because of any action taken in contemplation or furtherance of a trade dispute, unless the action would have been criminal if committed by one person. The Criminal Law Amendment Act of 1871 was repealed, and peaceful picketing was now thought to be legalized. In the same year the Employers and Workmen Act limited the penalty for breach of contract by workmen to payment of civil damages. It had been a long-standing grievance that workmen had been open to criminal prosecution and imprisonment, whereas employers were liable only for civil damages. The law had been much used by employers as a means of punishment or for strike-breaking.

An Act of 1876, which redefined a 'trade union', completed the Conservative Government's labour relations legislation. George Howell, secretary of the Parliamentary Committee of the TUC until 1875, remarked how trade unions had become 'public institutions'. It was 'useless to abuse them, to put them down is impossible . . . they are now protected by law, as well as being amenable to the law'.[21] This protection was not to prove as certain as Howell imagined; but over the next few years the unions were to find themselves concerned not so much with their legal standing as with their survival in economic hard times. The stonemasons' and ironfounders' unions both came near to collapse in 1879, and in the same year the engineers' union spent more on strike benefit in opposition to threatened wage reductions than it had spent on strikes during a generation.

Did strikes pay? The question was much discussed. The majority report of the 1867 Royal Commission thought probably not. Trade unionists argued that on balance they did. An article by George Howell in *Fraser's Magazine* for December 1879 pointed out how a partial strike was often used to test a question, so that not all workmen lost wages; also how the very threat of strike action could achieve results without any stoppage. From the incomplete evidence available, it seems that (as Mill argued) the market rate for labour was most likely to be reached – or at least more quickly adjusted upwards and more slowly adjusted downwards – in trades where unions were strong.[22] Not all strikes were about wages. The nine hours movement of the early 1870s demanded the reduction of the working week to fifty-four hours, though with the possibility of longer employment at overtime rates. The way to nine hours had been led by a prolonged but successful strike of Tyneside engineers in 1871. This attracted the support of *The Times* and of much 'respectable' opinion. Henry Fawcett, the Liberal economist and politician, praised the Tyne workmen for acting on their own, without expecting state help through legislation.[23]

The 1860s and 1870s witnessed a notable growth of arbitration and conciliation machinery to soften industrial conflict.[24] A. J. Mundella, a Nottingham hosiery manufacturer and Liberal politician, helped to start the Nottingham Board of Arbitration for the hosiery trade, which consisted of equal numbers of employers and workpeople. This came to cover over 60,000 workers, and it served as a model for other industries. By 1875 nearly every trade where unions existed possessed either a standing joint committee with provision for arbitration, or the experience of arbitration on an ad hoc basis. The trade unions had thus secured recognition by employers, but at some sacrifice of freedom of action. This restriction was especially apparent in the coal and iron trades, where during the 1870s agreed sliding scales began to relate wages to selling prices.

5

Dissatisfaction among working-class voters with the Criminal Law Amendment Act of 1871 was one reason why Gladstone lost the February 1874 general election.[25] Dislike of his Government's education policy by Nonconformist supporters of the National Education League may have led many of them to abstain from voting, though the league had called off its campaign of intervention in by-elections some six months before the general election. Gladstone himself asserted that his party had been 'borne down in a torrent of gin and beer' as landlords used their influence in favour of the Conservatives because of the 1872 Licensing Act. This exaggerated claim was coloured by the fact that Gladstone himself had been pushed into second place in his own Greenwich constituency by a Conservative candidate who was a distiller. The most important single cause of the Liberal defeat was probably the swing among middle-class urban and suburban voters, who had previously voted Liberal but who now abstained or voted Conservative. They were alarmed at the amount of reform which the Gladstone Government had undertaken, and fearful that there was more to come. 'We had exhausted our programme,' admitted Lord

Kimberley, 'and quiet men asked, What will Gladstone do next? Will he not seek to recover his popularity by extreme radical measures?'[26] Gladstone's election promise to abolish the income tax, which might have appealed to middle-class voters, was little noticed. He had called the election suddenly, without preparing the electorate or his party for the offer. Jingoistic regret for the 'weakness' of Liberal foreign policy – especially towards the United States over the Alabama arbitration – probably also cost votes. So did the Collier and Ewelme cases, where Gladstone was thought to have used improper means to make appointments. In general, Liberal ministers gave an impression of tiredness and division, 'a range of exhausted volcanoes' as Disraeli had dubbed them in 1872.

J. E. Gorst had brought Conservative election machinery to a peak, whereas Liberal organization proved weak. The Liberals nominated some seventy fewer candidates than in 1868. The Conservatives won 350 seats, the Liberals 245, and the Irish Nationalists 57. Disraeli had been taunted before and during the election that he had no reform programme. He did not need one. His election address simply promised respite from 'incessant and harassing legislation', a restoration of British influence in Europe, and support for the British Empire. He formed an aristocratic cabinet, with six peers as members. In contrast, the Home Secretary was R. A. Cross, a successful Lancashire banker and barrister, who had never held office before but who proved to be highly competent. Although Disraeli had not promised reform, because of Cross and a few other ministers, the administration was destined to acquire a reforming reputation.[27] Cross was likened to a shopkeeper always ready to offer what the customers wanted. The most far-reaching Conservative measures were the trade union acts of 1875. The remainder were either consolidating statutes, or improvements which remained only permissive or partial – the Factory Acts of 1874 and 1878, the Artisans Dwellings Act (1875), the Public Health Act (1875), the Sale of Food and Drugs Act (1875), the Friendly Societies Act (1875), the Education Act (1876), the Rivers Pollution Prevention Act (1876), the Merchant Shipping Act (1876). Permissive legislation was described by one Liberal critic as Cross's 'panacea for all the ills that England is heir to'.[28]

Disraeli did not mention these social reforms in his 1880 election address, an indication of his limited interest. His main attention in government had gone into foreign policy. He might have won a general election called in 1878, immediately after his triumphal return from the Congress of Berlin (see below, p. 206). But by April 1880 many influences were combining to defeat the Conservatives.[29] Since the 1874 election the National Liberal Federation had sprung actively into life, whereas the Conservative National Union had been neglected. Chamberlain claimed in a letter to *The Times* (13.4.1880) that in 67 boroughs organized on 'caucus' lines the Liberals had been successful in 60. But 46 of the 67 boroughs had previously returned Liberals in 1868, long before the formation of the National Liberal Federation; and 10 places among Chamberlain's 60 still returned at least one Conservative. At the end of 1879 Gladstone had launched his Midlothian campaign against 'Beaconsfieldism', followed by a repeat campaign during the 1880 election. The most clear effect of the Midlothian campaigns was the train of Liberal victories elsewhere in Scotland, where only 7 Conservative Members of Parliament were left against 50 Liberals. But writing to Granville during the election, Gladstone himself did not claim that his speeches had made conversions 'at the moment in the place – though I believe they have a good deal of silent and slower effect on the tone of the public mind generally'. This cumulative effect was probably most powerful in ensuring that Liberals actually voted. The Nonconformists voted for Gladstone in 1880, whereas in 1874 many seem to have abstained. In those constituencies where firm comparisons can be made between the two elections the numbers of votes cast for Conservative candidates fell only in Scotland, but the Liberal total rose largely elsewhere – from 558,045 to 758,883 in English and Welsh boroughs, and from 159,972 to 215,512 in county constituencies.

Most floating voters were probably drawn towards Liberalism in 1880 neither by revulsion with Beaconsfieldism nor by liking for the National Liberal Federation and its radicalism, but by the impact of deepening agricultural and industrial distress. The Conservatives tried to pass this off as a temporary phase. Yet even well-to-do families were becoming affected by business anxieties; and Disraeli's South African and Afghanistan misadventures were probably disliked by many such people more because income tax had risen from 2*d*. in the £ in 1874 to 5*d*. in 1880 than because Gladstone had denounced them on moral grounds. Gladstone himself admitted privately how it was 'very sad' but 'in these guilty wars it is the business of paying which appears to be the most effective means of awakening the conscience'. A Farmers' Alliance had been formed in 1879 to voice the grievances of tenant farmers about land tenure, compensation for improvements, and game rights. The alliance put questions to candidates in agricultural constituencies, and evoked most response from the Liberals. This may have contributed towards the Conservative loss of as many as nineteen rural English county seats, in which they were traditionally strong. 353 Liberals were elected, 238 Conservatives, and 61 Irish Nationalists – which meant a comfortable Liberal majority overall of 54. Gladstone's election address had taken the Irish question as its chief theme. Disraeli's warned against Home Rule, but in rambling prose which lacked inspiration. A year later he died. Gladstone, by contrast, still had far to go in policy and in time.

Notes

1. R. Blake, *Disraeli* (1966), p. 487.
2. E. D. Steele, *Irish Land and British Politics, Tenant-Right and Nationality, 1865–1870* (1974), p. 67.

3. H. J. Hanham, *Elections and Party Management, Politics in the Time of Disraeli and Gladstone* (1959), pp. 209–17.
4. *Ibid.*, p. 217.
5. E. Ashley, 'Mr. Gladstone – Fragments of Personal Reminiscences', *National Review*, June 1898, pp. 539–40.
6. See especially N. Mansergh, *The Irish Question, 1840–1921* (3rd edn, 1975); and P. O'Farrell, *England and Ireland Since 1800* (1975).
7. See L. P. Curtis, Jr., *Apes and Angels, The Irishman in Victorian Caricature* (1971), esp. Ch. IV.
8. Ethel Drus (ed.), *Journal of Events during the Gladstone Ministry, 1868–1874*, Camden Miscellany, XXI (1958), pp. 9–10.
9. J. L. Hammond, *Gladstone and the Irish Nation* (2nd edn, 1964), p. 51.
10. See especially P. M. H. Bell, *Disestablishment in Ireland and Wales* (1969), Chs. 1–6.
11. See especially E. D. Steele, *Irish Land and English Politics, Tenant-Right and Nationality, 1865–1870* (1974).
12. J. L. Hammond, *Gladstone and the Irish Nation* (2nd edn, 1964), pp. 80–1; Agatha Ramm (ed.), *Political Correspondence of Mr. Gladstone and Lord Granville, 1876–1886* (1962), I, p. 58.
13. See especially F. Adams, *History of the Elementary School Contest in England* (1882; reprinted 1972), introduction by A. Briggs; and H. Roper, 'W. E. Forster's Memorandum of 21 October, 1869: A Re-Examination', *British Journal of Educational Studies*, XXI (1973).
14. See W. R. Ward, *Victorian Oxford* (1965), Ch. XI.
15. See R. A. Cosgrove, 'The Judicature Acts of 1873–1875; A Centennial Reassessment', *Durham University Journal*, LXVIII (1976), and references there.
16. See A. E. Musson, *British Trade Unions, 1800–1875* (1972), Chs. 7, 8, and references there. Also W. H. Fraser, *Trade Unions and Society, The Struggle for Acceptance, 1850–1880* (1974).
17. S. and Beatrice Webb, *History of Trade Unionism, 1666–1920* (1920), appendix VI; H. A. Clegg *et al.*, *History of British Trade Unions Since 1889*, I (1964), pp. 1–4, 466–7.
18. See especially H. J. Hanham, *Elections and Party Management, Politics in the Time of Disraeli and Gladstone* (1959), Ch. 15; and R. Harrison, *Before the Socialists* (1965), Ch. IV.
19. See especially B. C. Roberts, *The Trades Union Congress, 1868–1921* (1958); and A. E. Musson, *Trade Union and Social History* (1974), Ch. 3.
20. E. J. Feuchtwanger, *Gladstone* (1975), p. 164.
21. G. Howell, *Conflicts of Capital and Labour* (1878), p. xii.
22. See S. Pollard, 'Trade Unions and the Labour Market, 1870–1914', *Yorkshire Bulletin of Economic and Social Research*, Vol. 17 (1965).
23. H. Fawcett, *Essays and Addresses* (1872), p. 110. See especially E. Allen *et al.*, *The North-East Engineers' Strikes of 1871* (1971).
24. See especially V. L. Allen, 'The Origins of Industrial Conciliation and Arbitration', *International Review of Social History*, IX (1964); and J. H. Porter, 'Wage Bargaining under Conciliation Agreements, 1860–1914', *Economic History Review*, second series, XXIII (1970).
25. See H. J. Hanham, *Elections and Party Management, Politics in the Time of Disraeli and Gladstone* (1959), pp. 220–7.
26. Ethel Drus (ed.), *Journal of Events during the Gladstone Ministry, 1868–1874*, Camden Miscellany, XXI (1958), p. 43.
27. See especially P. W. Clayden, *England under Lord Beaconsfield* (1880: reprinted 1971); and P. Smith, *Disraelian Conservatism and Social Reform* (1967).
28. T. Wemyss Reid, *Politicians of Today* (1879; reprinted 1972), I, p. 288.
29. See H. J. Hanham, *Elections and Party Management, Politics in the Time of Disraeli and Gladstone* (1959), pp. 227–32; and T. Lloyd, *The General Election of 1880* (1968).

Chapter 9

Imperial policy: *'Vastness of dimension'*

1

Victorian England stood at the centre of a far-flung and ever-growing empire.[1] In 1871 its total population (including that of the United Kingdom) amounted to some 235 million people, spread across 7,770,000 square miles in five continents. It was literally 'an empire upon which the sun never sets'. It made Britain uniquely a world political power, at the same time as she was the world's leading industrial power. In forms of government overseas the British Empire ranged from self-governing white colonies of settlement (Canada, Australia, New Zealand) to dependent black, brown, and yellow colonies, protectorates, and protected states of many sizes and many races – with India as the greatest dependency of all. The white colonies were being peopled by a great emigration from the United Kingdom (see above, p. 9). The motives behind emigration varied – to find a better life, to make money, to employ skills (for example in railway building), to escape disgrace at home, even (it has been suggested) to sublimate frustrated sexual drive. Admittedly, the majority of emigrants travelled not to the empire but to the United States, for the thriving and diversified American economy – particularly the lure of free land – offered better prospects than any British colony. But great numbers remained under the British flag. The population of British North America increased from 1,282,000 in 1838 to 3,689,000 in 1871; of Australia from 52,000 in 1825 to 1,647,000 in 1870; of New Zealand from 59,000 in 1858 to 256,000 in 1871.[2] This high rate of growth was expected to continue far into the future.

The eighteenth-century justification for empire in terms of profitable trade in tropical commodities had been rivalled during the nineteenth century by a new sense of the value of the empire as a market, especially for surplus population and for surplus capital, which could be invested in railways and other instruments of colonization and also (first in Australia and then in South Africa) in gold and diamond mining.[3] Between 1865 and 1914 about £4,000 million was invested overseas, about 40 per cent of this in the British Empire.

Without heavy investment in improved communications – roads, railways, world-wide cable links, telegraphs – India, Australia, and Africa could not have opened up their interiors, nor could ideas of 'imperialism' have aspired to overcome separation of time and place. Indeed, *The Oxford Survey of the British Empire* (1914) declared that the empire was 'largely the outcome of the work of inventors and engineers'. In India a great sub-continental railway network of almost 25,000 miles, which was built between the end of the mutiny (1858) and the end of the century, transformed economic life. A global cable link was deliberately constructed, based entirely upon British territories. This provided fast communication for political and military purposes, and also for commercial intelligence.[4] Scores of shipping lines – of which the best known was the Peninsular and Orient (the P & O) – carried passengers and goods between all parts of the empire, greatly assisted by the opening of the Suez Canal in 1869 which cut communication between England and Australia to seven weeks. The improvement of armaments made a less attractive contribution to the advance of empire – more effective rifles, and the Maxim machine-gun of the 1880s, which could fire 666 shots a minute and was praised by H. M. Stanley, the explorer, as 'invaluable for subduing the heathen'.[5]

The British proved that they could usually conquer with ease and economy of men and money, and that they could also govern on the same terms. The administration of each colony rested in the hands of a few hundreds or thousands of expatriate white men, who were far outnumbered by the indigenous population. The success of white rule in many remote spots depended heavily upon strength of character and bluff. The government of India, however, presented problems all of its own. The Indian civil service necessarily became a large bureaucracy, led by white administrators recruited in Britain through open competition. These rulers of empire, and likewise its traders and missionaries, came from middle-class families which often retained an imperial connection through several generations. Sons were sent 'from many a quiet vicarage and rose garden into a journey far beyond the skyline to become the frontiersmen of all the world'.[6]

Real knowledge of the empire was confined to these comparative few men who served it. In his widely-read lectures on *The Expansion of England* (1883) Sir John Seeley, Regius Professor of Modern History at Cambridge, even remarked – in often remembered words – that 'we seem, as it were, to have conquered and peopled half the world in a fit of absence of mind'. Seeley meant only that in the eighteenth and early nineteenth centuries imperial expansion had not caught the popular interest. But the empire, though formed upon no system, had certainly not fallen into British hands without effort. Another historian explained in 1916 why Seeley's words had come to be so often quoted as if they meant that the empire had been acquired accidentally. 'Empire is congenial enough to the Englishman's temperament but it is repugnant to his political conscience. In order that he may be reconciled to it, it must seem to be imposed upon him by necessity – as a duty.'[7] This was 'the white man's burden', described by Rudyard Kipling in his famous poem (1899):

Take up the White Man's burden –
   Send forth the best ye breed –
Go bind your sons to exile
   To serve your captives' need.

Take up the White Man's burden –
   And reap his old reward:
The blame of those ye better,
   The hate of those ye guard.

Confidence was strong in the superiority of Christian and British institutions over those of non-whites, especially of African negroes. The Jamaican revolt of 1865 had greatly strengthened the conviction that the negroes were an inferior breed – of childlike irresponsibility – who required firm white government.[8] Ideas about the equality and perfectibility of all mankind were now largely abandoned. The highly popular books of H. M. Stanley – *Through the Dark Continent* (1878) and *In Darkest Africa* (1890) – did much to spread the view that negroes were irretrievably primitive.

2

This sense of imperial 'mission' usually came into play only when and where openings for profitable trade seemed to present themselves. During the first half of Victoria's reign much British trade was indeed conducted within an 'informal empire', which flourished alongside the growing formal empire.[9] Britain did not need to undertake the government of many remote regions, so long as they remained open to free trade; her industrial and commercial superiority guaranteed her a good share of the market. Latin America, China, and the Turkish Empire were all opened to free trade largely by British initiative – with only two formal colonial acquisitions, Aden (1839) and Hongkong (1841). The situation began to change, however, during the last quarter of the century when other powers, with protectionist trading intentions, began to colonize large areas, particularly in Africa. This eventually drove the British into making large additions of territory to the empire during the 1880s and 1890s in the name of 'imperialism'.

Significantly, the word was not used in this colonial context until 1868, and it was not commonly so employed for another decade.[10] During the 1850s and early 1860s the assumption was that the white colonies of settlement would always one day choose complete independence, although only a few theorists advocated the immediate break-up of the empire. By 1870, though, a change of emphasis was showing itself. The growing feeling now was that positive efforts should be made to retain an imperial connection with these white colonies, not by force but with their consent.[11] The Canadian Confederation was created by the British North America Act of 1867, and this stimulated thinking about the future relationship. The family image of 'mother country' and grown-up 'daughters' came into currency. 'We are all proud of our Empire,' wrote *The Times* (11.1.1867), 'and we all regard our Colonies and dependencies as the various members of such a family as earth never yet saw. That pride and that affection have undergone changes corresponding to the changed character and circumstances of the communities themselves.' This feeling was intensified in reaction against the seeming wish of Gladstone's Government after 1868 to abandon Canada and New Zealand. British troops were withdrawn from both territories, though the motive was financial economy not anti-imperial. The cry 'the Empire in danger' rang through sections of the press during 1869–70, and ministers found it necessary to emphasize their continuing support for the white colonial connection. When the Government belatedly agreed to guarantee a New Zealand loan, the *Spectator* (21.5.1870) remarked how ministers had changed their minds 'for the best of all reasons – because they had begun to discover that their line was not the line of the people of England'. Significantly, the Royal Colonial Institute was formed in 1868.

Attention about 1870 was centring upon the future of the white colonies of settlement. But what of the black, brown, and yellow dependencies? Few of them could provide good land or a good climate for emigrants, which meant that one leading motive for popular interest did not exist. India too was not a magnet for emigration. But it was the great special case of empire, a huge sub-continent with a population about 191 million in 1871.[12] It constituted a major centre of trade, and the growth of India's trade, and consequently of its revenue, maintained the large Indian army at no expense to the British Exchequer. A third or more of the British army was also stationed in India. The Indian sub-continent absorbed almost one-fifth of British exports, and supplied in return raw cotton, jute, wheat, and tea. By the end of the century India's trading surplus had come to play an essential part in covering Britain's balance of payments deficit. Not only did the Indian market absorb British goods which might not have been sellable elsewhere, Indian exports overcame foreign tariff barriers. A half and more of Indian exports to the United States, Germany, France, and Austria remained free from duty.[13]

But the value of India was psychological as well as economic. It was an empire within the empire. The government of this sub-continent was taken as the test of British capacity to rule native peoples elsewhere. 'The possession of India offers to ourselves that element of vastness of dimension which in this age is needed to secure width of thought and nobility of purpose.' So explained Sir Charles Dilke in *Greater Britain* (1868). In the language of late-Victorian popular journalism India represented 'the brightest jewel in the Empire's crown'. How unwilling the British were to lose India was shown by the ferocity with which the mutiny of 1857–8 had been suppressed. The East India Company was wound up, and the British Government assumed direct responsibility. The self-imposed commitment to 'reform' India continued, though now the British tried less to promote social and cultural changes – a policy which had encouraged the mutiny – and more to produce material improvement. Few now imagined that the Indians could do this for themselves through self-government – at least not in the foreseeable future. *The Times* (6.11.1878) explained the British position in India. 'We have conquered India, and we hold it, not for our advantage, but for its own welfare, because we can give it a Roman peace amid the discords of conflicting races and creeds. Our chief colonies are natural growths; India is an enforced acquisition.' Gladstone (as much as Disraeli) accepted the commitment to rule India. 'I hold, firmly and unconditionally, that we have indeed a great duty towards India, but that we have no interest in India, except the wellbeing of India itself.'[14]

India remained a mystery. This was fascinating – especially to Disraeli.[15] His whole interest in the empire centred upon the safety of India and the routes to it through the Near and Middle East. He showed little care for the colonies of settlement, and was bored by the details of administration of colonial dependencies. The 'imperialism' of his famous Crystal Palace speech of 1872 was clearly asserted, but it was also unspecific and defensive. He claimed that the Liberals wished to abandon the empire. The Conservatives, by contrast, wished 'to uphold' it. Yet Disraeli did not make imperialism a prominent issue at the 1874 general election. And the colonial policy of his 1874–80 Government amounted to little more than a series of improvisations and responses, some more successful than others.

In 1875 the Government bought the Egyptian Khedive's holding of Suez Canal shares for £4 million, in order to give Britain a leading voice in the running of this vital waterway to India and the Far East. The deal was kept secret until completed. Over 80 per cent of canal traffic was British by the 1880s. Disraeli was delighted at both the manner and the matter of his coup; but the purchase was criticized by Liberals as bound to lead to British involvement in Egypt. Even more criticized was Disraeli's introduction in 1876 of the Royal Titles Bill to allow Queen Victoria to be proclaimed Empress of India – as recognition to Indians of the major part played by their country within the empire. The bill was eventually passed mainly out of respect for the personal wish of the Queen to assume the title. The active part played by Disraeli during the Eastern question crisis of 1876–8 was chiefly motivated by his concern for India. Indian troops were dramatically transferred to Malta at the height of the confrontation with the Russians; and Cyprus was acquired to reinforce the British position in the eastern Mediterranean (see below, p. 204).

But the forward policies pursued in Fiji, Malaya, South Africa, and Afghanistan were not of Disraeli's own making. The annexation of Fiji had indeed already been set in motion by Gladstone's Government. Lord Carnarvon, the Conservative Colonial Secretary, was reluctant to proceed with annexation; but he found himself committed by the British representatives on the spot. Similar local initiatives led the Disraeli

Government into its two most costly colonial ventures – the Zulu and Afghan wars. Carnarvon, who a decade earlier had promoted the Canadian confederation, was keen for a confederation in South Africa, to include not only the four British territories but also the two Boer republics of the Orange Free State and the Transvaal. He believed that this would be the best way of checking the growing African unrest, and also of preventing the Boers from inviting investment from Continental powers. The Transvaal Government, bankrupt and hard pressed by the redoubtable Zulus, did accept British annexation in April 1877; but the Afrikaner farmers, led by Paul Kruger, remained opposed. The British now found themselves fighting the Zulus. Sir Bartle Frere, the High Commissioner in South Africa, acted recklessly, and a small British force was slaughtered at Isandhlwana in January 1879. Reinforcements had to be hurried out to defeat the Zulus at Ulundi in July. Carnarvon had resigned, Frere had been reckless; but Disraeli was accused of a lust for territory. In reality, the only valid charge against him was the quite opposite one – that he had taken too little interest in South African affairs.

Likewise on the north-west frontier of India the man in charge (Lord Lytton, the Viceroy) was responsible for expensive and damaging reverses. Lytton believed that the Russians were gaining the chief influence at Kabul, the Afghan capital. If allowed to consolidate their sway, they would be in a strong position to mount an attack upon India whenever they chose. Without approval from home, Lytton took a high line with the Afghans, and this led to war. A brilliant campaign by Major-General Roberts installed a British mission at Kabul. But in September 1879 its members were massacred; and a second punitive campaign had to be undertaken. At home Gladstone launched his first Midlothian campaign, during which he denounced Disraeli as an aggressive imperialist. Yet neither the tone of Disraeli's pronouncements about the empire since 1872, nor the nature of the colonial policy pursued by his Government, had shown him to be a deliberate imperial expansionist.

Notes

1. See, in general, especially B. Porter, *The Lion's Share, A Short History of British Imperialism, 1850–1970* (1975), Chs. I–VI; R. Hyam, *Britain's Imperial Century, 1815–1914* (1976); and C. C. Eldridge, *Victorian Imperialism* (1978).
2. C. C. Eldridge, *England's Mission, The Imperial Idea in the Age of Gladstone and Disraeli, 1868–1880* (1973), p. 121.
3. See especially A. R. Hall (ed.), *The Export of Capital from Britain, 1870–1914* (1968); and P. L. Cottrell, *British Overseas Investment in the Nineteenth Century* (1975).
4. See P. M. Kennedy, 'Imperial Cable Communications and Strategy, 1870–1914', *English Historical Review*, LXXXVI (1971).
5. A Bott, *Our Fathers* (1931), pp. 122, 212.
6. C. F. G. Masterman, *The Condition of England* (1909; reprinted 1961), p. 15. See especially L. H. Gann and P. Duignan, *The Rulers of British Africa, 1870–1914* (1978).

7. C. Gill, *National Power and Prosperity* (1916), p. xv; R. Hyam and G. Martin (eds.), *Reappraisals in British Imperial History* (1975), p. 4.

8. See Christine Bolt, *Victorian Attitudes to Race* (1970), esp. Ch. III.

9. See W. R. Louis (ed.), *Imperialism* (1976), and references there; especially R. Robinson and J. Gallagher, *Africa and the Victorians* (1961).

10. See R. Koebner and H. D. Schmidt, *Imperialism* (1964), Ch. II.

11. See C. C. Eldridge, *England's Mission, The Imperial Idea in the Age of Gladstone and Disraeli, 1868–1880* (1973), Chs. 1–3; and G. W. Martin, 'Anti-Imperialism in the Mid-Nineteenth Century and the Nature of the British Empire, 1820–70', in R. Hyam and G. Martin (eds.), *Reappraisals in British Imperial History* (1975).

12. See R. Hyam, *Britain's Imperial Century, 1815–1914* (1976), Ch. 7.

13. S. B. Saul, *Studies in British Overseas Trade, 1870–1914* (1960), pp. 62–3.

14. W. E. Gladstone, 'Aggression in Egypt', *Nineteenth Century,* August 1877, p. 153. See especially R. J. Moore, *Liberalism and Indian Politics, 1872–1922* (1966).

15. See R. Koebner and H. D. Schmidt, *Imperialism* (1964), Ch. V; and C. C. Eldridge, *England's Mission, The Imperial Idea in the Age of Gladstone and Disraeli, 1868–1880* (1973), Chs. 7, 8.

Chapter 10

Foreign policy: *'Peace, I hope, with honour'*

1

The conduct of colonial and foreign policy was necessarily influenced by the nature and limitations of British armed power. Until the last quarter of the nineteenth century the United Kingdom was spending more on its armed forces than any other state:[1]

		1870 (£)	1880 (£)	1890 (£)	1900 (£)
United Kingdom:	army	13,400,000	15,000,000	17,600,000	21,400,000
	navy	9,800,000	10,200,000	13,800,000	29,200,000
Germany:	army	9,600,000	18,200,000	24,200,000	33,600,000
	navy	1,200,000	2,400,000	4,600,000	7,400,000
France:	army	15,000,000	22,800,000	28,400,000	27,800,000
	navy	7,000,000	8,600,000	8,800,000	14,600,000
Russia:	army	18,600,000	26,000,000	24,600,000	32,100,000
	navy	2,400,000	3,800,000	4,400,000	8,400,000

The protection of Britain's world-wide imperial interests required a regular army which – though small by the standards of the Continent, where conscription prevailed – was bound to be comparatively expensive to maintain. After the ending of the Crimean War (1856) the size of the regular army was allowed to fall steadily under pressure for retrenchment; from an establishment over 200,000 in 1855 down to a low of 115,000 in 1870. Thereafter the total gradually rose again to reach over 150,000 during the 1890s.

The British army was not well regarded at home, except at moments of crisis or victory when 'the soldiers of the Queen' became briefly the objects of patriotic enthusiasm:

> And when we say we've always won,
> And when they ask us how it's done,
> We'll proudly point to every one
> Of England's Soldiers of the Queen.

To join the army was regarded as a last resort by working men out of employment, and recruiting figures rose in times of bad trade.[2] Edward Cardwell, the reforming War Secretary in Gladstone's 1868–74 Government, hoped that the suspension of the branding of deserters (with a large letter D), and the abolition of flogging as a punishment on home service would attract a superior category of men into the army;

but this did not happen. Pay remained low – less than a shilling a day – and barrack accommodation was primitive. Irishmen provided about a quarter of all army recruits in the 1870s, even though the Irish amounted to only about one-sixth of the total population. Professed Nonconformists, who would in general have been working men of a superior type, constituted only 3–4 per cent of recruits. During the early days of the Boer War the *Daily Mail* (28.12.1899) explained how fear of 'personal degradation' deterred the better-educated from joining the army. A clerk's black coat, however shabby, was the badge of a gentleman: 'but if he exchanges it for a red coat he sinks immediately into a condition of pupilage and servitude, with the prospect of promotion to be the valet of an officer'. The introduction of some form of compulsory service, though often discussed, never seemed likely. It was widely regarded as an infringement of traditional English liberty. Army officers came from the upper and upper-middle classes, especially from families with landed connections.[3] The Protestant Irish gentry provided a disproportionate number of officers, including the three leading late-Victorian army heroes – Lords Wolseley, Roberts, and Kitchener. These generals became household names through their victories in colonial wars; but the officer class at large remained remote from the Victorian business middle classes.

Cardwell's reforms represented a final stage in the quest for economy and efficiency which had been provoked by the expensive yet indifferent showing of the army during the Crimean War.[4] His great negative reform was the abolition from 1871 of the purchase of commissions or of promotion. This represented an attack upon privilege in the abstract; but promotion needed to be by merit for the sake of efficiency. Military conservatives, headed by the Duke of Cambridge, the Queen's cousin and Commander-in-Chief, wanted to 'leave well alone'. But Cardwell believed 'that the officers shall be made for the Army', not 'that the Army is made for the officers'. In the event, the composition of the officer class underwent little change. Resistance from the House of Lords was circumvented by pushing through abolition under royal warrant, on the ground that purchase had existed only by virtue of regulations established under earlier warrants.

Cardwell's three main positive reforms shaped the late-Victorian army: the Army Enlistment Act of 1870, the Regulation of Forces Act of 1871, and the localization and linked battalion scheme of 1872. The 1870 Act introduced a system of short service into the British army, inspired by the Prussian example, whereby after as little as six years' service men might be allowed to pass into the reserve. Cardwell hoped that this would eventually produce a reserve of 60,000 troops. The 1871 Act linked battalions of existing regiments together in a policy intended to provide one at home and one abroad. Cardwell was deterred from recommending complete mergers; but these followed ten years later when regiments were given territorial names in place of numbers. Localization had the double object of 'attracting the agricultural population to the Colours and encouraging the Militia to volunteer into their own Line regiments'. Sixty-six infantry 'brigade areas' were formed, with two line battalions and two militia battalions attached to each.

Unfortunately, despite a succession of late-Victorian 'scares' and official enquiries into the state of the army, little further improvement was attempted before the outbreak of the Boer War at the end of the century. Notably, no General Staff was created on the Prussian model. The linked battalion arrangement was thrown out of balance even by the small colonial campaigns of the 1870s and 1880s. The introduction of short service meant a much higher turnover of men, and this was not matched by the hoped-for big increase in recruiting. The home battalions – instead of constituting a significant home defence force – became mere training units for the battalions abroad. By 1878 not one home battalion stood ready for active service. To raise 20,000 men for the Egyptian campaign of 1882 10,800 reservists – not supposed to be used for small wars – had to be called out. To place some 450,000 men under the command of Lord Roberts during the Boer War all reservists and the cream of the militia, yeomanry, and volunteers (100,000 in all) had to be sent to South Africa.

The old militia and yeomanry, and the much newer volunteer force, were supposed to provide the part-time soldiers who would rally in support of the regular army for the defence of the British Isles against invasion. About 1870 the volunteers numbered some 200,000 men.[5] The force had come into existence in 1859 at a time of alleged invasion danger from France. About one Victorian male in twelve joined the volunteers to train without payment in spare time, with cost of uniforms met by the men themselves. At first one-half and later three-quarters of the volunteers were working men, especially artisans. Patriotic enthusiasm did not provide the whole explanation for the success of the volunteer movement in terms of numbers. It offered attractive recreational opportunities – fetes, dinners, outings, band playing, sport. Employers served as officers, foremen became non-commissioned officers, workmen were privates. The middle and upper classes gladly encouraged and financed their local units as expressions of class harmony. 'Too much cannot be said in favour of a pursuit which provides healthy and innocent amusement for the youth of our cities.' So claimed an article on 'English Physique' in *Macmillan's Magazine* for June 1870. 'Rifles and the suffrage are now in the hands of the people – the first as much of a trust as the last.' But it was probably fortunate that the half-trained volunteers were never called upon to fight Continental troops.

The defence of India was shared between the British regular army and the Indian army. A third or more of the regulars were usually stationed in India, with an especial responsibility to defend its north-west frontier from attack by tribesmen and perhaps, one day, by the Russians. The Indian army, led by British officers, contained 130,000 men in 1880; the armies of the princely states provided a further 350,000 troops. Apart from its Indian commitments, the British army was organized to fight a succession of 'small wars' on the frontiers of the empire. Lord Wolseley remarked in 1887 that foreigners might taunt the British with not being a military nation: 'but without doubt we are the most warlike people on earth. No other army has portions of it so constantly in the field'.[6] British troops became skilled and ruthless in fighting larger numbers of natives in faraway places, though not without some defeats. Imperial expansion or retrogression depended upon the exploits of a few hundreds or thousands of troops. Victory over the Egyptians at Tel-el-Kebir in 1882 – which led to the occupation of Egypt – cost 57 killed, 382 wounded, and 30 missing. Defeat by the Boers at Majuba in 1881, which was followed by the restoration of Transvaal independence. involved 93 killed, 133 wounded, and 58 taken prisoner.

The British army was inadequately trained to fight the white Boer farmers, and was certainly not ready to fight on the Continent of Europe. In 1868 the annual Mutiny Act was significantly altered. It still named the safety of the United Kingdom and the defence of overseas possessions as reasons for maintaining a standing army; but 'the Preservation of the Balance of Power in Europe' (inserted in the early eighteenth century) was now omitted. After the victory at Waterloo (1815) the prestige of the British army under the Duke of Wellington had long remained high on the Continent. But its performance during the Crimean War suggested that it would prove no match for the large and efficient Prussian army which won the Austro–Prussian (1866) and Franco–Prussian (1870–1) wars in dramatic succession. In 1887 Sir Charles Dilke remarked that Britain could not expect to land a force in Europe larger than the Belgian or Serbian armies; and certainly smaller (and not certainly more efficient) than the Roumanian army.[7]

Could the regular army, supported by the militia, yeomanry, and volunteers, even be expected to defend the British Isles successfully against invasion? The hope was that British naval supremacy would always prevent a large foreign landing. But suppose some mishap occurred to the fleet. Such a supposition was made in 'The Battle of Dorking', a story by G. T. Chesney, an engineer officer, which appeared in *Blackwood's Magazine* for May 1871.[8] This caused an immediate sensation. Over 80,000 copies of a sixpenny pamphlet reprint were sold within a month. British opinion had been impressed and alarmed by the recent Prussian victories only just across the English Channel. Chesney assumed that the Prussians had now landed in southern England. His story, written as a sad yet graphic retrospect, showed the nation cascading from apparent security to humiliating defeat. Chesney blamed the new rule by 'democracy'. 'The rich were idle and luxurious; the poor grudged the cost of defence. Politics had become a mere bidding for Radical votes.' In September 1871 at Cardwell's initiative the army held large-scale manoeuvres for the first time. These were felt to have demonstrated that the regulars, militia, and volunteers would together have won 'the battle of Dorking'; and for the moment fear of invasion faded.

2

Condescension mixed with contempt remained the common English attitude towards other Europeans, both among the working classes, who rarely travelled to foreign parts (except as soldiers or sailors), and among the upper and middle classes, who were much more likely to travel abroad. Notwithstanding her extensive family connections in Europe, Queen Victoria shared her subjects' distaste. 'We are the only honest people and therefore our task of dealing with others who are not so is dreadful.' A French visitor in the 1880s found Englishmen who believed that Nelson had been treacherously assassinated at Trafalgar.[9] Emerson, the American writer, remarked in *English Traits* (1856) that the French were disliked as frivolous, the Irish as aimless, and the Germans as professors. At the same time he found the English 'provokingly uncurious' about other nations. The great increase in opportunities for ordinary middle-class people to visit Europe apparently made no difference. *Punch* (24.10.1874) admitted that Cook's tours had not overcome insularity, but had simply begun to 'lower-middle-class-Englishize the Continent'. Continental ideas in the arts were treated with suspicion, even though Matthew Arnold praised French literature and Thomas Carlyle and George Eliot were Germanophiles. The careers of the English 'decadents' of the 1890s seemed only to confirm the worst fears about the danger of European influences. Mr Podsnap in Charles Dickens's *Our Mutual Friend* (1865) 'considered other countries a mistake'.

Attitudes towards the United States of America fell into a separate category. The United States – much the strongest magnet for emigrants – had never ceased to be accepted as part of the British 'family'. 'The Continent does not exist to them; but the United States is a sort of second home, and the older men who have not gone sigh and say, "If I had 'a emigrated, now you see, I should 'a done well".' So reported Richard Jefferies of the agricultural labourers.[10] Up to the time of the American Civil War (1861–5) the unruly and unpolished 'Yankees' were considered as juveniles. After the civil war, however, *Punch* began to portray 'Uncle Sam' as a vigorous young man. Awareness of growing American commercial power led to calls for closer co-operation, often with Anglo-Saxon racial overtones. 'You've only to pull together to lick all the world!' (*Punch*, 11.9.1869). By October 1878 Gladstone was accepting in an article called 'Kin Beyond Sea', written for the *North American Review*, that the United States would one day assume world commercial leadership. 'We have no more title against her than Venice, or Genoa, or Holland had had against us.' But Gladstone took satisfaction from the similarity of British and American institutions.

The *Alabama* arbitration of 1871–2 with the United States revealed Gladstone as a keen internationalist, eager to promote arbitration as a method of settling disputes.[11] It also showed him as very forbearing towards the brash Americans. Earlier attempts to settle by negotiation the much exaggerated claims for damage done by ships built in British yards for the Confederate rebels during the civil war had come to nothing. Gladstone knew that he was going against popular sentiment in accepting arbitration. The amount of damages awarded to the Americans – $15,500,000: £3,200,000 – though far less than they had demanded, was probably higher than the sometimes unscrupulous conduct of their case had deserved. Gladstone described the awards as both unjust in their grounds and harsh in amount; but he praised the 'moral value' of the example set by the two powers.

It was easy for Britain to take a high moral line in foreign relations because she was in general a satisfied power. She had no territorial ambitions in Europe, and she expressed reluctance to add to her overseas empire.[12] As the world's leading commercial nation she sought freedom for trade for everyone everywhere, in the expectation that this would bring her the greatest share of the profits. She also favoured peace, not only on moral grounds but because war often interfered with trade. Peace in Europe linked in British eyes with maintenance of the balance of power. Under the first Napoleon France had come near to preponderance on the Continent; and during the reign of Napoleon III in the 1850s and 1860s British foreign policy continued to be suspicious of French ambitions in Europe. France was also a colonial rival, with easy access to the world's oceans. British naval supremacy – which remained a basic assumption of British foreign policy throughout the century – was therefore measured especially with regard to the size of the French fleet (see below, p. 369). But Russia at the other end of Europe was also suspected as a potential enemy because of her aspirations to enter the Mediterranean by gaining control of Constantinople and the Straits. She would then threaten the Suez Canal and the short route to India. Increasingly, too, Russian expansion in Asia was seen as a threat to India itself. Into the twentieth century friction was to continue with France or Russia in areas where they were branching out from Europe – Morocco, Egypt, Turkey, Persia, Afghanistan, and China. Nearer home, the Low Countries constituted another sensitive area for British policy. No great power was to be allowed to gain control of the Dutch or Belgian ports, from which to mount a challenge to British naval or commercial supremacy.

British foreign policy through the nineteenth century tended to favour the central powers of Prussia (from 1871 at the head of the new German Empire) and Austria–Hungary. They were largely landlocked, and they were not colonial rivals. Yet Britain did not enter into alliance with them. She preferred non-commitment until the moment of a particular crisis, when she might then collaborate with one or more powers. Such collaboration could even be undertaken with the French or the

Russians, for association could sometimes constitute a form of control. Britain's island position and naval shield permitted what one French observer described in 1896 as her 'semi-detached policy', since she could not be suddenly attacked. [13] The 'democratic' character of the late-Victorian constitution was often given by foreign secretaries as one reason why Britain could not enter into alliances. War could only be declared if acceptable to public opinion, and ministers could not predict how it might react. 'Tell me what is the *casus belli* and I may be able to give a guess at the conduct which England will pursue. But without such information we not only cannot guess what England will do, but we cannot determine her course beforehand by any pledges or any arguments derived from general interests.' This line could of course be used to excuse the rejection of embarrassing overtures; but Lord Salisbury (who was writing here privately to the Permanent Under-Secretary at the Foreign Office) seems to have genuinely believed it.[14] Certainly, during the last quarter of the nineteenth century no treaty guarantees were made by Britain with respect to the territory or security of any foreign country. Charles Buxton remarked in *Ideas of the Day on Policy* (3rd edn, 1868) how 'a remarkable change' in public opinion had recently occurred with regard to foreign alliances. 'Instead of their being looked on as a source of strength, they are abhorred as possible causes of war.'

Although the power of public opinion was said to prevent the making of alliances, only limited official information was provided about the conduct of British foreign policy – a point of frequent complaint by radicals. Early-Victorian foreign secretaries had submitted much more evidence to Parliament in the shape of blue books than did their secretive late-Victorian successors. Requests for more information were regularly denied by ministers of both parties as 'not in the public interest'.[15] Paradoxically, as Parliament became more democratic in its election its influence over foreign policy seemed to have declined. Radical proposals for the creation of a House of Commons standing committee on foreign affairs were always resisted by the executive. The radicals came nearest to success in enforcing a check over foreign policy on 19 March 1886, when Henry Richard's motion that it was 'not just or expedient' to embark upon war, contract engagements, or add territories to the empire 'without the knowledge and consent of Parliament' was defeated by only six votes. Gladstone had argued that the executive must retain 'great discretion'. 'So far as foreign affairs are concerned,' complained the radical *Nation* (16.12.1911), 'this House of Commons and its two predecessors might never have met.'

3

Lord Palmerston – the great early-Victorian Foreign Secretary – had died in 1865. In his prime he had been, as *The Times* remembered in its obituary (19 October), 'the terror of the Continent'. But even before his death the European power political scene was being transformed. Britain and France had defeated Russia in the Crimean War, and had thereby checked her ambitions in the Balkans and Near East. But when in 1863 the Russians ferociously crushed a rising in Poland, British protests were starkly revealed as bluff. Russia, in short, was reasserting herself. During the Schleswig–Holstein crisis of 1863–4 British efforts to protect the territorial integrity of Denmark were exposed as further bluff. After a short war Schleswig and Holstein were ceded to Austria and Prussia. The Palmerstonian era in international relations had clearly ended: the Bismarckian era was beginning.

While Bismark was making united Germany the major power in Europe, British foreign policy took on a new quietness. France and Russia were still regarded as the main potential enemies; and in this belief the new prospect for Germany was even welcomed by Palmerston a few weeks before his death. 'With a view to the future, it is desirable that Germany, in the aggregate, should be strong, in order to control those two ambitious and aggressive powers, France and Russia.' Palmerston forecast that one day Russia would become 'almost as great as the old Roman Empire'. She could become 'mistress of all Asia, except British India, whenever she chooses to take it'.[16]

The word 'militarism' came into currency in the 1860s with especial reference to Prussia. Bismarck's methods, which involved the use of force abroad and the stifling of opposition at home, were not liked in England; but *The Times* (19.4.1867) remained optimistic about German unification. 'Let the people begin with unity; liberty cannot fail to follow in proper time.'[17] A distinction was also often drawn between militaristic Prussia and the rest of Germany, which was accepted as liberal and cultured. And the fact remained that Germany, unlike France or Russia, presented no immediate or prospective challenge to British overseas interests. The outbreak of the Franco–Prussian War in 1870 therefore found majority British opinion hostile to Napoleon III; but the rapid success of the German drive through northern France began to encourage shifts of attitude, for the extreme humiliation of France was not desired. Gladstone had negotiated agreements with both belligerent powers to respect the neutrality of Belgium during the war and for one year afterwards. When he learned that the Germans intended to annex Alsace–Lorraine, he wanted to rally the neutral European powers in protest, both because annexation would be against the wishes of the inhabitants and because it would give Germany a strategic advantage over France. But the cabinet refused to endorse his proposed initiative, and he was driven to writing an anonymous (but immediately attributed) article in the *Quarterly Review* for October 1870 on 'Germany, France and England'. The article remarked how Germany alone among modern states had made war pay. Happily, England's insular position allowed her to act with detachment, though not (Gladstone emphasized) without concern. Now that British diplomacy had given up trying to be the arbiter of Europe, it could take up the role of arbitrator: 'we should seek to found a moral empire upon the confidence of the nations, not upon their fears, their passions, or their antipathies'.

Gladstone wanted 'Public Right' to prevail on the Continent through the influence and exertions of the 'Concert of Europe'. 'It had censured the aggression of France; it will censure, if need arise, the greed of Germany.' Yet Gladstone was no pacifist. He was always prepared to support policies of intervention and force if these were recommended by the concert of powers. His sense of 'public right' was seriously upset when at the height of the Franco–Prussian War the Russians seized their chance to repudiate the Black Sea clauses of the Treaty of Paris, which had ended the Crimean War.[18] The treaty had neutralized the Black Sea by denying Russia the authority to maintain a fleet there. Gladstone resisted excited demands for immediate war with Russia; but he insisted that any relaxation of the treaty should be made by proper agreement among the powers. This was arranged through a diplomatic conference which met in London during the winter of 1870–1. Throughout the 1870s – with France weakened – Russia was regarded by British ministers as the main threat. Queen Victoria had become convinced by 1878 that war with Russia was 'inevitable now or later'.[19]

Disraeli returned to office in 1874 determined to uphold the interests of England, which he claimed had been neglected because of Gladstone's obsession with 'morality' in foreign relations. Yet Disraeli recognized as readily as his rival that peace constituted a major British interest, although his grandiloquent diplomatic tone contrasted with Gladstone's. He began with no particular foreign policy moves in mind, but waited upon events.

In the second half of 1875 the Eastern Question was reopened as a result of the virtual bankruptcy of the Turkish Government, and its inability to suppress revolts in Bosnia and Herzegovina along with unrest elsewhere. Although both Russia and Austria aspired to gain predominance over any new Balkan nation states, neither wished for an international crisis in the Near East at this stage. They therefore took the lead in suggesting that the troubles be ended by some very innocuous Turkish reforms and by the making of concessions to the insurgents. These were first put to the Turks by the European powers in the Andrássy Note of December 1875 and then in the Berlin Memorandum of May 1876. Disraeli reluctantly supported the first diplomatic intervention, but he refused to back the second. On 24 May a British fleet anchored outside the Dardenelles, nominally because of the unrest in Constantinople but actually as a warning to Russia to keep her hands off Turkey. Here was a gesture in the Palmerstonian manner, which was welcomed by Disraeli's supporters as an indication that Bismarck's control of European diplomacy had been ended. Disraeli claimed that the 'unnatural alliance' of the Three Emperors' League of 1872–3 (Germany, Austria, Russia) would never have arisen if Britain had asserted her 'just position' in Europe.[20]

Disraeli was determined to maintain a Turkish state strong enough to prevent a Russian threat to the British route to India; but he had no objection otherwise to the emancipation of Turkey's outlying provinces. He at once sought to assert Britain's 'just postion' by direct secret negotiations in June 1876 with Russia over autonomy for Bosnia. The Russians seem to have been too suspicious to take these approaches seriously. Disraeli's position at home was compromised by the news, which reached London late in June, of the suppression by Turkish forces in April of a Bulgarian rising, with the massacre of thousands of Christians. Gladstone had retired from politics; but after some hesitation he accepted what he felt to be a Christian 'call' to lead a great public outcry against the massacres, and against Disraeli's pro-Turkish policy which seemed to condone them.[21] Hundreds of public meetings were called during the second half of 1876 to denounce Disraeli's policy, in what became the greatest nineteenth-century agitation on a question of foreign policy. Feeling ran especially strong among Nonconformists in the provinces. Disraeli had become Earl of Beaconsfield in August 1876, and Gladstone equated 'Beaconsfieldism' with immorality and opportunism in foreign policy. The tone of his pamphlet on *The Bulgarian Horrors and the Question of the East* was indeed stronger than his actual proposals. He was widely thought to have recommended the expulsion of the Turks (in an immediately famous phrase) 'bag and baggage' from Europe. In fact, he had called only for the withdrawal of the governing class of Turks, political and military, from Bulgaria. 'Their Zaptiehs and their Mudirs, their Bimbashis and their Yuzbachis, their Kaimakams and their Pashas, one and all, bag and baggage, shall, I hope, clear out from the province they have desolated and profaned.' This meant, in effect, a call for Bulgarian self-government, but Disraeli also agreed to this in September. There was really very little difference between the two over the future of Bulgaria.

The extra-parliamentary agitation was easing by the end of 1876. When Parliament resumed in the spring of 1877 Gladstone found that his cause drew much less support at Westminster than in the country. The Liberals were divided, with the whig group decidedly cool. Gladstone turned again to opinion outside Parliament, and spoke at the foundation meeting of the National Liberal Federation on 31 May 1877. Nevertheless, Disraeli now regained the initiative, although only because Russia over-reached herself. The Russians declared war upon Turkey in April 1877; but their army made only slow progress, and not until March 1878 were they able to impose the Treaty of San Stefano upon the Turks. Disraeli ostentatiously moved Indian troops to Malta. War excitement in England found expression in the original 'jingo' music-hall song, first sung by 'the Great Macdermott' at the London Palladium:[22]

We don't want to fight;
   But, by jingo, if we do,
We've got the men, we've got the ships,
   We've got the money too.

But it was Gladstone, not the Tsar, who was burned in effigy, which may have meant that the jingoes were at least as much interested in domestic as in foreign politics.

The San Stefano treaty created a big Bulgaria as a Russian satellite in the Balkans; it also ceded territory to Russia in Asia Minor, and seemed to leave the Russians with the preponderant influence at Constantinople. All this was unacceptable to the British, and also to the Austrians, who now came together to demand a revision of the treaty. Bismarck, who hoped to restore the Three Emperors' League, and who was therefore keen to reconcile Austria and Russia, offered his services as 'honest broker'. The Congress of Berlin was convened in June 1878, and attended by Disraeli and Lord Salisbury (recently appointed Foreign Secretary) as British representatives. Bismarck tried to save appearances for Russia; but big Bulgaria was trisected, and Turkey-in-Europe re-emerged. Britain secured Cyprus as compensation for Russian acquisitions in the Caucasus, and as a base from which to watch over the Straits and from which to put pressure upon the Turks to introduce internal reforms. Disraeli returned home in triumph, to proclaim from a window of number 10 Downing Street (in a long famous phrase) that he had won 'peace, I hope, with honour'.[23] Gladstone, of course, totally denied this, as he explained in an article characteristically entitled 'England's Mission' (*Nineteenth Century*, September 1878). England, wrote Gladstone, which had helped Belgium, Spain, Portugal, Greece, and Italy to reach national freedom, had now at Berlin 'wrought actively to limit everywhere the area of self-government and to save from the wreck as much as possible of a domination which has contributed more than any other that ever existed to the misery, the debasement, and the extermination of mankind'. But another Liberal, John Morley, believed that the treaty of Berlin had meant the 'virtual ratification of the policy of bag and baggage'.

Notes

1. A. J. P. Taylor, *The Struggle for Mastery in Europe* (1954), p. xxvii.
2. See especially B. Bond, 'Recruiting the Victorian Army, 1870–92' *Victorian Studies*, V (1962); H. J. Hanham, 'Religion and Nationality in the Mid-Victorian Army', in M. R. D. Foot (ed.), *War and Society* (1973); and A. R. Skelley, *The Victorian Army at Home* (1977).
3. See especially G. Harries-Jenkins, *The Army in Victorian Society* (1977).
4. See especially B. Bond, 'Prelude to the Cardwell Reforms, 1856–68', *Journal of the Royal United Services Institution*, CVI (1961); and B. Bond, 'The Effect of the Cardwell Reforms in Army Organization, 1874–1904', *ibid.*, CV (1960). Also C. Barnett, *Britain and Her Army, 1509–1970* (1970), Chs. 13, 14.

5. See H. Cunningham, *The Volunteer Force* (1975).

6. T. H. Ward (ed.), *The Reign of Queen Victoria* (1887), I, p. 185. See especially B. Bond (ed.), *Victorian Military Campaigns* (1967); and D. Featherstone, *Colonial Small Wars, 1837–1901* (1973).

7. Sir C. Dilke, *The Present Position of European Politics* (1887), p. 306.

8. See I. F. Clarke, *Voices Prophesying War, 1763–1984* (1966), Ch. 2.

9. M. O'Rell, *John Bull et Son Ile* (1884), p. 4; R. Fulford (ed.), *Darling Child* (1976), p. 229.

10. R. Jefferies, *The Life of the Fields* (1892), pp. 218–9. See especially H. C. Allen, *The Anglo-American Relationship Since 1783* (1959); and R. L. Rapson, *Britons View America* (1971).

11. See especially A. Cook, *The Alabama Claims* (1975).

12. See, in general, C. J. Lowe, *The Reluctant Imperialists* (1967); and K. Bourne, *The Foreign Policy of Victorian England, 1830–1902* (1970). Also D. C. M. Platt, *Finance, Trade and Politics in British Foreign Policy, 1815–1914* (1968).

13. F. de Presenssé, 'England and the Continental Alliances', *Nineteenth Century*, November 1896, p. 684.

14. C. Howard, *Britain and the Casus Belli, 1822–1902* (1974), p. 131.

15. H. Temperley and Lillian M. Penson (eds.), *A Century of Diplomatic Blue Books* (1966), p. ix.

16. K. Bourne, *The Foreign Policy of Victorian England, 1830–1902* (1970), p. 382. See especially W. E. Mosse, *The European Powers and the German Question, 1848–1871* (1958); and R. Millman, *British Foreign Policy and the Coming of the Franco-Prussian War* (1965).

17. See especially R. J. Sontag, *Germany and England* (1969).

18. See W. E. Mosse, *The Rise and Fall of the Crimean System, 1855–71* (1963), Ch. VI.

19. *Letters of Queen Victoria*, second series (1926), II, p. 597. See especially R. W. Seton Watson, *Disraeli, Gladstone and the Eastern Question* (1962); W. N. Medlicott, *The Congress of Berlin and After* (2nd edn, 1963); and M. S. Anderson, *The Eastern Question* (1968), Chs. 6–8.

20. W. F. Monypenny and G. E. Buckle, *Life of Benjamin Disraeli, Earl of Beaconsfield* (2nd edn, 1929), II, p. 903. See especially W. N. Medlicott, 'Bismarck and Beaconsfield', in A. O. Sarkissian (ed.), *Studies in Diplomatic History and Historiography* (1961).

21. See especially R. T. Shannon, *Gladstone and the Bulgarian Agitation, 1876* (2nd edn, 1975). Also W. N. Medlicott, 'Gladstone and the Turks', *History*, XIII (1928).

22. See H. Cunningham, 'Jingoism and the Working Classes, 1877–78', *Bulletin of Labour History*, no. 19 (1969); and L. Senelick, 'Politics as Entertainment: Victorian Music-Hall Songs', *Victorian Studies*, XIX (1975), pp. 168–71.

23. *The Times*, 17 July 1878.

Fin de siècle, 1880–1900

Chapter 11

Introduction: *'An age of rapid results'*

1

As early as 12 November 1870 *Punch* was pointing out that the century was getting old, that it had already run the biblical three score years and ten. A pervasive sense of ending was apparent in society by the 1880s, not only in England but also in Europe. By 1890 the idea of 'fin de siècle' was sufficiently commonplace for it to become the title of a French play. When performed in the same year in London, the play publicized the phrase with such success that *Punch* was eventually to complain (29 August 1891) of 'that pest-term, and its fellow, "modernity"'.[1] The popularity of these expressions helped to exaggerate the mood which they were describing, encouraging a straining after pessimism on the one hand and after novelty on the other:

'Nowadays all the married men live like bachelors, and all the bachelors like married men.'
'*Fin de siècle*,' murmured Lord Henry.
'*Fin du globe*,' answered his hostess.

So ran the conversation in Oscar Wilde's *Picture of Dorian Gray* (1891).

The century was ending for an England that was becoming more and more urbanized and industrialized. By 1866, as noticed earlier, the editor of *Punch* was already asking for John Bull to be drawn with a more modern look. In 1883 John Ruskin went so far as to complain because this symbol of Englishness was still represented as a farmer, never as a manufacturer or shopkeeper.[2] Not that Ruskin liked the new life of the cities and towns. He complained in the *Nineteenth Century* for June 1880 of 'the disgrace and grief resulting from the mere trampling pressure and electric friction of town life'. Ruskin was here still thinking in the 'high pressure' steam-engine terms which have already been indicated as characteristic of the 1860s and 1870s, though he updated his remarks by adding a reference to electricity. Middle-class people of the 1880s were convinced that any pressure felt in earlier times had been much less than the pressure under which they found themselves – from the 'great depression' in business, from foreign competition in trade, from the Irish demand for Home Rule, from 'socialism'. Even the socialists themselves felt under strain. Beatrice Webb remarked in her diary (11.10.1889) how men talked of needing courage to meet death:

'alas, in these terrible days of mental pressure it is courage to *live* that we lack most'. An article on 'The Progress of Socialism' (*Contemporary Review*, January 1879) by William Cunningham argued that while the miseries of the poor were obvious, the 'cares of the rich' could be no less oppressive. 'The terrible anxieties of men of business, the harassing struggle against unceasing competition, the feverish excitements of speculative dealings, are surely signs of a most unhealthy social state.' The Registrar-General's *Annual Report* for 1885 pointed out how the death rate was rising among men over 35 and women over 45, even though it was falling at lower ages. 'That the struggle for existence is daily becoming more and more severe, and that feverish excitement and reckless expenditure are rapidly encroaching on repose and leisure, are matters of common observation. The wear and tear of life are greater, and vitality is sooner exhausted.'

In the 1860s J. A. Froude had drawn attention to the acceleration of change. It was still accelerating twenty years later. 'This is an age of rapid results,' wrote J. M. Whistler, the artist and wit, 'when remedies insist upon their diseases, that science shall triumph and no time be lost.'[3] Mental adjustment to such acceleration was proving difficult. Reactions were often exaggerated. 'Every accident is a "catastrophe"; every misfortune a "calamity"; every ailment a mortal disease.' So complained H. D. Traill in *Macmillan's Magazine* for November 1884. Did accelerating change always bring benefits? Had the Victorian experience demonstrated that 'progress' was certain? Tennyson's late poem, *Locksley Hall Sixty Years After* (1886) deplored the spread during Victoria's reign of industry, of town life, and of democracy:

> There among the glooming alleys Progress halts on palsied feet,
> Crime and Hunger cast our maidens by the thousand on the street.

How could progress be inevitable when scientists had now shown that time was not on man's side? The second law of thermodynamics, which became widely known in the 1890s, indicated that the solar system would eventually burn itself out. In *The Time Machine* (1895) H. G. Wells described the ultimate death of life on earth. Here then were three different voices – Wilde, who lived in the present; Tennyson, who preferred the past; Wells, who looked to the future – all sharing in the *fin de siècle* mood of unsettlement. Of course, optimists could still be found. Wells himself refused to be a pessimist. He concluded *The Time Machine* with the admission that 'the Advancement of Mankind' might end in nothingness. But he added a brave qualification. 'If that is so it remains for us to live as though it were not so.' Courage would be needed to find happiness while the century was dying.

Notes

1. *Notes & Queries*, 10 January 1891, p. 40. See also M. Nordau, *Degeneration* (1895), esp. book 1.
2. E. T. Cook and A. Wedderburn (eds.), *Works of John Ruskin*, XXXIII (1908), p. 365.
3. J. M. Whistler, *The Gentle Art of Making Enemies* (3rd edn, 1904), p. 285.

Chapter 12

Economic life: *'What makes the difference between good and bad times?'*

1

The population of England and Wales, and of the United Kingdom as a whole, was still growing fast during the last twenty years of the nineteenth century:

	England and Wales	United Kingdom
1881	26,000,000	34,900,000
1891	29,000,000	37,700,000
1901	32,500,000	41,500,000

In 1881 births in England and Wales numbered 884,000, deaths 492,000: by 1901 these totals had reached respectively 930,000 and 552,000. But the birth rate was now falling rapidly:[1]

	Births per thousand	Deaths per thousand
1876–80	35.4	20.8
1881–5	33.5	19.4
1886–90	31.4	18.9
1891–5	30.5	18.7
1896–1900	29.3	17.7

Both birth and death rates still varied widely from place to place:[2]

	1871-1881		1881-1891		1891-1901	
	Birth-rate	Death-rate	Birth-rate	Death-rate	Birth-rate	Death-rate
Towns:						
Large:						
London	34.7	21.4	32.9	19.3	29.8	17.9
8 Northern	38.7	24.6	34.6	21.8	31.9	20.4
Textile:						
22 Northern	36.9	23.8	31.5	20.8	27.8	19.4
Residential:						
9 Northern	30.6	20.7	27.7	18.5	25.3	17.9
26 Southern	29.4	18.2	27.3	16.4	24.5	15.6
Colliery districts:						
9 Northern	41.9	23.1	36.9	19.8	35.9	19.2

	1871-1881		1881-1891		1891-1901	
	Birth-rate	Death-rate	Birth-rate	Death-rate	Birth-rate	Death-rate
Rural residues:						
12 Northern	32.0	19.4	29.5	17.5	27.6	17.1
12 Southern	31.3	18.2	29.3	16.7	26.0	15.8

The decline of the birth rate in rural England was influenced by heavy emigration of young potential parents. In the textile districts the birth rate changed from being one of the highest to one of the lowest. The colliery districts, by contrast, maintained a birth rate well above the national average, though even here it was falling.

The large families of middle-class mid-Victorian England were often regarded by parents with more dismay than satisfaction. Queen Victoria, who herself bore four sons and four daughters, found childbearing distasteful and large families unappealing. When the Princess of Wales produced her fourth child and Victoria's fourteenth grandchild in 1868 the queen dismissed the event as 'very uninteresting – for it seems to me to go on like rabbits in Windsor Park!'[3] The trend in family size was indeed about to move downwards. Marriages of the 1860s which lasted twenty or more years produced an average of 6.16 live births; those of the 1870s 5.8; of the 1880s 5.3; and of the 1890s 4.13.[4] The widely read story of *Ginx's Baby, His Birth and Other Misfortunes*, first published in 1870 and often reprinted, was about the thirteenth child of a London navvy. It began life as an unwanted infant, and ended it by committing suicide as a surplus adult who could not find work. The working-class ideal was for children to work early and regularly; and the complaint against large families was not (as often with middle-class parents) about the cost of education but about shortage of child employment.

Excessive childbearing remained one cause of the high death rates both for children and for mothers, high even among the middle and upper classes. The mortality rate for infants under one year was 160 per 1,000 births in England and Wales in 1870; this figure dropped to the 130s during the 1880s, but by the end of the century it had returned to the level of thirty years earlier. On the mother's side, puerperal fever (septic poisoning) was the most common cause of death from childbirth. Since this infection was not a consequence either of poverty, overcrowding, or poor nutrition, middle-class women were as much at risk as working-class women. Indeed, the doctors whom only better-off mothers could afford were likely carriers of infection. Puerperal fever reached epidemic proportions in the early 1870s, and its toll thereafter was only reduced to the still high rate of 1.9 per 1,000 births, which persisted into the 1890s. In the middle-class London suburb of Camberwell in the 1880s the maternal death rate from childbirth remained at an average of 3.65 per 1,000 births. Yet delayed mortality from exhaustion and ill-health caused by excessive childbearing was not counted in these sad statistics. After Gladstone's sister-in-law, Lady Lyttleton, had borne eleven children, she was told by her doctor that she would probably die if she conceived again. Asked why she did not tell her husband of this warning, she replied, 'My dear, we never spoke about anything so nasty.' She gave birth to a son (a future Colonial Secretary) in 1857, but never recovered and died six months later. 'All her strength was given to her twelve children,' wrote her husband with affection but also with acquiescence, '. . . and the twelfth baby was the last gallant effort of the high mettled racer.'[5]

There was obviously no question here of discussion between husband and wife about attempting some form of family limitation. Nevertheless, from the 1850s, if not earlier, the practice of limitation seems to have been spreading among the middle classes.[6] Professional men and their wives – barristers, bankers, physicians, and the like – seem to have led the way. After mid-century in middle-class Camberwell the birth rate per thousand females aged 20–44 was well below the London average:[7]

	1851–60	1861–70
Camberwell	1.23	1.15
London	1.41	1.51

These were years of predominant prosperity, so this reduction in middle-class fertility cannot have been extensively encouraged by business uncertainties. But economics probably played a major part in the sense that middle-class expectations seem to have been growing fast during these years. Prosperity led the middle classes to seek an improving standard of living, bigger houses, more servants, private carriages – and fewer children.

The 1874 Births and Deaths Registration Act succeeded in enforcing almost complete registration for the first time. The published figures for all years before complete enforcement had not been corrected for under-registration.[8] With such correction, the birth rate seems to have reached its Victorian peak not in 1876 (as the official returns suggested) but in the early 1860s:

	Birth rate per thousand population	
	Registered births	Corrected
1851–5	33.8	35.5
1856–60	34.3	35.5
1861–5	35.0	35.8
1866–70	35.1	35.7
1871–5	35.4	35.7
1876–80	35.2	35.4

Among the working classes abortion continued to be widely practised. In addition, the Bradlaugh–Besant case of 1877–8 gave national and long-lasting publicity to the 'neo-Malthusian' argument for family limitation, and to the existence of contraceptive devices to assist such limitation.[9] *Coitus interruptus* had traditionally been the most usual method, and it remained the most popular even after mechanical and chemical contraceptives had become increasingly available. But these devices all seem to have come into greater use, and to have been steadily improved, during the second and third quarters of the nineteenth century. From the 1820s onwards works on methods of family limitation had always been available, even though their existence was never noticed in 'respectable' quarters. Charles Bradlaugh and Mrs Annie Besant were tried in 1877–8 for re-issuing one such work – Charles Knowles's *The Fruits of Philosophy*, originally published in the 1830s. This had been sold for over forty years; but in 1876 a Bristol bookseller was sentenced to two years hard labour for allegedly issuing an edition interleaved with obscene drawings. Bradlaugh, who had long been an advocate of family limitation for all classes, and Mrs Besant set out to force a test case by re-publishing the pamphlet and by telling the police of the fact. Why did the authorities decide to accept the challenge? Probably because Bradlaugh was already notorious as an atheist. The outcome was massive publicity for the pair and their cause. Sales of *The Fruits of Philosophy* jumped to perhaps 125,000 copies during the first half of 1877.

Bradlaugh and Mrs Besant were charged with intended incitement 'to indecent, obscene, unnatural, and immoral practices', and with obscene publication. In June 1877 they were found guilty of the latter offence, though not of intention to corrupt. They were subsequently sentenced to six months' imprisonment; but their conviction was overturned on appeal in February 1878. This reversal was only secured on technical grounds; yet the defendants persisted in publishing *The Fruits of Philosophy* until certain that no further action would be taken against them. The pamphlet was then withdrawn in favour of a new work by Mrs Besant, *The Law of Population*. By 1891 this had sold 175,000 copies. The 'respectable' press was generally hostile to Bradlaugh and Mrs Besant. Fear of 'consequences' was regarded by many papers as the main check upon mass immorality. Other papers rejected the Malthusian assumption that the world could become over-populated; and even those which accepted the existence of the over-population danger felt that they could not fully discuss family limitation. The Malthusian League was formed in 1877. Although it always remained an organization of only a few hundred enthusiasts, it reiterated throughout the late-Victorian and Edwardian years the 'truth' that over-population was '*the* cause of poverty'.[10]

By the 1880s advertisements for contraceptive devices were appearing in women's magazines and health manuals. Mass production was beginning.[11] Significantly, the words 'contraception' and 'contraceptive' came into use about this time. Not until the Edwardian period, however, was it widely suggested that family limitation (by whatever means) was the main cause of the steady fall in the birth rate. Two-thirds of women born between 1870 and 1884, who were wives of professional or salaried men, have been estimated as attempting some form of fertility control. Among the wives of wage earners and labourers nearly half were apparently making the attempt.[12] Very little evidence has survived about individual examples. But Hannah Mitchell, a pioneer socialist and feminist, remembered in her autobiography how ideas of family limitation were gaining circulation in the Lancashire cotton district by the 1890s. 'Limiting the population as a means of fighting poverty was one of the new ideas.' She herself had only one child.[13] Religious opinion remained firmly opposed to artificial interference with conception; but by the 1890s the Nonconformist *Christian World* (15.6.1893) was accepting use of the 'safe period' as a form of pregnancy control. Yet this practice can hardly have contributed to the fall in the birth rate, since prevailing medical opinion had placed the time of safety about the middle of the menstrual cycle, which was likely to have been for most women the time of highest risk.[14]

2

As the birth rate fell so did the death rate. It was still as high as 20.5 per thousand in 1880; but it started to drop markedly during the 1890s, and was down to 16.9 by 1901. At last, communicable diseases – tuberculosis, scarlet fever, diarrhoea, dysentry – were coming under control (even though their nature was not yet always medically understood) thanks to public health supervision, improved personal hygiene, and higher individual resistance to disease.[15] Much the largest part of this decline in mortality arose from a lessening of the incidence of tuberculosis. This seems to have followed not from medical measures but from improved resistance to infection, which came with better standards of nutrition and housing. Indeed, the infectious nature of the disease was not established until 1882, and comparatively few sanatoria had been opened by the end of the century. Only the control of smallpox through vaccination was directly a result of medical therapy. Diphtheria was even on the increase at the end of the century. And non-communicable diseases – of the circulation, digestion, respiratory system, and the rest – remained at least as threatening to life as fifty years earlier. Of lives saved in the 1890s which would not have been saved in the 1850s, it has been estimated that nearly half (47.2 per cent) were saved from death by tuberculosis. 22.9 per cent escaped death from typhus, enteric, and similar fevers, 20.3 per cent from scarlet fever, 8.9 per cent from diarrhoea, dysentry, and cholera, 6.1 from smallpox. The most marked reduction in tuberculosis deaths occurred among people in their twenties and early thirties. But by the end of the century everyone up to the age of 44 enjoyed a significantly better chance of survival, age for age, than at mid-century – with the important exception of infants under one year.

Awareness of the hazards of parenthood may have been one factor behind the late-Victorian decline in the marriage rate. The rate for England and Wales, corrected to take account of the proportion of marriageable persons in the population, fell markedly and steadily from 19.6 per 1,000 in 1871 to 17.6 in 1881 and down to 15.9 by 1901.[16] One of the longest remembered of *Punch*'s quips was its 'Advice to Persons About to Marry: Don't'. This had first appeared in *Punch*'s almanack for January 1845; but a historian of the journal remarked how it was still being frequently repeated in the 1890s.[17] The average age of marriage, which stood at 25.6 years for men and 24.2 for women in 1873, rose gradually thereafter to 26.5 and 25.0 by the mid 1890s. Among men, differences of several years in age at marriage continued between classes. Among women of all classes young marriage was becoming less frequent. The percentage of married females in the 20–24 age group fell from over one-third to less than one-quarter between 1871 and 1911. 'Dowager. "It's been the worst season I can remember, Sir James! All the men seem to have got married, and none of the girls!"' (*Punch*, 15.12.1884).

More commonly, though, it was the reluctance of bridegrooms that was the cause of complaint among all classes. Within the London working class the initiative in putting up the banns and in arranging a marriage was usually taken by the woman, often after she had become pregnant. Marriage celebrations rarely attracted as much expense and attention as a working-class funeral. The demands of employment meant that most working-class weddings took place on a Saturday or Sunday. The prospect of a lifetime of childbearing and poverty lay ahead for most girls. At the turn of the century the life expectation of a woman of 20 was 46 years. Approximately one-third of this was likely to be given to the physiological and emotional demands of childbearing and maternal care of infants.[18]

The livelier spirits, both married and unmarried, among the working classes could always think of emigration as a way of escape from dismal prospects in town or country. The 1880s witnessed a great surge overseas. The United States was still the favourite destination for both skilled and unskilled workmen, except for the years 1876–85 when agricultural labourers preferred Australia and New Zealand:[19]

	Emigration from the United Kingdom			Annual averages (nearest 1,000)		
	Total	USA	British North America	Australia/ New Zealand	South Africa	Total Empire	All other countries
1871–80	168	109	18	30	5	53	6
1881–90	256	172	30	37	8	75	9
1891–1900	174	114	19	13	17	49	11

Migration by countrymen and women into the towns was reduced in the 1880s because of this exodus overseas, but it revived in the 1890s:[20]

Net gain or loss by migration in England (in thousands)			
	London	Other towns	Colliery districts	Rural areas
1871–81	+307	+297	+84	—837
1881–91	+169	— 31	+90	—845
1891–1901	+226	+294	+85	—660

The magnetism of the north of England industrial towns was diminishing. London and its satellites were now regarded as offering greater opportunities for individual advancement:[21]

	Gain or loss by migration (in thousands)	
	1881–91	1891–1901
North of England		
8 large towns	+21.4	—143.6
22 textile towns	+3.7	—40.6
14 industrial towns	—88.6	—51.4
7 old towns	—17.1	—10.3
9 residential towns	+21.7	+59.7
South of England		
London	+168.9	+226.5
11 industrial towns	—5.9	+25.4
13 old towns	—24.3	+1.5
26 residential towns	+44.8	+83.4
16 military towns	+13.1	+72.5

This heavy population movement from country to town or overseas meant that the numbers employed in agriculture continued to decline during the last quarter of the nineteenth century. Manufacturing continued to absorb more labour, though its percentage share of the employed labour force did not increase much further. In proportionate terms trade and commerce were becoming more important, as were the service industries, government employment, and the professions:[22]

	Percentage distribution of the labour force in Great Britain (as percentages of the total occupied population)				
	Agriculture, forestry, fishing	Manufacture, mining, industry	Trade and transport	Domestic and personal	Public, professional and all other
1871	15.1	43.1	19.6	15.3	6.8
1881	12.6	43.5	21.3	15.4	7.3
1891	10.5	43.9	22.6	15.8	7.1
1901	8.7	46.3	21.4	14.1	9.6

The occupied population of England and Wales has been estimated at:[23]

1881		1891		1901	
Male	Female	Male	Female	Male	Female
7,800,000	3,400,000	8,800,000	3,800,000	10,200,000	4,200,000

In 1891 the major occupations offered employment as follows:

	Male	Female	Total	1871 Total
Agriculture	1,141,000	51,000	1,192,000	1,436,000
Mining	559,000	5,000	564,000	377,000
Building and roadmaking	833,000	3,000	836,000	664,000
Manufacturing	2,609,000	1,530,000	4,139,000	3,358,000
Transport	816,000	10,000	826,000	523,000
Dealing	851,000	298,000	1,149,000	838,000
Banking and insurance	291,000	19,000	310,000	119,000
Public service and professions	563,000	265,000	828,000	578,000
Domestic service	359,000	1,632,000	1,991,000	1,683,000

3

These were the years of the 'great depression' in British industry and agriculture, so-called at the time and since.[24] Exports were now growing only slowly, in contrast to the rapid growth of earlier years:[25]

	Textiles		Cottons		Iron and Steel		Machinery		Coal		Total
	£m.	%	£m.	%	£m.	%	£m.	%	£m.	%	£m.
1860-9	98.5	62	57.6	36	24.0	15	4.6	3	4.5	3	159.7
1870-9	118.6	55	71.5	33	34.9	16	7.7	4	8.8	4	218.1
1880-9	114.1	49	73.3	32	35.3	15	11.8	5	10.5	5	230.3
1890-9	104.3	44	67.2	28	32.5	14	16.1	7	17.5	7	237.1

(At current prices: annual averages)

Imports, on the other hand, were still increasing, even if no longer so fast as in the 1850s and 1860s:[26]

| | Grain and Flour | | Groceries | | Meat, dairy produce | | Textile raw materials | | Other raw materials | | Manu-factured goods | | Total |
	£m.	%	£m.	%	£m.	%	£m.	%	£m.	%	£m.	%	£m.
1855–9	19.6	12	24.7	15	5.0	3	50.4	30	26.3	16	2.8	2	169.5
1860–9	31.9	12	33.9	13	12.0	5	90.7	35	32.1	12	5.0	2	260.9
1870–9	52.0	14	49.4	14	23.4	7	95.8	27	44.2	12	9.9	3	360.6
1880–9	55.1	14	44.7	11	36.8	9	94.9	24	45.5	12	12.3	3	393.6
1890–9	55.1	13	42.1	10	51.7	12	89.8	21	52.0	12	15.7	4	435.8

(Annual averages)

The imbalance on visible trade was extending, although the overall balance of payments was kept favourable through repeatedly larger invisible earnings:[27]

	Balance of visible trade	Net shipping earnings	Profits, interest, dividends	Insurance, brokerage, commissions	All other	Balance of invisible trade	Net balance
1871–5	−64	+51	+83	+16	−12	+139	+75
1876–80	−124	+54	+88	+16	−9	+149	+25
1881–5	−99	+60	+96	+16	−11	+161	+61
1886–90	−89	+57	+115	+15	−11	+177	+88
1891–5	−134	+57	+124	+15	−10	+186	+52
1896–1900	−159	+62	+132	+16	−11	+199	+40

(Annual averages in £m.)

How 'depressed' then was the British economy during the last quarter of the nineteenth century? The wheat-growing branch of agriculture was forced to contract rapidly and painfully in the face of cheap American competition; but no major sector of manufacturing industry suffered so severely as wheat farming. The eight to ten year trade cycle still brought upswings in industrial activity as well as downturns, even though these upswings could not equal the great boom of the early 1870s. Alarmists tended to make their comparisons with these very exceptional years. Certainly, the later 1870s, middle 1880s, and middle 1890s were all periods of deep economic depression. This was reflected in the unemployment statistics, which were collected at that time only for workmen in certain skilled trades where unemployment benefit was paid. Unemployment among these workers rose from under 1 per cent in the boom year of 1872 to heights of 11.4 per cent in 1879 and 10.2 per cent in 1886. Industrial output fell in the worst years to below 90 per cent of capacity.

Such was the measure of the late-Victorian depression. Yet those fortunate enough to remain in work found their standards of living not depressed but rising. Cutbacks in prices and profit margins, plus the influx of cheap foreign food, meant that overall real wages rose fairly steadily. They were improving even while labour leaders were complaining bitterly in the 1880s about unemployment. At this same time employers, for their part, were bemoaning the decline in prices and profits. These various complaints all encouraged the feeling that the depression was much more general and permanent than was really the case. 'Businessmen say that never has trade been so bad or its prospects so gloomy,' wrote Mrs Craik, the novelist, in the *Contemporary Review* for September 1886. 'Is this only a temporary crisis? Or a warning of that decadence which comes to all nations?'

Some detached observers did try to emphasize the circumscribed nature of the crisis. 'The so-called depression of trade in recent years would seem to be more correctly described as a fall in the value of investments and capital employed in industry; it is a genuine depression as regards capital and profits, but wages on the whole have advanced, and goods have been cheapened.' So argued G. Armitage-Smith, an economist, at the turn of the century.[28] Statistics showed the truth of this distinction. Wholesale prices fell almost continuously from the mid 1870s till the mid 1890s:

	Coal and metals	Textile fibres	Grains	Animal products	Sugar, tea, tobacco, coffee and cocoa	Total index
	Board of Trade wholesale price indices (1871–5 = 100)					
1871–5	100	100	100	100	100	100
1876–80	66.7	85.4	95.4	102.6	90.2	92.0
1881–5	60.7	76.9	83.7	98.6	75.1	83.6
1886–90	61.5	66.5	67.7	84.8	56.8	70.6
1891–5	63.6	60.3	66.0	84.6	53.7	68.3

Prices of milk, butter, meat, eggs, and fruit held up best because of growing demand from people who found themselves able to diversify their diet thanks to price falls for other foodstuffs and necessities. Profits fell roughly in step with prices, to a low point in the mid 1890s:[29]

	Profits/industrial income (%)	Profits/national income (%)
1865–9	46.0	26.4
1870–4	47.7	29.4
1875–9	43.3	26.1
1880–4	42.6	25.7
1885–9	42.2	25.2
1890–4	37.8	22.7

On the other hand, real wages were moving up:[30]

Money wages and real wages in the United Kingdom (1850=100)

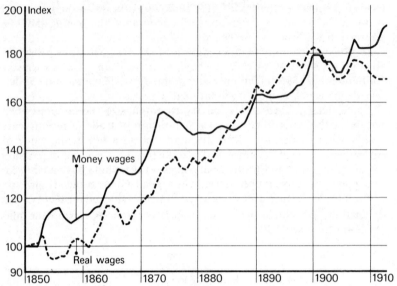

These figures make no allowances for unemployment

Here was an 80 per cent rise in real wages between the middle and the end of the century. And about half of this remarkable upsurge occurred during the years of 'depression':

	Wages (%)	Prices and rent (%)	Real wages (%)
1850–4 to 1873–7	+41	+11	+32
1873–7 to 1880–4	−4	−7	+3
1880–4 to 1900–2	+21	−8	+32
1873–7 to 1900–2	+17	−14	+36
1850–4 to 1900–2	+70	−5	+80

Armitage-Smith, the contemporary economist already quoted, came near to denying the existence of depression at all. He admitted that businessmen had been complaining strongly about 'dulness in trade'. He preferred, however, to describe trade not as dull, merely as 'quieter but steadier than formerly; while there have been no periods of violent excitement and huge profits, commercial crises, once frequent and very acute, have been fewer and less disastrous in their effects during the past twenty-five years.' It was certainly true that the disastrous impact of the Gurney crash of 1866 was remembered in 1890 when the great finance house of Barings was about to collapse. This time the Bank of England led a bold and successful rescue operation. Nevertheless, Armitage-

Smith had to admit that business profits had 'steadily declined' during recent years; and under ,uch pressure neither landowners nor industrialists could be expected to share his sober satisfaction. Their political influence secured the appointment of Royal Commissions on Agricultural Depression (1879–82 and 1893–7) and on Depression of Trade and Industry (1885–6).

Despite the proneness of businessmen to gloom, industrial output was still growing. This was emphasized in an optimistic article by a statistician, M. G. Mulhall, on 'Ten Years of National Growth' in the *Contemporary Review* for December 1886. 'So far from any falling-off in commerce, there has been a healthy increase, and the decline of prices, however injurious to some interests, has been on the whole advantageous to the country.' United Kingdom coal production, for example, as Mulhall explained, had increased rapidly even during the years from the end of the boom of the early 1870s through the trough of the late 1870s and into the second trough of the mid 1880s. It grew from under 127 million tons in 1874 to about 160 million tons during the mid 1880s. The coal export trade, especially in steam coal for ships, was responsible for much of this increase. Exports first passed 10 million tons per year in 1867, reached double this by 1883, and treble by 1894. Yet coalowners still complained about low prices and profits.[31]

Increasing coal exports certainly brought no benefit to manufacturing industry. Cotton had long been the biggest export industry, but during the last quarter of the century it seemed to have lost much of its dynamism.[32] The value of textile exports (including cottons) actually fell. This happened admittedly at a time of falling prices; but the cotton industry was plainly no longer a growth centre. Its response to heightened foreign tariffs and competition was not so much to modernize its products or methods as to switch exports increasingly to traditional-style markets in India and the Far East. On the technical side most cotton spinners preferred to continue with mule spinning as against the newer ring spinning developed in the United States. There may have been a case for this – balancing returns on capital already invested against fresh capital outlay needed for change, and bearing in mind that mule spinning was well suited for the medium and fine counts in which Lancashire specialized. But psychologically it was damaging. Innovation no longer set the pace.

This was true of other industries besides cotton. In the steel industry the case was particularly striking, in that many key inventions were British in origin and yet their application gave increasing advantage to foreign rivals.[33] These were the years when large-scale production of steel at low cost first became possible, and it began to replace iron. The railways changed to steel rails in the 1870s, and shipbuilders from iron to steel hulls in the 1880s. Henry Bessemer's invention of the converter in 1856 was the first breakthrough. Eleven years later the Siemens open-hearth process was made commercially practicable by a Frenchman, Pierre Martin. William Siemens was a German-born metallurgist who became a British subject. Both these processes required non-phosphoric ores, which were scarcer than ordinary phosphoric ironstone. Then at the end of the 1870s Gilchrist Thomas found a way to make cheap steel from phosphoric ore. British steelmakers, however, proved reluctant to adopt this process. As late as 1900 only about 16 per cent of the United Kingdom output of steel ingots and castings was made by the Thomas 'basic' process, the rest by the 'acid' process which required non-phosphoric ore.

Up to the end of the 1870s British steel production kept well ahead by volume. Output more than tripled during the decade, to reach 1 million tons for the first time in 1879. This was more than the production of Germany, France, and Belgium combined. But the Gilchrist Thomas process was now eagerly adopted on the Continent. British output still grew steadily during the 1880s, but that of Germany and the United States bounded forward. In 1886 United States steel output first passed that of Britain, and from 1893 so did that of Germany. At the end of the nineteenth century Britain, which into the 1880s had led the world in steel manufacture, found herself well down in third place:[34]

| | Steel production as percentage of world production | | |
	United Kingdom	Germany	United States
1875–9	35.9	16.6	26.0
1880–4	32.7	17.7	28.4
1885–9	31.8	17.8	31.4
1890–4	24.6	21.4	33.7
1895–9	19.8	22.5	35.4

As striking as the expansion of steel making in the late nineteenth century was the development of large-scale production of chemicals.[35] Britain clung to the Leblanc method of alkali manufacture into the twentieth century, long after Germany and France had adopted the cheaper Solvay process. In the synthetic dyestuffs branch of the industry the Germans gained such predominance that on the outbreak of war in 1914 they supplied the British market with 80 per cent of its artificial dyes; and all the khaki used for soldiers' uniforms was found to come from the enemy town of Stuttgart. For some chemical products, admittedly – such as soap, paint, certain fertilizers and heavy chemicals – Britain rivalled the German output both in quality and quantity.

Even newer than the chemical industry, and equally important for continuing economic advance, was the electrical industry.[36] Many of the pioneers had been British – Michael Faraday, J. W. Swan, James Clerk-Maxwell. Yet by 1913 the output of British electrical products and equipment was less than half that of Germany. Moreover, three of the four largest manufacturers of electrical goods in Britain were offshoots of giant American or German firms. The development and use of machine-tools was another field where foreign rivals seemed generally more enterprising by the end of the century.[37] The Americans were encouraged to find new machines and methods by the growing size of their engineering firms; in Britain, by contrast, small general engineering jobbing shops remained numerous. Such firms did not provide a strong market for new machinery, especially as they tended to think in terms of one-off orders rather than standardized long production runs. The bicycle industry, however, did make the breakthrough to large-scale production in the 1890s; and this created a big demand for machine-tools to make bicycles for the world. In 1909 Britain overtook Germany as the leading exporter, and by 1913 British exports were worth over £600,000 against Germany's £350,000.[38]

British businessmen were thus not always lacking in enterprise. To take a notable example, Britain continued to lead the world in shipbuilding, both for British shipowners and for foreigners.[39] These were the years when sail gave way to steam, and iron to steel; but this made no difference to Britain's predominance. Sales of British ships abroad doubled between 1892–6 and 1909–13, from just under 500,000 gross tons per year to just over 1 million. German competition had to be watched, but German costs remained too high for world markets. The huge size of the British mercantile marine – about one-third of world tonnage from the 1860s right to 1914 – provided a strong home market. This made possible the extensive specialization necessary for success. Not that the industry hurried into modernization. Here was a case where caution and attachment to tried methods proved economically advantageous.

Through the Edwardian years Britain was building about 60 per cent of all ships launched. British ships were carrying about one-half of world seaborne trade in the early 1900s, including nearly all the trade within the British Empire. German competition was growing on world long-haul routes; but only on the North Atlantic passenger services did the German lines come near to capturing an equal share of the traffic.[40]

Another successful expression of late-Victorian and Edwardian enterprise centred round the processing, distribution, and sale of food and consumer goods for the new mass urban market.[41] The early Victorians had been served by simple local haberdashers, chandlers, mercers, and like retailers. Now these old local outlets began to be challenged by 'multiple' stores, which sold nationally-marketed products such as Pears' soap, Cadbury's chocolates, and Player's cigarettes. All this new enterprise depended upon managerial skills of a high order, and upon the services of a large new workforce.

4

Though the blanket idea of a 'great depression' was misleading, Britain's overall economic performance during the last quarter of the nineteenth century was certainly much less lively than during its first three-quarters. The industrial growth rate dropped by about one-half:[42]

	Percentage growth rates of industrial production (corrected for unemployment)
1860s–1870s	33.2
1870s–1880s	20.8
1880s–1890s	17.4
1890s–1900s	17.9

This cannot be explained as an inevitable consequence of the ending of Britain's industrial hegemony, for after the First World War the growth rate was to revive again. It happened because Britain's industrial base remained too narrow. As late as 1907, 46 per cent of total output and 70 per cent of all exports, came from the coal, iron and steel, and textile industries. It was inevitable that these old industries should lose at least some ground in the face of foreign competition, for their growth potential was not unlimited.

The report of the Royal Commission on Depression of Trade and Industry (1886) praised the Germans for their enterprise, and warned of the 'increasing severity' of their competition both in home and overseas markets. The commission concluded that there was 'some falling off among the trading classes of this country from the more energetic practice of former periods'. Yet there could be no conclusive evidence about this. The number of firms with unsatisfactory products or sales techniques may not have increased at all compared with earlier years. The difference may simply have been that, with Britain no longer dominating all the markets, unsatisfactory performance was now more likely to lead to lost orders. Both employers and workmen were accused, however, of working less hard than in the past. Businessmen were criticized for complaining about foreign tariffs, and for wanting outside help instead of helping themselves. 'All concerned – merchants and workmen together – are tempted to take life too easily.'[43] Trade union restrictive practices were often blamed as burdens upon industry. But these had operated even in the days of mid-Victorian prosperity. If they were burdens, they were not new ones.

Was Britain's early start upon industrialization the cause of novel difficulties by the late-nineteenth century? The problem here may have been not simply obsolescent machinery, but an inefficient social and economic infrastructure. Unhealthy towns, poor roads and bridges, a railway network which had grown piecemeal, the English class system, inadequate mass education – such was the late-Victorian inheritance. Some of these difficulties were not shared by the Germans or the Americans.

For example, the belated introduction of compulsory elementary education into England compared unfavourably with the elaborate provision in Germany and the United States from the early nineteenth century. England remained well behind Germany in the organization of scientific education and technical instruction. Ignorance of science was often defended on the ground that British success in the Industrial Revolution had been based upon 'practical' knowledge without much reference to theory. From the 1860s onwards repeated warnings were made both by a succession of official enquiries and by scientific publicists such as Lyon Playfair and T. H. Huxley. But it took the rest of the century even to clarify objectives and terminology.[44] When Huxley argued for 'technical education' he described it as 'simply a good education, with more attention to physical science, to drawing, and to modern languages than is common'; there was 'nothing specially technical about it'. In respect of practical knowledge he was a traditionalist. 'The workshop is the only real school for a handicraft.' But was it? During the 1880s practical instruction at last began to be recognized as a legitimate branch of technical education, at least for workmen. For 'the higher ranks of industry', however, Alfred Marshall could still remark in his *Principles of Economics* (1890) that 'according to the best English opinions' 'technical education' must be general not particular. Marshall was here really advocating 'technological education', a term which duly emerged by the turn of the century.

This terminological confusion reflected the uncertainty in the minds of late-Victorians about what they should do. Not surprisingly, therefore, despite widespread admissions of deficiency, the action taken was still hesitant and piecemeal. Small beginnings were made by the Department of Science and Art in the 1850s and 1860s with grants in support of local evening classes. The Science and Art Department examinations eventually became popular not only for evening-class students but also for schools venturing upon secondary teaching.[45]

	Total examined	Pure mathematics	Inorganic chemistry		Metallurgy	
			theory	practical	theory	practical
1870	16,515	3,995	2,694	—	160	—
1880	34,678	11,179	5,529	1,937	277	—
1890	83,070	25,261	17,769	8,238	514	253
1895	108,193	29,692	23,787	15,128	534	391

Despite the success of this scheme the cost caused successive governments to view it with suspicion. Private enterprise was still expected to undertake as much or more in education as the national and local authorities. The London Livery Companies were persuaded in the 1870s to spend some of their great wealth upon setting up the City and Guilds of London Institute for the Advancement of Technical Education. The City and Guilds' examinations in vocational technical subjects were soon well established, and over 14,500 candidates sat in 1900.

The Royal Commission on Technical Instruction (1881–4) carried out a world-wide survey of technical education. Eventually there followed the Technical Instruction Act of 1889, which empowered (but did not compel) local authorities to open technical schools. From 1890 the long-famous 'whisky money' became available from national taxation to assist local efforts. The budget of that year proposed a tax of 6*d.* per gallon on spirits to help create a fund of nearly £750,000 for the compensation of holders of surplus liquor licences. Powerful opposition, however, both from the liquor trade and from the temperance lobby caused this money to be diverted instead to support for technical education.

5

Statistics of the percentage distribution of manufacturing output among the major powers showed how the United States and Germany were advancing during the last quarter of the nineteenth century:[46]

	United States	United Kingdom	Germany	France	Russia
1870	23.3	31.8	13.2	10.3	3.7
1881–5	28.6	26.6	13.9	8.6	3.4
1896–1900	30.1	19.5	16.6	7.1	5.0

Britain's falling share of world production was reflected in her overseas trade.[47] Though British exports were still increasing in value overall, the British proportion of world export trade in manufactured goods was declining – from 41.4 per cent in 1880 to 32.5 per cent in 1899, and down to 29.9 per cent by 1913. Over the same period the German share rose from 19.3 per cent to 26.5 per cent, and the United States share from 2.8 to 12.6 per cent. Britain's share of world trade in such major items as iron and steel manufactures, metal goods, and transport equipment fell heavily. In iron and steel the fall was from 60.5 per cent of world trade in 1880 to 35.6 per cent in 1913.

Britain's foreign trade was also changing significantly in its character. Up to 1873 about two-thirds was of the type appropriate to a great imperial power – the exchange of manufactured goods for raw materials. By the end of the century, however, this had dropped to one-third. A quarter of her foreign trade now comprised the exchange of manufactures for manufactures, and almost another quarter was financed through her surplus on invisible earnings. Here was another indication of how Britain had ceased to be the workshop of the world:[48]

Percentage distribution of United Kingdom foreign trade				
	Commodities against invisible items	Raw materials and food against raw materials and food	Manufactures against manufactures	Manufactures against raw materials and food	Total value (£m.)
1864–73	12.1	10.9	13.2	63.8	4,553
1874–83	20.1	12.1	17.2	50.4	5,486
1884–93	18.2	14.3	20.1	47.4	5,675
1894–1903	23.9	16.3	25.3	34.5	6,723

Both the Germans and the Americans were developing their home industries and markets and their overseas trade under the protection of tariff barriers. Cobdenite hopes that the world would follow Britain in adopting full free trade were sharply disappointed during the last quarter of the nineteenth century. The freer trade trend of the 1860s and early 1870s in Europe was reversed at the end of the decade when Germany began to reimpose tariffs. France, Austria, Italy, and Russia all increased their tariffs in the 1880s. The United States had persisted with high protection even through the 1860s, and from the 1890s American barriers became very high. *The Times* (13.10.1890) called the McKinley tariff an 'act of unfriendliness'. In 1904 it was calculated that the average *ad valorem* equivalent of import duties levied on the chief manufactures exported from the United Kingdom was approximately: Germany 25 per cent, Italy 27 per cent, France 34 per cent, Austria 35 per cent, United States 73 per cent, Russia 131 per cent.[49] By the end of the century even the self-governing colonies within the British Empire, headed by Canada, had adopted tariffs not only for revenue purposes but also to protect their infant industries.

To what extent, then, was British industry and trade injured by the imposition of tariffs?[50] How much did it matter that, while Britain's home markets were left wide open under free trade, the home markets of other powers were protected? Certain industries, or branches of industries, did suffer severely at certain times – wool and worsted textiles, for example, more than cottons. But in general the level of European tariffs was not prohibitive. On the eve of the First World War the major industrial countries were still each other's best customers, despite tariffs. Through her commercial treaties with most-favoured-nation clauses, Britain was in a no less favourable position to trade with the Continental powers than they were with one another. Under this system any reduction of duty made by one nation for another was automatically extended to every nation in the network. In 1908 Britain had forty-six such treaties. They at least prevented positive discrimination against her exports. If Britain began to fall behind in European and world markets at this time it was mainly because of lack of competitiveness. Other European countries even managed to increase their shares of the highly protected United States market, but Britain could not emulate them.

By the late 1870s pressure for modification of the free trade policy was beginning to be voiced by businessmen affected by the prevailing deep trade depression.[51] *The Times* (23.6.1879) remained unimpressed. 'The doctrines of free trade are ... verities as certain as the axioms of mathematical science, and, like them, are above the accidents of time and place.' But the same paper did emphasize a few weeks later (20 August) that Britain was now more dependent than ever before upon the competitiveness of her goods. 'What makes the difference between good and bad times?' Fluctuating foreign and colonial demand, answered *The Times*. Some businessmen, however, put the chief blame upon foreign tariffs. They asked not so much for the erection of a permanent system of British tariffs as for a policy of 'reciprocity' or 'retaliation' to force a lowering of foreign tariff barriers. With these objectives in view the Fair Trade League was formed in 1881. Its leaders included W. Farrer Ecroyd, a Yorkshire worsted manufacturer; Samuel Cunliffe-Lister, a Yorkshire silk manufacturer and agricultural landlord; S. S. Lloyd, a Birmingham banker and chairman of the Association of British Chambers of Commerce (1862–80); David McIver, a Liberal shipowner; and Howard Vincent. Ecroyd, Lloyd, and McIver all served as Conservative Members of Parliament for periods during the 1880s. Vincent represented Sheffield Central between 1885 and 1908, and received strong working-class support from his constituency for his fair trade views. Many of the Fair Trade League leaders were associated with areas and industries (the midlands metal trades, Sheffield steel, the West Riding worsted trade) which felt that they were under 'unfair' foreign pressure. At first the League made little impact, for trade revived during the early 1880s. Moreover, the fair traders met strong opposition from the Liberals, the traditional party of free trade, who were then in government. Conservative chiefs such as Lord Salisbury and Lord Randolph Churchill were at least prepared to listen and to enquire. When the Conservatives returned to office in 1885 they immediately set up a Royal Commission on Depression of Trade and Industry. Its minority report came out in favour of fair trade. All the commissioners agreed that foreign tariffs were among the causes of depression; but the majority argued that these lay outside British control.

Fair trade was an issue at the general election of 1885. Liberals declared that it would mean a return to the 'dear loaf' of the days of the Corn Laws, since taxation of foreign grain must raise bread prices. Fair traders answered that any slight increase would be more than balanced by the wage rises which would result from increased colonial demand for British manufacturers. In the 1886 general election Home Rule largely submerged the fair trade cry. Nevertheless, the Cobden Club admitted that more Members of Parliament critical of free trade had been returned than at any election since 1852. Yet the new alliance of the Conservatives with the Liberal Unionists against Home Rule now made it unlikely that Salisbury's Government would respond to demands for fair trade unless they were shown to be widely and urgently supported outside Parliament, for the Liberal Unionists were committed free traders. The Fair Trade League tried to rally such outside pressure during the late 1880s. At the annual conference of the Conservative National Union in November 1887 the movement reached its highest point of success when Howard Vincent secured the adoption by an overwhelming majority of a resolution which called for 'speedy reform in the policy of the United Kingdom as regards foreign imports'. The Conservative leaders, however, still refused to accept this as present policy. Soon trade again began to revive, and thereafter the fair trade movement rapidly lost ground. Many leading members shifted their interest to the cause of imperial federation, and founded the United Empire Trade League in 1891. The demand now was for some form of customs union which would cement the unity of the empire. It was hoped that this positive approach would prove more attractive both to party leaders and to electors than the negative policy of 'retaliation'. But little impression was made at the general election of 1892; and discussion both of imperial federation and of trade protection continued without much effect until Joseph Chamberlain brought them together under the banner of 'tariff reform' in 1903.

6

Lady Bracknell in Oscar Wilde's *The Importance of Being Earnest* (1895) exclaimed how landownership had 'ceased to be either a profit or a pleasure. It gives one position and prevents one from keeping it up'. Yet support for fair trade was never especially strong in rural England. Some large landowners came out in favour; but many tenant farmers and farm labourers seem to have suspected that it would divert attention from desired rent reductions, or from the 'land question' in general. Such was the view, for example, of the Farmers' Alliance.

The population of the English countryside had begun to fall because of overseas emigration and townward migration even before the onset of depression. This process continued to the end of the century, leaving some villages visibly depopulated. But the relative decline of rural numbers, compared with the rapidly expanding town population, was much more striking than the absolute decline:[52]

Urban and rural populations, England and Wales		
	Rural	Urban	Rural percentage
1871	8,700,000	14,000,000	38.2
1881	8,300,000	17,600,000	32.1
1891	8,100,000	20,900,000	28.0
1901	7,500,000	25,100,000	23.0

Agriculture marked time in terms of overall income, whereas income from manufacture and trade continued to grow, thereby illustrating how depression was much more persistent in the countryside:[53]

Industrial distribution of the national income of Great Britain			
	Agriculture, forestry, fishing	Manufacture, mining, building	Trade and transport	Total national product
1871	130.4	348.9	201.6	916.6
1881	109.1	395.9	241.9	1051.2
1891	110.9	495.2	289.6	1288.2
1901	104.6	660.7	383.0	1642.9

Wheat acreage in Great Britain dropped from a peak of 3,688,000 acres in 1869 to a minimum of 1,375,000 acres in 1904. Wheat had sold at an average of 55*s.* per quarter during 1870–4; but it was down to an all-time low of 22*s.* 10*d.* in 1894. Reductions in acreage had brought no improvement in price because British markets remained wide open to importation from overseas. From the mid 1870s wheat was rushing in from the United States, Canada, and Russia; and from the mid 1880s it poured in also from Argentina, India, and Australia. The railways had opened up the American mid-west, and the completion of the Suez Canal in 1869 had much shortened the route to Australasia. Cargo-carrying costs across the Atlantic and other oceans were falling fast because of improved ship and marine-engine design. In the late 1860s it had cost 15*s.* 11*d.* to transport a quarter of wheat from Chicago to Liverpool: by the early 1900s it cost 3*s.* 11*d.* Imported wheat, which had provided half of Britain's consumption in the early 1870s, was providing four-fifths by the 1890s: 30,901,000 Cwts. (1870), 55,262,000 (1880), 60,474,000 (1890), 68,669,000 (1900). In respect of meat supplies the development of canning and refrigeration processes played a vital part, enabling Argentina, Australia, and New Zealand to enter the markets. The first cargo of frozen mutton left New Zealand in 1882. By the mid 1890s about one-third of the United Kingdom's meat was imported, compared with only one-fifth twenty years earlier:[54]

	Home Produce (1,000 tons)				Imported meat (1,000 tons)		
	Beef and veal	Mutton and lamb	Pig meat	Total	Dead	Live	Total
1876–8	657	404	265	1,326	246	90	336
1893–5	731	382	261	1,374	532	157	689

The wheat farmers of the eastern and southern counties of England were the group most seriously hit by agricultural depression.[55] Livestock farmers – most numerous in the north and west – fared better. The fall in grain prices reduced fodder costs. And although refrigerated imports came to supply much of the new mass demand for cheap meat, home-grown meat continued to be preferred by the rest of the market. Prices for wool farmers slumped by a half or more; partly because of changes in fashion, but more because imports of Australian wool quadrupled from about 100 million lbs. in the mid 1860s to over 400 million by the mid 1880s. Averaged overall, the incentive income of United Kingdom farmers has been calculated to have fallen one-half between 1873 and the early 1880s.[56]

Between 1875 and 1895 the amount of land left to grass in the arable counties of the south and east rose from 3,500,000 to 5 million acres. Here was a major landscape change. Hedges and fences were now more often left untended in order to save labour, and crops remained unweeded. But within reach of the growing cities and towns it proved profitable to turn from arable farming to milk production. Market gardening also greatly extended, using cheap manure from the towns themselves as the basis for intensive cultivation. The railways delivered manure in one direction; and milk, fruit, vegetables, and flowers in the other. Between 1875 and 1895 the area of market gardens in England increased from 35,000 to 85,000 acres, and of orchards from 151,000 acres to 213,000 acres. Market gardening became the speciality of wide areas of the Thames valley, Kent, and the east midlands. The vale of Evesham, and parts of Cambridgeshire and Essex, developed large-scale fruit-growing, with jam factories on hand. Tomatoes began to be extensively cultivated under glass, and ceased to be luxuries. The Lincolnshire bulb industry expanded dramatically. Spalding had only one bulb grower in 1885, but twenty-two by 1892.

For those engaged in these activities there was no depression. But for many wheat farmers the price decline of as much as one-half proved to be insupportable. Their high-cost production methods left little room for economies without rapid falls in output. About one farmer in 150 was forced into liquidation in Huntingdonshire, compared with only about one in 500 in livestock-farming Lancashire. Rent remissions and reductions could give some easement to tenant farmers at the expense of landlords. Rents fell perhaps 40 per cent in the depressed south and east between the 1870s and the 1890s.

The hope at first had been that the depression was temporary. A succession of wet years – 1875, 1877, 1878, and above all 1879 – were blamed for raising costs of harvesting and for lowering the quality of grain. 1880 was another wet summer, while that of 1882 was almost as cold and wet as that of 1879. It was not surprising that at first landlords and farmers looked more to the effects of the weather than to the growing volume of overseas imports. The report of the first Royal Commission on agricultural depression, published in 1882, finally brought the two factors together by remarking that 'if it had not been for the enormous competition from America, prices in bad seasons would necessarily have gone up, and English produce would have thus found compensation for deficient yield'. The weather improved again, but wheat prices continued to fall. Since a return to any form of protection was outside practical politics, the Government could help only indirectly. The 1883 Agricultural Holdings Act did give farmers better assurance of compensation for improvements made at their own expense, if they left at the end of a tenancy. This meant that they were no longer discouraged from farming as efficiently as possible. And it was the efficient landlords and farmers who survived. The second Royal Commission (1893–7) noticed how men of energy and capital had even continued to grow wheat competitively; how market gardening and fruit farming had prospered; and how milk production had been made to pay by Scottish immigrants on the former wheatlands of Essex. Too many wheat farmers had been set in their ways – willing to grow nothing else, and letting the high profits of the early 1870s fix their expectations.

Where tenants fared badly so might their landlords. The chief sufferers among landowners seem to have been among the gentry, who had less margin of income to spare than the great aristocratic landowners. The incomes of some big landlords were greatly augmented by ownership of valuable urban land and property, or of coal or other mineral deposits. The mineral receipts of the Duke of Northumberland, for example, had reached £73,000 per annum by 1914, so that after deductions for estate expenditure they were providing nearly 60 per cent of his net income.

Certainly, the fabric of landlord life did not collapse under the pressure of bad times. 'Socially, not less than geographically, the County continues to exist. The wives and daughters of the country gentlemen who are County J.Ps. set the fashion in their neighbourhood and are still regarded as moulded out of clay slightly superior to that of which their neighbours consist.'[57] The introduction of county councils in 1889 changed the form of county government, but landed gentlemen were elected to the new bodies in large numbers. Some landowners had indeed sold or rented their estates to newcomers, who might be commercial or colonial plutocrats with little understanding of country life – 'rich vulgarians', 'billiard marker gentry'. But much of the old rural order survived right up to 1914.

The circumstances of agricultural labourers improved in most parts of England despite the depression, except for men who were laid off. Money wages did not fall much, even in the wheat-growing counties:[58]

Weekly cash wages of English agricultural labourers							
Northern counties	East midlands	West midlands	South-west	South-east midlands	South and south-east	East Anglia	Average
s. d.	s. d.	s. d.	s. d.	s. d.	s. d.	s. d.	s. d.
1879–81	16 2	14 5	13 4	12 4	13 0	13 10	12 6	13 9
1892–3	16 5	15 2	12 6	11 8	12 4	12 10	11 10	13 4
1898	16 10	16 2	13 10	12 7	13 0	14 10	11 11	14 5
1907	17 3	16 3	14 8	13 8	13 11	15 9	12 10	14 11

The 1882 Royal Commission report remarked that the drop in food prices had even raised rural real wages. The report emphasized, however, the continuing poor quality of much rural housing. A social survey of fifty-six Warwickshire villages in the early 1890s complained of the housing, but noted how money wages had fallen less than the cost of living. The curate of a Cambridgeshire parish in the early 1850s returned to the countryside to become a Norfolk rector in 1879; and he found great improvements in the standards and aspirations of labourers and their families. Children were cleaner and better educated. Norfolk wives no longer worked, but gave their time to making their homes more habitable.[59]

Rural trade unions revived at the start of the 1890s, chiefly in East Anglia, though never on the scale of the 1870s. Arch's national Agricultural Labourers' Union was now mainly confined to Norfolk and Essex. Some wage increases were won because of a temporary revival in wheat prices. But when prices slumped from 1892 wages were again cut; and during the mid 1890s the unions almost all collapsed.[60]

7

The onset of agricultural depression gave added importance to demands for 'land reform'. Disraeli told the House of Lords (30 August 1880) that two subjects occupied the mind of the country. One was the government of Ireland: the other was 'the principles upon which the landed property of this country should continue to be established'. The two topics were indeed connected through the Irish land question. Reformers and their opponents both realized that the weakening of the rights of landlords under the Irish Land Acts of 1870 and 1881 might carry implications for land law in England. How far should the state interfere with rights to landed property? 'Land may be treated as private property, held so as not to prejudice the public welfare, but not to be taken from owners without fair compensation; or it may be distinguished from private property, and the principles which guard private property held inappropriate to land. On which line was land legislation to proceed?' So asked R. E. Prothero, a future President of the Board of Agriculture, in 1888.[61]

The demand for land reform went back at least to the Levellers of the seventeenth century.[62] Continuous pressure for land reform carried through from the agitation of the Anti-Corn Law League in the 1840s. The successful demand for Corn Law repeal was only one expression of the deep hostility to 'feudalism' of the League leaders, Richard Cobden and John Bright. Cobden complained that a few thousand large landowners owned most of the soil, and that in no other country were the peasantry so deprived of land. Cobden exclaimed in 1864 that if he had still been a young man he would have formed 'a League for free trade in land just as we had a League for free trade in corn'.[63] He died in 1865; but the Cobden Club published the textbooks of the movement for 'free trade in land' during the 1870s and 1880s – a symposium on *Systems of Land Tenure in Various Countries* (1870), Arthur Arnold's *Free Land* (1880), and G. C. Brodrick's *English Land and English Landlords* (1881).

In Cobden's time opponents of land reform denied that large owners held as much land as reformers claimed. Lord Derby, himself one of the largest landlords, pressed in 1871 for the compilation of a modern Domesday Book, which he believed would reveal that ownership of land was more extensive than was often admitted. Gladstone's Government responded, and the results of a full-scale enquiry were published in 1876. The evidence was somewhat confused; but it was eventually clarified to show that 4,217 owners of large estates of a 1,000 acres or more possessed over half the land of England. The reformers were thus now armed with striking official statistics. Of 62 Members of Parliament listed as land reformers in Dod's *Parliamentary Companion* of 1880, 43 were connected with industry, commerce, or finance. Among these were John Bright and Joseph Chamberlain. Membership of the land reform organizations – J. S. Mill's Land Tenure Reform Association (1869), the Land Nationalization Society (1881), and the Land Reform Union (1883) – included significant numbers of professional men.

The land nationalizers were socialists, but the majority of land reformers stopped short of nationalization. All reformers were agreed, however, that the great estates must in some way be broken up and the land 'given back' to the people. They accepted that these estates had been created in the past by 'force and fraud'. This process had included the abrogation of the manorial rights of labourers through enclosure and other devices. But how was the break-up of the great estates to be achieved? The Cobdenite free traders in land favoured a gradualist approach. Pointing to American and European examples, they wanted abolition of primogeniture and entail, of discrimination between realty and personalty, and of all other practices which restricted the division of large estates. Primogeniture and entail were really more symbols than major problems in themselves. The law of primogeniture only applied in cases of intestacy, and family lawyers ensured that such instances were rare. The custom of making settlements at the marriage of the eldest son in each generation constituted the main obstacle to the break-up of the great estates by natural means. Such settlements made land 'owners' in effect only life tenants, since they could not sell their property outright at least until their eldest son came of age, by which time a fresh settlement was in prospect. Meanwhile, estates were often charged with payments to younger sons or brothers, to sisters or daughters, married, unmarried, and widowed – all of which made it the more difficult to sell. The free traders wanted, in Bright's words, to make it almost as easy to buy and sell land as anything else, 'that the natural forces of accumulation and dispersion shall have free play'. This gradualist approach, it was argued, would strengthen, not weaken, the idea of property. Communistic ideas were most likely to spread 'when the social contrast between the owner and cultivator of the soil is too flagrant, and when the former, enriched by the foresight and industry of others, is content to be a mere drone or absentee'.[64]

The minority of land reformers who wanted more urgent intervention were divided into several groups. Some sought nationalization; some preferred municipalization; some thought compensation should be paid, others not. And some concentrated upon the appropriation of rent. The ideas put forward by the American Henry George in *Progress and Poverty* (first published 1879, English edition 1881) were widely and earnestly discussed by land reformers of all shades, and also by their opponents.[65] George described the continuing existence of poverty in the midst of plenty as 'the great enigma of our times'. He claimed to have found a solution in 'recognition of the common right to land . . . to be reached by the simple and easy method of abolishing all taxation save that upon land values'. Since economic progress had always produced a growing shortage of land, idle landowners had always unfairly reaped increasing returns from the labour and capital of others. The state should tax away all economic rent, that unearned increment which had been created not by the landowners themselves but by society. The state need not then take the land itself – 'We may safely leave them the shell, if we take the kernel.' In this sense George separated himself from the outright land nationalizers, though he did not always make the distinction clear.

By the end of 1882, thanks in part to the influence of George, radicals such as John Morley and Joseph Chamberlain were beginning to wonder if comprehensive land reform, so long discussed, was at last moving from the stage of discussion to the stage of action. Morley accepted that George, Mill, and other advanced land reformers had been right in arguing that 'the mere legal reformers – the removers of restrictions on transfer – do not touch the root of the matter'. Both Morley and Chamberlain were interested in George's ideas, though without fully accepting them.[66] Chamberlain did not proscribe all landlords, only the 'indolent and inefficient'. 'They must give place to others who will do full justice to the capabilities of the land.' But he was often accused of wanting to apply George's ideas, especially after a famous speech to Birmingham working men in January 1885. Chamberlain then assured his audience that the recent extension of the franchise to rural householders under the Third Reform Act had given workers 'in factory or in field' power to control the Government. Privilege would now be restrained: 'what ransom will property pay for the security which it enjoys'. This seemed to hint at confiscation, though in reality Chamberlain did not wish to go so far. He only wanted local authorities to be given powers to buy land compulsorily at fair prices. In the towns he wanted local councils to be able to insist upon higher standards of planning and building, though he hoped that the mere threat of compulsory purchase would be enough to check private landlords. And in the countryside he was an enthusiast for the provision of allotments and smallholdings. Here the call became 'three acres and a cow', a cry made popular by Jesse Collings, who had entered Parliament as one of Chamberlain's closest Birmingham associates and who became the particular advocate over the next forty years of smallholdings for sale or rent, bought from state or municipal funds.[67] Land reformers of all persuasions insisted that the rural labourers were 'hungry' for land of their own, or at least would become so if encouraged. Acts were passed to allow the creation of allotments (1887) and smallholdings (1892, 1907, 1908) under county council auspices. But the number of labourers who became successful smallholders always remained comparatively small. Success required capital, fertile and easily worked soil, good access to profitable markets, and also enterprise and endurance.

The legislative outcome of all the efforts of the land reformers was modest. In particular, they failed to secure any major changes in land law or landownership. Legislation of the early 1880s removed some of the expense and complication from buying and selling land. But the Settled Land Act of 1882 even strengthened the large estates system by facilitating completion of restrictive covenants. At the 1885 general election land questions were prominent as never before; but at the 1886 election they were submerged by the Home Rule issue. Chamberlain left the Liberal Party. In a 1905 *Law Quarterly Review* article on 'The Paradox of the Land Law' A. V. Dicey remarked that, though 'democracy' now prevailed in political life, English land law remained 'appropriate to an aristocratic state'.

Notes

1. N. L. Tranter, *Population Since the Industrial Revolution* (1973), p. 53. See especially Rosalind Mitchison, *British Population Change Since 1860* (1977), and references there.
2. A. K. Cairncorss, *Home and Foreign Investment, 1870-1913* (1953), p. 82.
3. R. Fulford (ed.), *Your Dear Letter* (1971), pp. 186, 200-1, 264.
4. H. J. Habbakuk, *Population Growth and Economic Development Since 1750* (1972), p. 54.
5. Lord Chandos, *From Peace to War* (1968), pp. 15-19; Betty Askwith, *The Lyttletons* (1975), Ch. 10.
6. See T. H. C. Stevenson, 'The Fertility of Various Social Classes in England and Wales from the Middle of the Nineteenth Century to 1911', *Journal of the Royal Statistical Society*, LXXXIII (1920); and J. W. Innes, *Class Fertility Trends in England and Wales, 1876-1934* (1938). Patricia Branca, *Silent Sisterhood* (1975), convincingly challenges arguments in J. A. Banks, *Prosperity and Parenthood* (1954); and in J. A. and Olive Banks, *Feminism and Family Planning in Victorian England* (1964).
7. Patricia Branca, *Silent Sisterhood* (1975), p. 121.
8. See D. V. Glass, 'A Note on the Under-Registration of Births in Britain in the Nineteenth Century', *Population Studies*, V (1951-2).
9. See J. A. and Olive Banks, 'The Bradlaugh-Besant Trial and the English Newspapers', *Population Studies*, VIII (1954-5); D. V. Glass, *Population Policies and Movements in Europe* (1967), Ch. I; Patricia Knight, 'Women and Abortion in Victorian and Edwardian England', *History Workshop*, no. 4 (1977); and A. McLaren, 'Women's Work and Regulation of Family Size: The Question of Abortion in the Nineteenth Century', *ibid*.
10. See R. E. Dowse and J. Peel, 'The Politics of Birth-Control', *Political Studies*, XIII (1965).
11. See J. Peel, 'The Manufacture and Retailing of Contraceptives in England', *Population Studies*, XVII (1963-4).
12. See J. Matras, 'Social Categories of Family Formation: Data for British Female Cohorts born 1831-1906', *Population Studies*, XIX (1965).
13. Hannah Mitchell, *The Hard Way Up* (1968), pp. 88-9, 102.
14. Patricia Branca, *Silent Sisterhood* (1975), p. 130.
15. See T. McKeown and R. G. Record, 'Reasons for the Decline of Mortality in England and Wales during the Nineteenth Century', in M. W. Flinn and T. C. Smout (eds.), *Essays in Social History* (1974); and T. McKeown, *The Modern Rise of Population* (1976), esp. Ch. 3.
16. G. U. Yule, 'On the Changes in the Marriage- and Birth-Rates in England and Wales during the Past Half Century', *Journal of the Royal Statistical Society*, LXIX (1906), pp. 90-1.

17. M. H. Spielmann, *History of Punch* (1895), pp. 141–2.
18. See G. Stedman Jones, 'Working-Class Culture and Working-Class Politics in London, 1870–1900', *Journal of Social History*, VII (1974), pp. 491–2; and R. M. Titmuss, 'The Position of Women: Some Vital Statistics', in M. W. Flinn and T. C. Smout (eds.), *Essays in Social History* (1974), Ch. 12.
19. See B. Thomas, *Migration and Economic Growth: A Study of Great Britain and the Atlantic Economy* (2nd edn, 1973), esp. Ch. V.
20. Phyllis Deane and W. A. Cole, *British Economic Growth, 1688–1959* (2nd edn, 1967), p. 10.
21. B. Thomas, *Migration and Economic Growth: A Study of Great Britain and the Atlantic Economy* (2nd edn, 1973) p. 459.
22. Phyllis Deane and W. A. Cole, *British Economic Growth, 1688–1959* (2nd edn, 1967), p. 142.
23. See D. C. Marsh, *The Changing Social Structure of England and Wales, 1871–1961* (2nd edn, 1965), pp. 117–30; and W. A. Armstrong, 'An Industrial Classification, 1841–1891', in E. A. Wrigley (ed.), *Nineteenth-Century Society* (1972), Ch. 6, part 2.
24. See S. B. Saul, *The Myth of the Great Depression, 1873–1896* (1969), and references there.
25. P. Mathias, *The First Industrial Nation* (1969), p. 468.
26. *Ibid.*, p. 467.
27. Phyllis Deane and W. A. Cole, *British Economic Growth, 1688–1959* (2nd edn, 1967), p. 36.
28. G. Armitage-Smith, *The Free-Trade Movement and its Results* (1898), pp. 197–8.
29. S. B. Saul, *The Myth of the Great Depression, 1873–1896* (1969), pp. 14, 42.
30. See G. H. Wood, 'Real Wages and the Standard of Comfort Since 1850', *Journal of the Royal Statistical Society*, LXXIII (1909), reprinted in E. M. Carus-Wilson (ed.), *Essays in Economic History*, Vol. 3 (1962).
31. See A. J. Taylor, 'The Coal Industry', in D. H. Aldcroft (ed.), *The Development of British Industry and Foreign Competition, 1875–1914* (1968), and references there. Also M. W. Kirby, *The British Coalmining Industry, 1870–1846* (1977), Ch. 1.
32. See R. E. Tyson, 'The Cotton Industry', in D. H. Aldcroft (ed.), *The Development of British Industry and Foreign Competition, 1875–1914* (1968), and references there. Also L. G. Sandberg, *Lancashire in Decline* (1974).
33. See P. L. Payne, 'Iron and Steel Manufactures', in D. H. Aldcroft (ed.), *The Development of British Industry and Foreign Competition, 1875–1914* (1968), and references there. Table from 'Iron and Coal Trades Review Diamond Jubilee issue'. 1927.
34. *Ibid.*, p. 72.
35. See H. W. Richardson, 'Chemicals', *ibid.*, and references there.
36. See I. C. R. Byatt, 'Electrical Products', *ibid.*, and references there.
37. See S. B. Saul, 'The Market and the Development of the Mechanical Engineering Industries in Britain, 1860–1914', in S. B. Saul (ed.), *Technological Change: The United States and Britain in the Nineteenth Century* (1970). Also R. Floud, *History of Machine Tool Industry* (1976).
38. See A. E. Harrison, 'The Competitiveness of the British Cycle Industry, 1890–1914' *Economic History Review*, second series, XXII (1969).
39. See S. Pollard, 'British and World Shipbuilding, 1890–1914', *Journal of Economic History*, XVII (1957).
40. D. H. Aldcroft, *Studies in British Transport History, 1870–1970* (1974), Chs. 3, 4.
41. See C. Wilson, 'Economy and Society in Late Victorian Britain', *Economic History Review*, second series, XVIII (1965).
42. Phyllis Deane and W. A. Cole, *British Economic Growth, 1688–1959* (2nd edn., 1967), p. 297.
43. T. H. Ward (ed.), *The Reign of Queen Victoria* (1887), II, pp. 39–40.
44. See especially P. W. Musgrave, 'The Definition of Technical Education, 1860–1910', in P. W. Musgrave (ed.), *Sociology, History, and Education* (1970). Also S. F. Cotgrove, *Technical Education and Social Change* (1958).
45. P. W. Musgrave (ed.), *Sociology, History, and Education* (1970) p. 268.

46. B. Thomas, *Migration and Economic Growth: A Study of Great Britain and the Atlantic Economy* (2nd edn, 1973) p. 120.

47. See especially S. B. Saul, *Studies in British Overseas Trade, 1870–1914* (1960); and S. B. Saul, 'The Export Economy, 1870–1914', *Yorkshire Bulletin of Economic and Social Research*, Vol. 17 (1965).

48. B. Thomas, *Migration and Economic Growth: A Study of Great Britain and the Atlantic Economy* (2nd edn, 1973), p. 122.

49. J. H. Clapham, *The Economic Development of France and Germany, 1815–1914* (4th edn, 1936), p. 322.

50. See S. B. Saul, *Studies in British Overseas Trade, 1870–1914* (1960), esp. Ch. VI.

51. See especially S. H. Zebel, 'Fair Trade and English Reaction to the Breakdown of the Cobden Treaty System', *Journal of Modern History*, XII (1940); and B. H. Brown, *The Tariff Reform Movement in Great Britain, 1881–1895* (1943).

52. R. Lawton, 'Rural Depopulation in Nineteenth Century England' in D. R. Mills (ed.), *English Rural Communities* (1973), p. 195.

53. Phyllis Deane and W. A. Cole, *British Economic Growth, 1688–1959* (2nd edn, 1967), p. 166.

54. *Royal Commission on Agricultural Depression, Final Report*, C.8540 (1897), p. 64.

55. See especially Christabel S. Orwin and Edith H. Whetham, *History of British Agriculture, 1846–1914* (1971), Chs. 9–12; P. J. Perry (ed.), *British Agriculture, 1875–1914* (1973); and P. J. Perry, *British Farming in the Great Depression, 1870–1914* (1974).

56. J. R. Bellerby, 'National and Agricultural Income 1851', *Economic Journal*, LXIX (1959), p. 103.

57. T. H. S. Escott, *Social Transformations of the Victorian Age* (1897), p. 97.

58. R. M. Hartwell (ed.), *The Long Debate on Poverty* (2nd edn, 1974), p. 44.

59. A. Jessop, 'My Return to Arcady', *Nineteenth Century*, August 1881; J. Ashby and B. King, 'Statistics of Some Midland Villages', *Economic Journal*, III (1893).

60. J. P. D. Dunbabin (ed.), *Rural Discontent in Nineteenth-Century Britain* (1974), pp. 82–4, 259–62.

61. R. E. Prothero, *The Pioneers and Progress of English Farming* (1888), p. 179.

62. See especially F. M. L. Thompson, 'Land and Politics in England in the Nineteenth Century', *Transactions of the Royal Historical Society*, fifth series, Vol. 15 (1965); H. J. Perkin, 'Land Reform and Class Conflict in Victorian Britain', in J. Butt and I. F. Clarke (eds.), *The Victorians and Social Protest* (1973); and R. Douglas, *Land, People, and Politics* (1976).

63. D. Read, *Cobden and Bright* (1967), esp. pp. 188–91.

64. G. C. Brodrick, *English Land and English Landlords* (1881), pp. 452–3.

65. See especially E. P. Lawrence, *Henry George in the British Isles* (1957).

66. D. A. Hamer, *John Morley* (1968), p. 140; P. Fraser, *Joseph Chamberlain* (1966), esp. Ch. 2.

67. See J. Collings and J. L. Green, *Life of the Right Hon. Jesse Collings* (1920), part II. Also J. P. D. Dunbabin (ed.), *Rural Discontent in Nineteenth-Century Britain* (1974), pp. 245–51.

Chapter 13

Social life: *'The mistress never converses with her servants'*

1

The total occupied population of the United Kingdom towards the end of the nineteenth century has been estimated as follows:[1]

	Working class	Middle and upper classes
1881	11,840,000	2,610,000
1901	13,800,000	3,940,000

In this categorization shop assistants were taken as the humblest members of the middle class. Middle-class numbers overall were not only continuing to grow fast, they were also increasing proportionately within the workforce. 'From above, the younger sons of the aristocracy have been dropping into the more active ranks of the middle class – "going into trade." From below, the best men of the working class are still pushing up.'[2]

Growth of the middle class. England and Wales. Males. Numbers occupied in certain groups (in thousands)

	1881	1901
Professions and administration	248	343
Commerce, clerks, and miscellaneous	397	694
Dealers and assistants	652	915
Employers not included above	169	217
Farmers	203	203
Total	1,669	2,372
Others occupied	6,090	7,785
All occupied	7,759	10,157
Percentage middle class of all	21.5	23.3

The middle classes were not only more numerous but also better off than ever before. United Kingdom taxable income – that is, income over the exemption limit and therefore clearly belonging to the middle and upper classes – had averaged just over £200 million per annum in the 1860s; but by the early 1870s it had doubled, and by the early 1890s it had passed £600 million. The number of middle-class persons in the United Kingdom with taxable incomes has been estimated at rather more than 300,000 about 1860, over 500,000 by the mid 1870s, and about 850,000 by the mid 1890s.[3]

The numbers of women schoolteachers continued to rise steadily, while the ranks of women secretaries and typists were now expanding at a remarkable rate:[4]

	Schoolteachers (all grades)		Clerks (all types)	
	Men	Women	Men	Women
1881	46,074	122,846	229,705	6,420
1901	58,675	171,670	461,164	57,736
1911	68,670	183,298	561,155	124,843

But most middle-class married women still remained at home as mistresses of more or less large households. Jokes of complaint about servants had appeared in *Punch* since its earliest days in the 1840s; but by the 1880s grumblings about 'the servant problem' were attaining a new intensity. The *General Report* upon the 1881 census remarked that 'the frequently heard complaints of householders as to the increasing difficulty of finding suitable servants may have a real foundation'. The numbers of indoor female servants were still rising; but at a much slower rate than the rise in middle-class numbers and demand – the 1,230,400 female domestics of 1881 had grown only to 1,285,600 by 1901, and to 1,296,000 by 1911. In 1881 there had been about 218 female domestics per thousand families in England and Wales: by 1911 this figure had fallen to 170.

Women of every age, and especially teenage girls, were becoming less ready to enter or to stay in 'service' as the new urban mass society offered them more opportunities for employment in factories or shops. Though this alternative labour might be hard and long, it was less demanding than the all-day work and discipline imposed upon domestic servants. One lady's maid complained in 1913 how she was 'not expected to be tired'. Many mistresses seem to have been very cold in their dealings with servants. Mrs Beeton's *Everyday Cookery* (edition *c*.1900) was fearful lest household discipline should be relaxed by casual conversation. 'The mistress,' advised Mrs Beeton, 'never converses with her servants; never speaks but to gently give an order, ask a question, or say good morning and evening.'

The wages of domestic servants still varied widely between households and between districts; but all had increased faster than the general wage rise. Between the 1861 and 1906 editions of Mrs Beeton's *Book of Household Management* recommended annual wages (without beer money) for cooks had risen from £14–£30 to £20–£60, and for maids-of-all-work from £9–14 to £12–£28. The increased cost of domestic service reduced the numbers that could be afforded by any one household. Whereas in 1861 Mrs Beeton had considered that an income of £1,000 a year could support a cook, two housemaids, a nursemaid, and a male servant, her 1906 edition accepted that this would now only pay for a cook, one housemaid, and perhaps a manservant. The turnover rate continued high, a fact memorably noticed in 1904 by Saki, the short-story writer. 'On a raw Wednesday morning, in a few ill-chosen words, she told the cook that she drank . . . The cook was a good cook, as cooks go; and as cooks go she went.'

Did the cook move to a better job? The ideal of self-improvement was still frequently praised. Yet the chances for self-made men were declining within a business world increasingly controlled by established firms. The late-Victorian cotton trade remained one of the few spheres where individuals could still set up on credit or on small capital and hope to prosper. An enquiry undertaken in 1912 showed that over two-thirds of cotton millowners, directors, and managers had begun as manual workers or in lowly clerical positions.[5] Social rising at a higher level – of wealthy businessmen into the peerage – was ceasing to be exceptional by the end of the century. About seventy of approximately 200 new peers created between 1886 and 1914 depended for their wealth upon business profits. On the other hand, over half of the new peers still came from landed backgrounds.[6] While many members of the landed aristocracy and gentry were struggling through the 'great depression' in agriculture, the plutocracy was flourishing. In the 1860s only one or two millionaires had died each year; but by the turn of the century the annual total had reached four or five, and by 1910–13 eight or nine. The majority of millionaires were financiers or businessmen, especially bankers and brewers.[7]

The plutocrats introduced new blood and new money into late-Victorian 'Society'. So also did American heiresses. Winston Churchill's mother – Jenny Jerome – who married Lord Randolph Churchill in 1874, was among the first of a wave of American brides. Joseph Chamberlain and Sir William Harcourt were among other politicians who formed domestic transatlantic alliances. This 'American invasion' was much noticed, not always with approval. But, as one journalist remarked, perhaps with innuendo, the Prince of Wales was 'an habitual worshipper at American shrines'.[8] The Prince also welcomed into 'Society' a new breed of 'professional beauties'. These were headed by Lillie Langtry, who became his mistress.

2

The conventional three-class division provided only a crude separation of Victorian society. In his great social survey of *Life and Labour of the People in London*, undertaken during the last two decades of the century, Charles Booth, a Liverpool shipowner by family connection but a social statistician by inclination, used an eight-fold categorization of the 900,000 inhabitants of the East End. Four of these categories lived above the 'poverty line', and four below:

A.	The lowest class of occasional labourers, loafers, and semi-criminals.	
B.	Casual earnings – 'very poor'	
C.	Intermittent earnings	together the 'poor'.
D.	Small regular earnings	
E.	Regular standard earnings – above the line of poverty.	
F.	Higher class labour.	
G.	Lower middle class.	
H.	Upper middle class.	

Booth fixed his poverty line at an income of 18*s.*–21*s.* per week 'for a moderate family'. About 30 per cent of London's population were found to be living below this line. Booth described 'the poor' as those 'whose means may be sufficient, but are barely sufficient, for decent independent life'; the 'very poor' were those 'whose means are insufficient for this according to the usual standard of life in this country'. Booth's 'poor' were 'living under a struggle to obtain the necessaries of life and make both ends meet'; while the 'very poor' lived 'in a state of chronic want'. Class A, Booth's 'residuum', comprised a relatively small (though alarming) number; but class B amounted to over 100,000 of the population of east London.

At the turn of the century Seebohm Rowntree's social survey of York – *Poverty, A Study of Town Life* (1901) – showed that for York as for London some 30 per cent of the population were living in poverty. London was plainly not a special case; and what was true for York was likely to be true for other provincial towns of its size (75,000) and bigger. The main weakness of Booth's description of poverty and unemployment had been his failure to take account of the trade cycle. His picture of poverty had remained static. Rowntree's was dynamic, making allowance for variations both in general economic and in family circumstances. He showed how an individual born into poverty could expect a period of prosperity when he left school and started work; how this would decline when he married and had children, rise again as his offspring began to earn, and finally worsen when his children left home and his strength began to fail with old age. Here was dynamic poverty, presented not as a snapshot but as a moving picture. This Rowntree life cycle had of course been described by earlier writers, but never against a firm background of statistics:

> 'A labourer is thus in poverty, and therefore underfed –
> (a) In childhood – when his constitution is being built up.
> (b) In early middle life – when he should be in his prime.
> (c) In old age.'

Women, added Rowntree, were in poverty during the greater part of the childbearing period.

Rowntree carefully defined two levels of poverty: 'primary' ('families whose total earnings were insufficient to obtain the minimum necessaries for the maintenance of merely physical efficiency'), and 'secondary' ('families whose total earnings would have been sufficient for the maintenance of merely physical efficiency were it not that some portion of it was absorbed by other expenditure, either useful or wasteful'). Nearly 10 per cent of York's population lingered in primary poverty, nearly 18 per cent in secondary poverty.

Though poverty was still extensive at the end of the century, it had probably been still more widespread in the 1860s. Certainly, the percentage of the population in receipt of poor relief was falling markedly from the 1870s:[9]

	Indoor paupers		Outdoor paupers		Total	
	Mean number	Per cent of population	Mean number	Per cent of population	Mean number	Per cent of population
1870	156,800	0.71	876,000	3.9	1,032,800	4.6
1880	180,817	0.71	627,213	2.5	808,030	3.2
1890	187,921	0.66	587,296	2.1	775,217	2.7
1900	215,377	0.68	577,122	1.8	792,499	2.5

The numbers receiving relief during the course of each year were about double these totals, which were the mean of the numbers granted relief in England and Wales on 1 January and on 1 July preceding. The cost of poor relief was kept well under control, despite population increase. Expenditure for London, which had reached £2 million by 1882, did not pass £3 million until 1896; expenditure for the rest of England and Wales, which had first exceeded £6 million in 1868, did not exceed £7 million until 1896.[10]

It was often asserted that the working classes were now more widely prosperous than ever before. *The Times* Golden Jubilee survey (21.6.1887) claimed that 'every class down to the poorest, and not excluding even absolute paupers, has adopted a standard of living very much higher than that which contented our grandfathers or even our fathers'; life had been 'sweetened at every step by improvements purchased either by private or public expenditure of which they could hardly have dreamed'. The *Final Report* of the Royal Commission on Depression in Trade and Industry (1886) spoke of 'the immense improvement' in the condition of the working classes over the previous twenty years. Often-cited statistical support for these optimistic generalizations was provided by two leading contemporary social statisticians – Sir Robert Giffen, who lectured in 1883 to the Statistical Society on 'The Progress of the Working Classes in the Last Half-Century'; and Leon Levi, who in 1885 published a new edition of his 1867 book on *Wages and Earnings of the Working Classes*. Giffen argued that the rich, though more numerous, were not richer than in earlier times, and that the poor were on average twice as well-off as fifty years earlier. 'The "poor" have thus had almost all the benefit of the great material advance of the last fifty years.' But this comforting measurement was based upon errors in the selection and comparison of statistics.[11] In reality, business profits assessed under income-tax schedule D for the same fraction of the population as paid tax in 1850 had risen some 60 per cent by 1880. During the same period average money wages had increased only some 47 per cent and real wages 34 per cent, both figures without subtraction for unemployment. In other words, the better-off classes were benefiting not least but most of all from 'the great material advance' noticed by Giffen. Nevertheless, the position of the working classes was certainly improving. United Kingdom average real wages rose a further 30–40 per cent between 1880 and the end of the century.

3

By the 1880s enough of the working classes were becoming sufficiently prosperous to constitute a mass market for a widening range of consumer goods and of foods other than bare necessities. Between 1870 and 1900 United Kingdom personal expenditure upon consumer goods increased by half, while spending upon services more than doubled:[12]

	Expenditure on tea, coffee, alcohol, tobacco, fish, coal, motor cars, and cycles at current retail prices (£m.)	Total consumption finished consumer goods at current retail prices (£m.)	Consumption of services at current prices (£m.)	Total personal consumption of goods and services at current prices (£m.)
1870	183.7	715.3	238.8	954
1880	224.5	835.2	310.8	1,146
1890	250.2	851.7	401.4	1,253
1900	313.2	1,087.4	521.1	1,609

The inrush of cheap imported food from the 1870s transformed the cost, quality, and range of working-class diet:[13]

| Commodity (in lb) | Food imports per head of United Kingdom population (annual averages) | | | | |
	1861–5	1871–5	1881–5	1891–5	1901–5
Wheat and wheat flour	127	171	231	259	276
Total, all grains	224	335	423	488	527
Sugar	41	57	74	82	84
Tea	2.8	4.0	4.7	5.4	6.1
Coffee	1.2	1.0	0.9	0.7	0.7
Cocoa	0.1	0.2	0.3	0.6	1.1
Butter and margarine	3.9	4.8	7.2	10.4	13.2
Lard	1.3	1.8	2.5	3.8	4.9
Cheese	2.9	4.7	5.7	6.3	6.8
Currants	3.8	4.4	4.3	4.8	4.3

Commodity (in lb)	Food imports per head of United Kingdom population (annual averages)				
	1861–5	1871–5	1881–5	1891–5	1901–5
Rice	5.8	9.9	13.3	8.6	13.7
Ham and bacon	4.2	7.8	11.8	14.1	18.0
Eggs (no.)	9	19	26	36	53
Fresh meat	0.1	0.2	3.5	12.4	23.0

Between 1870 and 1913 United Kingdom annual consumption of tea rose from about 4.0 lb per head to about 6.5 lb. By the 1890s strong-flavoured Indian and Ceylon teas – preferred by the working classes – had taken three-quarters of the enlarged market, displacing the more delicate Chinese and Japanese leaves. One expert wrote in 1893 that he now felt 'almost justified in calling tea the English national drink'.[14]

Significantly, consumption per head of wheat had ceased to rise – a sign that the basic appetite for bread was now met for the majority. The consumption of potatoes per head was even declining, especially in the towns. The diet of working-class families above the poverty line was now becoming adequate for health:[15]

Estimated budget of the median family

Date: Wage:	Unit	Cal. per unit	1880 26s. 6d.		1914 35s. 6d.	
			No. of units	Cost	No. of units	Cost
				s. d.		s. d.
Bread	4 lb	5,000	11	4 7	10½	5 3
Meat	1 lb	1,200	4	2 4	10	7 1
Bacon	1 lb	2,685	1	11½	1½	1 5½
Suet, etc.	1 lb	3,540	1	6	1	7
Butter	1 lb	3,605	1	1 3	1½	1 9¾
Margarine	1 lb	3,525	—	—	½	3
Cheese	1 lb	2,055	½	4½	¾	6¾
Milk, fresh	1 pt	406	10	1 8	12	1 9
Potatoes	1 lb	310	28	1 10	21	1 3
Vegetables	—	—	—	—	—	3
Rice, etc.	1 lb	1,630	2	4	3	6
Tea	1 oz	0	6	1 0¾	8	10¾
Sugar	1 lb	1,860	4	1 2	5	11¼
Total for food	—	—	—	16 0¾	—	22 7
Rent	—	—	—	3 6	—	5 0
Fuel, etc.	—	—	—	1 6	—	1 6
Clothing	—	—	—	2 0	—	2 6
Sundries	—	—	—	3 5¼	—	3 11
Total	—	—	—	26 6	—	35 6
Calorie value	—	—	94,100	—	106,900	—
Calorie value per 'man' per day	—	—	3,470	—	3,900	—

More meat, butter, and milk were being eaten by working people; and fruit was being added to their diets, especially in the form of jam. During the Edwardian period bananas were first imported in large quantities, and quickly achieved popularity as the cheapest fruit for the urban poor. Not all was advance, however. Margarine first became familiar on English tables in the 1870s. Its palatability was gradually improved, but its nutritional quality remained low. Tinned condensed skimmed milk – much inferior in food value to fresh milk – also became very popular with working-class families by the end of the century. Ignorance about food values and about diet balance was widespread, even among the middle classes. One meal which became very popular with the urban working classes was fried fish and chips. This did offer a balanced intake, especially if bought with peas. The first fish and chip shop was probably opened in Lancashire, perhaps in Oldham, soon after 1870.

An article by J. A. Hobson, the radical economist and social reformer, in the *Contemporary Review* for April 1896 took as its title the key question 'Is Poverty Diminishing?'. Hobson concluded that in material terms it was indeed lessening; but that expectations were expanding at an even faster rate. Here lay 'the peculiar danger of our recent civilisation'. Improved education, the spread of cheap reading matter, railways and the growth of easy communication, 'and, most potent of all, the experience of new sensations and the stimulation of new ideas provided by city life, have constantly and rapidly enlarged the scope of desires of the poorer classes'. As want diminished, a new problem of 'felt poverty' was arising.

Notes

1. A. L. Bowley, *Wages and Income in the United Kingdom Since 1860* (1937), p. 91.
2. F. Greenwood, 'What has become of the Middle Classes?', *Blackwood's Magazine*, August 1885, p. 177; A. L. Bowley, *Wages and Income in the United Kingdom Since 1860* (1937), p. 128.
3. Sir J. Stamp, *British Incomes and Property* (1922), pp. 318–19, 448.
4. Lee Holcombe, *Victorian Ladies at Work* (1973), pp. 203, 210.
5. See S. J. Chapman and F. J. Marquis, 'The Recruiting of the Employing Classes from the Ranks of the Wage-Earners in the Cotton Industry', *Journal of the Royal Statistical Society*, LXXV (1912).
6. See R. E. Pumphrey, 'The Introduction of Industrialists into the British Peerage', *American Historical Review*, LXV (1959); and F. M. L. Thompson, *English Landed Society in the Nineteenth Century* (1963), Ch. XI.
7. H. S. Maclauchlan, 'Ten Years of Millionaires', *Contemporary Review*, March 1897. See also W. D. Rubinstein, 'British Millionaires, 1809–1949', *Bulletin of the Institute of Historical Research*, XLVII (1974).
8. T. H. S. Escott, *Society in London* (1885), pp. 97–100. See also H. Pearson, *The Pilgrim Daughters* (1961).
9. M. E. Rose, *The Relief of Poverty, 1834–1914* (1972), p. 53.
10. *Royal Commission on the Poor Laws and Relief of Distress*, appendix Vol. I, minutes of evidence, Cd. 4625 (1909), appendix V (17).
11. H. Perkin, *The Origins of Modern English Society, 1780–1880* (1969), pp. 410–23.

See also S. Meacham, *A Life Apart, The English Working Class, 1890–1914* (1977).

12. J. B. Jefferys and Dorothy Walters, 'National Income and Expenditure of the United Kingdom', *Income and Wealth*, series V (1955), p. 27.

13. P. Mathias, *Retailing Revolution* (1967), p. 30. See especially J. Burnett, *Plenty and Want, A Social History of Diet in England from 1815 to the Present Day* (1966); T. C. Barker *et al.*, *Our Changing Fare* (1966); and D. J. Oddy and D. Miller (eds.), *The Making of the Modern British Diet* (1976).

14. See C. H. Denyer, 'The Consumption of Tea and Other Staple Drinks', *Economic Journal*, III (1893).

15. A. L. Bowley, *Wages and Income Since 1860* (1937), p. 36. See also R. N. Salaman, *The History and Social Influence of the Potato* (1949), pp. 532–6.

Chapter 14

Town life: *'A nice little back garden'*

1

By the end of the nineteenth century the English people had visibly become a nation of city and town dwellers. Significantly, the expression 'the man in the street' now came into general use; so also did the verb 'to urbanize' in the sense of to make a town rather than in the old sense of to render urbane.[1] The American A. F. Weber in his pioneering survey of *The Growth of Cities in the Nineteenth Century* (1899) declared that the tendency towards urban concentration was 'all but universal in the Western world', 'the most remarkable phenomenon of the present century'. In other Western countries, however, it was still a tendency, whereas in England it was already a preponderant reality. In 1801 little more than one-third of the population of England and Wales had lived in an urban environment, but by mid-century this had risen to one-half of a doubled population. Then by 1901 it had passed three-quarters of a population which had nearly doubled again:[2]

	Population		Urban percentage
	Total	Urban	
1801	8,900,000	3,100,000	34.8
1851	17,900,000	9,000,000	50.2
1881	26,000,000	17,600,000	67.9
1901	32,500,000	25,100,000	77.0

Between 1871 and 1901 the number of towns in England and Wales with more than 50,000 inhabitants rose from 37 to 75. In 1901, 14,200,000 people – well over half the urban population – lived in cities with populations greater than 100,000. These cities formed the cores of six large urban areas which were so extensively and intensively urban as to require a new word to describe them. This word – 'conurbation' – was duly coined by Patrick Geddes, the pioneering town planner, in his book *Cities in Evolution* (1915):

Population of conurbations

	Greater London	South-east Lancashire	West Midlands	West Yorkshire	Merseyside	Tyneside
1871	3,890,000	1,386,000	969,000	1,064,000	690,000	346,000
1881	4,770,000	1,685,000	1,134,000	1,269,000	824,000	426,000
1901	6,586,000	2,117,000	1,483,000	1,524,000	1,030,000	678,000

Greater London formed much the biggest conurbation. By 1901 it contained one-fifth of the entire population of England and Wales, and during the preceding decade it absorbed (from reproduction or immigration) one-quarter of all population increase. During the last quarter of the nineteenth century – while the provincial cities were losing some of their attractiveness as social and political centres – London was becoming a world city, the hub of an empire of unprecedented size.[3]

Not all was praise of London, however. Observers frequently contrasted the glitter of its high life with the darkness of its low life, its 'vortices of prosperity and misery'. Charles Booth's great survey of *Life and Labour of the People in London* was started in the late 1880s; but the squalor of much working-class life in the capital had sprung quite suddenly into heightened middle- and upper-class notice some five years earlier. At that time came the publication, successively, of Walter Besant's East End novel *All Sorts and Conditions of Men* in the summer of 1882; of a series of newspaper articles on London slum life by G. R. Sims and others during 1883; and in October 1883 of a small anonymous pamphlet with the compelling title of *The Bitter Cry of Outcast London*. This pamphlet, was chiefly the work of the Reverend Andrew Mearns, secretary of the London Congregational Union. It contained little new evidence; but it went beyond the usual descriptions of externalities into a powerful account of the almost animal nature of life in overcrowded slums. 'Every room in these rotten and reeking tenements houses a family, often two. In one cellar a sanitary inspector reports finding a father, mother, three children, and four pigs!' The confident assertion that immorality was 'but the natural outcome of conditions like these' was probably what gave the pamphlet its particular impact, especially after it had been re-published in adroitly condensed form in the *Pall Mall Gazette*. 'Incest is common.' W. T. Stead, the *Gazette*'s flamboyant editor, used *The Bitter Cry* as a basis for pressing the housing question to the forefront of social politics, in language which deliberately kept the moral (or rather, the immoral) aspect at the centre of discussion. 'The man who lives by letting a pestilential dwelling-house is morally on a par with a man who lives by keeping a brothel.'[4]

Articles on working-class housing by Lord Salisbury, the Conservative leader, and by Joseph Chamberlain, the radical leader, followed respectively in the *National Review* for November and the *Fortnightly Review* for December 1883. Both articles were widely read. Daringly for a Conservative, Salisbury advocated the granting of a public loan to the

Peabody Trustees. Chamberlain in reply accused Salisbury of thereby wishing to place a burden upon the community which ought to be borne by landowners. 'The expense of making towns habitable for the toilers who dwell in them must be thrown on the land which their toil makes valuable, and without any effort on the part of its owners.' A Royal Commission on the Housing of the Working Classes (1884-5) resulted from this upsurge of public interest, with the Prince of Wales as a member. Its report described the limited success both of legislation and of charitable effort in combating the slum problem. Overcrowding was named as the central evil. But few remedies were proposed beyond urging more decisive use of the existing powers of local authorities.

The 1890 Housing of the Working Classes Act was mainly a codifying measure. Nevertheless, by simplifying procedures it did encourage the initiation of some municipal housing schemes. By 1904 over eighty towns had borrowed about £4,250,000 under the act, compared with only £2,500,000 borrowed during 1875-90. But local authorities were often still inhibited by having to buy slums dear even though they wished to re-house slum dwellers cheap. Moreover, the places with the biggest slum problems were usually too poor to raise large sums through the rates or from borrowing. No national housing subsidies were available to overcome these local difficulties. Rents charged for the limited amount of municipal housing which was offered had therefore to be set too high for most of the slum families ejected to make space for it. Demolition costs for the new London County Council's first major scheme in Bethnal Green (1893-1900) averaged over £300 per family. There was no acceptance yet that local authorities might undertake house building as a social service quite apart from slum clearance.

The volume of national house building passed through a trough in the mid 1880s and reached a peak at the turn of the century:[5]

	Houses built in Great Britain (annual averages per quinquennium)
1875-9	113,500
1880-4	81,700
1885-9	78,000
1890-4	83,200
1895-9	128,200
1900-4	145,300

The housing stock of England and Wales stood at 5,218,000 in 1881, and 6,710,000 in 1901. The 1894 London Building Act laid down the first fully effective building code, and its standards came to be nationally adopted. 'Bye-law streets', built to a minimum regulation standard of sanitation and construction, were becoming a noticeable feature of the working-class districts in England's cities and towns. They were straight and wide, often gas-lit, adequately drained and supplied with water; but repetitive, bleak, and often treeless.

The regulation of new building did nothing to reduce overcrowding.

The 1891 census showed that 11.23 per cent of the people of England and Wales lived more than two persons per tenement. The worst area was the industrial north-east, where Gateshead had over 40 per cent of its population overcrowded, Newcastle over 35 per cent and Sunderland nearly 33 per cent. Yet not all towns faced a major overcrowding problem. Nottingham, Derby, and Leicester reported only 2–4 per cent overcrowding. Local factors were said to have caused these contrasts, 'such as the inherited habits of the people in this and that district, the architectural history of this and that town, and the nature of the ground on which it is built'.[6] But by the time of the 1901 census a distinct overall improvement was apparent. The national percentage of the population overcrowded had now fallen to 8.20 per cent of a larger total, though the chief towns of the north-east still suffered from more than 30 per cent overcrowding. The London figure was still 16 per cent, with double that percentage in the worst localities. The article on 'Housing' in the 1910 edition of the *Encyclopedia Britannica* attributed the improvement of the 1890s to the spread of electric tramcars, which had made the suburbs more accessible to the working classes; to the decline in the birth rate, which had reduced the pressure upon housing; and to the influence of public health regulations. Much of the overcrowding that remained, claimed the article, was 'voluntary', because many large families took in lodgers and because foreign immigrants chose to herd together in London, the ports, and a few manufacturing towns.

Were the crowded and unhealthy conditions of town life producing not merely mass individual ill-health but permanent deterioration of the physique of the new race of town dwellers? This was a question which began to be urgently asked, especially in relation to London and the big cities. It was often asserted that Londoners died out in the second or third generation. Charles Booth and his fellow investigators contended that country-born immigrants were taking over all the jobs in London which required good physique and intelligence. But analysis by Weber in the 1890s, and by historians since, has found no such simple pattern.[7] Costermongers and dock labourers continued to be mostly London-born, whereas gas workers, busmen, railway labourers, and domestic servants were often immigrants from the country. In one trade which demanded great physical strength – brewing – less than four out of ten workers had been born in London; but among coal labourers, another physically demanding job, six out of ten were Londoners by birth. It was certainly true, however, that London's East End – with its reputation for poverty – attracted a low proportion of rural immigrants, who preferred instead the inner ring of suburbs.

Weber emphasized in *The Growth of Cities* how city types were neither irretrievably caught up in physical decline nor were they bound to slip into moral decline and a life of crime. Town crime was increasing less rapidly than town population. Indictable offences known to the police in England and Wales actually fell by almost a quarter from over 100,000 in 1882 to 76,000 in 1899. Admittedly, they again averaged about 100,000 per year during the later Edwardian years; but the population of England and Wales then stood some 10 million higher than in the early 1880s. The spread of elementary education had checked the recruitment of youngsters into the criminal classes of London and the large towns. Those who did take to crime were no longer given brief prison sentences, but were confined to reformatories for long periods. Assaults on police in ten north of England police districts fell by one-half between the early 1870s and the late 1880s.[8]

Policemen were now being recruited from among working men of a superior type compared with recruits of the early-Victorian period. But the Criminal Investigation Department of the Metropolitan Police was not formed until 1878, and long thereafter the calibre of English detectives was said to fall well below that of the French. The CID was much criticized for its failure to solve the 'Jack the Ripper' murders of the last months of 1888.[9] The bodies of five women, all prostitutes, were discovered in Whitechapel, London, disembowelled and mutilated; and the similarities of technique strongly pointed to a single murderer. The newspapers roused public fear and fascination to a remarkable level all over the country. Numerous public figures – from the Duke of Clarence, second in line to the throne, downwards – were rumoured to be responsible. The privileged position of the murderer, it was suggested, could explain the failure of the police to make an arrest. The real reason was that forensic science barely existed at this date. Even an acceptable method of taking and comparing fingerprints was not adopted until the 1890s. A maniac sexual killer was, moreover, a morbid type – at war with urban society – to which the police had not yet grown accustomed. While the professionals were faltering, the reading public turned for reassurance to a fictional amateur – Sherlock Holmes. The first of Arthur Conan Doyle's Holmes short stories, 'A Scandal in Bohemia', appeared in the *Strand Magazine* for July 1891. Detective stories became highly popular, and Holmes soon had many imitators.

2

In 'A Defence of Detective Stories' (1901) G. K. Chesterton wrote of 'that thrilling mood and moment when the eyes of the great city, like the eyes of a cat, begin to flame in the dark'. City lights exerted a fascination over the late-Victorians. Not only were the lights often cheerful in their brightness, they extended by many hours the length of every man's day both for work and (increasingly) for recreation. Whistler's *Nocturnes*, painted in the 1870s, expressed his liking for London in the twilight when 'tall chimneys become campanali' and at night when warehouses seemed like palaces.[10] The 'decadent' writers and artists of the 1890s enthused about the city, and especially about London, because it amounted to a re-shaping of the natural world:[11]

Ah, London! London! our delight,
Great flower that opens but at night,
Great City of the Midnight Sun,
Whose day begins when day is done.

But the 'counter-decadents' likewise praised city life, because it showed man's mental and physical power. The gradual spread between 1880 and the end of the century of electric street and shop-window lighting – intense and steady, in contrast to gas light – only added to this sense of power. And the introduction of electric tramcars from the 1890s offered the excitement of bright moving lights along the night-time streets. W. S. Jevons explained in 1882 how the brightly lit streets of poor neighbourhoods formed 'the promenade ground of those who have few pleasures . . . To those who live in crowded dirty lodgings unsavoury streets may be a breathing-place, and the well-filled shop windows the only available museum of science and art.'[12]

'Shopping' was becoming a new leisure activity, especially for middle-class women.[13] Shoppers now came forth not only to buy what was known to be needed but also to be tempted into purchasing goods on display. Large and lavish department stores grew up rapidly in city shopping centres from the 1870s. In London Whiteleys and Harrods led the way. William Whiteley had opened his haberdashery shop in 1863; but within a few years he had become 'the Universal Provider'. Prices of goods in department stores were fixed and known. The days of haggling were passing, even in small shops. Osbert Lancaster has remembered the prominent part played by the big stores in the Edwardian life of his family. 'All my female relatives had their own favourites, where some of them had been honoured customers for more than half a century and their arrival was greeted by frenzied bowing on the part of frock-coated shopwalkers, and where certain of the older assistants stood to them almost in the relationship of confessors.'[14] Shop service was thus still personalized. Then in 1909 the American Gordon Selfridge opened his Oxford Street store. This was elaborate both in its architecture and in its provision for customers; and it offered the ultimate service – which, paradoxically, meant the absence of service unless asked for. Customers could come and go without being expected to buy. Here, proclaimed Selfridge, was 'freedom of the stores'.

Department stores could only be sited at or near the centres of cities and big towns; but the other major innovators in retailing – the multiple chain stores – set out to establish themselves along every significant urban and suburban high street.[15] They often specialized in selling goods which had just begun to be mass produced: footwear (Freeman, Hardy, and Willis), men's clothing (Burton's), books (W. H. Smith), chemists' items (Boot's), and cheap imported foods (Lipton's; Home and Colonial; and others). These multiple firms played a significant part in raising the standard of living and diet among the late-Victorian lower middle and working classes. Aggressive advertising enabled the multiples to capture large numbers of customers, and thereby to trade at very low profit margins. The grocery chains concentrated upon a few lines – tea, sugar, cheese, ham, bacon, butter, eggs, margarine.

In middle-class areas and in working-class backstreets family-owned shops could hold out against the multiples by offering (at higher prices) a more personal service and bigger choice. In 1915 about 80 per cent of all retail sales were still being made by small, mainly single-shop businesses. Nevertheless, the economic impact of the multiples was striking; as also was their visual impact, with their arresting, standardized shop fronts and skilful window displays. The estimated number of multiple shop branches in the United Kingdom grew from just over 1,500 in 1880 to more than 22,750 by 1915. Department stores then took 2–3 per cent of retail trade, multiples 7–8.5 per cent, and co-operative stores 7.5–9.0 per cent.

The 'co-ops.' thus constituted the biggest single retailing group in the late-Victorian and Edwardian periods.[16] Their members and customers were almost entirely working class. The Industrial and Provident Societies Act of 1862 had allowed local societies to federate, and this had made possible a national network. The Co-operative Wholesale Society was formed in 1863. By 1881 membership of United Kingdom retail associations totalled almost 550,000, with sales over £15 million; and by 1914 membership had reached well over 3 million, and turnover £88 million. The movement was especially strong in the north of England, particularly in the smaller industrial towns. In 1894, for example, it was estimated that three-quarters of the retail trade of Crewe passed through the local co-operative society. Certain middle-class groups also ventured upon co-operation. The Civil Service Supply Association was formed in 1865, the Civil Service Co-operative Society Ltd in 1866, and the Army and Navy Co-operative Society Ltd in 1872.

To serve the needs of the new shops and their customers, the number of shop assistants grew rapidly, especially of women assistants. Their conditions of work were often poor, and their hours stretched from early morning to late evening.[17] The Early Closing Association (1843) fought a long battle. At first it hoped for voluntary limitation of hours (which some West End stores did introduce), but before the end of the century it was pressing for legislative intervention. The 1911 Shops Act, though it provided for inspection and for a weekly half-holiday, still did not fix maximum hours of work; and clauses in the original bill about ventilation and provision of lavatories were deleted. 'Living in' was commonplace for assistants of both sexes, especially in the south of England. The regimented atmosphere of Edwardian shop work and residence was sensitively evoked by H. G. Wells in his novel *Kipps* (1905).

3

Many of the new department-store women shoppers had travelled up to town from the suburbs. The rate of suburban growth round London and the big provincial cities during the 1880s and 1890s was dramatic:[18]

	Inner London	Outer London
1881	3,830,000	940,000
1891	4,228,000	1,410,000
1901	4,536,000	2,050,000

One observer described London in 1888 'as to its greater part – a new city'. Between 1881 and 1891 the three English counties with the largest population increases were the Home Counties of Middlesex (51 per cent), Essex (38 per cent), and Surrey (24 per cent). In the next ten years the towns with the largest rates of growth were all on the edges of great cities – East Ham, Walthamstow, Leyton, West Ham, Willesden, Hornsey, Tottenham, and Croydon (round London), King's Norton, Handsworth, Smethwick (round Birmingham), and Wallasey (near Liverpool). In an article on 'The Rise of the Suburbs' in the *Contemporary Review* for October 1891 Sidney Low answered the fears of those who thought that town life was producing racial degeneration. Low had no doubt that 'the townsman of the middle classes, who has learned to live healthily in his suburb' was 'physically quite the equal of his rural competitor. The perpetual going and coming, the daily journeys by rail or tram or steamer, have not affected his health, while they have sharpened his faculties. He is more alert, more active, and more elastic than the rustic.' Low was the more optimistic because, thanks to shorter hours of work plus cheap trains and trams, working-class families were also beginning to move out. 'The life of the suburb may do for the town artisan in the future what it has already done for the clerk.' Low was thus restating the hopeful view of suburban spread, which had been voiced a generation earlier by Charles Kingsley. The opposing pessimistic view of Bagehot in the 1860s was likewise still being pressed in the 1890s. Frederic Harrison thought it 'a national calamity' that one-sixth of the English people were, as Londoners, 'cut off at once both from country life and city life'.[19]

But these were the opinions of intellectuals, who were not themselves representative suburbanites. Mrs Panton's advice to young married couples in her domestic guidebook *From Kitchen to Garrett* (1888) was a more typical suburban voice.

To young people, like my couple, I would strongly recommend a house some little way out of London. Rents are less; smuts and blacks conspicuous by their absence; a small garden, or even a tiny conservatory . . . is not an impossibility; and if Edwin has to pay for his season-ticket, that is nothing in comparison with his being able to sleep in fresh air, to have a game of tennis in summer, or a friendly evening of music, chess, or games in the winter, without expense.

Mrs Panton remained well aware of the poor quality of some suburban building, as she made clear eight years later in her book ominously entitled *Suburban Residences and how to Circumvent Them*. Mr Pooter, the anti-hero of George and Weedon Grossmith's *Diary of a Nobody* (1892), worked as a head clerk in the City of London, and withdrew each evening to his house in Holloway. 'After my work in the City I like to be at home. What's the good of a home, if you are never in it? "Home, Sweet Home", that's my motto.' Here was the home-centred suburban family. Distance from the 'culture' of the urban centre did not trouble such people. They welcomed the 'dullness' of suburban life and called it 'quiet'. The very names favoured for suburban villas suggested satisfaction, a sense of having arrived at a desired place. The most common were either rural, such as 'The Limes', 'Roselands', or 'The Laurels' (favoured by the Pooters); or romantic, such as 'Kenilworth', 'Iona', 'Malabar'.[20]

The Pooters lived near a suburban railway line – too near. But Mr Pooter characteristically made the best of it. 'We have a nice little back garden which runs down to the railway. We were rather afraid of the noise of the trains at first, but the landlord said we should not notice them after a bit, and took £2 off the rent.' In 1881 almost 800,000 people, including many Mr Pooters, were entering the City of London daily on foot or in vehicles; a total raised to nearly 1,122,000 by 1891. In 1881 twelve London railway stations were disgorging 176,000 passengers daily.[21] In short, the business life of London was becoming increasingly linked with suburban commuting. Many Londoners still walked to work; but by the turn of the century perhaps one in four – and probably a majority of the middle classes – were reaching their employment by some form of public transport:[22]

	Passenger traffic in Greater London			
	Railway (local companies)	Tramways	Bus (LGOC and LRCC)	Number of journeys per head
1880	133,877,485	64,817,361	57,722,231	54.8
1890	167,299,200	191,041,904	148,531,099	91.5
1902	273,767,648	358,119,754	279,466,557	136.0

These were contemporary estimates, to be taken as an indication of the rapid rate of growth rather than as accurate in detail. Commuters travelling into London for work, and others (especially women) engaged in search of shopping and entertainment were mixed together in the statistics. But it has been estimated that 410,000 people were reaching London each day by rail from the suburbs in 1901, of whom about 250,000 were commuters. 25,569 travelled at the workmen's 2*d*. fare, and 86,495 at other workmen's fares up to 11*d*. Workmen's trains had been in limited operation since the early 1860s. Legislation which allowed the destruction of housing for the sake of line extensions had begun to include clauses which bound the railway companies to help alleviate the slum problem which their demolitions were aggravating.[23]

They were required to offer cheap travel to the suburbs by way of compensation. The Great Eastern Railway Act of 1864 stimulated that company to give a lead. By 1903 it was running ten workmen's trains each day from a large number of stations at 1*d.* per journey, starting as much as 11 miles out from its terminus at Liverpool Street. From 1883 the Cheap Trains Act gave the Board of Trade general powers to compel railway companies to meet whatever demand might arise for such trains, or for cheap accommodation on other trains. Passenger duty was removed from all fares charged at not more than 1*d.* per mile. But other railway companies remained much less keen than the Great Eastern to encourage workmen to undertake train travel. The companies feared – with some justice – that contact with large numbers of working men would drive middle-class passengers to other suburbs and other lines. Of an estimated 27,569 commuters travelling at 2*d.* workmen's fare in 1901, over two-thirds came from east London suburbs served by the Great Eastern.

Travel within central London had been much accelerated with the opening of the world's first underground railway, the Metropolitan Line, in 1863. This had developed into the Inner Circle by 1884. In 1890 the first electric 'tube' line was built, free from the choking smoke of the underground's steam engines.[24] The further rapid development of London's tube lines during the Edwardian years came to be largely controlled, in the absence of British initiative, by the American transport millionaire, C. T. Yerkes, and his company, Underground Electric Railways of London.

While the railways were still expanding, many canals, now often owned by the railway companies themselves, were falling into neglect, despite expressions of concern at such waste of a national asset. But the greatest inland waterway of all – the Manchester Ship Canal – was opened in 1894. Mancunians had objected to allegedly extortionate rates levied at the port of Liverpool, and by the railways and the Bridgewater Navigation. The new canal allowed ocean-going ships to reach Manchester, which aspired to become a major port in its own right.[25]

Just as many canals were decaying, so most main roads had fallen into poor repair once long-distance traffic had switched to the railways. Late-Victorian trunk roads were much quieter than they had been fifty years earlier in the days of coaching. But by the 1890s revival was beginning, at the instance first of the bicycle and then of the motor car. In 1896 H. G. Wells published his bicycling story, *The Wheels of Chance*, which showed how lower middle-class men such as Mr Hopdriver (a draper's assistant), and young women also, were putting the main roads back into use for cycling tours. The first bicycles – the penny farthings – of the early 1870s had been for enthusiasts only. But the development of the low-built, chain-driven 'safety' bicycle during the 1880s, and of the pneumatic tyre at the end of the decade, opened the way for cycling as a mass activity among both sexes and all classes.[26] Between 1895 and 1897 came the 'bicycle boom' when cycling in Rotten Row and elsewhere even became briefly popular with younger 'Society' folk. Large-scale investment in bicycle manufacture eventually brought prices well down – to as low as £10 by the turn of the century, and to half that within a decade. All but the poorest came to afford at least second-hand 'bikes'.[27]

For the first time in history men and women of modest means could command their own private transport. Cycling, exclaimed A. J. Balfour, soon to become prime minister and himself an enthusiast, had helped to counter the problem of urban concentration. 'The cycle has saved us.' Village life also gained from this new mass mobility. The bicycle, it was written in 1909, 'far more than the railway, has put an end to the isolation of the village'.[28] The lives of young women who took to cycling had quite suddenly become much freer. Richard Le Gallienne's *Cycle Songs* (1896) suggested that women's emancipation was being achieved much more by the bicyclist than by the suffragist:

No, 'twas not constitutional –
    It came of a little wheel.

Yet the coming of the late-Victorian bicycle was only the start of the road-transport revolution. It was preparing the way technologically and psychologically for the advent of Edwardian motor car.

Notes

1. E. Partridge, *Words, Words, Words!* (1933), p. 70. See also E. E. Lampard, 'The Urbanizing World', in H. J. Dyos and M. Wolff (eds.), *The Victorian City* (1973).
2. R. Lawton, 'Rural Depopulation in Nineteenth Century England', in D. R. Mills (ed.), *English Rural Communities* (1973), p. 195. See also D. C. Marsh, *The Changing Social Structure of England and Wales, 1871–1961* (1965), pp. 66–71; and C. M. Law, 'The Growth of Urban Population in England and Wales, 1801–1911', *Transactions and Papers of the Institute of British Geographers*, XLI (1967).
3. See especially A. Briggs, *Victorian Cities* (1963), Ch. VIII; G. Stedman Jones, *Outcast London* (1971), Chs. 6, 11; and J. N. Tarn, *Five Per Cent Philanthropy* (1973), Chs. 7, 8.
4. See R. L. Schults, *Crusader in Babylon, W. T. Stead and the Pall Mall Gazette* (1972), pp. 49–61; and A. S. Wohl, *The Eternal Slum* (1977), Ch. 8. Also A. S. Wohl's 1970 edition of *The Bitter Cry of Outcast London*.
5. P. Mathias, *The First Industrial Nation* (1969), p. 490.
6. W. H. Mallock, *Classes and Masses* (1896), pp. 134–8.
7. See A. F. Weber, *The Growth of Cities in the Nineteenth Century* (1899: reprinted 1963), esp. Ch. VII; and G. Stedman Jones, *Outcast London* (1971), Ch. 6.
8. See especially T. A. Critchley, *A History of Police in England and Wales, 900–1966* (1967), Chs. 4, 5; J. J. Tobias, *Crime and Industrial Society in the 19th Century* (1967), Ch. 13; and R. D. Storch, 'The Policeman as Domestic Missionary: Urban Discipline and Popular Culture in Northern England, 1850–1880', *Journal of Social History*, Vol. 9 (1976).
9. See especially D. Rumbelow, *The Complete Jack the Ripper* (1975).
10. See E. H. D. Johnson, 'Victorian Artists and the Urban Milieu', in H. J. Dyos and M. Wolff (eds.), *The Victorian City* (1973).
11. See R. K. R. Thornton (ed.), *Poetry of the Nineties* (1970), Ch. 2.

12. W. S. Jevons, *The State in Relation to Labour* (1882), p. 84.
13. See especially J. B. Jefferys, *Retail Trading in Britain, 1850–1950* (1954); and Alison Adburgham, *Shops and Shopping, 1800–1914* (1964).
14. O. Lancaster, *All Done from Memory* (1963), pp. 35–6.
15. See P. Mathias, *Retailing Revolution* (1967).
16. See especially P. H. J. H. Gosden, *Self-Help, Voluntary Associations in the 19th Century* (1973), Ch. 7; and Julia Hood and B. S. Yamey, 'The Middle-class Co-Operative Retailing Societies in London, 1864–1900', *Oxford Economic Papers*, new series 9 (1957).
17. See W. B. Whitaker, *Victorian and Edwardian Shopworkers* (1973); and Lee Holcombe, *Victorian Ladies at Work* (1973), Ch. V.
18. See especially W. Ashworth, *The Genesis of Modern British Town Planning* (1954), Ch. VI; H. J. Dyos, *Victorian Suburb* (1961); and D. J. Olsen, *The Growth of Victorian London* (1976), Chs. 5, 8.
19. F. Harrison, *The Meaning of History* (1894), pp. 250–6.
20. M. Robbins, *Middlesex* (1953), p. 207.
21. *The Times*, 16 July 1881, 3 July 1891.
22. *Royal Commission on London Traffic, Appendices to the Evidence* (1906), Cd. 2752, appendix no. 6, p. 127. See also J. R. Kellett, *The Impact of Railways on Victorian Cities* (1969), pp. 377–81.
23. See H. J. Dyos, 'Workmen's Fares in South London, 1860–1914', *Journal of Transport History*, I (1953).
24. See T. C. Barker and M. Robbins, *History of London Transport* (1975–6), I, Ch. X; II, Chs. III–V.
25. See D. A. Farnie, 'The Manchester Ship Canal, 1894–1914', in W. H. Chaloner and B. M. Ratcliffe (eds), *Trade and Transport* (1977).
26. See especially C. F. Caunter, *The History and Development of Cycles* (1955); J. Woodforde, *The Story of the Bicycle* (1970); and D. Rubinstein, 'Cycling in the 1890s', *Victorian Studies*, XXI (1977).
27. See A. E. Harrison, 'The Competitiveness of the British Cycle Industry, 1890–1914', *Economic History Review*, second series, XXII (1969).
28. W. M. Short (ed.), *Arthur James Balfour as Philosopher and Thinker* (1912), p. 537; H. D. Traill and J. S. Mann, *The Building of Britain and the Empire* (n.d.), VI, p. 1041.

Chapter 15

Religious life: *'Post-Christian days'*

1

Until near the end of the nineteenth century most Anglican and Nonconformist leaders continued to believe that Christianity was prospering in England. Membership was still growing, and churches and chapels continued to be built to match the progress of urbanization[1]

	Church of England in England		
	Easter Day communicants	Churches	Clergy
1881	1,225,000	16,300	20,341
1891	1,490,000	16,956	22,753
1901	1,945,000	17,368	23,670

	Methodist membership in England					
	Wesleyan	New Connexion	Primitive	Bible Christian	United	Total
1881	349,695	25,797	168,807	21,209	65,067	630,575
1891	387,779	28,756	181,518	25,769	67,200	690,022
1901	412,194	32,324	187,260	28,315	72,568	732,661

	Congregational and Baptist membership in England			
	Congregational	Particular Baptist	General Baptist	Baptist Union
1880	—	176,500	24,489	
1890	—	194,500	26,805	
1900	257,435			239,114

	Roman Catholic in England and Wales			
	Estimated Catholic population	Churches	Priests	Mass attenders
1881	—	1,175	1,979	—
1891	1,357,000	1,387	2,604	726,000
1901	—	1,536	3,298	—

The Presbyterian Church of England expanded from 46,450 members in 1876 to 78,087 by 1901. Membership of the Society of Friends grew from 15,101 in 1881 to 17,476 in 1901.

Here was steady growth; but the sense of progress was misleading. Up to about 1885 church and chapel membership nearly kept pace with rising population. But this meant that in terms of absolute numbers more and more Victorians were staying outside the churches and chapels. And then from about 1885 attendances ceased even to keep in proportion to population size. Admittedly, unofficial religious censuses taken in various towns showed that great local variations could be expected within the general trend.[2] Over one-third of the population of Bristol attended church or chapel in the early 1880s, a much higher proportion than in the large industrial towns of the north and midlands. In middle-class centres of resort and retirement such as Bath and Hastings as many as half the population were church or chapel attenders. But most of the working classes were still keeping away from church or chapel, as they had done at the time of the 1851 religious census. This was confirmed for London of the 1880s and 1890s by Charles Booth's social survey: 'the great masses of the people remain apart from all forms of religious communion'. Certainly, the Sunday schools flourished in London and in many other towns, especially in the north. But, as Booth observed, 'the very choir boys when their voices crack promptly claim the privileges of men and give up churchgoing'. *Punch* (17.2.1894) suggested that board school religion had been made so carefully non-sectarian as to lose all Christian content and appeal. It composed a mock 'Universal Hymn for School Board Hymnals':

> Arise my soul – if soul I've got –
>   And, vaguely vocal, thank
> For all the blessings of my lot
>   The – Unknown Eternal Blank.
>
> I thank the – Streak of Azure Haze
>   That on my birth has smiled,
> And made me, in post-Christian days,
>   A happy School-Board child.

An ominous sign by the end of the century was the decline in the numbers of men coming forward for training as Anglican clergymen. Those annually ordained reached a peak of 814 in 1886, but the total had fallen to 569 by 1901. Opportunities for careers in the secular professions had much increased. Teachers in universities and public schools were no longer required to be in holy orders. The restless career of one fictional clergyman was portrayed by Matthew Arnold's neice, Mrs Humphry Ward, in her best-selling novel *Robert Elsmere*, published in 1888.[3] It showed Elsmere variously influenced by Darwin, by Ruskin, by William Morris, and (most notably) by T. H. Green, the Oxford idealist philosopher. Elsmere quit the Church of England to found a 'New Brotherhood' in London's East End, where he sought to make contact with the new urban realities. 'What does the artisan class, what does the town democracy throughout Europe, care any longer for Christian checks or Christian sanctions as they have been taught to understand them? Has Christianity brought us to this: that the Christian nations are to be the first in the world's history to try the experiment of a life without faith?' Gladstone discussed '*Robert Elsmere* and the 'Battle of Belief' in the *Nineteenth Century* for May 1888; and his intervention helped to raise sales as high as 70,000 copies by the end of 1891. The devout statesman found Elsmere's non-Christian deism more baffling than even agnosticism or atheism. How could it be consistent, he asked, to wish the retention of 'what was manifested, but to thrust aside the manifesting Person'? Elsmere's readiness to start a new religious group in response to spiritual uncertainty and social change was characteristic of the period. An article in *Blackwood's Magazine* for May 1890 described the contemporary rage for starting new religions, which it thought had originated with mid-Victorian positivism. 'To aspirants for fame in London drawing-rooms, I say without hesitation, "Start a New Religion, and start it at once".' Positivism had been followed by spiritualism, and the Society for Psychical Research had begun its investigations in 1882. Then had come theosophy, with Mrs Besant as its publicist. 'Just now Hypnotism is all the rage.'[4]

Migration from country to town, or from town to town, or within town – all of which were now occurring on a scale never before experienced – could easily break habits of churchgoing. Moreover, new forms of Sunday amusement and recreation were spreading – including the popularization of the bicycle.[5] Details of hours of church services first began to appear in rural church porches in the 1890s, in the hope of attracting cycle-excursionists who had wandered far from their home places of worship. Many churches and chapels tried to come to terms with these new influences by incorporating them into their routines. Cycling clubs, sporting clubs, music societies, youth groups, women's groups, excursion and holiday groups, and the like were formed as church or chapel extensions. But this effort brought with it the danger that secular activity would begin to seem more important than worship or belief. The Congregational *British Weekly* remarked in 1891 that 'those who come to church because there is amusement to be found in connection with it, remain only as long as this attraction lasts for them. You do not find such persons eager to attend the services'.[6]

2

Another complaint of the late 1880s and 1890s was that clergymen no longer preached the gospel because they had turned to preach instead about social questions. The rise of the condition of England question, and of 'socialism', to prominence meant that the denominations had to decide how to respond. Christian Socialism had been advocated by

F. D. Maurice and others in the 1850s and 1860s; but the Maurice party had attracted only limited response within the Church of England. In the next generation, however, Anglican clergymen who had been inspired by Maurice's example gained considerable influence.[7] The Guild of St Matthew, formed in 1877 and dominated by the Reverend Stewart Headlam, an East End clergyman, never rose above 450 members at its peak in 1894–5, over a quarter of them Anglican clergy. But it broke ground for other organizations – notably for the Christian Social Union, started in 1889. Headlam's list of questions to candidates at the 1885 general election showed how the Guild of St Matthew advocated not only social reform but was also inclined to support political radicalism. He believed that the state constituted a sacred organism which ought to be used for Christian ends; Christian duty required agitation in support of free elementary education, land reform, an eight hours bill, universal suffrage, and Lords reform.

The social service idealism of the Christian Social Union was less precise and less politically radical, and therefore more widely supported within the Church of England. Its leaders were upper-class and successful – Brooke Foss Westcott, Charles Gore (both of whom became bishops), and Henry Scott Holland (canon of St Paul's, and later Regius Professor of Divinity at Oxford). All three had been influenced at Oxford by T. H. Green. In 1889 Gore, Holland, and others published *Lux Mundi*, a symposium of essays designed to demonstrate that God intended the new secular knowledge to reveal the essential truth of incarnational religion. The book provoked a strongly hostile reaction from old-fashioned Anglicans – the more so because the authors did not admit to being innovators, but claimed to be expounding Anglican orthodoxy. Gore was unfairly charged with putting interest in social questions before faith. The CSU reached a maximum membership of about 6,000 including many bishops. Its programme remained vague; but it did establish that the Church of England was bound to take account of the disorders of the social system, and that well-meaning support for charity and other palliatives was not enough.

Unfortunately, the CSU spoke almost entirely to the middle classes. The Church of England still found it difficult to understand urban working-class culture and values. City 'settlements' were started during the 1880s in the East End of London and elsewhere by dedicated clergymen and lay volunteers; but even these foundations exuded university and middle-class culture (see below, p. 298). Charles Booth concluded that the churches and chapels could enrol only those working-class Londoners who were able and willing to adopt middle-class ways. 'As those of them who do join any church become almost indistinguishable from the class with which they then mix, the change that has really come about is not so much *of* as *out of* the class to which they have belonged.'

Certainly, the 'Nonconformist conscience' – first so named by a

Wesleyan minister in *The Times* of 28 November 1890 – was decidedly not a working-class way of regarding life and religion.[8] It placed heavy emphasis upon social negatives – strongly against drinking, against gambling, against the music halls. The Parnell divorce case of 1890 had brought the 'Nonconformist conscience' into clamorous action. It insisted that Parnell, as an adulterer, must resign his leadership of the Irish Nationalists in Parliament if British Liberals were to continue to work with them for the enactment of Home Rule (see below, p. 355). In the same spirit Sir Charles Dilke had been driven from a leading place in the Liberal Party in 1886 when his alleged adultery became a matter of court action. 'All impure men must be hounded from public life,' proclaimed the *Methodist Times* (10.9.1885), expelled by 'the Supreme Court of the Public Conscience of the Nation'.[9] The editor of the *Methodist Times* was Hugh Price Hughes, a Wesleyan minister who became the best-known voice of the 'Nonconformist conscience'. In 1896 he was elected the first president of the National Free Church Council. Nonconformists were now increasingly calling themselves by the more positive name of 'Free Churchmen.'

The 'Nonconformist conscience' did try to develop a positive social side, even though traditional evangelical influence within the chapels preferred to emphasize the next rather than the present world. 'Modern Methodism feels that, besides being an ecclesiastical organization and a spiritual power, it must also be a social force striving, by the application of a practical Christianity, to lengthen the lives, improve the homes, educate the minds, and raise the moral and physical standard of the people.' So claimed Skeats and Miall's *History of the Free Churches in England* (1891). The Wesleyans began to modify their circuit system to meet the needs of densely populated areas by opening central mission halls in London and other towns, as part of what Price Hughes called 'the Forward Movement'. But the 1898 Wesleyan conference admitted that contact with the working classes remained generally weak. 'The supreme question is, who shall capture the unconverted millions, the seventy-five per cent of the population outside any place of worship.' R. W. Dale, the Congregational leader, contended, however, that the special mission of his denomination was to the middle classes, 'to draw to Christ those who are never likely to be reached by the Salvation Army'.[10]

The Salvation Army had been formed by William Booth, a one time Methodist preacher, with the aim of bringing Christianity to the tens of thousands who lived in urban squalor beyond the reach of more conventional religious approaches. It deliberately set out to be different – noisy but disciplined. It adopted military organization and uniforms, and marched behind brass bands.[11] 'General' Booth remained in absolute command through to his death in 1912. In an unpolished midlands accent he preached a simple and evangelistic message, 'Blood and Fire' – 'the precious blood of Christ's atonement by which only we were saved, and the Holy Spirit who sanctifies, energizes, and comforts the true soldiers of God.' The movement had begun in London during the 1860s; but not until the late 1870s did it start to be called the Salvation Army and to adopt military forms. Growth of membership was then rapid until the end of the century; from 127 'officers' in 1878 to 2,260 by 1886, and 4,170 by 1899.[12] Recruits came chiefly from the artisan and lower middle classes, and men and women were treated equally. At first the police and magistrates viewed the movement with suspicion. Salvationists were imprisoned on charges of obstruction or provocation to riot because of their insistence upon street preaching. Roughs, organized in some places as the 'Skeleton Army', also broke up meetings. Gradually during the 1880s, however, the Salvation Army gained acceptance. The Church Army, started in 1882, represented a mild Anglican imitation, which sent mission groups into slum parishes.

At first William Booth had wanted to place heavy emphasis upon spiritual salvation; but by the late 1880s he had come to accept the importance of social work as a step towards saving souls. In 1890 he published *In Darkest England, and The Way Out*. This book described the vast extent of contemporary poverty, and then offered a scheme for solving the problem of the unemployed by sending them through a succession of self-sustaining communities – a City Colony, a Farm Colony near London, and the Oversea Colony in one of the colonies. Only thus, argued Booth, could the 'submerged tenth' be saved for Christianity. The book aroused widespread interest, and £100,000 was subscribed. A farm colony was opened in Essex, but the overseas colony never materialized. The Salvation Army persisted with relief work among the very poor and the residuum, which no other sect was equipped to undertake. But in terms of converting large numbers to Christian belief and practice it proved to be no more successful than the conventional churches and chapels. Some thousands had found their own salvation in becoming officers; but (as Charles Booth emphasized in his London survey) 'not by this road . . . will religion be brought to the mass of the English people'.

Notes

1. See O. Chadwick, *The Victorian Church*, II (2nd edn, 1972), esp. Ch. V; A. D. Gilbert, *Religion and Society in Industrial England* (1976), esp. Ch. 2; and R. Currie *et al.*, *Churches and Churchgoers* (1977).
2. See H. McLeod, 'Class, Community and Region: the Religious Geography of Nineteenth-Century England', *Sociological Yearbook of Religion in Britain*, Vol. 6 (1973), Ch. 2; and H. McLeod, *Class and Religion in the Late Victorian City* (1974).
3. See especially, W. S. Peterson, *Victorian Heretic* (1976).
4. See especially A. H. Nethercott, *The First Five Lives of Annie Besant* (1960), part V; W. M. Simon, 'Auguste Comte's English Disciples', *Victorian Studies*, VIII (1964); and A. Gauld, *The Founders of Psychical Research* (1968).
5. See especially O. Chadwick, *The Victorian Church*, II (2nd edn, 1972), part VIII; and O. Chadwick, *The Secularisation of the European Mind in the Nineteenth Century* (1976).

6. K. S. Inglis, *Churches and the Working Classes in Victorian England* (1963), pp. 78–9. See also S. Yeo, *Religion and Voluntary Organisations in Crisis* (1976).

7. See especially K. S. Inglis, *Churches and the Working Classes in Victorian England* (1963), Ch. 7; P. d'A. Jones, *The Christian Socialist Revival, 1877–1914* (1968); and G. Kitson Clark, *Churchmen and the Condition of England, 1832–1885* (1973).

8. See especially J. F. Glaser, 'Parnell's Fall and the Nonconformist Conscience', *Irish Historical Studies*, XII (1960–1); and J. Kent, 'Hugh Price Hughes and the Nonconformist Conscience', in G. V. Bennett and J. D. Walsh (eds.), *Essays in Modern Church History in Memory of Norman Sykes* (1966).

9. E. Trudgill, *Madonnas and Magdalens* (1976), pp. 199–200. See especially, R. Jenkins, *Sir Charles Dilke* (1958).

10. A. W. W. Dale, *Life of R. W. Dale* (1899), p. 613. See especially K. S. Inglis, 'English Nonconformity and Social reform', *Past and Present* no. 13 (1958); and K. S. Inglis, *Churches and the Working Classes in Victorian England* (1963), Ch. 2.

11. See especially K. S. Inglis, *Churches and the Working Classes in Victorian England* (1963), Ch. 5; R. Robertson, 'The Salvation Army: the Persistence of Sectarianism', in B. R. Wislon (ed.), *Patterns of Sectarianism* (1967); and Christine Parkin, 'The Salvation Army and Social Questions of the Day', *Sociological Yearbook of Religion in Britain*, Vol. 5 (1967). Also R. Sandall and A. R. Wiggins, *History of the Salvation Army*, 4 vols. (1947–64).

12. R. Currie *et al.*, *Churches and Churchgoers* (1977), pp. 208–9.

Chapter 16

Cultural life: *'Art for art's sake'*

1

The first half of the reign of Queen Victoria had been the heyday of the Victorian sages: Carlyle had spoken powerfully on social and political questions, Newman on theology, Ruskin on art and society.[1] During the second half of the reign Matthew Arnold was trying to speak with a similar authority in advocating the pursuit of 'sweetness and light'. Perhaps the influence of the sages had never been so great as some sympathetic twentieth-century commentators have liked to imagine. Certainly, Anthony Trollope – a representative figure – remarked in his autobiography, written in the mid 1870s, how contemporaries were refusing to be influenced by the pessimism of Carlyle or Ruskin. 'The loudness and extravagance of their lamentations' seemed 'so contrary to the convictions of men who cannot but see how comfort has been increased, how health has been improved, and education extended.' Had the sages been wrong in their warnings? Or was it that society – increasingly urbanized, commercialized, and democratized – now lacked the capacity to accept their guidance because it had become irretrievably corrupted? Materially, as Trollope emphasized, many late-Victorians were becoming much more satisfied. And satisfaction was a suspect state of mind according to Matthew Arnold, since (as he argued in *Culture and Anarchy*) culture properly understood 'begets a dissatisfaction'. It was an ideal standard to be earnestly pursued, and yet never to be attained. 'Not a having and a resting, but a growing and a becoming.'

   Arnold was heard but not followed. One difficulty was that, despite his advocacy of a whole culture embracing all classes and all knowledge, he sounded too much like an 'intellectual', a person apart. It may have been significant that the very word 'intellectual' seems to have first come into use during the third quarter of the century. After Arnold, intellectuals began to withdraw from public advocacy, to concentrate instead upon the private development and enjoyment of their separate interests. The growing volume of specialized knowledge associated with each discipline was making it increasingly difficult to comprehend the whole range of the arts and sciences. Lord Acton, the historian – who continued to try – died in 1902 surrounded by unread books. By this date all the other leading English historians had succumbed to 'specialization' – another significant new word – not only upon their subject but increasingly by period within it. Specialization in historical and other studies at the universities was also in part a response to pressure for more thorough teaching and examination. The growth of the professions had increased the demand for paper qualifications.

H. T. Buckle's broadly-conceived *History of Civilisation in England* (1857–61) had been so popular that it was bracketed by Bernard Shaw in 1894 with Marx's *Capital* as one of the two most influential books of the century.[2] The histories of J. A. Froude, E. A. Freeman, and J. R. Green had all sold well when published between the 1860s and the early 1880s. But in the next generation F. W. Maitland, the brilliant legal historian, declined the regius chair at Cambridge in 1902 in part because he refused to meet the expectation that he should 'speak to the world at large'. History was now proclaimed as a 'science'. 'Style and the needs of a popular audience,' argued the regius professor at Oxford, 'have no more to do with history than with law or astronomy.'[3] Fortunately, young G. M. Trevelyan's 1904 essay on 'Clio, a Muse' sounded a counter-call for historians to return to writing for intelligent general readers. Trevelyan himself pursued this course with his books on the unification of Italy (1907–11), which became highly acclaimed.

It was not only late-Victorian historians who were retreating from social commitment. During the 1870s 'aestheticism' came into vogue in painting and literature, under the slogan of 'art for art's sake'.[4] This cry was taken from Gautier, the French writer, who had first used it in the 1830s and who in 1857 published his poem *L'Art*:

Tout passe – L'art robuste
Seul a l'éternité;
      Le buste
Survit à la cité.

Ruskin had wanted art and literature to be part of life; but for Walter Pater, the Oxford don who became the prophet of aestheticism, they offered a retreat from life.[5] Art for art's sake as expounded by Pater offered no message to society, no sense that artists in paint or in words should speak either to their age or for it. Pater's views were given influential expression in his book *Studies in the History of the Renaissance* (1873), and especially in its conclusion. Aestheticism offered itself as a substitute both for belief in political progress and for religious expectation. An informed appreciation of beauty was to Pater the highest satisfaction open to man. 'Not the fruit of experience but experience itself is the end . . . For art comes to you proposing frankly to give nothing but the highest quality to your moments as they pass, and simply for those moments' sake.' Life was short, and (to use a favourite word of the aesthetes) it needed to be lived 'intensely'.

In both painting and poetry D. G. Rossetti provided a link between the Pre-Raphaelite and aesthetic movements. In the 1860s Rossetti lived a few doors away in Chelsea from the American James McNeil Whistler, who was emerging as the most original painter of the aesthetic period as well as being a wit and a publicist.[6] Whistler scorned narrative painting and insisted that it was not the subject that was most important – not even his own mother, of whom he painted a notable portrait – but the arrangement of forms, colours, light and shade. This concern shaped his *Nocturnes* and *Symphonies* of the 1860s and 1870s. Ruskin made an unbalanced attack upon *Nocturne in Black and Gold* as an 'ill-educated conceit' which amounted almost to 'wilful imposture'. This led Whistler in 1878 to sue for libel, which brought into full publicity the contrast between the naturalist and narrative painters and Whistler's version of impressionism. Whistler won a significant moral victory, though he received only one farthing damages. In 1885 he delivered his *Ten O'Clock Lecture*, which expounded his view of art. He contended that great artists had never set out to be social reformers. It was wrong to confound beauty with virtue, and to ask before a work of art, 'What good shall it do?' It was wrong, also, to expect painters to represent nature exactly. Their function was to offer not reproduction but interpretation. Since Whistler's time (as one twentieth-century art historian has observed) 'few critics have ventured to state roundly that a picture was good or bad, or to attempt to see in it anything beyond the qualities the painter himself intended'.[7] In 1886 the New English Art Club was founded by Walter Sickert (who had worked with Whistler), John Singer Sargent, and other impressionists. Sargent was indeed only marginally an impressionist, and his facility in the grand manner was to make him the fashionable portrait painter of the turn of the century, though his best portraits showed some impressionistic skill in the handling of light. Sickert's work remained fresher, especially in his many evocations of music-hall interiors, which conveyed not detail but a sense of life and action.[8]

The man who came to personify aestheticism in the eyes of the public was Oscar Wilde – poet, playwright, and poseur.[9] Wilde and Swinburne provided the models for Bunthorne, 'a Fleshly Poet', in the Gilbert and Sullivan opera *Patience* (1881), which ridiculed all exaggerated affection for sunflowers, lilies, blue and white china, and other symbols and enthusiasms of the movement. In *Punch* George du Maurier's cartoons had been laughing at aesthetic long-haired men and short-haired women for several years before Gilbert's attack.

The aesthetic movement was too intellectual and too foreign in its inspiration ever to attain wide popularity. Yet the movement did exert visible influence. 'No drawing room under its sanctions was complete without an array of blue and white ginger jars, bowls of lilies, peacocks' feathers, Japanese fans, and – culminating proof of true discipleship – a dado.' So remembered H. J. Jennings in a book called *Our Homes and How to Beautify Them*, which looked back from 1902. Despite its exaggerations, concluded Jennings, the aesthetic movement did good. 'People began to realise that it was possible to make their homes more beautiful.' The adjective 'art' came into use as an indicator of sensitive design. Art textiles, art pottery, art wallpaper, art furniture, and art jewellery made during the 1870s and 1880s brought lasting benefit to design, even though the output of the art craftsmen proper was necessarily limited. The retailer most closely associated with the aesthetic movement was Liberty of London, whose 'art fabrics' quickly achieved an international reputation.[10] Under aesthetic influence colours for dress and decoration became softer. Heavy dark mahogony furniture went out of fashion. Four-poster beds gave way to brass and iron bedsteads. Rugs, which could be easily cleaned, replaced carpets which (before the days of vacuum cleaners) could not. Unfortunately, failures in taste were still frequent. Cheap materials and hurried workmanship were too often substituted for careful craftsmanship. And by the 1890s the reaction against heaviness and bleakness had over-reached itself. Rooms were now being filled with too many pieces of furniture and littered with ornaments. These were sometimes tasteful in themselves, but the effect became too cluttered to express good taste overall. Such conspicuous consumption and display were tellingly analysed in Thorstein Veblen's *Theory of the Leisure Class* (1899).

Art for art's sake could easily slip into art for the artist's sake. This was an attitude strongly repudiated by William Morris, the brilliant craftsman, critic, and socialist – the successor of Ruskin.[11] In a lecture on *The Art of the People* (1879) Morris denounced art for art's sake as 'a piece of slang that does not mean the harmless thing it seems to mean . . . An art cultivated professedly by a few, and for a few, who would consider it necessary – a duty, if they could admit duties – to despise the common herd'. Morris believed deeply in the personal element in art and design; but his belief in self-expression led him not to self-centred individualism (art for one's own sake) but to open-hearted socialism (art for everyone's sake). He wanted 'an Art made by the people and for the people, a joy to the maker and the user'. He argued that such a generous collaboration would establish a natural unity between function, form, and decoration. Art should be 'man's expression of his joy in labour . . . the chief accusation I have to bring against the modern state of society is that it is founded on the art-lacking or unhappy labour of the greater part of men'.

From the early 1860s Morris worked with great originality inside his 'Firm' of fellow craftsmen in the making of fabrics, wallpapers, glass, furniture, and the like. In the 1890s he won, through the Kelmscott Press, a further reputation as a printer. More generally, Morris helped to inspire the Arts and Crafts movement of the 1880s and 1890s, which brought together some outstanding designers and workmen.[12] This movement was to come into contact with *art nouveau* ideas, which suddenly erupted on the Continent in the early 1890s. The sinuous curves of *art nouveau*, based on leaf patterns and other natural forms, represented a distinctive and exciting style of design exclusive to the decade.

In architecture Morris's ideas were first expressed through the Red House at Bexleyheath, completed in 1860 with Philip Webb as architect. The house was built in a friendly red brick and tile at a time when stucco and slate predominated in districts without local stone; and the external elevations were dictated by the internal arrangements, not vice versa. The Red House example was to influence English country house architecture until well into the twentieth century. Unfortunately, public building came much less under the Morris influence. By the end of the century a neo-baroque style, thought suitable to an imperial power, found some favour. One notable exponent was Sir Aston Webb, architect of the Royal Naval College, Dartmouth.[13]

Morris and his friends deplored not only the Victorians' lack of an architectural manner, but also their determination to 'restore' old buildings in what they believed to be improved versions of the original. In 1877, after hearing that Sir Gilbert Scott was contemplating an attack upon Tewkesbury Abbey, Morris wrote to the *Athenaeum* warning against restoration as currently practised. He argued that when in previous centuries men had wished to repair or to alter buildings they had done so not in sham versions of the original, but in the style of their own times. Given that the nineteenth century regrettably possessed no style to add of its own, Morris pleaded for 'Protection in place of Restoration'; and to this end he helped to found the Society for the Protection of Ancient Buildings.[14]

2

By the late 1880s 'aestheticism' was changing into 'decadence', which constituted the extreme expression of the *fin de siécle* mood. Pater in his essay on 'The School of Giorgione' in *The Renaissance* had remarked how a great painting amounted to 'fallen light, caught as the colours are in an Eastern carpet, but refined upon, and dealt with more subtly and exquisitely than by nature itself'. This vision had been turned by Wilde and others into a preference for the artificial over the natural. When Pater realized that his counsels of hedonism were being distorted, he suppressed the conclusion from the second edition of *The Renaissance*, and re-presented his argument in *Marius the Epicurean* (1885). But by this date Pater was losing the leadership of advanced artistic opinion. His approach had always been constructive and helpful, whereas the decadent approach was to be destructive and disparaging, especially of the middle classes:[15]

> 'What is civilization, Mr. Wilde?'
> 'Love of beauty.'
> 'And what is beauty?'
> 'That which the middle classes call ugly.'

Yet the decadents were themselves in reaction against the admiration of beauty. They professed to prefer pessimism to optimism, the decayed to the living, the abnormal to the normal. They were suspected of drug-taking and homosexuality. A sense of corruption certainly pervaded the sickly but powerful drawings of Aubrey Beardsley, who – along with several of the decadent poets – was to die young. Time seemed short, and decadence involved a restless search for 'the new'. The 'new hedonism', the 'new woman', the 'new drama', and the like were excitedly discovered and proclaimed.

The decadent writers of the 1890s always remained a minority. And this minority was expressly opposed by the 'counter-decadents', who gathered round the *National Observer*, edited by W. E. Henley.[16] Henley, himself a cripple, advocated athleticism of mind and body. Max Beerbohm – wit, cartoonist, and essayist – dubbed Henley's group the 'Henley Regatta'. Beerbohm himself associated with the decadents, but he was not committed to them. W. B. Yeats, the Irish writer, contrived to write both decadent and counter-decadent poetry. Grant Allen, a busy novelist and essayist, emphasized in an article on 'The New Hedonism' in the *Fortnightly Review* for March 1894 the importance of good physical health ('each man and each woman holds his virility and her feminity in trust for humanity'); but also the need for a lively popular understanding of the arts. 'Every unit of gain in the aesthetic sense, every diffusion of a wider taste for poetry, for art, for music, for decoration, is to the good of humanity.'

The *Yellow Book*, which started in 1894 with a lurid cover drawn by Beardsley, was regarded by the public at large as the very epitome of decadence. Yellow became the corrupt colour of the hour. Yet the *Yellow Book*'s contributors included Henley; and even a few such 'respectable' names as Sir Frederick Leighton, President of the Royal Academy, and Henry James, the novelist. The press, however, persisted in regarding the publication as, in the words of *The Times* (20.4.1894), 'a combination of English rowdiness with French lubricity'. It was indeed the foreign, French connections of the decadents which made them especially suspect. Decadence in France looked back to Baudelaire's *Les Fleurs du Mal*, which had been dedicated to Gautier, the advocate of art for art's sake.

The English decadent movement subsided rapidly after the imprisonment of Oscar Wilde for homosexual practices in 1895. The *Yellow Book* ceased publication in 1897. Beardsley died in 1898, Wilde in 1900. As one contemporary, Holbrook Jackson, concluded in his study of *The Eighteen Nineties* (1913), the general public had only fully realized the existence of the decadence with the arrest of Wilde. 'And the suddenness with which the decadent movement in English literature and art ceased, from that time, proves ... the tremendous power of outraged public opinion in this country.'

Yet the *fin de siècle* mood in general did not fade with the fading of decadence. The most popular poetic expression of pessimism at the end of the century was not a decadent piece at all, but Edward Fitzgerald's free translation of the *Rubaiyat of Omar Khayyam*, first published in 1859. Sales of this haunting sound of sadness built up strikingly as the century ran out, even among people who read little other poetry:

Ah, make the most of what we yet may spend,
Before we too into the Dust descend;
    Dust unto Dust, and under Dust to lie,
Sans Wine, sans Song, sans Singer, and – sans End.

The widely publicized linking of homosexuality with literature added to working-class suspicion of the arts. As late as the First World War the ribald cry 'Watch out for oscarwhile' was addressed in Manchester factories to mystified new apprentices.[17] But the vigorous sentiments of W. E. Henley appealed to middle-class readers, as did the books of Robert Louis Stevenson, author of *Treasure Island* (1882) and of *Kidnapped* (1886). And in 1890 the best known by name of all late-Victorian writers first sprang into prominence – Rudyard Kipling.[18] Kipling came to mean different things to different people. To the late-Victorians at large, many of whom had hardly read him, his was taken as the voice of imperial achievement and confidence. To others more sophisticated – aware of such warnings as the *Recessional* (1897)

God of our fathers, known of old,
Lord of our far-flung battle-line,
Beneath whose awful Hand we hold
    Dominion over palm and pine –
Lord God of Hosts, be with us yet,
Lest we forget – lest we forget!

– Kipling was the prophet not of imperial confidence but of imperial responsibility and concern. And to his most dedicated readers he was the great Anglo-Indian writer, who searchingly captured the atmosphere of the late-Victorian raj. It was in this role that he first achieved notice, with tales about the Anglo-Indian governing class and songs and stories about the daily lives of common soldiers in India, foremost among them Tommy Atkins. His brilliantly idiomatic cockney *Barrack Room Ballads* (first volume 1892) were reprinted some fifty times in thirty years.

3

The writing profession was expanding rapidly by the end of the nineteenth century. The 1881 census listed over 3,400 men and women engaged in literature and journalism in England and Wales. By 1891 this total had reached nearly 5,800, by 1901 about 11,000, and by 1911 nearly 13,800. Manufacturing costs for paper and printing were falling markedly, and this greatly helped the publication of low-priced books and magazines. *Cassell's Library of English Literature*, started in 1875 as a weekly-part series of extracts from the classics, with editorial commentary, has been claimed as probably the most successful feat of popularization ever offered to the English mass market. Contents ranged from Beowolf to Browning. Many other rival cheap series, priced at a few pence per volume, soon followed.[19]

During the 1880s fiction overtook theology as the largest category among new books and new editions published each year. By 1889 out of 6,067 new titles and new editions fiction's total amounted to 1,040 plus 364 new editions, compared with 630 plus 134 for theology.[20] The development of international copyright laws had checked literary piracy, and had opened up an enormous royalty-earning market for English writers in the United States. Walter Besant, himself a successful novelist and one of the founders of the Society of Authors (1884), claimed that the increase of literacy at home alongside the growth of the United States and of the white colonies had extended the potential English-speaking and reading market from about 50,000 people in 1830 to some 120 million sixty years later.[21] With such a market even moderately successful authors could prosper as never before. Yet no later novelists seemed able to reach all classes, as Dickens had done. Certainly not George Meredith nor Henry James, who were publishing their best work during the last quarter of the nineteenth century but who were appreciated by only a comparatively small part of the reading public. Thomas Hardy's novels, from *Under the Greenwood Tree* (1872) to *Jude the Obscure* (1895), came nearest to attracting an all-class audience.[22]

The mid 1890s saw the sudden end of the old-style three-volume novel (the 'three-decker'), priced at 31*s*. 6*d*. This format had ceased to suit the big circulating libraries, for the re-sale value of copies was being undermined by the speedy publication of cheap reprints of successful titles.[23] Many authors had long wanted single-volume first editions, in the belief that they had lost sales by expensive three-volume publication. Novels were henceforward usually first issued at 6*s*. Novel reading had now become entirely 'respectable'. Discussion of the moral usefulness or danger of such reading ceased to be prominent after about 1880.[24] Criticism came to concentrate upon technique and content. Content was indeed now sometimes quite daring, as novelists began to discuss relations between the sexes with a new frankness. French influence was felt in this connection, although George Moore was soon allowing himself more freedom than either Zola or Maupassant had shown. Hardy's *Tess of the D'Urbervilles* (1891) was the first major English novel to allow a seduced woman to appear as an unqualified heroine.[25]

Whereas the novel had been the most successful Victorian literary form, contemporary English play writing long continued at a much less satisfactory level. 'The plays, as a rule, which have been good literature have either never been acted or have seldom succeeded as plays; the plays that have been acted and have been successful have seldom been good literature.' So wrote George Saintsbury, a prominent academic, in his *History of Nineteenth Century Literature* (1896). But Saintsbury was taking no account of the revival which had at last arrived. The 1890s saw British dramatists, for the first time since the days of Sheridan, writing highly actable plays which were also significant literature. William Archer, a leading critic, pointed out in *The Theatrical World of*

1895 how the plays of writers such as Oscar Wilde, A. W. Pinero, and Henry Arthur Jones had advanced beyond the level of Tom Robertson, the pioneering dramatist of the 1860s. Robertsonian comedy had usually ended with a happy marriage: 'the new drama is much more apt to take marriage (if not the Divorce Court) for its starting point.'

This shift towards realism owed much to the example of Ibsen, the Norwegian dramatist, whose plays were first heard in England from 1889. Ibsen was ruthless in his revelations of social hypocrisy, which were the more disturbing for being set in an atmosphere of nordic gloom. *Ghosts*, with its theme of syphilis transmitted from father to son, drew a storm of hostile comment when first performed in 1891. It was condemned as subversive, both morally and politically – fit to be admired only by 'long-haired, soft-hatted, villainous or sickly-looking socialists'. 'The most loathsome play,' concluded the *Licensed Victuallers' Mirror*, 'that was ever put upon any stage'.[26] Understandably, these Norwegian drawing-room tragedies made critics and audiences feel uncomfortable. To their credit, both critics and audiences rapidly overcame their inhibitions, and recognized the social relevance and dramatic cogency of Ibsen's message. When *An Enemy of the People* was played in 1893 it was widely acclaimed as significant drama. Four years later Queen Victoria herself attended a performance of *Ghosts*. Bernard Shaw, an Ibsen enthusiast – not yet himself known as a major dramatist – pointed out in 1895 how the Norwegian had raised by example the standard of contemporary British drama. Recent successes such as Wilde's *Lady Windermere's Fan* (1892), Pinero's *The Second Mrs Tanqueray* (1893), and Jones's *The Case of Rebellious Susan* (1894) were very much better plays than previous box-office draws. 'The change is evident at once . . . a modern manager need not produce *The Wild Duck*; but he must be very careful not to produce a play which will seem insipid and old-fashioned to playgoers who have seen *The Wild Duck*, even though they may have hissed it.'[27] Wilde's plays were indeed called watered-down Ibsen by superior critics; but his wit on stage was sparkling.

Admittedly, the new drama of the 1890s could not match in popularity the light operas of Gilbert and Sullivan.[28] By the time of Sir Arthur Sullivan's death in 1900 *The Times* was recognizing that the Savoy operas were 'the one form of dramatic and musical art which this generation has evolved – the only form which can be called in any sense characteristic'. Sullivan's tuneful music and Gilbert's matching words had produced a form which bridged the gap between the music halls and 'severely classical music', and which could be enjoyed by all classes. Gilbert's plots and characters, however burlesque, were deliberately shaped to give no moral offence; and this opened the way for the great family appeal of the operas. The collaboration began in 1871, and continued into the nineties – with *H.M.S. Pinafore* (1878), *The Mikado* (1885), and *The Gondoliers* (1889) accepted by *Punch* (4.1.1890) as the best operas of the series. Grove's *Dictionary of Music and Musicians*

(1883) asked 'whether the ability so conspicuous in these operettas is always to be employed on works which from their very nature must be even more fugitive than comedy in general?' In the event, this apparently ephemeral work has lived on long after most of Sullivan's more pretentious compositions have been forgotten. His serious opera *Ivanhoe* (1891) enjoyed some success, and his oratorio *The Golden Legend* (1886) for a time rivalled *Elijah* as second in popularity to *The Messiah*. *The Lost Chord* (1877), a test piece for tears, was sung in countless drawing rooms, and sold 500,000 copies in twenty-five years.

Before or after attending a theatre or concert, meals could now be readily taken in public, as restaurants sprang up extensively in London and other centres. Dining out became a popular middle and upper-class activity on its own account, most notably at such fashionable London restaurants as the Café Royal, the Gaiety, the Tivoli, and Romano's. At a lower level of provision, tea-rooms opened in most cities and large towns about the turn of the century, run especially by J. Lyons and Co. and by the Aerated Bread Company (ABC). These firms offered a standardized but pleasant atmosphere in which to eat acceptable food at modest prices.[29]

4

The 1880s witnessed the rise of the 'new journalism', so named by Matthew Arnold in 1887. Arnold's article went on to repeat the complaint which he had voiced in *Culture and Anarchy* twenty years earlier about the unsatisfactory cultural tone of all three social classes. The new journalism, he admitted, was 'full of ability, novelty, variety, sensation, sympathy, generous instincts; its one great fault is that it is *feather-brained* . . . the democracy, with abundance of life, movement, sympathy, good instincts, is disposed to be, like this journalism, *feather-brained*; just as the upper class is disposed to be selfish in politics, and the middle class narrow'.[30]

Arnold was here referring particularly to W. T. Stead, editor from 1883 to 1889 of the penny London evening paper, the *Pall Mall Gazette*.[31] Stead introduced many innovations into English journalism – crossheads, short paragraphs, signed articles, interviews with celebrities – most of which he took from journalistic practice in the United States. These new methods were then further developed by other pioneers, most notably by T. P. O'Connor and by Alfred Harmsworth. As a result, a further great widening of the market both for newspapers and for magazines was achieved. Stead's success, however, lay not in permanently increasing the readership and profitability of the *Pall Mall Gazette*, but in winning mass publicity for his successive publicity campaigns. He even persuaded himself in 1885 at the height of his most famous campaign against 'The Maiden Tribute of Modern Babylon' that he was 'the man of most importance now alive'. This campaign revealed how easy it was for men of means to buy young virgins in London, or for such girls to be trapped into 'white slavery' on the Continent. Stead himself arranged to buy the virginity of one girl. This, and every other revelation, he trumpeted dramatically in the *Gazette* – 'I order Five Virgins', 'A Child of Thirteen Bought for £5'. 'If the daughters of the people must be served up as dainty morsels to minister to the passions of the rich, let them at least attain an age when they can understand the nature of the sacrifice' – 'the hour of Democracy has struck'. The age of consent still stood as low as thirteen, and bills to raise it had always failed in Parliament. Stead's campaign, by dramatizing the whole issue, was probably decisive in securing the enactment of the Criminal Law Amendment Bill which was being debated in the summer of 1885, and which raised the age of consent to sixteen. But because of carelessness with regard to the law in his demonstration purchase of a girl, Stead found himself imprisoned for three months.

Stead had introduced the 'new journalism'; but T. P. O'Connor, editor from 1888 to 1890 of the new halfpenny London evening *Star*, first made it pay for a daily paper.[32] O'Connor was a keen radical politician – indeed an Irish Nationalist; but he made sure that his paper was not swamped by political news. He promised in his first number (17.1.1888) to give his readers 'plenty of entirely unpolitical literature – sometimes humorous, sometimes pathetic; anecdotal, statistical, the craze of fashions, and the arts of housekeeping – now and then, a short, dramatic, and picturesque tale'. The *Star*'s gossip column, 'Mainly About People', set a new standard in personalized news reporting: 'the men and women that figure in the forum or the pulpit or the law court shall be presented as they are – living, breathing, in blushes or in tears – and not merely by the dead words that they utter'. The coverage given by the *Star* to the Jack the Ripper murders briefly pushed circulation as high as 300,000; but normal sales had reached the substantial figure of 120,000–150,000 daily by the end of 1888. The *Star*, the *Echo* (1868), and the *Evening News* (1881) were all halfpenny evening papers which aimed lower down the market than the penny morning papers. In the provincial towns numerous halfpenny evenings were started from the seventies. These gave especial attention to racing, football, and other sports news. By 1900, thirty-four English provincial towns had at least one morning and one evening paper, while twenty-nine others possessed evening papers only.

Alongside new evening papers for the masses came a new breed of popular weekly journals. The way was led here by George Newnes's *Tit-Bits*, started in 1881, followed in 1888 by Alfred Harmsworth's *Answers to Correspondents*.[33] As their titles suggested, these halfpenny publications were carefully shaped to satisfy half-educated readers eager for scraps of simple amusement and information. 'Any person who takes in *Tit-Bits* for three months will at the end of that time be an entertaining companion, as he will then have at his command a stock of smart sayings and a fund of anecdote.' 'What the Queen Eats' was one

Answers headline which compelled attention. 'A Pound a Week for Life' was offered to the reader who guessed how much gold and silver coin remained in the bank of England at the close of business on 4 December 1889. More than 700,000 entries were received. A succession of new Harmsworth magazines followed in the wake of *Answers* – *Comic Cuts* (1890), *Illustrated Chips* (1890), *Forget-Me-Not* (1891), and several more. Total sales of all Harmsworth publications soon passed the million. A new market had been found, and was being profitably exploited; but the new readers seemed to be well satisfied. By the mid 1890s *Answers* and its two main rivals – *Tit-Bits*, and *Pearson's Weekly* (1890) – were each selling 400,000–600,000 copies every week.

These new prints were shallow and trivial, but at least they were not corrupting. Gladstone was even persuaded to say in an interview that he considered 'the gigantic circulation of *Answers* an undeniable proof of the growth of sound public taste for healthy and instructive reading. The journal must have vast influence'. Flora Thompson remembered the influence exerted by the new publications even in remote Oxfordshire, where countryfolk became as eager as townsfolk to know how many years of life were spent in bed, or how far all the sausages eaten on one Sunday morning would stretch if placed end to end.[34] The success of these halfpenny weeklies certainly reduced the sale of the less wholesome 'penny bloods', such as *Ally Sloper's Half Holiday*. This had been started in 1884 to exploit the appeal of a saucy cartoon character originally created in the 1860s. His adventures were boisterous, and his thirst for gin unquenchable.[35] Harmsworth, by contrast, took particular care to avoid any encouragement of impropriety. 'The spoken word vanishes, the printed word remains. Every word of the 100,000 we print every week is carefully considered.' Care even reached the point of refusing any advertisements which contained the words 'constipation' or 'rupture'.

George Newnes published not only *Tit-Bits*, but also the most popular monthly magazine of the turn of the century – the *Strand Magazine* (1891).[36] Priced at sixpence, its role among the middle classes was in some respects similar to that of *Tit-Bits* among the working classes. It combined unusual or informative articles with good fiction, well illustrated. Many of the leading writers of the day contributed to the *Strand*, though it was especially known for its association with Conan Doyle and Sherlock Holmes. It reached the very high sale of nearly 500,000 copies per month at the turn of the century.

5

The 1870 Education Act carried with it the implication that the children of the working classes could not be left as 'hands' – the nation needed their brains. The subsequent introduction of compulsion significantly limited parental authority. The 1889 Prevention of Cruelty to Children

Act gave the courts power to intervene in cases of parental brutality, and even to remove children from parental control. Appropriately, the National Society for the Prevention of Cruelty to Children was formed in 1889. Childhood was coming to be accepted as an autonomous stage in human development, and child psychology was starting to teach that children's minds were different from and not just smaller than adult minds.[37] Adolescence, too, was beginning to be recognized as a stage in life, and potentially a difficult stage; not only for upper and upper middle-class children deliberately withdrawn into public schools and universities, but also for lower middle and working-class boys and girls who left school in their early teens. The old assumption had been that when working-class children entered employment they became young adults. But from the 1880s increased notice began to be taken of the 'youth' problem. This seems to have been especially stimulated by regret that the good behaviour taught in the elementary schools often rapidly disintegrated as soon as children left school. Youth organizations made attempts to counter this. The Boys' Brigade, started in Glasgow in 1883, had 35,000 members in the United Kingdom by 1899.[38] The Church Lads' Brigade, started in London in 1891, reached a peak of 70,000 members about 1908. In the East End and other deprived areas of the big cities numerous boys' clubs were opened during the 1880s and 1890s, sponsored by various public schools. The aim was to bridge the class gulf, to the benefit of higher and lower classes alike.

How successful was the new nationwide but patchwork system of denominational and board school elementary education introduced from 1870?[39] The development of the new system was certainly impressive in terms of the number of new school places which were rapidly provided – initially to fill gaps, and then to keep up with the increasing and shifting population. Progress was not equally satisfactory everywhere; but by 1882 school places were available at inspected schools for one in six of the population of England and Wales, and by 1895 for one in five. By this latter date all working-class children had a school reasonably close to hand. In London the school population was growing at 10,000 a year, and by the end of the century 531,000 new elementary school places had been created. In Lancashire between 1870 and the end of the century there was a 56 per cent rise in population, an 80 per cent increase in the number of schools, a 177 per cent rise in average attendance, and a 500 per cent increase in state expenditure. In 1870 one Lancastrian in twenty-five had been attending school at a parliamentary cost of 5*d.* per head: by the end of the century the percentage had reached one in seven at 3*s.* per head. Total Education Department expenditure grew from £760,561 in 1870 to £6,661,640 in 1895. 1,879,218 children were then attending board schools, and almost equal numbers (1,850,545) were being taught at Church of England schools. Roman Catholic schools served 230,392 pupils, Wesleyan schools 129,724, and undenominational 'British' schools (mainly Nonconformist) 235,151.

The provision of a sufficient number of elementary school places did not in itself ensure regular attendance.[40] Attendance at inspected primary schools in the 1860s had rarely exceeded 65 per cent of children nominally on the rolls. It took a generation before satisfactory levels – 80–90 per cent – were achieved in country and in town. Good attendance medals were offered by many schools; but such incentives could not deal with incorrigible truants, nor help those whose parents needed (or at least wanted) the income from child work. The school attendance officers became familiar figures in working-class districts. 'Part-timers' and 'early leavers' (before 13) were allowed at the discretion of local school boards. 29,000 boys and 33,000 girls under 14 were working half-time in cotton factories in 1878; as late as 1907 9,000 boys and 10,000 girls were still cotton half-timers. An Inter-Departmental Committee on the Employment of School Children found in 1901 that some 300,000 combined paid work with school attendance. The committee accepted that employment up to twenty hours per week was suitable for children; but it found that many children worked longer than this. Country children were often kept from school at harvest and other busy times. But in the towns the main cause of non-attendance was illness. School log books recorded the almost continuous tyranny exercised by childhood infections.

Country labourers were said not to value education. But urban trade unionists had come out strongly in favour of free and compulsory elementary education.[41] The National Education League published 20,000 copies of Robert Applegarth's *Compulsory Attendance at School: The Working Man's View* (1870). The intensified working-class movement of the 1880s and 1890s showed a deep interest in educational questions. William Morris was convinced that improved education would lead the masses to support socialism. The Social Democratic Federation contested London school Board elections in the 1880s, and the Independent Labour Party followed suit in the north of England from the 1890s. Some town boards were vigorous and innovating; others, especially in the countryside, were feeble and cheeseparing. 'I have not given a blackboard lesson for more than a fortnight,' complained one west country board school head teacher in 1873, 'on account of having no chalk.'[42] To raise a significant sum for education in sparsely populated country districts meant the levying of a much higher rate than was necessary in the towns.

As the new board schools spread over England they were taken as symbols of the progress of the age. E. R. Robson, architect to the London School Board, set a high standard of quality and suitability in his designs.[43] His schools adopted a yellow brick version of the Queen Anne style, secular and civic, in deliberate contrast to the Gothic style which had become associated with denominational rivalries. Robson's influence helped to ensure that by the end of the century the new board schools throughout the country were generally much superior in building to most voluntary schools. Sidney Webb praised London's 500 board schools as 'by far the greatest of our municipal assets'.[44] Webb went on to praise the quality of board school teaching. Here he was treading more disputed ground. Little more than half of all elementary teachers at the turn of the century were qualified – the rest were assistant teachers and pupil teachers. An article in the *Graphic* (7.11.1885) explained how the great majority of elementary school teachers came 'by a sort of process of natural selection from the ranks of the children who attend these schools'. Their performance was sometimes praised ('Labouring in the midst of depressing influences the teachers are found full of zeal and enthusiasm'), sometimes attacked. An article on 'The Teacher Problem' (*Fortnightly Review*, May 1899) complained that because elementary school teachers were themselves products of the elementary system they lacked breadth and depth of knowledge; and so they were unable to raise the level of teaching beyond more 'instruction' in a limited range of 'subjects'.

The Revised Code of 1862 had certainly left teachers with much less discretion in what they taught, and at the mercy of managers and inspectors. In self-defence the National Union of Elementary Teachers was formed in 1870.[45] The union campaigned for security of tenure and adequate salaries, for control of entry into the profession; for promotion of teachers into the inspectorate, and for a comprehensive pension scheme. By 1890 it was apparent that no major reform in the schools could be promoted against the opposition of the NUET. There was indeed some truth in the charges of narrowness made against elementary teachers. And yet their achievement was apparent. As early as 1883 one Birmingham employer was remarking how the more than 1,000 boys taken by his firm since 1870 had proved markedly superior to earlier intakes – 'more orderly, more amenable to discipline, and much more intelligent'.[46] The improvement in cleanliness and dress of elementary school children between the 1870s and the end of the century was strikingly illustrated by contrasting photographs in the report of the Inter-Departmental Committee on Physical Deterioration (1904). The influence of elementary education seems to have been cumulative. As the board school children of the 1870s and 1880s themselves became parents they set higher standards for their children.

The brightest working-class children could climb the educational 'ladder'. Four or five in 1,000 could expect – by winning a series of scholarships – to progress from elementary school to grammar school and then to university. Most late-Victorians accepted this as sufficient; but the ladder concept continued to be questioned by radical thinkers. One Golden Jubilee survey of educational progress recognized that it would be a problem for the future 'whether, in addition to the comparatively easy task of opening a career to great talent springing from humble homes, they shall in any degree advance us in the solution of that far deeper human problem, how the lives of the broad mass of the ungifted and the unambitious may be redeemed from barrenness'.[47] In the meantime from the late 1870s a few able children in a few industrial towns could progress to new 'higher grade schools', which consisted of senior pupils taken from the top standards of elementary schools. These schools were financed partly by the school boards and partly by the Science and Art Department. During the 1890s school boards also began to organize evening continuation classes. The Bryce Commission on Secondary Education praised the higher grade schools in 1895 for meeting 'a demand for Secondary Education from the lower social strata'. Its report emphasized the importance of a large further extension of secondary education, both to improve the quality of individual lives and to counter foreign rivalry in trade and industry.

Ernest Barker has left a moving account in *Father of the Man* (1948) of his own progress from a Cheshire village school via Manchester Grammar School to Balliol College, Oxford. 'To serve as an educational ladder between the public elementary school and the universities,' noted the *Manchester Guardian* (24.2.1906), 'has become a point of honour with the Grammar School and with its present High Master.' Barker was exceptionally lucky in his school. Slightly less able or fortunate boys could hope to reach one of the provincial universities.[48] Owen's College, Manchester, which dated from 1851, became linked with colleges in Liverpool and Leeds to form the federal Victoria University in 1880. Then at the beginning of the century the three colleges separated into individual universities (1903–4). Joseph Chamberlain had already decided that Birmingham deserved a full university of its own, and Birmingham University duly received its charter in 1900.[49]

From the first these new universities determined to become more than glorified technical colleges. Though they willingly developed close contacts with local industry, they carefully maintained a balance between the arts on the one hand and science and technology on the other. This was notably the case at Manchester University, where A. W. Ward and T. F. Tout were historians of international reputation, and where Ernest Rutherford, the great atomic physicist, did much of his best work (1907–19). About 1890 the provincial civic universities were producing about 100 graduates per year; twenty years later the total had reached 500 to 600. In addition, the provincial universities catered for many non-degree students. The overall number of full-time students at English and Welsh universities in 1913–14 was 19,458. This included Oxford with 4,025; Cambridge 3,679; London 4,026; Manchester 1,014; and Birmingham 869. From 1889 the Treasury began to pay annual grants to universities. These were allocated by a special committee, which in 1919 was to become the University Grants Committee. The total grant rose from only £15,000 in 1889 to £170,000 by 1914.

6

Only a handful of working-class youths were reaching the universities by the turn of the century, whereas over 1,000,000 spectators were reaching the football terraces as spectators every winter Saturday. Soccer was now firmly established as a mass spectator sport. Over 100,000 attended the 1901 cup final at Crystal Palace. Social commentators were sharply divided about the desirability of this mass enthusiasm. Some welcomed it as a social safety-valve, which helped to avoid strikes and even revolution; but others regarded it as a sign of decadence. 'Paid players and vast hordes of idle spectators – these were symptoms of the decline of Rome.'[50] An article on 'The New Football Mania' in the *Nineteenth Century* for October 1892 complained that the names and faces of local professional footballers were now much better known than those of local Members of Parliament. Industrial town life was drab, but enthusiastic support for local football teams added excitement, and even encouraged a sense of working-class solidarity. Rowdyism, though, soon became a problem. Small numbers of spectators, complained the *Manchester Guardian* (21.2.1906), were inclined 'to stone the referee or to mob the visiting team'. None the less, the ultimate accolade, if not of social 'respectability' at least of social tolerance, was given to the game in 1914 when George V became the first sovereign to attend the cup final and present the cup.

George V's own favourite sports were shooting and yachting, both predominantly upper-class pastimes. Golf had now become very popular with the upper and upper middle classes in England. It was a game which – like lawn tennis – could be played with satisfaction at various levels of skill, especially after the introduction of the rubber-core ball from the beginning of the century. 'Golf, of course, had long been in fashion,' explained *Punch* (19.7.1911) in its survey of the preceding decade, 'but it was only now that not to play put one outside the pale'. Even Lloyd George, the scourge of the aristocracy, played golf enthusiastically, though not well. By the end of the 1890s bridge was displacing whist as the fashionable card game. 'Possibly golf and bridge combined,' grumbled Lord Esher, the confidant of kings and politicians, in his journal for 1908, 'may help us to succumb to the Germans when the day of trial comes.'[51]

Notes

1. See especially J. Holloway, *The Victorian Sage* (1953); and G. Watson, *The English Ideology* (1973), Ch. 13.
2. D. H. Laurence (ed.), *Bernard Shaw, Collected Letters, 1874–1897* (1965), p. 456.
3. C. H. S. Fifoot (ed.), *Letters of Frederic William Maitland* (1965), pp. 349, 351; O. Elton, *Frederick York Powell* (1906), II, pp. 1–13. See also R. Langhorne, 'Historiography', in C. B. Cox and A. E. Dyson (eds.), *The Twentieth-Century Mind*, I (1972).
4. See especially Elizabeth Aslin, *The Aesthetic Movement* (1969); and R. V. Johnson, *Aestheticism* (1969).
5. See especially R. L. Stein, *The Ritual of Interpretation, The Fine Arts as Literature in Ruskin, Rossetti, and Pater* (1975).

6. See especially D. Sutton, *James McNeil Whistler* (1966).
7. W. Gaunt, *The Aesthetic Adventure* (2nd edn, 1975), p. 110.
8. See especially D. Sutton, *Walter Sickert* (1976).
9. See especially H. Pearson, *Life of Oscar Wilde* (1946); and H. Montgomery Hyde, *Oscar Wilde* (1976). Also K. Beckson (ed.), *Oscar Wilde* (1974).
10. See Alison Adburgham, *Liberty's* (1975).
11. See especially J. W. Mackail, *Life of William Morris* (1899; reprinted 1950); P. Henderson, *William Morris* (1967); and P. Thompson, *The Work of William Morris* (1967).
12. See especially S. T. Madsen, *Art Nouveau* (1967); and Gillian Naylor, *The Arts and Crafts Movement* (1971).
13. See A. Service (ed.), *Edwardian Architecture and Its Origins* (1975); and A. Service, *Edwardian Architecture* (1977).
14. J. W. Mackail, *Life of William Morris* (1899; reprinted 1950), I, pp. 350-7.
15. See especially H. Jackson, *The Eighteen Nineties* (1913).
16. See J. H. Buckley, *William Ernest Henley* (1945); and A. Guillaume, *William Ernest Henley et Son Groupe* (1973).
17. R. Roberts, *The Classic Slum* (1971), pp. 36-7; Flora Thompson, *Lark Rise to Candleford* (1973), p. 498.
18. See especially J. I. M. Stewart, *Rudyard Kipling* (1966); C. Carrington, *Rudyard Kipling* (2nd edn, 1970); and J. Gross (ed.), *Rudyard Kipling* (1972).
19. V. E. Neuburg, *Popular Literature* (1977), pp. 207-12.
20. *Journal of the Royal Statistical Society*, LIII (1890), pp. 151-3.
21. W. Besant, *The Pen and the Book* (1899), pp. 28-35.
22. See, in general, M. Bradbury, *The Social Context of Modern English Literature* (1971), part one. In particular, I. Williams (ed.), *Meredith* (1971); R. Gard (ed.), *Henry James* (1968); and R. G. Cox (ed.), *Thomas Hardy* (1970).
23. See Guinevere L. Griest, *Mudie's Circulating Library and the Victorian Novel* (1970), Chs. 7, 8.
24. K. Graham, *English Criticism of the Novel, 1865-1900* (1965), pp. 5-6.
25. I. Gregor and B. Nicholas, *The Moral and the Story* (1962), p. 135. See especially T. Hardy, 'Candour in English Fiction', *New Review*, January 1890, in H. Orel (ed.), *Thomas Hardy's Personal Writings* (1967).
26. See M. Egan (ed.), *Ibsen* (1972), esp. p. 202.
27. G. B. Shaw, *Our Theatre in the Nineties* (1932), I, p. 165.
28. See especially H. Pearson, *Gilbert and Sullivan* (1935); and A. Jacobs, *Gilbert and Sullivan* (1951).
29. D. J. Olsen, *The Growth of Victorian London* (1976), pp. 93-111; D. J. Richardson, 'J. Lyons and Co. Ltd.: Caterers and Food Manufacturers, 1894-1939', in D. J. Oddy and D. Miller (eds.) *The Making of Modern British Diet* (1976).
30. *Nineteenth Century*, May 1887, pp. 638-9. See especially S. Morison, *The English Newspaper* (1932), Ch. XV; A. Hutt, *The Changing Newspaper* (1973), Ch. 4; and A. J. Lee, *The Origins of the Popular Press, 1855-1914* (1976).
31. See especially R. L. Schults, *Crusader in Babylon* (1972).
32. See especially H. W. Massingham, *The London Daily Press* (1892), Ch. VII.
33. See especially R. Pound and G. Harmsworth, *Northcliffe* (1959), book one; and P. Ferris, *The House of Northcliffe* (1971), Chs. 4-6.
34. Flora Thompson, *Lark Rise to Candleford* (1973), pp. 498-9.
35. G. Perry and A. Aldridge, *The Penguin Book of Comics* (2nd edn, 1971), Ch. 2; V. E. Neuburg, *Popular Literature* (1977), pp. 231-3.
36. See R. Pound, *The Strand Magazine, 1891-1950* (1966).
37. See Ivy and Margaret Pinchbeck, *Children in English Society*, II (1973), esp. Ch. XX; and D. Wardle, *The Rise of the Schooled Society* (1974), pp. 34-8.
38. See B. Simon, *Education and the Labour Movement, 1870-1920* (1965), pp. 64-70; and J. Springhall, *Youth, Empire and Society* (1977).
39. See especially Gillian Sutherland, *Policy-Making in Elementary Education, 1870-1895* (1973). Also E. C. Midwinter, 'The Administration of Public Education in

Late Victorian Lancashire', *Northern History*, IV (1969); and S. Maclure, *One Hundred Years of London Education, 1870–1970* (1970), part one.
40. See especially D. Rubinstein, *School Attendance in London, 1870–1904* (1969); and Pamela Horn, *The Victorian Country Child* (1974), Chs. 2–4.
41. See B. Simon, *Education and the Labour Movement, 1870–1920* (1965), Ch. 1; and W. P. McCann, 'Trade Unionists, Artisans and the 1870 Education Act', *British Journal of Educational Studies*, XVIII (1970).
42. Muriel Goaman, *Never So Good* (1974), p. 132.
43. See D. Gregory-Jones, 'The London Board Schools, E. R. Robson', in A. Service (ed.), *Edwardian Architecture and Its Origins* (1975); and M. Seaborne and R. Lowe, *The English School*, II (1977), part one. Also E. R. Robson, *School Architecture* (1874: reprinted 1972).
44. S. Webb, *London Education* (1903), p. 6.
45. See A. Tropp, *The School Teachers* (1957).
46. W. H. B. Court (ed.), *British Economic History, 1870–1914* (1965), pp. 162–3.
47. T. H. Ward (ed.), *The Reign of Queen Victoria* (1887), II, p. 306. See especially A. E. Dyson and J. Lovelock, *Education and Democracy* (1975), part four.
48. See especially M. Sanderson (ed.), *Universities in the Nineteenth Century* (1965); and M. Sanderson, *The Universities and British Industry, 1850–1970* (1972).
49. J. Amery, *Life of Joseph Chamberlain*, IV (1951), Ch. LXXXIV.
50. P. A. Welsby (ed.), *Sermons and Society* (1970), p. 347.
51. M. V. Brett (ed.), *Journals and Letters of Reginald, Viscount Esher* (1934), II, pp. 321, 330. See especially G. Cousins, *Golf in Britain* (1975).

Government

Developments: *'We are all socialists now'*
1

'We Englishmen pass on the Continent as masters of the art of government; yet it may be doubted whether, even among us, the science which corresponds to the art, is not very much in the condition of Political Economy before Adam Smith took it in hand.' So claimed Henry Maine in his book on *Popular Government* (1885). Certainly, neither by art nor by science had government yet devised means of overcoming the problem of widespread and persistent poverty in the midst of national plenty. By the 1880s many of the poor were indeed visibly improving their standards of living; but many others still were not. An additional dangerous problem was therefore arising – poverty in the midst of improvement. Yet even those who were making overall economic gains were not necessarily content; for cyclical trade depression still brought periods of high unemployment. 'Periods of flash prosperity, speedily followed by depression, which pinches and starves even the best artisan class.'[1]

The higher classes were beginning to learn much more about working-class life. The impact made by *The Bitter Cry of Outcast London* (1883), and by other accounts of bad housing conditions in the capital, has already been noticed. But assertion and sentiment often took the place of evidence until the publication from 1889 of the successive large volumes of Charles Booth's *Life and Labour of the People in London*. This compilation placed social enquiry upon a new basis of carefully collected facts, objectively assembled.[2] Booth himself shared the contemporary middle-class sense of bafflement in the face of the problem of poverty. 'To relieve this sense of helplessness, the problem of human life must be better stated. The *a priori* reasoning of political economy, orthodox and unorthodox alike, fails from want of reality. At its base are a series of assumptions very imperfectly connected with the observed facts of life.' Booth set out to provide evidence rather than to propose remedies. But he did suggest the mass removal of the casual poor (his category B) to industrial or labour colonies.[3] He argued that 'the poverty of the poor' was 'mainly the result of the competition of the very poor'; and that the distress of his categories C and D – labourers in intermittent work, and those in regular employment at no more than 21*s*. per week –

was the direct consequence of the existence of category B. If this last group were removed from the labour market, its work could easily be absorbed by categories C and D. Booth (who regarded himself as a Conservative in politics) contended that this limited degree of 'socialist' intervention was necessary for the overall benefit of individualism. 'Our individualism fails because our Socialism is incomplete ... The Individualist system breaks down as things are, and is invaded on every side by Socialistic innovations, but its hardy doctrines would have a far better chance in a society purged of those who cannot stand alone.' Fortunately, the impracticality of Booth's removal scheme did not affect the validity of the social discoveries which had provoked it.

Booth's survey of London was eventually complemented by Seebohm Rowntree's survey of York, published in 1901. Rowntree came to similar conclusions about the extent of poverty, but showed greater sophistication in fixing the poverty line. The revelations of Booth and Rowntree undermined the old assumptions that individual poverty was usually the result of character weakness. Booth still accepted that a substantial proportion of those in distress must be weak or vicious; but he argued that it was their circumstances, and especially unemployment, which had most often degraded them. Rowntree made the striking discovery that half the working men of York who suffered primary poverty were 'in regular work but at low wages'; there was no blameworthy idleness in such cases. One household in every six or seven in primary poverty had fallen into distress because of the death of the chief wage-earner, which was again not a cause for blame. Rowntree emphasized that though many unskilled workers lacked ideas they did not lack sound moral qualities. Poverty, he concluded, was in large part 'the result of false social and economic conditions'.

Reformers began to hope that once the causes of poverty had been isolated by social investigation distress might be removed, or at least controlled, by legislation inspired by social science – just as the spread of disease had come to be checked by legislation influenced by medical science. In particular, unemployment, which Booth and Rowntree had demonstrated to be the main cause of poverty among the able-bodied, became the subject of intense discussion.[4] In practical terms it could be shown to be a frequent outcome of ill-health, bad housing, and poor environment; in theoretical terms, it could be expressed as the consequence of a highly imperfect market for labour and an often erratic consumer demand. Among members of trade unions which paid out-of-work benefit, monthly unemployment peaks sometimes as high as 10 per cent were reached during 1884–5, 1887, 1892–5, 1904–5, and 1908–9, with an average of 10.2 for the whole year of 1886.

Significantly, the very word 'unemployment', with its neutral note, not attaching blame, only came into common use from the 1880s, though coined earlier. Between the 1880s and 1914 three distinct approaches to the unemployment problem were canvassed. The most ambitious method wanted to eliminate the condition through fundamental changes in the organization and control of industry. Other policies sought to remove the unemployed from the labour market, either by occupying them upon artificial relief works or by subjecting them to compulsory training schemes. A third approach aimed to minimize the extent and effects of unemployment without removing the out-of-work from the market and without making changes in the industrial system.

The first approach, favoured by socialists, never became practical politics up to 1914. But the provision of relief works was tried and found wanting between 1886 and 1905. In March 1886 Joseph Chamberlain issued a circular as President of the Local Government Board which urged local authorities to plan the undertaking of necessary public works to coincide with periods of trade depression, and to co-operate with the Poor Law authorities in providing non-pauperizing work for the deserving unemployed. This circular was issued five times up to 1893, but comparatively little was achieved at its prompting. Suitable work proved difficult to find and costly to finance. Moreover, most applicants seem to have been not skilled artisans unluckily out of jobs (as Chamberlain envisaged), but chronically irregular workers who turned relief work into another form of casual employment. The Unemployed Workmen Act of 1905 constituted the last and most ambitious attempt to deal with unemployment through job creation schemes. This act formally established a Central (Unemployed) Body for London, with Distress Committees in every metropolitan borough and in all urban districts of at least 50,000 population. These committees were empowered not only to put men to work if no other jobs were available, but also to aid emigration, to establish farm colonies, and to open labour exchanges. As a stimulus to social experiment the Act achieved something; but in numerical terms it did little to alleviate hardship among the thousands of good workmen who needed to be saved from the demoralizing Poor Law. The Act in operation, concluded young William Beveridge in his pioneering book *Unemployment, A Problem of Industry* (1909), had demonstrated 'beyond question its own essential inadequacy'. By this date Beveridge and Winston Churchill were putting into practice the third type of unemployment policy through their notable Labour Exchanges Act of 1909 (see below, p. 466).

Interventionalist approaches to the problem of unemployment, and to the poverty problem of which it formed a part, found encouragement during the last quarter of the nineteenth century from the rapid decline in the influence of old theoretical prohibitions. Admittedly, the case for minimum intervention was still being voiced by Herbert Spencer in *The Man Versus the State* (1884), one of the last of a long series of books which he had published since mid-century.[5] Spencer's wide range of reference to biology and psychology as well as to politics and economics, and his facile terminology, had given a 'scientific' cover to his thoughts which greatly impressed mid-Victorian readers. But by the time of the publication of *The Man Versus the State* he was on the defensive. His views which had once seemed liberal were now regarded as conservative. His book came to be grouped with Henry Maine's study of *Popular Government* (1885), which took a melancholy view of the prospects for rule by democracy.[6] Maine contended that the delicate fabric of modern society required freedom, variety, and security for property. But he feared that the new democratic electorate would not understand this. Rapid changes would be attempted; and since rapid yet orderly change was unattainable, the result would be chaos. A reaction might then follow in favour of totalitarian government; and this was the last thing which Maine desired, for he was a conservative not an authoritarian. 'The possibilities of reform are strictly limited . . . all organic life in the world is only possible through the accident that temperature in it ranges between a maximum of 120 degrees and a minimum a few degrees below zero of the Centigrade. For all we know, a similarly narrow limitation may hold of legislative changes in the structure of human society.' W. E. H. Lecky's *Democracy and Liberty* (1896) re-stated some of Maine's fears, giving particular emphasis to the democratic threat to middle-class interests. Both Maine and Lecky favoured a strong House of Lords, with full power to check the passage of dangerous legislation sent up by a democratic House of Commons.

These negative approaches to the problem of individual liberty in a democratic society were rejected by the idealist philosophers, who came to dominate academic English philosophy during the last years of the century.[7] The idealists believed, with varying emphasis between themselves, not in negative liberty but in the need to promote conditions favourable to the enjoyment of positive liberty.

When we speak of freedom as something to be so highly prized, we mean a positive power or capacity of doing or enjoying something worth doing or enjoying, and that, too, something that we do or enjoy in common with others. We mean by it a power which each man exercises through the help or security given him by his fellow-men, and which he in turn helps to secure for them.

So argued T. H. Green, the Oxford philosopher, in a lecture on *Liberal Legislation and Freedom of Contract*. Green's ideas were influenced by the thought of Kant and Hegel; but for him state power was important as a means not an end of government. State intervention was necessary to provide support and opportunities for individuals to lead fuller lives, to develop their 'social capacity'. How far Green was prepared to go in support of state intervention was left unclear at the time of his early death in 1882. Certainly, some of his followers – writing after the further large increase of the electorate under the Third Reform Act – put bold glosses upon his ideas. D. G. Ritchie's *Principles of State Interference* (1891) dismissed the belief that all power gained by the state was power taken from individuals. 'The explicit recognition of popular sovereignty tends to abolish the antithesis between "the Man" and "the State". The State becomes, not "I" indeed, but "we".' J. H. Muirhead's *The Service*

of the State, Four Lectures on the Political Teaching of T. H. Green
(1908) contended that there was 'an old-world air' about 'controversy as
to the right, and even as to the limits of State interference with any of the
actions of individuals'. The idea of a 'fixed liberty-fund', claimed
Muirhead, had gone the way of the wage-fund. Yet Bernard Bosanquet,
the ablest idealist after Green, worked for the Charity Organisation
Society, which remained a body decidedly hostile to collectivism. His
Philosophical Theory of the State (1899) set limits to intervention
which even enabled him to reconcile state action with the COS purpose
of helping individuals to help themselves.[8]

2

New approaches in political philosophy, which gave more or less
encouragement to policies of increased intervention, were being
matched by new ideas in economics.[9] The article on 'Political Economy'
in the 1885 edition of the *Encyclopedia Britannica* noted how *laissez-
faire* had 'now for some time lost the sacrosanct character with which it
was formerly invested'. Some of the leading tenets of classical political
economy came under heavy attack from about 1870: notably,
Malthusian population theory, the wage-fund theory, and labour or
cost of production theories of value. The sometimes bitter conflict
between employers and trade unions had provoked a new search for the
'law that determines the stable equilibrium of work and wages', which
the old political economy had failed to find. J. K. Ingram, speaking as
president of the economics section of the British Association in 1878,
admitted that political economy had erred in habitually regarding the
labourer from an abstract point of view as 'an instrument of
production'. It was 'too often forgotten that he is before all things a man
and a member of society'. The impact of the 'great depression' from the
mid 1870s provoked widespread complaints at many levels of discussion
about the trade cycle, about wages and distribution, about profits and
competition, and even about the workings and wisdom of the free trade
system.
    Discussion of Malthus's population theory – the contention that
without individual moral restraint population increase would tend to
outrun expansion of food supplies – was deleted from the 1899 edition of
Newsholme's *Elements of Vital Statistics* as of only historical interest.
Growth of population was visibly not outstripping the food and other
resources available to the late-Victorians. H. M. Hyndman, the
socialist, emphasized that the problem of the times was not over-
population, 'but the miserable system of distributing the wealth which
the population creates'.[10] The supplement to the Thirty-Fifth *Annual
Report* of the Registrar-General argued sharply in 1875 that Malthusian
restraint would have kept national population down to that of a second-
rate power – with industry crippled for want of labour, commerce

limited by shortage of ships, and the colonies unpeopled. This dismissal of the 'Malthusians difficulty' greatly encouraged the liberation of social thinking; for it could no longer be argued that state aid would only increase the numbers of the poor to the danger of society.

In 1869 John Stuart Mill had publicly abandoned the classical wage-fund theory. Under Darwinian influence the whole idea of 'unbending necessities' in economic life was to be discarded during the 1870s and 1880s. C. F. Bastable explained why this had happened in a lecture which compared the position of economic science in 1894 with that of 1860. 'Just as in biology the older inelastic views as to the nature of species and types gave way before the idea of innumerable gradations and transitional forms, so rigidity of definition and isolation of the study of wealth became no longer possible. Economic problems were found to be in contact at many points with social and political ones.'

In 1871 appeared the first edition of W. S. Jevons's *Theory of Political Economy*, which gradually became accepted as marking a new beginning in economics.[11] Jevons emphasized how economists must refuse to be constricted by 'the great influence of authoritative writers'. His main contribution consisted of the idea of marginal utility, which repudiated the classical labour or cost of production theories of value. 'Value depends solely on the final degree of utility.' The emphasis placed by the classical economists upon the creation of aggregate wealth had been appropriate in a period of rapid economic growth; but Jevons and the new economists were living in less buoyant times economically, and also in an age of expanding political democracy. They were therefore more interested in demonstrating how costs could be minimized; and also how individual satisfaction could be measured and maximized Marginal utility theory set the individual at the centre of analysis by arguing that market exchange values were determined by subjective assessments, not (as the classical economists had claimed) by the value of the factors of production. Jevons's marginal utility theory, and his fresh use of mathematical concepts, helped to prepare the way for Alfred Marshall's *Principles of Political Economy* (1890), which became the leading English textbook up to 1914 and after.[12] Marshall accepted that state action could sometimes promote social improvements more successfully than individual action; for example, in the provision of working-class education, and in the control of the urban environment. 'In this sense,' he wrote in 1907, 'nearly every economist of the present generation is a socialist.'

3

Darwinian biology obviously lent itself to application by analogy in social science. Nevertheless, T. H. Huxley, the great Darwinian publicist, emphasized in an important article on 'The Struggle for Existence' (*Fortnightly Review*, February 1888) and in his 1893

Romanes Lecture on *Evolution and Ethics* how the principle of natural selection could not be used to justify a free-for-all in human society. The natural process, Huxley argued, must be controlled by rational and ethical thinking. Right social conduct required self-restraint. 'In place of thrusting aside, or treading down all competitors, it requires that the individual shall not merely respect, but shall help his fellows.' Social policy should be directed 'not so much to the survival of the fittest, as to the fitting of as many as possible to survive. It repudiates the gladiatorial theory of existence'. By definition, contended Huxley, the establishment of human society implied the setting of limits; and the more complex that society became the more would the state need to intervene in the common interest. For example, increased foreign competition in trade required sanitary reform to create a healthy environment, plus improved educational and recreational facilities to improve the mental quality of the workforce. Beyond this Huxley does not seem to have wanted to go in state intervention; but an article by Julia Wedgwood called 'The Old Order Changeth' (*Contemporary Review*, September 1896) showed how Darwin had encouraged a way of thinking about society as an improvable entity, a way which could lead logically to support for comprehensive social reform. The Darwinian doctrine, concluded Miss Wedgwood, could be 'compressed into the statement that the world was not made 6,000 years ago, but is making still'.

Huxley was eager to counter the extreme views of the social Darwinians.[13] He knew that the criterion of 'survival of the fittest' (an expression coined not by Darwin but by Spencer) lacked the strength to support the glosses which extremists put upon it. It meant no more than that those who survive are fit, those who are fit survive. It gave no justification for the theories of interference with individual life in the name of racial improvement or survival. The social Darwinians, however, were convinced that abnormal conditions within the new urban industrial society were tending to produce an ever greater proportion of births from the least physically and mentally 'fit' stock – an unnatural situation of the survival of the unfittest. They regarded this as a main cause of Britain's declining competitiveness in world trade, especially in competition with the Germans and Americans who allegedly had remained racially more dynamic thanks to less distorted reproduction patterns. If the unfittest came to dominate British society, the social Darwinians saw no hope for Britain as a major power. Karl Pearson's *National Life from the Standpoint of Science* (1901) was committed to the thesis that civilization had resulted from 'the struggle of race with race, and the survival of the physically and mentally fitter race'. Leading social Darwinians such as Pearson, Benjamin Kidd, and (most notably) Francis Galton did not believe that general welfare reform would by itself reverse the tendency towards racial degeneration. They advocated 'eugenics', the calculated encouragement of high quality human breeding from good stock. The word was coined by Galton in the 1880s. Cash bonuses were recommended to encourage marriages and births among the 'fit': segregation and sterilization were proposed for the 'unfit'. Social Darwinians readily accepted that individual liberty might have to be curtailed for the sake of the 'race'.

Yet reliable statistics of physical unfitness were few. An article by Lord Brabazon on 'Decay of Bodily Strength in Towns' (*Nineteenth Century*, May 1887) noted how 30,000 out of 64,000 men who offered themselves for the army in 1884 were rejected as physically unfit. Rowntree's survey of York included figures which showed how nearly half of would-be army recruits in York, Leeds, and Sheffield were found to be medically unacceptable between 1897 and 1901. The *Manchester Guardian* (29.10.1906) pointed out that in the Manchester area in 1899 only just over 1,000 fully fit recruits had been available out of 11,000 volunteers. The *Guardian* explained that only 'the lowest class of the population' tried to join the army, those who could not otherwise find food and shelter. Social Darwinians, however, could answer alarmedly that it was precisely this lowest class which was the most prolific. Though social Darwinian remedies were too extreme to attract large support, the discussion which they provoked did help to prepare the way for the Edwardian welfare reforms.

In the 1880s Arnold Toynbee, an ardent pupil of T. H. Green, had helped to introduce the methods of the great German school of economic history into England.[14] His course of lectures delivered to working men during 1881–2 on *The Industrial Revolution of the Eighteenth Century* (published in 1884) offered a view of history coloured by close awareness of present social and economic problems. The Industrial Revolution in Toynbee's view, and his book put the expression into lasting currency in England, had been a destructive event. His interpretation discounted the impersonal economic gains, and emphasized instead the social losses of large-scale industrialization – the squalor of the new town life, the separation of workmen from masters brought about by the substitution of the factory for the domestic system. Industrialization, argued Toynbee, had created middle-class wealth only at the price of a century of working-class suffering. Along with significant numbers of other young middle-class university men of his generation, he felt a deep sense of guilt about the persistence of poverty and misery among the working classes. This showed strongly in his lecture on Henry George's *Progress and Poverty*, which he delivered to workmen shortly before his death in 1883.

We – the middle classes, I mean, not merely the very rich – we have neglected you; instead of justice we have offered you charity, and instead of sympathy, we have offered you hard and unreal advice . . . you have to forgive us, for we have wronged you . . . if you will forgive us – nay, whether you will forgive us or not – we will serve you, we will devote our lives to your service, and we cannot do more.

The old political economy, argued Toynbee, had failed as a guide towards the equitable distribution of the wealth produced by the

Industrial Revolution. 'For such an end a gospel of life is needed, and the old Political Economy had none.'

Toynbee put his social concern to the test in the East End of London, where he worked with Samuel Barnett, Rector of St Jude's, Whitechapel. After Toynbee's early death in 1883, Barnett promoted the opening of the first 'settlement' – Toynbee Hall – as a memorial to his friend.[15] Settlements were experiments in religious and social action conducted by men who accepted a call as Christians, and as fortunate members of the higher classes, to live and to work for a time among the urban working classes. Edward Denison and other Christian Socialists had shown the way in the 1860s; but the influx from the 1880s of hundreds of university men into the East End and elsewhere achieved a significance out of all proportion to the relatively small numbers involved. Barnett's idea was for a permanent presence, not just for a temporary 'mission'. Graduates and undergraduates came to live close to the people. Settlement running costs were met by subscriptions raised at the universities. Barnett regarded close contact between university men and the East Enders as beneficial to both. The working classes would gain the opportunity – despite their bleak surroundings – to raise their level of culture, both social and intellectual. University men would learn about the dark realities of life and labour for the urban poor, and they would carry their impressions with them into their later careers. Almost all the civil servants and junior politicians who were involved in the great Edwardian social reforms had participated in the settlement movement – Robert Morant, C. F. G. Masterman, William Beveridge, W. J. Braithwaite, and others.

Toynbee Hall, which was opened in 1884, was especially linked with Balliol College, Oxford. It was soon followed by Oxford House, which was especially the care of Keble College. Other settlements followed – Nonconformist and Roman Catholic as well as Anglican, in the provincial towns as well as in London. By 1913, twenty-seven settlements were counted in the capital and twelve in the rest of England, most of them with university connections. Of all the activities undertaken by settlement residents their participation in local government brought the most obvious benefits. The residents helped to rouse local bodies – town councils, Poor Law guardians, school managers, and others – to awareness of their social responsibilities. As teaching centres the settlements offered education up to secondary standard for self-improving workers. The settlements also helped to spread radical social and political ideas by providing respectable platforms and responsive audiences for socialist, trade union, and other advanced speakers. Not that the settlement movement was socialist in itself. Barnett's aim was to narrow class differences rather than to remove them. A poor man, he explained in *Practicable Socialism* (1888), might seem deprived compared with the owner of some stately mansion, and yet be the head of a happy home and family. Such a man's poverty was not an evil to be cured. 'It is a sign that life does not depend on possessions.' The existence of poor men alongside rich allowed a pleasing variety of earthly experience. 'The poverty which has to be cured is the poverty which degrades human nature.' Barnett believed that pensions should be paid to those who had kept out of the workhouse up to the age of sixty. And he was a strong advocate of working-class participation as guardians in the running of the Poor Law, 'where by experience they would learn how impossible it is to adjust relief to desert, and how much less cruel is regular sternness than spasmodic kindness'. A well-administered Poor Law remained in Barnett's view 'the best weapon in hand for the troubles to come, and such is impossible without the sympathy of all classes.'[16]

The settlement movement was only one intense expression of the strong and widely-remarked stirring of 'social conscience' among the middle and upper classes during the 1890s. An article entitled 'Since 1880' in the *Nineteenth Century* for April 1885 by G. J. Goschen, the Liberal politician, described the 'general awakening of the public conscience . . . a growing dissatisfaction, not on the part of the suffering classes alone, but on that of the richest and most cultivated classes, with much in the present social system.' Thomas Hughes, the writer and radical, argued in 1887 how the national conscience was 'wonderfully better in all ways . . . On the whole there is not, nor ever was, a nation that kept a more active conscience.'[17] The old belief that the workers ought to be able to manage through self-help and thrift aided by charity from the higher classes was no longer so confidently held. Too many people were seen to be suffering through no fault of their own – notably because of fluctuations in the trade cycle. Many workmen could never hope to save enough out of low wages to carry them through long periods of unemployment. Yet, as the first Fabian socialist tract *Why are the Many Poor?* (1884) complained, 'with the smallest of chances the poor are expected to display the greatest of virtues'. At Christmas 1875 the *Manchester Guardian* (27 December) had still been voicing the old charitable view that 'in the battle of life' it was necessary 'that now and then there should be a truce in which the wounded may be succoured . . . Bumble himself would not grudge the paupers their Christmas dinner.' But nineteen years later (24.12.1894) the *Guardian*'s attitude had changed completely: 'that the world must be made a better place for the unprivileged many is a conviction which has come home to most of us, however little of Socialists we may be, and the old easy contentment with a social system largely unjust but tempered by "charity" and Christmas effusion has passed away, never to return.' The *Manchester Guardian* was a Liberal newspaper, but Conservatives could also feel the pricking of social conscience. John Bailey, who opposed Sidney Webb, the Fabian, at a London County Council election in 1892 and was a Conservative parliamentary candidate in 1895 and 1900, made a revealing confession in his private journal for 5 December 1894:[18]

To-night took up a horrid Socialist book which made me very uncomfortable.

Nothing else ever really depresses me but this hideous doubt which comes now and then, of whether one is justified in living on rents and interest at all. I shall not act on it, no doubt, and indeed I am generally convinced of its unreasonableness, but the awful inequality of our social conditions is enough to give one pause ... The solution to all such questions is, I hope, this: that it is better to accept the amazingly rapid improvement that is going on than to plunge into any Socialist Medea's cauldron!

Those of the propertied classes who were not moved by conscience could still be moved by fear of social explosion from below. Both altruism and fear had led to wide recognition of the need to draw what Charles Booth called the 'true working classes' away from the degraded and potentially violent 'residuum' at the bottom of society.[19] In the mid 1880s the danger seemed real and immediate that sufficient numbers of the ill-housed and unemployed would join with the residuum to engulf civilized London. The 'condition of England question' began to be discussed with an intensity unequalled since the Chartist crisis of the 1840s. *The Bitter Cry of Outcast London* (1883) and subsequent housing revelations, the London unemployed riots of February 1886 and November 1887, the matchgirls' strike of 1888, the Jack the Ripper murders in 1888, and the London dock strike of 1889 all evoked great fear and great sympathy in varying proportions. *The Times* of 9 February 1886 had reported that the West End 'was for a couple of hours in the hands of the mob'. In this unsettled situation the *Daily Telegraph* (10.2.1886), the most popular middle-class newspaper, voiced a dismissive attitude towards old dogmas. 'Ministers may rest assured that the public are not just at present in a mood to scrutinise with too severe an eye any deviation from the high doctrines of political economy which may be found desirable.'

The politicians had to adjust their approaches to suit this new climate of opinion. Gladstone in his old age still viewed with alarm the encroachments of 'socialism'. Liberals had no wish to abandon their traditional concern for individual freedom; on the other hand, could they deny the need to help those who could not help themselves? John Stuart Mill had himself forecast in his *Autobiography* (1873) that 'the social problem of the future' would be 'how to unite the greatest individual liberty of action with a common ownership of the raw material of the globe, and an equal participation of all in the benefits of combined labour'. How far then had Mill moved towards 'socialism'?[20] Sidney Webb and other socialists of the 1880s claimed him as one of themselves, making reference especially to the 1852 edition of his *Political Economy* and to his posthumous *Chapters on Socialism* (1879). But Mill had spoken favourably only of a decentralized co-operative economy, not of a planned society. Nevertheless, during the early 1870s his advocacy through the Land Tenure Reform Association of taxation of the unearned increment did help to prepare the way for the radical and socialist programmes of the 1880s.

The question 'why are the many poor?' could be made to carry with it the hostile supplementary question 'why are the few rich?' And the next question then was to ask whether social reform should set out to make the poor less poor by making the rich less rich. Philip Snowdon, the socialist, expressed no hesitation during the Commons debates on old-age pensions (9.7.1908) that social reform was 'a question of making the rich poorer and the poor richer'. Socialist literature made frequent reference to the 'idle rich'. Sidney Webb's Fabian tract *Facts for Socialists* (1887) noted how in 1881 over 400,000 adult men (1 in 21) 'did not even profess to have the shadow of an occupation'. 'The natural interests of the small nation privileged to exact rent for its monopolies, and of the great nation thereby driven to receive only the remnant of the product, are permanently opposed.'

The Fabians demanded the restitution to public use of all 'rent' and interest.[21] The level of these, according to the Fabian theory of differential rent, was determined not by the efforts of owners but by the difference in yield between the poorest land (or capital, or human skills) in use, and the yield of a superior example. Factors for which owners could claim no credit (good land, inherited capital, a hardworking labour force) could thus bring them great profits, even while leaving their workers with low wages. The unfairly rich, moreover, could grow even richer. As society developed, the demand for land intensified, and its value therefore rose. This rise resulted entirely from social factors, not from the efforts of owners. Here was the idea of the 'unearned increment'. This had been briefly discussed by J. S. Mill; but (as already noticed) it was Henry George through his *Progress and Poverty* (1879) and his subsequent lecture tours who brought the concept into wide discussion in England. George wanted to concentrate all taxation upon the unearned increment. This single-tax formula did not win extensive support; but many of the social problems of late-Victorian England could be blamed upon the working of unearned increment, especially after the Fabians had extended its application to include the profits of capital as well as the profits of land. W. H. Dawson's *The Unearned Increment* (1890) complained of 'fabulous land-values and rents in towns, with terrible overcrowding and degradation of the working classes in large centres of population; the over-burdening of agriculture and the harassing of industry, entailing dear production and high prices; unhealthy land speculation, deranging commerce and often inflicting ruin upon the labouring classes; with social and political evils of many kinds.'

The emergence of the idea of the unearned increment was soon reflected in the language of the politicians. In March 1883 Joseph Chamberlain made his long-remembered attack upon Lord Salisbury, the Conservative leader, as the spokesman of landowners 'who toil not neither do they spin'; whose fortunes had originated 'in times gone by for the services which courtiers rendered kings', and had subsequently grown 'while they have slept by levying an increased share of all that other men have done by toil and labour to add to the general wealth and prosperity'.[22] The Queen's private secretary, Sir Henry Ponsonby, remarked in November 1883 that most recent major political speeches had dealt with 'socialism'. 'I don't exactly know what it means. It don't mean the Socialism of the German Revolutionists, but means I suppose Associationalism as opposed to Individualism.'[23] Ponsonby was here accepting 'socialism' in its broadest and loosest sense, as meaning a willingness to consider with favour interventionist policies intended to benefit the masses. Significantly, the contrasting words 'collectivism' and 'individualism' both came into common currency during the 1880s. So also from about 1887 did the cry 'we are all socialists now'. This was attributed to Sir William Harcourt, the Liberal. Harcourt, and most others who used the expression, were not claiming that many Englishmen had become converts to Marxism or to any advanced socialist dogma which involved the abolition of capitalism. Harcourt's 'socialists' wanted no more than to control in varying degrees the workings of the capitalist system. Joseph Chamberlain even claimed in 1885 that the Poor Law was socialism, as well as the 1870 Education Act. 'The greater part of municipal work is Socialism; and every kindly act of legislation.'[24] The Liberals were probably wiser than they knew in taking up the word 'socialism' in their own diluted sense. If they had presented a total negative to the word and to the new mood, socialism might well have attracted larger support in the purer versions which were being publicized by the new organizations of the 1880s and 1890s – the Social Democratic Federation, the Fabian Society, and the Independent Labour Party. As it was, these bodies, though important in stimulating discussion and in developing working-class politics, attracted only a few thousand members (see below, p. 327). Meanwhile large numbers of late-Victorians went round agreeing that 'we are all socialists now'.

4

One symptom of the advance of 'socialism' was the abandonment by the Liberal Party of its old cries of cheap government and low taxation. The new mass electorate felt no inhibitions about spending taxpayers' money. Income tax was now established as a permanent tax, though not yet a heavy one.[25] From 1870 it became an annual levy, instead of being voted for a block of years. This had been intended by Gladstone to emphasize its temporary nature; in practice it enabled the tax to become a highly flexible instrument of policy, its level adjustable year by year. Gradually, the revenue came to depend less upon indirect and more on direct taxation. *The Times* Golden Jubilee survey (21.6.1887) noticed the 'curious irony' that 'when the mass of the population were directly taxed in a hundred ways they had no voice in the direction of policy', whereas 'now that every addition to the expenditure is met by raising the income-tax those who pay it are outvoted twenty times over by electors who pay nothing but duties upon one or two luxuries'. But not until the beginning of the twentieth century did income-tax receipts become the largest item in gross public revenue, forced up by the costs of the Boer War:

	Direct taxation (£m.)			Indirect taxation (£m.)		
	Income and property tax	Land and assessed taxes	Death duties	Customs	Excise	Stamps
1880	9.2	2.7	6.2	19.3	25.3	4.2
1890	12.8	3.0	9.1	20.4	27.2	5.0
1900	18.8	2.5	18.5	24.1	37.3	8.5
1910	38.8	2.6	18.1	34.7	37.4	8.2
1913	41.2	2.7	25.2	33.5	38.0	10.1

The standard rate of income tax moved from as low as 2*d*. in the £ in 1874–5 to as high as 8*d*. by the late 1890s. The Boer War then drove the rate for 1903 to 1*s*. 3*d*.; and in the immediate pre-war years (1910–14) the cost of the Liberal welfare reforms and of the naval race with Germany kept the level at 1*s*. 2*d*.

The new readiness of governments to spend taxpayers' money was regretted and yet accepted by Sir William Harcourt, Chancellor of the Exchequer in Gladstone's 1892–4 Ministry.[26] Harcourt complained in 1893 how the War Office was demanding more arms, the Admiralty more ships. 'The Board of Trade are bound to satisfy the demands of the Labour Party. The Home Office has requirements on behalf of factories and workshops. Ireland is a bottomless pit'; and so on. In his 1893 budget speech Harcourt pictured Gladstone and himself as the last surviving advocates of economy in government. 'The saying has been attributed to me that every one is a socialist now. I do not know whether I ever said that, but this I will say – there are no economists now. Financial economy has gone the way of political economy.' The great wealth of the nation, admitted Harcourt, had encouraged free spending, because revenue from taxation was growing even apart from increases in tax rates. Harcourt's 1894 budget became famous for introducing graduated estate duties, payable at death, in place of various existing duties which had worked unfairly.[27] Graduation was an old radical idea, which had begun to win increasing support during the last quarter of the century. The principle, claimed Harcourt in his budget speech, was 'a most equitable and politic principle. Every writer on political economy has laid down the doctrine that taxation should be proportionate to the ability to bear it'. The burden of the new estate duty was still very light, rising from 1 per cent on property worth £500 or under to 8 per cent on property worth over £1 million. Harcourt may not have fully understood the potential of the weapon which he had put into the hands of later Chancellors for levelling down the ownership of property.

Up to 1890 higher state spending had not taken a higher percentage of the gross national product. But thereafter it grew from about 8.8 per cent (at 1900 prices) in 1890 to about half as much again in the immediate pre-war years.[28] Between 1890 and 1910 the amount of money spent by United Kingdom central and local government more than doubled:

	Central government (£)	Local government (£)	Total (£)
1890	80,500,000	50,100,000	130,600,000
1910	141,800,000	130,200,000	272,000,000

In 1900, during the Boer War, total expenditure temporarily reached £280,800,000. Then by 1910 total peacetime spending was again approaching this wartime level. In other words, the extra money which the late-Victorians had raised to spend upon armaments the Edwardians also raised – partly to spend on arms, but partly also for welfare purposes. Defence expenditure grew from £34,900,000 in 1890 to £91,300,000 in 1913, social service spending from £27,300,000 to £100,800,000.

This intensifying government activity required an increasingly rapid growth in the numbers of permanent non-industrial civil servants: 50,000 (1881), 116,000 (1901), 280,000 (1914). This 1914 civil service remained comparatively small by later twentieth-century standards, but a 'new bureaucracy' was already seen to be emerging. 'The professional administrator', concluded Sydney Low's *Governance of England* (2nd edn, 1914), had become 'a characteristic product of modern conditions like the professional politician'.

Notes

1. H. M. Hyndman, *England for All* (1881; reprinted 1973), p. 3.
2. See especially T. S. and M. B. Simey, *Charles Booth* (1960); and G. Stedman Jones, *Outcast London* (1971), Ch. 16.
3. See J. Brown, 'Charles Booth and Labour Colonies, 1889–1905', *Economic History Review*, second series, XXI (1968); and T. Lummis, 'Charles Booth: Moralist or Social Scientist?', *ibid.*, XXIV (1971).
4. See especially José Harris, *Unemployment and Politics, A Study in English Social Policy, 1886–1914* (1972).
5. See especially Sir Ernest Barker, *Political Thought in England, 1848–1914* (2nd edn, 1947), Ch. IV; D. Macrae's 1969 edition of *The Man Versus the State*; and J. D. Y. Peel, *Herbert Spencer* (1971).
6. See especially B. E. Lippincott, *Victorian Critics of Democracy* (1938), pp. 167–243; and N. Pilling, 'The Conservatism of Sir Henry Maine', *Political Studies*, XVIII (1970).
7. See especially D. Nicholls, 'Positive Liberty, 1880–1914', *American Political Science Review*, LVI (1962); M. Richter, *The Politics of Conscience: T. H. Green and His Age*

(1964); A. M. Quinton, 'Absolute Idealism', *Proceedings of the British Academy* LVII (1971); and M. Freeden, *The New Liberalism* (1978).

8. See S. Collini, 'Hobhouse, Bosanquet and the State: Philosophical Idealism and Political Argument in England, 1880–1918', *Past & Present*, no. 72 (1976).

9. See especially R. L. Smyth (ed.), *Essays in Economic Method* (1962); T. W. Hutchison, *A Review of Economic Doctrines, 1870–1929* (1962), part I; and T. W. Hutchison, 'Economists and Economic Policy in Britain after 1870', *History of Political Economy*, Vol. 1 (1969).

10. A. L. Thorold, *Life of Henry Labouchere* (1913), p. 415.

11. See especially Lord Robbins, *The Evolution of Modern Economic Theory* (1970), Ch. 9; R. D. Collison Black's 1970 edition of *The Theory of Political Economy*; and R. D. Collison Black *et al.* (eds.), *The Marginal Revolution in Economics* (1973).

12. See especially A. C. Pigou (ed.), *Memorials of Alfred Marshall* (1925); and C. J. Dewey, '"Cambridge Idealists": Utilitarian Revisionists in Late Nineteenth-Century Cambridge', *Historical Journal*, XVII (1974).

13. See B. Semmel, *Imperialism and Social Reform* (1960), Ch. III; R. J. Halliday, 'Social Darwinism: A Definition', *Victorian Studies*, XIV (1971); D. W. Forrest, *Francis Galton* (1974), Ch. 17; and M. S. Helfand, 'T. H. Huxley's "Evolution and Ethics": the Politics of Evolution and the Evolution of Politics', *Victorian Studies*, XX (1977).

14. See especially Beatrice Webb, *My Apprenticeship* (1926), Ch. IV.

15. See especially J. A. R. Pimlott, *Toynbee Hall* (1935); and K. S. Inglis, *Churches and the Working Classes in Victorian England* (1963), Ch. 4.

16. S. Barnett, 'Distress in East London', *Nineteenth Century*, November 1886, p. 691.

17. E. C. Mack and W. H. G. Armytage, *Thomas Hughes* (1952), p. 260.

18. J. Bailey, *Letters and Diaries* (1935), p. 53.

19. See especially G. Stedman Jones, *Outcast London* (1971), Ch. 16.

20. See especially L. Robbins, *The Theory of Economic Policy* (1952), Ch. V; and W. Wolfe, *From Radicalism to Socialism* (1975), Ch. 2.

21. See especially A. M. McBriar, *Fabian Socialism and English Politics, 1884–1918* (1962), pp. 29–47; and D. M. Ricci, 'Fabian Socialism: A Theory of Rent as Exploitation', *Journal of British Studies*, IX (1969).

22. J. L. Garvin, *Life of Joseph Chamberlain*, (1932), p. 392.

23. A. Ponsonby, *Henry Ponsonby* (1942), p. 379.

24. J. L. Garvin, *Life of Joseph Chamberlain*, II (1933), p. 78. See also T. H. Marshall, *Sociology at the Crossroads* (1963), pp. 271–3; and M. Freeden, *The New Liberalism* (1978), Ch. II.

25. See especially B. Mallet, *British Budgets, 1887–1913* (1913); Ursula K. Hicks, 'The Budget as an Instrument of Policy', *Three Banks Review*, June 1953; and B. E. V. Sabine, *A History of Income Tax* (1966), Chs. 7, 8.

26. A. G. Gardiner, *Life of Sir William Harcourt* (1923), II, pp. 226–32.

27. *Ibid.*, Ch. XVI; and B. E. V. Sabine, 'Harcourt's Budget of 1894', *British Tax Review*, 1974.

28. See Ursula K. Hicks, *British Public Finances* (1954), esp. Ch. 1; and A. T. Peacock and J. Wiseman, *The Growth of Public Expenditure in the United Kingdom* (1961), esp. Ch. 3.

Personalities: *'That indefinable something'*

1

The most striking new political personality of the 1880s was Lord Randolph Churchill (1849–95), the expositor of 'Tory Democracy'.[1] The meteoric career of the 'Grand Young Man' was substantially concentrated within this one decade. Churchill, younger son of the seventh Duke of Marlborough, had entered Parliament for the family borough of Woodstock in 1874; but he did not come to the fore until the Gladstone Government took office in 1880. The audacious and humorous sallies of the group which became known as the 'Fourth Party' – it comprised Churchill, Sir Henry Drummond Woolf, J. E. Gorst, and A. J. Balfour – then began to attract national notice. Despite their nickname the quartet remained within the Conservative ranks; but they were dissatisfied with what they rightly regarded as the feeble opposition offered to Gladstone by Sir Stafford Northcote and other Conservative leaders in the Commons. Churchill led the Fourth Party in Gladstone-baiting, to the dismay of Gladstone's admiring private secretary. 'Its aim is to turn into ridicule grave statements of Mr. Gladstone and others; to scoff and laugh; to "draw" the Prime Minister; to lay a trap for the Government; to have in short a bit of "sport"; to get up a row; to provoke a scene.'[2]

Churchill was overflowing with restless energy. He became a popular platform speaker, even though he remained aristocratically aloof. His speeches were polished, colourful, amusing, and consequently widely reported. But their content remained limited, and much less original than their presentation. Nevertheless, simply by his activity on behalf of Tory Democracy Churchill played a vital part in putting the Conservative Party in touch with the mass electorate. 'He made the people believe in us.' Churchill's health was never good, and this made him often irritable in his dealings with colleagues. But by the time of his appointment as Secretary of State for India in 1885 he had become accepted as a major figure in the Conservative leadership. When he took office as Chancellor of the Exchequer in 1886, however, he soon showed himself to be unwilling to compromise. 'He must be Chief, Supreme, a Bismarck.'[3] He overplayed his hand; and Lord Salisbury, the Prime Minister, was glad to accept his resignation from the chancellorship after only five months. Churchill died in 1895, perhaps from syphilis, after a sadly prolonged and public deterioration of mind and body. His elder son, Winston, though he had hardly known his father, wrote an admiring biography (1905).

2

Arthur James Balfour (1848–1930) – Conservative Prime Minister, 1902–5 – comprised one-quarter of the Fourth Party; but he always remained its least committed member.[4] He retained a strong family loyalty to his uncle, Lord Salisbury, the Conservative leader in the Lords; not that this prevented Balfour from participating in the discomfiture of Sir Stafford Northcote, the party leader in the Commons, who was Salisbury's main rival to become the next Conservative premier. Salisbury, who with patrician disregard of criticism was always ready to appoint his relatives to high office, made Balfour Chief Secretary for Ireland in 1887; and in this demanding job he unexpectedly established his reputation. Previously, he had seemed to be an urbane but languid dabbler in politics. Now he showed that he could be calculating and tenacious in support of a policy in which he believed. 'Mr. Balfour's courage and resolution,' enthused *The Times* review of 1888, 'his imperturbable temper, his skill in oratorical fence, and his trenchant powers of reasoning have brought him into the very front rank of contemporary statesmen.' Balfour's urbanity had been found to conceal strength of mind, not weakness. In 1902 he finally succeeded his uncle as Prime Minister; and in that year he again showed his tenacity by his determined support of the Government's highly contentious but valuable Education Bill.

Balfour never became a popular political figure, for he made no effort to understand the urban middle and working classes. 'He has no comprehension of the habits or thoughts of his countrymen,' remarked Austen Chamberlain, 'and no idea of how things strike them.'[5] This failure of understanding contributed to his loss of the premiership in 1905, and to his virtual deposition as Conservative Party leader in 1911. A sharp questioning mind beneath his casual manner made Balfour into an amateur philosopher. *A Defence of Philosophic Doubt* appeared in 1879, and *Foundations of Belief* in 1895. For relaxation he much enjoyed the exclusive round of country house entertaining, to which he brought ease and wit in conversation, knowledge of music, and an enthusiasm for lawn tennis and golf. During the 1880s and 1890s he was the leading member of the coterie known as 'The Souls', a youngish group of well-born but lively and intelligent people who discussed literature, art, and ideas with a seriousness unusual in high social circles. Balfour, in short, possessed an interesting personality. He was more than a politician: yet much more of a politician than he seemed.

3

Whereas Balfour was brilliant and happy in politics, Lord Rosebery (1847–1929) – Liberal Prime Minister 1894–5 – was brilliant and unhappy. He was described in the Edwardian twilight of his career as possessing 'all the gifts except the gift of being able to apply them'.[6] Rosebery had been born the heir to a great title and much land in Scotland and England. This high inheritance, plus his outstanding intelligence, combined to win him early acceptance as a coming man in politics. In 1879–80 he organized Gladstone's Midlothian campaigns. But Rosebery's own electrifying speeches were soon attracting audiences second in size only to his leader's. Yet Gladstone found Rosebery a difficult follower. His introspective temperament always magnified difficulties, and he found the compromises of politics hard to take. He refused a succession of junior offices in Gladstone's second administration before in 1881 finally accepting a Home Office under-secretaryship, with responsibility for Scottish affairs. But he resigned in dissatisfaction two years later. A world tour during 1883–4 helped to make Rosebery into a Liberal imperialist. He finally entered Glad-stone's cabinet in February 1885, but it fell in June. As one of the few great landowners to stay with Gladstone over Home Rule – and the ablest among them – Rosebery's standing among the Liberals now reached new heights. He served as Foreign Secretary in 1886 and again during 1892–4 – although during the interim his wife had died, a loss which nearly drove him out of politics. He succeeded Gladstone as Prime Minister in February 1894. The queen wanted him; and Sir William Harcourt, the abrasive Liberal leader in the Commons, could not rally sufficient support. But Rosebery's cabinet was always divided and unhappy, and the aloof Prime Minister, plagued by insomnia, which always overcame him at times of pressure, was not the man to pull it together. Consolation of sorts came when his horses won the Derby in 1894 and again the next year. Rosebery gladly resigned in June 1895, and he never held office again, although into the new century he was regarded as a major political figure. He gradually drifted out of touch with practical Liberal politics and towards Conservatism. He left no major legislative contribution behind him, although he did introduce the practice of party political continuity into the conduct of British foreign policy. His literary achievement included polished and perceptive biographical studies of Napoleon (1900) and of several great English statesmen. Rosebery himself might have joined their ranks. 'He was endowed with all the elements of greatness; but the elements are not enough. They must be compounded into unity by that indefinable something, constant and purposeful, which we call character.'

4

James Keir Hardie (1856–1915), another Scotsman prominent in the politics of the 1890s stood at the opposite end of the social scale to Lord Rosebery.[7] Hardie was the founding father of the Independent Labour Party (1893), and the best-known late-Victorian and Edwardian socialist. Of illegitimate birth, he began work as a Lanarkshire miner, was dismissed as an agitator, and became a miners' trade union leader. He first entered Parliament in 1892 as independent Labour member for South West Ham. He arrived at the House of Commons wearing a deer-stalker hat – headgear which he happened to like. It was not typical working-class wear; but his widely publicized 'cloth cap' was taken as symbolizing the new working-class political independence. Hardie was not a deep thinker, nor was he more than a competent speaker and journalist. Yet he came to enjoy in his own lifetime a unique intensity of respect within the Labour movement, which was often highly critical of its leaders. He won this position by his singlemindedness, and by his patent and unbounded faith in the common people. The fact that his socialism was not based upon an intellectual position – such as an economic analysis of the failings of society – but upon a moral vision, helped him to develop a broad appeal within the Labour movement and beyond. He did not threaten class war. He remained a convinced but undogmatic Christian, who regarded socialism as the best political expression of Christian brotherly love.

Hardie's unique standing was much assisted by his bearded patriarchal appearance, which made him look much older than his actual age. He was not sixty when he died, yet for years he had been known as the 'grand old man of Labour'. Implicit in this soubriquet, however, lay the admission that by Edwardian times Hardie no longer stood quite at the centre of working-class politics. From 1906 Labour in Parliament acted as an established party, whereas Hardie remained in spirit always a pioneer. 'He is the only man who could have created the Labour Party,' explained one acute Liberal journalist in 1908, 'for concentration and intensity are the creative impulses. But he is almost the only man in the party who is not fitted to lead it.'[8] He died in 1915, deeply distressed that the international socialist movement had proved unable to prevent the outbreak of the First World War.

Notes

1. See especially Lord Rosebery, *Lord Randolph Churchill* (1906); W. S. Churchill, *Lord Randolph Churchill* (2nd edn, 1951); and R. Rhodes James, *Lord Randolph Churchill* (1959).
2. D. W. H. Bahlman (ed.), *Diary of Sir Edward Walter Hamilton, 1880–1885* (1972), I, p. 276.
3. Lord Chilston, *W. H. Smith* (1965), p. 227.
4. See especially Blanche E. C. Dugdale, *Arthur James Balfour* (1936); K. Young, *Arthur James Balfour* (1963); and S. H. Zebel, *Balfour* (1973).
5. Sir A. Chamberlain, *Politics From Inside* (1936), p. 464.
6. A. G. Gardiner, *Prophets, Priests and Kings* (1908), p. 278. See especially R. Rhodes James, *Rosebery* (1963).
7. See especially K. O. Morgan, *Keir Hardie* (1975); and I. McLean, *Keir Hardie* (1975).
8. A. G. Gardiner, *Prophets, Priests and Kings* (1908), p. 218.

Democracy: *'Is this democracy to prove fatal to England?'*

1

The Representation of the People Act, 1884, and the Redistribution of Seats Act, 1885, came to be known together as the Third Reform Act. These two Liberal measures, plus the Corrupt and Illegal Practices Prevention Act of 1883; and the 1885 Registration Act, amounted to the largest single instalment of parliamentary reform undertaken during the nineteenth century; and the electoral system which they created remained in operation until 1918.[1] Most commentators and politicians assumed that 'democracy' had now arrived. In his preface to *The*

Radical Programme (1885) Joseph Chamberlain welcomed 'government of the people by the people'. 'At last the majority of the nation will be represented by a majority of the House of Commons.' Yet this democracy stopped well short of 'one man one vote'; and no women at all were allowed the suffrage in parliamentary elections.

The most noticed feature of the Representation of the People Act was its extension of the franchise to agricultural labourers who were householders. Just as Gladstone had convinced himself during the 1860s that working-class householders in the towns were skilled workmen who deserved to be trusted with voting privileges, so he had now convinced himself that agricultural labourers possessed the same qualities.[2] He told the Commons while introducing the bill that he believed 'the peasant generally to be, not in the highest sense, but in a very real sense, a skilled labourer' because he was required to undertake 'many things which require in him the exercise of active intelligence.' In articles on 'The County Franchise' in the *Nineteenth Century* (November 1877, January 1878) Gladstone had emphasized the conservative qualities of the skilled labourers both in country and town. 'It is this great safeguard, the love of inequality, which has made safe the changes past, and will make safe the changes yet to come.' The 1884 Franchise Act put the county and borough suffrage upon the same basis for the first time. This meant that male householders were now given equal rights to vote whether they happened to live in country or in town. Lodgers could also claim votes if they occupied lodgings valued at £10 per annum unfurnished. But this high valuation excluded many working-class lodgers. Paupers remained disfranchised, as did living-in servants, or any sons living with parents who could not claim exclusive use of a room, which was unlikely in working-class families. Connection with property thus remained the basic test for a vote, though it had now been much broadened in application. The Second Reform Act had enfranchised one out of three adult males in England and Wales: the Third Reform Act extended this to two out of three. Gladstone both welcomed this wider extension and remained glad to keep the propertyless and rootless outside the electoral system.

Enfranchisement required not only possession of a voting right but also acceptance upon the electoral registers. The 1885 Registration Act reformed the system; but enough complexities remained to keep many potential working-class voters off the lists. A year's residence was necessary to qualify for the householder, lodger, or service franchises; but a quarter or a third of urban working-class families were likely to move house each year as jobs were changed or as different accommodation was needed. The registers, moreover, always began several months out of date, and remained effective for a year thereafter. Constituency party agents always had to work hard to keep working-class voters on the registers. The lodger vote was particularly difficult to organize, and was often collected only in marginal seats. The fact that registration 'should depend on the activity, and be undertaken in the interests of a political party' was rightly criticized as 'an indefensible anomaly'.[3]

Though on average about one adult male in three in England and Wales still lacked a vote after 1884, in some working-class constituencies this proportion reached as high as one in two. On the other hand, while the poor often remained voteless, owners of businesses and university graduates (who were represented through university constituencies) could gain additional votes. Gladstone, indeed, had welcomed the continuation of plural voting as recognition of the importance of property. Plural voters perhaps numbered upwards of 500,000 in 1914. Total electoral numbers increased as follows:[4]

	England and Wales		United Kingdom
	County electorate	Borough electorate	Total electorate
1883	966,721	1,651,732	3,152,912
1885	2,538,349	1,842,191	5,708,030
	England		
1906	3,116,339	2,359,654	7,266,708

In 1906 the English electorate comprised the following spread of voters:

	County electorate	Borough electorate
Owners	479,443	—
Occupiers and householders	2,578,859	2,216,894
Lodgers	57,073	119,513
Others	—	23,247

Perhaps 60 per cent of these voters came from the working class, and 40 per cent from the middle class. In other words, the middle classes retained about twice the electoral weight which they would have carried within a 'one man one vote' system.[5]

Under the 1885 Redistribution Act 142 seats in England and Wales – mostly in small boroughs under 15,000 population – were redistributed. Sixty-eight were given to English and Welsh county constituencies, seventy-four to boroughs. Thirty-nine of these last were in greater London. The capital and the industrial districts were now at last accorded representation more nearly in proportion to population. Most of the old county divisions and the larger borough seats were divided into single-member constituencies. These more or less artificial units replaced the old representation of communities, a change strongly attacked both by traditionalists and by some reformers. Liberal newspapers such as the *Manchester Guardian*, *Birmingham Post*, and *Leeds Mercury* protested against the 'vivisection of the great boroughs'. These papers rightly foresaw that, though the representation of Manchester was now increased from three to six seats, no one would be able to speak powerfully in future as 'Member for Manchester (or

Birmingham, or Leeds)'.[6] A few enthusiasts (notably Leonard Courtney, who resigned from Gladstone's Government over the issue) argued
in vain for a system of proportional representation, which would have
allowed a democratic redistribution without disturbing local community representation.[7] Predominantly single-class constituencies now
emerged in the cities and large towns – working-class inner urban seats,
middle-class suburban seats. The former were eventually to become
likely Labour strongholds, the latter often became Conservative safe
seats. The House of Commons now contained 670 members, allocated
as follows:

	England	Wales	Scotland	Ireland
Counties	234	19	39	85
Boroughs	226	11	31	16
Universities	5	—	2	2

The creation of equal electoral districts was only partly attempted in
1885. Many anomalies in representation remained, and new ones were
soon produced by shifts in population. For example, Durham city
contained only 2,600 electors in 1910, whereas the expanding suburban
constituency of Romford had 52,984. The decline or stagnation of rural
population meant that by 1906 a county vote in Great Britain had
become worth almost double a borough vote in terms of electoral
weight.

The *Economist* (6.12.1884) remarked how the franchise and
redistribution Acts together amounted to 'a pacific revolution', which
disturbed existing interests as never before. 'What with the disfranchise-
ments, and the new franchise, and the increase in Members for large
places, and the adoption throughout nine-tenths of the Kingdom of the
one-member principle, every sitting Member will find himself, for one
reason or another, addressing a new constituency.' Many new local
associations had to be created by the political parties to match the big
increase in the number of constituencies – from 416 in 1880 to 643 in
1885. The old-style political agent, who practised manipulation from
behind the scenes, was coming to seem unsuited to the new electoral
numbers and the new 'programme' politics. Cox and Hardy's *Hints to
Solicitors for the Conduct of Elections*, long a standard work, was being
described by 1887 as 'strange old-world reading . . . so rapid has been the
revolution'.[8] Electorates had grown too big for handling by bribery or
by lavish payments for services and generous 'treating'. Even before the
enlargement of the electorate the Corrupt and Illegal Practices Act of
1883 had at last severely and effectively tightened the rules for the
conduct of elections. Members of Parliament were coming to accept
high standards of political morality. Corruption at elections was made
punishable by up to two years' imprisonment, and for the first time a
limit was set to election expenses. In broad terms, candidates could not
spend more than £1,000 per 5,000 voters. The number of party workers

who could be paid was also drastically reduced. At the 1885 election expenditure fell in many constituencies by two-thirds compared with 1880.

Local electioneering now acquired a new character. Unpaid party volunteers – women as well as men – took over much constituency work both during elections and at other times. By 1894 an American observer was remarking how the most striking feature of English elections was

the number of women and men who worked for the different candidates with no other incentive than the desire to see their man and their party win. The shopkeepers, after a long day behind the counter, worked in the committee-rooms until two in the morning, folding and mailing circulars and other campaign matter. The women of the village, led by the rector's wife, directed forty-five thousand envelopes in one week; and the ladies from the Castle rose early and canvassed the town in rain and storm.[9]

The number of successful petitions for election bribery dropped from sixteen in 1880 to three in 1885. Corruption still lingered into the twentieth century in a few old towns. And Members of Parliament and candidates were expected to circulate money in their constituencies, notably through generous subscriptions and donations to local bodies. But purity of election had at last been achieved. The coming of democracy coincided not with the debasement of constituency politics but with its elevation.

The representatives chosen by the late-Victorian and Edwardian mass electorate remained predominantly upper- and middle-class in origins and business interests. Comparable numbers of Unionist and Liberal candidates were returned at the December 1910 election. Their main business connections (with some individuals counted under more than one heading) were as follows:[10]

	Unionist	Liberal
Landowners	123	38
Heavy industries	43	47
Transport industries	48	45
Finance	124	92
Merchants	20	40
Coalowners	10	14
Textiles	5	18

66 Conservatives and 62 Liberals were qualified as solicitors or barristers. One hundred and ninety-six Conservatives had attended public schools (90 at Eton), and 104 Liberals (23 at Eton). Eighty-seven Liberals had been educated at secondary schools, but only 23 Conservatives.

Should Members of Parliament be paid salaries, so that more working men might be elected? After the passing of the Second Reform Act this began to be seriously albeit spasmodically discussed; and late-Victorian Liberals (including Gladstone) came to favour it. Sir Henry

Campbell-Bannerman, as Liberal Prime Minister, argued in the Commons (7.3.1906) that payment of a salary would raise the quality of members elected by widening the range of choice, and would also strengthen their independence once returned. But the Liberals long hesitated to act, in the belief that a decision by politicians to pay themselves would be unpopular, even though the £252,000 needed each year was no more than the cost of one battleship. In the end, however, the Osborne Judgement (1909), which prevented expenditure by trade unions for political purposes (such as payment of trade union Members of Parliament) forced the Liberals to move, especially as from 1910 they needed Labour support in the Commons. From the start of the financial year 1911–12 all Members of Parliament became entitled to £400 per year, a quarter of which was allocated for necessary parliamentary expenses free of income tax. Traditionalist critics grumbled that this would encourage 'professional politicians'. But Campbell-Bannerman had answered by asking, 'What do you mean by a professional politician? If you take a man who devotes himself to his work, to the study of public affairs, in order to qualify himself here, and contrast with him a man who came here as a pastime or a means of social advancement, which of the two is the better man?' Traditionalists feared that the House of Commons would lose its character as 'the best club in London'. The House still liked to think of itself as a place where gentlemen met to discuss the country's affairs, rather than as a debating chamber on the Continental model. Doubts whether Labour members, who were not 'gentlemen', would cause difficulties were to prove groundless, for most of them came to accept not only the written but also the unwritten rules of the House.

2

Late-Victorian and Edwardian Members of Parliament found themselves much busier than their predecessors. Legislation had assumed a novel importance, as successive governments tried to meet the needs of the new urban industrial society and the expectations of the new mass electorate. Gladstone's secretary noted in 1882 how 'every year the demands on the Executive and for legislation increase at a frightful ratio'.[11] Gladstone had been reluctant to press the demands of ministers upon the House of Commons; but his 1868–74 administration introduced frequent 'morning' sittings (2 p.m. to 7 p.m. on Tuesdays and Fridays). Then in 1872 the rights of private members to move amendments on a motion to go into committee of supply were restricted, even though this was the established procedure whereby they could voice grievances ('grievances before supply'). Deliberate Irish obstruction of Commons business from the late 1870s gave additional urgency to the case for further changes in procedure. Obstruction was not itself new, but the Irish practised it with a novel persistence for the sake of disrupting business in general rather than because they were necessarily opposed to the measures which they prevented from passing. The first counter-move was made in 1880 by Disraeli's Government, which secured a standing order giving power to the Speaker or Chairman of Committee to suspend individual members. But the main crisis came after Gladstone had resumed office. From a quarter to four in the afternoon of Monday 31 January 1881 the House of Commons was kept in continuous session until the debate on leave to introduce an Irish coercion bill was terminated by the intervention of the Speaker at nine-thirty on the morning of Wednesday 2 February. 'The dignity, the credit and the authority of this House,' the Speaker solemnly announced, 'are seriously threatened and it is necessary they should be vindicated.' This intervention was widely welcomed, inside the Commons and out. The rules of debate were now changed. In 1882 the Speaker was formally given power to close a debate, and from 1887 any member could move the closure with the consent of the Speaker. The 'guillotine' was first employed in the same year to accelerate progress through a bill. Further tightening of the rules still proved necessary during the 1890s, ending with Balfour's 'parliamentary railway timetable' of 1902. From this date private members were left with only Friday afternoons for their business, and the Government was able to arrange virtually all the work of the Commons, and to fix the times by which motions were to be carried. The contentious 1902 Education Act could not have passed but for the new procedure.

The new standing orders meant that backbench Members of Parliament could no longer aspire to exert a regular public check upon the executive. The cabinet had taken the initiative, and the opportunity to mount a regular challenge was now confined to the official Opposition, which was itself led by the alternative cabinet. It has indeed been suggested that during the 1880-5 Liberal administration the two front benches deliberately worked together to restrict the influence of uncomfortable minorities – not only the wild Irish, but also the Fourth Party on the Conservative side and the radicals within the Liberal ranks. In 1883 the Liberal and Conservative leaders voted on the same side in 46 per cent of divisions for which the whips operated.[12] Still, as Government control of the parliamentary timetable grew, expectations of party solidarity in voting grew with it. The Conservatives cast party votes in only 71 per cent of all Commons divisions in 1881 and the Liberals in 66 per cent; but by 1894 these proportions had reached 91 per cent and 81 per cent respectively. A change in attitude was noted by Lord Salisbury, who wrote to the Queen in 1889 about the disappearance of 'the old judicial type of Member, who sat rather loose to his Party and could be trusted to be fair'; now they were 'all partisans'.[13] Private Members of Parliament did retain some influence behind the scenes. 'In the lobbies, in the smoke-room, on the terrace many a man who will vote straight speaks his mind plainly enough.' Different sections of each party could be expected to show varying degrees of enthusiasm for different policies or measures. The party whips were expected to understand these variations, and to know the limits beyond which the party could not be pushed by its leaders. Open backbench revolt was still possible, but it represented last resort action which was as much likely to destroy a Government as to control it. Balfour's administration was disintegrating throughout 1905 because of backbench disillusionment. 'Old-fashioned Tories, who, in the whole course of their parliamentary lives, had never entertained the thought of voting against their party, now left the House swearing that nothing would induce them to stay and vote. They swept past the Whips at the doors.'[14]

The practice of putting questions to ministers grew rapidly during the second half of the nineteenth century; and while other rights of private members were being curtailed it provided (as was said) a 'safety-valve', which did not absorb too much parliamentary time.[15] The rise of constituency democracy brought a greater need for local Members of Parliament to be seen to be active at Westminster, not least on behalf of their constituents. The number of questions on the order paper rose from some 200 per year about 1850 to 4,000–5,000 by the end of the century.

3

The power at the command of the British Government had now become enormous. *The Times* (5.5.1880) exclaimed how ministers found before them 'the most varied and extensive field of action ever enjoyed by a governing power'. As well as the interests of the people at home, they had the care of new communities throughout the British Empire. The effective authority of Roman emperors had been limited by slow communications, but the development of the telegraph had now placed the British Cabinet 'within speaking distance of every city and every colony with which it has to deal'. And to carry out the wishes of ministers the reformed and expanded civil service provided 'the most effective machinery of public administration in the world'.

The British cabinet ruled widely; but it was itself led by the Prime Minister.[16] To the end of his career Gladstone liked to leave his fellow cabinet ministers – whom he had selected with great care – largely free in their own departments. He was always reluctant to seek the removal of a cabinet minister against his will, half accepting the old idea that all ministers were equal servants of the Crown. It was not indeed until 1905 that the office of Prime Minister was constitutionally recognized to exist, when its holder was given precedence after the Archbishop of York. But throughout the nineteenth century the Prime Minister had been developing a particular constitutional relationship with the sovereign; and he alone gained the right to ask for a dissolution of Parliament. Then as politics came to demand more and more public speaking outside Parliament the Prime Minister – or the Opposition leader who was the alternative Prime Minister – began to be taken as the personification of their respective parties. Disraeli achieved this position even without much campaigning outside Westminster. Gladstone's campaigns became dramatic progresses – to which Lord Salisbury, a reluctant but effective public speaker, was forced to respond.

The new democracy liked to be addressed by strong personalities. But would it allow the politicians to rule effectively? Or would it prove changeable and difficult to govern? The Niagara figure of speech was again used in discussion of the political future after the passing of the Third Reform Act as after the passing of the Second. 'Are we being swept along a turbulent and irresistible torrent which is bearing us towards some political Niagara, in which every mortal thing we know will be twisted and smashed beyond all recognition?' So asked Lord Randolph Churchill in 1885. 'Or are we, on the other hand, gliding passively along a quiet river of human progress that will lead us to some undiscovered ocean of almost superhuman development?' T. H. S. Escott put the same questions more concretely. 'What productive forces are there inherent in the democracy? What power has it of implanting energy, and inspiring action, in individuals? How is the principle of authority at home and abroad to be maintained under its supremacy? How are its passions to be curbed or its inertness to be dispelled? Who or what will be adequate to its discipline? Or is this democracy to prove fatal to England as an imperial State, and as a pattern and mother of constitutions to the world?'[17]

Joseph Chamberlain had no doubts that the new democracy would accept a firm lead, as he explained in 1886:[18]

I think a democratic government should be the strongest government, from a military and Imperial point of view, in the world, for it has the people behind it ... The problem is to give the democracy the whole power, but to induce them to do no more in the way of using it than to decide on the general principles which they wish to see carried out and the men by whom they are to be carried out. My Radicalism, at all events, desires to see established a strong government and an Imperial government.

John Morley agreed about the need for 'statesmen who have made up their minds ... The English democracy will follow leaders, and has no dislike of authority'.[19] James Bryce, the Liberal historian and politician, analysed the nature of late-Victorian political public opinion in his book on *The American Commonwealth* (1888). He suggested that a small group of practising politicians, journalists, and thinkers – numbering hundreds rather than thousands – exchanged ideas and devised policies. A larger second group followed public affairs with some continuous interest, reading political speeches in the press, occasionally attending political meetings, and probably enrolling as members of political organizations.

When an election arrives they go to vote of their own accord. They talk over politics after dinner or coming into town by a suburban train. The proportion of such persons is larger in the professional classes (and especially among the lawyers) than in the mercantile, larger in the upper mercantile than among the working men of the large towns, larger among skilled than unskilled artisans, larger in the North than in the South, larger among the town workmen than among the newly enfranchised agricultural labourers.

Such people, thought Bryce, comprised less than a third of the electorate, though their numbers were growing. The rest of the electors possessed almost no informed knowledge of politics, though they might well vote at elections 'because they consider themselves to belong to a party, or fancy that on a given occasion they have more to expect from the one party than from the other'.

As Bryce also emphasized, the new mass electorate exercised not a continuous but an occasional control, expressed at general elections which were called only at intervals of several years. The introduction of some form of referendum – as practised in Switzerland and elsewhere – found some advocates but no wide support from the 1880s as a means of obtaining clear expression of the popular will upon specific important constitutional issues, such as Home Rule or Lords reform. A. V. Dicey argued that 'the Referendum, or the People's Veto' was 'in absolute harmony with the democratic principles or sentiment of the day'.[20] But the whole idea of government by 'mandate', whether implied or whether directly expressed through referendum, was roundly rejected by Gladstone. He drew a deep distinction between seeking support from the electors and being under mandate to them. Similarly, he always insisted upon the right of ministers to initiate legislation or to take action without previous electoral approval. When in April 1886 he introduced his Home Rule proposals in the Commons, he was challenged by Lord Hartington on the ground that the voters had not been consulted on this contentious issue at the general election five months earlier. Gladstone's reply was emphatic. He pointed out that the First Reform Bill had been introduced in 1831 soon after a general election in which parliamentary reform had been little discussed. 'My noble friend complains that this was a question which had not been referred to the public.' This seemed to suggest 'that the Government has committed fault in bringing forward this question at the present time because it had not brought the matter under public consideration. It seems to me that this is an extraordinary doctrine. I want to know where it is to be found in any Constitutional authority.'[21]

Was it constitutionally proper for the Lords to reject measures passed by the Commons on the ground that the electorate needed to be consulted? The late-Victorian House of Lords, with its now permanent Conservative majority, began to claim this right and more with respect to Liberal legislation. By 1900, 466 Conservative peers sat in the Lords but only 69 Liberals. Most of the former were not regular attenders; but they comprised a 'band of non-political Conservatives' always ready to vote against Liberal measures on critical occasions.[22] The peers defeated or mutilated Liberal bills during every Liberal administration from 1868 to 1914, despite the increasing anger of the Liberal leaders. Most notably, in 1893 the upper house dismissed Gladstone's Second Home Rule Bill by 419 votes to 41, even though the Liberals had won a majority at the recent general election with this at the top of their programme. In his famous *Fortnightly Review* article of May 1883 Lord Randolph Churchill expressed satisfaction that the upper house now gave the Conservatives a reserve power. 'Under present circumstances it is to the House of Lords alone that the Conservatives in the Commons and in the country look for the maintenance of their principles, for the rejection or modification of existing legislation, and for an effective control of a Government which is believed to aim at great constitutional changes.' This arrogant attitude was to persist among Conservatives up to the 'peers versus people' crisis of 1909–11. It was expressed openly by Balfour, the Conservative leader, after the crushing electoral defeat of 1906. He then assured a meeting of provincial Conservatives that it was 'the bounden duty of each and every one of you in his separate sphere and with such power and influence as he has been endowed with to do his best to see that the great Unionist party shall still control, whether in power or whether in opposition, the destinies of this great Empire'.[23]

In face of these arrogant assumptions the question whether the House of Lords should be 'mended or ended' (an expression inspired by John Morley in 1884) became a matter of active discussion among Liberals. Many ideas for reform were aired. In 1908 a committee of the Lords itself proposed a membership reform scheme, but one too limited to begin to satisfy the advocates of change. The alternative – and the course followed in the 1911 Parliament Act – was to leave membership intact (at least in the first instance), but to allow the upper house only a delaying power over legislation. Such a course had been advocated by John Bright in 1883. Apart from a deliberate wholesale creation of peerages, there was no hope that a Liberal majority could ever again be found in the Lords. The defections caused by Gladstone's policies even before his conversion to support for Home Rule in 1885 had been too many. Not only did almost all the whig peers refuse to support the 1893 Home Rule Bill, but also thirty-eight of the sixty-two holders of peerages which Gladstone had himself recommended during his years as Prime Minister.[24]

Gladstone had long held the peerage in high esteem as a stabilizing social and political force; but during his last years he fell into despair about the attitude of the House of Lords. This may have been one reason why he gave countenance in the 1890s to the beginning of the virtual sale of honours (including peerages) in return for contributions to party funds.[25] The Conservatives eventually came to follow the same practice. The costs of the new-style mass electioneering were very high. About £30,000 had sufficed for central party election funds in 1880, but for

Edwardian elections up to four times that amount was needed. It also now cost as much as £100,000 per year to run party headquarters. By 1914 Lord Selborne was explaining to the House of Lords itself (23 February) why honours had to be sold for party purposes. Paradoxically, he blamed this upon the democratic electors, large numbers of whom 'would not take the trouble to vote' unless roused by expensive electioneering.

4

To win the support and to meet the aspirations of the new mass electorate Lord Randolph Churchill offered 'Tory Democracy'.[26] He claimed to have coined the term himself. In fact, it was already known in the 1870s, although Churchill certainly made it into his own. Walter Bagehot (*Economist*, 15.1.1876) had described Disraeli as the inventor of 'Democratic Conservatism'; and Churchill was glad to claim that Tory Democracy was a continuation of Disraeli's policy of '*Sanitas sanitatum, omnia sanitas*'. 'Such was the quotation in which a careful mind will discover a scheme of social progress and reform of dimensions so large and wide-spreading that many volumes would not suffice to explain its details.' So asserted Churchill in his widely noticed *Fortnightly Review* article of May 1883, which had been inspired by the unveiling of the Disraeli statue. Churchill was the first leading Conservative positively to enjoy participating in the new mass politics. He was ready to deliver exciting speeches to party followers all over the country, and not only at election times. These speeches attracted wide publicity, as did the sallies of the Fourth Party in the Commons. Yet Tory Democracy depended for its appeal much more upon Churchill's personality than upon the weight of his matter. As a Conservative he was not in a position to propose bold and expensive social reforms. These would have seemed to threaten the pockets and property of those members of the upper and middle classes whose support the party needed to keep or to win. Tory Democracy had perforce to walk a tightrope – offering strong government with economy to the middle classes, at the same time as it offered strong government with 'reform' to the working classes. A speech at Dartford on 2 October 1886, after Churchill had become Chancellor of the Exchequer, was the nearest that he ever came to outlining a full programme. The proposals for domestic reform made in this speech, though valuable enough in themselves, remained circumscribed and familiar. They did not constitute a complete programme for social progress. Churchill advocated changes in parliamentary procedures, land reform for the benefit of agricultural labourers, and a large reconstruction of local government; but he spoke most strongly in favour of economy in government and of close ties with Germany and Austria. 'I will not conceal from you that my own special object, to which I hope to devote whatever energy and strength and influence I may possess, is to endeavour to attain some genuine and considerable reduction of public expenditure and consequent reduction of taxation.'

In a speech at Birmingham on 16 April 1884 Churchill had raised the cry 'Trust the People'. In itself this sounded ultra-democratic. Churchill was always happy to catch the headlines. But its meaning in his definition was sober enough – trust the people to trust their aristocratic 'natural' rulers in the Conservative Party, in particular Randolph Churchill, son of a duke. '"Trust the people" – I have long tried to make that my motto ... To rally the people round the Throne, to unite the Throne with the people, a loyal Throne and a patriotic people, that is our policy and that is our faith.' Churchill had used the National Union of Conservative and Constitutional Associations as a base for his own advancement.[27] Conservatives in the constituencies were glad to be told that they ought to be allowed to play a bigger role through the National Union in determining party policy and party strategy at Westminster. In 1883 Churchill gained control of the Union's council. He then challenged Sir Stafford Northcote and Lord Salisbury to grant real influence to the National Union in accordance with the democratic spirit of the times. A prolonged behind-the-scenes struggle ensued, during which Churchill at one point resigned as council chairman, was reinstated, won a majority on the council at its Sheffield conference in July 1884, but then unexpectedly came to terms with Salisbury. In effect, Churchill secured his own entrance into the ruling circles of the party by abandoning the National Union's claim to an influential role in party affairs. From 1885 every constituency Conservative association was automatically affiliated to the National Union, and Union conferences were allowed to pass policy resolutions. But these carried no weight. 'The action of the Conference is not fettered; it is ignored.'[28]

Lord Salisbury and other party leaders were not so blind as Churchill liked to claim to the need for widening the organization and the appeal of the Conservative Party in the country. They gave encouragement – admittedly at first hesitant – to the Primrose League, a curious body started at the end of 1883 and named after what was allegedly Disraeli's favourite flower.[29] Churchill and his Fourth Party friends played a leading part in the early stages; but the Primrose League soon outgrew their tutelage and became an expression of largely uncritical support for the party leadership. It developed a neo-Gothic hierarchy of membership copied from the friendly societies, which brought together artisans, middle classes, and aristocracy. The higher classes could subscribe as knights and dames; the working classes could become associates. By 1891 total membership exceeded 1 million, grouped in 2,143 'habitations'; and by 1910 numbers had passed 2 million. The Primrose League became especially strong in the country districts and small towns, where it was noteworthy for the political role which it found for women members: 'an artisan will often tell a lady about his political opinions and his domestic affairs, when he would resent being questioned by a man'.[30] League fetes and other entertainments became regular events at which all classes could join in celebration of a common political faith.

The National Liberal Federation, which had begun in a spirit of great independence from party leaders in 1877, eventually became no more independent than the Conservative National Union. It stayed loyal to Gladstone in 1886, after its founder, Joseph Chamberlain, had left the Liberal Party over Home Rule. Its rambling Newcastle programme of 1891, which tried to offer something to every section of the party, was apparently accepted by Gladstone; but such a programme was too shapeless to make a successful electoral appeal (see below, p. 355). By the end of the 1890s the NLF had tacitly abandoned its claim to shape Liberal Policy; and in 1906 formulation of the Liberal programme for the landslide election victory was left to Campbell-Bannerman, the party leader.[31]

The Liberals held office for only three years between 1886 and 1905. In this period the Conservatives became the 'natural' ruling party. The movement of the propertied middle classes towards the Conservative side had begun even before Gladstone came out in favour of Home Rule in 1885. But the Conservatives could not have won so many elections after the passing of the Third Reform Act if they had not also attracted between a third and a half of the working-class vote. Into the 1880s the Conservatives had been anxious about the predominance of Liberal opinions in the press; but only the *Daily News* among London morning papers stayed with Gladstone over Home Rule.

In the House of Commons the Conservatives gained a predominance in English seats from the time of the 1886 Home Rule election, and this predominance was only temporarily broken in 1906:[32]

	England	United Kingdom
1885		
Conservative	213	249
Liberal	238	319
1886		
Conservative and Lib. Unionist	333	393
Liberal	122	191
1892		
Conservative and Lib. Unionist	261	314
Liberal	190	271
1895		
Conservative and Lib. Unionist	343	411
Liberal	112	177
1900		
Conservative and Lib. Unionist	332	402
Liberal	121	183

	England	United Kingdom
1906		
Conservative and Lib. Unionist	122	156
Liberal	306	399
1910 (Jan.)		
Conservative and Lib. Unionist	233	272
Liberal	188	274
1910 (Dec.)		
Conservative and Lib. Unionist	234	272
Liberal	186	271

The Conservatives had thus now become particularly the English political party. Home Rule was described in one National Union pamphlet as 'a direct attack upon England and the English race'.[33] Of ninety-eight British seats never won by the Conservatives between 1885 and 1910 seventy-seven were in Scotland, Wales, the West Riding, and the far north of England. Only in these two last areas, plus Devon and Cornwall and the east midlands, could the Liberals be confident of gaining the greater part of English working-class support at every election. Elsewhere potential Liberal voters among the working men could not be relied upon to go to the polls.[34] Overall the Liberals had become heavily dependent upon Celtic fringe seats outside England:[35]

Liberal majority among members of Parliament from the Celtic fringe

1868	1874	1880	1885	1886	1892	1895	1900
84	66	132	60	101	113	81	79

When from 1912 to 1914 the Liberal/Irish majority in the Commons persisted with the Third Home Rule Bill, it became a matter of alarming uncertainty whether the Conservative Opposition, which represented a clear majority of English seats, would acquiesce in this re-casting of the union in favour of the most restless of its Celtic parts.

5

It was not surprising that the growth of an urban industrial class society should bring with it the growth of an independent working-class political movement, leading eventually to the formation of the Labour Party.[36] By the last quarter of the nineteenth century working-class families were becoming massed together in cities and towns as never before. Large-scale factory industry – monotonous and impersonal – was becoming established as the way of work for millions. The new politicians of the 1880s and 1890s offered a way through socialism to much more congenial conditions of working and living. Life for the masses, exclaimed Keir Hardie in 1894, had become 'arid and barren'.

Our children grow up in great cities divorced from the great forces of Mother Nature . . . Our strong men pass their manhood under a veritable reign of terror, lest the opportunity to work for a living be suddenly denied them . . . The instincts after better things are ruthlessly killed out by the overmastering demands of supplying mere physical requirements.[37]

At the theoretical level Henry George's *Progress and Poverty* (1879) had widely publicized the idea of the unearned increment. This offered a simple explanation for the oppression of the poor by the propertied. It gave, explained J. A. Hobson, 'definiteness to the feeling of discontent by assigning an easily intelligible cause'. During the 1880s George made four lecture tours of the British Isles, and his sweeping eloquence, added to his persuasive literary style, drew interest at all levels of society. Gladstone's daughter, Mary, read *Progress and Poverty* in 1883 – 'supposed to be the most upsetting, revolutionary book of the age' – and found it 'most brilliantly written'.[38] Gladstone himself did not share his daughter's enthusiasm. Nevertheless, the unhappy course of his second ministry from 1880 contributed to the climate of dissatisfaction which prompted men to listen to new ideas. Trade depression, coercion in Ireland, military involvement in Egypt, the absence of social reform – all helped to encourage disillusionment with the Liberals.

The new socialists of the 1880s had to make a fresh start in organization, for only a few local radical clubs had survived from earlier working-class movements; and despite the fears of the higher classes, the European example of the first International and of the Commune had left no lasting mark in England. 'Socialism' indeed had seemed to be a foreign phenomenon, and one of the major achievements of the socialists of the 1880s was to put it into English dress. The first new socialist body to emerge was the Social Democratic Federation, led by H. M. Hyndman.[39] Hyndman was the comfortably-off son of a London merchant, who adopted socialism only after a period as a Tory radical. Throughout his career he liked to address audiences in a frockcoat and top hat. His conversion to socialism began when he read the first volume of Karl Marx's *Capital* in a French translation while crossing the Atlantic in 1880. In June 1881 a group of working men from the London radical clubs joined with Hyndman and other middle-class radicals 'to unite the various organisations of Democrats and workers throughout Great Britain and Ireland for the purpose of securing equal rights for all, and forming a centre of organisation in times of political excitement'. So was launched the Democratic Federation, a radical (but not yet a socialist) body, especially interested in promoting adult suffrage, land reform, and Irish self-government. By 1883 Hyndman had recruited a number of able young lieutenants – H. H. Champion, a former army officer; Eleanor Marx, youngest daughter of Karl (who died that March in London); Tom Mann and John Burns, both skilled working men; and William Morris, the great craftsman. 'Socialist ideas are growing rapidly among the educated class,' Hyndman assured Henry George in

March 1883. In the next year the Democratic Federation was renamed the Social Democratic Federation, and its shift to the left was complete.

But what was its socialism to mean, and what strategy should it follow? Should it preach the Marxist doctrine of class war and lead the working classes into early conflict, or should it concentrate upon anti-capitalist propaganda until the capitalist system reached its inevitable collapse? Throughout the remaining forty years of his career Hyndman never quite made up his mind between these alternative courses. The Social Democratic Federation did produce a programme of short-term reforms – 'palliatives' or 'stepping-stones', as they were called – which included nationalization of land and of all means of production, free compulsory education for all, and Home Rule for Ireland. But Hyndman forecast the collapse of capitalist society as likely to take place in 1889; and when this failed to happen he simply changed the date to 1900. As early as December 1884 a small group, irritated by Hyndman's dictatorial manner and led by Eleanor Marx and William Morris, seceded to form the Socialist League. In 1887 H. H. Champion, disillusioned with the ineffective use of threats of force, came out strongly in favour of a widely based socialist party which would co-operate with the trade unions. Hyndman never understood the importance of the trade union movement, and treated its leaders coldly. Champion left the SDF and John Burns and Tom Mann soon followed suit. The SDF continued under Hyndman's leadership into the twentieth century; and its active campaigning, especially in London and Lancashire, kept the advanced socialist message well before the public. Its uncompromising spirit was reflected in its 1906 programme, which began with 'Abolition of the Monarchy' and included 'Repudiation of the National Debt', 'Abolition of all indirect taxation', 'The abolition of standing armies', and much more intended 'to carry on the class war'.[40]

How far did the socialist leaders of the 1880s and 1890s, middle-class and working-class, come under the influence of Marx?[41] Hyndman had consulted Marx at the time of the formation of the Democratic Association. Marx had not been impressed; but Hyndman adopted his own version of Marxism. He accepted Marx's theory of surplus value – the contention that all value arose from human labour. Land and capital constituted the means of labour, and yet these lay under the control of the bourgeoisie, who paid wages below the true value of labour. The theory thus demonstrated to its own satisfaction how the working classes were exploited, and how class war was inescapable. Most of the leading British socialists of the 1880s owed something to Marx, but few of them (even those who claimed to be Marxists) followed him without qualification or with full understanding. No English translation of *Capital* appeared until 1887, and even thereafter Marx continued more often spoken about than read. Moreover, many late-Victorian readers of Marx, convinced that final utility determined value, decided that he had fallen into irretrievable error at the very beginning of *Capital* by making the validity of all his subsequent arguments depend upon acceptance of his theory of surplus value.

Marxist theory exerted only a limited influence even within the most intellectual of the new socialist bodies of the 1880s – the Fabian Society.[42] This started in London in January 1884 as an offshoot of the ethical Fellowship of the New Life. Its purpose was defined as 'the reconstruction of Society in accordance with the highest moral possibilities'. Its leading members were Frank Podmore, E. R. Pease, and Hubert Bland, soon joined by Bernard Shaw and Mrs Annie Besant, and in 1885 by Sydney Webb. Only gradually did this galaxy of lively middle-class minds conclude that the reconstruction of society would require the application of socialism. Though provincial branches were formed, the dominant Fabian note was always sounded by the London society. Its motto was ambiguous: 'For the right moment you must wait, as Fabius did most patiently when warring against Hannibal ... but when the time comes you must strike hard, as Fabius did, or your waiting will be in vain.' Did this imply support at the right moment for violent revolution? This was certainly not ruled out during the society's first socialist phase; but the ineffectiveness of the unemployed agitation led by the SDF during 1886-7 convinced the Fabians that persistent peaceful propaganda would prove the best way of advancing socialism. They organized extensive and intensive programmes of meetings and lectures. But the most influential Fabian weapon was the political pamphlet. The series of Fabian tracts covered the whole range of domestic political questions – *Facts for Socialists* (1887), *An Eight Hours Bill* (1889), *The New Reform Bill* (1890), *Reform of the Poor Law* (1890), *The Unearned Increment* (1891), and dozens more. These tracts came to circulate in thousands, not only among committed socialists but among all reformers. The symposium of *Fabian Essays* (1889), which included essays by Shaw and Webb – the one the most brilliant, the other the most penetrating of Fabian writers – had sold 27,000 copies by the beginning of 1893. The Industrial Revolution, wrote Webb, had 'left the labourer a landless stranger in his own country. The political evolution is making him its ruler'.[43]

The Fabians became committed to propaganda and to 'permeation'. They were unenthusiastic about attempts to start an independent Labour Party, because they believed that the leaders of the established political parties could be persuaded to adopt socialist policies one by one. 'This permeation is apparently destined to continue,' claimed Webb in *Socialism in England*, 'and the avowed Socialist party in England will probably remain a comparatively small disintegrating and educational force, never itself exercising political power, but applying ideas and principles of social reconstruction to each of the great political parties in turn.' Webb, and his able but calculating wife, Beatrice, whom he married in 1892, were dedicated practitioners of permeation at the personal level, as they entertained many of the leading politicians of the day – Balfour, Asquith, Haldane, Churchill, and others – at their London home.[44] The Webbs, Shaw, and the other Fabians over-rated their own direct influence upon politics and politicians. But as writers and propagandists they raised issues and provided arguments with a persistence and a clarity which certainly assisted the progress of social reform – even if (as happened over the Poor Law) such reform sometimes took shapes which they disliked.

Both the Fabian Society and the Social Democratic Federation exerted influence through activity, not through large membership. The London Fabians totalled only 130 members in 1889, and some 800 by the late 1890s. The provincial Fabian branches had about 1,300 members in 1893. The SDF, which had been largely London-centred in the 1880s, began to attract greater numbers of provincial members in the 1890s. In 1886 it had 11 London branches with 390 members; by 1897 it had reached a peak of 42 London branches with 1,124 members; 32 Lancashire branches with 989 members, and 36 other branches with 1,068 members.[45]

6

The idea of a separate national Labour Party, distinct from the Liberal Party, and with its own Members of Parliament, was discussed in the 1880s; but not until after the formation of the Independent Labour Party in 1893 did real progress begin to be made. In the early 1870s the positivist intellectuals, who had given valuable help to the reform and trade union movements, advised the formation of an independent party – though they were also interested in Chamberlain's plans for the transformation of the Liberal Party.[46] In 1887 Champion had left the SDF to campaign for the election of a group of Members of Parliament who would represent the working-class cause at Westminster in the same singleminded spirit as the Irish Nationalists. 'Lib-Lab' members had sat in the Commons since the first two appeared in 1874; but they had remained few in number and cautious in argument. Liberal constituency parties were predominantly middle-class in character, and usually reluctant to adopt working-class candidates. The most notable Lib-Lab, Henry Broadhurst, served briefly as Under-Secretary at the Home Office in Gladstone's 1886 ministry. But working-class admiration for Gladstone was beginning to flag by the 1890s. In 1885, as already noticed, Andrew Reid had edited *Why I am a Liberal*, a partisan symposium which opened with Gladstone's definition of Liberalism as 'Trust in the People, qualified by Prudence'. By 1894 as editor of another symposium called *The New Party* – to which Keir Hardie and other leading socialists contributed – Reid referred back to the Gladstonian shibboleth; but only to abandon it as 'more diplomatic than democratic'. 'You have stolen my property, and now you tell me that you will return it with prudence. Prudence? Impudence I call it.'

Champion wanted to develop an independent Labour Party by bringing the trade unions into close contact with the socialist political bodies. The Trades Union Congress had formed a Labour Electoral Committee in 1886, which by 1887 had become the Labour Electoral Association. With help from this election machinery, Champion candidates intervened, or threatened to intervene, in several by-elections during 1888. In the process Champion brought working-class questions to the fore, and sought gradually to develop a programme for an independent party. He also launched a new paper, the *Labour Elector*. One of the 1888 by-elections was at Mid-Lanark, where Keir Hardie – a local miner – first stood for Parliament. In retrospect, though Hardie came bottom of the poll with 617 votes and the Liberal won with 3,847, this by-election can be seen as a turning point. It had drawn attention to the question of working-class representation as no previous contest had done. Hardie had taken only 8.4 per cent of the poll, but even such a small percentage put Liberal seats at risk in some constituencies. Hardie soon moved on to form the Scottish Labour Party; and in 1892 he was elected as independent Labour candidate without Liberal opposition for the strongly working-class London constituency of South West Ham – 'a very microcosm of the nineteenth-century world . . . On one side, lines of endless docks and on the other, lines of endless misery'.[47]

But it was in the north of England, and especially in the West Riding of Yorkshire, that the social and political atmosphere was most extensively suitable for launching a new working-class party. The woollen, worsted, and cotton mills of Yorkshire and Lancashire were run on methods which sharply separated bosses from 'hands'. In the Bradford worsted district strikes, notably at the great Manningham Mills, had broken out in response to wage cuts resulting from the effects of the United States McKinley tariff of 1890. Small socialist clubs had grown up, and in the spring of 1891 the Bradford Labour Union was formed. Similar activity was also spreading through other West Riding towns and villages, and across the Pennines to Manchester and the cotton district. The new bodies were strongly socialist in programme and working-class in membership, and determined to remain independent from the Liberal or Conservative Parties. 'We have two parties in the past; the can'ts and the won'ts, and it's time we had a party that will.'[48]

When he entered Parliament in 1892 Hardie was convinced that the moment was right for starting such a party, and that Bradford was the best centre for the initiative. The new party was always to remain strongly provincial, suspicious of the middle-class socialists of London, who were themselves cool towards the new move. The inaugural conference of the Independent Labour Party therefore duly assembled at Bradford on 13 January 1893. About 120 delegates attended, over a third of them from the Yorkshire woollen and worsted area. Bernard Shaw represented the London Fabians, but no national leader of the SDF attended. Six Lancashire branches of the SDF sent delegates, as did eleven north of England Fabian groups. The conference was dominated, however, not by these organizations of the 1880s but by the new Labour clubs, and by Hardie with his demand for a new organization in the country to promote a large independent working-class voice in Parliament. 'We maun gang oor ain gait,' Hardie summed up from the chair. 'The demand of the Labour Party is for economic freedom. It is the natural outcome of political enfranchisement.' The 'object' of the new party was defined as 'collective ownership of the means of production, distribution and exchange'. But the conference recognized that the party would need to win the votes of workers and others who were unwilling to call themselves 'socialists'; and to this end the undogmatic name of Independent Labour Party was chosen. This name also emphasized the wish of the new party to attract the support of the trade unions. Few trade union leaders had yet accepted the need for independent working-class political action. Hardie from the first recognized the importance of winning them over, not only on account of the votes of their members but also with a view to using their funds for political purposes.

The ILP was committed to socialism, but neither Hardie nor most of its members dwelt much upon political theory. 'The idol-breaking of Carlyle', 'the ideal-making of Ruskin' were preferred to the inspiration of Marx. So explained Robert Blatchford, who became the great journalist of the new political upsurge.[49] Blatchford's paper, the *Clarion* – started in Manchester in 1891, and written in a plain but compelling man-to-man style – was selling 40,000 copies per week by 1894. His book *Merrie England* (1893), which invited 'John Smith', a working man, to become a socialist, sold 750,000 copies in its penny edition within one year. The working classes, argued Blatchford, comprised seven-eighths of the population but received little more than one-third of the national income. Society needed to be transformed. Socialism 'would provide cheap and pure food. It would extend and elevate the means of study and amusement . . . It would demolish the slums . . . It would compel all men to do some kind of useful work'. The details of Blatchford's proposals mattered less than the revivalist spirit of his writings. Many of these early socialists were active Nonconformists, who regarded their politics as an expression of true Christianity. Others (such as Blatchford) were secularists, who had transferred to politics the enthusiasm which might have been given to religion.

'More inspiration for the work,' claimed Hardie, 'has been drawn from the teachings of Jesus than from any other source.' Striking expression of this religious spirit was given in the Labour Church movement.[50] This was started by John Trevor of Manchester, who in 1893 inspired the formation of the Labour Church Union. This declared that the religion of the Labour movement was 'not Sectarian or Dogmatic; but Free Religion', which united all classes 'in working for the Abolition of Commercial Slavery'. By 1895 over fifty Labour churches – chiefly in Lancashire and Yorkshire – had become affiliated to the Labour Church Union. The extent of Christian observance at meetings varied widely. Bible readings might be replaced by readings from socialist writers, Christian hymns by socialist songs. But all followed the forms of a religious service, with an uplifting political sermon at the centre of the proceedings. The Labour churches disappeared rapidly after the mid 1890s. The secularization of society was proceeding fast, and the need to justify political action in religious terms was ceasing to be felt even in the close communities of the textile towns and villages.

Blatchford inspired the formation of Clarion cycling clubs, which soon claimed to have 7,000 members. These enthusiasts distributed the *Clarion* and other socialist propaganda, and at the same time enjoyed healthy exercise together. The social side of this early socialist movement was enmeshed with the political. Many conversions were made or strengthened through formal or informal group discussion of Blatchford's writings or through hearing the rousing speeches of Philip Snowden of Keighley. These writings and speeches gave expression to aspirations which working men could not articulate for themselves.

A lecture by Mr. Snowden, in a provincial town, is an event of some importance; his coming is announced beforehand on every hoarding, and his speech is well reported in the local press next day. The people who hear it are a sufficient proportion of the total population to reappear in little groups next morning in every workshop in the town; and are sufficiently delighted with what they have heard to ensure that the principal topic on Monday among the working classes, after Saturday's football match, shall be Sunday's Socialist lecture.[51]

Paid-up membership of the ILP reached 10,720 by 1895, but had fallen to about half this by the end of the century. Members seem to have been chiefly skilled manual workers, clerks, and supervisors. Hardie claimed over 50,000 supporters in June 1895, almost certainly a large exaggeration. 1895 was to prove a disappointing year. All twenty-eight ILP candidates – including Hardie – were defeated at the general election. The party had to make almost a new beginning; but its local strength proved strong enough to carry it through. Labour candidates had begun to win election to local councils and school boards; and (fortified by numerous Fabian tracts which explained the powers of local bodies) the new members began to demand public housing programmes, improved sanitation, provision of public baths, better pay for council workmen, the municipalization of tramways, and other benefits. In 1898 Labour even briefly gained a majority on West Ham Council. Between 1900 and 1905 ILP representation upon town councils increased from sixty-three members to 153, and on county councils from four to ten. Clearly, thousands of local electors, who were not themselves members of socialist organizations, were now ready to vote for socialist candidates.

7

According to *The Times*, the Trafalgar Square riots of February 1886 excited more alarm in London even than the Chartist meeting on Kennington Common in 1848.[52] It was widely believed that the socialists were attempting to start a revolution. In reality, they were not sure how far they wanted to commit themselves – as Hyndman, the SDF leader, even admitted at the time. The winter of 1885–6 had been exceptionally severe. In addition to unemployment caused by the trade depression, the bad weather had brought outdoor work to a halt, and distress was especially intense among the London dockers and building workers. A meeting of the unemployed had been called for the afternoon of 8 February in Trafalgar Square by the Labourers' League – a small organization of unskilled workers, linked with the Fair Trade League – to demand public works and protective tariffs as a solution for unemployment. This meeting was broken up by a rival SDF demonstration, headed by Hyndman, Champion, and Burns (who carried a red flag). These socialist speakers denounced the Conservatives (the Fair Trade League was Conservative-dominated), and preached socialism and revolution. Burns described Members of Parliament as 'capitalists who had fattened upon the labour of the working men'; to hang such parasites 'would be a waste of good rope'. Hyndman asserted that 500 determined men out of the thousands present could soon make a change in society. The crowd, estimated by *The Times* at 20,000, consisted mostly of dockers and building workers. The fair traders' platform was wrecked; but real trouble only began after the SDF leaders, on police advice, agreed to lead off their procession for dispersal in Hyde Park. In Pall Mall, where some members of clubs shouted abuse at the marchers, this parade turned into a riot. Club windows were broken, and looting of shops in Piccadilly began. The police proved too few to restore order for several hours. The SDF leaders were eventually prosecuted for sedition, but acquitted. They had been glad to witness what they hoped would be the beginning of the end of the capitalist system. But they had become alarmed when the process lost its character, and became instead an excuse for violence by the criminal classes.

Few of the London unemployed had become converts to socialism. Some of the rioters even on one occasion sang *Rule Britannia*. None the less, 'respectable' citizens all over London, including skilled working men, were ready to believe that the socialists were massing to overthrow society. They seemed the more threatening for being, in the words of *The Times*, 'under concealed leaders'. On 9 February a dense fog fell over the city, which added to the uncertainty. 'Roughs' again gathered in Trafalgar Square. It was cleared in the afternoon; but the rumour then spread that hundreds of dockers were marching from the East End to attack property in the West End. Nothing happened. Nevertheless, the panic on 10 February was greater than ever. Rumour this time said that thousands were marching from Deptford, destroying property as they came. Shops and offices were closed all over the capital. The Deptford marchers never materialized, but a large crowd did gather at the

Elephant and Castle in expectation of joining them. Eventually the police broke up this and other mobs, and tension subsided. But throughout the rest of 1886 and 1887 fear of further outbreaks remained. Subscriptions to the Lord Mayor's Mansion House Fund for the Unemployed, which had been languishing, shot up after the February troubles. Another crisis came on 13 November 1887 when an intended socialist meeting in Trafalgar Square was prohibited by the police. The socialists determined to assert the right to free protest. Processions organized by the SDF and other bodies converged on the square, but their way was violently blocked by soldiers and mounted police. John Burns and Cunningham Graham, a sympathetic radical Member of Parliament, were imprisoned for their parts in this encounter; and 'Bloody Sunday' became a long-remembered date in the socialist calendar.

The new socialist politicians had attracted much publicity during 1886–7, but they gained little else. On the one hand, they had confirmed 'respectable' opinion in its belief that socialism meant violence. On the other hand, though the unemployed had been glad to attend socialist demonstrations they had not necessarily become converts. Moreover, they were too poor to pay subscriptions to socialist organizations. As trade began to improve during the late 1880s pressure through political protest began to be replaced by a great upsurge of trade union activity.[53] Socialists played prominent parts in this movement – John Burns, Will Thorne, Ben Tillett, Tom Mann, and others; but their influence stemmed from their skill as leaders rather than from their commitment to socialism. The right of trade unions to exist was now generally accepted, though the legitimate extent of their role was still disputed. 'If artisans combine (as they well may),' wrote Gladstone in 1887, 'partly to uphold their wages, it is also greatly with the noble object of keeping all the members of their enormous class independent of public alms.'[54] Trade unions were now praised by sympathetic observers as organs of 'industrial democracy' – the title of a comprehensive and influential analysis published by the Webbs in 1897. The Royal Commission on Labour (1891–4) discussed with equanimity the consolidation of both employers' and workers' organizations. It found that 'powerful trades unions on the one side and powerful associations of employers on the other had been the means of bringing together in conference the representatives of both classes, enabling each to appreciate the position of the other'.

The Trades Union Congress met each year, praised by *The Times* (1.9.1888) for its respectability. During the early 1880s its affiliated unions contained about 500,000 members, a drop of over one-half from the economic boom days of the early 1870s. Affiliated union membership reached a new peak of 1,470,000 in 1890, before steadying about 1 million through the 1890s. The first official figure of total trade union membership in Great Britain gave 1,576,000 members for 1892. This total had risen to just over 2 million by the start of the twentieth century. These were substantial numbers, even if trade unionists still comprised not more than 20 per cent of the adult male working class. Unionists tended to be concentrated within certain industries and localities, where they often formed a majority of the workforce. The seven counties of the north of England contained almost half the total union membership in 1892. The industrial midlands accounted for another 210,000 members. London, with less than 200,000, remained proportionately weak as a trade union centre.[55]

The craft trade unions had proved best able to survive during the hard times of the late 1870s and 1880s. The six major craft unions represented 134,000 members in 1883. The cotton unions had also held much of their ground; but the miners had been driven to accept sliding-scales, which had meant a lowering of wages. Most of the non-craft unions which had been formed in the boom of the early 1870s were hardly a memory by the time of the economic upturn of the late 1880s. The 'new unions' of this period, were both new foundations and new in their types of membership. They were not craft unions but 'general' unions, catering for more or less wide ranges of workers who might possess some skills but who were not specialist artisans. They tended to start with particular workers – gasworkers, dockers – but then to broaden out more or less deliberately to increase their potential for action and survival. Socialists, who preached the need for solidarity among all wage-earners, were likely to encourage 'general' unionism and militancy. But not all 'new unions' were militant. They covered perhaps 200,000 workers in 1892, out of more than 1,500,000 union members altogether – a reminder that much of the trade union growth occurred within old-style bodies in the cotton, engineering, and mining industries.

Nevertheless, certain 'new unions' attracted much publicity by their strikes at the end of the 1880s; and the propertied and governing classes came to regard these unions as voicing 'industrial democracy'. Because the 'new unions' represented less skilled and less well-paid workers they could not charge large membership fees to finance unemployment or other benefits; and so they were bound to be offensive not defensive bodies. Their prime interest lay in higher wages, for which they were prepared to strike. Such aggressive strike action could, of course, only hope to be successful at times of high trade prosperity when employers found it difficult to recruit alternative labour. The outstanding example of such action was the great London dock strike of 1889. But a prelude to the dock strike had been provided in 1888 when the matchgirls at Bryant and May's East London factory formed a union, organized by Annie Besant, and successfully struck for better conditions. The victory of these miserable few score matchgirls provided a spur for efforts on a larger scale elsewhere. Early in 1889 Will Thorne, a stoker at the Beckton gasworks in East Ham, started the National Union of Gasworkers and General Labourers. Thorne demanded an eight-hour day for gasworkers in place of the existing twelve-hour shift system. Astonishingly, victory came almost without a struggle. This London success was soon repeated at provincial gasworks. The gas companies had suddenly found that they could not hope to maintain supplies without experienced workmen. The eight-hour day now became a general aspiration among most trade unionists, preferably to be enforced by legislation.

Gasworkers laid off in the summer regularly went to work in the docks, where casual labour predominated and where Ben Tillett had begun to organize a General Labourers' Union. In August 1889 a trivial dispute provided the occasion for the whole dock labour force (including the skilled stevedores and watermen, who possessed their own strong unions) to strike for the 'dockers' tanner' (sixpence an hour, instead of fivepence or less), plus improvements in working conditions. Tillett's union increased its membership dramatically; and when the owners refused to respond he was joined in leading the strike by Tom Mann and John Burns. They succeeded both in maintaining peace and in skilfully attracting nationwide sympathy, notably through well-organized processions of strikers through the City of London. Australian trade unions sent £30,000 just when funds were running low. The Lord Mayor of London and then Cardinal Manning acted as mediators, and early in September the 'dockers' tanner' and most other demands were conceded. The propertied classes had been much impressed and relieved by the orderliness of this strike, in contrast to the rioting of 1886 and 1887.[56] The system of casual and low-paid labour in the docks was suddenly regarded as 'barbarous and unchristian' (*The Times*, 26 September). The dock directors tried to defend themselves by saying that enough men had always been available to work for fivepence an hour. 'In an earlier and perhaps ruder age this defence would have been thought conclusive as against a summons to raise their scale of wages at a few hours' notice, and without any antecedent change in the supply of labour. But public sympathy declined to pay the smallest attention to their plea.'

The success of the dockers brought a great rush of unionization. But as soon as business and the demand for labour again began to slacken in the early 1890s trade unions once more found themselves on the defensive. Tillett's union was driven from the docks within little more than a year of its 1889 victory. Unfortunately, public interest in the dockers had now faded. Nevertheless, some of the new unions did survive, especially in industries such as gas and transport which were still growing and which needed a steady supply of experienced workmen, even if they were not skilled in the old craft sense. Some of the new unions now began to introduce social benefits after the example of the craft unions. The contrast between 'old' and 'new' unions was thus beginning to be blurred.

Not all employers were yet prepared to accept that 'labour' was the equal of 'capital'. The 1890s witnessed several well-publicized confrontations between major employers and large trade unions. To counter foreign competition many firms were seeking to introduce new machinery and new methods. This modernization brought some of them into sharp conflict with workpeople who often found themselves facing redundancy, downgrading, or wage cuts. Powerful employers' associations were formed, and also the National Free Labour Association, which provided blackleg labour during strikes. In 1893 two major lockouts occurred when the coal and cotton employers sought wage reductions. The coal conflict was only ended by the notable mediation of Lord Rosebery, the Foreign Secretary; and the cotton spinning crisis by the dramatic negotiation of the wage-fixing Brooklands agreement. During 1897–8 came a six-month engineering lockout, when the strongest of employers' federations faced the greatest craft union, in a contest over the union demand for an eight-hour day and the employers' counter-demand for an end to restrictive practices. This was the first major national strike or lockout in British history. The engineers spent nearly £500,000 of their own funds, plus further large sums from other unions and from public subscriptions. The employers won in the short term; but the self-awareness of the whole trade union movement had been permanently heightened by this costly confrontation.

The 1899 appeal court judgement in *Lyons v. Wilkins* severely limited the rights of pickets, which had been thought secure since 1875. Trade union leaders now recognized that further legislation would be needed both to protect their organizations and to improve conditions of work. The 1899 Trades Union Congress therefore called for a conference 'of all the co-operative, socialistic, trade union, and other working organizations ... to devise ways and means for securing the return of an increased number of labour members to the next Parliament'. This meeting took place in London on 27 February 1900. One hundred and twenty-nine delegates attended, and they accepted Keir Hardie's motion to form 'a distinct Labour group in Parliament, who shall have their own whips, and agree upon their policy'. The conference then formed a Labour Representation Committee to organize candidatures. This committee comprised two ILP and two SDF representatives, one Fabian, and seven trade unionists. In October 1900 Parliament was suddenly dissolved, and fifteen LRC candidates stood in the mid-Boer War 'khaki election'. Only Keir Hardie and Richard Bell (a trade unionist who was almost a Lib-Lab) were successful. But the socialist politicians and the trade union leaders were coming together, and this was a vital development for the future. In this process of adjustment some of the first freshness of socialist enthusiasm was perhaps beginning to be lost, as good administration and careful electoral calculation became increasingly important, both at local and national levels. Keir Hardie's enthusiastic pioneering contribution had now been made. Ramsay MacDonald, the personable yet moderate secretary of the LRC, was to be the rising working-class politician of the new century.

8

Democracy in local government had been consolidated by the end of the nineteenth century. 'As with the national Parliament, so with the local councils. They are elected by the people of the locality; they work under the censorship of local opinion.'[57] Reform of county government, which had been often discussed and several times attempted since the great reform of municipal government in 1835, was at last enacted in 1888. The Local Government Act and the County Electors Act of that year together established a system of county councils to replace the county magistrates meeting at quarter sessions. The new councils comprised a chairman, councillors and aldermen, and were elected on a franchise equivalent to that in the boroughs – twelve months' occupation, twelve months' residence, twelve months' rating. Sixty-one county boroughs – many more than originally proposed – were kept separate from the counties, some because they were important urban centres, others for historical reasons. The county landlords were glad to keep apart from the town radicals, and vice versa.[58]

The 1888 legislation was introduced by Lord Salisbury's Conservative Government. Gladstone's 1880-5 Liberal Ministry had not found time for the reform of county government to match the extension of the parliamentary franchise to agricultural labourers under the Third Reform Act (1884-5). The first Gladstone Government had discussed such reform in terms of financial and administrative improvement, but his second ministry spoke also in terms of democracy. 'The point to be immediately kept in view and attained is the substitution of a Council mainly or entirely elective for a rural House of Lords.' So emphasized J. G. Dodson, President of the Local Government Board. But the efforts of the Liberals became concentrated upon the difficult enactment of parliamentary reform. Then came Gladstone's preoccupation with Irish Home Rule, and the Conservative election victory in 1886. Salisbury's Government found it prudent, however, to tackle the question despite continuing lack of enthusiasm among its landed supporters. Pressure for change came from the Tory democrat Lord Randolph Churchill, and from Joseph Chamberlain – now a Liberal Unionist ally of the Conservatives. Salisbury pursued a middle course by offering a bill which satisfied the reformers, but which did not go beyond what the landlords were prepared to tolerate, albeit reluctantly. In the event, fears that the new county councils would fall under the control of radical spendthrifts were not realized.[59] Political contests took place at the first elections in only a minority of counties. Those landlords who – as magistrates – had controlled quarter sessions found themselves, for the most part, elected as councillors or chosen as aldermen to control the new county councils. In twenty-two counties the chairmen of quarter sessions were elected chairmen of the county councils; in six counties the lord lieutenants were chosen. Admittedly, in counties near to industrial areas significant numbers of businessmen were also elected; but these had begun to infiltrate the county hierarchies before 1888, and they were not radicals. It had become necessary to follow the forms of democracy, but that was all. 'Not many years ago it was a virtue "to stem the tide of democracy". We are all Democrats now and rush with pride to own it.'

Control of county police was deliberately left with the magistrates. 'The civilisation of many English counties,' explained Salisbury to Chamberlain, 'is sufficiently backward to make it hazardous for the Crown to part with power over the police.' Proposals for district councils, which Chamberlain wanted, were dropped. These were eventually created under the Local Government Act of 1894. This Liberal measure established a new network of parish councils, rural district councils, and urban district councils in place of the old confusion of authorities. The vote for these bodies was given to all county and parliamentary electors on the principle of one man one vote.

The 1888 Act had set up the new London County Council. In 1899 the Conservatives promoted a London Government Act, which added twenty-eight Metropolitan Borough Councils to the London scene. The Conservatives had disliked the radical policies pursued by the Progressive majority on the LCC, and wished to trim its powers, though as finally amended and passed the Act was a sensible measure of devolution which the Liberals found it hard to discredit.[60] This measure completed the nineteenth-century reform of local government in England and Wales. Most ad hoc authorities had now been absorbed. The 1902 Education Act was to merge the school boards with the local authorities, although the boards of Poor Law guardians were to continue for a further generation. The local electorate now included about three-quarters of all adult males in England and Wales, plus several hundred thousand women. The first women to hold local office seem to have been school board members elected from 1870, followed by a woman Poor Law guardian elected in 1875, and two women elected to the London County Council in 1889. The courts eventually ruled that these two last were disqualified by their sex. An Act allowing women to sit on county and borough councils was finally passed in 1907.

Local authority spending was increasing rapidly about the turn of the century. A Local Government Board report in 1909 listed the causes: growth of population; new statutory duties in health and education; the grant of discretionary powers to provide local services; the development of more elaborate and costly methods of road-making, sewage disposal, and hospital provision; and, in general, the growth of public expectation. Expenditure other than out of loans by local authorities in England and Wales grew from £43,500,000 in 1883 to £129,400,000 in 1911. Loan-financed expenditure increased from £9,400,000 to £18,200,000. Exchequer grants-in-aid rose from £3,300,000 in 1883 to £21,900,000 in 1913. Sidney Webb praised such grants as 'the hinge in the flap' which preserved local freedom while stimulating good government.[61]

By 1900 large local authorities were likely to be deeply engaged in 'municipal trading', especially with the provision of water, gas, and electricity, with municipal transport, and (in a few places) with housing for the working classes. Receipts from main trading services grew from £3,200,000 in 1880 to £12,200,000 in 1900 and to £40,200,000 in 1913. Conservative critics remained distrustful of 'municipal socialism'. *The Times* in a long series of articles under this title (19 August–11 November 1902) emphasized that 'the primary duty of a local governing body is to govern not to trade'. Avowed socialists such as Bernard Shaw, author of *Commonsense of Municipal Trading* (1904), were enthusiastic about this 'highly desirable and beneficial extension of civilization'. The mass of local electors – drawing their water, lighting their gas, and catching their trams – enjoyed the benefits of 'municipal socialism' while ignoring the accompanying political ideology, desirable or dangerous.

Was it expecting too much from unpaid local councillors to ask them to run municipal enterprises? *The Times* claimed this as one reason why leading local figures seemed to be increasingly reluctant to participate in local government. 'The men of wealth, of large affairs, the leading citizens, have been gradually replaced by people with perhaps as much spirit and as good intentions, but with an experience less broad and of a smaller calibre.' Yet participation by leading figures may never have been so high in many places as Edwardian pessimists liked to assume. On the other hand, increasing numbers of professional men seem to have been joining the councils in Birmingham, Leeds, and elsewhere.[62] Certainly, the municipal lead which in the 1870s had come from Chamberlain's Birmingham was coming by 1890s from the new London County Council.[63] The inadequacy, confusion, and corruption of London local government – headed by the Metropolitan Board of Works, established in 1855 – had long remained one of the great scandals of Victorian England. Before 1889 no one authority could speak for London as a whole – certainly not the privileged, unrepresentative but ever unreformed, ancient Corporation of the City of London. 'Is the capital of the British Empire to be the only space in that Empire in which the nation cannot speak through its local representatives?' The LCC therefore found much to do both in material and in psychological terms. The Progressives (a loose coalition which ranged from Liberal Unionists to Fabians) won a majority at the first election in 1899, a predominance retained until 1907. Lord Rosebery, who had been elected as a Progressive, was made chairman of the council. But the major influence upon the new body came from the Fabian socialists; their tract, *Facts for Londoners*, was published on the eve of the first elections.[64] National attention had already begun to centre on London during the 1880s with the appearance there of the socialist societies, followed by the unemployed demonstrations of 1886–7, and by the 1889 dock strike. What was thought and done in London had become important in the provinces, even in Birmingham or Manchester which had long prided themselves upon their superior coherence and influence. The formation of the LCC created an institutional focus for this attention, as London's new rulers embarked upon large schemes of municipal trading. Sidney Webb's *London Programme* (1891) took as its leading principle 'the promotion of the interests of London as a whole, rather than those of individual Londoners'. Even so, the Fabians failed to persuade the Progressives to attempt municipal intervention outside the obvious fields. The Fabians wanted municipal participation in baking, milk supply, the sale of intoxicating liquors, pawnshops, and fire insurance.

In London and elsewhere municipal independence began to weaken during the Edwardian years as the central government extended its activities. The new social services introduced by the Liberals were national in scope, control, and finance. With the unemployed, the elderly, and the sick partly taken off poor relief – and with the increasing importance of specific exchequer grants – local ideas began to count for less and central direction to matter more. At the beginning of the century the Association of Municipal Corporations had been pressing for wider powers, more flexible procedures, and longer time for loans; but by the immediate pre-war years it was no longer seeking independence, only more money from central government. In the words of one expert writing in the 1920s, during the Edwardian period there occurred an 'increasing transfer of the *thinking* from the local to the central government'.[65]

Notes

1. See especially N. Blewett, 'The Franchise in the United Kingdom, 1885–1918', *Past & Present*, no. 32 (1965); H. Pelling, *Social Geography of British Elections, 1885–1910* (1967); N. Blewett, *The Peers, The Parties and The People* (1972), parts I, IV.

2. See N. McCord, 'Some Difficulties of Parliamentary Reform', *Historical Journal*, X (1967), pp. 387–90.

3. S. Buxton, *Handbook to Political Questions of the Day* (8th edn, 1892), p. 118.

4. C. Seymour, *Electoral Reform in England and Wales, 1832–1885* (1915), p. 533; A. K. Russell, *Liberal Landslide, The General Election of 1906* (1973), p. 16; F. W. S. Craig (ed.), *British Electoral Facts, 1885–1975* (3rd edn, 1976), p. 75.

5. N. Blewett, *The Peers, The Parties and The People* (1972), pp. 363–4; H. C. G. Matthew *et al.*, 'The Franchise Factor in the Rise of the Labour Party', *English Historical Review*, XCI (1976), p. 733.

6. *Pall Mall Gazette*, 4 December 1884; *Annual Register, 1884*, pp. 255–7. See also D. Read, *The English Provinces, 1760–1960* (1964), pp. 183, 227–8.

7. G. P. Gooch, *Life of Lord Courtney* (1920), Ch. X. See also Sir W. R. Anson, *Law and Custom of the Constitution*, part I, Parliament (3rd edn, 1897), pp. 134–41.

8. *Westminster Review*, Vol. 128 (1887), p. 104. See especially C. O'Leary, *The Elimination of Corrupt Practices in British Elections, 1868–1911* (1962).

9. R. H. Davis, *Our English Cousins* (1894), in H. S. Commager (ed.), *Britain Through American Eyes* (1974), p. 567.

10. See J. A. Thomas, *The House of Commons, 1906–1911* (1958). Also W. L. Guttsman, *The British Political Elite* (1963), Ch. 4; N. Blewett, *The Peers, The Parties and The People* (1972), Ch. 11; and A. K. Russell, *Liberal Landslide, The General Election of 1906* (1973), pp. 60–3.

11. D. W. R. Bahlman (ed.), *Diary of Sir Edward Walter Hamilton* (1972), I, p. 236. See especially E. Hughes, 'The Changes in Parliamentary Procedure, 1880–1882', in R.

Pares and A. J. P. Taylor (eds.), *Essays Presented to Sir Lewis Namier* (1956); P. Fraser, 'The Growth of Ministerial Control in the Nineteenth-Century House of Commons', *English Historical Review*, LXXV (1960); Valerie Cromwell, 'The Losing of the Initiative by the House of Commons, 1780–1914', *Transactions of the Royal Historical Society*, fifth series, Vol. 18 (1968); and H. J. Hanham (ed.), *The Nineteenth Century Constitution* (1969), Ch. 3.

12. H. Berrington, 'Partisanship and Dissidence in the Nineteenth-Century House of Commons', *Parliamentary Affairs*, XXI (1968). See also A. L. Lowell, *The Government of England* (1917), II, Ch. XXXV.

13. *Letters of Queen Victoria*, third series (1930), I, p. 510.

14. W. D. Green, 'First Impressions of the House of Commons', *Windsor Magazine*, February 1896, p. 125; H. J. Hanham (ed.), *The Nineteenth Century Constitution* (1969), Ch. 3.

15. See D. N. Chester and Nona Bowring, *Questions in Parliament* (1962), esp. Ch. 2.

16. See especially J. P. Mackintosh, *The British Cabinet* (2nd edn, 1968), part four; H. J. Hanham (ed.), *The Nineteenth Century Constitution* (1969), Ch. 2.

17. W. S. Churchill, *Lord Randolph Churchill* (2nd edn, 1951), p. 231; T. H. S. Escott, *Society in London* (1885), pp. 257–8.

18. J. L. Garvin, *Life of Joseph Chamberlain*, II (1933), p. 191.

19. *Macmillan's Magazine*, January 1885, pp. 233–4.

20. A. V. Dicey, 'The Referendum', *National Review*, March 1894, p. 69.

21. C. S. Emden, *The People and the Constitution* (2nd edn, 1956), pp. 216–22.

22. A. Ponsonby, *The Decline of Aristocracy* (1912), p. 105. See especially Emily Allyn, *Lords Versus Commons* (1931); and H. J. Hanham (ed.), *The Nineteenth Century Constitution* (1969), pp. 169–99.

23. *The Times*, 16 January 1906.

24. D. Southgate, *The Passing of the Whigs, 1832–1886* (1962), pp. 412–13.

25. See H. J. Hanham, 'The Sale of Honours in Late Victorian England', *Victorian Studies*, III (1959–60).

26. See, in general, E. J. Feuchtwanger, *Disraeli, Democracy and The Tory Party* (1968), esp. Ch. VII; and E. J. Feuchtwanger, 'The Rise and Progress of Tory Democracy', in J. S. Bromley and E. H. Kossmann (eds.), *Britain and the Netherlands*, V (1975). In particular, W. S. Churchill, *Lord Randolph Churchill* (2nd edn, 1951); and R. Rhodes James, *Lord Randolph Churchill* (1959).

27. See especially F. H. Herrick, 'Lord Randolph Churchill and the Popular Organization of the Conservative Party', *Pacific Historical Review*, XV (1946); and R. T. Mackenzie, *British Political Parties* (2nd edn, 1963), Ch. IV.

28. A. L. Lowell, *The Government of England* (1917), I, p. 577.

29. See especially Janet H. Robb, *The Primrose League, 1883–1906* (1942).

30. A. L. Lowell, *The Government of England* (1917), II, p. 11.

31. *Ibid.*, Ch. XXIX; and S. H. Beer, *Modern British Politics* (2nd edn, 1969), pp. 54–61.

32. F. W. S. Craig (ed.), *Electoral Facts, 1885–1975* (3rd edn, 1976), pp. 6–8.

33. R. T. Mackenzie and A. Silver, *Angels in Marble, Working Class Conservatives in England* (1968), pp. 54–5. See also J. Cornford, 'The Transformation of Conservatism in the Late Nineteenth Century', *Victorian Studies*, VII (1963); and J. P. D. Dunbabin, 'Parliamentary Elections in Great Britain, 1868–1900: A Psephological Note', *English Historical Review*, LXXXI.

34. N. Blewett, *The Peers, The Parties and The People* (1972), esp. Chs. 1, 18; E. Allardt and S. Rokkan (eds.), *Mass Politics* (1970), p. 108.

35. J. P. D. Dunbabin, 'Parliamentary Elections in Great Britain, 1868–1900: A Psephological Note', *English Historical Review*, LXXXI (1966), p. 92.

36. See especially H. Pelling, *The Origins of the Labour Party, 1880–1900* (2nd edn, 1965); and P. P. Poirier, *The Advent of the Labour Party* (1958).

37. A. Reid (ed.), *The New Party* (1894), pp. 259–60.

38. J. A. Hobson, 'The Influence of Henry George in England', *Fortnightly Review*, December 1897; Mary Gladstone, *Diaries and Letters* (1930), p. 293.

39. See especially C. Tsuzuki, *H. M. Hyndman and British Socialism* (1961); and P.

Thompson, *Socialists, Liberals and Labour, The Struggle for London, 1885–1914* (1967), esp. Ch. VI.
40. R. C. K. Ensor (ed.), *Modern Socialism* (2nd edn, 1907), pp. 351–5.
41. See especially S. Pierson, *Marxism and the Origins of British Socialism* (1973); and K. Willis, 'The Introduction and Critical Reception of Marxist Thought in Britain, 1850–1900', *Historical Journal*, Vol. 20 (1977).
42. See especially A. M. McBriar, *Fabian Socialism and English Politics, 1884–1918* (1962); W. Wolfe, *From Radicalism to Socialism* (1975); and N. and Jeanne MacKenzie, *The First Fabians* (1977).
43. See especially A. Briggs's introduction to 6th edn (1962).
44. See especially Beatrice Webb, *Our Partnership* (1948).
45. H. Pelling, *Origins of the Labour Party, 1880–1900* (2nd edn, 1965), appendix A; P. A. Watmough, 'The Membership of the Social Democratic Federation', *Bulletin of Labour History*, no. 34 (1977).
46. R. Harrison, *Before the Socialists* (1965), pp. 299–302.
47. E. Hughes, *Keir Hardie* (1956), p. 54.
48. See especially J. Reynolds and K. Laybourn, 'The Emergence of the Independent Labour Party in Bradford',*International Review of Social History*, XX (1975).
49. A. Reid (ed.), *The New Party* (1894), p. 14.
50. *Ibid.*, p. 264. See especially K. S. Inglis, *Churches and the Working Classes in Victorian England* (1963), Ch. 6; and S. Pierson, *Marxism and the Origins of British Socialism* (1973), pp. 226–45.
51. B. Villiers, *The Socialist Movement in England* (1908), pp. 172–3. See also D. Hopkin, 'The Membership of the Independent Labour Party: A Spatial and Occupational Analysis', *International Review of Social History*, XX (1975).
52. See especially G. Stedman Jones, *Outcast London* (1971), Chs. 16, 19; and R. Mace, *Trafalgar Square* (1976), Ch. 7.
53. See J. Lovell, *British Trade Unions, 1875–1933* (1977), and references there; especially H. A. Clegg *et al.*, *A History of British Trade Unions Since 1889*, I (1964).
54. *Nineteenth Century*, January 1887, p. 16.
55. S. and Beatrice Webb, *History of Trade Unionism, 1666–1920* (1920), Ch. VIII.
56. See especially G. Stedman Jones, *Outcast London* (1971), Ch. 17.
57. J. Redlich and F. W. Hirst, *The History of Local Government in England* (ed. B. Keith-Lucas, 2nd edn, 1970), p. 220.
58. See especially B. Keith-Lucas, *The English Local Government Franchise* (1952), Ch. IV; and J. P. D. Dunbabin, 'The Politics of the Establishment of County Councils', *Historical Journal*, VI (1963).
59. See J. M. Lee, *Social Leaders and Public Persons* (1963), Chs. 1–3; and J. P. D. Dunbabin, 'Expectations of the New County Councils and their Realization', *Historical Journal*, VIII (1965).
60. See K. Young, 'The Politics of London Government, 1880–1899', *Public Administration*, Vol. 51 (1973).
61. J. W. Grice, *National and Local Finance* (1910), p. ix. See also Ursula K. Hicks, *British Public Finances* (1954), Ch. IV.
62. A. L. Lowell, *The Government of England* (1917), pp. 199–200; E. P. Hennock, *Fit and Proper Persons* (1973), pp. 34–5, 268–9, 350–2.
63. See especially A. Briggs, *Victorian Cities* (1963), Ch. 8; and K. Young, *Local Politics and the Rise of Party* (1975), Chs. 1–3.
64. See A. M. McBriar, *Fabian Socialism and English Politics, 1884–1918* (1962), Ch. VIII.
65. E. S. Griffith, *The Modern Development of City Government in the United Kingdom and the United States* (1927), I, pp. 373–4, 415–16.

Chapter 18

Domestic policy: *'Three millions are disloyal'*

1

The Liberals won the 1880 election by their attacks upon 'Beacons-fieldism'; but it was not clear what their positive purposes were, for they offered no detailed reform programme. The coalition character of the Liberal Party was reflected in Gladstone's cabinet. Alongside whigs such as Lords Granville (Foreign Secretary) and Hartington (Indian secretary), Gladstone had reluctantly accepted Joseph Chamberlain as President of the Board of Trade, even though the radical leader had no preliminary experience of junior office. John Bright became Chancellor of the Duchy of Lancaster, and W. E. Forster Irish Chief Secretary. Gladstone himself had retired from the party leadership in 1875; but after his Bulgarian agitation and Midlothian campaigns there was no real doubt who must head the Government, even though the queen made clear her strong preference for Hartington.

The tendency of the Liberals to sectional enthusiasms remained subdued during 1880; but unfortunately the Government made a slow start in proposing major reforms which might have held the ranks together. Gladstone deliberately postponed until later in the life of the Parliament proposals for extending household suffrage to the counties, in the belief that such a change ought to be quickly followed by a general election fought upon the new registers. To please the Farmers Alliance a Ground Game Act was passed in 1880, which made it obligatory to include in leases a clause allowing tenants equal rights with landlords to take hares and rabbits. This was followed in 1883 by the Agricultural Holdings Act, which was important in principle since it limited the rights of landlords by giving tenants claim to compensation for improvements. Gladstone's 1880 budget (he was Chancellor of the Exchequer as well as Prime Minister until December 1882) repealed the much disliked malt tax.[1]

The new House of Commons ran into immediate and unnecessary trouble – which was to persist through to the dissolution in 1885 – over the election of Charles Bradlaugh, the well-known atheist (and also advocate of republicanism and birth control) as Member of Parliament for Northampton.[2] Bradlaugh did not wish to take the oath upon the Bible, but to affirm. When this was denied him, he expressed his willingness to swear, although he made it clear that the Christian oath meant nothing to him. A majority of members, encouraged by the Fourth Party, which first came together over the affair, now refused to allow the atheist to take his seat at all. He was successively committed to the clock tower of Westminster, thrice re-elected by Northampton and thrice rejected by the Commons. Gladstone abhorred atheism, but he strongly supported Bradlaugh's right to affirm. None the less, a Government Affirmation Bill was defeated by three votes in 1883. Only after Bradlaugh's fifth victory at Northampton in the general election of 1885 was he at last allowed to take his seat undisturbed. Religious prejudice was weakening, and Bradlaugh's dignified behaviour under pressure had begun to win him support in the country. In 1888 he secured the passing of an Affirmation Act; and in 1891 the Religious Disabilities Removals Act deleted religious belief as one of the necessary qualifications for membership of Parliament. The Bradlaugh affair contributed to a growing sense during the early 1880s of the ineffectiveness – even the foolishness – of Parliament. Government proposals were regularly obstructed by the Irish in one house and by the Conservative peers in the other. The Irish question, reactivated by Parnell and by the Land League, absorbed more and more time both in cabinet and in Parliament. Military disasters, first in South Africa and then in Egypt, further diverted the attention of ministers from domestic reform.

The Conservatives' Afghanistan and South African involvements had been scathingly denounced by Gladstone; and the forward policy in Afghanistan was reversed when the Liberals returned to office. But Liberal intentions with regard to the conflict with the Transvaal Boers were at first much less clearcut.[3] Gladstone's hope was that the Transvaal might after all join the South African federation projected by the Disraeli Government. The Liberals therefore did not immediately abrogate the 1877 annexation as most Boers now wanted. Yet Gladstone had said during his first Midlothian campaign that no strength would come to the empire from ruling the Transvaal. By the end of 1880 the Government found itself in a corner with the choice between open war with the Boers – now in rebellion – or abandonment of the idea of federation. At the end of February 1881 Major-General Sir George Colley, the Governor of Natal, was heavily defeated and killed at Majuba Hill. It came as a shock to the British public to realize that their army could be worsted by a force of Boer farmers. The cabinet was divided between those members who wanted revenge and those who wanted peace. Gladstone worked towards peace, well aware of the loss of prestige but sure that Britain should not undertake the big and expensive effort which would be needed to overcome the Boers. The Pretoria Convention of August 1881 recognized the independence of the Transvaal under British 'suzereignty'. This was modified by the London Convention of 1884, which no longer mentioned suzereignty but remained vague about the precise status of the Boer republics.

The Gladstone Government had contrived to dismay not only

imperial expansionists by its South African vacillations but also the opponents of expansion. It was to achieve the same effect during the long-drawn-out course of the Egyptian crisis.[4] British interest in Egypt had been intensified by the opening of the Suez Canal in 1869, followed by Disraeli's purchase of the Khedive's canal shares in 1875, which Gladstone had criticized as likely to lead to political involvement. How then did Gladstone – despite his many attacks upon 'Beaconsfieldism' – end up by virtually annexing Egypt to the British Empire? He began by hoping to work closely with the French, and he always claimed to be acting in Egypt on behalf of the concert of Europe. An Anglo-French condominion had been established in 1878 to restore payments to European creditors, and the Khedive Ismail had been deposed in favour of his son Tewfik. Yet Egypt continued to drift into chaos; and in response a nationalist movement emerged. This was led by Arabi Pasha, who wanted to remove all foreign influence. France and Britian sent a fleet to Alexandria to protect European interests and to protect the Khedive. Rioting broke out, Europeans were killed, and the British Consul was assaulted. The French withdrew, but on 11 July 1882 the royal navy bombarded the forts of Alexandria. This gesture, which resulted from a misunderstanding by the admiral of his orders, only strengthened the nationalist movement; and to defend British rights and to ensure the security of the Suez Canal the Gladstone Government now found it necessary to send a British army into Egypt. On 13 September Arabi was smashingly defeated at Tel-el-Kebir. Commonsense – and care for the canal – committed the British to remaining in occupation until the Egyptian state and its finances had been put upon a secure footing. In September 1883 Sir Evelyn Baring (later Lord Cromer) was sent as British Consul-General with plenipotentiary powers. He was destined to remain in Egypt as virtual ruler for almost a quarter of a century. The Gladstone cabinet had thus found itself moving step by step into full military involvement. Privately, it was racked by doubts and divisions about its own actions. John Bright had refused to countenance the bombardment of Alexandria and had resigned. In a speech in October 1882 Gladstone tried to draw a distinction between his own decision to order the invasion of Egypt and Disraeli's imperial adventures. 'We have carried on this war from a love of peace, and I may say on the principles of peace. We have been pulling down a military anarchy. It is impossible for any country to prosper under a military tyranny.'[5]

But the worst was yet to come, as the trouble-centre shifted from Egypt to the Soudan. In 1881 the Soudanese, under the leadership of the Mahdi, a religious fanatic, had revolted against Egyptian rule. The Egyptians tried to regain control in 1883, but their army was destroyed in November. Egypt itself now seemed to be in danger, and the British Government was asked for help by the Egyptians. The London press clamoured for action, but the cabinet was split. Eventually, Major-General Charles Gordon – who as the energetic Governor-General of the Soudan during the 1870s had attempted to suppress the slave trade – was sent to help organize the evacuation of the beleagured Egyptian garrisons. In terms of experience Gordon was the obvious choice for this role, but in terms of temperament he was not the man to command a withdrawal operation. His earlier career in Africa and Asia had already made him into a popular hero, 'Chinese Gordon'. He was a fearless, evangelical Christian, ready tenaciously to adhere to the right course as he saw it. At the time of his appointment even Gladstone's private secretary described him as 'a half cracked fatalist'.[6] Gordon soon persuaded himself that evacuation of the whole Soudan was undesirable, and that Khartoum could not be evacuated but could be held. By March 1884 the town was under siege. The Gladstone cabinet hesitated to send a relief expedition. Gladstone himself had been away ill when Gordon was chosen, and the Prime Minister did not feel fully committed once Gordon had defied orders to assist an evacuation. A relief expedition was finally sent in September. After many delays it reached Khartoum on 28 January 1885, only to find that the garrison had been overrun two days earlier. Gordon had been killed and decapitated.

When the news reached England a wave of noisy hostility erupted, especially against Gladstone. He was more bitterly attacked at this time than ever before. The GOM became the 'MOG', 'the Murderer of Gordon'. The queen telegraphed identical reprimands to Gladstone, Granville, and Hartington unprecedentedly *en clair* – 'These news from Khartoum are frightful, and to think that all this might have been prevented and many precious lives saved by earlier action is too frightful.'[7] A Commons censure motion was defeated by only fourteen votes. But Gladstone remained unrepentant. He remarked in 1888 that Gordon had 'remained in utter defiance of the whole mind and spirit of our instructions. I do not know what could have justified him except (like Nelson at Trafalgar) a great success. To remain beleaguered in Khartoum was only the proof of his failure'. If the relief expedition had reached the city in time, Gladstone believed that Gordon would have refused to withdraw, 'and the dilemma would have arisen in another form'.[8]

Gladstone had been ill and contemplating retirement at the beginning of 1885; but Gordon's death and its effects – far from depressing the septuagenerian Prime Minister – restored his will to continue, despite spreading demoralization within his cabinet and despite plots to oust him. Gladstone indeed had come almost to relish the tensions. He described to his wife the early career of the ministry as 'a wild romance of politics with a continual succession of hairbreadth escapes and strange accidents pressing one upon another'. Gladstone added that Russia and Ireland were the 'two *great* dangers remaining'.[9] His firm initial handling of the Penjdeh crisis did much to draw public and parliamentary attention away from the Soudan (see below, p. 372). The reality of the Russian danger confirmed Gladstone in the belief that he had been right to resist other entanglements. But what did he have in mind for Ireland?

2

The agricultural depression of the later 1870s had given a new dimension and intensity to the Irish problem.[10] Irish tenants could not pay their rents. Evictions resulted; but evictions led to 'boycotting' of those who took over farms from evicted tenants, and to cattle-maiming, arson, and attempts on the lives of landlords and agents. The Irish National Land League, inspired by Michael Davitt but with Parnell as president, began to campaign for 'the land of Ireland for the people of Ireland'. Agitation in Ireland reached a new intensity when in the summer of 1880 the Lords rejected a bill to award compensation out of the Irish church surplus to certain classes of evicted tenants. The Gladstone Government felt bound to restore law and order. A coercion bill was met in the Commons by unprecedented obstruction from the Irish members, but was eventually passed. At the same time Gladstone had come to accept the need for a second Irish Land Act, more thoroughgoing than the measure of 1870. The new Act passed in 1881 gave tenants the 'three Fs' – fair rents, free sale, and fixity of tenure. The measure was extremely complicated in operation, and more than half the tenants with holdings of over one acre were not within its range. None the less it represented a radical interference with property rights. It introduced a system of dual ownership of land, which reduced landlords to little more than receivers of rents, the 'fairness' of which was to be fixed by the courts.

Gladstone genuinely wished to meet Irish needs. But his Act did look like a belated concession to violence. Moreover, it soon seemed to have been a concession which Parnell would not accept as sufficient. Once again the Liberal Government was contriving to satisfy no one. The continuance of disturbance in Ireland now convinced Gladstone that Parnell wanted to wreck the Land Act; and in October 1881 the Irish leader was imprisoned in Kilmainham Jail, Dublin. Parnell may have been glad to be arrested, for the Land League was losing momentum. He was kept in jail until May 1882. By then he was anxious for release, both on personal and political grounds, and Gladstone was ready to be conciliatory. An understanding – the so-called Kilmainham 'treaty' – was reached with Parnell by Chamberlain on Gladstone's behalf. Parnell promised to support Liberal policies both in Ireland and on the floor of the Commons in return for promises of improvements to the Land Act, along with the implication that coercion would be ended. However, the Gladstone Government was not yet out of trouble either in Ireland or within its own ranks. The Irish Viceroy (Lord Cowper) and the Chief Secretary (W. E. Forster) both resigned. Then on 6 May 1882, the day after Parnell's release, Forster's successor (Lord Frederick

Cavendish) and his Permanent Under-Secretary (W. H. Burke) were assassinated while walking in Phoenix Park, Dublin. The two men were stabbed with long surgical knives and their throats cut. An Irish extremist group claimed responsibility. British opinion was outraged. Gladstone was shaken, and Parnell also was aghast. But the Irish leader was able to use the murders to draw support away from violent courses. The defunct Land League was succeeded by the Irish National League, which placed Home Rule in the forefront of its programme.

How did Gladstone now regard Home Rule? 'Not the least chance of any question as to any sort of assembly (for Ireland) in Dublin. That question if anywhere is not in the nearer future.' So wrote Gladstone to Granville in November 1882. Perhaps significantly, Gladstone was not entirely ruling out the concession of Home Rule at some future date. For the present, however, he was eager to concentrate upon a wide extension of Irish local government. Good government for Ireland, he told Granville in January 1883, required more devolution of power both on psychological and on practical grounds, so as to remove the sense of grievance and so as to make the Irish bear the full cost of the reforms which they demanded.[11]

3

But before the onset of the next crisis in Anglo-Irish relations the Gladstone Government found time to turn at last to parliamentary reform. This produced a curious crisis on its own account.[12] The National Liberal Federation conference in October 1883 had called for parliamentary reform; and backbench Liberals – tired of the Irish question and of Government failures – wanted a striking legislative success. Gladstone's franchise bill, introduced in February 1884, aimed largely to assimilate the county and borough franchises throughout the United Kingdom. The electoral effect of this would be especially striking in Ireland, with its mainly rural electorate. A redistribution bill was promised for the next session. The Representation of the People Bill passed the Commons in June; but the Conservative majority in the Lords refused to accept franchise extension until the Government's redistribution plan was also known. The Conservative leaders complained that once the franchise measure had been passed the Liberals would have gained total control of redistribution. If the Lords amended a redistribution bill, the Government could drop it or hold an election under the existing system; and Salisbury had estimated that this was unfairly weighted against the Conservatives to the extent of about thirty-five seats in Parliament.

Rather than oppose the principle of franchise extension, the Conservatives began to work for redistribution on terms favourable to themselves. The behind-the-scenes manoeuvring between politicians became intense throughout the autumn of 1884. Both Gladstone on the

Liberal side and Salisbury on the Conservative side deliberately manipulated the crisis to keep their restless supporters united behind them. They treated the spate of partisan meetings in the country during the autumn recess as justification not for intransigence but for compromise. Though Gladstone refused to accept that the upper house possessed the right to dictate either the conduct of Government business or the calling of a general election, he did not want to force (in Chamberlain's phrase) a 'peers versus people' confrontation. So a deal was eventually worked out in private discussions between the party leaders whereby the franchise bill would pass both houses with an agreed redistribution measure to follow. Complications were much reduced by agreement to go for single-member constituencies. Gladstone's secretary noted how Salisbury showed 'no respect for tradition'. The Conservative leader had realized that his party stood to gain from a thorough redistribution, which would remove small borough constituencies and create large numbers of middle-class suburban seats. These were now more likely to return Conservatives than Liberals. All small boroughs under 15,000 population were eliminated.

Salisbury was satisfied, and so were the radicals on the Liberal side. They now expected to gain a predominant position within the Liberal ranks in Parliament. They were ready with their programme. 'We have been looking to the extension of the franchise in order to bring into prominence questions which have been too long neglected. The great problem of our civilization is still unsolved. We have to account for and to grapple with the mass of misery and destitution in our midst, co-existent as it is with the evidence of abundant wealth and teeming prosperity.' So exclaimed Joseph Chamberlain at Warrington on 8 September 1885. This speech formed part of his autumn exposition of the 'unauthorized programme' (so named by Goschen) which Chamberlain was pressing upon Gladstone and the Liberal Party.[13] The second Gladstone Government had finally fallen in June, when a Conservative amendment to the budget was passed by a majority of twelve – with Parnell's Irish voting against the Liberals. Tired and more than ever divided about future policy, the Liberal ministers were glad to quit office. Salisbury reluctantly formed a minority Conservative administration; and the parties prepared for a general election in the late autumn when the new registers were ready.

Chamberlain's 'unauthorized programme' was never finalized. But it variously included free elementary education; democratic local government for the counties; some form of devolution (but no Home Rule) for Ireland; financial reform (including graduated taxation) to lighten the pressure of indirect taxation on the masses, and to pay for housing and other social reform; compulsory land purchase by local authorities to create a body of smallholders ('three acres and a cow'); disestablishment of the state churches in England, Scotland, and Wales; Lords reform; and triennial parliaments. Chamberlain presented this programme in bold language which made it sound much more extreme than its content in detail justified. It did not mention old-age pensions, health and unemployment insurance, or other measures which were to be part of twentieth-century social reform. It envisaged that local authorities would play a leading part. Its old-style radical emphasis upon land reform as the key to social progress also proved difficult to make appealing to the urban electorate. Chamberlain argued that the enforced flight of rural workers to the towns was a main cause of urban unemployment, housing shortage, and high rents. He also attacked the monopolistic ownership of urban land. Landed property both in town and country was pictured as 'stolen' from the people; but ownership of capital was not challenged at all. A modern radical, exclaimed one SDF leader, was an 'Artful Dodger' who told the people 'to take hold of the landlord thief, but to let the greater thief, the capitalist, go scot-free'. But then Chamberlain himself was a business capitalist.[14]

Chamberlain's programme attracted great attention and much denunciation from Conservative leaders, who berated him as a communist or anarchist, 'Jack Cade', 'Dick Turpin'. The whigs were equally alarmed. Chamberlain would have been glad to drive them out of the Liberal Party. But what did Gladstone think? He disliked Chamberlain as a political careerist, and he disliked his 'socialism' just as much. The Liberal leader therefore gave no public approval to the programme, even though Chamberlain proved willing after private discussions at Hawarden to limit his immediate demands to compulsory land purchase. Gladstone simply hinted at 'an instinct that Irish questions might elbow out all others'.

The vote of Irish electors in England was not, however, given at the general election to the Liberals. At the last moment in November 1885 Parnell instructed Irish voters outside Ireland to support Conservative candidates. He had gained the impression from secret contacts with Lord Carnarvon, the Irish Viceroy, and from Randolph Churchill that the Conservatives might be prepared to contemplate some measure of internal self-government for Ireland. He knew that the Conservatives, with their control of the Lords, were in a better position than the Liberals to carry such a reform if they wished. Lord Salisbury remained uncommitted; but his minority Government did not renew the current coercion Act, and a useful Land Purchase Act was promoted. Chamberlain estimated that Parnell's advice swung about twenty-five seats to the Conservatives. If these seats had gone to the Liberals, Gladstone's Home Rule Bill might have just passed the Commons in the following summer.

The elections gave the Liberals 335 seats, the Conservatives 249, and the Irish Nationalists 86. The results disappointed the Liberals, who were denied a clear majority. Chamberlain was proved wrong in his expectation of a great increase in the number of urban radical representatives; for the Conservatives won 54 of the 87 new seats in England. Even among the new rural voters the appeal of 'three acres and a cow' may not have been unusually strong. The Liberals did well in the English counties, but much of their success may have resulted simply from the absorption of already Liberal small boroughs into adjacent county constituencies.[15] Gladstone attributed the urban defeats to 'Fair Trade + Parnell + Church + Chamberlain.' Chamberlain had agreed with Gladstone that Church disestablishment could not be an immediate issue, but his advocacy in principle may have cost Anglican votes. Certainly, Chamberlain had now lost influence within the Liberal Party: the initiative remained with Gladstone.[16]

4

Salisbury did not resign until defeated in the Commons on 26 January 1886, and not until he had made it clear that the Conservatives now proposed to revert to coercion in Ireland. Irish hopes of Salisbury had collapsed, but their hopes of Gladstone had suddenly rocketed. In mid-December Gladstone's son, Herbert, had leaked to the press the news of his father's conversion to support for Home Rule. Gladstone himself had not planned the flying of this 'Hawarden kite', though his opponents immediately interpreted this as a deliberate bid for power. Gladstone had hoped to convert his party gently, not by shock tactics. He had also thought that the Conservatives might be privately encouraged to take up Home Rule in the national interest. Both hopes were now ended by this dramatic revelation. Yet Salisbury would never have been ready to split his party for the sake of Home Rule. He was convinced that such a policy would lead to complete separation and to military danger. 'It would be an act of political bankruptcy, an avowal that we were unable to satisfy even the most sacred obligations, and that all claims to protect or govern any one beyond our own narrow island were at an end.'[17]

As early as August 1885 Hartington was warning Granville, his fellow whig, that Gladstone's 'state of mind about Ireland is extremely alarming'.[18] Gladstone had now realized that the Irish were more than a problem: they were a nation. He had come to regard their right to Home Rule almost in the same spirit as he had earlier supported Italian or Balkan nationalism. Hartington had still supposed in August 1885 that, since party unity over Home Rule would be 'an impossibility', Gladstone would not press the point. But Gladstone could claim that the cause mattered more than party. On a lower plane, he was well content to risk shedding Chamberlain and his group. A purged Liberal Party, Gladstone assumed, would be more effective in pursuit of Home Rule. He was to be proved wrong. His failure to keep Chamberlain within the Liberal ranks did much to ensure that Home Rule had no chance of enactment for a generation. Chamberlain might just conceivably have been persuaded if Gladstone had spared pains to conciliate him. To Gladstone's disgust Chamberlain briefly joined the new Liberal Cabinet in January 1886, only to resign as soon as he heard the outline of the

Irish proposals. Hartington had refused to join at all. He nursed hopes of taking over the Liberal leadership; but Gladstone manoeuvred adroitly to keep control. Gladstone's Irish plan involved not only Home Rule, but also a scheme of land purchase. Chamberlain professed to dislike the land scheme; but his main concern was that Home Rule would lead to Irish independence and to danger of foreign attack upon the British Isles. This was also Salisbury's view – the Conservative leader and the radical leader were coming together.

The Home Rule Bill was introduced by Gladstone to the Commons on 8 April 1886 with one of his greatest speeches. He explained how Home Rule would restore the dignity of Parliament by removing the reason for Irish obstruction. 'We stand face to face with what is termed Irish nationality ... Is this a thing that we should view with horror or apprehension?' Because Irishmen were even more influenced by 'local patriotism' than were Scotsmen, this did not mean that they were incapable of 'Imperial patriotism' at the same time. The concession of 'local self-government' would not undermine the unity of the three kingdoms but strengthen it. The bill envisaged a separate Irish legislature and executive, in control of all Irish affairs but not of such imperial matters as the Crown; defence; foreign relations; trade, customs, and navigation; the post office; and coinage. As first proposed, no Irish members were to sit at Westminster; but Gladstone soon changed his mind on this. The Irish contribution to the imperial budget would amount to some 40 per cent of the Irish tax yield, and complete Irish exclusion from Westminster would therefore mean taxation without representation. Exclusion was also seen by others as a step towards complete separation. Yet to retain even a reduced number of Irish representatives at Westminster would give them influence – perhaps the deciding say in a vote – over the internal affairs of Great Britain. This question of Irish representation proved to be a major technical difficulty in 1886, and again with the Second Home Rule Bill of 1893. Many English supporters of Home Rule were persuaded as much or more by the prospect of removing Irish obstruction as by enthusiasm for the principle of separate government. They were not happy to be told that some Irish would remain at Westminster after all, to give their restless countrymen a double representation not enjoyed by Englishmen.

The Home Rule Bill made no mention of Ulster, with its Protestant majority. Gladstone was insufficiently aware of the problem. It was new in the sense that up to 1885 the representation of Ulster had divided on normal political lines between Liberals and Conservatives. But the advent of Home Rule nationalism in southern Ireland had provoked an upsurge of Orangeism in the north.[19] When Lord Randolph Churchill exclaimed dramatically 'Ulster will fight, Ulster will be right', his words became a rallying cry both for the present and for the future. Less excitedly, John Bright's considerable influence was cast against the Home Rule Bill, in part because of its disregard of the 'loyal and protestant' people of Ulster. G. J. Goschen, another leading Liberal Unionist, included the Ulster question and the problem of Irish representation at Westminster among what he called the 'bundle of impossibilities' associated with Home Rule. Bright's decision helped to tip the scales against the bill in the Commons. It was defeated on 8 June by 341 votes to 311, a larger hostile majority than Gladstone had expected. Hartington, Bright, and Chamberlain led 93 Liberals into the opposition lobby. 131 radicals voted for Home Rule, but 32 voted against or abstained.[20]

Outside Parliament the majority against Home Rule was probably much greater than inside. Numerous intellectuals were opposed – Matthew Arnold, Herbert Spencer, Benjamin Jowett, and many more who might have been expected to take a liberal view. The apparent suddenness of Gladstone's decision was not a recommendation. He appeared to be willing to chance a new constitution for the United Kingdom at a few weeks' notice. Randolph Churchill cuttingly described him as 'an old man in a hurry'. Why should so much be risked for the violent Irish? The English middle classes, with their ingrained respect for law and order, had been horrified by the violence of the Land League period.[21] John Morley in an article called 'Irish Revolution and English Liberalism' (*Nineteenth Century*, November 1882) had remarked on 'the honourable English abhorrence of systematic crime. To us a murder is a murder whether it is committed in Yorkshire or in Kerry, in Kent or in Connemara'. Englishmen refused 'to enter into distinctions of motive, of historical tradition, of local circumstance'. Gladstone appeared to be over-ready to give way to force, and also too ready to lavish taxpayers' money through his land purchase bill. Attitudes might have changed if a spirit of crusading enthusiasm had been aroused in England, as had been worked up over the Bulgarian question. But Gladstone gave himself no time to achieve this in 1886.

After the defeat of the Home Rule Bill, Gladstone immediately appealed to the country. The result of the 1886 general election was conclusive for the present. The Conservatives won 317 seats, the new Liberal Unionists 77, the Liberals 191, and the Irish Nationalists 85. Gladstone was once more replaced as Prime Minister by Lord Salisbury. Many former Liberal voters seem to have abstained at the 1886 election; but they might vote Liberal again next time. However, even if the 1886 Home Rule Bill had passed the Commons it would have been heavily defeated in the Lords. To hope to overawe the upper house, the Liberals would need to return to power with an emphatic majority in the Commons, and one which did not depend upon the votes of the Irish members.

Could the Liberal Unionists be brought back into the Liberal Party? During the course of the Home Rule debates they had started to form their own separate group – an unexpected parliamentary combination of about fifty whigs and moderates led by Hartington with about twenty Chamberlainite radicals. At the 1886 elections the Conservatives nearly everywhere honoured a pledge not to oppose those Liberals who had voted against the Home Rule Bill. As a result, seventy-seven Liberal Unionists were returned. An unsuccessful last effort at Liberal reunion was initiated by Chamberlain through a series of informal meetings in January and February 1887, the Round Table Conference.[22] Chamberlain was mainly concerned to show his Birmingham supporters that he had tried, and that he was not irrevocably committed to the Conservatives. Gladstone, who took no direct part in the talks, was probably not interested in getting the radical leader back. Henceforward Chamberlain became the most effective opponent of Home Rule in the Commons – even though he spoke from a seat on the Opposition front bench next to Gladstone himself. But Chamberlain's hopes of becoming Prime Minister – which he had certainly not abandoned when voting against Home Rule in 1886 – were being gradually destroyed by Gladstone's tenacious continuance in active politics for the sake of Home Rule. 'Thirty-two millions of people must go without much-needed legislation because three millions are disloyal.' So complained Chamberlain scathingly of Liberal policy.[23] Ireland, answered the Gladstonians, 'blocks the way'. An article with this title by Herbert Gladstone in the *Nineteenth Century* for June 1892 claimed that the removal of Irish business would save one-quarter of parliamentary time, which could then be devoted to reform. But the detailed provisions of the next Home Rule Bill were deliberately left wide open after the failure of 1886; for the Gladstonians differed among themselves over the thorny questions of Irish representation, Irish land reform, and Ulster.

5

Lord Salisbury's Cabinet, formed after Gladstone's defeat in the Home Rule election of 1886, was a competent but dull combination – with the important exception of Lord Randolph Churchill, who became Chancellor of the Exchequer. By November the restless Randolph was at odds with most of his colleagues over Irish policy, local government reform, reform of Commons procedure, foreign affairs, and economy. Salisbury decided that a breach was unavoidable. When in December Churchill tendered his resignation unless his demands for cuts in the army and navy estimates were met, Salisbury seized his chance and Churchill found himself out of office. He had chosen the wrong issue at the wrong time (over Christmas), and Salisbury's Government survived his departure with unexpected ease.[24]

Salisbury depended for his majority upon Liberal Unionist support, and this helped to prompt the introduction of several important reforms. Most notable was the legislation of 1888 which extended democratic forms of local government to the countryside, a reform which Chamberlain had wanted for years. In 1889 the Technical Instruction Act was passed, in 1890 the Housing of the Working Classes

Act, in 1891 an important Factory Act, and in 1892 a Smallholdings Act. Free elementary education – another cry from Chamberlain's unauthorized programme – was introduced from 1891. Yet Salisbury was not an enthusiastic reformer. He feared that even desirable limited change might whet the appetite for confiscation of property. He preferred to emphasize the 'constitutional' and 'national' role of Conservatism, in the face of the threat of Home Rule separation.[25] And in each of the four general elections after Gladstone's conversion – even including 1892 – the Conservatives won large majorities in England and clear majorities in Great Britain.

The Salisbury Government set out to prove to Englishmen (and hopefully even to Irishmen) that the union with Ireland could be made to work.[26] The Conservative Party added 'Unionist' to its title so as to emphasize this determination, an adjective suggested by Randolph Churchill. In 1887 Balfour became Chief Secretary, and he immediately embarked upon a policy of strong coercion alongside remedial legislation. Agrarian depression had returned to Ireland, and depression had led to the 'plan of campaign' – an organized refusal of rents in order to provide money for the support of evicted tenants. The imperturbable Balfour – unmoved by the soubriquet 'Bloody Balfour' which he was soon given – employed every device to combat the campaign: a strong coercion act without limit of time, frequent use of police and sometimes of troops, prompt and repeated imprisonment of leaders, contact with the Pope, financial and psychological support for landlords. These methods at least contained the outbreak, which Parnell had not supported. Balfour believed that Gladstone's land reforms had produced an unhappy system of 'dual ownership'. The Land Purchase Acts of 1888 and 1891 accepted that the peasants must be effectively helped to buy out their landlords. Balfour was confident that this would undermine the demand for Home Rule, since he refused to accept that the Irish were moved by genuine national sentiment. The existence of Protestant Ulster demonstrated to him how 'no single nationality' existed in Ireland. In an address on 'Nationality and Home Rule' in 1913 he condemned what he called 'exclusive' Irish patriotism, and looked forward 'to a time when Irish patriotism will as easily combine with British patriotism as Scottish patriotism combines now'.[27] Conservative land reform was further developed during Salisbury's 1895 ministry, and it came to a successful culmination with the 1903 Land Purchase Act, which marked the prospective end of privileged landlordism in Ireland. But this policy of 'killing Home Rule by kindness' never looked like smothering Home Rule, as Salisbury had promised in 1886. He had offered enforcement of the Conservative alternative 'honestly, consistently and resolutely for twenty years'.

The Salisbury Government made one big early blunder in its Irish policy, when it became indirectly associated with the Pigott forgeries.[28] In March and April 1887 *The Times* published articles on 'Parnellism and Crime' which culminated in the printing of a facsimile of what purported to be a letter from Parnell in May 1882 in which he privately condoned the Phoenix Park murders, even though he had publicly denounced them. The Conservative Home Secretary had secretly helped *The Times* to collect information for these articles. In response to the uproar caused by the disclosures, and under pressure from Joseph Chamberlain, the Government set up a special commission of enquiry. This became in effect a trial of Parnell and the Nationalists. But the hoped-for exposure of Parnell backfired with maximum publicity when Richard Pigott dramatically confessed in February 1889 that he had forged the letters.

The prospects for a large Liberal majority at the next general election now seemed promising, and Parnell became popular in England as never before. But not for long. In December 1889 the O'Shea divorce suit began, which in the following November revealed that the Irish leader had been living with the wife of Captain O'Shea – a former Irish Member of Parliament – intermittently since 1881 and continuously since 1886, and that three children had been born to them.[29] As the case proceeded a web of deception was revealed. The English 'Nonconformist Conscience' was outraged. Hugh Price Hughes, the Methodist leader, exclaimed that it would be 'an infamous thing for any Englishman to compel his chaste and virtuous Queen to receive as her first Irish prime minister an adulterer of this type'. Others were disturbed not because Parnell was living in adultery but because he had been found out. Gladstone felt unable to continue the Liberal association with the Irish Nationalists while an adulterer remained their leader. Yet Parnell refused to retire, and his party eventually split. In October 1891 he died, but only after making threats of violence which further damaged the Home Rule cause in England. 'His character for moderation was a pretence; his desire to reconcile England and Ireland was a sham; his alliance with the Liberal party was a fraud; his admiration for Mr Gladstone was a deception.'[30] Hopes of a Liberal majority large enough perhaps to overawe the House of Lords had faded.

The year of Parnell's death was also the year of the Liberal 'Newcastle Programme'. This variously proposed Church disestablishment in Wales and Scotland, local option, abolition of plural voting, triennial parliaments, land reform, encouragement of allotments, the creation of district and parish councils, and employers' liability for accidents; along with vague references to limitation of working hours, payment of Members of Parliament, and Lords reform. All these proposals – placed in no particular order behind Home Rule – were endorsed by the annual conference of the National Liberal Federation, and were apparently accepted by Gladstone as the party programme for the next general election. But the programme always looked improvised, an attempt to please the many crotchetmongers within the Liberal ranks. This might have mattered less if the main objective – Irish Home Rule – had been about to receive enthusiastic electoral endorsement. But this was not the case. At the 1892 general election the Liberals gained a majority, but only with Irish support – Liberals 272, Irish Nationalists 81, Conservatives 268, Liberal Unionists 46. Gladstone realized that, though he might now carry Home Rule in the Commons, the Lords would feel free to reject it. He formed his last Government in August 1892, and introduced his Second Home Rule Bill in March 1893. He now recommended the retention of eighty Irish representatives at Westminster. The initial intention to allow them no vote on matters concerning Great Britain alone was abandoned during the long passage of the bill through the Commons over the summer. It was brilliantly piloted by the aged Gladstone, tenaciously opposed by Chamberlain. 'The Prime Minister calls "black" and they say "it is good". The Prime Minister calls "white", and they say "it is better" . . . Never since the time of Herod has there been such slavish adulation.' The Irish answered with shrieks of 'Judas', scuffling broke out, and the Speaker had to return to the chamber to restore order. On 8 September 1893 the House of Lords threw out the bill by 419 votes to 41.

Gladstone wanted Parliament to be dissolved immediately, so that the Lords question could be put to the electorate. But his colleagues would not agree. They knew that the majority of English voters were not upset by the peers' action. Gladstone finally retired in March 1894, in protest over increased naval estimates but also because of old age and dissatisfaction with his colleagues. Who was to succeed him as prime minister? Sir William Harcourt stood second in the Commons, but his personality was too abrasive to make him acceptable as Prime Minister. The queen chose Lord Rosebery. Unfortunately, he remained aloof and despairing, and his cabinet was always disunited. A policy of 'filling up the cup' was tried with respect to the Lords. Bills were sent up in full expectation of rejection; yet in hopes that the electorate would become angered by the presumption of the upper house. But the defeat of its measures only made the ministry seem the more ineffective. In June it was suddenly defeated in the Commons over a comparatively minor vote. Rosebery seized the chance to resign. Salisbury again took office, and a general election followed. The Conservatives refused to commit themselves to a detailed programme, simply attacking Home Rule and other Liberal policies. This gained them a comfortable victory: Conservatives 340 seats, Liberal Unionists 71, Liberals 177, Irish Nationalists 82.

Salisbury formed a coalition Government with the Liberal Unionists. Chamberlain therefore now entered the cabinet of the selfsame aristocrat whom he had fiercely denounced in the early 1880s as the arch-representative of feudalism. He had decided, however, that the empire needed him. He chose to become Colonial Secretary – not previously regarded as one of the principal offices – because he wanted vigorously to promote the prosperity and the unity of the empire for the benefit of the people both of the United Kingdom and of the colonies. Chamberlain's policies in South Africa reached a violent climax in the

Boer War of 1899–1902 (see below, p. 365). In the middle of the war he persuaded Salisbury to risk an early 'khaki' general election (October 1900), at which the Conservatives campaigned as the 'patriotic' party. The Conservatives and Liberal Unionists retained their pre-election majority; but they made no further advance despite serious divisions about the war within the Liberal ranks – Conservatives 334 seats, Liberal Unionists 68, Liberals 184, Irish Nationalists 82. Chamberlain was forced to defend himself during the elections for the failure of the Government to introduce old-age pensions and other social reforms which he had earlier advocated. The only major social enactment had been the 1897 Workmen's Compensation Act.[31] This gave automatic compensation for accidents at work, though certain industries and certain accidents were still excluded. Over the next generation the Act was gradually amended to remove these exceptions. It represented a significant step in social intervention, for if workmen needed statutory protection against accidents did they not also require protection against illness or old age?

At the 1900 general election the Liberals spoke with several voices. Liberal imperialists, led by Rosebery and Asquith, supported the war; 'pro-Boers', led by Sir Wilfrid Lawson and young Lloyd George, opposed it; and Sir Henry Campbell-Bannerman, the party leader, tried to find a middle position, 'anti-Joe but never pro-Kruger'[32] The *Annual Register* for 1900 estimated the number of anti-war Liberal Members of Parliament as about 68, the Liberal imperialists as about 62, and Campbell-Bannerman's group as about 30 – with the remaining Liberal members uncertain. 'There are some who hold the war is just and necessary, some that it is just but unnecessary, some that it is not unjust but unnecessary, some that it is both unjust and unnecessary.' So explained the NLF executive committee in the spring of 1900. Lord Rosebery had resigned as Liberal leader in 1896 in order to give himself more room for manoeuvre. His Liberal imperialist group hoped to recapture for the party the middle ground of politics, which they felt had been lost by recent over-commitment to sectional 'fads' and 'crotchets'. The 'Limps' coupled 'sane Imperialism' with reform, to promote what Rosebery – in a key speech at Chesterfield in December 1901 – called 'efficiency', 'the condition of national fitness equal to the demands of our Empire'. The Liberal imperialists were especially keen for improved national education at all levels from elementary school to university; and also for some social reform on 'new Liberal' lines. What was the use of the empire, asked Asquith, if it did not breed 'an Imperial race'? What was the use of talking proudly about the empire 'if here, at its very centre, there is always to be found a mass of people, stunted in education, a prey of intemperance, huddled and congested beyond the possibility of realizing in any true sense either social or domestic life?'[33]

In 1902 the Liberal imperialists formed the Liberal League. But neither they nor the pro-Boer Liberals really wanted to break up the party. Meanwhile, the quietly astute Campbell-Bannerman, who had been elected as stop-gap leader in 1899, showed himself increasingly skilful in asserting his authority over all shades of party opinion. By 1905 he was able to form a strong cabinet which included both former pro-Boers and erstwhile Liberal imperialists.

Notes

1. J. P. D. Dunbabin (ed.), *Rural Discontent in Nineteenth-Century Britain* (1974), pp. 174–5.
2. See W. L. Arnstein, *The Bradlaugh Case* (1965).
3. See especially R. Robinson and J. Gallaher, *Africa and the Victorians* (1961), Ch. III; C. F. Goodfellow, *Great Britain and South African Confederation, 1870–1881* (1966); and D. M. Schreuder, *Gladstone and Kruger* (1969).
4. R. Robinson and J. Gallaher, *Africa and the Victorians* (1961), Chs. IV, V.
5. *Manchester Guardian*, 4 October 1882.
6. D. W. R. Bahlman (ed.), *Diary of Sir Edward Walter Hamilton* (1972), II, p. 545. See especially J. Symons, *England's Pride, The Story of the Gordon Relief Expedition* (1965).
7. See Elizabeth Longford, *Victoria R. I.* (1964), Ch. XXXI.
8. Lord E. Fitzmaurice, *Life of Granville George Leveson Gower, Second Earl Granville* (1905), II, pp. 401–2; J. Morley, *Life of William Ewart Gladstone* (1905), II, pp. 408–9.
9. A. T. Bassett (ed.), *Gladstone to His Wife* (1936), p. 246.
10. See especially F. S. L. Lyons, *Ireland Since the Famine* (1971), part II, Ch. 2; F. S. L. Lyons, *Charles Stewart Parnell* (1977), Chs. 4–7; and A. O'Day, *The English Face of Irish Nationalism* (1977).
11. Agatha Ramm (ed.), *Political Correspondence of Mr. Gladstone and Lord Granville, 1876–1886* (1962), I, p. 461; II, p. 10.
12. See especially A. Jones, *The Politics of Reform, 1884* (1972); and Mary E. J. Chadwick, 'The Role of Redistribution in the Making of the Third Reform Act', *Historical Journal*, Vol. 19 (1976).
13. See especially J. L. Garvin, *Life of Joseph Chamberlain*, II (1933), Chs. XXVII, XXVIII; and C. H. D. Howard, 'Joseph Chamberlain and the "Unauthorised Programme"', *English Historical Review*, LXV (1950). Also *The Radical Programme* (1885; edited 1971 by D. A. Hamer).
14. H. A. Clegg *et al.*, *History of British Trade Unions Since 1889*, I (1964), p. 53.
15. M. Barker, *Gladstone and Radicalism* (1975), pp. 24–40, 257–8.
16. A. B. Cooke and J. Vincent, *The Governing Passion, Cabinet Government and Party Politics in Britain, 1885–86* (1974), pp. 5, 14–15, 40.
17. 'Disintegration', *Quarterly Review*, October 1883, in P. Smith (ed.), *Lord Salisbury on Politics* (1972), p. 374.
18. B. Holland, *Life of Spencer Compton, Eighth Duke of Devonshire* (1911), II, pp. 77–8.
19. See P. J. Buckland, *Irish Unionism, 1885–1922* (1973), and references there.
20. T. W. Heyck, *The Dimensions of British Radicalism, The Case of Ireland, 1874–95* (1974), pp. 143–4.
21. See R. C. K. Ensor, 'Some Political and Economic Interactions in Later Victorian England', *Transactions of the Royal Historical Society*, fourth series, XXXI (1949).
22. See M. C. Hurst, *Joseph Chamberlain and Liberal Reunion* (1967).
23. *Ibid.*, p. 286.
24. See W. S. Churchill, *Lord Randolph Churchill* (2nd edn, 1951), Chs. XV–XVII; and R. Rhodes James, *Lord Randolph Churchill* (1959), Ch. 10.
25. See especially R. Blake, *The Conservative Party from Peel to Churchill* (1970), Ch. V.

26. See especially L. P. Curtis, jr., *Coercion and Conciliation in Ireland, 1880–1892* (1963); and F. S. L. Lyons, *Ireland Since the Famine* (1971), part II, Ch. 4.
27. Lord Balfour, *Opinions and Argument* (1927), pp. 79–80.
28. See T. W. Moody, '*The Times* versus Parnell and Co., 1887–90', *Historical Studies*, VI (1968); and F. S. L. Lyons, '"Parnellism and Crime", 1887–90', *Transactions of the Royal Historical Society*, fifth series, Vol. 124 (1974)
29. See especially F. S. L. Lyons, *Charles Stewart Parnell* (1977), Chs. 15–18.
30. E. Dicey, 'The Rival Coalitions', *Nineteenth Century*, January 1891, p. 174.
31. See W. C. Mallalieu, 'Joseph Chamberlain and Workmen's Compensation', *Journal of Economic History*, XX (1950); and D. G. Hanes, *The First British Workmen's Compensation Act, 1897* (1968).
32. See especially H. C. G. Matthew, *The Liberal Imperialists* (1973); S. Koss (ed.), *The Pro-Boers* (1973); and J. W. Auld, 'The Liberal Pro-Boers', *Journal of British Studies*, XIV (1975).
33. B. B. Gilbert, *The Evolution of National Insurance in Great Britain* (1966), p. 77.

Chapter 19

Imperial policy: *'Pegging out claims for the future'*

1

'The maintenance of the British Empire makes it possible, at a cost which is relatively small, compared with the whole number of British subjects, to secure peace, good order, and personal freedom throughout a large part of the world. In an age, further, of huge military States it is of the highest importance to safeguard against foreign aggression one of the two greatest free commonwealths in existence.' So wrote A. V. Dicey in 1905.[1] 'The day of small States appears to have passed ... Great empires are as much a necessity of our time as are huge mercantile companies.' Here was the voice of the 'new imperialism' of the last quarter of the nineteenth century, which produced a world-wide spread of new colonial empires, French, Russian, German, Belgian, Italian, and – most extensive of all – British. By 1901 the British Empire covered some 12 million square miles, more than one-fifth of the world's land surface: over 4 million square miles in America, 3 million in Australasia, and (with large recent additions) 3 million in Africa. The population of the empire now totalled about 400 million, of which nearly three-quarters lived in India. The population of the United Kingdom stood at 41,500,000, of Canada 5,400,000, of Australia 3,800,000, and of New Zealand 800,000. So only about one-eighth of the empire's citizens were white-skinned.

The word 'imperialism' had acquired a new meaning since mid-century, as Dicey explained. In the 1860s it had meant Caesarism, autocracy such as that of Napoleon III, and the word was always used unfavourably. 'In 1905 imperialism means the wish to maintain the unity and increase the strength of an empire which contains within its limits various more or less independent States.'[2] In 1868 the *Spectator* (11 January) gave an early lead to this shift in meaning when it defended imperialism 'in its best sense'. Such beneficent imperialism involved not only encouragement of white colonial self-government, but also acceptance of 'a binding duty to perform highly irksome or offensive tasks'. In this spirit, desire to bring 'civilization' (including Christianity) to backward coloured races was often advanced during the last quarter of the century as a main reason for taking territory. In reality, the prime motivation behind late-Victorian colonial expansion was never so altruistic.[3]

The 'scramble for Africa' – first so-named by *The Times* (15.9.1884) –

started in the late 1870s and the main stage was over by the end of the century, along with a similar scramble in the Pacific. Britain gained much territory; but the onset of these scrambles meant a real decline in her world power. Before this period only Britain and France had shown much interest in Africa; and a tacit working arrangement had left the French predominant in the north, but a British 'informal empire' supreme along most of the coastline of West, South, and East Africa. This had enabled Britain to trade without the responsibilities of government. But from the 1870s the French repudiated this tacit arrangement, and began a competition for African territory in which they were soon joined by other powers, most notably by the new Germany.[4] British claims to 'paramountcy' were brushed aside; the test now became 'effective occupation'. Britain found herself joining in the rush for formal control of large areas, sometimes to secure strategic points, sometimes for reasons of trade or hoped-for trade, or for the exploitation of raw materials. Britain's increasing involvement in Egypt and the Nile valley gave her a particular interest in East Africa, while in South Africa she wanted to consolidate British predominance. Contemporaries were engaged, exclaimed Lord Rosebery in 1893, in 'pegging out claims for the future ... We have to look forward beyond the chatter of platforms and the passions of party to the future of the race – to take our share in the partition of the world which we have not forced on, but which has been forced on us'.[5]

Of all the new African acquisitions of the 1880s only British Bechuanaland was annexed outright. The rest became 'protectorates' or 'spheres of influence'. This nomenclature reflected British regret at the need to extend formal rule.[6] In employing this approach Gladstone liked to think that he was still minimizing British commitments. In reality, the process of imperial expansion was both irresistible and irreversible, and it went forward as much under Liberal as under Conservative Governments.

2

Punch (21.2.1885) pictured opinion about colonies as divided into two schools – 'scuttle v. grab'. The word 'scuttle' had first come into use in this sense about 1883 with reference to the suggested evacuation of Egypt. Seeley's *Expansion of England*, published in that year, contrasted the 'bombastic' and the 'pessimistic' schools. Late-Victorian Liberals were often charged by Conservatives with being 'Little Englanders'. In fact, very few Liberals wanted to abandon the empire, though many followed Sir William Harcourt in wanting 'consolidation', not further expansion: 'it is a greater and a wiser policy to cultivate an Empire than to boom an Empire'.[7] On the other hand, no responsible British statesman wanted unlimited annexation. Only Cecil Rhodes – the thrusting imperialist businessman and politician in southern Africa

– had dreamt in his youth of Britain settling not only the whole of Africa, but also the whole of South America, much of the Middle East, and the Pacific islands, before ultimately reuniting with the United States.[8]

'Your empire, if we mean it to live, must grow, must steadily grow. If it ceases to grow it will begin to decay.' So proclaimed Lord Salisbury, the Conservative leader, in 1884. The empire, in his view, provided 'the necessary condition of that commercial prosperity and of that industrial activity which are the bread of life to millions of our people'. Salisbury seemed to be accepting (in an often used contemporary expression) that 'trade follows the flag'.[9] The statistics of exports, imports, and investment can now be shown not to have justified this belief:

	Percentage share of exports of British produce				
	Europe	USA	British Empire	South America	China and Japan
1880–4	33.7	12.2	34.5	6.9	3.1
1910–13	33.6	6.2	35.8	9.6	5.0

The proportion of British imports from empire countries varied little between 1870 and 1900. From 1900 the share of empire imports – especially of foodstuffs – did begin to rise, reaching nearly one-quarter of total imports by 1910. But some 80 per cent of these imports came from long-established white colonies and from India, not from the new tropical colonies. Sixty per cent of overseas investment went to foreign countries; and of the 40 per cent invested in the empire nearly all went to settled colonies. In 1914 over two-thirds of imperial investment lay in Canada, Australasia, and South Africa, and a further one-fifth in India and Ceylon.[10]

Joseph Chamberlain, Colonial Secretary from 1895 to 1903, looked forward to a more or less self-sufficient British Empire, which would flourish upon the exchange of British manufactures for colonial foodstuffs and raw materials. He came to believe that such an empire would need tariff protection, and also some new form of government. Eventually in 1903 he launched his 'tariff reform' campaign (see below, p. 457). Schemes for imperial federation between the United Kingdom and the white self-governing colonies had been discussed by enthusiasts since the 1870s.[11] Some proposals envisaged the colonies sending representatives to the Westminster House of Commons, and perhaps peers to the House of Lords. But true federationists wanted the formation of a new Imperial Parliament, to which the Westminster and colonial assemblies would all be subordinate.

The Imperial Federation League was formed in 1884, with W. E. Forster as its first president. Its only lasting achievement was to persuade the Salisbury Government to hold an official conference when the colonial ministers came to London for the 1887 Golden Jubilee

celebrations. A similar Colonial Conference was held at the time of the
Diamond Jubilee; and thereafter conferences were called every four or
five years.[12] This was as far as the colonial politicians were prepared to
go in accepting formal links. When in 1897 Chamberlain pressed the
idea of an Imperial Council, the colonials refused to commit themselves
to taxation by an imperial body upon which representation would be
related to population; and Chamberlain could not accept any scheme by
which the United Kingdom might be outvoted. Even Chamberlain's
alternative proposal for a consultative body received insufficient
support. The colonial politicians were jealous of their freedom of action.
They were also reluctant to contribute towards the costs of imperial
defence. Their loyalty to the idea of empire was not a loyalty which was
willing to be institutionalized or (still less) to be taxed.

Could this loyalty be encouraged by some other means? In 1884
during a speech in Australia Lord Rosebery had exclaimed that there
was 'no need for any nation, however great, leaving the Empire, because
the Empire is a commonwealth of nations'. In *Oceana, or England and
Her Colonies* (1886) J. A. Froude, the historian, remarked how 'the
English race do not like to be parts of an empire. But a "commonwealth"
of Oceana held together by common blood, common interest, and a
common pride in the great position which unity can secure – such a
commonwealth as this may grow of itself if politicians can be induced to
leave it alone.'[13] The way forward to an informal association of self-
governing states – all recognizing the same sovereign – had been pointed
by Lord Durham's famous report on Canada (1839), which had
provided the necessary political ideas; and by the British North America
Act of 1867, which had established the first 'Dominion'. At the 1897
Colonial Conference Lord Salisbury accepted that 'a great experiment'
was being attempted, 'trying to sustain such an empire entirely upon the
basis of mutual goodwill, sympathy, and affection'[14]

The 1897 jubilee celebrations represented the peak of imperial
enthusiasm in England.[15] The special golden issue of the *Daily Mail* (23
June) was rhapsodic about the white colonial troops in the jubilee
parade through London, 'every man such a splendid specimen and
testimony to the Greatness of the British Race . . . the sun never looked
down until yesterday on the embodiment of so much energy and power'.
The *Mail* was impressed too by the good humour and orderliness of the
watching crowds, which (it suggested) reflected 'the qualities of
government and organization which have made the Empire great'. 'We
send out a boy here and a boy there and the boy takes hold of the savages
of the part he comes to, and teaches them to march and shoot as he tells
them, to obey him and believe in him and die for him and the Queen.'
The British Empire, the *Mail* concluded with satisfaction, was a 'world-
shaping force'.

The correct attitude towards the coloured citizens of the new tropical
empire was discussed by Joseph Chamberlain at the Royal Colonial
Institute in 1897. The white colonials were 'part of ourselves'; the

coloured millions, on the other hand, were ruled as a duty under 'the great *Pax Britannica*', which brought them security and 'comparative prosperity'.[16] Chamberlain tried hard while Colonial Secretary to encourage the development of the tropical colonies along efficient business lines. He knew that private capitalists were reluctant to invest in such places, and he wanted to employ Government money for the exploitation of their soils and products. Some useful West Indian colonial development grants were made; but Chamberlain found it impossible to extract more than small amounts from a parsimonious Treasury, which was not stirred by his vision of an ultimately self-sufficient empire.

3

Chamberlain was much more successful in carrying opinion with him in support of his South African policies.[17] By the end of the century British predominance in southern Africa was being challenged by the growing strength of the Boers. Vast quantities of gold had been found near Johannesburg in 1886, and this had transformed the Transvaal into a prosperous state. The hope was receding that the Boers would one day again join a British-led federation within the empire, as they had briefly done in the 1870s. Left to itself the Transvaal now seemed likely to become the dominant force in southern Africa – especially if given support by the Germans, whom the Boers preferred to the British. The efforts of Cecil Rhodes to extend British control by means of the British South Africa Company (1889) were running into difficulties during the early nineties. Hopes of an 'all red on the map' Cape to Cairo railway route had been frustrated by the German occupation of Tanganyika; and many of the potential settlers of the new 'Rhodesia' had gone instead to seek their fortunes as *uitlanders* in the Transvaal goldfields. The chartered company idea was a characteristic British compromise, which allowed intervention without the expense of colonial adminis-tration. Other chartered companies had been formed in Borneo (1881), Nigeria (1886), and East Africa (1886). But such private enterprise on the frontiers of empire could lead to irregular behaviour; and this was to be strikingly demonstrated by the damaging episode of the Jameson raid.

On 29 December 1895 Dr L. S. Jameson, an associate of Rhodes, galloped into the Transvaal at the head of an armed body of mounted men – variously numbered between 350 and 500. His ostensible purpose was to protect British women and children during an expected rising of the *uitlanders*.[18] They now numbered as many as 44,000, and they certainly felt dissatisfied about their status. They had not been given full voting equality by the Boers, who were understandably determined to retain control of their republic. Yet, despite strong prompting from Rhodes and his friends, the *uitlanders* did not rise; and their failure to do so suggested that their second-class position was really neither unbearable nor unprofitable. Jameson's action was exposed the more clearly as an inexcusable incursion into a foreign state. It had not even been glorious in its failure, for he soon surrendered. Chamberlain had known of the efforts to encourage a rising, though he was not directly responsible for the raid. The extent of the Colonial Secretary's indirect involvement was not admitted at the time. A House of Commons select committee of inquiry in 1897 failed to press hard for the truth; perhaps because two Liberals, Rosebery and Harcourt, had themselves been involved with Rhodes before they left office in June 1895. The inquiry was described by one undeceived observer as 'the lying-in-state at Westminster'.

The German Kaiser sent a congratulatory telegram to President Kruger of the Transvaal on the failure of the raid. This undiplomatic act served only to emphasize the potential for mischief of German policy in southern Africa. Chamberlain's determination to secure federation was only strengthened by the failure of Rhodes and Jameson. An important Colonial Office memorandum in March 1896 described the Transvaal as 'the richest spot on earth'.[19] Henceforward the British Government abandoned indirect methods, and began to press the Transvaal Government directly. In 1897 a vigorous and aggressive new High Commissioner was sent out to the Cape, Sir Alfred Milner. From this point – given that the Boers were a proud, even an obstinate people – war became probable, though Milner and Chamberlain seem until a late stage to have believed that Kruger was bluffing. He made some concessions over the *uitlander* franchise; but he refused to accept any electoral system under which the Boer electorate could be outweighted by the *uitlander* voters, and he also demanded the abandonment of British claims to 'suzereignty'.

By the autumn of 1899 the Boers had decided to act while they still retained local superiority in numbers of fighting men. They delivered an ultimatum which set off hostilities on 12 October 1899. The British army was not yet ready for war, as large reinforcements were still on their way to South Africa. The army, moreover, was unprepared for conflict with the mounted Boer farmers on the veldt, who immediately used their mobility and skill as horsemen to inflict a series of defeats upon the British.[20] The Boers invaded the Cape and Natal, and besieged the strategic towns of Kimberley, Mafeking, and Ladysmith. During 'black week' (10–15 December) British relieving forces suffered three separate reverses at Stormberg, Magersfontein, and Colenso. Lord Roberts was hurried out as commander-in-chief, with Kitchener as his chief-of-staff. Eventually some 450,000 men were collected under their command to fight a maximum of 60,000 Boers. 7,792 imperial troops were killed or died of wounds; 20,811 were wounded; and as many as 13,000 died from disease, chiefly from enteric fever. The Boers lost some 4,000 men killed in action. In money terms the war cost the British over £200 million – a huge sum by the standards of Victorian 'little wars'.[21]

By the autumn of 1900 the main fighting was over. The sieges had been raised, and Pretoria taken. But guerilla warfare, at which the Boers proved highly resourceful, unexpectedly dragged on for a further eighteen months. To hunt down the Boer raiders the British army was forced into a policy of farm-burning, along with the confinement of Boer families in concentration camps. Deficiencies in sanitation and diet caused the deaths of some 20,000 women and children in the camps. In a widely noticed public speech Campbell-Bannerman, the Liberal leader, fiercely attacked 'methods of Barbarism' in South Africa – words which were intended not as an attack upon the British army but upon its political masters.[22] Peace was eventually concluded at Vereeniging in May 1902. The Transvaal and Orange Free State were absorbed into the British Empire; but the Boers were promised future self-government. Though they had finally lost the war, they were soon to win the peace.

'The War' had filled the newspapers for months on end. *Soldiers of the Queen* and *Good-Bye Dolly Gray* became the songs of the day, played and sung everywhere. The relief of Mafeking was celebrated in May 1900 with unprecedented enthusiasm verging upon hysteria by large crowds in London and other towns. 'We accepted Waterloo and Trafalgar more calmly than this deliverance of a few hundred Colonial volunteers besieged in a Bechuanaland village. The electric rapidity with which the populace of London poured into the streets the moment the news of the relief became known was, in itself, an astounding phenomenon. At ten o'clock on Friday evening, 18 May, the main public thoroughfares presented their usual aspect. By half-past ten they were blocked and choked by seething crowds, waving flags, blowing horns, shrieking and howling in a frenzy of delight.' So remarked the *Anglo-Saxon Review* (June 1900). Left-wing intellectuals and 'pro-Boers' deplored this jingoism. 'Vainglory is a characteristic which a jingo-ridden people exhibits in common with the child and the savage.' So contended J. A. Hobson in *The Psychology of Jingoism* (1901). Yet the jingoism of Mafeking night was perhaps an expression of relief rather than of vainglory. The *Anglo-Saxon Review* thought that the public was celebrating a danger escaped as much as a victory won. 'There have been many much greater wars than this South African Campaign, but perhaps no other which so tended to "get upon the nerves" of large populations.' Jingo feeling was perhaps most strongly sustained among the lower middle classes – white collar workers and the like – for whom the *Daily Mail* was the favourite newspaper.[23]

4

Victory in South Africa had been preceded by victory in the north.[24] Gordon's death was avenged by a crushing victory over the dervishes of the Soudan at Omdurman in September 1898. The triumph of 8,200 British and 17,600 Egyptian soldiers over double the number of Soudanese represented an achievement of planning and technology.

River steamers were used as transports, a railway was built, and 80 big guns and 44 Maxim machine-guns were deployed. As a result, 9,700 Soudanese were killed for the loss of only 20 British officers and 462 men. Control of the Soudan and Nile valley was at last assured. A final French challenge in Africa faded away a few weeks later when a small military expedition which had reached Fashoda, on the Nile 400 miles upstream from Khartoum, was forced to withdraw by a show of force. The French found themselves in a weak position both militarily and in diplomatic terms. Lord Salisbury had recently ensured the acquiescence of the Germans by making an agreement with them about the future disposal of the Portuguese Empire in the event of its collapse. War with France seemed possible; but the French finally accepted humiliation and gave up their claims.[25]

In May 1900 at the annual conference of the Primrose League Lord Salisbury looked back – at the height of the Boer War – upon the imperial history of the previous twenty years. 'All the wide territories which the Mahdi ruled with barbarous and atrocious cruelty have now been brought under the civilizing influence of the British Government.' The 'great blunder' of the death of Gordon had been 'erased'. The even greater humiliation of defeat by the Boers at Majuba was now being avenged. Lord Roberts was retaking 'the territories which ought never to have been released', and was restoring to South Africa 'the only chance it has of peace, of development, and of tranquillity'.[26] Salisbury was trying to sound confident. Nevertheless, imperial assurance had been shaken by the size of the effort needed to defeat the Boers. Kipling's poem, *The Lesson*, appeared in *The Times* of 29 July 1901:

We have forty million reasons for failure, but not a single excuse.
So the more we work and the less we talk the better results we shall get –
We have had an imperial lesson; it may make us an Empire yet!

Notes

1. A. V. Dicey, *Law and Opinion in England* (1905), pp. 455–6.
2. *Ibid.*, p. 450. See especially R. Koebner and H. D. Schmidt, *Imperialism* (1964), pp. 28–9, 95, 148–9.
3. See especially C. C. Eldridge, *Victorian Imperialism* (1978) and references there.
4. See especially E. F. Penrose (ed.), *European Imperialism and the Partition of Africa* (1975); and W. R. Louis (ed.), *Imperialism* (1976), and references there – notably R. Robinson and J. Gallaher, *Africa and the Victorians* (1961).
5. G. Bennett (ed.), *The Concept of Empire* (2nd edn, 1962), pp. 310–11.
6. B. Porter, *The Lion's Share, A Short History of British Imperialism, 1850–1970* (1975), p. 114.
7. A. G. Gardiner, *Life of Sir William Harcourt* (1923), II, pp. 496–7.
8. J. G. Lockhart and C. M. Woodhouse, *Rhodes* (1963), pp. 69–70. See also J. S. Galbraith, 'Cecil Rhodes and his "Cosmic Dreams", A Reassessment', *Journal of Imperial and Commonwealth History*, I (1972–3); and J. Flint, *Cecil Rhodes* (1976).

9. *The Times*, 5 April 1884. See especially S. B. Saul, *Studies in British Overseas Trade, 1870–1914* (1960), part II; D. K. Fieldhouse, *Economics and Empire, 1830–1914* (1973); and F. Crouzet, 'Trade and Empire: the British Experience from the Establishment of Free Trade until the First World War', in B. M. Ratcliffe (ed.), *Great Britain and Her World, 1750–1914* (1975).

10. See A. R. Hall (ed.), *The Export of Capital from Britain, 1870–1914* (1968); and P. L. Cottrell, *British Overseas Investment in the Nineteenth Century* (1975).

11. See especially G. W. Martin, 'The Idea of Imperial Federation', in R. Hyam and G. Martin, *Reappraisals in British Imperial History* (1975).

12. See especially J. E. Kendle, *The Colonial and Imperial Conferences, 1887–1911* (1967).

13. G. Bennett (ed.), *The Concept of Empire* (2nd edn, 1962), p. 283; R. Koebner and H. D. Schmidt, *Imperialism* (1964), pp. 182–3, 233. See especially N. Mansergh, *The Commonwealth Experience* (1969), part one.

14. G. Bennett (ed.), *The Concept of Empire* (2nd edn, 1962), pp. 321–2.

15. See J. Morris, *Pax Britannica, The Climax of an Empire* (1968); and B. Porter, *The Lion's Share, A Short History of British Imperialism, 1850–1970* (1975), Chs. IV, V.

16. G. Bennett (ed.), *The Concept of Empire* (2nd edn, 1962), p. 318.

17. See A. Porter, 'Lord Salisbury, Mr Chamberlain and South Africa, 1895–9', *Journal of Imperial and Commonwealth History*, I (1972).

18. See especially Jean van der Poel, *The Jameson Raid* (1951); J. S. Marais, *The Fall of Kruger's Republic* (1961); J. Butler, *The Liberal Party and the Jameson Raid* (1968); and D. Judd, *Radical Joe* (1977), Ch. 9.

19. R. Robinson and J. Gallagher, *Africa and the Victorians* (1961), p. 434.

20. See especially B. Farwell, *The Great Boer War* (1977). Also J. Symons, *Buller's Compaign* (1963).

21. L. S. Amery (ed.), *The Times History of the War in South Africa, 1899–1902*, VI (1909), pp. 605–7, VII (1909), pp. 24–5.

22. J. Wilson, *C–B: A Life of Sir Henry Campbell-Bannermann* (1973) pp. 349–51.

23. See especially H. Pelling, *Popular Politics and Society in Late Victorian Britain* (1968), Ch. 5; and R. Price, *An Imperial War and the British Working Classes* (1972).

24. R. Robinson and J. Gallaher, *Africa and the Victorians* (1961), Ch. XII; R. Hyam, *Britain's Imperial Century, 1815–1914* (1976) pp. 108–9.

25. See especially G. N. Sanderson, *England, Europe and the Upper Nile, 1882–99* (1965).

26. *The Times*, 10 May 1900.

Chapter 20

Foreign policy: *'Regard him as insane'*

It was a basic assumption of Victorian foreign policy, and of Victorian public opinion, that 'Britannia rules the waves'.[1] An article by Sir Robert Giffen, the statistician, on 'The Standard of Strength for Our Army' (*Nineteenth Century*, June 1901) started from an expectation of naval supremacy. 'The condition of the British Empire without command of the sea is hardly conceivable ... We should be liable to blockade at home and to the ruin of our foreign commerce, nor could we keep India or any other dependency by force.' The generals often argued that a naval disaster might allow an invader to land, and that therefore the army needed to be strong; but they were answered variously that British naval strength made disaster unlikely; that a small enemy landing could be defeated by the existing regular, militia, and volunteer troops in the United Kingdom; and that without conscription (which was unacceptable) no British army could be raised which would be large enough to resist a foreign landing in strength. This last point made it the more necessary to ensure the continuance of naval supremacy in home waters – at the same time as supremacy over the world's oceans remained hardly less essential for the protection of the British Empire and of British trade. A large part of this trade now consisted of food importation. Admiral Sir John Fisher, the dynamic Edwardian First Sea Lord, contended that if the navy were not supreme, no army however large would be of any use. 'It's not *invasion* we have to fear if our Navy is beaten. IT'S STARVATION!'

Naval supremacy gave Britain her position as the only world power. Foreigners might be envious, but British opinion was satisfied that this widespread strength was being used for the promotion of international peace and prosperity. The main challengers to British supremacy at sea were the French and the Russians. About 1860 the French took the lead in the introduction of ironclad warships; and a scare erupted about the possible superiority of the French navy, and about Napoleon III's supposed plans for an invasion of southern England. Technical change always posed problems of timing for the Admiralty, which could not afford to fall behind but which did not wish to waste money by scrapping ships until the last safe moment. Foreigners were often left to take initiatives, but British superiority in speed of shipbuilding and in technology was then used to make up lost ground. The French averaged five years to complete a battleship, the British three years three months.

The changeover to ironclads was successfully made in the 1860s and the French challenge faded. For some twenty years British naval predominance was maintained with ease and economy. But then in 1884 came another naval scare. W. T. Stead, editor of the *Pall Mall Gazette*, revealed in a series of articles on 'The Truth about the Navy' that France had been engaged upon a major ship construction programme. He claimed that the French and British fleets now stood about equal in numbers of first-class battleships. The resultant clamour forced the Gladstone Government to increase the naval estimates. In 1880 these had stood at £10,200,000: by 1890 they were to reach £13,800,000, and by 1900 £29,200,000. The mid 1880s certainly marked a low point in terms both of the quality and numerical superiority of the British navy. The possibility of war with Russia in 1885 found the Admiralty far from ready. The fleet was too miscellaneous – a collection of often inefficient ships of different sizes and capabilities, almost impossible to organize for mutual support in battle. Moreover, sailors had become too absorbed in a peacetime round of 'spit and polish'. This revealing expression was apparently coined within the Victorian navy.

By the late 1880s the prospect of a Franco-Russian alliance was growing. There emerged the danger of a simultaneous challenge to the Mediterranean fleet from two directions at once – as it tried to protect the lifeline of empire to Suez and India. In 1889 the Salisbury Government announced its intention of adopting a two-power standard. This meant the maintenance of a fleet of battleships and first-class cruisers not merely equal in numbers to those of the next two largest navies (the French and Russian), but with a sufficient further margin to be sure of defeating them in combination. The 1889 Naval Defence Act provided £21,500,000 for the construction of ten new battleships. Standardization of design in classes of ships was also introduced. The Act, however, only stimulated France and Russia to more construction of their own; and by 1893–4 another naval scare forced a further round of British building. The French and Russian navies were much less efficient than alarmists claimed, but the British were in no mood to take chances. The writings of the American Admiral Mahan – notably, *The Influence of Sea Power upon History, 1660–1783* (1890) and *The Influence of Sea Power upon the French Revolution and the Empire* (1892) – had exercised a powerful effect upon lay as well as upon professional naval opinion. Mahan demonstrated by historical example how sea power, silent but far reaching, had shaped the rise and fall of nations in peace and war. In war he was an advocate of concentration of force. Command of the seas, he believed, would be decided as in Nelson's day by pitched battle between opposed fleets of capital ships. In 1895 the Navy League was formed to publicize the truth that continued British command of the seas was essential for the survival of Britain and the British Empire.

By the time of the Diamond Jubilee naval review at Spithead in June 1897 naval supremacy seemed for the moment to be firmly assured. 165

British warships, including 21 first-class battleships and 54 cruisers, were reviewed by the Queen. The press waxed enthusiastic about this greatest-ever naval spectacle – 'witnessed by the ships sent by all the great powers of the world, and, without unseemly boasting, we may assume that they have taken the lesson to heart' (*The Times*, 29 June). Yet in relative numerical terms British superiority was much less than at the start of Victoria's reign; and in terms of guns and armour, strategy or tactics, the British advantage had become – after so many years of peace – an uncertain quantity. And now the Germans, with all their energy and their new industrial strength, were about to enter the naval race.

2

By the 1880s Europe was moving into the era of competing alliances, which was to continue until the ultimate confrontation of 1914. The rival groupings – of Germany and Austria (1879), joined by Italy (1882), on the one hand; and of France and Russia (1894), on the other – were evidence of a deadlock which preserved a general peace in Europe for a generation. But this was at the price of making general war the only alternative.

The Berlin settlement of 1878 had left much undecided with regard to Balkan frontiers and to future Turkish policy.[2] The Turks proved difficult allies, and during 1879 Disraeli and Salisbury sacrificed much of their credit at Constantinople by pressing hard for reforms. On his return to office in 1880 Gladstone set out to conduct his diplomacy through the concert of powers. In his third Midlothian speech of 1879 he had defined six principles of 'right policy':

1. good government at home;
2. the preservation of peace abroad;
3. 'to keep the Powers of Europe in union together';
4. the avoidance of entangling alliances;
5. acknowledgment of the equal rights of all nations;
6. 'sympathy with freedom'.[3]

The powers did work together during 1880–1 over frontier rectifications for Montenegro and Greece, but only Gladstone was truly committed to the idea of concert. Bismark regarded it as a direct challenge to his own plan to dominate Europe with the help of allies. Paradoxically, concerted coercion of Turkey – which Gladstone recommended to secure tranquillization of the Balkans and of the Near East – proved likely to produce more disturbance than peace; for the Turks obstinately resisted pressure. In Turkey, as in South Africa and Egypt, Gladstone's lofty Midlothian policies were soon going astray.

In 1881 Bismarck succeeded in re-constituting the Three Emperors' League on a formal basis. He was thereby able to keep France without an ally for a few more years. He remained contemptuous of Gladstone's high moral pretensions in foreign affairs, though fearful that his

Liberalism might encourage progressive forces in Europe. In 1884 the German Ambassador at St Petersburg was assured by Bismarck that Gladstone was 'devoid of all qualities of a statesman – apart from his disastrous rhetorical gift – to such a degree that I feel inclined to regard him as insane'. Each month of Gladstone's regime, claimed Bismarck, was bringing the British Empire closer to collapse into a republic.[4]

Lord Salisbury returned to office in 1885 as Prime Minister and Foreign Secretary in the middle of the Penjdeh crisis with Russia. He was much concerned that Gladstone's policies in Europe and Asia had left Britain in damaging isolation. This had been demonstrated during the international conferences of 1884–5 to settle the Egyptian finances. Bismarck had worked with the French to retain maximum control for the Continental powers. The Liberals, Salisbury concluded, had 'at last achieved their long desired "Concert of Europe". They have succeeded in uniting the Continent of Europe – against England.'[5] Yet it was the danger to security in the Mediterranean and on the frontiers of India which most worried Salisbury, not isolation as such. He skilfully set out during his 1885–6 and 1886–92 administrations to protect Britain's imperial position by seeking support and by making agreements on specific issues, while at the same time avoiding long-term commitments. This was a difficult course to follow successfully because the European powers were now putting their trust in alliances and were anxious to gain permanent benefits from British co-operation.

Even the Gladstone Government had prepared for war during the Penjdeh crisis of 1885, in opposition to further Russian encroachments towards the frontiers of India. On taking office, Salisbury tried to secure diplomatic support from Bismarck, but with little success. Fortunately, although the Russians were seeking maximum diplomatic advantage, they did not want to press to the point of war; and Salisbury was eventually able to settle the crisis on acceptable terms, with the Russians yielding up the important Zulficar pass.[6]

Europe was soon involved in a fresh crisis following the unification of the two Bulgarian provinces in September 1885, with the Bulgarians making anti-Russian gestures which infuriated the Tsar. The alarming possibility of Russian intervention in the Balkans drew Britain and Austria together, though for a time each waited for the other to take the lead. Then Bismarck, who was facing a quite different crisis because of the refusal of Austria and Italy to accept each other's terms for the renewal of the Triple Alliance, prompted the Italians to seek agreement with England.[7] Upon Italian initiative a secret agreement was signed between Italy and Britain on 12 February 1887 in the form of an exchange of notes, which pledged the two powers to prevent the domination of any other great power over territories adjacent to the Mediterranean. Six weeks later Austria acceded to this understanding, which has become known as the first Mediterranean agreement. It made the renewal of the Triple Alliance possible, and it suited Salisbury admirably. During the negotiations Bismarck had undertaken to keep

France quiet, for he welcomed the prospect of Britain joining in the maintenance of the status quo. By skilful diplomacy Salisbury contrived later in the year to negotiate a second agreement from a stronger diplomatic position, even forcing Bismarck to admit that Germany now needed British friendship. This second agreement of December 1887 was more explicit in support of Turkey, and was aimed at Russia.

The likely enemies of the British Empire remained France and/or Russia, not Germany. In military and economic terms the Triple Alliance outweighed France and Russia taken together. The balance of power had lost its equilibrium. But France and Russia were the restless powers of Europe, whereas Bismarck's Germany had become committed to maintaining the status quo. British policy therefore still tended to favour Germany and Austria, though not to the point of wanting formal alliance. Salisbury declined an alliance offer from Bismarck in January 1889. Even so, on the death of the old German Emperor in 1888 W. H. Smith, as Leader of the House of Commons, had described the German people as 'our allies and our friends'. In 1890 a settlement was made with Germany whereby, in return for the cession of Heligoland, which Britain had held off the north German coast since the beginning of the century, the Germans gave up claims to large parts of East Africa, including Zanzibar. Again the word 'alliance' was loosely used, this time by Salisbury himself. He warned the Queen that postponement of a settlement in Africa would make it difficult to retain German friendship, 'and would force us to change our systems of alliance in Europe. The alliance of France instead of the alliance of Germany must necessarily involve the early evacuation of Egypt under very unfavourable conditions'.[8]

3

The 1890s were to witness a more strident atmosphere than the 1880s, in diplomacy as in the arts. Bismarck was dismissed by the unpredictable young Kaiser William II in 1890. Russia broke away from Germany to form the Dual Entente with France (1894). In 1896 the Kaiser sent his congratulatory telegram to Kruger on the failure of the Jameson raid. And at the end of the decade Germany began to build a large navy. She was, in short, asserting herself in a challenging new way, not simply as the strongest Continental power but as an aspiring world power. All this was being attempted without the skilled hand of Bismarck in control. He had been cool towards colonial expansion by Germany; but from the mid 1880s domestic political necessities had led him to countenance the acquisition of colonies. He then began to use colonial aspirations and disputes as counters in his diplomatic manoeuvres, especially with Britain.[9] In general, Salisbury was willing to keep Bismarck's friendship by giving way in Africa and elsewhere except where imperial strategic interests were involved.

During the 1890s, however, fears of German ambitions in Europe and beyond were growing. In September 1897 the new *Daily Mail* sent its star reporter, G. W. Steevens, to describe life 'Under the Iron Heel' in sixteen articles. 'Rivalry in projects of colonisation and empire – these, beyond question, are the chief springs that feed German hostility towards England . . . Both as a nation and as individuals the Germans detest us . . . It is idle to ignore it.' An anonymous article about Germany in the *Contemporary Review* for December 1898 was entitled plainly 'The Arch-Enemy of England'. 'The plan of the German Emperor is the revival of the Continental alliance against England.' Growing German commercial rivalry was regarded as part of a deliberately hostile plan, and was therefore much more resented than American rivalry.

By the mid 1890s Britain could again be described as 'isolated'. Was this a cause for concern or satisfaction? The expression 'splendid isolation' was first used by Canadian politicians early in 1896, and it immediately gained currency in England. G. J. Goschen, the First Lord of the Admiralty, proclaimed that isolation was chosen and 'splendid' – it allowed 'freedom to act as we choose', not like other powers 'bartering favour for favour'.[10] On the other hand, Lord Salisbury always denied that a policy of chosen isolation was being followed, splendid or otherwise. In the middle of the Boer War when the German Ambassador referred to Britain's diplomatic isolation, Salisbury simply asked 'Have we ever felt that danger practically?' Not since the Napoleonic wars, noted the Prime Minister, had the British Isles themselves been in real danger. Yet he never denied the need to work with other powers to protect British interests at a distance, notably in the Near and Far East.

In 1886 and again in 1892 Salisbury was succeeded as Foreign Secretary by the Liberal Lord Rosebery. A bi-partisan tradition in foreign policy now began to develop. Britain's place in the world was less comfortable, and continuity of policy had become the more desirable. Yet changes in the past had often been more a matter of style and emphasis than of basic alteration. Even Gladstone on return to office in 1880 had 'sought for a ground of action which might be common to both political parties', and had found it 'in the unfulfilled clauses of the Treaty of Berlin'. Regardless of differences in domestic politics, declared Rosebery in 1895, 'we should preserve a united front abroad' so that foreign statesmen would realise that they were dealing not with a temporary Ministry 'but with a great, powerful, and united nation'.[11] Nations were indeed now speaking unto nations – with momentous implications for future peace and war. Dynastic foreign policy had become a thing of the past, explained the *Manchester Guardian* (2.4.1887). 'No two Continental Powers will henceforth quarrel about trifles, but where the national welfare – or, in cynical language, the national interests – are seriously in question every Continental nation will stake the whole of its resources in their defence.'

Notes

1. See especially A. J. Marder, _The Anatomy of British Sea Power_ (1964); G. S. Graham, _The Politics of Naval Supremacy_ (1965); and P. M. Kennedy, _The Rise and Fall of British Naval Mastery_ (1976), Ch. 7.
2. See especially W. N. Medlicott, _Bismarck, Gladstone, and the Concert of Europe_ (1969).
3. W. E. Gladstone, _Midlothian Speeches, 1879_ (1879; reprinted 1971).
4. W. E. Medlicott, _Bismarck, Gladstone, and the Concert of Europe_ (1969), appendix II.
5. Lady Gwendolen Cecil, _Life of Robert, Marquis of Salisbury_, III (1931), p. 136. See especially Lillian Penson, _Foreign Affairs under the Third Marquis of Salisbury_ (1962); and J. A. S. Grenville, _Lord Salisbury and Foreign Policy_ (1970).
6. See especially R. L. Greaves, _Persia and the Defence of India, 1884–1892_ (1959); and D. Gillard, _The Struggle for Asia, 1828–1914_ (1977), Ch. 7.
7. See especially F. H. Hinsley, 'Bismarck, Salisbury and the Mediterranean Agreements of 1887', _Historical Journal_, I (1958); and C. J. Lowe, _Salisbury and the Mediterranean, 1886–1896_ (1965).
8. K. Bourne, _The Foreign Policy of Victorian England, 1830–1902_ (1970), p. 429. See especially D. R. Gillard, 'Salisbury's African Policy and the Heligoland Offer of 1890', _English Historical Review_, LXXI (1960).
9. See especially W. R. Louis, 'Great Britain and German Expansion in Africa, 1884–1919', in P. Gifford and W. R. Louis (eds.), _Britain and Germany in Africa_ (1967), Ch. 1.
10. _The Times_, 27 February 1896; K. Bourne, _The Foreign Policy of Victorian England, 1830–1902_ (1970), p. 463. See especially C. Howard, _Splendid Isolation_ (1967).
11. C. J. Lowe, _The Reluctant Imperialists_ (1967), II, p. 9; H. J. Hanham (ed.), _The Nineteenth Century Constitution_ (1969), p. 99.

Edwardian England, 1901–14

Chapter 21

Introduction: *'They place the golden age behind them'*

1

The Edwardian age strictly defined ran from the accession of Edward VII in 1901 to his death in 1910. In certain contexts, however, it can be taken as continuing until the outbreak of the First World War in 1914. Because it was followed by this unprecedented and terrible war of attrition, the world before 1914 came to be remembered by many surviving well-to-do Edwardians with indulgence and nostalgia. 'So placid was this brief golden halt that often as a small child, passionately addicted to reading books of history, I used to wonder whether its stream had not altogether dried up ... Nothing had happened for so long, and nothing would happen again ... Everything was calm and still and kindly.' So claimed Sir Osbert Sitwell at the beginning of his first volume of memoirs, published in 1945. Sitwell looked back to a golden age which had never been. In period the Edwardians were very well aware of their many pressing problems, economic, social, and political. 'They place the golden age behind them,' wrote *The Times* (19.1.1909), 'and assume that no generation ever had to deal with evils so great and perplexing as those of the present day.'

The death of Queen Victoria on 22 January 1901 had almost coincided with the start of the new century. This double change had left contemporaries with a strong sense of a new beginning. Very few could remember life without Victoria on the throne. 'It is like the roof being off the house to think of England queenless.'[1] When on the day after Victoria's death *The Times* compared the twentieth-century present with the nineteenth-century past it felt uneasy about Britain's position in the world. 'At the close of the reign we are finding ourselves somewhat less secure of our position than we could desire, and somewhat less abreast of the problems of the age than we ought to be, considering the initial advantages we secured.' In the *Fortnightly Review* for January 1901 J. L. Garvin published an article with the stark questioning title, 'Will England last the Century?' Another article in the *Westminster Review* for June was entitled 'What should England do to be Saved?' 'England has grown old, her national vitality is exhausted. She has arrived at the stage of senile decay, while the United States is just entering upon that of vigorous puberty.' The *Daily Mail*'s welcome to the new century had admitted that 'at this very critical moment in some inscrutable manner the old fire of energy seems to be waning within us.

We are entering stormy seas, and the time may be near when we shall have to fight in very truth for our life.' Optimism could still sometimes be found in competition with pessimism. But thirty years earlier it had been pessimism which had competed with optimism.

Pessimists or not, most of the younger generation seem to have been glad to be making a new beginning, to be putting the Victorians behind them. Within a very few years Victorian values had become almost incomprehensible, as G. K. Chesterton explained as early as 1904: 'It will appear to many a somewhat grotesque matter to talk about a period in which most of us were born and which has only been dead a year or two, as if it were a primal Babylonian empire of which only a few columns are left crumbling in the desert. And yet such is, in spirit, the fact. To the early Victorian period we have in a moment lost the key.' So wrote Chesterton in his study of G. F. Watts, the Victorian painter. 'Mr. Max Beerbohm waves a wand and a whole generation of great men and great achievement suddenly look mildewed and unmeaning.'. 'Debunking' the Victorians was to receive its ultimate expression in Lytton Strachey's *Eminent Victorians*, which was not published until 1918. But Strachey had started work before the outbreak of war in 1914; and his book was a product of the Edwardian mood, only reinforced by wartime disillusionment.[2] In 1901 an *Anglo-Saxon Review* article by Edmund Gosse on 'The Custom of Biography', published only two months after Victoria's death, had anticipated Strachey in deploring the Victorian custom of writing voluminous but piously uncritical biographies. Gosse's own *Father and Son* (1907), which analysed his relationship with his puritanical Victorian father, was to serve as a masterly example of critical sensitivity in biography and autobiography.

Nevertheless, Gosse in 1907 had to describe his book as a 'document'. The Victorians were already part of history. The process of change, which they themselves had sensed to be accelerating, had soon left them behind. The Edwardians were now sure of what their fathers and grandfathers had only begun to suspect, that accelerating and inescapable alteration did not necessarily mean improvement. Rupert Brooke, the poet, was impressed in 1910 by the contrast between his own environment and that of his Victorian uncle of seventy. 'The whole machinery of life, and the minds of every class and kind of men, change beyond recognition every generation. I don't know that "Progress" is certain. All I know is that change is.'[3] Change, pressure for change, and fear of change were widely apparent in Edwardian England – in dealings between men, between men and women, between classes; in relations between states; in economic life, in society, in politics, and in the arts. In 1909 Edmund Gosse published verses with the scarcely poetic but significant title of *Social Revolution*:

> We spoke of coming claims for social sway,
>   Of rising horde and shattered citadel,
>   And one thought all things surely must be well,
> And one had little faith, and murmured 'Nay!'

In the same year C. F. G. Masterman, a young Liberal minister and perceptive social observer, concluded his widely-read book on *The Condition of England* by emphasizing how social separation was as serious and as international a problem as diplomatic and military rivalry: 'with the vertical division between nation and nation armed to the teeth, and the horizontal division between rich and poor which has become a cosmopolitan fissure, the future of progress is still doubtful and precarious ... We are uncertain whether civilization is about to blossom into flower, or wither in a tangle of dead leaves and faded gold'.

Notes

1. A. C. Benson, *Diary* (n.d.), p. 43.
2. M. Holroyd, *Lytton Strachey*, I (1967), p. 13, II (1968), pp. 66–7, 230.
3. C. Hassall, *Rupert Brooke* (1964), p. 238.

Chapter 22

Economic life: *'An old man's world would not be a beautiful one'*

1

The population was still growing significantly during the Edwardian period:

	England and Wales	United Kingdom
1901	32,500,000	41,500,000
1911	36,100,000	45,200,000

But though numbers were continuing to increase, the total population was beginning to contain proportionately less young people and proportionately more middle-aged. The 1911 census *Report* illustrated this movement, which was marked even within the short span between the two censuses of 1901 and 1911:

Ratio of the proportional numbers enumerated at each age (1911 = 100)

	1881	1901	1911
Under 5	127	107	100
5–10	118	105	100
10–15	111	106	100
15–20	106	108	100
20–25	102	109	100
25–30	92	102	100

In the higher age groups the ratios moved the other way:

30–35	84	94	100
35–40	82	91	100
40–45	87	92	100
45–50	83	91	100
50–55	89	92	100
55–60	88	91	100

In 1881 almost 16,400,000 out of a population of nearly 26 million had been aged under 30; by 1911 the corresponding totals were 20,600,000 out of 36,100,000. At first the consequences of the late-Victorian decline in the birth rate had even been advantageous, since the economy was required to support proportionately fewer unproductive children. But by 1911 this temporary advantage had passed, and the census *Report* warned of the economic consequences of a lessening proportion 'of workers at the most economically efficient ages', and also of its worrying implications for the future supply of army and navy recruits. If the birth rate continued to fall alongside a falling death rate, *The Times* (1 May 1901) warned that the end would be a change in the whole atmosphere of society: 'an old man's world would not be a beautiful one. It would not be one with variety, sparkle, sunshine, mirth, and the charm of the unexpected ... we might begin to regret the advances of sanitary science'.

The fall in the birth rate for England and Wales, which had begun in the 1860s and was obvious from the 1870s, had still not been arrested. It steadied at 28.5 per thousand population during 1901–3, but then began to drop again to 24.1 by 1913. The rate per 1,000 women aged 15–44 fell in the same way. In the 1860s and 1870s this had exceeded 150 per thousand; by 1901 it was down to 114.5, and by 1913 it was 97.1. Although total population was still increasing, the annual number of births began to fall after reaching a peak of 948,000 in 1903. In 1913 it was 882,000 – the same as in 1880, when the population of England and Wales had been over 10 million less. The death rate improved markedly during the Edwardian years, from 16.9 per 1,000 in 1901 down to 13.8 in 1914. There were 552,000 deaths in England and Wales in 1901, only 505,000 in 1913. In particular, the infantile death rate – which at the end of the 1890s had slipped back to the high level of 1870 – was at last beginning to improve permanently. The death rate for male children under 5, which was never below 50.00 per 1,000 up to 1906, had fallen about one-quarter by 1914. The Edwardians had quite suddenly begun to succeed where the late-Victorians had tried but failed:[1]

Death rate under 1 year per 1,000 live births

	1891–1900	1910
All causes	153.30	105.44
Common infectious diseases	10.00	7.22
Tuberculous diseases	7.92	3.91
Diarrhoea and enteritis	27.05	12.64
Congenital, developmental and wasting diseases	44.44	40.46
All other categories	63.89	41.21

Some cities and towns remained much less healthy than average:[2]

Birth and death rates, England and Wales

	1891–1901		1901–1911	
	Birth rate	Death rate	Birth rate	Death rate
Towns:				
Large:				
London	29.8	17.9	27.5	14.6
8 Northern	31.9	20.4	29.8	17.3

Birth and death rates, England and Wales

	1891–1901		1901–1911	
	Birth rate	Death rate	Birth rate	Death rate
Textile:				
22 Northern	27.8	19.4	23.5	16.2
Residential:				
9 Northern	25.3	17.9	22.0	15.4
26 Southern	24.5	15.6	21.2	13.4
Colliery districts:				
9 Northern	35.9	19.2	32.9	19.5
Rural residues:				
12 Northern	27.6	17.1	24.5	14.6
12 Southern	26.0	15.8	22.7	13.4

These figures indicated how the birth rate remained relatively high among coal-mining families and low among textile families. Almost everywhere, however, it had fallen by one-quarter to one-third over thirty years. The Registrar-General published figures for the legitimate birth rates in 1911 among the various social classes:[3]

	Per thousand married males under 55
Upper and middle class	119
Intermediate class	132
Skilled workmen	153
Intermediate class	158
Unskilled workmen	213
Textile workers	125
Miners	230
Agricultural labourers	161
Working class overall	175

Use of contraceptives had now spread beyond the middle classes to aspiring working-class families. Such parents were keen for their limited numbers of children to rise into the middle class. The children benefited, but did the nation as a whole? The lowest classes were being left to produce proportionately more and more of the population. The Registrar-General remarked concernedly how 'the population is being recruited out of due proportion from its least successful and progressive elements'. Sydney Webb wrote a Fabian tract on *The Decline in the Birth-Rate* (1907) in which he estimated that preventive measures had deprived England and Wales of some 200,000 babies per year during the previous twenty years. A low-grade or foreign quarter of all parents, Webb concluded, was producing one-half of the next generation. 'This can hardly result in anything but national deterioration; or, as an

alternative, in this country gradually falling to the Irish and the Jews.'
But even these prolific races were beginning to reproduce less quickly.
'The ultimate future of these islands may be to the Chinese.' After thirty
years with an almost continuously falling official birth rate, the fear was
growing that by the middle of the twentieth century population growth,
which had been so fast during the nineteenth century, might have
stopped altogether. This had already almost happened in France. How
then would British industry compete? How then would the empire be
peopled and defended?[4]

Some alarmists added to the concern by suggesting that the
reproductive capacity of the more 'respectable' classes was actually in
decline. If this were correct, the birth-rate fall among such people could
not be reversed. The semi-official National Birth-Rate Commission,
appointed in 1913, eventually dismissed these alarms; but its report was
not published until 1916. It then demonstrated that the fall in the birth
rate resulted only from 'conscious limitation of fertility', plus the still
widespread practice of abortion among the industrial population. The
age of first marriage for women was still edging upwards, thereby
making smaller families the more likely. Whereas in 1871 almost 37.5
per cent of females under 25 were married, by 1911 the proportion was
only 25.35 per cent.[5]

Emigration overseas continued at a high level throughout the first
decade of the twentieth century, and in the years just before 1914 it
reached unprecedented levels. The empire now overtook the United
States as the main destination; for the Americans no longer wanted
unskilled workers. This shift offered some consolation to Edwardians
who 'thought imperially', and who believed that emigrants to the empire
might still contribute to the maintenance of Britain's position in the
world:[6]

	Total	USA	British North America	Australia/ New Zealand	South Africa	Total Empire	All other countries
Emigration from the United Kingdom. Annual averages (nearest thousand)							
1901–10	284	126	85	23	28	136	22
1911–13	464	123	189	85	28	302	39

Heavy emigration overseas helped to reduce the volume of internal
migration within England. This now showed chiefly as a movement into
the area round London, including movement from inner London to
suburbs beyond the boundaries of the London County Council. The
colliery districts were still absorbing fresh outside workmen; but old
staple industries such as textiles no longer needed even all the extra
labour provided by local natural increase:[7]

	Population aged 20–44, England and Wales (in thousands)			
	Migration		Natural increase and migration	
	1901–5	1906–10	1901–5	1906–10
North-western England	−18.9	−20.8	+133.5	+102.2
Northern England	−16.9	−27.6	+62.8	+48.8
Midlands	−27.0	−51.9	+139.6	+99.1
London (aged 15–44)	−96.0	−130.1	−9.5	−53.0
Counties round London	+92.4	+71.6	+212.3	+188.2
South Wales and Mon.	+36.6	+35.7	+87.4	+80.7
Yorkshire	−13.1	−17.8	+98.1	+68.5
Totals	−42.9	−140.9	+724.2	+534.5

The rapid expansion of commerce, the consumer industries, the distributive trades, and government – already noticed as a striking new feature of the last years of the nineteenth century – continued through the Edwardian years:[8]

	Occupation Index Numbers (1901 = 100)		
	1881	1891	1911
General or local government	69	83	130
Commerce	70	81	119
Food, tobacco, drink, lodging	87	98	115
Gas, water, electricity	48	69	113
Defence	83	86	109
Professional and subordinate	91	96	105
Conveyance	82	91	101
Mines and quarries	86	93	115
Metals, machines, etc.	87	89	106
Textiles	124	117	101
Agriculture	148	123	96

The number of coalminers in England and Wales increased from about 450,000 in the early 1880s to almost 1 million before 1914. But at the 1911 census the distributive trades emerged as the largest occupational grouping, followed by agriculture (widely defined and including market gardening):[9]

	Workers	Percentage
Distributive trades	2,133,000	11.9
Agriculture	1,499,000	8.4
Transport and communications	1,416,000	7.9
Textiles	1,359,000	7.6
Clothing	1,159,000	6.5
Mining, quarrying	1,128,000	6.3
Building	950,000	5.3

	Workers	Percentage
Engineering and shipbuilding	878,000	4.9
Professional services	798,000	4.4
Public administration and defence	701,000	3.9
Food, drink, and tobacco	554,000	3.1
Metal manufacture	509,000	2.8

2

The 1907 census of production set a value upon the output of British industry (selling value less cost of materials and work put out). For England and Wales this amounted to £603 million, and for the United Kingdom £712 million. Perhaps £50 million should have been added for trades not covered by the census. The largest values were:[10]

	(£)
Mining and quarrying	115,000,000
Textiles	95,000,000
Food, drink, and tobacco	87,000,000
Engineering, shipbuilding, and electrical goods	72,000,000
Metal manufacture	45,000,000
Building and contracting	43,000,000
Clothing	40,000,000
Public utilities and government departments	36,000,000
Paper and printing	33,000,000
Gas, electricity, and water	32,000,000
Chemical and allied trades	27,000,000

The 'great depression' – in so far as it had ever happened – was now over, although the trade cycle still had its upswings and downswings. The twentieth century opened in boom, another followed in 1905–7, and a strong boom (1910–13) had just faded before the outbreak of the First World War. The value of British exports rose again in the new century, after stagnating during the 1880s and 1890s:[11]

	Textiles		Cottons		Iron and steel		Machinery		Coal		Vehicles		Total
	£m.	%	£m.	%	£m.	%	£m.	%	£m.	%	£m.	%	£m.
1880–9	114.1	49	73.3	32	35.3	15	11.8	5	10.5	5	—		230.3
1890–9	104.3	44	67.2	28	32.5	14	16.1	7	17.5	7	1.1	0	237.1
1900–9	126.2	38	86.4	26	45.7	14	23.8	7	32.9	10	8.4	3	333.3

(At current prices: annual averages)

But the value of imports increased more than the value of exports:[12]

	Grain and flour		Groceries		Meat, dairy produce		Textile raw materials		Other raw materials		Manu-factured goods		Total
	£m.	%	£m.	%	£m.	%	£m.	%	£m.	%	£m.	%	£m.
1880–9	55.1	14	44.7	11	36.8	9	94.9	24	45.5	12	12.3	3	393.6
1890–9	55.1	13	42.1	10	51.7	12	89.8	21	52.0	12	15.7	4	435.8
1900–9	66.1	12	40.0	7	73.2	13	107.2	19	77.4	14	31.7	6	570.4

(Annual averages)

Moreover, the rate of growth of United Kingdom industrial production remained at the reduced level to which it had fallen in the 1880s and 1890s:[13]

	Percentage rate of increase
1860s–1870s	33.2
1870s–1880s	20.8
1880s–1890s	17.4
1890s–1900s	17.9
1895/1904–1905/14	18.0

The balance of payments was kept favourable by the continuous strengthening of invisible items, including the income from Britain's now huge foreign investments:[14]

	Balance of visible trade	Net shipping earnings	Profits, interest, dividends	Insurance, brokerage, com-missions	Emigrants, tourists, smugglers, govern-ment, all other	Balance of invisible trade	Net balance
1891–5	−134	+57	+124	+15	−10	+186	+52
1896–1900	−159	+62	+132	+16	−11	+199	+40
1901–5	−177	+71	+149	+18	−13	+226	+49
1906–10	−144	+89	+196	+22	−18	+290	+146
1911–13	−140	+100	+241	+27	−22	+346	+206

(Annual averages in £m.)

Cotton exports revived during the Edwardian years.[15] Unfortunately, the industry missed the chance to modernize upon this basis of prosperity. Instead, it hurried into building new mills by the hundred but filled them with traditional machinery. World demand for cottons was strong, which allowed the diversion of exports to undemanding markets in Asia and Africa; and this masked the increasingly exposed position of the industry. Production of steel ingots and castings in 1913 totalled 7,664,000 tons, compared with only 329,000 tons in 1871. At last the 'basic' process was gaining acceptance, being responsible for about 38 per cent of the 1913 output. But by this date Britain was making less than half as much steel as Germany and less than one-quarter as much as the United States:[16]

	Production of steel expressed as percentages of world production		
	United Kingdom	Germany/Saar	United States
1900–4	15.1	22.3	41.0
1905–9	12.4	22.1	43.5
1910–13	10.3	22.7	42.3

In 1912 German iron and steel exports first exceeded the British. Moreover, British imports of iron and steel were now running as high as 45 per cent of exports.

Coal exports were certainly booming, with an increase from just over 40 million tons per annum at the turn of the century to 73,400,000 tons in 1913.[17] This amounted to at least one-quarter of total production, whereas in the 1870s only about one-tenth had been exported. Nevertheless, massive exports of a basic raw material were not evidence of industrial good health. As Alfred Marshall, the economist, remarked, any generation which exported coal 'in order to pay for those manufactures in the production of which Britain should hold her own, will inflict an injury on coming generations'.[18] Productivity in the coal industry had been falling since it reached a peak of 319 tons per man employed in the 1880s. The easily-dug seams were running out; and this – along with the high proportion of new recruits at the coalface, and perhaps also because of reluctance to work as hard as in the past – had brought productivity at the end of the Edwardian period down to 257 tons per man. This meant a large rise in costs both to industry and to domestic consumers, for coal remained the fuel for most firms and most households. Productivity in United States coalmines, where machinery was extensively used, reached double or treble the British average. Overall American labour productivity was continuing to grow fast, whereas British productivity improvement had slowed right down:[19]

	Annual percentage increase in physical output per worker	
	United Kingdom	United States
1870–90	1.0	0.9
1890–1907	0.1	2.0

The value added in 1907 to the cost of materials by a worker in certain British manufacturing industries averaged £100; the comparable United States average was nearly £500.

One cause of this striking contrast may have been the small size and private character of most British firms. In 1914 nearly 80 per cent of British companies remained in private hands.[20] This meant that they could not appeal to the public for modernization capital. Owners were reluctant to enter the capital market for fear of losing control. The still small proportion of public companies did, indeed, contain a number of very large firms by the Edwardian period.[21] Amalgamations had been undertaken sometimes to improve competitiveness in home and world markets (as with the Imperial Tobacco Company, formed in 1901), but sometimes to control competition (as with many late-Victorian brewery mergers). Seventeen breweries and distilleries featured among the fifty largest companies in 1905. Imperial Tobacco was the largest of all, with a capital of over £17,500,000. Large size did not guarantee large returns. The level of business profits revived slightly at the end of the 1890s, but then fell back again. The high profit levels of the early 1870s had now receded into history:[22]

	Profits/industrial income (%)	Profits/national income (%)
1870–4	47.7	29.4
1890–4	37.8	22.7
1895–9	40.6	24.9
1900–4	39.0	23.7
1905–9	39.5	23.5
1910–14	39.2	23.2

With a view to stimulating profits, methods of 'scientific management' began to be discussed from the 1890s, especially in the engineering industry.[23] The world's first book on factory organization seems to have been *The Commercial Organization of Factories* (1896) by J. Slater Lewis, head of the electrical engineering department at Salford Rolling Mills. Trade union leaders were assured that increased efficiency in factory and office methods could be made to raise wages as well as profits. But the lead in the movement was taken by the United States, where F. W. Taylor developed the system which came to be known as 'Taylorism'. In the United Kingdom Taylor's methods were little applied up to 1914, in part because they had been circulated in over-simplified versions which encouraged the belief that 'scientific management' involved a callous disregard of human limitations and also of hard-earned skills.

3

Though her manufactures were increasing by volume, Britain was still losing ground in terms of her percentage share of world production:[24]

	United States	United Kingdom	Germany	France	Russia
1870	23.3	31.8	13.2	10.3	3.7
1881–5	28.6	26.6	13.9	8.6	3.4
1896–1900	30.1	19.5	16.6	7.1	5.0
1906–10	35.3	14.7	15.9	6.4	5.0
1913	35.8	14.0	15.7	6.4	5.5

Likewise, though her exports were growing by volume, Britain was fast giving way in proportionate terms to foreign trade competitors, led by the Germans and the Americans. The British competitive performance in the markets of industrial countries was particularly disappointing. In 1899 the value of Britain's exports to these markets was still slightly higher than Germany's; but by 1913 German exports had more than doubled, whereas British exports had increased by less than one-third. Tariff barriers cannot have been a main cause of this contrast, for the Germans also faced them:[25]

		Exports by value (million dollars at 1913 prices)					
		To industrial countries		To semi-industrial countries		To rest of world	
		Manu-factures	All exports	Manu-factures	All exports	Manu-factures	All exports
United	1899	479	912	477	544	371	522
Kingdom	1913	624	969	810	927	526	660
Germany	1899	437	691	75	84	270	346
	1913	925	1,285	227	238	574	882
United	1899	272	1,366	83	113	68	182
States	1913	535	1,850	137	246	174	388

Germany was also very successful in the markets of primary producing countries, to which in 1899 she had exported much less than Britain and to which by 1913 she was exporting much more. Only in the markets of semi-industrial states did Britain maintain a big advantage. Though still in 1913 the world's largest exporter, her lead was now only small and diminishing:

		Manufactures	All exports
United Kingdom	1899	1,327	1,978
	1913	1,970	2,556
Germany	1899	782	1,121
	1913	1,726	2,405
United States	1899	423	1,661
	1913	846	2,484

(Million dollars at 1913 prices)

Not only was Germany likely soon to take first trading place in terms of value, her export mix was more balanced and up-to-date than Britain's. In 1913 German exports included much higher proportions of metal goods, chemicals, and machinery, and a much lower proportion of textiles:[26]

	United Kingdom (%)	Germany (%)
Coal	13.3	11.0
Metals	16.7	28.9
Machinery	10.0	17.7
Transport equipment	6.1	4.2
Chemicals	5.1	14.4
Textiles	48.8	23.9

German competition, which had helped to provoke the 'fair trade' movement of the 1880s, once more came under discussion during the depression of the mid 1890s. This concern was epitomized in E. E. Williams's vigorously written book, *Made in Germany* (1896), which received widespread notice. Williams had assembled statistics and evidence from consular reports and trade journals to demonstrate the growing reality of the German trade menace, 'a deliberate and deadly rivalry'. German goods, contended Williams, were flooding both British home and overseas markets, though it was German competition within the United Kingdom that was most apparent. The Merchandise Marks Act of 1887 had required foreign goods to be marked with their country of origin, hence 'made in Germany'. 'Roam the house over, and the fateful mark will greet you at every turn, from the piano in your drawing-room to the mug on your kitchen dresser, blazoned though it be with the legend, *A Present from Margate*.' What was to be done? Williams emphasized that both state help and individual effort would be needed. 'Fair trade, Commercial Consuls, Technical Colleges – good and necessary as they are – will not avail to stem the inroad of the German, unless our manufacturers and merchants brace themselves.' Britain's industrial predominance was gone, and was not likely to be regained. 'At least let us see to it that she fares no worse.' In 1901 Williams returned to the subject of foreign competition in an article called 'Made in Germany – Five Years After' (*National Review*, September 1901). He contended that his forecasts had been confirmed. And what, he now asked, of growing American competition? American industrial growth, however, though viewed with increasing concern at the turn of the century, never provoked quite the same agitation in Britain as did German rivalry. The Harmsworth press did issue warnings under the headline 'Uncle Sam takes his coat off'.[27] But whereas Germany was of comparable size to the United Kingdom, the obviously much greater economic potential of the United States had to be admitted. The Americans, moreover, could be regarded as 'cousins', thrusting and brash but also Anglo-Saxon. Finally, though the industry of the United States had become the world's biggest by the end of the nineteenth century, the greater part of its output was absorbed by the large American home market. Germany remained Britain's main rival in overseas trade.

At the end of 1901, on his return from a tour of the British Empire, the future King George V warned that even in traditional empire markets the foreign challenge would have to be met: 'the Old Country must wake up if she intends to maintain her old position of pre-eminence in her Colonial trade'.[28] The United States had come to dominate the Canadian market, and German intrusion was especially feared in Australia and Cape Colony. Yet at the turn of the century the value of German trade with the British Empire still totalled less than 5 per cent of that of the United Kingdom; and up to 1914 the foreign threat to empire markets remained more prospective than immediate. Nevertheless, the royal warning was widely noticed in the press under the headline 'Wake Up England!', a cry which was frequently recalled down to 1914.

Not all contemporary observers were pessimistic about the prospects for British industry and trade, nor have all historians written unfavourably about the Edwardian economic performance. The case has been argued, for example, that the British iron and steel industry really performed as well as could be expected after 1870.[29] The American and German iron and steel industries expanded much faster behind tariff protection because of their greater potential for growth, not because of any lack of enterprise on the British side. And was the increasing dependence of the cotton trade upon 'easy' markets evidence of failure of initiative, or was it simply a commonsense response to fierce competition and foreign tariff barriers? Even Britain's slowness to extend her industrial range into important new industries such as chemicals and motor-car manufacture has been at least partly excused.[30] Such expansion did take place after the First World War; and in the case of cars, W. R. Morris was just beginning large-scale production of cheap British models to compete with American Fords when the war broke out. Only now had demand built up sufficiently to justify the British car industry turning from concentration upon expensive luxury vehicles. Right timing of expansion was all-important: it was not necessary to be first. The *Manchester Guardian* (14.8.1907) praised English businessmen's 'remarkable gift for taking up a new thing just at the right time for making money out of it. France may invent the motor car and Italy perfect it, but one is convinced that in the long run it will be England that will make most profit out of it . . . she is rarely the pioneer in taking up a new idea either in machinery or methods of business organization. Yet she seldom seems to be too late'.

Most Edwardians had accepted that Britain could no longer lead the way in many branches of industry. The hope now had to be (as the *Guardian* suggested) that British businessmen could still make good profits while competing with foreigners as equals. Robert Giffen, and other free-trade opponents of protection, began to argue during the depression of the 1880s that industrial predominance did not always bring prosperity, and that conversely prosperity did not require predominance. Edwin Cannan made the same point in his presidential address to the economics section of the British Association in 1902. 'Commercial supremacy', argued Cannan, was a meaningless expression. 'Is it selling goods dear? Is it selling them cheap? Is it selling a large quantity of goods in proportion to the area of the country? or in proportion to its population? or absolutely, without any reference to its area or population? It seems to be a wonderful muddle of all these various and often contradictory ideas.' Foreign trade could not provide a measure of the wealth and prosperity of a country: 'the economic ideal is not for the nation any more than for the family that it should buy and sell the largest possible quantity of goods. The true statesman desires for his countrymen, just as the sensible parent desires for his children, that they should do the best paid work of the world.'[31]

Such a view took no account of the power-political competition mixed with competition in trade. Certainly, Britain was still very prosperous; but by giving ground in relative economic terms she had given ground in political terms. 'Does it hurt us?' asked E. E. Williams in his 1901 article. Free traders such as Cannan or Giffen claimed that the advance of other nations must only increase the demand for goods made by British workmen. 'Why should it injure them?,' asked Giffen. Because, answered Williams, in political terms wealth was 'a matter of comparison'. 'If a nation would be powerful it must root itself upon a production of wealth correspondent with the wealth production of other nations.' In these political terms any loss of economic ground was to be regretted. Hence the fear – not only among 'fair traders' and 'tariff reformers', but also among some free traders of wider vision than Giffen or Cannan – that more had been yielded than ought to have been. One such was Alfred Marshall, the Cambridge economist. He accepted that Britain was bound to cede some advantage 'to the great land which attracts alert minds of all nations to sharpen their inventive and resourceful faculties by impact on one another'. It was inevitable, too, 'that she should yield a little of it to that land of great industrial traditions which yoked science in the service of man with unrivalled energy'. But, concluded Marshall, 'it was not inevitable that she should lose so much of it as she has done'.[32]

4

During the Edwardian period English agriculture at last found a basis for stability and reviving prosperity.[33] Imports continued to grow, but prices recovered slightly. The price of wheat, for example, which had averaged little over 27s. per quarter during 1900–4, improved to almost 33s. for 1910–14. Wheat imports increased from under 70 million quarters per annum at the turn of the century to over 100 million quarters in the last years before the war. Yet wheat acreage in Great Britain, after touching a minimum of 1,375,000 acres in 1904, had recovered to 1,756,000 acres by 1913. Tenant farmers who had taken over farms at exceptionally low rents during the worst of the depression were especially well placed to benefit from even modest price improvements. The agricultural share of United Kingdom national income had fallen from 15.7 per cent during 1867–74 to 6.8 per cent by 1895–1904, and to 6.6 per cent by 1900–9. But this meant that the contribution of agriculture to the economy was steadying itself during the first decade of the twentieth century.

The census of production showed that in 1908 about one-third by value of the gross agricultural output of Great Britain came from the sale of crops and horticultural produce (£51,800,000), one-fifth from dairy products, (£30 million), and the rest from livestock and poultry (£69 million). Dairy output included over 1,000 million gallons of milk per year, 85 per cent of which was sold liquid, the rest for butter and cheese making. The *Review of Reviews* for May 1906 carried an enthusiastic article on 'The Revolution in British Agriculture', which noted how special trains now delivered London's milk from an average distance of 80 miles. 'In the North an interesting experiment is being tried of supplying milk in sealed bottles, so that its absolute purity can be guaranteed.' Fruit also had now become 'a more regular article of food for all classes'. The countryside round Wisbech had been transformed from wheatfields to orchards. Market gardening was flourishing. Labour migration from the Evesham district, for example, had almost stopped. 'Scores of active and intelligent workers, who might otherwise have been lost to their country, have settled down in holdings varying in size from two to ten or more acres.' Much more labour was absorbed by market gardening 'than in the old wheat days'.

The population of rural England and Wales began to grow again between 1901 and 1911 after forty years of decline, though admittedly some of this growth reflected outward movement by urban 'commuters':[34]

	Population		
	Rural	Urban	Rural percentage
1861	9,100,000	11,000,000	45.4
1901	7,500,000	25,100,000	23.0
1911	7,900,000	28,200,000	21.9

According to one contemporary calculation, between 1901 and 1911 the number of men aged over 20 at work on the land in England and Wales rose from 977,000 to 1,056,000. Farmers, along with their adult male relatives, had increased from 257,700 to 271,400; shepherds and labourers from 458,000 to 498,200.

Farmers' incentive income, which may have fallen by as much as one-half during the depression, has been estimated to have returned to the level of the early 1870s by 1906–10.[35] The earnings of agricultural labourers were certainly continuing to improve, though the cost of living was now also increasing. Part-payment in kind (which varied widely in form and value from county to county) provided some cushion against higher living costs:[36]

	Value of agricultural labourers' earnings (including payments in kind)					
	Earnings per week			Index when G.B. = 100		
	1867–70	1898	1907	1867–70	1898	1907
	s. d.	*s. d.*	*s. d.*			
London and Home Counties	16 6	18 5	18 6½	115	107	102
South West	12 5	15 7	16 10	87	91	92
Rural south-east	14 4½	15 9	16 5	101	92	90
Midlands	14 1	17 10	18 4½	99	104	101
Lincs, Rutland, E. and N. Riding	17 1	18 0	18 10	120	105	103
Lancs, Cheshire, W. Riding	17 1	18 8	19 7	120	108	108
Cumberland and Westmorland	18 6	18 9	19 2	129	109	105
Northumberland and Durham	18 9	20 5½	21 5½	131	119	118
G.B. average	14 3½	17 2½	18 2½	100	100	100

In 1913 Seebohm Rowntree published *How the Labourer Lives*. He estimated that the minimum expenditure needed to maintain 'physical efficiency' for a farm labourer's family of two adults and three children was 20s. 6d. per week. This allowed nothing for luxuries or emergencies. Nevertheless, he claimed that only in five northern counties of England and Wales did wages (including payments in kind) reach or exceed this modest level. Admittedly, Rowntree was comparing 1913 prices with 1907 earnings, and by 1913 wages had risen. In perhaps twenty-one counties 1913 earnings crossed the poverty line, but in seventeen counties they still did not. In terms of extent, therefore, poverty in the countryside probably exceeded even that of the towns.[37]

George Bourne commented in *Change in the Village* (1912) upon the new importance of cash in rural life. In the past, labourers had required money only occasionally. But now it had to be found each week 'not only, as of old, for rent and boots, and for some bread and flour, but also for butter or margarine, sugar, tea, bacon or foreign meat if possible, lard, jam, and – in the winter, at least – coal'. Only clothes were still not bought regularly. Rural industries were declining. Agricultural implements were ceasing to be made by village blacksmiths; milling was becoming concentrated at the ports, malting near the big breweries. In the small agricultural county of Rutland this process of decline has been strikingly measured:[38]

	1871	1911
Millers	43	22
Brickmakers	37	15
Sawyers	37	10
Cabinet makers	24	10
Coopers and turners	8	2
Wheelwrights	69	42
Blacksmiths	114	83
Saddlers	34	24
Tailors	114	63
Shoemakers	183	138

Town-made goods were driving out local products. But some of the increased contact with the outside world was clearly beneficial. For example, the easy circulation of newspapers now brought a new awareness, as Bourne recognized. 'Shackleton and the South Pole are probably household words in most of the cottages.'

Trade union activity revived again gradually in the countryside from 1906, beginning in Norfolk, which had been a strong centre of earlier movements.[39] The revival was led by George Edwards, who had participated in several unions since the 1870s. He was himself a farm worker and a strong Methodist, as Joseph Arch had been. Edwards made up with commitment and organizing ability what he lacked of Arch's fire. His Eastern Counties Agricultural Labourers' and Small-holders' Union had attracted 4,000 members by the end of 1909. At first the union accepted a Liberal Member of Parliament as president, and it was as much concerned with capturing the rural vote as with improving conditions of work. But in 1911 its name was changed to the National Agricultural Labourers' and Rural Workers' Union, and it became affiliated to the TUC. Socialists came to the fore, and Edwards retired from the secretaryship in 1913. From 1912 the Workers' Union – which had been formed in 1898 to organize unskilled workers – began to offer membership to agricultural labourers. Branches had been formed in fourteen counties by 1914. Successful strikes were conducted during 1913–14 in Lancashire, Somerset, and elsewhere by one union or the other. By the middle of 1914 the National Union comprised 360 branches in England and Wales with 15,000 members. Most agricultural labourers were still non-unionists. But, encouraged by the great expansion of industrial unionism during the immediate pre-war years, the trade union idea was at last gaining a permanent influence within the English countryside.

Notes

1. A. H. Halsey (ed.), *Trends in British Society Since 1900* (1972), p. 340.
2. A. K. Cairncross, *Home and Foreign Investment, 1870–1913* (1953), p. 82.
3. *Seventy-Fifth Annual Report of the Registrar-General* (1914), in N. L. Tranter (ed.), *Population and Industrialization* (1973), p. 280.
4. See D. Read (ed.), *Documents from Edwardian England* (1973), Ch. 2.
5. D. V. Glass, *Population Policies and Movements in Europe* (1967), p. 17.
6. B. Thomas, *Migration and Economic Growth: A Study of Great Britain and the Atlantic Economy* (2nd edn, 1973), p. 57. See also S. C. Johnson, *A History of Emigration* (1913; reprinted 1966), Ch. XIV.
7. B. Thomas, *Migration and Economic Growth; A Study of Great Britain and the Atlantic Economy* (2nd edn, 1973), pp. 452–3.
8. D. C. Jones, 'Some Notes on the Census of Occupations for England and Wales', *Journal of the Royal Statistical Society*, LXXVIII (1915), p. 58.
9. G. Routh, *Occupation and Pay in Great Britain, 1906–60* (1965), p. 40.
10. B. R. Mitchell and Phyllis Deane (eds.), *Abstract of British Historical Statistics* (1962), p. 270. See also G. H. Perris, *Industrial History of Modern England* (1914), appendix III.

11. P. Mathias, *The First Industrial Nation* (1969), p. 468.
12. *Ibid.*, p. 467.
13. Phyllis Deane and W. A. Cole, *British Economic Growth, 1688-1959* (2nd edn, 1967), p. 297.
14. *Ibid.*, p. 36.
15. See R. E. Tyson, 'The Cotton Industry', in D. H. Aldcroft (ed.), *The Development of British Industry and Foreign Competition, 1875-1914* (1968).
16. See P. L. Payne, 'Iron and Steel Manufactures', *ibid.*
17. A. J. Taylor, 'The Coal Industry', *ibid.*
18. A. Marshall, *Industry and Trade* (1919), p. 628.
19. A. Levine, *Industrial Retardation in Britain, 1880-1914* (1967), p. 15.
20. D. H. Aldcroft and H. W. Richardson, *The British Economy, 1870-1939* (1969), pp. 163-5.
21. See P. L. Payne, 'The Emergence of the Large-Scale Company in Great Britain, 1870-1914', *Economic History Review*, second series, XX (1967).
22. S. B. Saul, *The Myth of the Great Depression, 1873-1896* (1969), p. 42.
23. See L. H. Jenks, 'Early Phases of the Management Movement', *Administrative Science Quarterly*, V (1960), and references there. Also L. Urwick and E. F. L. Brech, *The Making of Scientific Management* (1963-4), esp. II, Chs. VI, VII.
24. B. Thomas, *Migration and Economic Growth: A Study of Great Britain and the Atlantic Economy* (2nd edn, 1973), p. 120.
25. D. H. Aldcroft (ed.), *The Development of British Industry and Foreign Competition, 1875-1914* (1968), p. 18.
26. A. L. Levine, *Industrial Retardation in Britain, 1880-1914* (1967), p. 135.
27. P. Ferris, *The House of Northcliffe* (1971), p. 109.
28. H. Nicolson, *King George the Fifth* (1952), pp. 73-4.
29. See D. N. McCloskey (ed.), *Essays on a Mature Economy: Britain After 1840* (1971), esp. Ch. 12. Also D. N. McCloskey, *Economic Maturity and Entrepreneurial Decline, British Iron and Steel 1870-1913* (1973).
30. See S. B. Saul, 'The Motor Industry in Britain to 1914', *Business History*, V (1962); and T. C. Barker, 'History: Economic and Social', in C. B. Cox and A. E. Dyson (eds.), *The Twentieth-Century Mind*, I (1972).
31. T. H. Ward (ed.), *The Reign of Queen Victoria* (1887), II, p. 41; R. L. Smyth (ed.), *Essays in Economic Method* (1962), pp. 198-9.
32. A. Marshall, *Official Papers* (1926), p. 405.
33. See Lord Ernle, *English Farming Past and Present* (6th edn, 1961), pp. 385-92; and Christabel S. Orwin and Edith H. Whetham, *History of British Agriculture, 1846-1914* (1971), esp. Ch. 13.
34. R. Lawton, 'Rural Depopulation in Nineteenth Century England', in D. R. Mills (ed.), *English Rural Communities* (1973), p. 195. See also A. L. Bowley, 'Rural Population of England and Wales', *Journal of the Royal Statistical Society*, LXXVII (1914).
35. J. R. Bellerby, 'National and Agricultural Income 1851', *Economic Journal*, LXIX (1959), p. 103.
36. E. H. Hunt, *Regional Wage Variations in Britain, 1850-1914* (1973), p. 64.
37. R. Lennard, *Economic Notes on English Agricultural Wages* (1914), pp. 94-5. See also G. Mingay, 'The Transformation of Agriculture', in R. M. Hartwell (ed.), *The Long Debate on Poverty* (2nd edn, 1974), pp. 48-51.
38. J. Saville, *Rural Depopulation in England and Wales, 1851-1951* (1957), pp. 21-3, 73-4.
39. See G. Edwards, *From Crow-Scaring to Westminster* (1922); and R. Groves, *Sharpen the Sickle!* (1949), pp. 98-149.

Chapter 23

Social life: *'New expenses have come into the category of necessities'*

1

The first attempt at a sociological breakdown of the whole spread of English society was made in an article on 'Present Tendencies of Class Differentiation' by F. G. D'Aeth, which appeared in the *Sociological Review* for October 1910.[1] This established seven social groupings by reference to income, occupation, housing, social customs, and education. Category A, 'The Loafer', lived in a slum on about 18s. per week – 'irregular labour, or drinks a higher wage'. Category B embraced 'low-skilled labour', earning approximately 25s. per week – 'some change clothes and put on collar in evening'. Category C represented the artisans, comfortably housed, earning about 45s. per week – 'table set for meals'. Category D covered smaller shopkeepers, clerks, elementary schoolteachers and the like, who earned perhaps £3 per week – 'furnish their houses; entertain visitors; some have young servant'. Category E comprised smaller businessmen, earning at most £300 per year, probably grammar-school educated – 'visiting cards; some dine late'. Category F included the heads of firms, professional men and administrators, earning at least £600 per annum, who had usually received a university education. And finally Category G meant 'The Rich', with £2,000 a year or more. D'Aeth suggested that two standards of living existed and could be measured: 'the standard of simple necessities, and the standard of refined and educated necessities'. For an average family the former could be secured by earnings of about 25s. per week, but the latter required £600 per year. A. L. Bowley, the leading Edwardian social statistician, accepted as upper middle-class those with an annual income of £1,000 to £5,000; he regarded those with between £300 and £999 as the solid middle class, and those earning less than £300 down to £120 he perceptively described as 'uncomfortably off'. The family of young George Orwell, for example, found its aspirations difficult to sustain on £400 a year. He was born into 'the lower-upper-middle class'; people in this class (he remembered) owned no land, but 'felt they were landowners in the sight of God'. They went into the professions or the services rather than into trade. To belong to this class on £400 a year 'meant that your gentility was almost purely theoretical'.[2]

The number of middle and upper-class persons in the United Kingdom with taxable incomes over £150 per year has been estimated at about 1,250,000 in 1909–10, compared with about 850,000 in the mid 1890s.[3] Middle-class numbers were thus continuing to grow fast; and middle-class numbers at work were increasing faster in the new century than working-class numbers, not only proportionately but absolutely:[4]

	Occupied population of the United Kingdom	
	Working class	Middle and upper classes
1891	12,810,000	3,210,000
1901	13,800,000	3,940,000
1911	14,710,000	4,990,000

	Males occupied. England and Wales (in thousands)		
	1891	1901	1911
Professions and administration	289	343	408
Commerce, clerks, and miscellaneous	514	694	908
Dealers and assistants	765	915	1,105
Employers not included above	190	217	239
Farmers	202	203	209
Total	1,960	2,372	2,869
Others occupied	6,846	7,785	8,587
All occupied	7,759	10,157	11,456
Percentage middle-class of all	22.3	23.3	25.0

The rate of increase in the numbers of middle-class working women accelerated markedly during the Edwardian period:

	Females occupied. England and Wales (in thousands)		
	1891	1901	1911
Professions and administration	191	236	271
Commerce, clerks and miscellaneous	89	151	263
Dealers and assistants	300	343	561
Employers not included above	27	27	29
Farmers	22	22	20
Total	629	779	1,144
Others occupied	3,317	3,393	3,687
All occupied	3,946	4,172	4,831
Percentage middle-class of all	16.0	18.7	23.7

Plutocratic materialism – about which both traditionalists and social reformers had been complaining since the mid-Victorian period – had spread widely among the well-to-do, even among old-established families. C. F. G. Masterman regretted in *The Condition of England* (1909) how the standard of life had been raised 'not so much in comfort as in ostentation'. He found steam yachts, luxury hotels, and motor cars to be the particular toys of the rich. 'We fling away in ugly white hotels, in uninspired dramatic entertainments, and in elaborate banquets of which everyone is weary, the price of many poor men's yearly income.' This process had been brilliantly described by the American Thorstein Veblen in his famous book on *The Theory of the Leisure Class* (1899) as 'conspicuous consumption'. This could only be fully practised by the wealthy. But the middle classes – and not least the lower middle classes – could try 'keeping up with the Joneses'. This expression was apparently an Americanism, coined as late as 1913; but social competition between neighbours was not new. 'We were finding our feet in the social world, making the best show we could. The brass knocker, the bay window, the dining and drawing rooms, establish the fact; whilst the Study gives evidence that already we had in view the great surburban ideal of being superior to the people next door.' So remarked the leading character in Shan Bullock's *Robert Thorne, The Story of a London Clerk* (1907). C. F. G. Masterman regretted that the suburban middle classes, after winning the 'struggle to live', had substituted only a materialistic 'struggle to attain'.

A survey taken in 1912–13 of 665 working-class households in Northampton, Warrington, and Reading with children out at work counted 472 families where the job status of all children remained the same as their fathers', 128 where some children had improved their status, and 65 where children had lost job status.[5] A social rise or fall thus remained a distinct possibility for many Edwardians; but the majority retained the social position which they had inherited. 'Most people in this world seem to live "in character",' explained H. G. Wells at the start of his novel *Tono-Bungay* (1909). 'They have a class, they have a place, they know what is becoming in them and what is due to them, and their proper size of tombstone tells at last how properly they have played the part.' Other observers emphasized how social tension was more likely to arise from comparisons within classes than between classes. 'The Joneses' to be emulated were in the same class – across the road, not out of sight. The working classes, especially in the countryside, were still inclined to be respectful towards their social superiors. 'They envy one another; they never envy the rich.' When a workman wished to praise someone, he was likely to say that his hero had 'behaved like a gentleman'.[6]

Nevertheless, the spread of 'socialism' in general and of trade unionism and strikes in particular were making the Edwardian suburban middle classes increasingly fearful of what Masterman described as 'the vision of a "Keir Hardie" in caricature – with red tie and defiant beard and cloth cap, and fierce, unquenchable thirst for Middle Class property'. Could the propertied classes hope to retain their economic and social advantages in a changing world? Max Beerbohm pointed out the significance of the butler in J. M. Barrie's play *The Admirable Crichton* (1902), who in a changed environment – when an upper-class family was shipwrecked on a desert island – soon took social charge. 'Crichton, the butler, is the type – the fantastically faked type – of the potential monsters blindly created by us.' But another leading essayist, G. K. Chesterton, refused to be surprised by this prospective turnround; for (concluded Chesterton) the perpetuation of existing social arrangements had not been secured by upper-class superiority, nor even by upper-class oppression, but by working-class deference. 'It rests on the perennial and unfailing kindness of the poor to the rich.'[7]

2

Poverty, complained Masterman in *The Condition of England*, was 'the foundation of the present industrial order', even though it was now poverty removed from 'actual lack of physical necessities'. The mean number of paupers was continuing to fall in proportionate terms; but they remained a very large absolute number, especially in years of economic depression such as 1909–10:[8]

Year ending Lady Day	Indoor paupers		Outdoor paupers		Total	
	Mean number	Per cent of popn.	Mean number	Per cent of popn.	Mean number	Per cent of popn.
1900	215,377	0.68	577,122	1.8	792,499	2.5
1910	275,075	0.78	539,642	1.5	916,377	2.6
1914	254,644	0.69	387,208	1.0	748,019	2.0

Booth and Rowntree had suggested that some 30 per cent of the urban population were living in poverty. A succession of local surveys inspired by Rowntree's example, plus a series of official inquiries into the cost of living among a wide-range of working-class occupations, provided evidence which could be related to Rowntree's suggested minimum income. This minimum – sufficient to keep a family of two adults and three children in a state of spartan physical efficiency – stood at 21*s*. 8*d*. in 1901, but had been raised by inflation to 23*s*. 8*d*. by 1911. In that year, as Rowntree explained in an article, almost one-third of all adult men in the United Kingdom were earning less than 25*s*. per week even when in full employment:[9]

Wage	Number of men	Percentage
Under 15*s*.	320,000	4
15*s*. to 20*s*.	640,000	8
20*s*. to 25*s*.	1,600,000	20
25*s*. to 30*s*.	1,680,000	21
30*s*. to 35*s*.	1,680,000	21
35*s*. to 40*s*.	1,040,000	13
40*s*. to 45*s*.	560,000	7
Over 45*s*.	480,000	6

The social survey taken in 1912–13 of Northampton (N), Warrington (W), and Reading (R) confirmed Rowntree's conclusion in his York inquiry that permanently inadequate wages were a main cause of poverty:[10]

Principle immediate causes of poverty

Immediate cause	Percentage of households below the Rowntree standard			
	N.	W.	R.	York 1899
Chief wage-earner:				
dead	21	6	14	27
ill or old	14	1	11	10
out of work	—	3	2	3
irregularly employed	—	3	4	3
regularly employed – wage insufficient for 3 children:				
3 children or less	21	22	33	
4 children or more	9	38	15	57
wage sufficient for 3 but family more than 3	35	27	21	

Nevertheless, the majority of working men did now earn more than 25*s.* per week; and Rowntree recognized in 1911 how even a small measure of income above the minimum brought a striking difference in living standards. 'The advantage which a family with 30*s.* a week has over one with £1 a week is greater than it ever was before.' United Kingdom personal consumption of goods and services, which had already grown from a value well under £1 million in 1870 to over £1,600,000 by 1900, had reached more than £2 million by 1913:[11]

	Expenditure on tea, coffee, alcohol, tobacco, fish, coal, motor cars, and cycles	Total consumption Finished consumer goods	Consumption of services	Total personal consumption
1900	313.2	1,087.4	521.1	1,609
1913	335.2	1,370.5	669.9	2,040

(current retail prices at £m.)

Yet expectations within working-class families were still growing, as Philip Snowden, the socialist, emphasized in his book on *The Living Wage* (1913).

New expenses have come into the category of necessities. The development of tramways, the coming of the halfpenny newspaper, the cheap but better-class music hall and the picture palace, the cheap periodicals and books, the very municipal enterprise which was intended to provide free libraries, free parks, free concerts, has added to the expenditure of the working classes, who cannot take advantage of these boons without incurring some little expense in sundries. The features of our advancing civilisation are always before the eyes of the working classes, and they fall into the habit of indulging in the cheaper ones.

Wages were now stationary, complained Snowden, even though prices had been increasing. The widespread rise in money wages alongside falling prices during the second half of the nineteenth century had come to a halt by 1900. Edwardian prices had turned upwards because of the increase in money supply caused by gold discoveries in Australia, South Africa, and the United States; and perhaps also because of the withdrawal of the United States from world markets as a major supplier of food. Most workers, who had grown to expect steady improvement in their purchasing power, now found the cost of living moving against them:[12]

| | Income per head of | | Index numbers | | | | | |
| | | | Income | | | | Real | |
	Popn (£)	Occupied (£)	Per head	Per occupied person	Wage rates	Cost of living	Income per occupied person	Wages per earner
1880	31.5	76.1	65	69	73	103	67	70
1901–5	41.7	97.3	85½	88½	92	89½	99	103
1906–10	43.8	100.6	90	91½	95	92	100	103
1911	45.6	104.9	93½	95½	96	95	100	100
1912	47.3	108.3	97	98½	99	98	100	100
1913	48.8	110.1	100	100	100	100	100	100

Certain categories of workers, and some localities, fared better than others in this new family-income pattern. Some coal miners and cotton workers, for example, still contrived to improve their standards of living. But the widespread inability of wage-earners to maintain their real incomes, explained Snowden, 'and to add the small additional indulgences to which they feel they are entitled', was largely responsible for the labour unrest of the years before 1914. 'The working classes, on the average, enjoy a higher standard of living than was the case sixty years ago, but the struggle to support the average standard of working-class life was never so hard as it is at the present time.'

Socialists such as Snowden, and 'new Liberals' such as Winston Churchill, often argued that while the poor were now finding themselves poorer in real terms, the rich were still growing richer. Leon Chiozza Money's *Riches and Poverty* (1905), which became a socialist textbook carried a striking diagram frontispiece which illustrated 'British Incomes in 1904'. This showed how 1,250,000 'Rich' drew incomes totalling £585 million; 3,750,000 'Comfortable' persons drew £245 million; while the remaining 38 million people had to make do with £880 million. Money's totals were only approximations; but Churchill, as President of the Board of Trade, estimated more surely in 1909 that in ten years the return to the income-tax-paying classes (only 1,100,000 people) had increased by £109 million. He found it 'melancholy' to compare this with the wages of the 10 million workers covered by the annual Board of Trade returns. Their annual wage total had grown by only £10 million, against which must be set the increase in rents and food prices. Subsequent calculations have suggested that in 1911–13 more than 85 per cent of the population of England and Wales aged over 25 (about 16,500,000 people) lived in families which owned £100 or less capital. Another 8–10 per cent (about 750,000 people) possessed over £100 but not more than £1,000. All the rest of the private capital of England and Wales was held by some 3 per cent of the population aged over 25, not more than 600,000 people.[13]

Notes

1. M. Abrams, 'Some Measurements of Social Stratification in Britain', in J. A. Jackson (ed.), *Social Stratification* (1968), pp. 133–4. See also D. Read (ed.), *Documents from Edwardian England* (1973), Ch. 4; and S. Meacham, *A Life Apart, The English Working Class, 1890–1914* (1977).
2. A. L. Bowley, *The Nature and Measurement of Social Phenomena* (1915), p. 98; G. Orwell, *The Road to Wigan Pier* (1937), Ch. 8.
3. Sir J. Stamp, *British Incomes and Property* (1922), p. 448.
4. A. L. Bowley, *Wages and Incomes Since 1860* (1937), pp. 91, 128–9.
5. A. L. Bowley, *The Nature and Measurement of Social Phenomena* (1915), p. 89.
6. E. Boutmy, *The English People* (1904), pp. 133–4; E. L. Gales, *Studies in Arcady* (1910), pp. 13, 23–6, 45.
7. M. Beerbohm, *Around Theatres* (1953), pp. 232–3; G. K. Chesterton, *Heretics* (1905), pp. 202–3.
8. M. E. Rose, *The Relief of Poverty, 1834–1914* (1972), p. 53.
9. B. S. Rowntree, 'The Industrial Unrest', *Contemporary Review*, October 1911, p. 453.
10. A. L. Bowley and A. R. Burnett-Hurst, *Livelihood and Poverty* (1915), p. 40.
11. J. B. Jeffreys and Dorothy Walters, 'National Income and Expenditure of the United Kingdom', *Income and Wealth*, series V (1955), p. 27.
12. A. L. Bowley, *Wages and Income Since 1860* (1937), p. 94.
13. R. S. Churchill, *Winston S. Churchill*, volume II, companion part 2 (1969), pp. 924–6; G. W. Daniels and H. Campion, *The Distribution of National Capital* (1936), pp. 29–30, 53.

Chapter 24

Town life: *'The largest secular change of a thousand years*

1

Edwardian Englishmen were a town generation, the first to predominate within any large state. In 1901, 25,100,000 (77 per cent) out of 32,500,000 people in England and Wales lived in a more or less urban environment: ten years later the figures were 28,200,000 (78.1 per cent) out of 36 million.[1] The conurbations were continuing to grow both in population and in area:

	Greater London	South-East Lancashire	West Midlands	West Yorkshire	Merseyside	Tyneside
1901	6,586,000	2,117,000	1,483,000	1,524,000	1,030,000	678,000
1911	7,256,000	2,328,000	1,634,000	1,590,000	1,157,000	816,000

Cities with over 100,000 inhabitants absorbed 15,800,000 people in 1911. This was 1,600,000 more than in 1901, but it constituted a slightly smaller percentage of the total urban population. More and more Edwardians were moving from within the formal big city boundaries to outlying suburbs and to captured commuter towns. John Burns, President of the Local Government Board, remarked when introducing the Housing and Town Planning Bill (12.5.1908) how every two-and-a-half years there was 'a county of London converted into urban life from rural conditions'.

Reformers such as Burns and C. F. G. Masterman, his Liberal ministerial colleague, were aware that the urban population was now taking on not merely a new magnitude but also a new character. 'It is a people which, all unnoticed and without clamour or protest, has passed through the largest secular change of a thousand years: from the life of the fields to the life of the city.' Nine out of ten families had migrated within three generations. 'How will they expand or degenerate in the new town existence, each in the perpetual presence of all?' So asked Masterman in an anxious chapter on 'The Multitude' in *The Condition of England* (1909). The volume of migration from country to town was now diminishing. The great majority of the urban masses were destined henceforward to be born in the towns. Fewer and fewer Englishmen had personal memories of country life, a rural experience to compare with their town experience. Mentally their horizons were becoming completely urban. Would they remain content? Would the town crowd prove stable? Or would the urban middle and working classes alike be shallow and excitable, without any rural sense of continuity, open to exploitation by charlatans and demagogues in commerce and in politics? Radicals such as Masterman were much disturbed by the over-excitement of Mafeking night. The new verb 'to maffick' was defined by the *Oxford English Dictionary* (1908) as 'to indulge in extravagant demonstrations of exultation'.

John Burns walked round some of London's poorer streets in 1905. He noted in his diary (21 March) that the London County Council had made them sanitary, but he thought that the houses needed painting and renovating. The fault lay with landlords. 'Oh you thrifty vergers, stingy deacons, pious shopkeepers who in your indecent haste to occupy the tawdry heaven of villadom consign your rack-rented tenants to the lower depths of a jerrybuilt hell.' Another expert observer had suggested how slums were produced by two influences. Firstly, by the existence of a localized demand for casual labour, which forced workers to crowd near the demand. Secondly, by the avarice of landlords who exploited this immobility by charging high rents for bad accommodation. 'House-knackers' aggravated London's slum problem by taking over properties near the end of lease, subdividing and rack-renting them without undertaking any repairs until 'a pretty imitation of a civic hell' was produced.[2] At the 1911 census the housing stock of England and Wales consisted of 7,550,000 houses. Housebuilding fell from a peak early in the twentieth century to a level lower just before 1914 than for fifty years:

Houses built in Great Britain (annual averages per quinquennium)

1895–9	128,200
1900–4	145,300
1905–9	115,800
1910–14	61,900

The severe slump in housebuilding seems to have been a direct result of Lloyd George's 1909 budget. Builders of small houses, whose profit margins on the houses themselves were often tiny, found Lloyd George threatening their compensating profit on land. By 1914 a 'house famine' prevailed in England, despite heavy overseas emigration – a shortage (according to one contemporary estimate) of at least 120,000 houses. In Crewe, where the shortfall in working-class accommodation was severe, discussion of the possibility of starting municipal housebuilding stood on the council's agenda for its meeting on 4 August 1914, the very day that war was declared.[3] Most local authorities still regarded municipal building as a last resort, and 95 per cent of the working classes still lived in privately-owned property. But in 1900 the LCC had begun (at Tooting) its first estate built not as a measure of slum clearance but on fresh land out in the suburbs. This represented a significant extension of commitment: the council was becoming a willing rather than a reluctant landlord. Within a decade about 7 per cent of London working-class families had become tenants of the LCC. The 1909 Housing and Town Planning Act compelled local authorities to adopt the housing provisions of the 1890 Housing of the Working Classes Act. Even so, by the end of 1913 fewer than 200,000 houses had been rendered fit for habitation under the Act, and less than 50,000 had been closed or demolished.

Would unskilled working men ever be able to afford rents high enough to tempt private builders into constructing for them houses sufficient both in numbers and in quality? Lloyd George's Land Enquiry Committee (1912–14), though unofficial, conducted the most thorough survey ever undertaken into housing conditions, both in town and country. Its report confirmed that a minimum of nearly 3 million people in England and Wales were still living in overcrowded conditions 'although not actually insanitary', while the environment of millions more was 'of almost unrelieved monotony'. And yet by the Edwardian years working-class housing and living conditions were visibly better for the majority than they had been a generation earlier. In 1906 John Burns praised 'the wonderful metamorphosis' supervised by the LCC. He met three men who had returned from abroad and who were 'startled' at the changes over fifteen years 'in streets, houses, offices and demeanour of people'. In 1900 a leading journalist had noted in his diary how central London was improving yearly. It was 'a perfect fairyland compared with ten years ago'. The journalist remembered when it was unwise to walk down Tottenham Court Road and the Strand after eight p.m. Drunkenness was now much less evident, and Burns remarked that he had been out all day on Easter Monday 1906 without seeing a single drunken person.[4]

Yet the fear of irreversible physical and moral degeneration caused by urban living – which had already been voiced in the 1880s and earlier – was widely shared and discussed in the first years of the new century. There was no denying that most of the town-born millions had grown up in polluted, crowded, noisy conditions, and that many of them remained ill-fed and ill-housed. 'The sphinx of the twentieth century,' concluded a book on *The Town Child* (1907), had 'propounded the riddle as to what England will do with this town population, or perhaps more truly, what this town population will do with England'. Was the poor performance of the British army in the Boer War a reflection of racial decay? Major-General J. F. Maurice, a veteran of several African campaigns, asserted in 1902 that 60 per cent of Englishmen were physically unfit for service, a figure apparently confirmed in the following year by the Director-General of the Army Medical Service. In response to these alarms the Balfour Government set up an Inter-Departmental Committee on Physical Deterioration (1903–4). This came to partly reassuring conclusions. It found Maurice's statistics to be misleading, and it did not discover evidence of racial degeneration. But it collected much expert testimony about ill health and bad conditions among the Edwardian working classes. It took evidence on the effects of urban overcrowding, about air pollution, working conditions, the care of infants and schoolchildren, venereal disease, and physical defects. The committee's report was 'emphatic in recommending that a systematised medical inspection of children at school should be imposed on every school authority as a public duty'. It also urged local authority feeding of hungry schoolchildren. In other words, answers to problems of urban living were now beginning to be given in terms of social welfare provision.

The famous series of Liberal welfare measures, initiated from 1906, had only just begun to show benefits by 1914; but already by the opening of the twentieth century hospital care for the sick poor was becoming much more available and effective.[5] The total of hospital beds in England and Wales grew from 112,750 in 1891 to 197,494 in 1911, an improvement from 3.89 to 5.48 per thousand population. Voluntary hospitals were no longer found only in large towns, for many small cottage hospitals were being opened. Even so, the proportion of voluntary hospital beds declined. Poor Law infirmaries, which had offered only 22,452 beds in 1891 were providing 74,013 by 1911; and the standard of treatment at the best of them was matching that of the best voluntary hospitals. But it needed the enforced experience of wounded officers in hospital during the First World War before most of the middle classes came to accept that hospital care need not be regarded as a form of relief suitable only for the working classes.

2

Suburbia continued to extend rapidly during the Edwardian years round the cities and large towns of England.[6] Revealingly, the population of inner London even began to fall between 1901 and 1911, while that of outer London continued to grow fast:

	Inner London	Outer London
1891	4,228,000	1,410,000
1901	4,536,000	2,050,000
1911	4,521,000	2,734,000

Continuing suburban growth of numbers meant continuing suburban spread (see pp. 410–11).[7]

An article in *The Times* (25.1.1904) on 'The formation of London Suburbs' remarked how the custom of living at a distance from work had 'spread from the merchant and the clerk to the artisan'. 'The substitution of small houses for large in the older suburbs, and the streets of cottages in new extensions' demonstrated 'that the suburb is now mainly the residence of the family of small means – say, from £100 to £300 per annum'. The suburbs round London and other big cities were certainly graded socially; in general, those furthest out were the

London-built up area

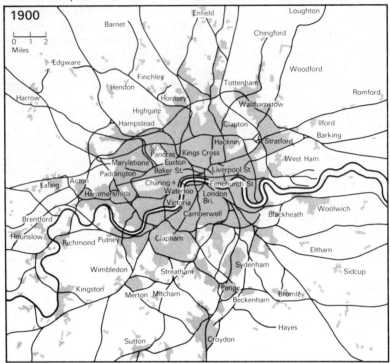

most spacious and superior. 'Dalston, Brixton, New Cross, Forest Hill, Walthamstow, Tottenham, contain many miles of small houses, which accommodate an immense number of clerks. Kennington, Stockwell, Camberwell, contain a large number of City tradesmen. Such suburbs as Balham, Sydenham, Highgate, Hampstead, Barnes, Richmond, and others contain the richer sort.'[8] *Punch* (16.1.1907) published 'The Song of Six Suburbs', which gently mocked suburban lifestyles:

> Supreme am I, Suburbia's guiding star,
>   And when I speak let lesser tongues be dumb;
> The prefix 'Upper' shows the class we are;
>   Where Tooting Beckons, Come!

Many of the upper middle classes were now moving out beyond suburbia to towns and villages entirely separate from the main urban complexes, commuting by train from the Home Counties into London, from Cheshire into Manchester and Liverpool, and from Wharfedale into Leeds. 'Like the Arab,' exclaimed the *Birmingham Mail* (26.11.1903), 'they are folding their tents and stealing silently away in the direction of Knowle or Solihull ... a little revolution is in progress.'

London-built up area

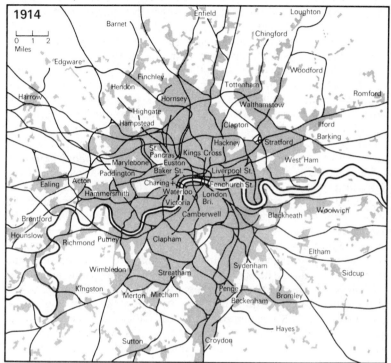

1914

0 1 2
Miles

Loughton
Enfield
Barnet
Chingford
Edgware
Woodford
Finchley
Hendon
Tottenham
Romford
Harrow
Hornsey
Walthamstow
Highgate
Hampstead
Clapton
Ilford
Hackney
Barking
St. Pancras
Kings Cross
Stratford
Marylebone
Euston
West Ham
Paddington
Baker St.
Liverpool St.
Ealing
Acton
Charing +
Fenchurch St.
Hammersmith
Waterloo
London Bri.
Victoria
Camberwell
Blackheath
Woolwich
Brentford
Hounslow
Clapham
Eltham
Richmond
Putney
Wimbledon
Streatham
Sydenham
Sidcup
Kingston
Penge
Merton
Mitcham
Beckenham
Bromley
Hayes
Sutton
Croydon

Masterman and other reformers were severe critics of the quality of much suburban building. The *Manchester Guardian* (2.7.1906) described jerry-builders as 'one of the worst social pests of today'. Two months later (17 September) the same paper discussed 'Some Shortcomings of Suburban Villas'. It noted how the chief aim of designers was to make houses look worth £100 more than was really the case by adding curved brickwork, elaborate cast-iron railings, bright terra-cotta finials, and other trimmings when it would have been better to spend a few pounds on thicker roofing to keep the houses cooler in summer and the water pipes from freezing in winter. Despite such criticisms the Pooters were no doubt still living happily in Edwardian Holloway.

Reformers were now pressing not simply for improved building standards but for 'town planning'.[9] 'We have forgotten that endless rows of brick boxes, looking out upon dreary streets and squalid backyards, are not really homes for people, and can never become such, however complete may be the drainage system, however pure the water supply, or however detailed the bye-laws under which they are built ... There is needed the vivifying touch of art which would give completeness.' So wrote Raymond Unwin, a leader of the town planning movement, in

Town Planning in Practice, An Introduction to the Art of Designing Cities and Suburbs (1909). In the same spirit, the *Manchester Guardian* (3.6.1906) complained about the Victorians' lack of colour sense, which (along with their toleration of smoke pollution) had made their cities and towns blacker and drabber than any before in history. 'We laboriously educated ourselves to the creed that virtue is only in work, and that where work and virtue are, drabs and browns must be the only wear.' Victorian expectations had been set especially low in respect of working-class housing. Gladstone had sternly told his Greenwich constituents in 1871 that only 'quacks ... beguiled by a spurious philanthropy' would 'promise to the dwellers in towns that every one of them shall have a house and garden in fresh air, with ample space'.[10]

The Victorians made just a few attempts at urban planning. Sir Titus Salt built Saltaire, near Bradford, during the third quarter of the nineteenth century for his woollen factory workers. The housing and layout were sanitary but bleak, with little sense of need to make the overall environment positively attractive. In 1888 W. H. Lever, the soap magnate, began construction of Port Sunlight in the Wirral, and here at last the importance of good architectural design and environmental tone gained recognition. The example of Port Sunlight helped to encourage Cadburys, the chocolate firm, to begin the full development from 1895 of Bourneville, near Birmingham. This became a balanced community rather than an exclusive company town, for about half the inhabitants were employed by other concerns. Ideas for model planned towns – without any element of company control – had been published by (among others) James Silk Buckingham, who called his town 'Victoria' (1849); by Sir Benjamin Richardson, whose 'City of Health' (1876) laid emphasis upon the provision of bathrooms and hot water; and by General William Booth, founder of the Salvation Army, whose *In Darkest England and The Way Out* (1890), as well as publicizing his remedial farm colony plan, also briefly recommended the building of 'model suburban villages'. By the 1890s 'garden cities' were coming to be widely advocated. The author of the most practical large scheme was Ebenezer Howard, who in 1898 published *To-Morrow: A Peaceful Path to Real Reform*. This was reissued in 1902 as *Garden Cities of To-Morrow*. Howard was a romantic, inspired by Ruskin, Carlyle, and Morris, who wanted to restore the people to the land; but he expressed his romanticism with a rare and engaging mixture of enthusiasm and sound sense. His book also benefitted from appearing at a time when leaders of opinion were becoming more than ever concerned about the possible 'degeneration' of the new town populations.

Howard's garden cities, sited in open country, aimed to attract people back from the overcrowded conurbations into a planned environment which would combine the best of both town and country. He summed up his ideas in the illustration of 'the three magnets' (opposite).

Howard's most original suggestion was that when a city had grown to full size – about 32,000 inhabitants – further development should be

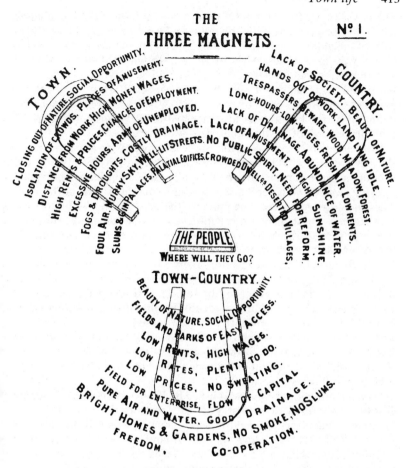

THE THREE MAGNETS

switched to a nearby new site. In time a cluster of cities, separated by rural zones, would thus be created. He also advocated permanent municipal ownership of land, which was to be leased to private developers but with the unearned increment reserved to the community. He hoped that industries would be attracted to the garden cities, though without pollution of the environment. 'The smoke fiend is kept well within bounds in Garden City; for all machinery is driven by electric energy.' In 1899 the Garden City Association was formed to discuss and to publicize Howard's ideas. Four years later the first garden city was started at Letchworth in Hertfordshire.[11] Within a few years, despite some financial difficulties, it was apparent that Letchworth was becoming a success. By 1914, 9,000 people were living there, and over £600,000 had been spent on new buildings. A typical Letchworth house consisted of a living-room, scullery, bathroom, and three bedrooms.

Such dwellings could be built for not much more than £150 (excluding land cost), and rented (including rates) for 5s. 6d. per week. The cottages were often laid out in short blocks of not more than four, and were set in broad tree-lined roads. Howard demonstrated at Letchworth that superior living and working conditions could be provided for the lower paid, and that this could even be done profitably through regulated private enterprise. The town so built was, moreover, a balanced community; for Letchworth also included middle-class housing, and a high proportion of local employment was created.

The success of Letchworth did not lead, however, to any attempts in the Edwardian period to copy it elsewhere. But garden city influence did encourage more concern for street layout, greater emphasis upon good housing design, and acceptance of land-use control by local authorities. These new attitudes were exemplified in the 'garden suburbs' built by the Edwardians. These were not brand-new towns but planned extensions of existing ones, the most notable being Hampstead Garden Suburb, started in 1907. Its architect, Raymond Unwin, had drawn the first plan for Letchworth. Hampstead's promoters emphasized how they wished 'to do something to meet the housing problem' by providing cottages only a 2d. bus ride from central London. They also hoped to encourage social integration by building residences for the wealthy on 'some of the beautiful sites round the Heath'. They promised to preserve every tree and to retain 'the foreground of the distant view'. The Hampstead estate quickly prospered, and it attracted international attention. But socially it disappointed one of the main hopes of its founders by becoming a mainly middle-class district.

'Town planning' was well established by 1914, and the Town Planning Institute was founded in that year as a joint professional body for architects, engineers, surveyors, and lawyers engaged in the new activity. Their separate work was not of course new; but by linking it together they found a new creative dimension. In 1909 the Liberal Government responded to the new mood by promoting the Housing and Town Planning Act. This was a pioneering measure for which John Burns, as President of the Local Government Board, made large claims. Its purpose, he announced, was to secure 'the home healthy, the house beautiful, the town pleasant, the city dignified, and the suburb salubrious'. It aimed to 'abolish, reconstruct, and prevent the slum'. Yet on the town-planning side the act was very limited. It addressed itself to the controlled development of new suburbs; yet it was not concerned with existing built-up areas, nor with towns taken as a whole. A town-planning scheme might be prepared with respect to any land which was undergoing (or was likely to undergo) building development; but already developed land could only be included if it was inextricably involved with this further building. By 1915 only 74 local authorities had been empowered to prepare schemes under the town-planning provisions of the act; and these schemes covered less than 168,000 acres. The 1909 Act, in short, remained inadequate in itself; but it was important as the first legislative recognition of the importance of town planning. It had been passed as a Liberal measure less than forty years after Gladstone, as Liberal prime minister, had denied the right of every town dweller to 'a house and garden in fresh air, with ample space'. From the beginning of the twentieth century it was coming to be recognized that national and local government must strive towards the translation for the new urban millions of this abstract right into physical reality.

3

Town planning included transport planning. London's transport problems were first comprehensively studied by a Royal Commission on London Traffic, which reported in 1905. It recommended the creation of an advisory Traffic Board, and some consolidation of railway and tramway management. But the Edwardians were reluctant to accept even this limited degree of control. By 1914, however, commercial pressures had established virtually one motor-bus network in London, with management of the tramways in the hands of local authorities. Rides per head of London population on public transport were rapidly increasing through the Edwardian years:[12]

	Underground and road services	All services (including main-line railways)
1901	142	177
1911	210	250

The spread of electric tramcars had made regular and cheap public transport available to all but the very poorest, both in London and in the provincial towns. C. F. G. Masterman exclaimed in 1906 that 'the two greatest boons which have come to our workingpeople' were 'the gas stove and the fast electric tram'. To these he might have added the bicycle. Another sympathetic observer forecast enthusiastically that 'as steam has concentrated people in towns, electricity will spread them over the land'. Tramlines were not stopping at urban boundaries, but were penetrating into the countryside round and between towns.[13]

The breakthrough in the development of electric traction for trams had been made in the United States. The opening in 1895 of the Bristol electric tramways system, using American equipment, marked the beginning of successful large-scale operation in Britain.[14] A tramways boom followed at the turn of the century, which coincided with and encouraged a suburban building boom. The provincial towns led the way at first. Not until 1901 did London United Tramways start the capital's first service – in the western suburbs. Operating costs for electric trams were perhaps 40 per cent lower than for horse trams, and workmen could be charged very cheap fares. In London and the big cities 1*d.* journeys could extend up to two-and-a-half miles. London passenger journeys by tram grew from 394 million in 1903 to 704 million in 1910.

Tramcars ran mainly on town roads which were more or less well maintained; but the coming of bicycles, followed by the introduction of motor cars, meant that rural roads were once again becoming important for through traffic.[15] The condition of many country roads at the end of the nineteenth century was poor. Clouds of dust were thrown up by the speeding pneumatic tyres of bicycles and cars – to the discomfort of travellers and bystanders alike, and to the detriment of the road surfaces and of adjacent property. Local authorities, and especially the county councils, slowly took action to cover main roads with a hard new 'Tarmac'. But the Edwardians did little else to meet the present and future needs of road transport. The main road from London to Carlisle, for example, was left in charge of no fewer than seventy-two separate local authorities. No overall national road policy was implemented, even after the 1909 Development Act – part of Lloyd George's financial revolution – had set up a Central Road Fund and a Road Board. The influence of vested interests and divided authority discouraged all but a small amount of road construction and re-aligning, though the Road Board was said to be ready with big schemes to be introduced when the next trade recession occurred.

The motor car had begun to be recognized as a coming force during the mid 1890s.[16] The editorial in the first number of *Autocar* (2.11.1895) remarked that 'the automatic carriage movement has come somewhat suddenly before the notice of the British public'. Bicycles had indeed prepared the way by accustoming people 'to the sight of wheeled vehicles without horses'. But what, asked *Autocar*, were the new vehicles to be called? 'Horseless carriage – automobile carriage – automatic carriage – autocar.' In the end none of these was accepted: 'motor car' became the usual English noun. The lead in the new development had come from Germany, France, and the United States. The first number of the *Daily Mail* (4.5.1896) admitted that 'Britannia's task of ruling the seas has left her a little careless of the rule of the road, as applied to horseless vehicles.' The main reason for this, as was often emphasized, had been restrictive legislation. Until 1896 the legal road speed limit for powered vehicles – fixed only with steam threshing and ploughing machines in mind – was a mere 4 miles per hour, set by an Act of 1865. This Act had also required a man with a red flag to walk in front, though an amendment of 1878 had dispensed with the red flag except where a local authority insisted upon it.

A well-connected motoring interest was already emerging, and its pressure secured the passing of the 1896 Locomotives on Highways Act. This raised the speed limit to 14 miles per hour, though the Local Government Board (through powers given to it under the Act) immediately lowered this to 12. To celebrate the initiation of the new rules the first London to Brighton run was organized; but only ten of the thirty-three starters finished the course. Nevertheless, the reliability of cars, and the confidence – even arrogance – of the pioneer motorists soon grew. A perceptive article by Joseph Pennell on 'Motors and Cycles: the Transition Stage' (*Contemporary Review*, February 1902) pointed out how only the wealthy could yet afford cars, and how car ownership was emphasizing class divisions. 'It is only since the coming of the automobile that I have known what it is to be poor.' Motorists soon became widely unpopular because of the noise, dust, and danger which they created. Significantly, Kenneth Grahame's Mr Toad in *The Wind in the Willows* (1908) was a reckless motorist. Bicycles had brought a liberating mobility, but wealthy motorists could now add speed to that mobility. W. E. Henley's *A Song of Speed* (1903) was a poem about a journey in the Mercedes of Alfred Harmsworth, owner of the *Daily Mail*:

> Speed as a chattel:
> Speed in your daily
> Account and economy;
> One with your wines
> And your books, and your bath –
> Speed!
> Speed as a rapture:
> An integral element
> In the new scheme of Life.

The number of road accidents increased rapidly as cars 'scorched' (the Edwardian word) along narrow and winding roads in town and country. The coincidence of the development of the motor car with the spread of female emancipation meant, as Osbert Sitwell remembered, that his was the first generation of young men able to take their girls for exciting fast drives.[17] The police soon had recourse to speed traps, disregarding complaints that they were 'un-English'. The immediate occasion for the establishment of the Automobile Association in 1905 was the ardour of the Sussex police in trying to curb speeding. The Association's scouts warned approaching members by not giving them the customary salute. In 1900 only 2,548 persons had been found guilty of traffic offences in England and Wales; by 1910 the total had reached 55,633. This amounted to over 9 per cent of all offences. For the first time, large numbers of the upper and middle classes were finding themselves on the wrong side of the law.[18]

The Motor Car Act of 1903 raised the speed limit to 20 miles per hour, and required the registering, numbering, and lighting of all cars. Cars could already far exceed this speed limit, but at least they were now recognized as a serious form of transport. The number in use in Great Britain was still only 8,465 in 1904; but this total had reached 32,451 by 1907. In 1914, 132,015 cars were registered, within a total of 388,860 motor vehicles of all kinds – private cars, motor cycles, buses, coaches, taxis, and goods vehicles. 23,151 'motor car attendants' were at work in England and Wales according to the 1911 census.

The first cars were all hand-built pieces of skilled engineering, and British makers gradually emerged who were able to compete with the foreign firms.[19] The Rolls-Royce partnership – of a dashing aristocratic enthusiast and a dedicated Manchester engineer – began in 1904. Rolls-Royce Silver Ghost models cost almost £1,000 from the first; and much more ordinary cars cost £300 upwards. *The Economist* (16.11.1907) commented shrewdly that a car was as yet only a substitute for a carriage and pair, and that it would not come into general use until it could compete in price with the horse and trap. The Edwardian car market did steadily widen, at least to the extent of reaching many of the solid middle classes. But this depth of demand did not constitute a real mass market, such as had already grown up in the United States after Henry Ford began production of his cheap Model T. In 1910 Ford did start manufacture in Manchester; but his English output of 6,000 vehicles in 1913 (Model T price £133) was insignificant compared with his American total of nearly 250,000. The whole British yearly output was then running at only 34,000 cars and commercial vehicles. An article on 'The Coming of the Cheap Car' in *The Times* (20.8.1912) warned of British unpreparedness. 'Much less would be heard of Juggernauts and road-hogs in the Press and elsewhere if motoring became more democratic ... If a valuable market is not to a large extent to be lost at the outset, the British manufacturer will have to set himself seriously to work to produce small cars as good and cheap as those now imported from abroad.' Fortunately, this challenge was about to be accepted by W. R. Morris. His Morris Oxford car, basic price £175, was announced at the 1912 motor show, though it had hardly gone into mass production when the 1914 war broke out.[20]

Many better-off Edwardians gained their first experience of motor travel through riding in a 'taxi', a quickly adopted abbreviation for 'taximeter car'.[21] Taxis became numerous on London's streets from 1907, and by 1914 receipts from motor cabs were exceeding those from horse cabs for the first time. Motor buses also displaced London's horse buses over much the same period.[22] The first motor buses were suitable only for rural routes with few stops; but the B type bus, introduced by London General from October 1910, quickly proved itself able to survive constant stopping and starting in city traffic. Within a year the company had withdrawn all its horse buses from service. Other companies gradually followed suit, and the last London horse bus in regular operation ran on 4 August 1914, the day of the declaration of war.

Between 1896 and 1913 the number of journeys in London by train grew from about 400 million to 710 million; but those by bus and tram had shot up from about 600 million to 1,545 million. Indication of how motor transport – which was already driving out the horse and even threatening the electric tramcar – would one day undermine the supremacy of the main-line train was first given during the great railway strike of 1911. In that year a significant number of middle-class people, unable to travel by rail, set out on their holidays for the first time by motor car. The railways were ceasing to be the undisputed masters in the provision of longer distance transport.

The continuing transport revolution was also taking on a new international dimension during these last pre-war years. At sea, huge turbine-driven luxury liners – such as the ill-fated *Titanic* (46,000 tons) – aimed to average twenty-five and more knots across the Atlantic. The sinking of this 'unsinkable' vessel on its maiden voyage in 1912 shook confidence not only in contemporary technology but also in contemporary society. The *Manchester Guardian* (11.4.1912) had described the ship before the tragedy as built for 'cosmopolitan millionaires' who regarded the sea as merely 'a dreary slum surrounding a Grand Babylon Hotel'. Left-wing commentators were unsurprised yet angered to note how 63 per cent of the first-class but only 23 per cent of the third-class passengers had been saved. Over 1,500 passengers and crew drowned, just over 700 survived.[23]

In the air the dream of centuries had at least been realized – the Edwardians could fly. An article on 'Flying Motor-cars' in the *Spectator* for 31 August 1901 had remarked how 'the usual telegram' had not yet arrived from the United States. But two years later it duly came, announcing the Wright brothers' first flight in a heavier-than-air machine. Yet even the normally perceptive *Daily Mail* (19.12.1903) only carried the news down page under the headline 'Balloonless Airship'; and the significance of this American achievement was not fully appreciated by the English public until 1909. Then the Frenchman, Louis Blériot, flew across the Channel from Calais to Dover. A hundred and twenty thousand people queued to see his plane on exhibition at Selfridge's store in London. H. G. Wells immediately drew the power political implications of Blériot's achievement. Britain was no longer safely protected by the sea. Here was great potential danger to the nation. But for individuals, continued Wells, here also was the removal of the last obstacle to personal mobility. Man had conquered land, sea, and now air.

The really wonderful thing in this astonishing development of cheap, abundant, swift locomotion we have seen in the last seventy years – in the development of which Mauretanias, aeroplanes, mile-a-minute expresses, tubes, motor-buses and motor-cars are just the bright, remarkable points – is this: that it dissolves almost all the reason and necessity why men should go on living permanently in any one place or rigidly disciplined to one set of conditions.

Man, concluded Wells, was 'off the chain of locality for good and all'.[24]

Notes

1. R. Lawton, 'Rural Depopulation in Nineteenth Century England', in D. R. Mills (ed.), *English Rural Communities* (1973), p. 195. See also C. M. Law, 'The Growth of

Urban Population in England and Wales, 1801–1911', *Transactions of the Institute of British Geographers*, XLI (1967).

2. See B. F. C. Costelloe, 'The Housing Problem', *Transactions of the Manchester Statistical Society*, 1899.
3. W. H. Chaloner, *The Social and Economic Development of Crewe* (1950), pp. 199–200. See also J. N. Tarn, *Five Per Cent Philanthropy* (1973), pp. 137–42; and A. S. Wohl, *The Eternal Slum* (1977), Ch. 10.
4. Burns Diary, 16 April, 14 July 1906, 3 October 1907 (B.L. Add. Mss. 46325).
5. See B. Abel-Smith, *The Hospitals, 1800–1948* (1964), Ch. 13.
6. See especially A. A. Jackson, *Semi-Detached London* (1973), Chs. 1–4.
7. T. C. Barker and M. Robbins, *History of London Transport* (1975–6), II, p. 4.
8. Sir W. Besant, *London in the Nineteenth Century* (1909), p. 28.
9. See especially W. Ashworth, *The Genesis of Modern British Town Planning* (1954), Chs. V, VII; and J. N. Tarn, *Five Per Cent Philanthropy* (1973), Ch. 9.
10. *The Times*, 30 October 1871.
11. See especially C. B. Purdom, *The Building of Satellite Towns* (2nd edn, 1949), parts I, II; and S. Bayley, *The Garden City* (1975).
12. See T. C. Barker and M. Robbins, *History of London Transport* (1975–6), II, Chs. I–VII.
13. Lucy Masterman, *C. F. G. Masterman* (1939), pp. 82–3; G. Haw, *Britain's Homes* (1902), p. 229.
14. See especially C. F. Klapper, *The Golden Age of Tramways* (1961); and J. P. McKay, *Tramways and Trolleys* (1976).
15. See S. and Beatrice Webb, *The Story of the King's Highway* (1913), Ch. X; and R. Jeffreys, *The King's Highway* (1949).
16. See especially A. Bird, *The Motor Car, 1765–1914* (1960); and W. Plowden, *The Motor Car and Politics, 1896–1970* (1971), part one.
17. Sir O. Sitwell, *Great Morning* (1948), pp. 234–5.
18. A. H. Halsey (ed.), *Trends in British Society Since 1900* (1972), p. 280.
19. See especially S. B. Saul, 'The Motor Industry in Britain to 1914', *Business History*, V (1962).
20. P. W. S. Andrews and Elizabeth Brunner, *Life of Lord Nuffield* (1959), esp. Chs. VI, VII; R. J. Overy, *William Morris, Viscount Nuffield* (1976), Ch. 1.
21. See G. N. Georgano, *History of the London Taxicab* (1972), Chs. 1–4.
22. See T. C. Barker and M. Robbins, *History of London Transport* (1975–6), II, esp. Chs. VI, VIII.
23. See G. Marcus, *The Maiden Voyage* (1969); and D. Read (ed.) *Documents from Edwardian England* (1973), pp. 50–1.
24. H. G. Wells, *An Englishman Looks at the World* (1914), Chs. 1–3. See also C. H. Gibbs Smith, *Aviation, An Historical Survey* (1970), and C. H. Gibbs Smith, *The Rebirth of European Aviation, 1902–1908* (1974).

Chapter 25

Religious life: *'A non-dogmatic affirmation of general kindliness'*

1

Church and chapel membership was still rising at the beginning of the twentieth century; but growth was not universal, and it was now heavily dependent upon recruitment of the children of existing members:[1]

	Church of England in England		
	Easter-Day Communicants	Churches	Clergy
1901	1,945,000	17,368	23,670
1911	2,293,000	—	23,193

	Methodist membership in England					
	Wesleyan	Primitive	New Connexion	Bible Christian	United	Total
1901	412,194	187,260	32,324	28,315	72,568	732,661
1906	447,474	203,103	37,701	32,317	80,323	800,234
				United Methodist		
1914	432,370	202,420		143,096		777,886

	Congregational and Baptist membership in England	
	Congregational	Baptist Union
1900	257,435	239,114
1914	289,545	264,923

	Roman Catholics in England and Wales			
	Estimated Catholic population	Churches	Priests	Mass attenders
1901	—	1,536	3,298	—
1913	1,793,038	1,845	3,650	960,000

The Presbyterian Church of England had 78,087 members in 1901, 88,166 in 1914. The Society of Friends expanded from 17,476 members in 1901 to 19,942 in 1914.

A religious census of London was taken by the *Daily News* in 1902–3.[2] This counted only some 830,000 worshippers in inner London compared with 1,400,000 non-attenders, persons available to attend divine service who did not do so. In outer London there were 420,000 worshippers compared with 460,000 non-attenders. This higher proportion of attendance reflected the greater practice of religious observance among the suburban middle classes than among the metropolitan working classes. Apart from Roman Catholics, and a comparative few Primitive Methodists, Baptists, and Salvationists, the London working classes continued to remain outside religious life. They lived defensively withdrawn inside their family circles. Attendance figures for the whole of London in 1902–3 totalled Church of England 538,000, Nonconformist 545,000, Roman Catholic 96,000, other 72,000. Comparison with the results of the 1886 *British Weekly* London census showed how religious observance in the capital had weakened, not simply in relation to population increase but even in absolute terms. Between 1886 and 1902–3, while the population of inner London was rising by well over 500,000 people, church and chapel attendance (even including 'twicers') fell by 164,000. The Church of England suffered most from this decline, with only about three London worshippers in 1902–3 for every four in 1886.

2

The noisy but unsuccessful opposition to the 1902 Education Act, which was alleged to favour the Church of England, proved to be the last powerful expression of Nonconformist militancy in England (see below, p. 435). Marriage with a deceased wife's sister – which nineteenth-century religious opinion had vehemently opposed on the ground that the Levitical Law forbade it – was at last allowed by an Act of 1907.[3] Even funerals were becoming less oppressive by the turn of the century. Queen Victoria's funeral in January 1901 had been conducted in white as a sign of joyfulness, as had Tennyson's in 1892. Mourning, remarked the *Manchester Guardian* (23.6.1906) had become 'as much out of date as Suttee'. Certainly, Courtaulds found their sales of crepe falling dramatically. Cremation was slowly gaining acceptance, and was regulated by the 1902 Cremation Act.[4]

How much did these changes in practice reflect a weakening of faith? In the autumn of 1904 the *Daily Telegraph* promoted a discussion on the theme, *Do We Believe?*, which attracted some 9,000 letters. Believers emphasized the importance of faith; unbelievers contended that men in an age of science knew where they stood without the aid of religion.[5] But Sir Oliver Lodge's popular *The Substance of Faith allied with Science* (1907) argued that acceptance of science was not incompatible with religious faith; on the contrary, it allowed 'a deeper insight into the Divine Nature'. Alternatively, J. A. Thompson contended in his *Introduction to Science* (1911) that science simply offered description; it remained for theology to offer interpretation.

In Edwardian theology immanentism became prominent, with its preference for 'the gospel of Jesus' against 'the gospel about Jesus'. R. J. Campbell, a popular Congregationalist preacher, published *The New Theology* (1907), which attracted considerable support, especially among the young and the left-wing.[6] Campbell emphasized, on the one hand, the immanence of God within human society; and on the other, the 'failure' of the churches within that society. He wanted to associate Christian profession closely with support for social reform. He described the Labour Party as 'in itself a Church, in the sense in which the word was originally used, for it represents the getting together of those who want to bring about the Kingdom of God'. Bernard Shaw in *Man and Superman* (1903) had publicized the idea of 'the Life Force', which impelled all living things. He described this as 'God in the act of creating Himself'. James Frazer's multi-volume *The Golden Bough* (1890–1915) collected a mass of information which illustrated the links between contemporary religion and ancient myths. This evidence could equally be used to demonstrate that Christian rites represented only a version of primitive superstition; or that the Christian message was the more relevant because it met a human need as old as man himself – that the 'will to believe' was perennial. William James, the influential American social psychologist, emphasized how there could be no certainty either in belief or disbelief. But he rejected the command 'that we shall put a stopper on our heart, instincts, and courage, and *wait* – acting of course meanwhile more or less as if religion were *not* true – till doomsday, or till such time as our intelligence and senses working together may have raked in evidence enough'.[7]

C. F. G. Masterman was pessimistic in *The Condition of England* (1909) about the future of Christianity. 'The drift is towards a non-dogmatic affirmation of general kindliness and good fellowship, with an emphasis rather on the service of man than the fulfilment of the will of God.' The religious bodies were concentrating more and more upon social and humanitarian improvement. The danger was that the clergy would obscure their special spiritual message without necessarily proving effective even as social workers. In the furtherance of social welfare clergymen were less well qualified than the specialists. Masterman noticed how schoolteachers were taking the influential position in the towns which had once been occupied by the clergy in the countryside. And J. A. Hobson remarked in *A Modern Outlook* (1910) how 'the care and cure of the body' had 'taken precedence of the care and cure of the soul. The doctor has largely displaced the priest.'

Notes

1. See A. D. Gilbert, *Religion and Society in Industrial England* (1976), Ch. 2, pp. 198–203; and R. Currie *et al.*, *Churches and Churchgoers* (1977).

2. R. Mudie-Smith (ed.), *The Religious Life of London* (1904). See also P. d'A. Jones, *The Christian Socialist Revival, 1877–1914* (1968), esp. Ch. III; O. Chadwick, *The Victorian Church*, II (2nd edn, 1972), esp. Ch. V: and H. McLeod, *Class and Religion in the Late Victorian City* (1974).

3. S. Buxton, *Handbook to Political Questions of the Day* (8th edn, 1892), pp. 358–60; R. Pearsall, *The Worm in the Bud* (1969), pp. 138–40.

4. D. C. Coleman, *Courtaulds*, I (1969), pp. 128–33, 194–6; J. Morley, *Death, Heaven, and the Victorians* (1971), Ch. 8.

5. See W. L. Courtney (ed.), *Do We Believe?* (1905).

6. See B. G. Worrall, 'R. J. Campbell and his New Theology', *Theology*, LXXXI (1978).

7. W. James, *The Will to Believe* (1897), pp. 29–30.

Chapter 26

Cultural life: *'I suffer nothing from reading the* Daily Mail'

1

An article on 'The Manufacture of Novels' in the *Spectator* for 31 October 1901 noted how the novel-reading public was continuing to grow, helped by the abolition of the three-volume novel. Novel reading had become 'the habitual recreation of the middle class . . . representatives of the same social stratum which a generation back perused with avidity the adventures of Jack Shephard are now devout readers of Miss Marie Corelli and Mr. Hall Caine.' These two late-Victorian romantic novelists published a succession of best-sellers, full of drama mixed with religiosity.[1] Hall Caine's *The Christian* (1897) sold 50,000 copies in a month, Marie Corelli's *The Master Christian* (1900) 260,000 in a few years. But best-sellers in the new century began to give less emphasis to religion or morality – novels such as Baroness Orczy's *The Scarlet Pimpernel* (1905), Edgar Wallace's *The Four Just Men* (1905), and Elinor Glyn's *Three Weeks* (1907). The popular preference in fiction was measured by a 1907 survey of the numbers of books held by twenty-one of the largest public libraries.[2] In all of them books by the leading Victorian popular novelists – Mary Elizabeth Braddon, Mrs Henry Wood, Ouida, Marie Corelli, and a few others – far outnumbered those by such 'serious' novelists as George Meredith, Henry James, or Joseph Conrad. The public library service was expanding rapidly about the turn of the century. Library authorities in England increased from 107 in 1886 to 438 by 1918. Public library stock grew from just over 1,800,000 volumes in 1885 to over 9,350,000 in 1914.

Lady Bell's *At The Works* (1907) calculated that more than a quarter of Middlesbrough workmen read books as well as newspapers; nearly a half read newspapers only; and a quarter did not read at all. Many self-improving workmen bought cheap editions of the classics.[3] W. T. Stead's Masterpiece Library, started in 1895, produced within two years 9 million copies of its condensed Penny Novels, and 5,276,000 of its Penny Poets. In 1906 J. M. Dent issued the first titles in his immediately successful Everyman's Library, which offered to the mass public classics of both the arts and the sciences in good quality format: 'a democratic library at the democratic price of one shilling'. Nearly 750 titles had been issued by 1914. Other important new series were the World's Classics (1901), Collins's Classics (1903), and the Home University Library of Modern Knowledge (1911). The *Manchester Guardian* (29.1.1906) commented that it would be 'not too fanciful to connect this increase in available literature with the great movement that has brought the accession of Labour Members to Parliament. It is all part of the widening of our national life'.

By this date the *Manchester Guardian* was providing almost daily book reviews and 'Books and Bookmen' articles. Middle-class interest in literature, and in literary gossip, was more extensive than ever before or since. 9,541 new books and new editions were published in 1913, over half as many again as at the beginning of the century. The written word had not yet to compete at home with the spoken word on radio or television. A handful of men of letters, who were also busy journalists, attracted a flattering degree of attention – notably, George Bernard Shaw, H. G. Wells, Arnold Bennett, G. K. Chesterton, and Hilaire Belloc. Old-fashioned critics complained that the quality of serious writing was being undermined, that writers were becoming propagandists. Certainly, many of the foremost names in Edwardian literature were well-known as advocates of social and political reform.[4] They were not sages in the Victorian manner of Carlyle or Ruskin – speaking powerfully at intervals from above – but pundits who could be read (or read about) in the newspapers almost every day. 'I have never taken my books seriously,' exclaimed Chesterton, 'but I take my opinions quite seriously.' Chesterton's fantasies and the satires of Belloc expressed the Anglo-Catholicism of the one and the Roman Catholicism of the other in social criticism which suggested remedies akin to those of the syndicalists. John Galsworthy's plays and novels – headed by *The Man of Property* (1906), the start of the Forsyte Saga – never seemed quite at ease either in their exposures of the upper middle class from which Galsworthy himself sprang, or in their advocacy of the working classes with which he felt sympathy. H. G. Wells, a genius of many parts, was in literary terms most notable as the author of *Kipps* (1905) and *The History of Mr Polly* (1910), novels which brilliantly combined social insight with readability.[5] When in 1914 one literary periodical polled its readers to discover their choice of the greatest living novelists, the winner was Thomas Hardy, with Wells second, and Joseph Conrad third. Conrad's *Chance* was the novel of the year – his first popular success, full of reflections upon life and especially upon the role of women, which had become a major contemporary concern.[6]

From the late-Victorian into the Edwardian years the novel continued as the favourite literary form. Nevertheless, the revival of English drama, which had begun during the 1890s, persisted into the new century. M. Borsa's *The English Stage of Today* (1908) claimed that the number of playgoers had risen by 44 per cent in ten years.[7] Melodrama was still very popular, and not only with the working classes. But Bernard Shaw had now become a middle-class favourite, especially with those of his plays which amused as well as lectured. 'Some day, when the laughter is forgotten, when the burlesque has dropped out of consciousness, he trusts that the idea will return and irritate, if not convince . . . Art for art's sake he loathes, as he loathes a childless marriage.'[8] Many of Shaw's more daring plays had been written in the 1890s; but they had mostly been performed only in private at that time. In the new reign they were at last widely seen, especially during the great Vedrenne-Barker repertory seasons at the Court Theatre, London, from 1904 to 1907. Shaw's most popular plays at the Court were *Man and Superman, You Never Can Tell, John Bull's Other Island, Captain Brassbound's Conversion, Major Barbara*, and *The Doctor's Dilemma*. The Court Theatre seasons were too good to last; but they had made a lasting impression. In Manchester Miss Annie Horniman's repertory company established itself at the Gaiety Theatre in 1907.[9] The aim, explained the *Manchester Guardian* (16 August), was to make playgoing 'as much a part of the mental life of educated people here as novel-reading is'. And, though always financially insecure, Miss Horniman's 'Manchester School' did succeed in this purpose. Before 1914 repertory companies had also been started at Liverpool, Bristol, and Birmingham.

English poets at the beginning of the twentieth century could not compare with English novelists or dramatists. The most popular contemporary poetry was not lyrical but narrative verse, notably that of Henry Newbolt and John Masefield. Not until 1912 did the first volume of *Georgian Poetry* appear, a sensitive selection from the work of younger poets. This set out to be fresh and realistic – deliberately post-Victorian – just as the novel and the drama had become realistic, both in subject and in language.[10] The refreshment of this approach gave the Georgians a sense of elation and new beginning. Rupert Brooke, destined through his war poems to become the best-known Georgian poet, described himself as 'given to the enchantment of being even for a moment alive in a world of real matter'. But in retrospect the Georgians still seem to relate to the Victorians whom they sought to reject.

2

As in drama so in serious music late-Victorian and Edwardian England enjoyed a burst of creativity by home-bred composers after a century and more of small achievement.[11] 'Much foreign music that was once greatly admired here has fallen into commendable disrepute.' So remarked Ernest Newman, a rising young music critic, in an article on 'English Music and Musical Criticism' in the *Contemporary Review* of November 1901. 'Only the outcasts of musical society – at each end of the social scale – now hanker after the worst products of Italian opera. Mendelssohn's influence and following are becoming smaller year after year. The passion for oratorio is dying.' Orchestral music was coming to take first place in popular appeal. Henry Wood had conducted the Promenade Concerts at the Queen's Hall, London, since 1895. A *Times* leading article (21.10.1910) on 'The Popularity of Music' claimed that the success of these concerts demonstrated how music was 'the one popular art of the present day, or rather the one art about which popular and cultivated opinions are not hopelessly at variance'. 'The land without music' now produced four composers of significance: Edward Elgar, Frederick Delius, Ralph Vaughan Williams, and Gustav Holst. Elgar was both the most important and the best-known of the group.[12] His major works – such as *The Dream of Gerontius* (1900), the first symphony (1908), or the violin concerto (1910) – conveyed a feeling of what he himself called 'stately sorrow', which seems in retrospect to have been appropriate to an end period in history. His music reflected both the self-doubt and self-assertion of the time. Assertion was expressed with least qualification in the *Pomp and Circumstance* marches (1901–7). The first of these was given the words of 'Land of Hope and Glory'; and so became Elgar's most popular work, virtually a second national anthem. The words were not Elgar's, but he rightly remained proud of the tune. 'I know that there are a lot of people who like to celebrate events with music. To these people I have given tunes. Is that wrong?' The music of Holst and Vaughan Williams was influenced by traditional English folk songs.[13] The English Folk Song Society had been founded in 1898 to develop and extend the work of collection begun by a few enthusiasts during Victoria's reign. The most pertinacious collector was Cecil Sharp, who recorded some 3,000 songs in England before his death in 1924.

But the Edwardians' own folk songs were being written for musical comedy and for the music hall.[14] Musical comedy emerged as a new light theatrical confection – a mixture of tuneful songs and lavish decor, with glamorous leading ladies and chorus girls. London's foremost musical-comedy manager was George Edwardes of the Gaiety Theatre, who was responsible for the first musical comedy, *In Town* (1892). This ran for 295 performances. A succession of even more successful shows followed through the Edwardian years. 'We went again for the *n*th time to see *The Merry Widow* last night,' wrote Lord Esher in his diary for 4 January 1908, 'one of the most charming plays with music that has ever been put on the stage.' Musical-comedy leading ladies could move (and marry) in the highest social circles. Esher's own younger son married Zena Dare, one such star.

The music hall had now become much more 'respectable' and much more organized than in its rough early days of the 1850s and 1860s.[15] Moss Empires opened a chain of halls with plush seats and no bars so that matrons could enjoy the show without fear of impropriety. They could watch such favourites as Harry Lauder, George Robey, and Vesta Tilley at the main theatres (where leading performers could earn several hundred pounds per week), and lesser names at the suburban houses. By 1908 London alone possessed over fifty music halls. Edward VII had visited the halls privately; but in 1912 George V formally attended the first Royal Command Variety Performance. With this event the music hall had finally achieved recognition as a national institution. The command performers included Lauder and Robey, but not the saucy

Marie Lloyd.

Yet the music hall was already past its best. Commercialization and 'respectability' were sapping its verve. Managers and performers started to play safe. As early as 1899 an article called 'The Blight on the Music Halls' by Max Beerbohm was complaining about attempts to eliminate vulgarity, 'an implicit element of the true Music Hall'. Managers tried to make up for vulgarity with 'variety', a succession of comedians, singers, dancers, jugglers, tumblers, male impersonators, female impersonators, soubrettes, ventriloquists, and any novelty acts available. Short cinematograph shows became one such novelty from the turn of the century. The Empire, Leicester Square, had led the way with these from 1896.[16] Not until some eleven years later were the first cinemas opened, for the seeing of films alone. The first London cinema was claimed for Balham in 1907, and thereafter the spread was rapid. Big business in the shape of Provincial Cinematograph Theatres Limited appeared in 1909, and by 1914 at least 3,500 cinemas were in existence.

Edwardian cinema audiences were youthful and predominantly working-class – with the middle classes adopting the same condescending line towards the new medium which they were to show towards television in the early 1950s. Many working-class cinemagoers had never been regular patrons of theatres or music halls. They constituted a brand-new public for mass entertainment. Courting couples could share not only the new experience of watching pictures that moved (though they did not yet talk), but also of sitting together in semi-darkness. When *The Drunkard's Reformation* (a 'great moral picture') was shown in full light at West Hendon in 1909, 'the dangers of darkness thus being avoided', attendances dropped sharply.[17] The earliest films were short sketches, often knockabout comedy. Newsreels were also much liked. By the immediate pre-war years full-length films were coming into popularity, and film stars were emerging. These were mostly American, for in 1913 only some 15 per cent of films shown were British-made. Charlie Chaplin, though London-born, achieved world fame from Hollywood, where he made his first comedy film early in 1914.

Edwardian films were silent, but recorded sound was adding its impact to the communications revolution.[18] The phonograph, or speaking machine (1877), and the motion picture camera (1889) were both inventions associated with the American, Thomas Edison. But Edison's phonograph, which used cylinders, was gradually displaced by the gramophone, which played discs and which gave much better reproduction. The Edwardian gramophone was able to reproduce vocal music with acceptable authenticity, though recorded orchestral music sounded tinny. A playing time of only three or four minutes per side further discouraged the recording of long orchestral works. Songs from opera and ballads were much favoured, as were comic songs and sketches. Two outstanding singers, Enrico Caruso and Nellie Melba, contributed greatly to establish the popularity of the gramophone, overcoming its limitations with performances in which strong character reinforced superlative technique. But Melba recordings cost as much as a guinea per disc in 1904. Record buyers presumably came from the middle and upper classes.

3

1896 had been a key year in the development of mass communications and mass entertainment in England. Within the space of a few months an Italian, Guglielmo Marconi, came to London to show the Post Office how he could transmit signals by wireless; the Empire music hall began to run cinematograph films; and on 4 May Alfred Harmsworth published the first number of the *Daily Mail*.

The same new technology which was developing wireless, the cinematograph, and the gramophone was also transforming newspaper production. Mechanical type-setting, and new presses capable of printing ten or twelve-page newspapers (compared with eight) at the high speed of 20,000 per hour cut the *Mail*'s production costs by a quarter or a half. As a result, it could appear as 'a Penny Newspaper for One Halfpenny'. The *Mail* also soon began to attract numerous profitable advertisements, including whole page spreads.[19] The classified newspaper advertisements of earlier days had been aimed at more or less small groups, whereas the appeal of the new display advertising was to a wide general public. *Mail* readers came chiefly from the middle and lower middle classes. The paper was designed to meet the needs, as Harmsworth shrewdly explained, not so much of comfortable £1,000 a year men as of men who vaguely hoped one day to reach £1,000. It was 'The Busy Man's Daily Journal' – a 'bright' morning paper which such readers could enjoy in the train or the tram on the way to work. Harmsworth discerningly separated news into two categories: 'actualities' and 'talking points'. The first, he explained, was 'news in its narrowest and best sense, reports of *happenings*, political resignations, strikes, crimes, deaths of famous people, wrecks and railway smashes, weather storms, sporting results, and so on. The second is getting the topics people are discussing and developing them, or stimulating a topic oneself.'[20] The most extreme way of stimulating a topic was to run a stunt. Some stunts were beneficial – like the prizes offered to encourage aviation progress, culminating in the £10,000 London–Manchester air race of 1910. Others were silly but harmless, like the campaign for the *Daily Mail* hat. But all made news, and news, not all serious, from far and wide was what the lower middle classes loved to read. Long-winded leading articles were rejected by the *Mail* in favour of short leaders. Politics were noticed when important; but Harmsworth emphasized that they were not to enjoy any 'divine right' to space. Long reports of political speeches were not found in the *Mail*. On the other hand, a lively political oration from a leading personality such as Lloyd George or Winston Churchill was likely to be awarded an appropriately lively summary.

Harmsworth's successful wooing of the lower middle classes gave the *Daily Mail* in its first decade the highest circulation ever attained by a daily newspaper. Sales were boosted to almost 1 million per day during the Boer War excitement of 1900. And they averaged over 750,000 during the Edwardian years before passing the 1 million mark in 1915, helped by the demand for war news. Journalism had now become much more a big business operation in search of profits, much less a gentlemanly pursuit of influence. Profits came not only from sales but also from advertising charges, which rose with rising circulation. Ownership was becoming concentrated in a few rival hands. By 1910 two-thirds of the London morning circulation and four-fifths of the evening circulation was controlled by three groups – Harmsworth's, Pearson's, and the *Morning Leader* group.[21] Yet, despite the success of the *Daily Mail* and its popular rivals, the older-established papers survived, albeit with some loss of circulation and some enlivening of presentation. This indicated the large extent to which Harmsworth was finding new newspaper readers. The total of daily newspaper readers has been estimated to have doubled between 1896 and 1906, and then to have doubled again by 1914.[22] Spending on newspaper-buying grew from under £8 million in 1901 to well over £13 million in 1913.

In terms of typography and layout the *Daily Express*, started by C. A. Pearson in 1900, was more innovating than the *Mail*. It carried news on the front page from the start, whereas the *Mail* followed the traditional practice of leaving the front page to advertisements. In 1903 Harmsworth started the *Daily Mirror*, intended to be a paper written by gentlewomen for gentlewomen, price one penny. It was an instant failure; but the venture was saved by transforming it in 1904 into a daily illustrated paper at one halfpenny, the first to make regular use of half-tone photographs. These could now be reproduced satisfactorily in newspapers. The *Mirror* eventually overtook the *Mail* in circulation – to become in 1912 the first daily paper to reach a million sale.

In 1908 Harmsworth bought *The Times*.[23] Since the retirement of J. T. Delane as editor in 1877 the paper had gone down steadily in influence and in circulation. But it remained a national institution; and Harmsworth was proud to use his wealth to restore its position. He gradually achieved this without (as was feared) either changing the tone of the paper or reducing the editor's independence. Sales grew from only 38,000 daily in 1908 to over 150,000 just before the war, helped by the price reductions from threepence to twopence in 1913 and then daringly to one penny in March 1914. Harmsworth's other 'quality' newspaper was the Sunday *Observer*, which he owned between 1905 and 1911.[24] Under the editorship from 1908 of J. L. Garvin, the *Observer* quickly gained great influence within Conservative circles. Its sales rose twelvefold to reach 60,000 weekly by 1911. The Edwardian press included several other publications of limited circulation but significant influence. The most successful politico-literary weekly was the

Conservative *Spectator*, edited by St Loe Strachey, which was selling about 23,000 copies per number in 1903. Two weeklies which lost money were the radical *Nation*, started in 1907 and with a circulation of only 5,000 by 1909; and the socialist *New Statesman*, launched by the Webbs and their friends in 1913 with a sale of 3,000–4,000 copies.

The 'quality' press held a low opinion of the lively *Daily Mail* and of the illustrated *Daily Mirror*. One jibe asserted that the *Mail* was designed 'for those who cannot think', and the *Mirror* 'for those who cannot read'.[25] Yet Harmsworth must be given credit for being the first daily journalist to address a large section of the urban and suburban lower middle class. The 'serious' Edwardian journals looked down upon this important audience. Such an attitude was the more odd because many of them were avowedly on the popular side in politics. But their journalism was too intellectual, too heavy. 'A people that never cared much for education, bred in towns and fond of sport, regards its newspapers as the handiest form of intellectual dissipation, cheaper, more varied, more amusing than the theatre or music hall, the recorder and appraiser of its pleasures.' So complained H. W. Massingham, editor of the *Nation*, 1907–23, in an article on 'The Materialism of English Life' (*Contemporary Review*, June 1904). Massingham wanted a committed political reading public. 'Clearly this is a different atmosphere from that which produced Chartism or the Reform Movement of the sixties and seventies, an atmosphere from which the elements of deep need and deep feeling are alike absent. This is a society made for cheap journalism.' Massingham forgot that the Chartist and Reform Bill periods were crisis moments of heightened political interest. The Edwardians could show strong political feelings when roused, as in the 1906 election or in the 'peers versus people' conflict. But the new mass reading public was unwilling to give continuous attention to political argument. In assuming that Harmsworth's approach was completely wrong, his critics forfeited all hope of making contact with the new readership. A. V. Dicey, the Oxford jurist, made a revealingly contradictory confession in 1905: 'I suffer nothing from reading the *Daily Mail* and often read it. I am quite sincere in believing the decline in the character of the press to be an evil, but nevertheless am often amused and interested by the *Daily Mail*.'[26]

4

By the end of the nineteenth century journalism for children was also flourishing, led by the *Boy's Own Paper*. This had been started by the Religious Tract Society in 1879. Under a skilful editor, G. A. Hutchison, who kept the religious and moral message clear but not too intrusive, the *BOP* quickly achieved remarkable success, reaching a sale of 200,000 copies per week. Among its contributors were Jules Verne and Conan Doyle.[27] The *BOP* and its rivals – such as *Chums* (1892) and *The*

Captain, 'A Magazine for Boys and Old Boys', started in 1899 – were published for middle-class and lower middle-class boys. Children in this social range were able to enjoy some outstanding new writing about the turn of the century. As well as G. A. Henty's many historical and contemporary adventure stories – such as *With Clive in India* (1884), *With Wolfe in Canada* (1886), and *With Roberts to Pretoria* (1902) – they could read Kipling's *Jungle Books* (1894–5), *Stalky and Co.* (1898), and *Just So Stories for Little Children* (1902); Kenneth Grahame's *The Wind in the Willows* (1908); and Beatrix Potter's animal fantasies. In addition, they could see J. M. Barrie's play, *Peter Pan* (1904). Edwardian middle-class children were also increasingly well supplied with toys. At the suggestion of H. G. Wells (a keen player of war games), toy soldiers were made to scale with the latest mechanical train sets manufactured by Frank Hornby. In 1907 Hornby marketed 'Meccano'. The Teddy Bear, inspired by President Theodore Roosevelt, first appeared in 1903.[28]

The *Manchester Guardian* (26.12.1906) wrote approvingly of a local production of *Peter Pan*. It was satisfied that middle-class children were well supplied both with education and enjoyment. But it was much less satisfied about the education and upbringing of working-class children. Admittedly, by the time they grew up they could now read and write; but many workmen then read 'little but betting news' and wrote 'little beyond betting slips'. The *Guardian* (22.10.1906) conceded that 'perhaps the enthusiasts for education hoped too much from it in 1870'. The paper remained convinced, however, that mass education would achieve the right results in the end. 'The educational system of 1870 has long been outgrown. The famous "Three R's" have grown into a complicated curriculum which aims at developing the mind along the right lines.' The 1890 code had marked the beginning of the end of 'payment by results'. By the close of the century teachers were enjoying a new latitude; and creative activities, games, physical education, and visits out of school were becoming customary, at least in the better elementary schools. The big expansion in the numbers of inspected elementary schools in England and Wales was now completed – 31,234 schools with 4,666,000 pupils in 1900, 32,480 schools with 5,393,000 pupils in 1914.

The board schools had emerged by the end of the nineteenth century as generally much superior to the voluntary denominational schools both in buildings and facilities. Voluntary effort had proved unable to keep up. By 1895 expenditure per child in average attendance had reached £2 10s. 1¾d. in board schools, but only £1 18s. 11¼d. in voluntary schools.[29] A large majority of the voluntary schools belonged to the Church of England, towards which the Conservative Governments in power at the turn of the century felt sectarian sympathy. But Conservative Ministers, including notably A. J. Balfour, Prime Minister from 1902, were also genuinely concerned to promote a high standard of elementary schooling in the national interest. Furthermore, they recognized the need for intervention to provide improved education at the secondary level, if the British Empire was to compete successfully in trade and in war during the new century. The 1895 Bryce Commission report on secondary education had emphasized how it was 'not merely in the interest of the material prosperity and intellectual activity of the nation, but no less in that of its happiness and moral strength, that the extension and reorganization of Secondary Education seem entitled to a place among the first subjects with which social legislation ought to deal'.[30] In 1896 the Conservatives introduced a bill which would have abolished the limit on the amount of state grant to denominational schools by removing the requirement for corresponding voluntary subscriptions. At the same time it proposed to restrict the sums which school boards could raise from the rates in support of their schools. It also wanted to permit 'reasonable arrangements' for separate denominational religious instruction in both voluntary and board schools, where enough parents of any denomination desired it. The bill, however, provoked diverse but widespread opposition from Nonconformists, Anglicans, and schoolteachers; and it was withdrawn. In the following year a much less ambitious measure was passed which exempted voluntary schools from payment of rates and increased the state grants to them. County and county borough councils, not the school boards, were recognized as the local education authorities for secondary education.

This last move was part of the Conservative attempt to simplify educational administration, which at both the local and national levels had drifted into muddle and overlap as a result of years of compromise and improvization. Some progress towards a unified central authority came with the bringing together in 1900 of the Education Department, the Science and Art Department, and the Charity Commissioners (in respect of their educational work) under a new Board of Education. Its President became in effect minister of education. At the local level Sir John Gorst – the last Vice-President of the Committee of the Privy Council on Education – determined to check the extension of school board activity into the secondary field. This had spread through the provision in some towns of higher grade schools, and in many places of evening classes. Gorst, abetted by his private secretary, Robert Morant, arranged for the whole of the London School Board expenditure on secondary education to be challenged through the auditor, T. B. Cockerton. Cockerton ruled that such provision could not lawfully be met from the rates. The London board appealed to the High Court, which at the end of 1900 ruled in favour of the auditor. The Cockerton decision was finally confirmed by the Court of Appeal in April 1901.

The Conservative Government was now able to move boldly forward to solve the crisis which it had deliberately brought to a head. Its plan was shaped by Morant (soon to become Permanent Secretary of the Board of Education) in association with Balfour, who was willingly carried along by the civil servant's purposeful energy. 'If we hesitate to do our duty,' concluded Balfour, 'and carry through this great reform, then I say we shall receive the contempt of the parents of the children living and to be born, for the next generation.'[31] The 1902 Education Act therefore insisted upon the need for unified control of public education. County and county borough councils were designated as the local education authorities, with paramount responsibility and rating powers both for secondary and for elementary schooling. Not only were the school boards abolished, the voluntary denominational schools were now to be supported from the local rates. The policy of 1870 was thus repudiated in two of its most important provisions. The managers of denominational schools were to include a minority (usually two out of six) of local authority representatives. Where 'management' ended and local authority control began was deliberately left vague. But managers were to continue to appoint teachers. Not surprisingly, the bitter old cry 'the Church on the rates' was revived by Nonconformist ultras, who refused to recognize the national need to sustain and improve Anglican education. A noisy campaign of opposition was promoted, led in the country by Dr John Clifford, a much respected Baptist minister, and with Lloyd George to the fore in the Commons. The bill took the unprecedentedly long time of nine months to pass through Parliament, where it came under fire not only from the Liberals but also from some Anglicans on the Government side who had reservations of their own.[32] An amendment – intended to curb the influence of ritualist Anglican clergy – which gave control of religious instruction to school managers instead of to the parish clergyman, provoked one Anglican cleric to describe the change as 'the greatest betrayal since the Crucifixion'. Nonconformist feeling waxed equally bitter. In September over 100,000 people were said to have attended a protest rally on Woodhouse Moor, Leeds. After the Act had been passed, a National Passive Resistance Committee was formed to organize a mass Nonconformist refusal to pay education rates. By the end of 1904 over 37,000 summonses had been issued, and distraint of goods in lieu of payment had occurred in some 1,500 cases. Eighty resisters had been committed to prison. Resistance by otherwise respectable citizens continued even up to 1914, but never with sufficient effect to endanger the new education system.

Clifford was sure that the Church of England was unscrupulously seeking to extend its power. 'It is not the tolerant and inclusive Church of the days of Lord Shaftesbury, but the bigoted and persecuting Church of the times of Laud and Whitgift.' Balfour, however, was able to emphasize the national benefits to be expected from the 1902 Act, even while he remained well aware that he had saved the Anglican school network. 'The existing education system of this country is chaotic, is ineffectual, is utterly behind the age, makes us the laughing-stock of every advanced nation in Europe and America.' It was not possible, continued Balfour adroitly but sensibly, to provide schools within reach of all the children which gave religious instruction in every desired variation: 'the only possible alternative in which there is even a semblance of justice is one which, while it permits so-called undenominational teaching in schools entirely supported out of the public funds, permits denominational teaching in schools which are not so wholly supported out of public funds.'

The 1902 Act (plus the equivalent 1903 Act for London) certainly succeeded in giving a great impetus to the nationwide provision of secondary education, even though doubts have been expressed whether Balfour foresaw the expense and bureaucracy that would follow.[33] In 1905 the total of inspected secondary schools in England and Wales stood at 575 with 94,698 pupils; by 1914 the figures had reached 1,027 schools with 187,647 pupils. *Regulations for Secondary Schools* (1904) laid down guidelines for the content and spirit of state secondary education. The emphasis was to be upon a good general course, and arts subjects (including compulsory Latin) were favoured; but teaching of science and mathematics was also made compulsory. Though not an adventurous syllabus, it was a coherent one.

The complementary 1904 elementary code outlined a programme of education for the majority which has been characterized by one historian as 'training in followership rather than leadership training'.[34] On the other hand, it spoke of the 'important though subsidiary object' of elementary education 'to discover individual children who show promise of exceptional capacity', and to prepare them for entry into the secondary schools. The idea of an educational 'ladder' predominated, even after 1908 when the Liberals introduced the 'free place' system. Secondary schools which did not reserve one-quarter of their places, free of fees, for children educated in public elementary schools were to receive a lower state grant. Here was a limited but significant widening of selection. Working-class children of good ability, not just the outstandingly brilliant, could now win secondary school places. In the event, however, still only relatively small numbers of pupils from humble homes were to find room in the secondary schools. Of boys and girls born before 1910 an estimated 37 per cent from professional and managerial families received secondary education, only 8 per cent from the classes below; for the 1910–19 age group the proportions were to be 47 per cent and 17 per cent respectively.[35] In other words, the first beneficiaries of the new system were not so much the working classes as the lower middle classes. Nevertheless, this constituted in itself an educational extension of high importance.

Equality of opportunity was still assumed by most of its advocates to imply selection on Darwinian lines.[36] But the radical view that equality of opportunity ought to mean more than equal opportunities for becoming unequal – that it ought to mean equal education for all – was being voiced with increasing strength during the Edwardian period. 'It is a broad, easy stair, and not a narrow ladder, that is wanted, one which will entice everyone to rise, will make for general and not for selected culture.' So argued J. A. Hobson in *The Crisis of Liberalism* (1909). R. H. Tawney contended in the *Political Quarterly* for May 1914 that it was not enough for a few able working-class boys and girls to be admitted to universities, or even for many more to be admitted in the future. 'We want as much university education as we can get for the workers who *remain* workers all their lives . . . not simply equality of opportunity but universality of provision.' Tawney's article was reprinted as a pamphlet by the Workers' Educational Association. This had been formed in 1903 by a diverse group of bishops, dons, and self-educated working men; and it began to conduct tutorial classes five years later. Its guiding spirit was Albert Mansbridge. Tawney himself led a highly successful pioneering class at Rochdale.[37] University extra-mural classes also greatly increased in number during the Edwardian period until about 50,000 students were participating each year. Unfortunately, scientific and technological subjects could hardly be taught by such methods. Economics and economic history became the favourite WEA course subjects.

5

These Edwardian working-class men and women were earnestly seeking to join a cultural world which found itself in a state of growing flux. The new beginning of the 1890s in the arts had not lasted long in England; but after a few years 'modernism' had returned with a second wind.[38] Continental influences once more began to be strongly felt in literature, in poetry, in music, and in thought. They came at first only after long delays, but by 1914 much more urgently. The old idea of linear progress in history (which had been as much accepted by Marx as it had been by Macaulay) was now sharply rejected, under the influence of thinkers such as Henri Bergson, whose *Time and Free-Will* was translated into English in 1910. In this spirit, one of the most influential of the new politico-literary journals simply but boldly called itself the *New Age* (1907). It noticed (26.1.1911) the prevailing 'disposition to expect a new earth, if not a new heaven'.[39]

In painting, a succession of new 'isms', which deliberately and disturbingly cut off from traditional styles – post-impressionism, cubism, futurism, vorticism – made an assault upon the Edwardian imagination just before 1914. The Vorticist journal *Blast*, started in June 1914, celebrated the end of tradition and historical sense. Vorticists lived for the present. 'Our vortex is not afraid of the Past: it has forgotten its existence.' The aim was 'to make the rest of the community shed their education skin, to destroy politeness'. Looking back from 1924, Virginia Woolf, the novelist, decided that 'in or about December 1910 human character changed'. She remembered how attitudes to art, to life, and to human relationships were becoming much more flexible in the years just before 1914. 'All human relations have shifted – those between masters and servants, husbands and wives, parents and children. And when human relations change there is at the same time a change in religion, conduct, politics, and literature. Let us agree to place one of these changes about the year 1910.'[40]

Edward VII had died in May 1910; the 'peers versus people' constitutional crisis was raging throughout the year; Blériot had flown the English Channel in 1909. But Virginia Woolf chose December 1910 because during that month the post-impressionist exhibition was being held at the Grafton Galleries, London, organized by her friend Roger Fry, the art critic.[41] This display of paintings by Cézanne, Gauguin, Van Gogh, Vlaminck, Picasso, and others – artists already familiar in France but still little-known in England – was widely received as either a bad joke, attempted fraud, or covert foreign promotion of sedition. 'It professes to simplify, and to gain simplicity it throws away all that the long-developed skill of past artists had acquired and bequeathed.' So complained *The Times* (7.11.1910). 'Like anarchism in politics, it is the rejection of all that civilization has done.' But the *Manchester Guardian* (18 November) was more sympathetic, remembering the initial hostility shown towards the pre-Raphaelites and then towards Whistler. The uproar at least showed that people still cared about art. Fry himself tried to explain why paintings did not need to 'tell a story' in the Victorian manner. 'These artists do not seek to give what can, after all, be but a pale reflex of actual appearance, but to arouse the conviction of a new and definite reality ... to make images which by the clearness of their logical structure, and by their closely-knit unity of texture, shall appeal to our disinterested imagination.' Fry gradually made his point. By the time of a second post-impressionist exhibition at the end of 1912 the style no longer seemed so revolutionary. Nor was it, compared with the other 'isms' which were now reaching England in quick succession. English insularity in art was finding itself under irresistible challenge.

The post-impressionist exhibition was a triumph for the tiny, self-admiring but brilliant 'Bloomsbury group' of intellectuals, who helped Fry to stage it. The group included not only artists and critics such as Fry, Duncan Grant, and Clive Bell; but writers such as Virginia Woolf, Lytton Strachey, and John Maynard Keynes, the Cambridge economist. Bertrand Russell (who was himself somewhat older than the Bloomsburyites) remembered 'how great a change in mental climate those ten years had brought. We were still Victorian; they were Edwardian. We believed in ordered progress by means of politics and free discussion. The more self-confident among us may have hoped to be leaders of the multitude, but none of us wished to be divorced from it. The generation of Keynes and Lytton did not seek to preserve any kinship with the Philistine.' They aimed at a life, contended Russell tartly, of refined retirement, 'and conceived of the good as consisting in the passionate mutual admiration of a clique of the elite.' This doctrine they attributed to G. E. Moore, the Cambridge philosopher, whose *Principia Ethica* (1903) they claimed to admire, but whose views on morals (as Keynes later admitted) they chose to ignore.[42]

The new public awareness of French painting was soon matched by a new appreciation of Russian literature, and in particular of Russian ballet. Dostoevsky's *The Brothers Karamazov* was proclaimed by Arnold Bennett in the *New Age* (31.3.1910) as 'one of the supreme marvels of the world'. Chekhov's plays were also being discovered, though still only by small audiences. But Diaghilev's Russian ballet, which first reached Covent Garden in the summer of 1911 (and returned in 1912 and 1913), suddenly attracted full houses of enthusiastic admirers. The gorgeous settings and costumes for the company's new dances, the fresh and exciting music of Stravinsky and Debussy, the brilliant dancing of Nijinsky and Karsavina in ballets such as *Le Spectre de la Rose* and *L'Après Midi d'un Faune*, created an unprecedented experience for sober English audiences. A *Times* correspondent (5.8.1911) concluded that the Russian ballet had 'brought a positively new art, it has extended the realms of beauty'. Edward Marsh, the literary critic, rightly linked the new ballet with the new painting. 'It's a Post-Impressionist picture put in motion.'[43]

Of course, only a small minority could directly experience the sights and sounds of the Russian ballet. But a radical new sound of a different kind was being heard by many more – American ragtime music. This crossed the Atlantic in 1911. Rupert Brooke saw the review *Hello Ragtime* no less than ten times. Alongside this noisy new music came new undecorous dances – the turkey trot, the bunny hug, the chicken scramble. These dances encouraged and reflected an easier relationship between the sexes. The tango, in particular, shocked the old-fashioned – it was declared to be 'not a dance but an assault'.[44]

The tango could not have been danced in the voluminous women's dress of the Victorian period. But costume too had suddenly changed. During nearly a century the basic shape of women's clothes had consisted of more or less ample angles and curves. Then quite suddenly in 1910 a decisively vertical line with a high waistband became established, as women shaped themselves into a letter 'H'. Ankles began to show. Women's dress, in short, was reflecting their wish to find greater freedom. 1911 witnessed a rage for violent colours in place of the pastel shades of Edward's reign, perhaps a symptom of the new restlessness. One *Punch* cartoon (13.12.1911) called 'A Decade's Progress' summed up the whole trend. It showed a grandmother, mother, and daughter as they had been dressed in 1901 and as they were now attired in 1911. The dowdy voluminous clothes of the earlier date, which had turned the grandmother into an old lady and had made the mother seem plain, had been replaced by much simpler, looser wear, which gave a look of release to all three females. The 'flapper', the characteristic young women of the 1920s, had already been given that name by 1914.[45] As with women's dress so with interior decoration, a new simplicity was becoming the fashion – at least in upper and upper middle-class homes. Photographs taken by Bedford Lemaire of rooms in upper-class houses showed how by 1910 most of the Victorian knick-knacks had been removed, how heavy wallpapers had been replaced by plain paint, how the potted palms had disappeared, and how tables and chairs had been reduced simply to the numbers required for use.[46] In decoration, dress, music, art, and literature – as in social, economic, and political life – standards of what seemed desirable or proper were shifting. The First World War was only to accelerate a transformation which had already begun.

Notes

1. See D. Hudson, 'Reading', in S. Nowell-Smith (ed.), *Edwardian England* (1964); and C. Cockburn, *Bestseller* (1972), pp. 1–74.
2. E. A. Baker, 'The Standard of Fiction in Public Libraries', *Library Association Record*, IX (1907). See also T. Kelly, *History of Public Libraries in Great Britain* (1973), book II.
3. See especially J. Gross, *The Rise and Fall of the Man of Letters* (1969), Ch. 7.
4. See especially S. Hynes, *The Edwardian Turn of Mind* (1966); and J. Gross, *The Rise and Fall of the Man of Letters* (1969), Ch. 8.
5. See especially W. Bellamy, *The Novels of Wells, Bennett, and Galsworthy: 1890–1910* (1971); P. Parrinder (ed.), *H. G. Wells* (1972); and N. and Jeanne Mackenzie, *The Time Travelled, The Life of H. G. Wells* (1973).
6. F. Swinnerton, *Swinnerton, An Autobiography* (1937), pp. 213–14.
7. See also A. E. Wilson, *Edwardian Theatre* (1951); and J. C. Trewin, *The Edwardian Theatre* (1976).
8. J. McCabe, *George Bernard Shaw* (1914), pp. viii–ix. See also D. MacCarthy, *The Court Theatre, 1904–1907* (1907); and T. F. Evans (ed.), *Shaw* (1976).
9. See R. Pogson, *Miss Horniman and the Gaiety Theatre, Manchester* (1952).
10. See especially R. H. Ross, *The Georgian Revolt* (1967); and T. Rogers (ed.), *Georgian Poetry* (1977).
11. See especially F. Howes, *The English Musical Renaissance* (1966).
12. See especially P. M. Young, *Elgar O.M.* (2nd edn, 1973); and M. Kennedy, *Portrait of Elgar* (1973).
13. See A. L. Lloyd, *Folk Song in England* (1967); and F. Hawes *Music in Britain* (1969).
14. See R. Pearsall, *Edwardian Popular Music* (1975).
15. See especially R. Mander and J. Mitchenson, *British Music Hall* (2nd edn, 1974).
16. See especially Rachel Low, *History of the British Film, 1906–1914* (1948); and J. Barnes, *The Beginnings of the Cinema in England* (1976).
17. A. A. Jackson, *Semi-Detached London* (1973), p. 50. See also A. Briggs, *Mass Entertainment: The Origins of a Modern Industry* (1960); and L. Baily, *BBC Scrapbooks*, I (1966), pp. 179–81.
18. See R. Pearsall, *Edwardian Popular Music* (1975), esp. Ch. 7.
19. E. Field, *Advertising, The Forgotten Years* (1959), pp. 123, 127–36. See especially R. Pound and G. Harmsworth, *Northcliffe* (1959), book two; and P. Ferris, *The House of Northcliffe* (1971), Chs. 8–16.
20. T. Clarke, *My Northcliffe Diary* (1931), pp. 195–205.
21. A. J. Lee, *The Origins of the Popular Press in England, 1855–1914* (1976), pp. 180, 293.
22. R. Williams, *The Long Revolution* (1965), p. 227.
23. See *The History of the Times*, III (1947); and R. Pound and G. Harmsworth, *Northcliffe* (1959), esp. Ch. 12.
24. See A. M. Gollin, *The Observer and J. L. Garvin, 1908–1914* (1960), esp. Chs. I, IX.
25. F. W. Hirst, *The Six Panics* (1913), p. 146. See especially A. F. Havighurst, *Radical Journalist, H. W. Massingham* (1974).
26. R. S. Rait (ed.), *Memorials of Albert Venn Dicey* (1925), p. 191. See especially F.

Williams, *Dangerous Estate* (1957), Chs. X, XI; and A. J. Lee, *The Origins of the Popular Press in England, 1855–1914* (1976), esp. Ch. 7.

27. R. D. Altick, *The English Common Reader* (1957), pp. 362, 395.
28. P. Garner, *The World of Edwardiana* (1974), Ch. VII.
29. Gillian Sutherland, *Policy-Making in Elementary Education, 1870–1895* (1973), p. 356.
30. See E. J. R. Eaglesham, *The Foundations of Twentieth-Century Education in England* (1967), and references there. Also J. E. B. Munson, 'The Unionist Coalition and Education, 1895–1902', *Historical Journal*, XX (1977).
31. See especially B. M. Allen, *Sir Robert Morant* (1934), part III; and G. R. Searle, *The Quest For National Efficiency* (1971), pp. 205–16. Also D. Read (ed.), *Documents from Edwardian England* (1973), pp. 227–35.
32. See D. R. Pugh, 'The Church and Education: Anglican Attitudes 1902', *Journal of Ecclesiastical History*, XXIII (1972); and S. Koss, *Nonconformity in Modern British Politics* (1975), Chs. 2–4.
33. E. Halévy, *Imperialism and the Rise of Labour* (2nd edn, 1951), pp. 206–7; K. Young, *Arthur James Balfour* (1963), pp. 207–8; S. H. Zebel, *Balfour* (1973), pp. 119–20.
34. E. J. R. Eaglesham, *The Foundations of Twentieth-Century Education in England* (1967), p. 53.
35. E. Halévy, *Imperialism and the Rise of Labour* (2nd edn, 1951), p. 205; A. Little and J. Westergaard, 'Trend of Class Differentials in Educational Opportunity in England and Wales', *British Journal of Sociology*, Vol. 15 (1964).
36. See A. E. Dyson and J. Lovelock (eds.), *Education and Democracy* (1975), part four.
37. See especially J. F. C. Harrison, *Learning and Living* (1961), Ch. VI; and T. Kelly, *History of Adult Education in Great Britain* (1962), Ch. 15.
38. See, in general, M. Bradbury, *The Social Context of Modern English Literature* (1971), Chs. I–V; and M. Bradbury and J. McFarlane (eds.), *Modernism, 1890–1930* (1976).
39. See W. Martin, *The New Age Under Orage* (1967), esp. Ch. VIII.
40. Virginia Woolf, *Collected Essays* (1966), I, pp. 320–1. See also S. Hynes, *The Edwardian Turn of Mind* (1968), esp. Ch. IX; and S. Hynes, *Edwardian Occasions* (1972), introduction.
41. See especially I. Dunlop, *The Shock of the New* (1972), Ch. 4. Also Virginia Woolf, *Roger Fry* (1940), Chs. VII, VIII; and R. Fry, *Vision and Design* (1961), pp. 188–93.
42. B. Russell, *Autobiography* (1975), pp. 67–8; J. M. Keynes, *Two Memoirs* (1949), p. 82. See also Q. Bell, *Bloomsbury* (1968).
43. C. Hassall, *Edward Marsh* (1959), pp. 231–2.
44. L. Baily, *BBC Scrapbooks*, I (1966), pp. 170–4; R. Pearsall, *Edwardian Popular Music* (1975), Ch. 11.
45. C. W. Cunnington, *The Perfect Lady* (1948), pp. 70–2; J. Laver, *Costume* (1963), pp. 114–17.
46. See N. Cooper, *The Opulent Eye: Late Victorian and Edwardian Taste in Interior Design* (1976).

Chapter 27

Government

Developments: *'Privilege for the proletariat'*

1

The problem of poverty, and how to overcome it, remained the main
domestic problem of Edwardian as of late-Victorian government. 'The
social problem is always with us. That is the modern version of our
Lord's saying concerning the poor.' So remarked the *Contemporary
Review* in July 1910. The Victorian gospel of thrift and self-help was
now under continuous attack. How could the poor hope to be thrifty in
their miserable circumstances? 'If the poor were not improvident, they
would hardly dare to live their lives at all.'[1] Was it surprising that they
were often demoralized? Was the gospel of thrift itself demoralizing? The
Manchester Guardian (12.3.1906) reported a conversation with a group
of children who were asked why they were putting money into the
savings bank – '"For myol-dage," she said firmly . . . Poor little five-year
old! Why, instead of telling you to look forward to helplessness, should
not our educational system seek to give you weapons wherewith to make
helplessness unlikely?'

The Victorians had shown social concern; but now it was becoming
widely recognized that both social theory and social policy must go
beyond such condescension and must admit the right of the poor to
social justice.[2] The definition of applied social values was taking the
place of the discovery of abstract social laws. Thinkers such as William
James, the American social psychologist, Alfred Marshall, the
economist, and Graham Wallas, the political scientist and author of
Human Nature in Politics (1908), began to contribute towards a
behavioural social science which analysed concrete problems –
including notably the problem of poverty. At the beginning of his
Principles of Economics (1890) Marshall had asked: 'May we not
outgrow the belief that poverty is necessary?' Significantly, he had
phrased this key question in terms which implied both a rejection of old
economic certainties and the assertion of new social values. 'The answer
depends partly on the moral and political capabilities of human nature
. . . But the answer depends in a great measure upon facts and inferences,
which are within the province of economics; and this it is which gives to
economic studies their chief and highest interest.'

By the turn of the century some of the younger Liberal thinkers and politicians were formulating a 'new Liberalism', which advocated extended state intervention even while claiming to remain distinct from socialism.[3] Whereas the old Liberalism had been closely involved with the movement towards political democracy, the 'new Liberalism' thought of democracy in social terms. Though many of the poor now possessed the vote, they could not be said to possess social justice when their willingness to work might be thwarted by unemployment and when a lifetime of labour could easily end in a penniless old age. In his 1892 election address H. H. Asquith, the future Liberal Prime Minister, who had been influenced at Oxford by T. H. Green, expressed ideas about positive liberty taken from his mentor: 'the collective action of the community may and ought to be employed positively as well as negatively; to raise as well as to level; to equalize opportunities no less than to curtail privileges; to make the freedom of the individual a reality and not a pretence.'[4] 'New Liberal' ideas were perhaps not so new as they seemed. They can be linked back to utilitarianism, with its greater emphasis upon social happiness than upon individual liberty, an emphasis which could lead on from ideas of social 'utility' into policies of social welfare. Recent biological and evolutionary theories had also encouraged an organic view of society, which recognized policies of working-class improvement as of benefit to all, rather than merely as acts of indulgence by the higher classes. 'All expenditure which succeeds in improving the part,' wrote young Herbert Samuel in *Liberalism* (1902), 'benefits, not that part alone, but the whole of the community.' L. T. Hobhouse, the leading academic exponent of the 'new Liberalism' emphasized in *Democracy and Reaction* (1904) the helplessness of individuals in modern society, dominated as it was by impersonal forces. Self-help was often impossible in such circumstances. An individual workman was 'the last person to have any say in the control of the market ... That is why it is not charity but justice for which he is asking'.[5]

In *The Crisis of Liberalism* (1909) J. A. Hobson asserted bluntly that 'the majority of solid Liberals in the centre' must accept the case for bold social reform. From the standpoint of continuity with old Gladstonian Liberalism, the 'new Liberalism' could be justified 'as a fuller appreciation and realization of individual liberty contained in the provision of equal opportunities for self-development. But to this individual standpoint must be joined a just apprehension of the social, viz., the insistence that these claims or rights of self-development be adjusted to the sovereignty of social welfare.' In the same spirit, Winston Churchill defined the 'new Liberalism' as 'the cause of the left-out millions'. He saw no need to draw philosophical distinctions between individualism and collectivism. 'No man can be a collectivist alone or an individualist alone. He must be both an individualist and a collectivist.' But socialism, claimed Churchill, went too far. 'Socialism seeks to pull down wealth; Liberalism seeks to raise up poverty. Socialism would destroy private interests; Liberalism would preserve them in the only way in which they can be safely and justly preserved, namely reconciling them with public right.'[6]

Socialists and 'new Liberals' agreed, however, that a 'national minimum' of social provision should be established. This was a concept developed and publicized by Sidney and Beatrice Webb, the Fabians.[7] The 'new Liberals' were glad to accept the idea of a minimum, while at the same time emphasizing that above the minimum free competition must continue to operate. 'I do not want to see impaired the vigour of competition,' declared Churchill, 'but we can do much to mitigate the consequences of failure. We want to draw a line below which we will not allow persons to live and labour, yet above which they may compete with all the strength of their manhood.' This idea of the 'national minimum' included a minimum income or 'living wage'. L. T. Hobhouse's *Liberalism* (1911) accepted that 'the "right to work" and the right to a "living wage"' were 'just as valid as the rights of person or property'. They were all 'integral conditions of a good social order'. Hobhouse wanted the minimum wage set at a figure safely above the poverty line – 25s.–30s. per week. The Trades Union Congress of 1912 demanded a minimum wage fixed by law at 30s. per week for 48 hours' work.[8] Churchill's 1909 Trade Boards Act created machinery for fixing minimum wages in certain 'sweated' trades (see below, p. 467). Philip Snowden, the socialist, pressed in *The Living Wage* (1913) for a wide extension of trade boards; and also for a broad definition of need in fixing the minimum. 'The amount of the living wage must bear some relation to the growing civilisation and expanding aspirations of the people.'

Conservatives were horrified by many of these arguments and proposals. They remained ready to respond to the needs of the poor in a spirit of paternalism which did not cast doubts upon the wisdom of existing social arrangements. But they deplored the idea that the poor had a 'right' to state help far beyond the traditional grim Poor Law minimum. This was emphasized by Lord Hugh Cecil in his 1912 book on *Conservatism*. 'If the claim is one of justice, and be admitted as such, a foundation is at once laid on which the fabric of a complete system of State socialism might be erected.' And state socialism, in Conservative eyes, meant not only the end of private property and of established institutions, but also the collapse of Christianity and the disruption of morality and family life. The claim that the poor had a right to social reform in their own special interest meant, according to Conservative thinking, a return to 'class' legislation. The privileges of the aristocracy had been abolished, remarked Lord Lansdowne during the debate (4.12.1906) in the upper house on the Trade Disputes Bill. 'Do not let us create a privilege for the proletariat.'

Notes

1. Mrs Pember Reeves, *Round About a Pound a Week* (2nd edn, 1914), p. 146.
2. See especially F. H. Herrick, 'British Liberalism and the Idea of Social Justice', *American Journal of Economics and Sociology*, Vol. 4 (1944–5); and Reba N. Soffer, 'The Revolution in English Social Thought, 1880–1914', *American Historical Review*, LXXV (1970).
3. See especially H. V. Emy, *Liberals, Radicals and Social Politics, 1892–1914* (1973); P. F. Clarke, 'The Progressive Movement in England', *Transactions of the Royal Historical Society*, fifth series, Vol. 24 (1974); and M. Freeden, *The New Liberalism* (1978).
4. Earl of Oxford and Asquith, *Memories and Reflections* (1928), I, p. 113.
5. See P. F. Clarke's 1972 edition of *Democracy and Reaction*; and P. Weiler, 'The New Liberalism of L. T. Hobhouse', *Victorian Studies*, XVI (1972–3).
6. W. S. Churchill, *Liberalism and the Social Problem* (1909), pp. 79, 82–3, 155. See also W. S. Churchill, *The People's Rights* (1909; reprinted 1970).
7. A. M. McBriar, *Fabian Socialism and English Politics* (1962), pp. 107–8, 257–8.
8. L. T. Hobhouse, *The Labour Movement* (3rd edn, 1912), p. 38; C. Watney and J. A. Little, *Industrial Warfare* (1912), pp. 40–1.

Personalities: *'If a man does not inspire trust'*

1

When Edward VII (1841–1910) became king in 1901 he had waited for the throne longer than any previous Prince of Wales.[1] Queen Victoria had persisted in regarding her son as too frivolous to be given responsibility, and to a considerable extent this attitude had encouraged the fault which she blamed. Too much of the prince's time had perforce been occupied with visiting, womanizing, sport, and voracious eating. His involvement in the Mordaunt divorce case in 1870 – when he had appeared in the witness box – and in the Tranby Croft card cheating scandal of 1891–2 shocked the 'Nonconformist conscience'. But his rare combination of bonhomie with dignity gradually built up a fund of popularity, which was reinforced by his three Derby victories of 1896, 1900, and 1909. 'Good old Teddy' was clearly a man who enjoyed life to the full. As king he insisted upon absolute and detailed authority in matters of protocol, decoration, and dress. Otherwise, his influence was less than his mother's, even over foreign affairs and defence in which he showed some genuine interest. The popular press assumed that the sovereign still personally exercised power; and on the strength of his imagined large contribution to the making of the Anglo-French entente and to European diplomacy in general he was given the flattering soubriquet of 'Edward the Peacemaker'. The last months of his reign were clouded by the 'peers versus people' crisis – in which the king, though in favour of some Lords reform, by no means sided with 'the people'. His death in the middle of the constitutional crisis left the throne to his little-known son, George V (1865–1936).[2] Both Edward VII and George V were seriously tempted not to accept advice from their

Liberal ministers about a dissolution of Parliament or a mass creation of peers to swamp the Conservative majority in the Lords. In the end, however, George V had to give way. As a young man he had read Bagehot's *English Constitution* (1867), with its famous summary of the rights of the sovereign as 'the right to be consulted, the right to encourage, the right to warn'. Queen Victoria had tried to retain power to take initiatives or at least to exercise vetoes. George V came to accept his limited political role; but at the same time he set out to develop the symbolic side of monarchy, which had first begun to extend during his grandmother's later years. He presented himself as a gruff but likeable father figure at the head of the imperial family. He made frequent tours of the United Kingdom, and was much more seen by his subjects than any previous monarch.

2

Sir Henry Campbell-Bannerman (1836–1908) became the first of Edward VII's two Liberal Prime Ministers.[3] The son of a wealthy Glasgow wholesale draper, he had served in two Gladstone cabinets as War Secretary (1886, 1892–5) before in 1899 being unexpectedly chosen as Liberal leader in the Commons, mainly because of his genial capacity for reconciling differences. He narrowly kept the Liberal Party connected – even though divided – during the Boer War; but then with unobtrusive assurance he brought it back to unity in opposition to the 1902 Education Act and to tariff reform. On becoming Prime Minister at the end of 1905 he quickly established his authority both within his cabinet and in the Commons. But his health soon began to break up, and he retired and died in April 1908. His view of social reform was limited (chiefly land reform); and his longer continuance as leader might have begun to undermine that very party unity which he had worked successfully to restore.

His successor as Prime Minister was Herbert Henry Asquith (1852–1928), who blandly (and at times bibulously) but successfully led the Liberal Government up to 1914 through a succession of crises.[4] He had been born into a West Riding wool manufacturing family; but his Balliol connections (he took a double-first at Oxford) and his success as a barrister gained him entrance into aristocratic 'Society'. His second wife, Margot Tennant, had been one of 'the Souls'. He entered the Commons in 1886, and served as Home Secretary from 1892 to 1895. Though an able speaker in and out of Parliament, Asquith never attempted to become a popular figure. He did not feel emotional sympathy for suffering and underprivilege; instead – lawyerlike – he recognized the preponderant case for taking legislative action. 'He is the constructive engineer of politics, not the seer of visions.'[5] It was in this spirit that he regarded the social programme of the 'new Liberalism'. In cabinet he let his two brilliant but restless lieutenants, Lloyd George and

Winston Churchill, have their heads, asserting his authority by sometimes lending them support at critical moments. 'A sudden curve developed of which I took immediate advantage' was his characteristic description of his adroit solution of one cabinet clash in 1909. Unfortunately, his qualities of detachment both with regard to his colleagues and towards the public did not qualify Asquith to be a successful wartime leader. His phrase 'wait and see' – first used warningly during the 1910 budget debates – was now unfairly but damagingly presented as evidence of his preference for delay and apathy. In 1916 he was ousted as Prime Minister by Lloyd George, and he never held office again.

3

By this date David Lloyd George (1863–1945) had proved himself both in peace and in war as 'the man who gets things done'.[6] He was a Welshman, brought up by his maternal uncle, Richard Lloyd, a self-educated shoemaker and co-pastor of a strict Baptist chapel at Criccieth, Carnarvonshire. As a young man Lloyd George preached at this chapel, but his religious commitment later declined. The local landowners were chiefly English-speaking Anglicans and Conservatives; uncle Lloyd and his nephew were Welsh-speaking Liberals. After attaining local prominence as a solicitor, Lloyd George was elected Member of Parliament for the Carnarvon Burghs in 1890, which remained his seat for fifty-five years. During the 1890s he played the part of a Welsh politician; but his courageous opposition to the Boer War won him a national reputation, though he was bitterly denounced and even found his life in danger at one Birmingham meeting. Thereafter Welsh affairs dropped from the forefront of his interests, though he always continued to emphasize his Welsh origins and indeed to exaggerate their humbleness.

In 1905 he became President of the Board of Trade, and in 1908 Chancellor of the Exchequer. After a visit to Germany in 1908 to study its welfare services, his great energies were given to the promotion of the pre-war series of Liberal social reforms. Previously Lloyd George had believed that poverty could be controlled through the encouragement of temperance, through land reform, and through the provision of old-age pensions. Now he began to advocate a much broader 'new Liberal' approach. This switch was characteristic of his pragmatism. 'Mr. Lloyd George looks at life with the frank self-assertion of a child, free from all formulas and prescriptions, seeing the thing, as it were, in a flash of truth ... He is not modern: he is momentary. There is no past: only the living present; no teachers: only the living facts.' This approach to politics meant that Lloyd George could be inconsistent, but this did not trouble him. He could also be unscrupulous in his methods, which meant that he did not always inspire confidence. Nevertheless, he remained sincere in his overriding objective – what he once described to his mistress as 'this job I have taken up of bettering the lives of the poor'.[7]

Winston Churchill (1874–1965) became the second dynamic personality within the pre-war Liberal Cabinet.[8] Asquith liked young Winston, but he did not expect him to reach the top in politics: 'to speak with the tongue of men and angels, and to spend laborious days and nights in administration, is of no good if a man does not inspire trust.' Yet, unlike Lloyd George, Churchill was never devious. He was distrusted mainly for what was regarded as his instability. 'His steering gear is too weak for his horsepower.'[9] Churchill had been dogged by this opinion since entering the Commons in 1900, where his dead father, Lord Randolph Churchill, was remembered for his restlessness as well as for his brilliance. In 1904 Churchill's support for free trade led him to cross the floor of the Commons from the Conservative to the Liberal benches. This could be viewed either as commendable attachment to principle, or as recklessness reminiscent of his father. But, unlike his father, Churchill was capable of steady application and of learning from experience. In Asquith's cabinet he served successively as President of the Board of Trade (1908), Home Secretary (1910), and First Lord of the Admiralty (1911–15). The sincerity of Churchill's commitment to social reform was often questioned. But the great pains which he took to prepare and to promote his measures did not suggest mere opportunism. At the Admiralty Churchill supervised the growth of the navy to meet the German challenge. Trained as a soldier, he was fascinated by war, an insterest which soon led him to be dubbed a warmonger. But in reality Churchill was horrified by conflict even though fascinated by it. Both Churchill and Lloyd George were outstanding orators, who could rouse enthusiasm in peace and in war. Churchill's speeches were best when carefully prepared. Lloyd George was much more spontaneous, able at will to adjust his text and his tone.

4

Sir Edward Grey (1862–1933) served as Liberal Foreign Secretary from 1905 to 1916; and he became chiefly responsible for the foreign policy which led to Britain's involvement in the First World War.[10] Both Campbell-Bannerman and Asquith accepted Grey's judgement, and left him with a largely free hand. He came from a Northumberland landowning family, and he felt a deep love for country life and pursuits, to which he often referred longingly during his years in office. Nevertheless, he was a committed politician in the whig tradition – he was related to Lord Grey of the Reform Bill; and though he did not compete publicly for power, he certainly expected it to come to him. He did not believe in democratic control of foreign policy. It suited his withdrawn temperament to insist that the conduct of diplomacy must be secret. A Foreign Secretary of greater intellectual subtlety – he took a third-class degree at Balliol – would probably not have been able to bear the strain imposed by the ambiguity of the Anglo-French relationship as it developed between 1904 and 1914. Yet Grey was perhaps not so self-sufficient as he liked to pretend. After the outbreak of war, for example, he used to go out of his way to avoid the sight of recruits marching down the street. Though he always remained convinced that Britain had done right in 1914, his spirit was permanently weakened by his 'failure' to preserve the peace. 'I hate war, I hate war.'

Notes

1. See especially P. Magnus, *King Edward the Seventh* (1964); and C. Hibbert, *Edward VII* (1976).
2. See especially H. Nicolson, *King George V* (1952).
3. See especially J. Wilson, *C-B: A Life of Sir Henry Campbell-Bannerman* (1973). Also José F. Harris and C. Hazlehurst, 'Campbell-Bannerman as Prime Minister', *History*, XV (1970).
4. See especially R. Jenkins, *Asquith* (1964); and S. Koss, *Asquith* (1976). Also C. Hazlehurst, 'Asquith as Prime Minister', *English Historical Review*, LXXXV (1970).
5. A. G. Gardiner, *Prophets, Priests and Kings* (1908), p. 31.
6. See especially J. Grigg, *The Young Lloyd George* (1973); P. Rowland, *Lloyd George* (1975); and D. M. Creiger, *Bounder from Wales* (1977). Also K. O. Morgan, 'Lloyd George and the Historians', *Transactions of the Honourable Society of Cymmrodorion* (1971).
7. A. G. Gardiner, *Prophets, Priests and Kings* (1908), p. 157; Frances Stevenson, *Lloyd George, A Diary* (1971), p. 31.
8. See especially R. S. Churchill, *Winston S. Churchill*, II (1967); and H. Pelling, *Winston Churchill* (1974), Chs. 1–8. Also C. Hazlehurst, 'Churchill as Social Reformer: The Liberal Phase', *Historical Studies*, Vol. 17 (1976).
9. W. George, *My Brother and I* (1958), p. 253; R. Jenkins, *Asquith* (1964), pp. 339–40.
10. See especially G. M. Trevelyan, *Grey of Falloden* (1937); and K. Robbins, *Sir Edward Grey* (1971).

Democracy: *'The growth of a society, not the uprising of a class'*

1

'To England has been given the great historic mission of working out the methods on which the democracy has so far been realised . . . The British government is now substantially a democracy, modified so far by older forms, the monarchy and the House of Lords.' So declared the 1908 *Chambers's Encyclopedia* article on 'Democracy'. Yet over 30 per cent of adult males in the counties and over 40 per cent in the boroughs still lacked the vote.[1] In addition, the suffragettes were complaining noisily because all women were still excluded from the parliamentary franchise. About 500,000 male electors, on the other hand, could cast plural votes. The Liberals were convinced that most plural voters were Conservatives; but they were less sure that a mathematically democratic 'one man, one vote' system would work in their favour. Propertyless working men might vote Labour. And would women be more likely to vote cautiously Conservative than Liberal? The assumption had still not been entirely banished that possession of a vote was a privilege, preferably linked to ownership of property. 'All men are equal – all men, that is to say, who possess umbrellas.' So ran the contemporary remark, repeated in E. M. Forster's *Howards End* (1910). A Franchise and Registration Bill which was introduced by the Liberal Government in 1912 would have abolished plural voting, would have greatly simplified registration procedure, and would have added about 2,500,000 men to the electorate from among the 4 million to 5 million still voteless. Unfortunately, this bill was not enacted because of complications caused by amendments proposed in favour of women's suffrage.

Despite the existence of a substantial group of Labour Party Members of Parliament from 1906, the conduct of national business remained firmly in the hands of upper- and middle-class politicians. A. L. Lowell, the American political scientist, described it in his comprehensive survey of *The Government of England* (1908) as 'government of the people, for the people, by the best of the people'. Socialists denounced such exclusiveness; but there was no widespread demand for government by working men. Lowell indicated the advantages of a system whereby both main parties chose their leaders from the same social circle. It had meant that, at least so far, party politics had not become class politics. Moreover, in the hands of men of substance reform was unlikely to become revolution.

The House of Lords, with its massive permanent Conservative majority, had wrecked a succession of bills sent up by the Liberals from 1906, notably the 1906 Education Bill (which had been the main Liberal measure of the first parliamentary session after the party's landslide election victory) and the 1908 Licensing Bill. How were the Liberals, with their huge Commons majority behind them, to deal with this flouting of their wishes? Only slowly did they feel their way towards a successful counter-stroke – in the shape of Lloyd George's 1909 'people's budget', which forced the Conservative majority in the Lords to choose between accepting radical finance or rejecting the budget, with the latter course breaking supposedly established convention. When the Lords insisted upon rejection, the 'peers versus people' elections of 1910 left the Liberals with a working majority in the Commons committed to curtailing the power of the non-elected chamber (see below, p. 467).

On 24 June 1907 Campbell-Bannerman, as Prime Minister, had won a Commons majority of 285 for the principle of restricting the power of the Lords to a suspensory veto – a policy recommended by John Bright in 1883 and by other radicals as early as the 1830s. The House of Lords, declared Campbell-Bannerman, was being used 'as a mere annexe of the Unionist party'. It had become, asserted Lloyd George picturesquely, Mr Balfour's poodle: 'it fetches and carries for him, barks at and bites anybody he sets it on to'.[2] The 1911 Parliament Act centred upon the suspensory veto. It deprived the Lords of all power over finance; but, as in the case of their resistance to the 1912 Home Rule Bill, it left the peers still able to delay non-financial legislation for two years. But a measure sent up by the Commons in three successive sessions could now become law on the third occasion regardless of continuing Lords objection. For the future, the Parliament Act promised further reform to substitute 'a Second Chamber constituted on a popular instead of a hereditary basis'. But once the role of the upper house had been limited by the Parliament Act the question of reform of membership lost urgency, since it now seemed to matter much less who were members of a body with such reduced powers.

2

The Lords were characterized as defending class privileges. How intent were the working classes in claiming 'privilege for the proletariat'? There was no widespread support for ideas of class war. 'The class struggle, as manual workers in general knew it, was apolitical and had place entirely within their own society.' So remembered Robert Roberts of his Edwardian boyhood in Salford.[3] The Independent Labour party, led by Keir Hardie, emphasized that it was a working-class party always ready to welcome supporters from other classes until such time as the whole class system had melted away. Violent revolution was never Hardie's intention. 'That Socialism is revolutionary is not in dispute, but that it can only be won by a violent outbreak is in no sense true.' Ramsay MacDonald was a steady advocate of 'evolution' not 'revolution'. Socialism, he explained in *Socialism and Society* (1905), 'marks the growth of society, not the uprising of a class'.

On the way to the socialist millennium Hardie and MacDonald were ready to accept as much piecemeal social reform as the Liberal and Conservative parties might offer. This attitude came through clearly during the Edwardian years after the formation of the Labour Representation Committee in 1900.[4] This alliance of socialist bodies and trade unions had been formed to increase the number of working-class representatives in Parliament; but it did not amount in itself to a national political party. At the 1900 general election only Keir Hardie and Richard Bell had been elected on the LRC ticket. The LRC could hardly yet be sure of survival. Hardie and MacDonald, the committee's secretary, recognized the need to affiliate many more trade unions; and the 1901 Taff Vale Decision provided a timely and powerful stimulus towards this end.[5] The Taff Vale case arose out of picketing undertaken by the Amalgamated Society of Railway Servants with the intention of hindering the Taff Vale Railway Company from employing blackleg labour. The decision of the courts threatened the power of unions to call strikes, since it made their funds liable to meet damages which might result from an actionable wrong committed by a trade union officer or member. The Taff Vale Decision was soon reinforced by the final outcome of the *Quinn v. Leatham* case, in which judgement was given against a union for boycotting an employer. When on 1 August 1901 Hardie asked the Conservative Government to introduce legislation 'to give trade-union funds the protection they have had for thirty years', Balfour refused. On the same day MacDonald sent a circular to trade unions emphasizing that the Taff Vale Decision 'should convince the unions that a labour party in Parliament is an immediate necessity'. Trade union affiliations to the LRC now grew rapidly. Between 1900 and the summer of 1901, forty-one unions had affiliated with just over 350,000 members; between the spring of 1902 and the winter of 1903, 127 new unions joined, raising the total affiliated union membership to about 850,000. The textile workers' union brought an accession of over 100,000 affiliated members, the engineers almost as many.

These additional numbers brought strength and income to the LRC. Its electoral fund soon stood at £150,000. Labour might still not win many seats in Parliament, but it now had the power to subtract enough votes from Liberal candidates in many industrial constituencies to let the Conservatives in. Campbell-Bannerman, the Liberal leader, and Herbert Gladstone, his chief whip, realized that a deal must be done not to oppose LRC candidates where working-class voters were numerically strong and where the Liberals were comparatively weak, in return for LRC agreement not to promote candidates in other constituencies. Hardie and MacDonald saw that such a deal offered hope of securing the return of a significant block of Labour members to Parliament for the first time. The agreement made in 1903 was kept secret so that irreconcilables on both sides could not wreck it. But through quiet pressure constituency by constituency – and despite flat denials by Hardie and MacDonald that any compact existed – the ground was cleared in time for the 1906 general election. In England and Wales all but three successful LRC candidates were given clear runs against Conservative opponents. As a result, the satisfactory total of twenty-nine LRC candidates were elected. Twenty-four miners and Lib-Labs were also returned, which made a total of fifty-three working-class representatives in the House of Commons. The LRC men immediately decided to take the name of the Labour Party, and also to sit on the opposition benches. These were two significant gestures of independence from the Liberals. Nevertheless, the Labour members still did not represent a national political party. National Labour Party organization in the constituencies was not to come until 1918.

The 1906 LRC election programme (unlike the Liberal programme) had spoken plainly of the need for social reform, though it made no mention of socialism. 'The unemployed ask for work, the Government gave them a worthless Act, and now, when you are beginning to understand the causes of your poverty, the red herring of Protection is drawn across your path.' The LRC programme also demanded new trade union legislation. The Liberal Government withdrew its own limited 1906 measure, and accepted Labour's bill which became the Trade Disputes Act. Action by two or more persons in furtherance of a trade dispute could now give cause for a civil suit only when it could have been brought if a single individual had acted in the same manner. Inducement to break a contract of employment or to interfere with the trade or employment of other persons could not provide the basis for a suit. Pickets were allowed henceforward not only to give information but to attempt directly to persuade others not to work.

At the two 1910 general elections the Labour pact with the Liberals was tacitly continued. Labour held its ground, but no more.[6] In January forty Labour Members of Parliament were returned, but not one had faced official Liberal opposition. In December forty-two Labour candidates were successful, only two in contest with official Liberals. Without the Liberal–Labour arrangement both parties would certainly have lost more seats, and the Conservatives would have gained an overall election victory. Sixteen of the seats won by Labour in 1906 had been normally held by the Conservatives, and Labour kept twelve of these in 1910. Socialist militants, however, sometimes grew restless with prudent electoral calculations. In 1907 Pete Curran had won the Jarrow by-election against both Conservative and Liberal opponents; and Victor Grayson won Colne Valley in the same year while standing against the two main parties as a socialist without Labour Party endorsement.[7] Grayson's stirring oratory roused fears that the working classes might be about to turn to violent revolution. But in 1910 both the Jarrow and Colne Valley seats reverted to the Liberals.

Ben Tillett, the trade union leader, published a pamphlet in 1908 which asked *Is the Parliamentary Labour Party a Failure?* He had no doubts that it was. Certainly, the majority of Labour Members of Parliament were respectable trade unionists of no great ability. Hardie, MacDonald, Snowden, and a few others were the exceptions. In 1910 even the parliamentary Committee of the TUC remarked how 'from the legislative point of view Labour has so far gained little'.[8] Apart from the 1906 Trade Disputes Act, Labour had influenced legislation on workmen's compensation, provision of school meals, and medical inspection of schoolchildren. This was a useful record but not a notable one. Ideas of syndicalism and direct action by the workers began to gain circulation. The extensive labour unrest of the immediate pre-war years was partly an expression of dissatisfaction with parliamentary government, of which the new Labour Party had now made itself a part. In his speech as retiring chairman of the ILP in 1909 Ramsay MacDonald found himself defending the parliamentary approach to the unemployment problem. 'To protect the conditions and existence of democratic government is just as essential to the building of the Socialist State as is the solution of the problem of unemployment. The latter is our aim, the former is the only condition under which our aim can be secured.'[9]

3

The Osborne Judgement of 1909 had put Labour members in need of further trade union legislation. Trade unions found themselves prevented from imposing political levies to pay Members of Parliament. In 1911 the Liberals initiated payment of members in return for Labour support of Lloyd George's insurance Bill. But not until 1913 did the Trade Union Act partially counter the Osborne Judgement. This act allowed the charging of union political levies; but members could contract out of payment, and political funds were to be kept separate from other union funds. The Liberals had refused to go further, partly because they were alarmed by the great strike wave of 1911–12.

Not even the leaders of the Labour Party anticipated that within a dozen years Ramsay MacDonald would be forming the first Labour Government. Philip Snowden remarked in 1911 that it seemed 'doubtful whether we shall have in this country within the next generation an avowed Socialist Party, built up by the elimination or destruction of other political parties, which will be sufficiently strong to take up the reins of government'. The impact of the First World war – including the Asquith–Lloyd George split – did much to weaken the Liberal Party. It has also been argued that the further extension of the electorate in 1918 made the crucial difference to Labour's prospects, that its continuing minority position up to 1914 simply reflected the fact that at least 4 million working men still lacked the vote. Yet about the same number of working men were already enfranchised in 1914, when they constituted perhaps 60 per cent of the electorate. Most of them had still voted Liberal or even Conservative in 1910. How would they vote at the next general election?

Ramsay MacDonald probably hoped to negotiate another electoral pact with the Liberals in time for a 1915 general election, albeit a pact more favourable to Labour. He knew that his party would contest more seats next time than ever before; but he feared that without a deal Labour would lose some of the thirty-seven seats which it held in 1914.[10] Four seats had been lost since 1910 at by-elections, although it could be argued that all were special cases. In twelve other by-elections, however, which Labour's intervention had turned into three-cornered contests, the Labour poll had been large enough to remind the Liberals of Labour's power to split the anti-Conservative vote. The longer term outlook for Labour in 1914 may have been more hopeful than its immediate prospects. The party was now well established as an electoral alliance. In 1909 it had gained the support of 550,000 affiliated members, including their political contributions, when the Miners' Federation – the largest trade union – had instructed its Members of Parliament to transfer their backing from the Liberals to the Labour party.[11] Among the younger miners, and among some other working men, the sense was spreading that the Liberal Party could not be the future party for their class. Admittedly, in Lancashire – where during the late-Victorian years working men had tended to vote Conservative – the Edwardian Liberal party tried hard to project itself in 'progressive' terms, which were meant to be attractive to working-class voters.[12] Winston Churchill delivered some of his most important speeches in support of the 'new Liberalism' in Lancashire. In 1906 C. P. Scott of the *Manchester Guardian* and other local Liberal leaders had welcomed the return of thirteen Lancashire and Cheshire Labour Members of Parliament alongside thirty-three Liberal members. Yet this meant that Labour seemed to be growing especially strong in the very region where the Liberals were trying to be most actively sympathetic towards working-class interests.

In most parts of England the old shared attitude between urban middle and working-class Liberal voters – that Gladstonian celebration of a political faith which joined the classes morally without disturbing their social separateness – was losing its institutional basis with the decline of the churches, chapels, temperance organizations, and the like. The trade unions did indeed represent new institutions on the upgrade; but these were predominantly working-class. The Labour Party was offering itself as especially the party of the working classes, at the same time as the Conservative Party had transformed itself into a party for the propertied urban middle classes. Paradoxically, the very restraint of most Labour leaders in not advocating class war or violence probably strengthened their electoral appeal to working-class consciousness. Between the class-aware Labour and Conservative Parties stood the Liberal Party. How long could it continue to attract large numbers of votes from both the middle classes and the working classes? A perceptive article by C. F. G. Masterman on 'Politics in Transition' (*Nineteenth Century*, January 1908) wondered how the Liberal Party could retain 'its few men of wealth, without losing those adherents who demand direct taxation of that wealth in the interests of social reform? Can it continue to bridge over that wide chasm of interest which exists to-day between the lower-middle class and the working class, which leads the former always to associate itself in interest with the classes above, and alternately to fear and to despise the classes below?'

Notes

1. See especially N. Blewett, 'The Franchise in the United Kingdom, 1885–1918', *Past & Present*, no. 32 (1965); N. Blewett, *The Peers, The Parties, and The People* (1972), Ch. 17; and H. C. G. Matthew *et al.*, 'The Franchise Factor in the Rise of the Labour Party', *English Historical Review*, XCI (1976).
2. See Corinne C. Weston, 'The Liberal Leadership and the Lords Veto, 1907–1910', *Historical Journal*, XI (1968).
3. R. Roberts, *The Classic Slum* (1971), p. 14. See especially R. Miliband, *Parliamentary Socialism* (2nd edn, 1972), Ch. I; E. J. Hobsbawm (ed.), *Labour's Turning*

Point, 1880–1900 (2nd edn, 1974), pp. 64–8; K. O. Morgan, *Keir Hardie* (1975) esp. Ch. X; and D. Marquand, *Ramsay MacDonald* (1977), pp. 87–93.

4. See especially F. Bealey and H. Pelling, *Labour and Politics, 1900–1906* (1958); and P. P. Poirier, *The Advent of the Labour Party* (1958).

5. See J. Lovell, *British Trade Unions, 1875–1933* (1977), Ch. 3, and references there.

6. N. Blewett, *The Peers, The Parties, and The People* (1972), Ch. 12, pp. 389–95; R. McKibbin, *The Evolution of the Labour Party, 1910–1924* (1974), pp. 11–19.

7. H. Pelling, *Popular Politics and Society in Late Victorian Britain* (1968), Ch. 8.

8. H. A. Clegg *et al.*, *History of British Trade Unions Since 1889*, I (1964), p. 405. See especially H. Pelling, *A Short History of the Labour Party* (4th edn, 1972), Ch. II.

9. Lord Elton, *Life of James Ramsay MacDonald, 1866–1919* (1939), pp. 152–3; D. Marquand, *Ramsay MacDonald* (1977), pp. 113–15.

10. See especially H. Pelling, *Popular Politics and Society in Late Victorian Britain* (1968), Ch. 6; M. Petter, 'The Progressive Alliance', *History*, Vol. 58 (1973); R. Douglas, 'Labour in Decline, 1910–1914', in K. D. Brown (ed.), *Essays in Anti-Labour History* (1974); P. F. Clarke, 'The Electoral Position of the Liberal and Labour Parties, 1910–1914', *English Historical Review*, XC (1975); and H. C. G. Matthew *et al.*, 'The Franchise Factor in the Rise of the Labour Party', *ibid.*, XCI (1976).

11. See R. Gregory, *The Miners and British Politics, 1906–1914* (1968).

12. See especially P. F. Clarke, *Lancashire and the New Liberalism* (1971); and P. F. Clarke, 'Electoral Sociology of Modern Britain', *History*, Vol. 57 (1972), pp. 49–53. Also P. Thompson, *Socialists, Liberals, and Labour, The Struggle for London, 1885–1914* (1967).

Chapter 28

Tariff reform versus social reform:
'Untrodden fields of British politics'

1

In 1903 Joseph Chamberlain gave focus to the anxious but rambling debate about 'national efficiency' which had been provoked by the Boer War. He launched his 'tariff reform' campaign.[1] In reply, the Liberals – in office from the end of 1905 – came to advocate a bold programme of social reform.

Many Victorians had supported free trade with an almost religious fervour. The effects of the 'great depression' and of the increasingly protectionist policies pursued by the United States and by many European powers did arouse doubts among businessmen especially affected; but though the 'fair trade' movement of the late 1870s and 1880s attracted notice it always remained a small minority agitation. Otherwise Lord Salisbury's Conservative Party might well have come out in its support. The Liberals remained staunch free traders. So did the socialists, keen though they were for state intervention in other spheres. They dismissed tariff reform as a capitalist diversion. Chamberlain himself had opposed 'fair trade' in Birmingham in the 1880s; but the growing feeling among local industrialists in favour of some fiscal defence for the Midlands metal trades against foreign competition from behind tariff barriers had begun to impress him. Not that he ever presented tariff reform simply as an easy way of protecting profits; but many businessmen probably came to support him for this reason. Chamberlain launched his campaign on a lofty imperial note. The sense of community which he had notably fostered in Birmingham he was now eager to encourage throughout the whole British Empire. He promised benefits to all classes and for all citizens of the empire, at home and overseas. 'We have to cement the union of the states beyond the seas; we have to consolidate the British race; we have to meet the clash of competition, commercial now – sometimes in the past it has been otherwise – it may be again in the future.'

Chamberlain began his tariff reform movement after serving from 1895 to 1903 as Colonial Secretary. In 1896 he had called for a zollverein, a system of empire free trade. But the self-governing colonies were not willing to expose their infant industries to British competition and to act purely as suppliers of primary products for the mother country. Chamberlain therefore turned towards some form of imperial preference. In 1897 Canada had introduced tariff preference on imports from the United Kingdom; and the other colonies were keen to follow suit if Britain would abandon free trade and grant them preferences in return. The Boer War delayed Chamberlain's response, but foreign hostility during its course made him still more anxious to foster imperial unity. To his deep regret a corn registration duty, imposed in 1902 to meet the cost of the war, was abandoned in the 1903 budget. He had hoped that through its remission to empire countries a beginning might have been made towards a system of imperial preference. On 15 May 1903 in Birmingham town hall Chamberlain began to reveal his new policy. 'The Empire is in its infancy. Now is the time when we can mould that Empire.' Little Englanders played up the fact that empire trade amounted to less than foreign trade. Chamberlain countered that it was the duty of British statesmen 'to do everything they can, even at some present sacrifice, to keep the trade of the colonies with Great Britain'; and to increase it 'even if in doing so we lessen somewhat the trade with our foreign competitors'. Was the empire, he asked 'making for union, or are we drifting to separation? That is the critical issue.'

The response to this speech was much stronger than Chamberlain himself had expected. His intention had been only to open discussion, in hopes of leading the Government to adopt tariff reform as its policy at the next general election. Instead, the tariff question suddenly became the issue of the moment, with the cabinet under strong pressure to commit itself at once for or against. Ministers became split between Chamberlainites, free traders, and followers of Balfour, who strove to hold his Government and party together by not clearly committing himself.[2] At heart he seems to have genuinely favoured a middle position, sharing the free traders' dislike of food taxes but wanting some power of fiscal 'retaliation' against foreigners. Despite prolonged manoeuvring, Balfour eventually failed to keep his cabinet together. Chamberlain resigned on 14 September 1903. He emphasized, however, that he was not going into opposition but was simply taking the issue to the country, preferably as a national cause above party politics. From October to December he pursued his campaign in a succession of major speeches in big industrial centres.

Chamberlain's Birmingham speech in May had dwelt upon the need for tariff reform to unite the empire; and this was his high theme. But he remained well aware of the need to appeal to the pockets and the stomachs of the middle and working classes at least as much as to their imaginations. His autumn speeches were therefore full of appeals *ad hominem* and *ad locum*. All major industries, claimed Chamberlain, were suffering severely or were likely eventually to suffer severely from foreign competition. 'Agriculture, the greatest of all trades and industries, has been practically destroyed . . . Sugar has gone, silk has gone, iron is threatened, the turn of cotton will come . . . At the present these industries and the working men who depend upon them are like sheep in the field.' Chamberlain admitted plainly that it would be impossible to give colonial preferences without imposing food taxes. To tax foreign raw materials would raise British manufacturing costs: so the tariffs must go upon food. But this, he claimed, could be contrived so as not to increase the cost of living. He proposed a duty of not more than 2*s.* per quarter on foreign corn, a similar duty on foreign flour, a 5 per cent duty on foreign meat and dairy produce (except bacon), and an average duty of 10 per cent on foreign manufactured goods. To compensate for the effects of these imports on the cost of living he proposed to reduce the existing revenue duty on tea by three-quarters, the sugar duty by half, with cuts also in the coffee and cocoa duties. In return for these preferences the self-governing colonies would lower their tariffs in favour of British manufactures. This, concluded Chamberlain, would increase empire trade by £26 million and create employment for 166,000 workers. He promised also that revenue collected from tariffs imposed upon foreign products would be sufficient to finance old-age pensions and other social reforms.

To publicize his ideas and to organize support Chamberlain formed in June 1903 a Birmingham Tariff Committee, financed by local businessmen. In July the Tariff Reform League was started, with headquarters in London and soon with hundreds of branches throughout the country. Its aim was to campaign outside Parliament for tariff reform just as sixty years earlier the Anti-Corn Law League had campaigned for free trade. It attracted large financial backing from leaders of the iron and steel, engineering, and electrical industries, which were all facing strong foreign competition. The nature of this support soon began to give Tariff Reform League propaganda more of a purely protectionist emphasis than Chamberlain had planned, overshadowing his high imperial vision. League meetings were called all over the country; leaflets and pamphlets poured out by the million; verses and songs were published; even plays and pageants were produced to dramatize the tariff reform message.

Newspaper support came from *The Times* and the *Daily Telegraph* among the serious dailies; and from the *Daily Express* and (after some early criticism of 'stomach taxes') from the *Daily Mail* among the popular papers. Day after day the *Express* repeated the slogan 'tariff reform means work for all'. Chamberlain's autumn speeches were widely noticed in all newspapers. Yet by the end of 1903 it was becoming clear that, though converts had been won, tariff reform was not going to win a quick victory. It was also clear that it could not avoid becoming a party question. The Liberals had remained firmly attached to free trade, the more so as resistance to Chamberlain's proposals helped to restore party unity. Asquith answered Chamberlain in a series of powerful speeches which helped to mark him out as a future Prime Minister. He recommended greater business efficiency and improved technical education. 'Instead of raising the price of bread let us try to raise the standard of life.'

By the end of 1903 Chamberlain realized that he would have to plan for a long campaign. He now formed a Tariff Commission, a body of experts and business representatives who set out to collect detailed evidence. Between 1904 and 1909 it issued reports on the iron and steel, cotton, wool, hosiery, lace, carpet, silk, flax, engineering, pottery, glass, and sugar and confectionary trades, and also upon the state of agriculture. Free traders derided 'King Joseph's' copying of the forms of a royal commission. A majority of professional economists came out against Chamberlain; but W. J. Ashley, Professor of Commerce at Birmingham University, supported tariff reform in his widely read book on *The Tariff Problem* (1903). 'The struggle to create an effective British Empire,' concluded Ashley rather grimly, 'is, at bottom, an attempt to counteract, by human foresight, the working of forces, which, left to themselves, involve the decadence of this country.' Only tariff reform could ensure the British Empire a place alongside the United States and Russia as one of 'three world-powers', with resources far greater than those of all other states.

Most arguments on both sides passed over the heads of most Edwardian electors. But the free traders made effective play with the simple contrast between the 'little loaf' – which they claimed as the inevitable consequence of tariff reform – and the 'big loaf' of free trade. They argued that Chamberlain's policy would mean a return to the 'hungry forties', an expression coined in 1903 by Jane Cobden, daughter of the great Victorian free trader. Tariff reform was too detailed a policy to communicate fully to popular audiences. It was a complicated positive, whereas free trade remained an attractively simple negative. Many electors, moreover, did not feel especially hard pressed. 1903 was a year of economic depression, but by 1905 trade was booming. In December Balfour at last resigned. Campbell-Bannerman formed a Liberal Government, and a general election was called for January 1906.[3] Chamberlain had long since abandoned hope of a tariff reform victory first time; 'but when the reaction comes and we return with a big majority we shall be pledged up to the eyes to carry out the policy that I have advocated.' Yet Balfour's long postponement of the election greatly increased the size of the ultimate defeat. The contest between free trade and tariff reform supplied the main election issue, although the 1902 Education Act and 'Chinese labour' were also prominent. Indentured Chinese labourers had been brought into the South African mines, and many working-class voters, who had expected the Boer War to open up new opportunities for emigration and employment, felt cheated by what the Liberals assured them was a form of slave labour. Attacks upon 'Chinese slavery' therefore appealingly combined self-interest with morality. The Liberals won a large majority over all other parties combined – Liberals 400, Labour 29; Conservatives 133; Liberal Unionists 24; Irish Nationalists 83. The turnout was high, 83.2 per cent compared with 75.1 per cent in 1900. The swing to the Liberals was proportionately even greater in seats than in votes. 220 fresh Liberal members entered the Commons. The Liberals polled 2,751,057 votes; Labour 321,663; the Conservatives and Liberal Unionists 2,422,071.

While some former Conservative voters seem to have abstained, most potential Liberal electors seem on this occasion to have gone to the polls. The Liberals were helped by the newness of the electoral register, which minimized the disfranchising effects of working-class 'flitting'. Chamberlain found himself able to make only a muted appeal in the agricultural districts, since he could not risk too much emphasis upon food taxes. The farmers, moreover, were disgruntled by the Education Act, which had increased local rates. As a result, the Conservatives and Liberal Unionists did especially badly in the countryside.

Nevertheless, Chamberlain was left with the initiative among the much reduced ranks of the Opposition, for only a handful of Conservative free traders remained in Parliament. But then in July 1906 he was virtually removed from politics by a paralytic stroke. Balfour, the Conservative leader, had been impressed not so much by the victory of free trade as by the number of Labour members returned. He concluded that to win the working-class vote at future elections the Conservatives would need to offer some social reforms. But how could these be paid for? Since the property-owners who financed the Conservative Party certainly did not want higher taxation, revenue would have to be found from tariffs. In a speech at the Savoy Hotel on 15 February 1907 Balfour outlined a new 'safe, sound, sober policy of fiscal reform' – designed to broaden the basis of taxation, to safeguard the 'great productive industries' from unfair foreign competition, to recapture foreign markets, and to maintain British colonial trade.[4] So Chamberlain's cause began to prosper within the Opposition ranks, despite (almost because of) the election defeat and despite Chamberlain's own withdrawal from active politics. Balfour's starting point, though, lay in domestic necessities rather than in imperial aspirations. Revealingly, he was prepared to argue 'that some revision of our fiscal system – some broadening of our basis of taxation – would be absolutely necessary if we were the only commercial nation in the world, and did not have a single colony'. The Liberals, by contrast, were about to seek the revenue for social reform from higher direct taxation. Both parties at least agreed that more revenue was needed. In March 1910 *Blackwood's Magazine* presented the tariff reform alternative with a strong financial emphasis. 'We have to face the great economic question, which stretches from English unemployment at one end to Imperial defence at the other – the question of how we are to increase our national and Imperial assets, and provide the new wealth which alone can solve our social difficulties, and which no juggling with present wealth will provide.'

2

Balfour had resigned in December 1905 rather than request a dissolution of Parliament. He hoped that cabinet-making and election-eering would reopen the divisions within the Liberal Party which enthusiastic resistance to the 1902 Education Act and to tariff reform had gone far to close. But Campbell-Bannerman, the Liberal leader, kept his party firmly in line, defeating a preconcerted move by the Liberal imperialists – Asquith, Grey, and Haldane – to consign him as Prime Minister to the House of Lords. Asquith became Chancellor of the Exchequer, Grey Foreign Secretary, and Haldane War Secretary. Among the former pro-Boers, Lloyd George took office for the first time as President of the Board of Trade. The veteran John Morley became Indian Secretary. It was a strong cabinet, which reflected all shades of party opinion and mixed old with new talent. But what policies was it to propose? There was no early sign that bold social reform would become the Liberal answer to tariff reform. Herbert Gladstone congratulated Campbell-Bannerman upon the preponderance of 'centre' Liberals among the party's backbenchers.[5] The *Review of Reviews* (February 1906) noted that the Liberals in Parliament included 176 Nonconformists – mostly middle-class men 'whose sympathies are more with the employer than the employed'. During the election campaign Campbell-Bannerman had spoken in favour of land reform, but he had also promised large-scale retrenchment. Clearly, he was not thinking of expensive social expenditure.[6] Asquith spent his first year at the Treasury in restoring Gladstonian standards, without hint of any revolution in public finance. During the 1906 session legislative attention was concentrated upon the Education Bill, which was intended to eliminate Anglican influence in single-school rural areas. It was eventually emasculated by the Lords and withdrawn. A further Education Bill in 1908 proved unsatisfactory even to Nonconformists, and thereafter the Liberal Government tacitly accepted the 1902 reorganization.

In addition to promoting the 1902 Education Act, the Balfour Government had set up the Inter-Departmental Committee on Physical Deterioration (1903–4) to investigate claims that the physique of the nation was being permanently impaired by the new urban working-class way of life. It particularly recommended medical inspection of schoolchildren, and the provision of school meals for poor children. Before leaving office Balfour had also recommended the appointment of a Royal Commission on the Poor Law and the Relief of Distress. Under pressure from Government backbenchers an order had meanwhile been issued which permitted Poor Law guardians to give relief in the form of school meals. The guardians quickly proved unsuitable to undertake this function; and in 1906 an Act was carried which allowed local authorities to arrange school meals. This was followed in 1907 by legislation to authorize school medical inspection. Though only permissive, these two measures can be seen in retrospect as marking a new beginning in British social legislation. They were followed by the 1908 Children Act, which abolished commitment of children to prison, established juvenile courts, and provided penalties for parents found guilty of neglect. This Act passed with little opposition, whereas fifty years earlier, as the Lord Advocate remarked (24.3.1908), it would have been regarded as an interference with individual liberty. Now the state was prepared to intervene in family matters which the Victorians had assumed to stand outside its range, except under the stigma of the Poor Law. Intervention for the benefit of the young was soon to be extended to care for the old, in the form not of relief but of pensions (1908); and finally in 1911 the enactment of health and unemployment insurance recognized that the welfare of individuals of working age could also concern the state.

But the Liberals did not realize in 1906 just how far and how fast they were destined to advance. The Education (Provision of Meals) Act was introduced on Labour initiative, with the Government merely lending support. Although the Act was not mandatory, some 310,000 needy schoolchildren in England and Wales were being fed by 1913–14; and in 1914 the Board of Education was empowered to compel local authorities to provide meals. The 1906 Act stipulated that even if parents did not pay for such meals they should not suffer any deprivation of civil rights. The gradual establishment of a school medical service under one clause of the 1907 Education (Administrative Provisions) Act excited less controversy than the introduction of school meals. Yet here again the Liberal Government had been hesitant, for it only sponsored the proposal under backbench pressure. The Act required the introduction of medical examinations, and it permitted (though not explicitly) the provision of medical treatment. By 1914 three out of four education authorities in England and Wales were giving some treatment, and fifty-three local authorities were paying for the treatment of schoolchildren in about 100 hospitals.

With expectation of life extending, the problem of the aged poor was assuming increased importance. At least ten countries were already providing state pensions, and in Britain argument about both principles and possible schemes had continued intermittently over some thirty years. In 1891 Charles Booth had published his first old-age pension proposals, and thereafter his ideas were often under discussion. Booth was always keen to emphasize how his suggestions – pensions of 7*s.* (originally 5*s.*) at seventy for men, and of 5*s.* for women – would supplement rather than undermine the efforts of private charity and of the Poor Law. Critics claimed that the prospect of a pension would discourage thrift. The foremost agencies of working-class thrift were the friendly societies, which long remained suspicious of any state intervention and only slowly came to appreciate the advantage to them of tax-supported pensions payable to their members. Others complained of the 'huge cost' of Booth's scheme, perhaps £20 million per annum. Cost discouraged leading politicians of both main parties from committing themselves. Joseph Chamberlain came nearest to firm commitment when in 1891 he expressed general support for a voluntary state-backed scheme of 5*s.* pensions, payable only to those who had already made the effort partly to provide for themselves in old age.

Chamberlain and Booth played prominent parts in the proceedings of the Royal Commission on the Aged Poor (1893–5). A National Committee of Organized Labour on Old Age pensions was formed in 1899 to support Booth. It was matched by a Committee on Old Age Pensions, started in 1900 under the inspiration of the Charity Organisation Society.

The high cost of the Boer War reinforced the reluctance of the Conservatives to spend money on pensions. In 1903 Chamberlain promised during his tariff reform campaign that pensions could be financed by tariffs levied on foreigners; but this proposal soon fell from prominence. The Liberals had a clear opportunity when they entered office in 1905; but some Gladstonian ministers were as fearful as the Conservatives of increased expenditure. Not until 1907 could Asquith promise action, and then only after a further year when a budget surplus was anticipated. A cabinet paper of December 1906 had persuasively suggested that large savings in Poor Law costs would result if pensions were introduced. 18.3 per cent of the English population over 65 were paupers, already maintained at public expense. Most shades of opinion now agreed that it was harsh to mark citizens as paupers simply because they had lived past working age. Yet the practicality of all contributory pension schemes was increasingly doubted. The poor themselves heartily rejected the idea of paying for benefits which they might not live to enjoy. It could be claimed, moreover, that if pension contributions were avoided working-class money would not be diverted from investment in the friendly societies.

The Liberal plan finally announced by Asquith in 1908 – non-contributory pensions of 5s. for individuals and of 7s. 6d. for married couples – was not 'universal', as Booth had desired. Only persons with annual incomes not above £21 were to receive the full pension. A sliding scale operated beyond this figure, with no pensions payable on incomes over £31 10s. Only British subjects resident in the United Kingdom for twenty years and not in receipt of poor relief (other than medical relief) since 1 January 1908 were eligible, nor must they have been in prison within the previous ten years. Finally, a pensioner must not have 'habitually failed to work according to his ability, opportunity, and need'. Asquith's scheme, in short, represented a compromise between the demand for a simple universal system, and the attachment of Gladstonian Liberals, the COS, and many friendly societies to the Victorian gospel of thrift. However, the several restrictions upon payment did not affect the underlying intention to offer the poor a benefit as of right, without stigma. 'The receipt of an old-age pension under this Act shall not deprive the pensioner of any right, franchise or privilege.' The Poor Law disqualification survived only for two years, and the test of industry proved unworkable, being formally abandoned in 1919. 'God bless that Lord George' was the cry at backwoods post offices when the first pensions were paid at the start of 1909. Old-age pensions were one social reform generally and immediately popular among the Edwardian working classes. By 1912–13, 968,000 old people in the United Kingdom were receiving over £12,300,000 each year in pensions. Outdoor poor relief for this age-group almost disappeared, a sign that the new payments were meeting a major social need.[7]

On becoming Prime Minister Asquith had passed parliamentary supervision of the old-age pensions bill to Lloyd George, who succeeded him as Chancellor of the Exchequer. Winston Churchill became President of the Board of Trade. Asquith's advocacy of old-age pensions had been severely practical, with emphasis upon the limited funds available. Nevertheless, in his 1907 budget he had introduced the principle of differentiation with respect to income tax. Henceforward, the full rate of tax – then 1s. in £ – was to apply to all unearned incomes; earned incomes up to £2,000 would meanwhile pay at 9d. in £, and existing abatements (an old form of unavowed differentiation) would be reckoned from earned income only. The need now, Asquith told the Commons (18.4.1907), was for a steady revenue policy in order to provide money for social reform. He proposed, therefore, to plan 'not for one year, but for several years'.

Lloyd George and Winston Churchill had recently become convinced of the need for boldness in social matters, which Churchill enthusiastically described in a letter to the *Nation* (7.3.1908) as 'these untrodden fields of British politics'. The enactment of old-age pensions could be only a beginning; the next beneficiaries must be the sick and unemployed. Germany, which Lloyd George specially visited in the summer of 1908, had initiated social insurance as far back as the 1880s. 'She is organized,' Churchill warned Asquith, 'not only for war, but for peace. We are organized for nothing except party politics.'[8] Not that Churchill was indifferent to such politics. He emphasized how social legislation might 'not only benefit the state but fortify the party'. During 1908 the Liberals lost seven seats at by-elections. The 1906 Liberal programme had proved too negative to retain much enduring appeal. 'There is a tremendous policy in Social Organization,' Churchill assured Asquith; 'the very class of legislation which is required is just the kind the House of Lords will not dare to oppose.' Churchill and Lloyd George were well aware that social reform was viewed with apathy or even suspicion by many working men. The 'new Liberal' hope was that the masses might show election gratitude once they were feeling the benefits of reform, though Churchill admitted that even this was not certain.

Churchill believed in 1908 that unemployment was especially 'the problem of the hour'. Trade was again extensively depressed. In February 1909 appeared the reports of the Royal Commission on the Poor Laws, appointed in 1905. A majority report was matched by a minority report, signed by four socialist members led by Beatrice Webb.[9] The majority wanted to reform but to retain (even though to rename) the Poor Law: the Webbs wished to abolish it. Both reports agreed on the need to tackle poverty and unemployment more effectively. £60 million had been spent in 1905–6 upon poor relief, health care, and education; but with only limited success. 'Something in our social organization is seriously wrong,' admitted the majority report. The Webb-inspired minority advocated what has been called 'administrative functionalism'. This meant the organization of state services for specific purposes, not for special groups (such as 'the poor'). The poor required to be treated not as a separate race, but as ordinary human beings who were suffering from identifiable difficulties. This meant abolition of the separate Poor Law, and the distribution of its functions among other bodies, local and national, including a new Ministry of Labour. The Webbs organized a national agitation to publicize their ideas. But the main proposals of both the majority and minority Poor Law reports were ignored by Lloyd George and Churchill. Poor Law abolition would have involved a major reshaping of local government structure and finance; and the Liberals preferred to concentrate upon providing social benefits.

In 1909 young William Beveridge published *Unemployment, A Problem of Industry*. Beveridge, who had been recruited by Churchill as a Board of Trade civil servant, explained why the 1905 Unemployed Workmen Act had failed. It had merely toyed with the problem of casual labour. 'To give them temporary work in times of exceptional depression is to throw them back upon chronic poverty at its close; it is like saving men from drowning in order to leave them on a quick-sand.' The Webbs wanted to attack the root causes of poverty and unemployment; but Lloyd George and Churchill (aided by Beveridge) settled for tackling effects. As practising 'new Liberal' politicians they were conscious of the need not to get too far ahead of party and public opinion. The Webbs argued that labour exchanges should be made compulsory. If an employer could hire workers only through exchanges, and workmen could find work nowhere else, the Government would be able to organize the labour market. Unemployment insurance on a voluntary basis would then be sufficient. Instead, Churchill and Lloyd George preferred to make labour exchanges voluntary but unemployment insurance compulsory in certain trades. In other words, they acted to fight the problem of destitution by relieving the unemployed rather than by attempting to prevent unemployment.[10]

Beveridge argued in his book that compulsory unemployment insurance and labour exchanges were complementary. Exchanges were required 'to reduce to a minimum the intervals between successive jobs. Insurance is required to tide over the intervals that will still remain.' In the event, these complementary innovations were enacted only at a two-year interval because of the constitutional crisis provoked by the 1909 budget. The Labour Exchanges Act passed through Parliament with little difficulty during the early stages of the crisis. Churchill explained how the exchanges would lessen 'two main defects in modern industrial conditions', lack of labour mobility and lack of information. By 1914 well over 400 exchanges throughout the United Kingdom were registering more than 2 million workers each year. Some 10 per cent of vacancies filled fell outside the region of the exchange of first application. To this extent was the flexibility of the labour market increased.

Churchill also promoted the 1909 Trade Boards Act. This created machinery for fixing wages in designated 'sweated' trades. The problem of such trades had disturbed the public conscience since the 1880s. A National Anti-Sweating League, formed in 1906, had revealed the extent of overwork and under-payment in certain trades which used mostly female labour, often on a domestic basis. Such workers had proved unable to organize protective trade unions. The 1908 Act applied to four occupations – tailoring, box making, lace making, and chain making, which employed about 200,000 workers of whom 140,000 were women and girls. Wages were successfully raised; and six more trades were added in 1913, which involved 170,000 workpeople. In its immediate range the Trade Boards Act was a limited measure, but it represented a significant recognition that the state might intervene to fix wages.

3

Lloyd George deliberately set out to make his first (1909) budget a bold one.[11] Trade had slumped, unemployment was high, and the Liberals were losing by-elections. A 'people's budget', especially if hotly contested by the Conservatives, might catch the public imagination. Would the Opposition dare to use its overwhelming Lords majority (some 472 Conservative peers were faced by only 105 Liberals in 1910) to defeat the budget despite the long-standing constitutional convention to the contrary? Though neither Lloyd George nor Asquith could be sure what would happen, they were not surprised when eventually the budget was rejected. Lloyd George forecast that defeat would advance the Liberal cause even more than acceptance. Some of his proposals were disliked even within the Liberal cabinet, notably the land taxes. The Chancellor needed to find nearly £16 million to meet the cost of old-age pensions and of new battleship building. But in addition he wanted fresh sources of revenue to finance social insurance. While leaving rates of earned income tax unchanged up to £3,000, Lloyd George therefore increased the tax upon higher earned and all unearned incomes from 1*s.* to 1*s.* 2*d.* in the £. A £10 tax allowance was given to small income-tax payers who earned under £500; but a maximum of 6*d.* super tax was introduced upon incomes above £5,000. These top rates were thought to be exorbitant by the Edwardian rich. Death duties, liquor licensing duties, and tobacco and spirit duties were also increased, and taxes on cars and petrol were introduced. But the most contentious features of the budget were the new revenue taxes on land – 20 per cent on the unearned increment in land values, a capital tax of 2*d.* in the £ on the value of undeveloped land and minerals, and a 10 per cent reversion duty on any benefit falling to a lessor at the end of a lease. Lloyd George was determined to extract money from those landowners who could make great profits with no effort simply because chance of nature had endowed their land with valuable minerals or because urban development had raised site values. The yield from these land taxes was to prove disappointing; but the Opposition concentrated its fiercest attacks upon them. Such 'socialism' was denounced as 'the beginning of the end of the rights of property'. The taxes were made the more offensive by provision for an inquisitorial valuation of land.

Lloyd George defended his proposals as a 'war budget . . . for raising money to wage implacable war against poverty and squalidness'. But by July 1909 it was becoming clear that the Conservatives might well reject the budget in the Lords. Even the Commons took some seventy days of debate to pass it. In the country a Budget Protest League was matched by a Budget League, presided over by Winston Churchill, who made pugnacious speeches up and down the country. At Limehouse on 30 July Lloyd George delivered what was immediately hailed as a famous (or infamous) defence of his land proposals. He defined a landlord's 'sole function, his chief pride' as 'stately consumption of wealth produced by others'. On 30 November the Finance Bill was rejected in the Lords by 350 votes to 75. A general election was now bound to follow; for the peers had refused supply, without which no government could rule. The Lords had virtually claimed the right to decide when a Parliament should end. The Opposition tried hard to fix public attention upon the allegedly dangerous character of the budget, and upon the alternative merits of tariff reform as a means of enlarging the revenue. Balfour sincerely believed that it was Liberal policy – not Conservative resistance – which was constitutionally damaging. He thought that the motive of the Liberals in imposing the land taxes was 'to please the "mass" of the voters . . . This is precisely the crime that lies at their door. They have chosen a particular section of the community, and a particular kind of property which they think both unpopular and helpless, and have proceeded to mulct it – demagoguery in its worst aspect.'[12] The Lords rejection motion attempted a show of democratic virtue: 'That this House is not justified in giving its consent to the Bill until it has been submitted to the judgement of the country.'

In the January 1910 general election this judgement went against the peers. Though other questions were discussed – notably a Conservative scare about the alleged weakness of the navy in the face of the German threat – the action of the Lords dominated the election. 'Peers versus people' was the Liberal cry. One answering Conservative cry asserted how 'England expects that every foreigner will pay his duty'. The Conservatives did regain many seats, both rural and urban, which they had lost only because of the high swing against them in 1906. In general, England split between a Liberal industrial working-class north, and a Conservative midlands and south. But Liberal and Labour candidates still gained 50.5 per cent (3,371,814) of the votes cast in the United Kingdom, against only 46.8 per cent (3,104,407) for the Conservatives and Liberal Unionists – Liberals 275 seats, Labour 40; Conservatives 241, Liberal Unionists 32; Irish Nationalists 82. The Liberals thus lost their overall majority in the Commons, but they retained a clear margin with Labour and Irish support. This verdict was strengthened by the highest percentage turnout in election history (86.8), a reflection of the intensity of partisan feeling.

Asquith had announced that if his Government were confirmed in office acceptance of the budget by the Lords would not now be enough. The Liberals would insist upon a reduction of the powers of the upper house. Nevertheless, the path from the election of January 1910 to the passing of the Parliament Act in August 1911 proved to be long and difficult. At first Asquith seemed to be stumbling. The Cabinet wandered from the clear issue of the Lords veto to the much less clear question of reform of the composition of the upper chamber. Fortunately, the Prime Minister finally asserted himself by announcing on 18 March that the Government intended to proceed with both the 1909 budget and with a bill to limit the powers of the Lords. He introduced the Parliament Bill on 14 April. The peers were to lose all authority over money bills, but were to be left with power to delay other legislation for two years. Asquith had made it clear that if the Lords rejected these proposals he would again appeal to the country; but only if the king were willing to create, as required, enough Liberal peers to muster a favourable majority in the Lords after a further Liberal election victory. Without such a royal promise the Government would resign forthwith, and leave Balfour to try (if he would) to govern against the wishes of a majority of the Commons – with the king by implication condoning the attempt. On 28 April the Lords passed the budget in a few hours, accepting that the January election had settled the issue. The centre of dispute now shifted to the Parliament Bill.

The culmination of the crisis was delayed, however, by the death of Edward VII on 6 May. Asquith felt that it would be unfair to expect the new King, George V, to be ready to take drastic action until he had grown used to his new role and until one last effort had been made to reach a settlement. A constitutional conference was arranged between Government and Opposition leaders. Much ground was traversed; but the intermittent discussions ultimately foundered over Home Rule, to which the Conservatives remained passionately opposed. They wanted constitutional legislation of the Home Rule type, if twice rejected by the Lords, to be next submitted to a referendum. The Liberals refused to allow the peers this new power to force an appeal to the country. On 15 November 1910 the cabinet agreed to ask the king both for a dissolution of Parliament and for a promise of peerage creations if needed. With great reluctance the king agreed, on the understanding that his willingness to create hundreds of peers would not be made public until the need became urgent. So a second general election took place in

December 1910, dominated by the Lords question but without the certain knowledge that Asquith, if he won, would be able in the last resort to secure a massive creation of peers. In the event the election produced little overall change in the state of the parties – Liberals 271 seats, Labour 42; Conservatives 237, Liberal Unionists 36; Irish Nationalists 84. But this was sufficient; for even the Conservatives recognized that to force another general election would be 'unthinkable'.

Asquith introduced the Parliament Bill into the new House of Commons on 21 February 1910. Churchill urged his chief not to be afraid of making '500 peers if necessary'. Asquith and most ministers hoped earnestly, however, that such action could still be avoided. Everything depended upon the Conservative peers. Logically, since they claimed to have rejected the 1909 budget for good reasons they ought to reject a measure designed to prevent them from acting in the same manner again. But the first move had proved to be a blunder; and Balfour now realized that it would be an even greater mistake to force a dilution of the peerage in futile resistance to the Parliament Bill. If they gave way on the Parliament Bill, the peers would still be left with power to delay a Home Rule Bill for two years: if the Liberals acquired a Lords majority, Home Rule would pass at the first attempt. When early in July 1911 the Lords began drastically to amend the Parliament Bill, Asquith asked George V to be ready to offer a large number of peerages. 249 Liberals were listed by the Government chief whip, including Thomas Hardy, J. M. Barrie, and Bertrand Russell.[13] It now became known to the Opposition that the king was committed. This destroyed the position of those – including Lansdowne, the Conservative leader in the Lords – who had kept up resistance in the belief that Asquith was bluffing.

As July moved into August the Conservative peers were consumed by arguments and uncertainties. 'Hedgers' prepared to give way under protest: 'ditchers', led by the pre-Victorian Lord Halsbury, were ready to succumb in the last ditch. During 9–10 August the final Lords debate took place. A heatwave had raised the temperature well into the nineties. The result remained in doubt to the end. But Lansdowne and the bulk of Conservative peers were now for 'hedging'. They abstained. Meanwhile, 37 Conservatives – urged on by Lord Curzon to avoid 'pollution' of their order – actually voted for the bill. The Liberal peers mustered 81 votes; and 13 bishops supported them. Against these 131 votes, the 'ditchers' could only total 114. So the Parliament Bill was passed, thanks to Conservative voting for a measure which all Conservatives deplored. Into such a paradoxical situation had Balfour and Lansdowne trapped their party. Within three months Balfour had resigned as leader.

4

In the autumn of 1910 Lloyd George had privately aired vague but ambitious ideas about the formation of a coalition government to make a 'grand settlement' of all major questions of social and constitutional reform, which would strengthen the country in case war should come. This was only one of several occasions during his career when Lloyd George was to seek ways out of political crisis by thoughts of coalition. His manoeuvrings on this occasion seem to have been disingenuous; but Balfour's eventual negative was almost certain from the first. He was not prepared to repeat what he later described as the 'unforgivable sin' of an earlier Conservative leader, Sir Robert Peel – the abandonment of principles which he had long publicly defended.[14]

The reform uppermost in Lloyd George's mind at this time was the provision of social insurance. The 1911 National Insurance Act was a much bolder innovation than the provision of old-age pensions. It provided protection against both sickness and unemployment. The latter proposals attracted little debate, for they were actuarily sound – confined to certain trades such as building, shipbuilding, and engineering, which were exposed to cyclical unemployment but which were not chronically depressed. Lloyd George and the 'new Liberals' were hoping, however, that this limited scheme would be gradually extended trade by trade.

Health insurance was much more daring; and it was passed and introduced only after a struggle with powerful pressure groups. The friendly societies and insurance companies had to be placated, for Lloyd George knew that their armies of door-to-door collectors could exert great influence. Along with the trade unions, these bodies were therefore designated 'approved societies' through which much of the scheme operated. Insurance became compulsory for all manual workers, and voluntary for anyone earning less than £160 per year. Self-employed and non-employed people were not covered. Workmen contributed 4*d.* weekly, employers 3*d.*, and the state not quite 2*d.* This represented – in Lloyd George's phrase – 'ninepence for fourpence'. 10*s.* sickness benefit was provided for 26 weeks, backed by medical, maternity, and sanatorium care. Yet health insurance was not popular. The Liberals lost three by-elections while the Act was passing through its final stages. The Harmsworth press, and Opposition extremists, encouraged a short-lived but noisy agitation against the sticking of stamps upon insurance cards, especially by mistresses on behalf of domestic servants. More seriously, the scheme was presented to the working classes as an oppressive system of deduction from wages. Finally, after the Act had passed but before it came into operation in January 1913, extreme opinion tried to exploit the fears of the doctors. Throughout 1912 they grumbled about their prospects under the scheme. Lloyd George was described by the President of the British Medical Association as a 'national calamity'. But the Association overplayed its hand; and by making important concessions Lloyd George was able to enlist most of the less affluent doctors. In particular, he had taken care not to seem to be creating a salaried state medical service.

A 'social service state', in which certain minimum standards were assured, was beginning to emerge by 1914, although this minimum was not yet universally available. The true 'welfare state' – which was to embrace the idea of the optimum rather than the minimum – lay another forty years in the future.[15] But the principle of provision through insurance was already established. This contrasted with the socialist method, advocated by Keir Hardie and Philip Snowden in opposition to Lloyd George, of financing benefits entirely from the proceeds of graduated taxation. Why, it was asked, should it be 'ninepence for fourpence': why not 'fivepence for nothing'? But Ramsay MacDonald accepted the contributory principle in 1911; and the 1945 Labour Government followed MacDonald, not Hardie, when it came to construct the mid-century welfare state.[16]

In his 1913 budget statement Lloyd George looked back to the financial situation faced by Gladstone at the time of his 1861 budget. Gladstone had provided for a revenue of £70 million; now the total was £195 million. Expenditure on armaments had grown from £28 million to nearly £75 million; spending on the Post Office from £3 million to £24 million, on education from £1,200,000 to £19,200,000 (plus a further £16,600,000 from local rates); grants-in-aid to local authorities (unknown in 1861) now cost £11 million; and social expenditure (old-age pensions, labour exchanges, health and unemployment insurance), also unknown in 1861, now took £20 million. All this spending, concluded Lloyd George, was 'not an extravagance but a real economy – an economy of time, strength, nerve, and brain … It undoubtedly increases the efficiency of the nation.' Gladstonian Liberals had always been eager to reduce and restrain government spending; 'new Liberals' accepted some heavy expenditure as a necessity, even a virtue.

The Government had yet more spending plans in mind. Lloyd George's May 1914 budget proposed (albeit confusedly) to meet the expected high costs of educational reform and of reform of local government finance, along with yet further battleship building. The income-tax rate on all unearned incomes was to be raised from 1s. 2d. to 1s. 4d. This was also to be the rate upon earned income over £2,500 per year. Below this level, Lloyd George proposed the first fully graduated scale. The super tax threshold was to be lowered from £5,000 to £3,000. In nine years of Liberal rule the top tax rate would thus have grown from 9d. to 2s. 8d., and the maximum rate of death duty from 8 per cent to 20 per cent. Government expenditure had risen over the same period by one-third, and the 1914 budget was the first to contemplate a national outlay over £200 million.

Lloyd George was interested not only in revenue but also in land. During 1913 he launched a campaign for land reform, which he wanted to make the next great Liberal enterprise.[17] He had been closely acquainted with land problems all his life, well aware of the privileges of landlords in rural Wales and of the poverty of landless agricultural workers. His 1909 Development Act had established a Development

Commission to give financial help to agriculture and fisheries, especially in times of high unemployment. Before further reform could be undertaken Lloyd George recognized that firm statistical evidence would be needed; and to this end he had inspired the formation of a Land Enquiry Committee, which consisted of a group of interested Liberals including Seebohm Rowntree. It published two large reports, the first (1913) dealing with rural land problems and the second (1914) with town land. Rowntree also wrote *How the Labourer Lives* (1913), a rural survey similar to his influential book on urban poverty. Lloyd George built his speeches upon evidence taken from these sources, speaking first at Bedford in October 1913. Labourers' income, he claimed, now stood lower in real value than in the reign of Henry VII. He demanded a living wage for labourers, allotments for those who wanted them, the demolition of rural slums, an end to 'capricious eviction', protection against rent increases which arose because of improvements made by tenants, and defence against the destruction of farmers' crops by game preserved only for the pleasure of landlords. 'Labourers had diminished, game had tripled. The landlord was no more necessary to agriculture than a gold chain to a watch.' Lloyd George believed that a new uniform system of land valuation would greatly increase local authority rate income, and that this would make possible the introduction of wide new local responsibilities in education, housing, and other social provision. Land courts could fix higher wages for labourers and lower rents for tenant farmers, both benefits at the expense of landowners.

The land campaigners arranged lectures and meetings all over the country, and circulated pamphlets by the million. But what did land reform offer to urban voters, the majority of the electorate? Reformers contended that greater prosperity in the countryside would increase the demand for town-made goods. Moreover, land reform in the towns was to include slum clearance, compulsory acquisition and leasing of land, and rating reform. Nevertheless, not much impact seems to have been made in the towns up to August 1914. C. F. G. Masterman, Lloyd George's chief lieutenant in the Government, described him at the end of May 1914 as 'overworked and unhappy: disturbed at the unpopularity of insurance, at the failure of the Land Campaign to beat up a great emotional wave'. The 1914 budget, which was closely bound up with Lloyd George's land schemes, ran into procedural and other difficulties because he had not planned carefully ahead. Forty to fifty Liberal Members of Parliament were prepared to vote against important features of the budget. As a result, it was in process of being drastically and humiliatingly trimmed down when the war suddenly supervened. Lloyd George and the 'new Liberalism' had lost much prestige. Masterman had recently been twice defeated at by-elections caused by his promotion to the cabinet. Churchill had long since moved to the Admiralty, and away from social reform. If peace had continued during the second half of 1914 would the fortunes of Lloyd George have revived? Alternatively, without the 'new Liberalism' to provide rallying causes and crises could the Liberal Party have held its ground – in the short term, against the challenge from the Conservatives and tariff reform; and in the long term, against the competition of the Labour Party for working-class votes? 'We have nothing to offer positively to attract enthusiasm,' Masterman had written on 30 May, 'and *everything* we have done since 1910 has cost a certain number of votes.'[18]

5

The Conservatives had denounced land reform as confiscation of property. They continued to proclaim tariff reform – both as a policy which would bring prosperity to all classes and so reduce the need for state interference, and also as a means of finding money for any further social reforms which might prove necessary. But they remained uncertain about what such reforms might be. During the December 1910 election Balfour had unexpectedly suggested that tariff reform might be witheld by a Conservative Government until specifically approved at a referendum. Bonar Law, his successor as party leader, had been a keen tariff reformer; but in 1913 he agreed that, although he would introduce imperial preference upon gaining office, he would not propose food taxes without a further specific election mandate.

After ten years of tariff reform agitation the United Kingdom remained a free-trade country. This attachment was wise, even though most contemporaries were unaware of the best reasons for their attachment.[19] Economic conditions had much changed since the adoption of unilateral free trade by the early Victorians. Nevertheless, Edwardian England stood at the centre of an expanding multilateral system of international payments. The great expansion of world production during the late nineteenth century would have produced serious friction if exchanges of goods had been financed on the old unilateral basis. This would have involved serious encroachments by new competitors upon established trading patterns. Fortunately, these competitors did not now need to concentrate all their exports in direct competition with British exports. Britain did still develop an increasingly adverse balance of visible trade (at a peak of £177 million in 1901–5); but this was compensated by steadily rising income from invisible services (£346 million per annum in 1911–13) of benefit to the whole world economy. If Britain had attempted to raise tariff barriers and to develop imperial preference, this new system would have been upset. Industrial Europe and the United States would have been forced either further to intensify world competition in manufactures, or to adjust their internal economies and to seek new sources of supply through the development of colonies and spheres of influence. Those Edwardians who wanted Britain to concentrate upon empire trade failed to understand how the sale of British goods throughout the world smoothed the flow of British trade and how the flow of that trade irrigated the whole international system. Paradoxically, the international economy of the early twentieth century worked well precisely because it was a mixture of British free trade and foreign protection. 'If we hold fast to free trade,' concluded the president of the National Liberal Federation at its 1913 conference, 'we shall continue to prosper, if only the world does not destroy property by war.'

Notes

1. See especially B. Semmel, *Imperialism and Social Reform* (1960), Ch. V; and J. Amery, *Life of Joseph Chamberlain* (1951–69), Vols. IV–VI. Also D. Read (ed.), *Documents from Edwardian England* (1973), Ch. 8.
2. See A. Gollin, *Balfour's Burden* (1965); and R. A. Rempel, *Unionists Divided* (1972).
3. See especially N. Blewett, *The Peers, The Parties, and The People* (1972), pp. 36–42; and A. K. Russell, *Liberal Landslide, The General Election of 1906* (1973).
4. *The Times*, 16 February 1907.
5. B. L. Add. Mss. 41217 ff. 294–5.
6. See J. R. Hay, *The Origin of the Liberal Welfare Reforms, 1906–14* (1975), and references there; notably B. B. Gilbert, *The Evolution of National Insurance in Great Britain* (1966). Also D. Read (ed.), *Documents from Edwardian England* (1973), Ch. 10.
7. H. J. Hoare, *Old Age Pensions* (1915), Ch. IX.
8. R. S. Churchill, *Winston S. Churchill* (1969), Vol. II, companion part 2, pp. 863–4. See also H. Pelling, *Popular Politics and Society in Late Victorian Britain* (1968), Ch. 1.
9. See M. E. Rose, *The Relief of Poverty, 1834–1914* (1972), Ch. 5, and references there.
10. See especially B. B. Gilbert, 'Winston Churchill versus the Webbs: the Origins of British Unemployment Insurance', *American Historical Review*, Vol. 71 (1966); and José Harris, *Unemployment and Politics* (1972).
11. See especially N. Blewett, *The Peers, The Parties and The People* (1972); and B. K. Murray, 'The Politics of the "People's Budget"', *Historical Journal*, XV (1973).
12. K. Young, *Arthur James Balfour* (1963), p. 287.
13. R. Jenkins, *Asquith* (1964), appendix A.
14. Blanche E. C. Dugdale, *Arthur James Balfour* (1936), II, Ch. IV. See especially G. R. Searle, *The Quest for National Efficiency* (1971), Ch. VI; and R. J. Scally, *The Origins of the Lloyd George Coalition* (1975), Ch. VII.
15. See A. Briggs, 'The Welfare State in Historical Perspective', *European Journal of Sociology*, Vol. 2 (1961).
16. D. Marquand, *Ramsay Macdonald* (1977), pp. 138–41.
17. See H. V. Emy, 'The Land Campaign: Lloyd George as a Social Reformer, 1909–14', in A. J. P. Taylor (ed.), *Lloyd George, Twelve Essays*, (1971); R. Douglas, *Land, People and Politics* (1976), esp. Ch. 9; and B. B. Gilbert, 'David Lloyd George: The Reform of British Land-Holding and the Budget of 1914', *Historical Journal*, XXI (1978).
18. K. D. Brown (ed.), *Essays in Anti-Labour History* (1974), pp. 31–2.
19. See especially S. B. Saul, *Studies in British Overseas Trade* (1960); and F. Crouzet, 'Trade and Empire: the British Experience from the Establishment of Free Trade until the First World War', in B. M. Ratcliffe (ed.), *Great Britain and Her World* (1975).

Chapter 29

Imperial policy: *'Will the Empire live?'*

1

The Boer War put an end to the wilder expressions of late-Victorian imperialism.[1] 'The war has been the nation's Recessional after all the pomp and show of the year of Jubilee. It has transmuted the complacent arrogance and contempt of other nations begotten of long years of peace and prosperity to a truer consciousness both of our strength and of our defects, and has awakened an earnest desire to make those defects good.' So admitted the first volume of *The Times History of the War in South Africa* (1900). During the Edwardian years the British Empire ceased to provide excitement. Instead, its progress – even its ultimate survival – became a subject of sober concern. At the opening of the 1902 Colonial Conference Joseph Chamberlain remarked how 'the weary Titan staggers under the too vast orb of its fate. We have borne the burden for many years. We think it is time that our children should assist us to support it'.[2] Yet Chamberlain found little backing at the conference for his ideas of imperial unification. The sense of national differentiation was strengthening yearly within the white 'Dominions' (as the self-governing colonies were coming increasingly to be called), unchecked by the introduction of Rhodes Scholarships to Oxford (1902) or of Empire Day (1904). New generations were growing up overseas which had never known Britain as 'home'. New Zealand remained the most British of the Dominions; but when at the 1911 Imperial Conference her Prime Minister, Sir Joseph Ward, unexpectedly echoed Chamberlain's old proposals for formal links, he was opposed both by the other Dominion premiers and by Asquith, the British Prime Minister. Such a scheme, declared Asquith, would be 'absolutely fatal to our present system of responsible government'.[3]

Chamberlain turned after the 1902 Colonial Conference to his tariff reform campaign, in the hope that colonial preference might be made the basis for a more united empire. The Liberals would have none of this; but at the 1911 conference Asquith pointed to a middle way: 'we are, and intend to remain, units indeed, but units in a greater unity'. Balfour, the Conservative leader, was likewise beginning to explore the 'commonwealth' idea. 'Our experiment is new ... How are you going to carry out what is the ideal and the ambition of all the great self-governing millions in the Empire, which is a new ideal and a new ambition, that of at once combining the self-conscious national life with the consciousness of belonging to a yet larger whole?'

The white colonies proved almost as unwilling to make contributions towards imperial defence – first requested by Chamberlain – as to support schemes of formal federation.[4] Chamberlain wanted colonial support in money and men, especially for the royal navy. But only New Zealand made a direct grant, Australia and Canada preferring to form their own fleets. R. B. Haldane, the Liberal War Secretary, did succeed in creating an Imperial General Staff (1907); but colonial particularism was still accepted by the 1909 Imperial Defence Conference, and was not lessened even when greater consultation was arranged in the immediate pre-war years through the Committee of Imperial Defence. The self-governing colonies had sent 30,000 men to the Boer War, and were to send large forces to fight in the First World War; but they had refused to bind themselves in advance. Their commitment to the mother country was now much more sentimental than constitutional.

Radicals and socialists remained suspicious of the empire. They argued that it provided large profits for unscrupulous businessmen, but few benefits for the people either of the colonies or of the United Kingdom. They claimed that ministers were too much influenced by financiers and adventurers, and that seizure of territory was often virtually dictated by them. Attempts to influence ministers were certainly made, for example by Transvaal gold magnates. But the politicians always pursued their own objectives, though these did often include the opening up of opportunities for more trade. The most notable radical critic was J. A. Hobson, who published his analysis of *Imperialism* in 1902. He argued that the maldistribution of purchasing power in a capitalist society led to 'under-consumption' by the poor and to 'over-saving' by the rich, who invested their capital overseas where it could hope for higher returns than at home. Most of this investment went to developed countries outside the empire; but Hobson contended that sufficient went to unstable or new territories, both colonial and foreign, to create a national commitment to protect 'economic parasites' through British foreign or colonial policy. Yet, in reality, the profits from participation in the 'scramble' for Africa were not large, apart from the gold and diamond ventures in South Africa. Cecil Rhodes' British South Africa Company did not pay a dividend for years, and the British East Africa Company never did so.

2

The coloured citizens of the British Empire far outnumbered the whites. Were they to be regarded as equal to white men, or as inferior?[5] Sir Alfred Milner as High Commissioner in South Africa, and Lord Curzon as Viceroy of India, did not quite assert that coloured races were biologically inferior; but they assumed that it would take many generations to raise them up to the level of white civilization. Even J. A. Hobson's *Imperialism* accepted the need for continuing white rule of coloured peoples, though he wanted this to be under international auspices. 'Such interference with the government of a lower race must be directed primarily to secure the safety and progress of the civilization of the world, and not the special interest of the interfering nation.' But most Edwardians remained satisfied that Britain could carry out her imperial 'mission' without any need for internationalization. Moreover, white rule need not be everywhere intrusive. Too much territory had been acquired, especially in Africa, to make intensive government practicable with the limited resources available. 'Indirect rule' through existing native leaders was deliberately cultivated – notably by Sir Frederick Lugard in Nigeria.

Even Ramsay MacDonald, the socialist, accepted that there was 'a repulsion between the white and coloured races which becomes active when they live together and the conditions of social equality begin to arise'.[6] MacDonald hoped, therefore, that the races would keep apart. Where, regrettably, intermingling had occurred his hope was that as coloured people advanced in education they would be granted the franchise, as had happened in Cape Colony. Unfortunately, in the very year in which MacDonald was writing (1909) non-white rights and prospects in South Africa were coming under serious threat. In their last months in power in 1905 the Conservatives had drafted a constitution for the Transvaal which proposed representative but not responsible government, on the assumption that the Boers could not yet be expected to remain loyal. But in February 1906 the new Liberal Cabinet decided to go the whole way.[7] The story – spread later by Lloyd George – that Campbell-Bannerman suddenly converted the cabinet into making a 'magnanimous gesture' has now been discredited. Liberal ministers were not dramatically converted; nor did they anticipate that Boer politicians, rather than politicians of British descent, would gain a majority in the Transvaal assembly at the first elections in 1907. When this happened, the Liberals had to admit that they had miscalculated. In 1909 the Asquith cabinet accepted a South African proposal for a union of the old British colonies of the Cape and Natal with the two former Boer republics to form one Union of South Africa. The Liberals hoped that this would produce another strong Dominion within the British Empire in control of the strategic tip of Africa. The Boer leaders – Louis Botha and J. C. Smuts – pledged their loyalty to the imperial connection. It was assumed in England that the supposedly more vigorous and progressive attitudes of the English-speaking South Africans would gradually soften Boer rigidity. In particular, Liberals hoped that the advancement of non-white South Africans would continue. In Cape Colony some 22,000 non-white Africans and Indians already possessed the vote under a property qualification. But the Boer territories had not been compelled to establish such a franchise by the 1902 peace treaty. 'The question of granting franchises to natives,' the treaty agreed, 'will not be decided until after the introduction of self-government.' The Liberals were bound by this clause when they decided to grant Boer self-government in 1906. Liberal ministers were uncomfortably aware that they risked being generous towards the white Boers at the expense of the non-white Africans and Indians. By 1909 ministers felt still more uncomfortable when the draft bill sent from South Africa restricted membership of the Union Parliament to whites, and excluded the vast majority of non-whites from even the possibility of qualifying for the franchise. Nevertheless, ministers accepted that it was now too late to prevent discrimination by colour. If the British Government had tried to amend the colour-bar provisions, the white South Africans would have taken their stand on the principle of colonial self-government, and they would probably have been supported on such grounds by the Canadians and Australians. The goodwill of Botha and his friends would have been lost, and the influence of the Boer extremists strengthened. The Liberals had to take refuge in the sincere expectation that a united South Africa would soon come to recognize the injustice of a racially-restricted franchise. At the same time, Liberals believed that the economic progress which would be made possible by the union would benefit the natives much more than immediate possession of the vote. In summing up the South Africa Bill in the Commons, Asquith could do no more than hope that the South African whites would 'sooner rather than later' liberalize their franchise.

Only a handful of radicals and Labour men had wanted to take a strong line even to the point of risking the failure of the scheme for union. Keir Hardie argued in Parliament that the Boers would give way rather than lose the union. On the other hand, he saw no chance that they would ever concede votes to non-whites once the union had been secured. 'For the first time we are asked to write over the portals of the British Empire: "Abandon hope all ye who enter here".'

The conciliatory Liberal policy towards the Boers encouraged Indians to hope for some liberalization of the government of India. Lord Curzon – the able but autocratic Viceroy from 1898 to 1905 – had pursued a policy of good government and reform even at the cost of alienating educated Indian opinion.[8] His partition of Bengal on the ground that it was too large for effective administration had given particular offence, and had greatly strengthened the nationalist movement led by the Indian National Congress, which had been formed in 1885. Liberal policy under John Morley as Secretary of State for India (1905–10) and Lord Minto as Viceroy (1905–10) showed more sensitivity towards Indian feeling, though still ready to employ repression for the maintenance of law and order.[9] 'Reforms may not save the Raj,' wrote Morley to Minto, 'but if they don't nothing else will.' In this somewhat resigned spirit the Indian Councils Act was passed in 1909 after prolonged gestation. The legislative councils were enlarged to accommodate twice as many Indian members, who represented class and communal interests. Members were now permitted to debate budgetary matters. An Indian was appointed to the Viceroy's executive council, which was left as the only council with an official majority. Morley persuaded Minto that it would still be able to exercise a check upon the others. Certainly, Liberal policy was not democratic. It was designed, in the spirit of Macauley's famous 1835 memorandum on Indian education, to produce a consultative autocracy – analogous to the Prussian or Japanese autocracies – by opening participation in government to 'a class of persons, Indian in blood and colour, but English in taste, in opinion, in morals, and in intellect', Morley stated plainly that Indian self-government was not his objective; he was 'doing nothing to loosen the bolts'.

3

The Indian reforms worked well in the short term. So did the South African settlement. The British Empire seemed to be in much better order in 1914 than at the beginning of the century. But what of the long term? The example of the decline and fall of the Roman Empire was often in Edwardian minds. An anonymous pamphlet called *The Decline and Fall of the British Empire* (1905) was published in the form of a work supposedly issued in Japan in the year 2005. It listed eight causes of British decline during the twentieth century – the prevalence of town over country life; the weakening of British interest in the sea; the growth of luxury; the decline of taste; the debilitation of the physique and health of the people; the deterioration of religious and intellectual life; excessive taxation and municipal extravagance; and the inability of the British to defend themselves and their empire. Although the British Empire had revealed some capacity for adaptability during the Edwardian years, H. G. Wells was right still to be asking in 1914 – 'Will the Empire live? What will hold such an Empire as the British together?'[10]

Notes

1. See especially A. P. Thornton, *The Imperial Idea and Its Enemies* (1959), Ch. III.
2. G. Bennett (ed.), *The Concept of Empire* (2nd edn, 1962), p. 330. See, in general, M. Beloff, *Imperial Sunset* (1969), Chs. I–IV; B. Porter, *The Lion's Share* (1976), Ch. VI; and R. Hyam, *Britain's Imperial Century, 1815–1914* (1976).
3. See especially A. B. Keith (ed.), *Selected Speeches and Documents on British Colonial Policy, 1763–1917* (1918), Ch. IX; J. Kendle, *The Colonial and Imperial Conferences, 1887–1911* (1967); and N. Mansergh, *The Commonwealth Experience* (1969), Ch. 5.
4. See especially D. C. Gordon, *The Dominion Partnership in Imperial Defense, 1870–1914* (1965).
5. See, in general, J. Morris, *Pax Britannica* (1968), Ch. 8.
6. J. Ramsay MacDonald, *Socialism and Government* (1909), II, pp. 80–91.

7. See especially R. Hyam, *Elgin and Churchill at the Colonial Office, 1905–1908* (1968), Chs. 4, 11, 13; R. Hyam, 'African Interests and the South Africa Act, 1908—1910', *Historical Journal*, XIII (1970); and R. Hyam and G. Martin (eds.), *Reappraisals in British Imperial History* (1975), Ch. 8.
8. See especially D. Dilks, *Curzon in India* (1969–70).
9. See especially R. J. Moore, *Liberalism and Indian Politics, 1872–1922* (1966); S. A. Wolpert, *Morley and India, 1906–1910* (1967); and S. E. Koss, *John Morley at the India Office, 1905–1910* (1969).
10. H. G. Wells, *An Englishman Looks at the World* (1914), p. 33. See also S. Hynes, *The Edwardian Turn of Mind* (1968), Ch. II; and R. F. Betts, 'The Allusion to Rome in British Imperialist Thought of the Late Nineteenth and Early Twentieth Centuries', *Victorian Studies*, XV (1971).

Chapter 30

Foreign policy: *'Peace at that price would be a humiliation'*

1

Britain's relative power in the world – already visibly diminishing during the last quarter of the nineteenth century – was to decline still further during the first years of the twentieth century up to the outbreak of the First World War in 1914. Increasingly, albeit reluctantly and often uncertainly, British diplomacy began to make withdrawals and to enter into commitments. Both were now accepted as necessary for the protection of essential interests. Old Lord Salisbury forecast in 1902 'some great change in public affairs – in which the forces which contend for the mastery among us will be differently ranged and balanced'. The British Empire seemed to be threatened as never before in his lifetime. 'The large aggregation of human force which lies around our Empire seems to draw more closely together, and to assume almost un- consciously a more and more aggressive aspect.'[1]

Britain now felt the need for assistance to defend her commercial position in the Far East – hence the Anglo-Japanese alliance of 1902. And in the New World she found it necessary to recognize the predominance of the United States. This last was made psychologically easier by a sense of 'special relationship' with the Americans, based upon a common heritage and language.[2] This special feeling was always stronger upon the British than upon the American side. The patronizing British attitude of the early-Victorian period had now been replaced by a full sense of American potential power. It was accepted that Britain and the United States stood as equals; and perceptive observers were already admitting that Britain would soon become the weaker power. In 1902 W. T. Stead published *The Americanization of the World, or The Trend of the Twentieth Century*. From 1912 *Whitaker's Almanack* removed the United States out of alphabetical order among the foreign powers to a special place immediately after its section on the British Empire. Kinship made it easier to accept the prospect of American world leadership. The consoling sentiment that 'blood is thicker than water' was constantly repeated. By the later Edwardian years, however, this emphasis upon 'race' in Anglo-American relations seems to have diminished, influenced perhaps by realization that an increasing number of United States citizens did not come from Anglo-Saxon stock. Sir Edward Grey, the Liberal Foreign Secretary, admitted in a private letter to President Theodore Roosevelt in 1906 that the Americans were 'making a new race and a new type drawn from many sources'. Nevertheless, Grey still claimed a special relationship because 'some generations of freedom on both sides' had 'evolved a type of man that looks at things from a kindred point of view'.[3]

Three major diplomatic clashes with the United States had occurred during the eighteen nineties: over the Venezuelan boundary with British Guiana, over the Alaskan boundary with Canada, and over the projected Panama Canal.[4] The Venezuelan difficulty started in 1895, and the final boundary arbitration in 1899 worked out largely in Britain's favour. But the Americans had compelled Britain to accept arbitration by asserting their interest under the Monroe Doctrine in Latin American affairs. During the Spanish-American war of 1898–9 Britain pursued a policy of neutrality, but one which seemed to favour the United States. This encouraged a pro-British attitude among the American public during the Boer War. Kipling's famous poem on *The White Man's Burden* (1899), though applicable to all imperial powers, was in its immediate context an appeal to the United States to undertake the government of the Phillipines, which had been captured from Spain. The Americans took a high line over the Alaskan boundary dispute, which ended in 1903 with a settlement generously in their favour. They proved equally insistent in demanding sole control of the proposed Panama Canal. The consequent Hay–Pauncefote treaty of 1901 possessed general as well as particular importance. It signalized the abandonment of all claims to British equality with the United States in the Caribbean. This reflected not only the assumption that war with the United States had become unthinkable; it also represented a first withdrawal of British power from a distant part of the world.

A similar adjustment was about to be made in the Far East, the more striking because in this case it was contrived through a limited alliance with a non-white power – the newly half-westernized Japan.[5] At the turn of the century high hopes had arisen about the vast potential market for British goods in China. But during and after the Boer War Britain lacked the naval and military strength to feel confident about maintaining the 'open door', or even about securing a favourable share if partition of China into spheres of influence became unavoidable. Lord Lansdowne, who had succeeded Salisbury as Foreign Secretary in 1900, first tried to negotiate some working Far Eastern arrangement with the Germans; but they proved unwilling to risk offending the Russians – who stood on their European frontier – simply for the sake of the relatively small German interests in the Orient. With much hesitation, therefore, Lansdowne turned to Japan. The Anglo-Japanese treaty of 1902 constituted a real alliance, notwithstanding Salisbury's reiterated doubts whether British ministers could properly enter into long-term commitments. The treaty applied, however, only to the Far East. The British cabinet seems to have been swayed by Admiralty arguments that a Japanese alliance would ensure joint local naval supremacy over the French and Russians on relatively cheap terms. Otherwise, much increased spending on warship construction would become necessary. The treaty promised mutual aid if either country were attacked by more than one power in the Far East. The Japanese hoped to extend their influence in Korea, and the treaty in effect recognized this aspiration, despite complaints from Salisbury that Britain might be led into war. But the treaty did not expect British intervention in a war between Russia and Japan alone. When this duly broke out in 1904 British concern that the Japanese might be overwhelmed by their white enemies soon changed to satisfaction at the comprehensive Japanese victory, which included the elimination of Russia as a naval power. The alliance treaty was renewed in 1905, with each country now bound to assist the other if attacked in the Far East by even one power. This constituted a check upon Russian thoughts of revenge. In return, Japan undertook to send troops to help defend India if needed.

The Japanese alliance was the more daring for being concluded with a non-white power. The Japanese, however, were not yet feared. By contrast, the Chinese, even though their empire had lapsed into chaos, were much distrusted, at least for the long term. The Edwardians often spoke of the 'yellow peril', the prospect of western civilization being swamped by hundreds of millions of Chinese. The Boxer rising of 1900, which became an indiscriminate attack upon foreigners in China, was taken as a portent.[6]

Prejudice against foreigners was given focus by the large influx of refugees driven from eastern Europe by the Russian pogroms of the eighties and after.[7] 120,000 Jews came to England between 1870 and 1914. The number of residents in England and Wales who had been born in Russia or Russian Poland grew from 14,468 in 1881 to 95,541 in 1911, by which date they comprised one-third of all foreign-born residents. They tended to concentrate in a few areas, notably the East End of London (nearly 44,000 in Stepney alone by 1911) where the 'alien invasion' was alleged to have overcrowded the labour market and thereby to have reduced wages and to have lengthened hours of work. The Trades Union Congress passed motions condemning the influx of 'foreign pauper labour' in 1888, 1892, and 1894. The Conservative 1905 Aliens Act was intended to keep out 'undesirable and destitute aliens'. But generous application of the Act under the Liberals, who took office soon after its passing, largely nullified its intentions. Alarmists tended to associate foreigners – especially east Europeans – with anarchism or red revolution, which was always being presented as likely to spread from the Continent to England. The famous 'siege of Sidney Street', Mile End, in 1911 was attended by Winston Churchill as Home Secretary, after he had called out troops to help capture 'Peter the Painter'. Exchanges of fire ended when the house suddenly went up in flames. Two bodies were later recovered.[8]

2

In the cold world of the twentieth century British ministers came to accept that deals would have to be made with foreign powers. But with which powers and on what terms? Germany had been traditionally a friend throughout the nineteenth century: France and Russia had remained potential enemies, even while sometimes serving as allies. In 1898, first in private and then in public, Joseph Chamberlain pressed the idea of an alliance with Germany.[9] All the major powers of Europe, argued Chamberlain, had now joined alliances; 'and as long as we have interests which at one time or another conflict with the interests of all, we are liable to be confronted at any moment with a combination of Great Powers'. Lord Salisbury remained dubious about Chamberlain's fear of 'a quarrel with all the world at the same time'. Success later in the year in the Fashoda confrontation with France showed how much Britain could still achieve alone. In November 1899 Chamberlain tried again by appealing for some arrangement between Britain, the United States, and Germany – 'the Teutonic race and the two great branches of the Anglo-Saxon race'; but his speech was coldly received in all three countries. A mutually attractive basis for an Anglo-German alliance remained hard to find – given that the main German concern lay in Europe, with especial fear of the Russian danger, whereas Britain's pressing problems lay in the wider world. Germany would only consider support for British interests and aspirations in the Far East in return for full British adhesion to the Triple Alliance in Europe. This would have meant accepting the possibility of war with Russia and France for the sake of German or Austrian interests in eastern Europe. During 1901 a succession of schemes for some new Anglo-German relationship were aired by one side or the other, with more or less formality and authority.[10] Lord Lansdowne was certainly more ready to contemplate an alliance, even a secret alliance, than Salisbury had been as Foreign Secretary; but the cabinet – prompted by Salisbury, who was still Prime Minister – refused to move so far as to join the Triple Alliance. Salisbury could see no advantage for Britain. 'The liability of having to defend the German and Austrian frontiers against Russia is heavier than that of having to defend the British Isles against France.'[11] Could something less than a full alliance be contrived? Lansdowne continued to hope so; but when at the end of 1901 he suggested simply an entente – a declaration of common policy 'defining the interests which we shall jointly defend' – the German ambassador instantly rejected the proposal.

Neither British nor German ministers realized that this would be the last attempt of its kind. Within three years an entente with France had been signed. Paradoxically, Lansdowne had been prepared to offer the Germans in 1901 far more than he was ever to promise the French. But from 1902 German naval building began to alter the whole tone of Anglo-German relations. In that year the Admiralty for the first time drew up plans in case of hostilities with Germany. The First Lord warned the cabinet in October that 'the new German navy is being carefully built up from the point of view of a war with us'.[12] The German Navy Laws of 1898 and 1900 had begun the construction of a great battle-fleet. Britain found herself driven to build in reply, in order to maintain her traditional naval supremacy. Even so, by 1909 the two-power standard had perforce to be abandoned. It could be assumed, fortunately, that the next two largest navies – of Germany and of the United States – would never be allied against Britain. The objective now became a 60 per cent margin of superiority in capital ships over the Germans. And to exploit this margin most of Britain's battleships became concentrated in or near the North Sea to the plan of Sir John Fisher, the dynamic First Sea Lord (1904-10). At the same time Fisher ruthlessly scrapped over 150 obsolescent ships, useful only for 'showing the flag'. This world role for the navy was now diminishing before the necessity of defending the British Isles themselves. In 1906 *HMS Dreadnought* was launched, the first of a new type of all-big-gun battleship. This revolution in design, far from giving the Germans a chance to start on equal terms (as was sometimes claimed), threw their plans into temporary disarray. Nevertheless, the German challenge remained very serious, and Fisher seems to have considered at least half-seriously the making of a pre-emptive strike upon the German fleet. The *Daily Mail* had suggested this as early as 24 July 1902. It was understandable that the Germans should want a strong navy for reasons of prestige and commerce protection; but the short-range ships which were launched seemed to be designed only for war with Britain. Admiral Tirpitz's 'risk-fleet' theory required a German navy so strong that the British, even if superior in numbers, would not dare to risk an attack. Britain could then be placed under diplomatic pressure to follow a German lead. The plan failed, since the growth of the German fleet drove the British not into amenability but into increasingly close relations with the French and Russians. Sir Edward Grey, the Liberal Foreign Secretary from the end of 1905, explained how the combination of a large German navy with the leading army in Europe constituted a threat to Europe in general and to Britain in particular. 'We have to take into account not only the German Navy, but also the German Army. If the German fleet ever becomes superior to ours, the German Army can conquer this country. There is no corresponding risk of this kind to Germany: for however superior our Fleet was, no Naval victory would bring us any nearer Berlin.'[13] The navy was for Germany (in Winston Churchill's word) a 'luxury', whereas for Britain it was a necessity.

In November 1907 the Germans embarked upon a large dreadnought building programme. This was matched by extra British construction. Then early in 1909 the Germans were suddenly (albeit mistakenly) thought to be secretly accelerating their programme. The days when the British could catch up any foreign rival in shipbuilding were now gone; the Germans could build a battleship in the same time, a little over three years. The cry 'we want eight, and we won't wait' (coined by George

Wyndham, the Conservative politician) expressed the demand for an immediate response so as to ensure Britain's continuing lead in the future. The *Daily Telegraph* (18.3.1909) announced that it was 'not yet prepared to turn the face of every portrait of Nelson to the wall'. The German foreign minister offered to restrain further building if Britain would sign a mutual undertaking not to join any hostile coalition and to preserve a benevolent neutrality in case of war. Such an agreement, commented Grey, 'would serve to establish German hegemony in Europe ... an invitation to help Germany to make a European combination which would be directed against us when it suited her so to use it'.[14] The Liberal Government, though reluctant to spend so heavily, did eventually build the eight battleships, upon the excuse that Austria and Italy were entering the dreadnought race. When war came in 1914 Britain had 20 dreadnought battleships at sea against 13 German, plus 12 under construction against 7.

British army and navy expenditure rose steadily during the pre-war years:[15]

	1900 (£)	1910(£)	1914(£)
British army estimates	21,400,000	27,600,000	29,400,000
British naval estimates	29,200,000	40,400,000	47,400,000
German army estimates	33,600,000	40,800,000	88,400,000
German naval estimates	7,400,000	20,600,000	22,400,000

To help remedy the shortcomings of the British army revealed during the Boer War a major reorganization gradually followed during the Edwardian years. At Balfour's initiative the Defence Committee of the Cabinet was transformed into the Committee of Imperial Defence (1903), chaired by the Prime Minister and with its own secretariat.[16] The Esher Committee (1903–4) secured the creation of an Army Council as a policy-making body, along with the abolition of the old obstructive office of commander-in-chief. A General Staff, recommended by the Hartington Commission of 1888–90, was also at last established. The application of the Esher proposals, which had begun under the Conservatives, was completed by R. B. Haldane as War Secretary (1906–12) in the pre-war Liberal Governments. Unfortunately, the Committee of Imperial Defence did not develop into a strategic co-ordinating body between the army and navy, since neither of the Edwardian Liberal premiers (Campbell-Bannerman and Asquith) sought to use it to give a lead; but the committee found a valuable role in making war preparations over a wide range of previously little considered aspects such as food supply, censorship, and espionage. It also compiled the War Book, which laid down the sequence of action to be followed when hostilities seemed imminent.

Under Haldane the big decision was made to form an 'expeditionary force' which could be sent to France if the British Government decided to intervene in a Franco-German war. No longer was the British army to regard itself simply as a force for the defence of the British Isles and the British Empire. This meant acceptance of the 'blue water' thesis, that the navy could be trusted to keep the British Isles safe from invasion. 'It is not a problem of Home Defence,' Lord Esher had emphasized. 'The Navy can deal with home defence. It is a problem of foreign defence.'[17] Haldane planned to send six fully-equipped infantry divisions plus a cavalry division to Europe within fifteen days of the outbreak of war. This force would be provided by the regular army. But what about reserves? Haldane abolished the old militia and volunteers. In their place he formed in 1907 a 'special reserve' for the regular army, to which it was hoped men from the militia would transfer. A new Territorial Force was formed, liable for service anywhere in the United Kingdom but with strong local connections. The 'territorials' – with an establishment of 300,000 men, and their own artillery and services – were to undergo annual training for four years and were liable for service until the age of 30. Politicians of all parties recognized that the British public would not accept any army reorganization which required compulsory military service. This was despite the advocacy of Lord Roberts and the National Service League. Started in 1901, the league had 35,000 members by 1909. From 1908 Haldane promoted the formation of units of the Officers' Training Corps at universities and public schools. Even the Boy Scout movement – initiated in the same year by Lieutenant-General Baden-Powell, hero of the Boer War siege of Mafeking – saw itself partly in terms of preparation for war. One of the 'Camp Fire Yarns' in Baden-Powell's *Scouting for Boys* (1908) complained about Members of Parliament who wanted to make the army and navy smaller so as to save money. 'These men are called "politicians". They do not look to the good of the country.' The Boy Scout movement had 152,000 United Kingdom members by 1913.[18]

The army entered the First World War much better organized than at the outbreak of the Boer War. It now possessed a General Staff. Its officers and men had acquired a new sense of professional purpose. Credit for this must go especially to the energetic Haldane, and to the persistent and ubiquitous Esher, an influential figure mostly behind the scenes. The British army which was perforce comparatively small, and the British navy, which was perforce comparatively very large, were both sufficiently 'ready' by 1914.

3

In May 1903 Edward VII paid a state visit to Paris, which became a great personal success. The Parisian crowds, hostile at first, were won over by Edward's obvious bonhomie. Within a year the Anglo-French entente had been signed; and this helped to win for the king the name of 'Edward the Peacemaker'. Edward was certainly in favour of peace, but his contribution to British diplomacy was always marginal. He took a genuine though not detailed interest in foreign affairs, and he was always willing to use his European royal connections with the Kaiser and others in support of British policy. But he took no initiatives, and as a constitutional sovereign he could hardly have done so.[19]

Soundings about an Anglo-French settlement, first by Delcassé, the French Foreign Minister, and then by Lansdowne, the British Foreign Secretary, had begun months before the king's visit. Both powers were concerned about the deteriorating situation in the Far East and about unrest in Morocco, either of which might lead to conflict between them. In July 1903 during President Loubet's return visit to London Lansdowne and Delcassé discussed the framework of a settlement. As eventually agreed, Britain recognized France's preponderant position in Morocco in return for French acceptance of Britain's leading role in Egypt. In addition, long-standing colonial differences were settled around the world. French claims to fishing rights off Newfoundland were satisfied by territorial concessions in West Africa; British claims in Madagascar were abandoned; spheres of influence were delimited in Siam; and the New Hebrides were placed under joint administration. The entente treaty was finally signed on 8 April 1904.[20] It was designed to remove a potential enemy, not to make an ally. But over the next ten years pressure from Germany was to give the Anglo-French relationship a closeness hardly anticipated at its beginning.

In theory an entente – in the sense of an amicable settlement of differences – could still have been concluded with Germany. But the Germans insisted upon conducting their diplomacy with all the ruthlessness of war. At first they hoped that the Russo-Japanese War (1904–5), between an ally of France and an ally of Britain, would quickly break either the Franco-Russian alliance or the new French friendship with Britain. When this did not happen, the Germans began to meddle in Morocco, where they had previously claimed no interest. At the end of March 1905 the Kaiser visited Tangier and proclaimed his friendship for the sultan in a public speech. The Germans forced the resignation of Delcassé; but they pressed too hard, and British support for the French began to look beyond the diplomatic. Reluctantly in January 1906 Sir Edward Grey, the new Foreign Secretary, authorized the continuation of Anglo-French military staff talks, which had already begun unofficially. Grey told the German ambassador that British public opinion would not want to leave the French in the lurch if war broke out between France and Germany over Morocco. In a memorandum Grey emphasised how close the two countries had become. 'The *Entente* and still more the constant and emphatic demonstrations of affection (official, naval, political, commercial, Municipal and in the Press)' had added up to a moral commitment.[21] Eventually an international conference at Algeciras agreed a settlement which left the French position intact, but which frustrated French hopes of assuming immediate control of Morocco. Germany had asserted her right to be consulted; but in a manner which had confirmed Grey's suspicions about her ultimate aims. These fears were assessed with penetration and clarity by Eyre Crowe, senior clerk in the Foreign Office, in a long memorandum of 1 January 1907. Crowe argued that either Germany was 'consciously aiming at the establishment of a German hegemony at first in Europe, and eventually in the world'; or that 'the great German design is in reality no more than the expression of a vague, confused and unpractical statesmanship not realizing its own drift'. Either way the peace of Europe was threatened. Crowe argued for firmness with the Germans; the history of the previous twenty years had shown that the making of concessions was only taken as weakness.[22]

Grey's policy became increasingly pro-French, though never directly anti-German. Crowe and most senior Foreign Office officials during the pre-war years were certainly hostile towards Germany; but their influence over the Foreign Secretary was not total, and it diminished as Grey became more experienced. Grey wrote in 1909 how 'the real isolation of Germany would mean war; so would the domination of Germany in Europe. There is a fairly wide course between the two extremes in which European politics should steer'.[23] But in following this course Grey did not take the British public much into his confidence. The radical *Nation* (11.2.1811) complained how 'secret diplomacy has led inevitably to disingenuous armaments. The whole basis of such a position is anti-democratic and anti-Liberal'. The radical wing of the Liberal Party campaigned hard but ineffectively for open diplomacy and for more parliamentary control.[24] Yet Grey instinctively never took secret action out of tune with mass public opinion. This was to be demonstrated by the remarkable public enthusiasm for his speech on the eve of war in 1914, which at last fully revealed the British position.

Grey had inherited the Anglo-French entente from his Conservative predecessor. To this he added the Anglo-Russian entente of 31 August 1907.[25] This likewise took the form of an attempted settlement of long-standing differences and rivalries. The two Governments recognized China's sovereignty over Tibet, and promised to respect its independence and territorial integrity. Russia accepted Afghanistan as a British sphere of influence, but Britain agreed not to interfere in its domestic affairs. Persia was divided into three zones of influence – a British zone in the south-east on the Indian frontier, a large Russian zone in the north, and a neutral zone between. By a separate note Russia also recognized British predominance in the Persian Gulf. The hint was also given that Britain would not now oppose Russian control of Constantinople and the Straits. From the mid 1890s Lord Salisbury had come to realize that this could not be resisted without disproportionate naval and military effort, though he remained anxious to postpone the disintegration of the Turkish Empire as long as possible. British control of Egypt, which Salisbury had made semi-permanent, provided a strong base from which to protect British interests during any Turkish break-up.

The Anglo-Russian entente was never popular in England. Radicals and socialists disliked friendship with autocratic tsardom. And at the diplomatic level relations did not long remain smooth, especially with respect to continuing Russian encroachment in Persia. Nor were Anglo-French diplomatic exchanges all harmonious after 1906. Grey, however, insisted upon a conciliatory attitude. And the Agadir crisis in the summer of 1911 brought the two countries closer together than ever. Once again Germany showed herself over-assertive in Morocco, though not without some original justification for complaint. The French had taken advantage of internal disturbances to occupy Fez. The Germans demanded compensation, which was reasonable; but they also sent a gunboat to Agadir, which was threatening. The dispute had ceased to be simply a colonial quarrel. Lloyd George was authorized to warn the Germans in a speech at the Mansion House, London, on 21 July. His language was the more effective for being plain rather than diplomatic, even though the Germans were not directly mentioned and even though the British Government was really hoping for a compromise settlement. British power, claimed Lloyd George, had been 'many a time in the past, and may yet be in the future, invaluable to the cause of human liberty. It has more than once in the past redeemed Continental nations'. If peace could only be preserved 'by the surrender of the great and beneficent position Britain has won by centuries of heroism and achievement, by allowing Britain to be treated when her interests were vitally affected as if she were of no account in the Cabinet of nations, then I say emphatically that peace at that price would be a humiliation intolerable for a great country like ours to endure'.[26]

The Germans eventually moderated their demands; but the Agadir crisis stimulated the renewal of Anglo-French military staff talks, and the beginning of naval staff discussions. Only now did the whole cabinet hear of the 1906 contacts. In 1912 the French concentrated their fleet in the Mediterranean, and the bulk of the British Mediterranean fleet was withdrawn to meet the German threat in home waters. These moves were undertaken independently, to suit the best interests of each power; but it was widely assumed (and deplored in left-wing circles) that a firm agreement had been made. In reality, the Liberal Government refused to be committed to any firm naval or military obligations in the event of war between France and Germany. Preparation for what *might* be done, if Britain and France became allies in such a war, did not represent in official British eyes commitment necessarily to become allies.

In May 1914 the cabinet reluctantly agreed to enter into secret naval conversations with the Russians, at their request. A Commons statement by Grey on 11 June 1914 in answer to pointed parliamentary questioning about Anglo-Russian naval relations has been described as the only occasion when he was deliberately misleading.[27] Usually he contrived to avoid *suggestio falsi* even while practising *suppressio veri*. Pressure upon Grey both from backbenchers and from within the cabinet after the Agadir confrontation had forced a new British initiative towards the Germans in 1912. Haldane visited Germany in

February to seek agreement for some slowing down of the naval race. But again the Germans overplayed their hand. They demanded the signing of a non-aggression pact. Grey was willing to declare that 'England will make no unprovoked attack upon Germany and will pursue no aggressive policy towards her'; but he could not promise support or even benevolent neutrality in all future circumstances. A neutrality clause would have suggested to the French that Britain would not consider going to their aid even if the Germans tried to crush them.[28]

In 1911 at a meeting of the Committee of Imperial Defence attended by the Dominion delegates to the Imperial Conference Grey had underlined how Britain was 'not committed by entanglements which tie our hands'. But he also emphasized the unwisdom of allowing any one power to move towards the domination of Europe. 'If while that process was going on we were appealed to for help and sat by and looked on and did nothing . . . the result would be one great combination in Europe, outside which we should be left without a friend.' To retain command of the seas Britain would then have to build a fleet to match a possible combination of five European powers. Therefore, concluded Grey, if Germany ever tried to use her great strength 'to obtain the dominating position in Europe then I think there would be trouble'.[29]

Notes

1. J. A. S. Grenville, *Lord Salisbury and Foreign Policy* (1970), pp. 439–40. See, in general, C. J. Lowe and M. L. Dockrill, *The Mirage of Power* (1972), Vol. 1; and Zara S. Steiner, *Britain and the Origins of the First World War* (1977).
2. See M. Beloff, 'The Special Relationship: An Anglo-American Myth', in M. Gilbert (ed.), *A Century of Conflict* (1966); and B. Perkins, *The Great Rapprochement, England and the United States, 1895–1914* (1969).
3. G. M. Trevelyan, *Grey of Falloden* (1937), p. 116.
4. See especially A. E. Campbell, *Great Britain and the United States, 1895–1903* (1960).
5. See especially I. H. Nish, *The Anglo-Japanese Alliance, 1894–1907* (1966).
6. See V. G. Kiernan, *The Lords of Human Kind* (1969), Ch. 5.
7. See L. P. Gartner, *The Jewish Immigrant in England, 1870–1914* (1960); J. A. Garrard, *The English and Immigration, 1880–1910* (1972); and B. Gainer, *The Alien Invasion* (1972).
8. See especially D. Rumbelow, *The Houndsditch Murders and the Siege of Sidney Street* (1973); and C. Holmes, 'In Search of Sidney Street', *Bulletin of the Society for the Study of Labour History*, no. 29 (1974).
9. See especially J. L. Garvin, *Life of Joseph Chamberlain*, III (1934), Chs. LVIII, LXIX; and C. Howard, *Britain and the Casus Belli, 1822–1902* (1974), Ch. XVII.
10. See especially G. Monger, *The End of Isolation* (1963), Ch. 2; and J. A. S. Grenville, *Lord Salisbury and Foreign Policy* (1970), Ch. XV.
11. K. Bourne, *The Foreign Policy of Victorian England, 1830–1902* (1970), pp. 462–3.
12. *Ibid.*, p. 478. See especially E. L. Woodward, *Great Britain and the German Navy* (1935); A. J. Marder, *From the Dreadnought to Scapa Flow*, I (1961); and P. Padfield, *The Great Naval Race* (1974).
13. G. P. Gooch and H. Temperley (eds.), *British Documents on the Origins of the War, 1898–1914*, VI (1930), p. 779.
14. *Ibid.*, p. 266.

15. A. J. P. Taylor, *The Struggle for Mastery in Europe* (1954), p. xxvii.
16. See especially W. S. Hamer, *The British Army, Civil-Military Relations, 1885–1905* (1970); N. d'Ombrain, *War Machinery and High Policy* (1973); and J. Gooch, *The Plans of War, The General Staff and British Military Strategy, c. 1900–1916* (1974).
17. M. V. Brett (ed.), *Journals and Letters of Reginald, Viscount Esher* (1934), II, p. 33. See especially B. Bond, 'Richard Burdon Haldane at the War Office', *Army Quarterly*, Vol. 86 (1963); and M. Howard, *Studies in War and Peace* (1970), Ch. 5.
18. See J. Springhall, *Youth, Empire and Society* (1977), esp. Ch. 3.
19. See C. Hibbert, *Edward VII* (1976), Chs. 16–18.
20. See especially G. Monger, *The End of Isolation* (1963); and P. J. V. Rolo, *Entente Cordiale* (1969).
21. G. P. Gooch and H. Temperley (eds.), *British Documents on the Origins of the War, 1898–1914*, III (1928), p. 266. See S. R. Williamson, *The Politics of Grand Strategy* (1969), esp. Ch. 3.
22. G. P. Gooch and H. Temperley (eds.), *British Documents on the Origins of the War, 1898–1914*, III (1928), appendix A. See also Zara S. Steiner, *The Foreign Office and Foreign Policy, 1898–1914* (1969).
23. C. J. Lowe and M. L. Dockrill, *The Mirage of Power* (1972), I, p. 27. See especially F. H. Hinsley (ed.), *British Foreign Policy Under Sir Edward Grey* (1977).
24. See especially A. J. P. Taylor, *The Trouble Makers* (1957), Ch. IV; A. J. A. Morris, *Radicalism Against War, 1906–1914* (1972); and Zara S. Steiner, *Britain and the Origins of the First World War* (1977), Ch. 7.
25. See especially G. Monger, *The End of Isolation* (1963), Ch. II; and D. Gillard, *The Struggle for Asia, 1828–1914* (1977), Ch. 8.
26. K. Bourne, *The Foreign Policy of Victorian England, 1830–1902* (1970), pp. 495–6. See also K. Wilson, 'The Agadir Crisis, The Mansion House Speech, and the Double-Edgedness of Agreements', *Historical Journal*, XV (1972).
27. A. J. Marder, *From the Dreadnought to Scapa Flow*, I (1961), p. 310. See also Sir Edward Grey, *Twenty-Five Years, 1892–1916* (1925), I, p. 289; and S. R. Williamson, *The Politics of Grand Strategy* (1969), pp. 338–9.
28. G. P. Gooch and H. Temperley (eds.), *British Documents on the Origins of the War, 1898–1914*, VI (1930), p. 713.
29. *Ibid.*, appendix V.

Chapter 31

Crisis: *'Within measurable distance of civil war'*

1

Edward VII died on 6 May 1910: Britain entered the First World War on 4 August 1914. These four years were a time of social and political crisis in Great Britain and Ireland – a crisis with several aspects and phases, and with a persistence which led even some unexcitable and intelligent contemporaries to fear the outbreak of revolution. The bitter 'peers versus people' confrontation did not end until the defeat of the diehard peers in August 1911. And the passing of the Parliament Act was accompanied in its last stages by the Agadir crisis with Germany. The Parliament Act paved the way for the introduction in April 1912 of the third Irish Home Rule Bill, which the Liberals were bound to sponsor since their parliamentary majority now depended upon Irish support. Under the Parliament Act procedure, despite inevitable rejection by the Lords, Home Rule was likely to pass in 1914. But Protestant Ulstermen refused to accept inclusion in a united self-governing Ireland, and they showed themselves ready to take up arms in the name of 'loyalty'. The suffragettes – whose cry of 'votes for women' had been building up with increasing stridency since 1903 – were employing ever more violent methods. And while some women were restless, many more men – organized in trade unions as never before – were venturing upon a sequence of bitter strikes.

Under pressure from these threatening developments, the credit of parliamentary politicians and of parliamentary government came under increasing question. The reputation of Lloyd George, in particular, was nearly shattered by the Marconi scandal of 1912–13. Lloyd George and two other ministers were found to have dealt in the shares of the American Marconi Company, even while the Government of which they were members was entering into a lucrative contract with the British Marconi Company. The three men were self-damagingly evasive in their explanations; and they were lucky to escape through a party vote which accepted the indulgent majority report of a parliamentary select committee.[1] The persistence of crisis encouraged a demand from the far right for some 'strong man' (perhaps Milner, perhaps Kitchener) to put national affairs in order. In *The Party System* (1911) and *The Servile State* (1912) the Chesterton brothers and Hilaire Belloc offered, in place of what they described as a 'dying constitution', their own amalgam of Catholic authoritarianism with anti-semitism. At the other end of the political spectrum the syndicalists on the left of the trade union movement were also very active, with their demand for workers' control of industry. In December 1913 Sidney Low, a leading political commentator, summed up the problems and prospects of a society which knew that it was facing major internal tensions but did not know that it was on the brink of terrible war:[2]

We have a society in which political power rests with the mass of its poorer members; in which education, carried up to a certain level, is general; in which an unprecedented mental restlessness has been stimulated by the diffusion of reading matter, and the facilities for rapid communication; in which class barriers are still rigid, though the physical, temperamental, and personal differences, which formerly divided classes from one another, have been attenuated; in which moral sanctions and conventions, handed down by tradition, and based ultimately on Christian theology, have lost much of their force; in which the relations of the individual to the universal order, to the state, to the family, and to his fellow-citizens, are being freely examined in the light of new scientific discoveries and philosophical speculations; in which there is a rising belief that a system of industrialism, based on arduous toil for weekly wages by the majority of mankind, is as much opposed to reason and humanity as slavery itself. A revolution, as comprehensive as that which ultimately abolished predial and domestic servitude, seems to be entering upon its initial stages; the passion for material equality, which has succeeded that for political equality, will hardly be satisfied without many strenuous attempts to transfer property, and all the amenities and opportunities which go with property, from the Few to the Many.

The strength of the British constitution, Low rightly concluded, would be tested by its capacity to respond sensitively and without breakdown to these new aspirations.

2

The trade union movement was already well established by the first decade of the twentieth century. About 25 per cent of adult male manual workers belonged to unions in 1901 and about 30 per cent in 1910. But during 1910–14 the unions made a dramatic advance in support and in militancy:[3]

	Total union membership (GB & NI)	Number of stoppages beginning in year	Total working days lost by all stoppages in progress during year
1892	1,576,000	700	17,248
1901	2,025,000	631	4,130
1907	2,513,000	585	2,150
1910	2,565,000	521	9,870
1911	3,139,000	872	10,160
1912	3,416,000	834	40,890
1913	4,135,000	1,459	9,800
1914	4,145,000	972	9,880

Trade union membership thus rose about 60 per cent between 1910 and 1914. Membership of the large 'general' unions for the less skilled and unskilled grew especially fast. The Workers' Union, for example, progressed from less than 4,500 members in 1910 to 143,000 by 1914. It became especially strong among the new semi-skilled workers in engineering, where mass production methods were displacing the old craft ways. By 1914 semi-skilled men comprised about 20 per cent of the engineering labour force. In 1913 in the Black Country the Workers' Union was said to be 'not so much directing the strikes as following them, and is making members by the thousand'.[4]

By no means all Edwardian industry fell into turmoil just before 1914. The textile, engineering, and iron and steel trades, for example, suffered no major stoppages. But 'industrial warfare' overshadowed industrial peace. And among the upper and middle classes the fear was persistent that 'industrial anarchy' would lead on to economic and political breakdown; and that some at least of the strikers were deliberately working towards that end. *The Times* (10.9.1913) noted how in the past trade unions had usually been cautious organizations, 'with a far stronger inclination towards bargaining with employers than towards fighting them'. But now national union leaders were often remote from their membership, and they could not always control their local activists. In addition, *The Times* feared that Marxist ideas of class conflict had taken root. These factors were tending 'to make collective bargaining almost a waste of time and to secure for industrial anarchy and warfare a new lease of life'. Perhaps reason could not always be expected to prevail within the new mass urban industrial environment. The findings of the pioneering European social psychologists – Ferdinand Tönnies (author of *Community and Association*, 1887), Gustave Le Bon, and Gabriel Tarde – had suggested that the urban masses, without control by rural community systems, could be easily manipulated by skilful agitators. 'Let us face the fact,' wrote the *Sunday Times* (21.1.1912), 'that the unrest and ferocity of the masses arises neither from ignorance nor knowledge. It arises from innate defective civic instincts when these are incited by the invective and pungent harangues of professional demagogues.' Such leaders cared nothing for 'economic and natural laws'. 'In the long run – and the sands of our opportunity have already nearly run their measure – these inexorable laws will destroy a nation that is foolish enough to tolerate incitory and pyrocephalic demagogues any longer ... We are within measurable distance of civil war.'

But real problems and aspirations underlay the great strike wave. The most general grievance was the fall in real wages. Another factor was the loss of faith by some working men in the Labour Party in Parliament. A third influence, as Seebohm Rowntree explained in *The Way to Industrial Peace and the Problem of Unemployment* (1914), was increased working-class awareness of 'what life may be under more favourable circumstances'. Winston Churchill summed up this new mood as 'not towards inadequate hours of work, but towards sufficient hours of leisure'. Workmen were 'not content that their lives should remain mere alternations between bed and the factory'.[5] These forces had been accumulating for years before finally erupting just before 1914, when low unemployment levels provided a favourable opportunity for strong trade union pressure. The Liberal welfare reforms failed to prevent working-class restlessness. Old-age pensions were popular; but the bureaucracy associated with national insurance was distrusted, for the state functionaries previously best known to the poor were policemen and Poor Law officials. Lloyd George carefully involved the trade unions within his insurance scheme as approved societies; but many unions still disliked the scheme because it increased their administrative burdens and also seemed to compete with their own benefit functions.

The sequence of major Edwardian industrial disputes began in 1907 when the railwaymen demanded a general wage rise. The railway companies were adamant in their rejection, refusing (with one exception) even to recognize the existence of the railway trade unions. The companies emphasized how they were bound by legislation not to increase railway rates, despite increasing costs. The men, for their part, based their demands upon the rising cost of living. Under threat of the first-ever national railway stoppage, the Liberal Government deputed Lloyd George to intervene. This he did with characteristic decision, even though he was well aware of the slightness of his formal powers under the 1896 Conciliation Act. The railway directors persisted in refusing to negotiate directly with the union leaders, and Lloyd George had to act as an intermediary. In the end it was agreed to form a conciliation board for each railway company, upon which both management and workers would be represented; but the workmen's spokesmen were to be chosen by direct vote, thus avoiding any recognition of the unions by the railway employers. On this compromise basis a national railway strike was averted. In the summer of 1911, however, it proved to be impossible to avert a shutdown of the railways. Though it lasted for only two days (18–19 August) this first national railway strike added greatly to the tensions of a summer full of crises. Troops even appeared on the streets of London. The railwaymen were again incensed by lagging wages, by the ineffectiveness of the 1907 conciliation machinery, by the continuing non-recognition of their unions by the employers, and by the Osborne Judgement. After emphasizing the danger of war with Germany because of the Agadir crisis, Lloyd George persuaded representatives of the railway companies to meet the union leaders, and a modified conciliation system was ultimately agreed. The Railway Traffic Act of 1913 permitted the rises in railway rates which were needed to finance the cost of improved wages and conditions.

The seamen and dockers under Ben Tillett were also noisily on strike during 1911; but the stoppage which had first caught the headlines was the Cambrian coal strike in south Wales. As with the railway directors, the coal owners were not without a genuine case for tightness over wages. In many areas output per man had been falling and costs rising. The Liberal Government had conceded the miners' demand for a statutory eight-hour day in 1908, but the consequent rearrangement of working practices meant that this significant piece of state intervention produced as much discontent as satisfaction. The miners, moreover, still demanded legislation to fix a minimum wage. The south Wales miners were the most militant. Late in 1910 those at work in pits controlled by the Cambrian combine refused to accept new rates for difficult working, even though these had been negotiated by W. Abraham, the much respected chairman of the South Wales Miners' Federation. In November the miners began a ten-month strike which became marked by rioting, the despatch of police reinforcements from London, troop movements, and one fatal casualty at Tonypandy – for which Churchill, as Home Secretary, was long unfairly blamed by Labour.

1912 proved to be the worst of all pre-war years for industrial stoppages, dominated by a national coal strike of over 1 million miners from February to April in support of the minimum wage. A committee of four ministers, headed by Asquith, reluctantly intervened; and eventually the Government sponsored legislation to establish district boards for fixing wages. This was not the minimum wage demanded, but after an inconclusive ballot the miners' leaders called off the stoppage. Next came a bitter strike of London lightermen, dockers, and carters in the summer of 1912. Its failure illustrated the limitations of sectional pressure; and during 1913–14 the idea of a 'triple alliance' of miners, railwaymen, and port workers was under discussion.

Large unions spread throughout a whole industry on the American model would obviously maximize the pressure upon employers. But only the railway workers, with the formation of the National Union of Railwaymen in 1913, took decisive action in this direction. The amalgamation movement was recommended by some militants as a step towards syndicalism, a theory of industrial organization formulated especially in France. The most active English syndicalist leader was Tom Mann. The best known syndicalist publication was a pamphlet issued by a group of south Wales miners in 1912, *The Miners' Next Step*. It advocated the centralization of the miners' unions to create one national union; this union was then to ally with similar national unions formed in other industries to campaign for workers' control of all industry. Syndicalism repudiated traditional forms of working-class leadership, both industrial and political. 'They, the leaders, become "gentlemen", they become M.P.s, and have considerable prestige because of this power. Now, when any man or men assume power of this description, we have a right to ask them to be infallible. This is the penalty, a just one too, of autocracy.' The syndicalists were a-parliamentary, if not anti-parliamentary. The *Daily Herald*, started as a working-class newspaper in 1911, published its reports of parliamentary debates under the heading 'The House of Pretence'.[6]

The Miners' Next Step wanted to reduce the state to a Central Production Board, which 'with a statistical department to ascertain the needs of the people, will issue its demands on the different departments of industry, leaving to the men themselves to determine under what conditions and how the work should be done. This would mean real democracy in real life'. To achieve such a transformation *The Miners' Next Step* openly advocated 'extremely drastic and militant' action. The 'irritation strike' and the go-slow were recommended so as to reduce profits and thus make capitalists more amenable to their own abolition. A general strike was accepted as a further stage in the exertion of pressure. All these objectives and methods aroused intense concern in the press and in Parliament. One Conservative Member of Parliament moved a motion in the Commons (27.3.1912) 'that, in the opinion of this House, the growth and advocacy by certain labour agitators of an anti-social policy of Syndicalism based upon class warfare and incitement to mutiny constitute a grave danger to the State and the welfare of the community'. The syndicalists certainly hoped that the pre-war labour unrest would lead to a social and industrial transformation; but their real influence proved to be limited, though not negligible. The extremism of their policies reflected the unsettlement of the times, disillusionment with traditional methods and hostility towards still autocratic employers. Philip Snowden – a Labour politician who was otherwise very critical of the syndicalists – gave them credit for helping workmen to insist upon respect as human beings instead of treatment as mere 'hands'. 'Socialism has been so much concerned about the community that it has neglected the individual to some extent. Syndicalism comes to urge that aspect of the social problem . . . By some means or other an industrial system must be devised which will give the workman a direct interest in his work.'[7]

An Anglicized version of syndicalism which came to appeal to many left-wing intellectuals was guild socialism, an ingenious synthesis of political socialism and industrial syndicalism.[8] Guild socialists viewed the state with less suspicion than pure syndicalists, but they opposed the centralized bureaucracy so much admired by the Fabians. Under a guild socialist system the state was to retain ultimate power; but it was to delegate most of its authority to industrial guilds, with each guild paying a single tax or rent to the state. In the best spirit of medieval guild craftsmen guild responsibility would include the maintenance of high standards of workmanship. All guild members would be guaranteed continuous wages, full medical cover, and old-age pensions, without need for state involvement in the provision of welfare services.

The Liberal Government had pursued an unemployment policy, but it had not attempted to follow an overall labour policy. Ministerial intervention in the railway and coal disputes certainly showed that the Government was willing in extreme cases to take control of industrial affairs out of the hands of employers. But such intervention was reluctant. Moreover, by 1914 the major trade unions were not looking for more such intervention. After the passing of the 1913 Trade Union Act the unions were confident of their acceptance in law; they were also well aware of their growing numbers. They were becoming increasingly eager to be left alone, so that organized labour and organized management could contest together without outside interference under conditions of what one expert observer has paradoxically but perceptively named 'collective *laissez-faire*'.[9] In this spirit on the eve of war in 1914 the triple alliance of miners, railwaymen, and port workers was forming for another round of industrial agitation. A national outbreak of strikes was not so near, however, as the propertied classes alarmedly feared. Events after the war were to demonstrate the difficulty of taking strike action in concert. Nor was the triple alliance forming under syndicalist or other 'revolutionary' direction. Union leaders in all three industries – well aware of the expense of strike action – were still hoping in 1914 that simply the threat of concerted stoppages would win higher wages and better conditions. Yet organized labour was undoubtedly talking with a new confidence and assertiveness during the last weeks of peace, as one Kent railwayman made clear. 'We are big and powerful enough to fight our own battle without the aid of Parliament or any other agency. There could be no affection between the robber and the robbed. The workers were not employed for love, but for their share of their employers' profits. People might be sympathetic and charitable, but what the labourer required was not charity but justice, and he wanted it upon his legs, not upon his knees.'[10]

3

The emancipation of women – and especially of middle-class women – was accelerating by the turn of the century, as shown for example in the statistics of women at work in England and Wales:[11]

	1881	1911
Middle-class occupations	427,000	1,114,000
Working-class occupations	2,976,000	3,687,000

The numbers of women in middle-class employment thus rose 161 per cent in thirty years, compared with a rise of 24 per cent in working-class jobs. Paid work for working-class women, notably in domestic service, did not often provide opportunities for greater self-expression; but among middle-class girls the new opportunities for careers as schoolteachers, nurses, and in office work gave income and scope for shaping their own lives as never before.

These novel opportunities had been created by the expanding requirements of the economy and of society, rather than as a result of the pressure from the Victorian feminist movement. None the less, feminist demands gained strength and support from the new situation. One strong demand was for equal pay for equal work. In 1914 most women – from those in the professions down to unskilled manual workers – were paid only about half the equivalent male earnings (see above, p. 42). Ethel Snowden, wife of the Labour politician, explained in her book on *The Feminist Movement* (1913) how feminism was much more than a demand for the vote; and yet how it was not an expression of any desire to escape from the 'glorious responsibilities' of women as wives and mothers. 'She asks for freedom for women in the exercise of those gifts and in the use of those qualities of soul and mind which are apart from the consequences of the sex-act. She objects to the forcing of woman's interests into one groove.' Feminists, continued Mrs Snowden, demanded the establishment of one high code of sexual conduct, applicable equally to men and women. Men such as H. G. Wells agreed about the need for a common code, but preferred to advocate acceptance of more relaxed standards for women. His novel *Ann Veronica* (1909) – closely based upon a sexual escapade of his own – told of a clever yet beautiful girl who defiantly left home, became a suffragette, fell in love with an older man, and (not waiting to be seduced) seduced him, ran off with him to Switzerland, became pregnant, and yet lived happily ever after. The book was banned by many libraries. Nevertheless, writers found it much easier to gain notice for daring novels than for daring plays. A sustained campaign had to be waged during the Edwardian years to ease stage censorship, which was still exercised by the Lord Chamberlain. Though the system itself was not altered, a considerable relaxation of censorship standards was secured. A leading campaigner was Bernard Shaw. Beatrice Webb found his *Misalliance* (1910) 'brilliant but disgusting', 'everyone wishing to have sexual intercourse with everyone else'.[12]

Mrs Webb rightly emphasized how 'in the quiet intermediate area of respectable working-class, middle-class and professional life, and in much gentle society, there is not this over-sexed condition'. Still, the Edwardians were the first generation to begin to learn scientifically about sex. Sigmund Freud's psychological work was just becoming known outside specialist circles, though the first English translation of *The Interpretation of Dreams* (1913) still carried a publisher's note limiting its sale to members of the medical, scholastic, legal, and clerical professions. Havelock Ellis's *Man and Woman* (1894), which had reached its fifth edition by 1914, succeeded for the first time in explaining objectively and intelligibly to non-specialist English readers how and why the sexes differed, yet also how they were equal, female with male. Thanks in important part to the influence of Ellis, the subject of sex was now being acknowledged to exist, at least in print and among thinking people. One short story in the *New Age* of 22 May 1913 by a woman writer (Minna Withers) was entitled 'The Secretary, Sex, and a Dog'. It described, with a frankness which would have shocked 'respectable' Victorians, one physical exchange between an author and his virgin but willing secretary. 'I reached home, having experienced "everything", and I was feeling remarkably normal ... This was what half Society was fighting against, and the other half was hankering after ... It was such a little thing; it was absurd.'

Recognition of women's rights in law had been extending gradually since the passing of the 1857 Matrimonial Causes Act.[13] But women still found it much more difficult to secure a divorce than men; since a husband could divorce his wife for adultery alone, whereas a wife was required to furnish additional grounds such as cruelty or desertion. The Divorce Law Reform Association (1906) joined in pressure which eventually led to the appointment of a Royal Commission on Divorce and Matrimonial Causes (1909–12). The work of this commission attracted considerable attention and emotion. It recommended that women should be treated equally with men in respect of grounds for divorce; also that divorce should be made less costly, so that poorer people were not excluded from the protection of the law. A majority report further advised that desertion for more than three years, cruelty, incurable insanity, incurable drunkenness, and imprisonment under commuted death sentence should constitute grounds for divorce.

Women could not vote in parliamentary elections, though they could do so in local elections; and from 1907 they were allowed to serve on county and county borough councils. Such local political involvement could be distinguished from participation in national politics on the ground that local government directly affected women's domestic concerns. But in *The Feminist Movement* Mrs Snowden turned this old argument on its head: 'because the special sphere of woman is the home, women ought to have the vote'. Yet were women physically and psychologically capable of carrying the responsibilities of the parliamentary franchise? Some eminent Edwardian medical men said not. Sir Almroth E. Wright, a distinguished bacteriologist, published in 1913 *The Unexpurgated Case Against Women's Suffrage*. Wright contended that the militant suffragettes were sexually and intellectually embittered – drawn from the female surplus million 'which had better long ago have gone out to mate with its complement of men beyond the sea'. Government, argued Wright, ultimately depended upon force, and women were physically weak; it also required intellectual stability, in which women were deficient; and it needed appreciation of standards of abstract morality, whereas women thought only subjectively. 'The mind of woman is always threatened with danger from the reverberations of her physiological emergencies.'

Against this background of progress and prejudice, the suffragettes added their shrill voices to the pre-war discord – not least to demonstrate that women as much as men could sustain violence in politics.[14] In 1897 the National Union of Women's Suffrage Societies had brought together existing Victorian suffrage organizations. Then in 1903 the Women's Social and Political Union was founded by Mrs Emmeline Pankhurst, the widow of a radical Manchester barrister, supported by her daughters, Christabel and Sylvia. Mrs Pankhurst was a remarkable woman – not only good looking, but also an outstanding political speaker, and an able (though increasingly dictatorial) organizer. The *Daily Mail* dubbed her followers 'suffragettes' to distinguish them from the non-militant 'suffragists'. The WSPU raised the cry 'votes for women', but left it open whether this meant votes for all women or merely the franchise on the same (far from universal) terms as for men. The word 'social' in the WSPU title reflected Mrs Pankhurst's initial concern for the improvement of the lot of working-class women; but she was to move away from her early ILP connections towards Conservatism. Some working-class suffragettes did emerge – notably Annie Kenney, a cotton operative; but both the suffragette and suffragist movements were predominantly middle-class, with a topping of aristocratic support.

For two years the WSPU attracted little attention. It was ignored by the politicians and by the press. To gain notice it therefore turned in 1905 to militant action, to the interruption of political meetings. Sir Edward Grey was asked at a Manchester Liberal rally if he would support votes for women. When he declined to answer, Christabel Pankhurst and Annie Kenney caused a disturbance and had to be forcibly ejected. They were later arrested for trying to hold a protest meeting outside the hall, refused to pay fines, and spent a week in prison. The suffragettes wanted to know how much (or little) to expect from the new Liberal Government. Liberal and Conservative politicians were divided across party lines with regard to female suffrage. Campbell-Bannerman was inclined to be favourable, Asquith to be hostile. Churchill's attitude fluctuated. Balfour was friendly, Bonar Law less so. Even some Labour politicians hesitated, lest the grant of votes to some women should damage the prospect of gaining universal suffrage for all men. Against this uncertain background it was not surprising that between 1907 and 1912 a succession of private members' bills came to nothing. The suffrage organizations meanwhile continued to grow. The NUWSS increased from only 16 affiliated societies in 1903 to over 300 by 1911. The income of the WSPU rose from £2,700 in 1907 to £36,500 in 1914. The suffragette organ, *Votes for Women*, sold about 30,000 copies per week.

In 1912 the Liberal cabinet at last agreed to accept the insertion of female suffrage clauses into its Franchise and Registration Bill, if the Commons decided on a free vote to support such amendment. But unexpectedly the Speaker ruled that this would be inadmissible, since it would transform the character of the bill. The suffragettes were convinced that the Speaker had colluded with the Conservatives, who wished to save plural voting; or with Asquith, who remained personally unenthusiastic about votes for women. Thereafter suffragette militancy, which had already progressed from interruption of meetings to shop window smashing, was extended to arson of churches, hotels, railway stations, and other public buildings. Cabinet ministers were physically assaulted. During the 1913 Derby one suffragette fatally threw herself under the king's horse. In the same year Mrs Pankhurst was sentenced to three years' imprisonment for accepting responsibility for a bomb explosion in a house under construction for Lloyd George. Suffragettes in prison had contrived to secure early release by going on hunger strike. The Government therefore sponsored the 'Cat and Mouse' Act (1913), which allowed release for recuperation followed by rearrest. To such strange lengths had suffragette violence driven the legislature.

But the Pankhursts' extremism had begun to disgust even many friends of the women's cause. In 1913 Christabel Pankhurst published a widely-noticed pamphlet called *The Great Scourge and How to End It*. This warned women against marriage because three-quarters or more men were claimed to be infected with venereal disease contracted from prostitutes. Miss Pankhurst suggested a new rallying cry – 'Votes for Women and Chastity for Men'. The *Manchester Guardian* (9.6.1913), though always sympathetic to the women's cause, denounced such 'diseased emotionalism'. By this date defections and splits had left the WSPU as simply the tool of Emmeline and Christabel Pankhurst. Even Sylvia – who had stayed faithful to the early working-class sympathies of the agitation, and who campaigned from London's East End – was driven out of the WSPU early in 1914. Mrs Pankhurst claimed in her memoirs, published about that time, that militancy had been proved right because it had gained notice for the agitation. The limited militancy of the early years could be justified in this way; but later excesses only provoked sufficient anger to lose support without generating enough fear to force concession. The narrowness of the Pankhursts' demand – their concentration upon winning the vote – also drew too much attention away from the needs of women for equality in other respects, at work and in the home.

When war came in August 1914 the suffragettes quickly suspended their agitation. This saved them from continuing along an increasingly dangerous and futile course. The contribution made by women to the war effort greatly reinforced their claims to full citizenship. But paradoxically it was the absence of agitation which made it easy for Parliament in wartime finally to concede votes for women.[15] The 1918 Representation of the People Act extended the franchise to virtually all 13 million men in the United Kingdom and to 8,500,000 women over 30. The 'flapper vote' for young women had to wait until 1928. One major fear of Mrs Pankhurst's opponents was then realized – women electors thereafter outnumbered men.

4

On 10 March 1914 the *Rokeby Venus* in the National Gallery was slashed by a suffragette. On 4 June another suffragette, who was being presented at court, suddenly called upon the king to stop the forcible feeding of suffragettes on hunger strike in prison. 'I don't know what we are coming to,' commented the king characteristically in his diary.[16] These small but spectacular irregularities broke upon a 'respectable' public which was already full of fears not only about the threat from the triple alliance in industry, but also about the intensifying crisis in Ireland.[17]

After the rejection of the two Gladstonian Home Rule Bills, the Liberals had been cautious about further attempts at Irish legislation. With a clear majority in the 1906 Parliament independent of Irish support, the Campbell-Bannerman and Asquith Governments chose to pursue (in Asquith's phrase) a 'step by step' policy, hoping at least temporarily to satisfy the Irish by lesser reforms while at the same time preparing the British public for the possibility of the enactment of Home Rule at some future date. In 1907 they promoted an Irish Councils Bill, a modest measure of local government reorganization, so modest that Irish opinion repudiated it as derisory. More successful, however, were steps taken to end coercion, to protect evicted tenants, to improve housing and education, to encourage the Irish language, and to establish a national university. The 1910 elections left the Asquith Government dependent upon Irish support in the Commons. Ministers now had to accept that a Third Irish Home Rule Bill must follow once the Parliament Act had passed. Asquith finally introduced the measure in 1912. It was twice rejected by the Lords; but during 1914 it was in process of reaching the statute book under the Parliament Act procedure regardless of the disapproval of the upper house. Unfortunately, this was far from concluding the matter. Between 1912 and 1914 a growing prospect of civil war developed in Ireland, centred upon Ulster's refusal to be ruled by the south. Ulster, more accurately north-east Ulster, round Belfast, was Protestant, industrial as well as agricultural, and satisfied with the union: the rest of Ireland was Catholic, largely agricultural, and dissatisfied. The cry 'Ulster will fight and Ulster will be right', coined by Lord Randolph Churchill in 1886, now rang out with ominous intensity. Ulster's new leader was Sir Edward Carson, a former Solicitor-General (1900–5) and a stirring orator of implacable opinions.

Ulster's determination was firmly backed by the Conservatives at Westminster, who believed that Home Rule would soon lead to the break-up of the United Kingdom. The Liberals insisted that the Irish would remain satisfied with the limited independence envisaged in all three Home Rule Bills. When Austen Chamberlain told Winston Churchill in 1913 that his root objection to Home Rule was the idea of 'Ireland a Nation', Churchill chaffed him that this was to deny the Irish any satisfaction in the enjoyment of their parliament. 'You are like the RC Church which admits the necessity of the marriage bed but holds that you must find no pleasure in the enjoyment of it.' Churchill went on to add contradictorily, however, that 'there can be no "nation" as long as they accept a subsidy and we can always bring them back by withholding supplies'.[18] As with state socialism so with Irish nationalism the

Edwardian Liberals were trying to discover a middle position, without too much care for logic.

The Conservatives seemed unwilling to abandon the claim to a veto on Home Rule, which their House of Lords majority had previously given them. During the Parliament Bill debates Churchill had complained to the king of 'their claim to govern the country whether in office or in opposition and to resort to disorder because they cannot have their way'. On 27 July 1912 Bonar Law, now leader of the Conservative Party, was reported as asserting in a public speech at Blenheim Palace that he could 'imagine no length of resistance to which Ulster can go in which I should not be prepared to support them'. 'The veto of violence,' summed up Churchill in 1914, 'has replaced the veto of privilege.'[19] Unionists from southern Ireland exerted a disproportionate influence within the Conservative hierarchy. The Conservatives would not give up the belief that they were the 'natural' ruling party: yet by 1914 they had spent eight frustrating years in opposition. They convinced themselves that the Liberals had not been given a Home Rule mandate in 1910, and that therefore such a major constitutional change ought not to be enacted until a further general election had shown that a majority of the voters wanted it. The Conservatives were the more irritated because the Irish were over-represented in proportion to population by at least twenty Members of Parliament. The Liberals replied, firstly, that Home Rule had indeed been under discussion during the 1910 elections; secondly, that to admit the right of the Conservatives to force another general election would be to admit their continuing right of veto; and thirdly, that even if the Liberal Government won a favourable election verdict Ulster would still threaten violent resistance to the enforcement of Home Rule. Round these arguments and counter-arguments language and feelings grew steadily stronger during 1912–14. Social contact between the party politicians became increasingly strained. The English political compromise seemed to be disintegrating. The Opposition, in Churchill's words, was not 'playing the game' in trying to eject the Government by threat of civil war. 'Had British statesmen and leaders of great parties in the past allowed their thoughts to turn to projects of bloodshed within the bosom of the country, we should have shared the follies of Poland.' The strongest argument in Ulster's favour asserted that under the unwritten modern British constitution majorities had generally respected significant minority rights. Unfortunately, both the Conservatives and the Liberals began by assuming that, for economic reasons, separate Home Rule for southern Ireland would not be viable.

Faced with intransigent opposition, it was immaterial that Asquith's Home Rule Bill was extremely limited in its terms. Only restricted powers were to be conferred upon a Dublin Parliament, and much financial and other control was reserved for Westminster, where Irish representation was retained. Yet the modest nature of the measure even added to Conservative and Ulster alarms, since it clearly represented only a first step. John Redmond, the Irish leader in Parliament, immediately began to talk about 'revision'. Asquith nevertheless insisted that Home Rule was not a step towards separation: 'the application upon a large, I might say upon a colossal, scale of Imperial credit in the working out of Land Purchase and in the maintenance of Old Age Pensions makes the idea of separation between the two islands more unthinkable than ever it was.' On the other hand, Asquith was eager to claim Home Rule as a move towards more efficient government through the devolution of some of the powers of the Westminster Parliament. The idea of 'Home-Rule-all-round' – of separate legislatures for England, Scotland, and Wales as well as Ireland – had been linked with discussion of Home Rule since the 1880s. Asquith described the existing multifarious involvement of the House of Commons – in local, national, imperial, and international affairs – as a 'grotesquely impossible task'. He also cited the example of the Transvaal to show how the concession of self-rule to Ireland might make friends out of recent enemies. Over a score of self-governing legislatures within the empire owed allegiance to the Crown. 'They have solved, under every diversity of conditions, economic, social, and religious, the problem of reconciling local autonomy with Imperial unity. Are we going to break up the Empire by adding one more?'

In private, though not at first in public, ministers were prepared to admit that Ulster might need 'special treatment'; but they long hoped that the Ulstermen were only bluffing in their talk of civil war. Carson's followers were not bluffing, as the Government came gradually to realize. As early as 1911 Carson was emphasizing to Captain Craig, the chief organizer of armed resistance, that he was 'not for a mere game of bluff'.[20] On 28 September 1912 at a public ceremony in Belfast their supporters solemnly began to sign the Covenant, a pledge to use 'all means which may be found necessary to defeat the setting up of a Home Rule Parliament in Ireland'. Almost a quarter of a million men subscribed to this threat of force. By 1914 the Ulster Volunteers, Carson's army, had become well trained; and arms from Germany were being landed with little secrecy. In England a British Covenant was published in March 1914; and its first signatories included Kipling, Elgar, and Lord Roberts. Like Roberts, many army officers were Conservatives with Irish family connections. Early in 1914 Bonar Law even toyed with the idea of wielding the Conservative majority in the Lords to amend the annual Army Act – upon which all discipline depended – in order to prevent the use of troops against Ulster. In March the news that the Government had ordered military movements to counter possible violent outbreaks in northern Ireland provoked a spate of resignations among army officers. This so-called Curragh 'mutiny' was not a mutiny in the proper sense; but it did demonstrate the unreliability of the army in the excited atmosphere of the time.[21] When Churchill, as First Lord of the Admiralty, sent ships to the Irish coast 'in case of serious disorders arising' he was accused by the Conservatives of planning a pogrom of Ulster 'loyalists'. This exaggerated reaction probably reflected a sense that Churchill's great energy and taunting oratory were proving vital to the Liberal Government's steadfastness during these culminating months of Irish crisis.

After the Curragh episode Asquith himself took over as War Secretary. He was still hoping to avoid a final breakdown, either in Parliament or in Ulster. While proposing on 9 March 1914 the second reading of the Home Rule Bill (now on its third circuit), he offered an Amending Bill which would have postponed the application of Home Rule to Ulster for six years. This would have meant the calling of two general elections between the beginning of Home Rule in southern Ireland and its application in the north. Carson dismissed this gesture as 'sentence of death with a stay of execution for six years'. Nevertheless, he and Bonar Law, though not all their followers, were now prepared for some compromise. This was demonstrated in the summer when Carson, Craig, Bonar Law, and Lansdowne met Asquith and Lloyd George, plus Redmond and Dillon (the Irish leaders) in a Buckingham Palace conference (21–24 July). The idea of exclusion was now accepted by both sides; but the conference still broke down over the exclusion or inclusion of two Ulster counties with almost equal Protestant/Catholic populations. The conference never reached discussion of Conservative insistence upon the perpetual exclusion of Ulster.

Both sides had modified their positions since 1912; but because their remaining differences seemed irreconcilable, Ireland stood on the brink of civil war by the last days of July 1914. The Catholics of the south were now armed and organized to fight the Protestants of the north. 'There can no longer be the slightest doubt,' wrote *The Times* of 28 July about the Irish situation, 'that the country is now confronted with one of the greatest crises in the history of the British race.' Yet Asquith still remained hopeful. His mind was moving towards a proposal for the permanent exclusion of Ulster, within imposed boundaries. This would have forced both the Irish Nationalists and the Ulstermen to choose between acceptance or recourse to violence; and Asquith did not believe that the leaders on either side would want to risk civil war when each had gained so much. But before this late settlement could be pressed upon them quite a different war had broken out on the Continent.

5

British politicians may have been worrying about possible civil war in Ireland in July 1914, but 'the man in the tramcar' apparently was not. One *Daily Mail* reporter asked a tramload of Londoners for their opinions about the Ulster crisis. 'I don't think anything about it' was the answer from all.[22] Nor were passengers in English tramcars thinking much about the possibility of war in Europe in July 1914. The Archduke Franz Ferdinand, heir to the Austrian throne, had been assassinated at

Sarajevo in Serbia on 28 June. It was realized by the more knowledgeable that the Austrians would demand compensation; but only reluctantly was it understood in England that Europe was heading towards a general war between the rival alliance systems of Germany and Austria, on the one hand, and France and Russia on the other. Serbia was a backward, disreputable country; the archduke was unpopular. Would the great powers really want to fight each other with such uninspiring justification? The Balkans had been in tumult during 1912–13; but Sir Edward Grey, the British Foreign Secretary, had arranged joint diplomatic action by the great powers to contain and to end the wars. On 8 January 1913 the cabinet formally congratulated him upon 'the skill and success with which he is piloting the European ship through troubled waters'.[23] But there had been no fundamental improvement in relations between the main international rivals. Recent Anglo-German exchanges, for example, had been harmonious only because attention had concentrated upon relatively minor issues. In July 1914 a draft agreement was reached over the Baghdad railway question; and discussions had taken place during 1912–13 about the possible future of the Portuguese colonies. On the other hand, naval rivalry was continuing, even though after 1912 the Germans had begun to give more priority to army expenditure.[24]

As late as 23 July 1914 Lloyd George was assuring the House of Commons that relations with Germany were better than for years past. Yet on this same day the Austrians delivered an ultimatum to Serbia so strong that its acceptance would have put an end to Serbian sovereign independence. Grey had begun to grow concerned from 6 July, when during an interview with the German ambassador he had found that the Germans were disinclined to restrain the Austrians from taking an extreme line. The British cabinet was deeply occupied with the Irish crisis, and Grey worked on his own initiative to coax the Germans into a mood of willingness to check their ally. To no avail. On 24 July at the end of a meeting devoted to Ireland Grey gave the cabinet its first intimation of the seriousness of the European situation. Serbia, wrote Asquith, could never comply with Austria's 'humiliating ultimatum'. If Austria then attacked Serbia, Russia would come to the aid of the Serbs, 'and if so it is difficult both for Germany and France to refrain from lending a hand. So that we are within measurable distance of a real Armageddon.'[25] On 28 July Austria duly declared war against Serbia. Russia then mobilized. Germany sent an ultimatum to Russia, which was ignored. On 1 August Germany declared war against Russia, and on 3 August against France.

What was Britain to do? She was under no treaty obligations to intervene. Even if the Germans attacked France through Belgium, the cabinet decided on 29 July that the commitment to uphold the treaty of 1839 which guaranteed Belgian neutrality fell collectively not individually upon the five signatory powers – Britain, France, Germany, Austria, and Russia. Therefore, Asquith told the king, British intervention on behalf of Belgium 'if it arises will be rather one of policy than of legal obligation'. The Liberal cabinet was much divided and confused over whether Britain should intervene even if the Germans did not breach Belgian neutrality.[26] Knowing the extent of cabinet uncertainty, neither Asquith nor Grey asked for an unequivocal cabinet decision. Ministers did agree that, with the French fleet concentrated in the Mediterranean, the British navy should prevent a German landing on the French coast. The Germans, for their part, expressed willingness to accept this restriction provided Britain remained otherwise neutral. But the Germans also demanded passage for their troops through Belgium. The Belgians refused (which had not been certain in advance), and called for help. 'This simplifies matters,' commented Asquith. His cabinet was now almost united. But a majority of its members had been swinging towards an anti-German position even before the attack upon Belgium. Only John Morley and John Burns eventually pressed their resignations. A note was sent to Berlin which demanded respect for Belgian neutrality. A reply was requested by 11 p.m. on 4 August. When no reply was received, Britain stood at war with Germany.

The Germans had hoped for British neutrality. But the Schlieffen plan – which their armies followed in their sweep through Belgium and northern France – was intended to gain a quick victory, and the German army did not regard intervention by the comparatively small British Expeditionary Force as likely to make much difference. Even definite foreknowledge by the other powers of British reactions would probably not have checked the sequence of events. In any case, Grey was never sure in advance how far the cabinet, Parliament, and the country would be willing to go. Personally he had no doubts about the moral obligation towards France, as he made plain in his famous speech to the House of Commons on 3 August 1914. This immensely influential address carried the more weight because it seemed to be disarmingly little prepared in form. Grey emphasized, on the one hand, that Britain was bound by no secret commitments. On the other hand, he admitted that since 1906 Anglo-French staff talks had taken place. The 1904 entente had initiated a strengthening friendship between France and Britain. Had this friendship come to include a moral obligation to lend support in war? To answer that crucial question, insisted Grey, everyone must 'look into his own heart, and his own feelings and construe the extent of the obligation for himself. I construe it myself as I feel it'. In Grey's view British self-interest coincided with British moral obligation. The future of Belgium, the future in the Mediterranean, 'and what may happen to France from our failure to support France – if we were to say that all these things mattered nothing and to say we would stand aside, we should, I believe, sacrifice our respect and good name and reputation before the world and should not escape the most serious and grave economic consequences.' After the invasion of 'little Belgium' mass public opinion was sure that Britain ought to fight.

The outbreak of a general European war had been anticipated from the very beginnings of the alliance system in the days of Bismarck. The 'great war' of 1914 (as it quickly became known) was already being described in the 1880s. 'Whole nations will be in the field; the commerce of the world may be on the sea to win or lose; national existences will be at stake; men will be tempted to do anything which will shorten hostilities and tend to a decisive issue. Conduct in the next war will certainly be hard; it is very doubtful if it will be scrupulous, whether on the part of belligerents or neutrals; and most likely the next war will be great.' So forecast W. E. Hall in the preface to the 1889 edition of his standard work on *International Law*. A steady succession of popular books and plays appeared before 1914 which imagined German invasions of England – notably *The Riddle of the Sands* (1903) by Erskine Childers, *The Invasion of 1910* (1906) by William Le Queux, and Guy du Maurier's drama *An Englishman's Home* (1909).[27] In 1909 Robert Blatchford, the socialist journalist, contributed a nationally noticed series of articles to the *Daily Mail*, which recommended national service and preparation for war as the only hope of preventing a confrontation with Germany. Only such determination, argued Blatchford, had any chance of making the Germans realize that force would not pay. 'I write these articles because I believe that Germany is deliberately preparing to destroy the British Empire, and because I know that we are not ready to defend ourselves against a sudden and formidable attack.'[28]

Was war with Germany then widely expected during the years up to 1914? Social Darwinian writers certainly suggested that war with someone was desirable. On the other hand, Norman Angell's *The Great Illusion* sold 2 million copies between 1910 and 1913 in demonstrating not (as frequently misrepresented) that international commercial relationships had made war impossible, but that any major war would now prove economically disastrous – for victors and vanquished alike. Angell hoped that Europe's rulers would conduct their diplomacy under the restraint of this new reality.[29] Many socialists, such as Keir Hardie, contended that Europe's working men would prevent the politicians and soldiers from entering upon war; that the workers would strike and refuse to fight. Yet the German socialists did not do so. After the outbreak of hostilities G. D. H. Cole had to admit that much of Labour's 'somewhat artificial philosophy of international relations' had proved to be 'shallow and unreal'.[30]

Some Englishmen felt a strong sense of ending during the years before 1914, as they faced crises at home and abroad which seemed to be increasingly difficult to solve. In April 1914 Graham Wallas, the political scientist, remarked anxiously in *The Great Society* about the fear in twentieth-century politics and literature 'conscious or half-conscious, lest the civilisation which we have adopted so rapidly and with so little forethought may prove unable to secure either a harmonious life for its members or even its own stability'. On 28 April 1914 John Bailey, a leading literary critic and minor Conservative politician, wrote a private letter revealingly full of pessimism even in advance of the outbreak of war:[31]

The old ordered world in which one was brought up seems to be passing away, and a man of peace and stable ways like me finds the prospect most disquieting. I find myself sometimes half envying those who die, feeling that they at any rate are safe from the troubles that seem to be coming so thick upon us who still live. We woke up here this morning to find a large hotel fifty yards from this burnt to a ruin by these crazy women ... a terrible demonstration of how our social system exists by consent and is largely at the mercy of any fool or knave who will risk himself to destroy it ... it is positively painful to read the newspaper now – one dreads the depression which follows.

Yet Bailey and Wallas were middle-aged intellectuals. Young men of the time such as Harold Macmillan in London 'Society', and J. B. Priestley in provincial Bradford, were to claim in their memoirs that they had felt no expectation of coming war. They were too busy enjoying themselves. Hugh Dalton, another young man of 1914, remembered how he was 'intellectually aware of the tensions in Europe, and particularly of the threat to Britain of the ever-growing and highly efficient German fleet. But I was not emotionally aware of any close risk of catastrophe'.[32] Perhaps this was a widespread attitude. When the final crisis was breaking the *Manchester Guardian* (27 July) remarked how 'the European war which has been talked about for so long that no one really believed it would ever come is nearer embodiment than any of us can remember'. A *Daily Mail* journalist wrote in the same vein in his private diary on the day after the British declaration of war – 'The great war that we have always kept in reserve, in the belief that it would be for our children or our children's children to go through is here, and *we* are to go through it. The country is serious and sober and surprised.'[33] Any euphoria felt during the first months of fighting was gradually to be eroded by the terrible experience of total war:

> What passing-bells for these who die as cattle?
> Only the monstrous anger of the guns.
> Only the stuttering rifles' rapid rattle
> Can patter out their hasty orisons.
>
> (Wilfred Owen, *Anthem for Doomed Youth*, 1917)

Notes

1. See Frances Donaldson, *The Marconi Scandal* (1962).
2. S. Low, *The Governance of England* (2nd edn, 1914), pp. xxxvii–viii.
3. H. A. Clegg *et al.*, *A History of British Trade Unions Since 1889*, I (1964), pp. 466–7, 489; H. Pelling, *Popular Politics and Society in Late Victorian Britain* (1968), p. 149. See especially J. Lovell, *British Trade Unions, 1875–1933* (1977), Ch. 4 and references there. Also D. Read (ed.), *Documents from Edwardian England* (1973), Ch. 11.
4. R. Hyman, *The Workers' Union* (1971), p. 56.

5. W. S. Churchill, *Liberalism and the Social Problem* (1909), pp. 181–2.
6. R. Postgate, *Life of George Lansbury* (1951), p. 139. See also R. J. Holton, '*Daily Herald* v. *Daily Citizen*, 1912–15', *International Review of Social History*, XIX (1974).
7. P. Snowden, *Socialism and Syndicalism* (1913), pp. 243–4. See especially B. Holton, *British Syndicalism, 1900–1914* (1976).
8. See especially S. G. Hobson, *National Guilds* (1914); and A. R. Orage (ed.), *National Guilds* (1914).
9. M. Ginsberg (ed.), *Law and Opinion in England in the 20th Century* (1959), p. 227. See especially H. Pelling, *Popular Politics and Society in Late Victorian Britain* (1968), Ch. 4.
10. *Kentish Gazette*, 7 April 1914. See especially G. A. Phillips, 'The Triple Industrial Alliance in 1914', *Economic History Review*, second series, XXIV (1971).
11. Lee Holcombe, *Victorian Ladies at Work* (1973), p. 216.
12. Beatrice Webb, *Our Partnership* (1948), pp. 359–60. See especially S. Hynes, *The Edwardian Turn of Mind* (1968), Chs. V–VIII.
13. See especially O. R. McGregor, *Divorce in England* (1957), Ch. I.
14. See especially R. Fulford, *Votes for Women* (1957); Constance Rover, *Women's Suffrage and Party Politics in Britain, 1866–1914* (1967); A. Rosen, *Rise Up, Women!* (1974); and D. Morgan, *Suffragists and Liberals* (1975). Also Midge Mackenzie, *Shoulder to Shoulder* (1975).
15. See M. D. Pugh, 'Politicians and the Woman's Vote, 1914–1918', *History*, Vol. 59 (1974).
16. J. Gore, *King George V* (1949), p. 153.
17. See especially A. T. Q. Stewart, *The Ulster Crisis* (1967); F. S. L. Lyons, *Ireland Since the Famine* (1971), part II, Chs. 7, 9; and N. Mansergh, *The Irish Question, 1840–1921* (3rd edn, 1975), Chs. V, VI.
18. A. Chamberlain, *Politics from Inside* (1936), p. 576.
19. *The Times*, 29 July 1912; R. S. Churchill, *Winston S. Churchill*, II (1967), pp. 432–489.
20. St J. Ervine, *Craigavon* (1949), p. 185.
21. See A. P. Ryan, *The Mutiny at the Curragh* (1956).
22. P. Ferris, *The House of Northcliffe* (1971), p. 192.
23. C. J. Lowe and M. L. Dockrill, *The Mirage of Power* (1972), I, pp. 117–18. See especially F. H. Hinsley (ed.), *The Foreign Policy of Sir Edward Grey* (1977), Ch. 23; and Zara S. Steiner, *Britain and the Origins of the First World War* (1977), Ch. 9.
24. See V. R. Berghahn, *Germany and the Approach of War in 1914* (1973), and references there; notably, F. Fischer, *War of Illusions* (1973).
25. Lord Oxford and Asquith, *Memories and Reflections* (1928), II, p. 5.
26. See especially C. Hazlehurst, *Politicians at War* (1971), part I.
27. See I. F. Clarke, *Voices Prophesying War, 1763–1984* (1966), Chs. 3, 4.
28. T. Brex, '*Scare-Mongerings*' from the Daily Mail* (1914), pp. 66–9.
29. See H. Weinroth, 'Norman Angell and the *Great Illusion*: An Episode in pre-1914 Pacifism', *Historical Journal*, XVII (1974).
30. G. D. H. Cole, *Labour in War-Time* (1915), p. 2.
31. J. Bailey, *Life and Letters* (1935), p. 146.
32. H. Dalton, *Call Back Yesterday* (1953), p. 80.
33. T. Clarke, *My Northcliffe Diary* (1931), p. 64.

Further reading

References are given at appropriate points in the text to many relevant books and articles. Only the most important titles, or those most helpful as introductions, are listed here.

Bibliographies

H. J. Hanham, *Bibliography of British History, 1851–1914* (1975) provides a comprehensive survey both of contemporary works and of historical books and articles published up to about 1972. D. Nicholls (ed.), *Nineteenth-Century Britain, 1815–1914* (1978) is a more recent critical bibliography, which passes confident judgement upon nearly a thousand titles. The following offer detailed guidance to reading upon particular themes: Rosalind Mitchison, *British Population Since 1860* (1977); R. A. Church, *The Great Victorian Boom, 1850–1873* (1975); S. B. Saul, *The Myth of the Great Depression* (1969); P. L. Cottrell, *British Overseas Investment in the Nineteenth Century* (1975); E. L. Jones, *The Development of English Agriculture, 1815–1873* (1968); M. E. Rose, *The Relief of Poverty, 1834–1914* (1972); Martha Vicinus, *Suffer and Be Still* (1972), Ch. 10, and Martha Vicinus, *A Widening Sphere, Changing Roles of Victorian Women* (1977), Ch. 10; R. A. Soloway, 'Church and Society: Recent Trends in Nineteenth Century Religious History', *Journal of British Studies*, XI (1972); E. J. R. Eaglesham, *The Foundations of Twentieth-Century Education in England* (1967); Gillian Sutherland, *Elementary Education in the Nineteenth Century* (1971); Valerie Cromwell, *Revolution or Evolution, British Government in the Nineteenth Century* (1977); P. Adelman, *Gladstone, Disraeli and Later Victorian Politics* (1970); P. Adelman, *The Rise of the Labour Party* (1972); A. E. Musson, *British Trade Unions, 1800–1875* (1972); J. Lovell, *British Trade Unions, 1875–1933* (1977); P. J. Buckland, *Irish Unionism, 1885–1922* (1973); H. Browne, *Joseph Chamberlain, Radical and Imperialist* (1974); W. R. Louis, *Imperialism* (1976); C. C. Eldridge, *Victorian Imperialism* (1978).

Statistical evidence

B. R. Mitchell and Phyllis Deane, *Abstract of British Historical Statistics* (1962) is invaluable, as is Phyllis Deane and W. A. Cole, *British Economic Growth, 1688–1958* (2nd edn, 1967). For electoral and political statistics see the several compilations by F. W. S. Craig. C. Cook and B. Keith, *British Historical Facts, 1830–1900* (1975) supplies a diversity of information.

Selected source material

Selections of contemporary documents include W. H. B. Court, *British Economic History, 1870–1914* (1965); C. J. Lowe, *The Reluctant Imperialists* (1967); K. Bourne, *The Foreign Policy of Victorian England, 1830–1902* (1970); K. O. Morgan, *The Age of Lloyd George* (1971); D. M. Thompson, *Nonconformity in the Nineteenth Century* (1972);

J. Briggs and I. Sellers, *Victorian Nonconformity* (1973); D. Read, *Documents from Edwardian England* (1973); E. J. Hobsbawm, *Labour's Turning Point, 1880-1900* (2nd edn, 1974); P. Keating, *Into Unknown England, 1866-1913* (1976); W. D. Handcock, *English Historical Documents, 1874-1914* (1977).

Messrs Batsford have published selections of contemporary photographs locality by locality, starting with John Betjemen's *Victorian and Edwardian London* (1969). But the best edited books of this kind are those by Gordon Winter – *A Country Camera, 1844-1914* (1966); *Past Positive, London's Social History Recorded in Photographs* (1971); and *The Golden Years, 1903-1913* (1975). Gustave Doré and Blanchard Jerrold's *London* (1872), which contains many notable drawings, has been several times reprinted.

Contemporary descriptions and surveys

Diversely revealing are C. Buxton, *Handbook to Political Questions of the Day* (1880: nine edns to 1903); T. H. S. Escott, *England, Her People, Polity, and Pursuits* (1879); H. W. Lucy, *A Diary of Two Parliaments* (1885-6), and subsequent volumes; Charles Booth, *Life and Labour of the People in London* (1889-1902), from which A. Fried and R. M. Elman, *Charles Booth's London* (1969) is a convenient selection; G. W. Smalley, *London Letters* (1890); B. S. Rowntree, *Poverty, A Study of Town Life* (1901); Henry James, *English Hours* (1905); Lady Bell, *At The Works* (1907); and C. F. G. Masterman, *The Condition of England* (1909: new edn 1960).

Diaries and letters

The following convey both information and atmosphere within their respective contexts: Beatrice Webb, *My Apprenticeship* (1926), and *Our Partnership* (1948); M. V. Brett (ed.), *Journals and Letters of Reginald, Viscount Esher* (1934); W. Plomer (ed.), *Kilvert's Diary* (1960); R. Fulford (ed.), *Dearest Child, Letters Between Queen Victoria and the Princess Royal* (1964), and subsequent volumes; D. W. R. Bahlman (ed.), *Diary of Sir Edward Walter Hamilton* (1972); J. M. Winter and D. M. Joslin (eds.), *R. H. Tawney's Commonplace Book* (1972); A. B. Cooke and J. Vincent (eds.), *The Governing Passion* (1974).

Autobiographies

Notable among many others are Flora Thompson, *Lark Rise to Candleford* (1945); Mary V. Hughes, *A London Family, 1870-1900* (1946); Sir Ernest Barker, *Father of the Man* (1948); Katharine Chorley, *Manchester Made Them* (1950); Gwen Raverat, *Period Piece* (1952); L. E. Jones, *An Edwardian Youth* (1956); Hannah Mitchell, *The Hard Way Up* (1968); and R. Roberts, *The Classic Slum* (1971).

General histories

Throughout two generations the leading general histories of late-Victorian and Edwardian England have been E. Halévy's *Imperialism and the Rise of Labour, 1895-1905* (2nd edn, 1951), and *The Rule of Democracy, 1905-1914* (2nd edn, 1952); and R. C. K. Ensor's *England, 1870-1914* (1936). Halévy and Ensor were both born in the late nineteenth century about which they came to write as historians during the inter-war years. Their books brilliantly combine detailed knowledge with a sense of period. Subsequent research has of course provided much evidence not available to them, either as contemporaries or as historians. The second half of G. M. Young's *Victorian England: Portrait of An Age* (3rd edn, 1977) offers a stylish but disapproving sketch, first published in 1936, by another historian who was also a young contemporary. 'What failed in the late Victorian age, and its flash Edwardian epilogue, was the Victorian public.' J. B. Priestley's *The Edwardians* (1970) represents a successful mix of outline history with vivid personal memories, plus superb illustrations. Three histories by much younger late-twentieth-century historians are G. F. A. Best's *Mid-Victorian Britain, 1851–1875* (1971), enthusiastic yet perceptive; R. Shannon's *The Crisis of Imperialism, 1865–1915* (1974), which takes some knowledge for granted; and P. Thompson's *The Edwardians* (1975), which brings 'oral history' into belated but useful service. R. Rhodes James, *The British Revolution*, I (1976) concentrates upon high politics 1880–1914.

Late-Victorian economic history has been well and widely covered. See W. Ashworth, *An Economic History of England, 1870–1939* (1960); S. G. Checkland, *The Rise of Industrial Society in England, 1815–1885* (1964); P. Mathias, *The First Industrial Nation* (1969); and D. S. Landes, *The Unbound Prometheus* (1969). The history of political thought is still best surveyed by B. Lippincott, *Victorian Critics of Democracy* (1938); E. Barker, *Political Thought in England, 1848–1914* (2nd edn, 1947); and C. Brinton, *English Political Thought in the Nineteenth Century* (2nd edn, 1962). Intellectual and cultural history can be approached through W. E. Houghton, *The Victorian Frame of Mind, 1830–1870* (1957); R. Williams, *Culture and Society, 1780–1950* (1958); S. Hynes, *The Edwardian Turn of Mind* (1968); M. Bradbury, *The Social Context of Modern English Literature* (1971); and C. B. Cox and A. E. Dyson (eds.), *The Twentieth Century Mind*, I (1972).

Specialized histories

The following titles – which range more broadly than detailed monographs – all provide essential information, and most of them add valuable insights. W. Ashworth, *The Genesis of Modern British Town Planning* (1954); H. J. Hanham, *Elections and Party Management, Politics in the Time of Disraeli and Gladstone* (1959); R. Robinson and J. Gallagher, *Africa and the Victorians* (1961); A. Briggs, *Victorian Cities* (1963); F. M. L. Thompson, *English Landed Society in the Nineteenth Century* (1963); H. A. Clegg *et al.*, *A History of British Trade Unions Since 1889*, I (1964); H. Pelling, *The Origins of the Labour Party, 1880–1900* (2nd edn, 1965); D. C. Marsh, *The Changing Social Structure of England and Wales, 1871–1961* (2nd edn, 1965); B. B. Gilbert, *The Evolution of National Insurance in Great Britain* (1966); J. Gross, *The Rise and Fall of the Man of Letters* (1969); R. Blake, *The Conservative Party from Peel to Churchill* (1970); F. S. L. Lyons, *Ireland Since the Famine* (1971); O. Chadwick, *The Victorian Church*, I (3rd edn, 1971), II (2nd edn, 1972); N. Blewett, *The Peers, The Parties, and The People* (1972); D. A. Hamer, *Liberal Politics in the Age of Gladstone and Rosebery* (1972); José Harris, *Unemployment and Politics* (1972); H. J. Dyos and M. Wolff (eds.), *The Victorian City* (1973); N. Mansergh, *The Irish Question, 1840–1921* (3rd edn, 1975); P. O'Farrell, *England and Ireland Since 1800* (1975); A. D. Gilbert, *Religion and Society in Industrial England* (1976); R. Hyam, *Britain's Imperial Century, 1815–1914* (1976); A. J. Lee, *The Origins of the Popular Press, 1855–1914* (1976); J. Vincent, *The Formation of the Liberal Party, 1857–1868* (2nd edn, 1976).

Biographies

The most important biographies of the leading political figures are listed in the references to the sections on 'Personalities' in Chapters 7, 17, and 27. Other notable biographies are R. Jenkins, *Sir Charles Dilke* (1958); R. Pound and G. Harmsworth, *Northcliffe* (1959); M. K. Ashby, *Joseph Ashby of Tysoe* (1961); A. Briggs, *Social Thought and Social Action: A Study of the Work of Seebohm Rowntree* (1961); H. Pearson, *Bernard Shaw* (1961); R. Lambert, *Sir John Simon, 1816–1904* (1963); Lord David Cecil, *Max* (1964); C. Hassall, *Rupert Brooke* (1964); P. Henderson, *William Morris* (1967); M. Kennedy, *Portrait of Elgar* (1968); C. Carrington, *Rudyard Kipling* (2nd edn, 1970); N. and Jeanne Mackenzie, *The Time Traveller, The Life of H. G. Wells* (1973); and F. S. L. Lyons, *Charles Steward Parnell* (1977).

Addendum

The following relevant books have been published since the present text was completed: P. Clarke, *Liberals and Social Democrats* (1978); J. Complin, *The Rise of the Plutocrats*

(1978); J. Grigg, *Lloyd George, The People's Champion* (1978); B. Harrison, *Separate Spheres, The Opposition to Women's Suffrage in Britain, 1867–1928* (1978); P. T. Marsh, *The Discipline of Popular Government, Lord Salisbury's Domestic Statecraft, 1881–1902* (1978); M. Pugh, *Electoral Reform in War and Peace, 1906–18* (1978); F. B. Smith, *The People's Health, 1830–1910* (1979); R. N. Soffer, *Ethics and Society in England* (1978); D. Wiltshire, *The Social and Political Thought of Herbert Spencer* (1978).

Index

528   Index